Race, Poverty, and American Cities

Race, Poverty, and American Cities

Edited by John Charles Boger and Judith Welch Wegner

The University of

North Carolina Press

Chapel Hill & London

The paper in this book meets the guidelines for
permanence and durability of the Committee
on Production Guidelines for Book Longevity
of the Council on Library Resources.

Library of Congress Cataloging-in-Publication
Data

Race, poverty, and American cities / edited by
John Charles Boger and Judith Welch Wegner.
p.   cm.   Includes bibliographical references
and index.
ISBN 0-8078-2274-4 (cloth : alk. paper)
ISBN 0-8078-4578-7 (pbk. : alk. paper)
1. Cities and towns—United States. 2. Sociology, Urban—United States. 3. Urban policy—
United States. 4. Urban poor—United States.
5. United States—Race relations. I. Boger, John
Charles. II. Wegner, Judith Welch.
HT123.R23   1996   95-45056
307.76'0973—dc20   CIP

Publication of this work was aided by a
generous grant from the Z. Smith Reynolds
Foundation.

Apart from the Afterword, the essays in this
volume originally appeared, in somewhat
different form, in the *North Carolina Law
Review* 71, no. 5 (June 1993), a special issue
entitled *Symposium—The Urban Crisis: The
Kerner Commission Report Revisited,* © 1993 by
the North Carolina Law Review Association,
Chapel Hill, North Carolina.

00 99 98 97 96   5 4 3 2 1

Dedicated to
Julius LeVonne Chambers

Contents

Preface

This volume was conceived in the spring of 1992 in sober reflection on the urban crisis plaguing this nation. It came to birth in spring 1995 in the face of growing division between rich and poor, whites and "minorities," urban and suburban populations, "haves" and "have-nots."

In April 1992 America's imagination was gripped by the image of cities burning. A sense of the surreal suffused the nation. White police officers, videotaped in the act of severely beating a black man, Rodney King, were freed by the criminal justice system. Fires leveled South Central Los Angeles, and man-made devastation surpassed that wrought by earthquakes and other natural disasters. Racial tensions flared, sparking both anger and anguish. Political analysts' and broadcasters' words paled beside the poet's:

> Things fall apart; the center cannot hold;
> Mere anarchy is loosed upon the world,
> The blood-dimmed tide is loosed, and everywhere
> The ceremony of innocence is drowned;
> The best lack all conviction, while the worst
> Are full of passionate intensity.[1]

Los Angeles—land of fantasy—came to symbolize the grim realities of the new "urban crisis," one that drew the nation's attention, for a time, until it turned its head.

The South Central riots and their aftermath prompted myriad questions and provided few answers. Will forces such as those at work in Los Angeles in 1992 trigger a growing incidence of urban unrest in the days ahead? Is urban deterioration inevitable? If so, have our great cities outlived their time? Is poverty inextricably linked to race and ethnicity? Are the roots of racism deeper than we can or will acknowledge? Has our system of laws permitted inequity and injustice to persist or simply failed to provide a cure? Have intransigent afflictions such as these defeated our collective imagination or only our will? What lessons might be gleaned from prior incidents of urban strife to shape our policies for the future? No less troubling is the growing recognition that none of these questions can readily be answered in isolation. Instead, meaningful solutions to the problems plaguing America's cities must be premised on a better understanding of how attitudes about race and poverty, and the fate of evolving urban centers, are inextricably intertwined.

Nearly four years after the South Central riots, the country's urban crisis and the interrelated issues of race and poverty seem no less pressing and their solutions no more clear. If anything, these issues have grown more compelling and more complex. The economy has become more internationalized, and industrial jobs continue to flee the cities. Health care reform has been attempted with limited success, and center-city hospitals remain overwhelmed with the urban poor. Public concern about violent crime has led to calls for more prisons and longer jail terms. Growing frustration fuels initiatives to curb the rights of illegal immigrants and their children and to revamp the social welfare system. Protesting voices challenge the fairness and wisdom of affirmative action, while racial disparities in employment and educational opportunities continue to grow. The political system has been shaken by shifting partisan coalitions, and proposals to "reinvent" government have given way to ever simplified solutions and ever more profound distrust.

This volume is based on two fundamental premises. It was conceived in the belief that, when faced with such difficult questions, the nation needs the best answers its scholars can give—lest policymakers, in Yeats's words, "lack all conviction" in facing some of the foremost problems of our time. The essays in this volume bring together the views of those trained in a wide range of disciplines—law, economics, journalism, geography, business, urban planning, social welfare, and public health—in hopes that their varied insights will shed needed light on complex and intransigent problems facing our cities and their people.

This volume likewise reflects a firm belief that history is a powerful teacher, one whose lessons we dare not ignore. The editors and contributors to this volume have accordingly used as their stepping-off point the Kerner Commission Report,[2] commissioned by President Lyndon Johnson in July 1967 and issued in March 1968. The report offers an important context for the present discussion and remarkable measures by which to assess the nation's current plight. The Kerner Report provided careful, detailed findings regarding the status of African Americans[3] in cities in the late 1960s—their income and employment status, their educational opportunities, their access to health care, their relation to the public welfare system and to the criminal justice system, and their access to political power. This information serves as a useful benchmark for measuring the progress of African Americans and other racial minorities a generation later.

The Kerner Report also contained a series of remarkably clear and explicit policy prescriptions that it promised could revitalize urban America and avoid the development of "two nations, one black and one white, separate and unequal." The Kerner Report's strategies for "integration" and "enrichment" likewise provided a fruitful framework for discussing the status of African Americans in the late 1960s. That framework continues to provide an important template for assessing changes in the lives of African Americans as is discussed in a number of the essays in this volume. At the same time, that framework has been modified as appropriate in light of significant changes that have occurred as America's cities have become more multiethnic.

The essays that follow are arranged in six major sections:

(1) Looking Backward and Looking Ahead: Lessons and Questions from the Kerner Commission Report;

(2) An Urban Policy for America: Is Such a Framework Feasible?;

(3) Residential Mobility: Effects on Education, Employment, and Racial Integration;

(4) America's Social Policy: How Race Matters in Developing Health, Education, and Welfare Policies;

(5) The Dual Racial Reality of the Media's Message;

(6) Do We Have the Will to Change?: A Continuing Conversation between Academics and Policymakers.

Many of the essays were originally developed for publication in volume 71 of the North Carolina Law Review as part of a symposium titled "The Urban Crisis: The Kerner Commission Report Revisited." Contributors completed their essays in January 1993, and the symposium issue was printed in June 1993. Essays appearing in the present volume were edited and brought up to date as of the time of publication. Essays have been published in revised form with the consent of the authors and the editors of the North Carolina Law Review.

Notes

1. William Butler Yeats, "The Second Coming," in Collected Poems of William Butler Yeats (New York: Macmillan, 1956), 184–85.

2. Report of the National Advisory Commission on Civil Disorders (New York: Bantam Books, 1968).

3. The contributors to this volume have used the terms African American, black, and black American, often interchangeably, in their essays. The editors have elected to defer to the contributors' choices in the absence of any universally accepted racial or ethnic designation.

Part One   Looking Backward
and Looking Ahead

Lessons and Questions from the
Kerner Commission Report

John Charles Boger   Race and the American City

The Kerner Commission
Report in Retrospect

During the early 1960s, America's cities, especially the racial minorities
and poor within them, became a national focus of political, social, and intellectual concern. One major social force contributing to this rediscovery
of urban problems was the civil rights movement, which had moved the nation's conscience during the decade between 1954 and 1964 by its struggle
against segregation in the South, and which in 1965 began to redirect its
energies northward, toward the "dark ghettos" of the industrial East and
Midwest.[1]

At almost the same moment, American concern about poverty—concern that largely had abated following World War II—began to rekindle,
sparked in part by the passionate writings of Michael Harrington[2] and the
speeches of the nation's young president, John F. Kennedy.[3] Among the
many powerful images evoked by Harrington's writings, two stood out: impoverished, white mining families in rural Appalachia and desperate African American families languishing in the nation's central cities.

> There is a new type of slum. Its citizens are the internal migrants, the
> Negroes, the poor whites from the farms, the Puerto Ricans. They join
> the failures from the old ethnic culture and form an entirely different
> kind of neighborhood. For many of them, the crucial problem is color,
> and this makes the ghetto walls higher than they have ever been. All of
> them arrive at a time of housing shortage . . . and thus it is harder to es-
> cape even when income rises. But, above all, these people do not partic-
> ipate in the culture of aspiration that was the vitality of the ethnic slum.[4]

At the same time, leading sociologists who were studying "juvenile
delinquency" began in the early 1960s to develop explanatory theories that
focused less on the personal moral failings of juveniles and their families
and more on the dysfunctionality of urban neighborhoods:[5] "Cloward,
Ohlin, and Harrington emphasized that juvenile delinquency reflected a
broader deterioration in slum conditions. Their writings, in fact, helped

rediscover urban poverty. The older ethnic slum, they said, had been crowded and unsanitary, but the people had a vital community life and, most important, aspirations. . . . Most modern slums were populated by 'dregs' who could not get out and by ill-prepared migrants from the South, many of whom carried the added burden of racial discrimination."[6]

These social and intellectual currents emerged at a time when Democratic Party leaders were pondering how best to solidify political allegiance among southern black migrants who had streamed to northern cities after World War II; collectively these new urban immigrants promised to become a crucial political constituency in key industrial states by the mid-1960s.[7]

For different reasons, then, each of these related developments—the evolving civil rights movement, the reawakened national concern over poverty, revised theories on the cause of juvenile delinquency, and the Democratic Party's effort to consolidate its urban political base—focused attention on American cities, especially on their African American poor, among whom, Daniel Patrick Moynihan warned, a "tangle of pathologies" lay largely unaddressed.[8]

In response to these perceived challenges, President Kennedy directed his brother, Attorney General Robert Kennedy, to assemble a task force and charged it to develop a coordinated program to alleviate poverty.[9] This legislative program, ultimately completed after President Kennedy's assassination in 1963, became a declared War on Poverty. It was fully embraced by President Lyndon Johnson as a centerpiece of his Great Society initiative.[10] Principally an urban strategy, the War on Poverty took direct aim at the racial ghettos of the nation's cities. The legislative program included passage of (1) the Equal Opportunity Act of 1964, (2) the Housing and Urban Development Act of 1965, (3) the "Model Cities" program, formally known as the Demonstration Cities and Metropolitan Development Act of 1966, and (4) the Elementary and Secondary Education Act of 1965.[11] (Ironically, some of the most effective long-term weapons against poverty came not from the legislation originally designed as central to the War on Poverty, but from key components of Johnson's larger Great Society legislation, especially Medicare and Medicaid, inaugurated via the Social Security Amendment of 1965 and the subsequent expansion of Social Security benefits.)[12]

In his effort to implement the War on Poverty, President Johnson commissioned two major, interdisciplinary examinations of housing and urban policy: the National Commission on Urban Problems (the Douglas Commission)[13] and the President's Committee on Urban Housing (the Kaiser Committee).[14] When major racial riots tore across the urban landscape during the spring of 1967, President Johnson appointed a third commission, explicitly charged to explore the links between racial discrimination and urban policy: the Kerner Commission.

Nearly three decades have passed since the Kerner Commission issued its final report in March 1968, a searing indictment of America's urban and racial policies.[15] Even if the nation had somehow managed in the intervening decades to resolve its urban and racial challenges, this extraordinary document would invite historical reflection. Yet the problems outlined by the Kerner Commission continue to defy solution by the nation's policymakers, and reflections on the Kerner Commission Report have keen contemporary significance. As the 1992 Los Angeles rebellion emphasized,[16] millions of the urban poor still find themselves without full-time employment, adequate education, affordable health care, decent housing, or social welfare programs that meet their basic needs. Moreover, the black-white racial divisions that dominated the Kerner Commission's vision of urban life in 1968 remain sharp, although they have been complicated by the emergence of other ethnic groups—Cubans, Puerto Ricans, Mexican Americans, Latinos from Central and South America, Japanese, Chinese, Vietnamese, Cambodians, Thais, Koreans, and others—whose legitimate claims for participation in American urban life make political, social, and economic relationships more challenging.[17]

Meanwhile, America's cities in 1995 continue to face serious, burgeoning social ills, many of which are closely intertwined with race and ethnicity: a decline in manufacturing and other blue-collar jobs, inadequate public schools, an explosion of gang- and drug-related violence and crime among the young, the AIDS epidemic and other looming public health challenges, an increasingly impoverished citizenry, an inadequate tax base, and private disinvestment in urban projects. Many urban mayors today find themselves with less money than in 1968 and fewer clear ideas about what can be done.

To be sure, the urban scene has changed significantly since 1968, and in some respects, as we document below, conditions have improved. *Yet the principal theme of this essay is that the fundamental social and economic diagnoses of the Kerner Commission remain pertinent nearly three decades later, while its policy prescriptions remain largely ignored. Whether the Kerner Commission was correct and, if so, whether the policies proposed in 1968 have continuing relevance for the nation in 1995 are fundamental questions that the contributors to this volume must address in the pages to follow.*

In this essay I undertake two preliminary tasks: first, to review the Kerner Commission's principal findings and recommendations; second, to provide readers with a statistical snapshot of the altered circumstances that face African Americans and America's cities in 1995. With these data in mind, readers can move on to the essays of other contributors to this volume, probing their ideas and asking what policy prescriptions appear most promising for the decades to come.[18]

In a separate essay I summarize and address both the public policy changes proposed by the Republicans, who entered Congress after the 1994 midterm election promising a new "Contract with America," as well as the more modest changes proposed (and in a few instances, enacted) by the Clinton administration between 1993 and 1995. Although issues of race and urban policy have been conspicuously absent as express themes in these policy debates, few doubt that race and the cities form a major (though implicit) subtext behind the proposed Republican changes in national direction.

The Urban Crisis of the Mid-1960s and the Kerner Commission Report

During the mid-1960s the nation witnessed five consecutive summers of racial unrest in its cities.[19] These riots followed a decade of mounting white violence, targeted especially against African Americans who had challenged the South's system of legalized segregation. During the decade between 1954 and 1964 scores of southern black churches had been firebombed, and dozens of blacks had been killed in the civil rights struggle.[20] In July 1967, following the especially deadly and destructive riots by African Americans that spring and early summer, President Lyndon B. Johnson issued Executive Order No. 11,365,[21] creating the National Advisory Commission on Civil Disorders. The president charged the commission to investigate "the origins of the recent major civil disorders in our cities, includ[ing] the basic causes and factors leading to such disorders," and to propose "methods and techniques for averting or controlling such disorders," including "the appropriate role of the local, state and Federal authorities."[22] Nine months later, in March 1968, the commission, chaired by then-governor Otto Kerner of Illinois, delivered a comprehensive report to the American nation. The report began with a memorable warning:

> Our nation is moving toward two societies, one black, one white—separate and unequal. . . . Reaction to last summer's disorders has quickened the movement and deepened the division. Discrimination and segregation have long permeated much of American life; they now threaten the future of every American.

> This deepening racial division is not inevitable. The movement apart can be reversed. Choice is still possible. Our principal task is to define that choice and to press for a national resolution.

To pursue our present course will involve the continuing polarization of the American community and, ultimately, the destruction of basic democratic values.[23]

At first glance this warning of a deepening racial division seemed to point to a racial pattern as old as American history. From colonial times, America's white majority had insisted on and legally enforced the separate and unequal status of blacks.[24] The Constitution itself implicitly recognized chattel slavery,[25] ensuring the growth of a nation "half slave and half free." Even in the nonslaveholding areas outside the South prior to 1861, most free blacks endured intense social segregation and legally enforced discrimination.[26] The Civil War ended chattel slavery as an institution but brought no real end to the legal subordination of blacks. Instead, less than a decade after adoption of the Fourteenth and Fifteenth Amendments— garlanded with promises of equal protection under the laws, full citizenship, and political enfranchisement—national political and judicial leaders abandoned their short-lived experiment in racial equality, acquiesced in renewed racial discrimination, and collaborated to block further participation in the democratic process by millions of African American voters.[27] The white majority, in effect, repudiated the legal promises crafted during Reconstruction and chose instead to shape twentieth-century American life and law in the image of Jim Crow.[28]

Yet the Kerner Commission Report, in retelling this history,[29] made clear that its alarm in 1968 proceeded not merely from the perpetuation of these old racial divisions but from a dangerous new form of separation that was unfolding in the mid-1960s, one that would "threaten the future of every American." Some critics objected that the commission had failed to appreciate new and positive trends in America's racial relations. After centuries of oppression, African Americans appeared poised to achieve the equal rights denied them for 350 years. Decades of patient planning and struggle by National Association for the Advancement of Colored People (NAACP) lawyers[30] had culminated in 1954 in the remarkable success of *Brown v. Board of Education*, a decision in which the Supreme Court had formally renounced Jim Crow.[31] The Warren Court subsequently presided over a remarkable campaign to restore the Fourteenth and Fifteenth Amendments as guarantors of equal rights for black citizens.

Moreover, a decade of direct political activity organized by the Southern Christian Leadership Conference, the Congress of Racial Equality, the NAACP, and the Student Nonviolent Coordinating Committee[32] had prompted Congress in 1964 and 1965 to enact the two most sweeping civil rights statutes ever written into American law: the Civil Rights Act of 1964[33] and the Voting Rights Act of 1965.[34] Together these acts were designed to end racial discrimination in public education, employment, voting, and governmental programs. Surely, these observers reasoned, the promising developments from 1954 to 1965 spelled the end of America's history of racial division. Surely the nation was moving forward, not backward.[35]

Yet the Kerner Commission's verdict was strongly to the contrary. Neither *Brown v. Board of Education* nor the Civil Rights Act of 1964 nor the victories of Dr. King nor any of the hard-won accomplishments of the second civil rights revolution would suffice to heal America's racial wounds. Instead, the commission implied, the riots were clear proof that antidiscrimination laws alone could never fully redress the residual injuries of slavery and segregation. Ironically, after a decade of remarkable achievements in court and Congress, America faced a racial divide more profound than any in its segregated past.[36]

The Kerner Commission's Vision of the Future

The commission's stern analysis began with a description of two related social movements, each set in motion during the early 1900s, that had gathered force steadily after World War II.[37] The first was the migration of African Americans from the rural South to the urban North; the second was the almost simultaneous departure of urban whites from northern cities to suburban enclaves. According to the report the resulting residential separation was virtually absolute:

- Almost all Negro population growth (98 percent from 1950 to 1966) is occurring within metropolitan areas, primarily within central cities.
- The vast majority of white population growth (78 percent from 1960 to 1966) is occurring in suburban portions of metropolitan areas. Since 1960, white central-city population has declined by 1.3 million.
- As a result, central cities are becoming more heavily Negro while the suburban fringes around them remain almost entirely white.[38]

These demographic shifts, the commission observed, were not the product of private choice or other race-neutral explanations. "What white Americans have never fully understood—but what the Negro can never forget—is that white society is deeply implicated in the ghetto. White institutions created it, white institutions maintain it, and white society condones it."[39]

In a series of point-by-point forecasts, the commission urged that these developments, if unchecked, would undercut the positive effects of the Civil Rights Act and the judicial decrees of the Warren Court. First, the commission reasoned, the accelerating residential segregation would frustrate black efforts to secure equal employment,[40] since "most new employment opportunities . . . are being created in suburbs and outlying areas—and this trend is likely to continue indefinitely."[41] The exclusion of blacks from this emerging suburban workforce would be catastrophic; black un-employment (and underemployment) would become "the single most im-portant source of poverty among Negroes"[42] and a principal source of fam-ily and social disorganization as well: "Wives of these men are forced to work, and usually produce more money. If men stay at home without working, their inadequacies constantly confront them and tensions arise between them and their wives and children. Under these pressures, it is not surprising that many of these men flee their responsibilities as husbands and fathers, leaving home, and drifting from city to city, or adopting the style of 'street corner men.'"[43]

The adverse effects of the developing urban/suburban "mismatch" be-tween jobs and minority workers, the commission forewarned, would extend beyond individual family circles. Central cities, increasingly inhab-ited by low-paid or unemployed African Americans and other ethnic mi-norities, would experience—indeed, already were experiencing—the in-terrelated social effects of concentrated poverty: high rates of crime,[44] inadequate health care,[45] inadequate sanitation,[46] and exploitative retail services.[47]

The commission added that this concentrated poverty would seriously limit the educational prospects of urban children:

> When disadvantaged children are racially isolated in the schools, they are deprived of one of the more significant ingredients of quality educa-tion: exposure to other children with strong educational backgrounds. The Coleman Report and the Report of the Civil Rights Commission es-tablish that the predominant socio-economic background of the stu-dents in a school exerts a powerful impact upon achievement. . . . An-other strong influence on achievement derives from the tendency of school administrators, teachers, parents and the students themselves to regard ghetto schools as inferior. Reflecting this attitude, students at-tending such schools lose confidence in their ability to shape their fu-ture. The Coleman Report found this factor—destiny control—"to have a stronger relationship to achievement than . . . all the [other] 'school' factors together."[48]

The commission foresaw unhappy social consequences for urban hous-ing and municipal governance flowing from the increased racial isola-tion. While inadequate housing was not a problem faced solely by urban blacks,[49] the commission nonetheless contended that, because of their higher relative rates of poverty and the pervasive discrimination they faced in the broader urban housing market, African Americans would experi-ence the adverse effects of poor housing disproportionately.[50] "Discrimina-tion prevents access to many nonslum areas, particularly the suburbs, and has a detrimental effect on ghetto housing itself. By restricting the area open to a growing population, housing discrimination makes it profitable for landlords to break up ghetto apartments for denser occupancy, hastening housing deterioration. By creating a 'back pressure' in the racial ghettos, discrimination keeps prices and rents of older, more deteriorated housing in the ghetto higher than they would be in a truly free and open market."[51]

Having cataloged the adverse effects on individual citizens, the Kerner Commission next examined the cumulative effect of urban racial isolation on the financial health of the nation's cities:

> As a result of the population shifts of the post-war period, concentrating the more affluent parts of the urban population in residential suburbs while leaving the less affluent in the central cities, the increasing burden of municipal taxes frequently falls upon that part of the urban population least able to pay them. Increasing concentrations of urban growth have called forth greater expenditures for every kind of public service: education, health, police protection, fire protection, parks, sewage disposal, sanitation, water supply, etc. These expenditures have strikingly outpaced tax revenues.[52]

The commission found little consolation in the likelihood that African Americans soon would gain political power in urban centers. Black mayors and city councils, the commission reasoned, would lack both the will and the capacity to increase taxes on already overburdened city taxpayers.[53] Nor would additional sources of municipal revenues likely become available. Private industry was unlikely to make investments in the racial ghetto; the commission observed that "the withdrawal of private capital is already far advanced in most all-Negro areas of our large cities," and that even if "private investment continued, it alone would not suffice."[54] Only the federal government could command sufficient financial resources to step into the financial breach. Yet by the time African Americans came to power in urban centers, the commission predicted, "it is probable that Congress will be more heavily influenced by representatives of the suburban and outlying city electorate. These areas will comprise 41 percent of our total population by 1985, compared with 33 percent in 1960. Central cities will decline from 31 percent to 27 percent. Without decisive action toward integration, this influential suburban electorate would be over 95 percent white and much more affluent than the central city population."[55]

The commission specifically addressed the crucial role played by the national media in shaping the nation's racial and urban understanding.[56] It faulted the media less for their riot coverage than for their broader failure "to report adequately on the causes and consequences of civil disorders."[57]

The Kerner Commission's Prescriptions for National Action

The Kerner Commission insisted that these accelerating trends toward racial isolation required an immediate, comprehensive, national response. Only three basic strategies were possible: The nation could adopt a so-called Present Policies Choice that maintained the current allocation of resources to urban areas and the poor.[58] Alternatively it could pursue an Enrichment Choice that would offset the effects of continued Negro segregation with programs designed to improve the quality of life in disadvantaged central-city neighborhoods, a choice that "would require marked increases in federal spending for education, housing, employment, job training, and social services."[59] Finally, the nation could exercise an Integration Choice, "aimed at reversing the march toward two societies, separate and unequal."[60] This choice would provide strong incentives for African Americans to leave central-city residences, enlarging their choices in housing, employment, and education. It would also require large-scale public investments, on an interim basis, in the quality of central-city life for those residents who chose to remain behind.[61]

Having sketched out the alternatives, the commission urged the nation to make the Integration Choice. It expressed grave doubts about the underlying assumptions of an Enrichment Choice strategy:

> In the end . . . its premise is that disadvantaged Negroes can achieve equality of opportunity with whites while continuing in conditions of nearly complete separation. This premise has been vigorously advocated by Black Power proponents. . . .
>
> This argument is understandable, but there is a great deal of evidence that it is unrealistic. The economy of the United States and particularly the sources of employment are preponderantly white. In this circumstance, a policy of separate but equal employment could only relegate Negroes permanently to inferior incomes and economic status.[62]

The commission reserved even harsher judgment for the Present Policies Choice. Of the three, it declared, "the Present Policies Choice—the choice we are now making [by default]—is the course with the most ominous consequences for our society."[63] Because current social and policy efforts could not adequately address the employment, educational, and other needs of central-city residents, the commission warned, to continue along that course would risk heightened anger and renewed violence, especially among despairing, inner-city youth: "If large-scale violence resulted, white retaliation would follow. This spiral could quite conceivably lead to a kind of urban *apartheid* with semi-martial law in many major cities, enforced residence of Negroes in segregated areas, and a drastic reduction in personal freedom for all Americans, particularly Negroes."[64]

Even if widespread violence were averted, the commission argued, the Present Policies Choice would lead almost certainly to increased racial isolation and polarization, unless millions of African Americans were somehow to achieve rapid income advances or unless there occurred a "migration of a growing Negro middle class out of the central city[,] . . . [which] might diminish the racial undertones of . . . th[e] competition for federal funds between central cities and outlying areas." [65]

In casting its institutional weight behind the Integration Choice, the commission insisted that this choice was (1) responsive to the expected job growth in the suburbs, (2) compelled by evidence that "socio-class integration is the most effective way of improving the education of ghetto children," (3) best adapted to create an adequate housing supply for poor and moderate income citizens, and (4) most faithful to American political and social ideals. [66]

Many of the commission's specific policy recommendations to implement this strategy, however, actually focused on programs directed toward inner-city improvements. The commission proposed, for example, to improve employment prospects by (1) consolidating urban employment efforts, (2) increasing manpower and job training efforts in urban areas, (3) taking aggressive action against those employment practices with a racially discriminatory intent or effect, (4) providing tax credits to spur investment in rural as well as urban poverty areas, and (5) beginning "immediate action to create 2,000,000 new jobs over the next three years—one million in the public sector and one million in the private sector." [67] None of these employment proposals directly confronted the problem of residential segregation.

In the area of public education, while the commission supported general efforts to "reduce de facto segregation in our schools," especially the "racial discrimination in Northern as well as Southern schools," [68] it stopped short of calling for mandatory, interdistrict school desegregation. [69] Instead, most of its recommendations targeted inner-city schools and children for compensatory or supplemental aid. [70]

Only in the area of housing did the commission prescribe solutions tailored to address the urban/suburban racial segregation central to its analysis of the underlying problem. The commission's suburban housing strategy was twofold. First, it called for "a comprehensive and enforceable federal open housing law to cover the sale or rental of all housing, including single family homes." [71] To implement the law, the commission urged "voluntary community action" to disseminate information about suburban housing opportunities to urban minorities and to provide education in suburban communities about "the desirability of open housing." [72] Second, the commission urged an expansion of federal housing programs that would target more low- and moderate-income units in suburban areas, to be implemented through a revitalized federal housing program that would add 6 million units to the federal low-income housing inventory within five years.[73]

The National Response to the Kerner Commission Report

The Kerner Commission warned America that it must choose among three mutually exclusive policy alternatives. Yet within a month after the commission issued its report, President Lyndon Johnson renounced a second presidential term,[74] and later in 1968 Republican candidate Richard Nixon narrowly defeated the Democratic presidential candidate, Vice-President Hubert Humphrey. During the succeeding eight years, the urban and poverty programs crafted by Lyndon Johnson's administration—the War on Poverty and the Model Cities Program—gradually lost executive and legislative momentum. Gary Orfield has characterized the national political response as a near-total rejection of the basic Kerner prescriptions:

> With the election of Nixon and Reagan, whose administrations have set the basic social-policy agenda for the last twenty years, the country rejected the fundamental conclusions and recommendations of the Kerner Report. The issue of civil rights disappeared from national politics, and the idea that there was something fundamentally wrong with existing racial conditions, something that required strong governmental action, was rejected. . . . Presidential politics polarized on racial grounds with four of the five elections since the Kerner Report won by the candidate who received virtually no black votes.[75]

It would be inaccurate, however, to suggest that the nation took no steps at all to address the social ills of segregation and isolated urban poverty. Prior to the 1968 presidential election, Congress passed two major pieces of housing legislation, both of which were prompted in part by the riots and the themes of the Kerner Commission Report. One was the Fair Housing Act of 1968,[76] which had been hastily appended by Congress, after the assassination of Dr. Martin Luther King Jr. on April 4, 1968, to pending civil rights legislation that had been designed to protect citizens from violence or intimidation while exercising their civil rights.[77] Under the Fair Housing Act, it became "the policy of the United States to provide within constitutional limitations, for fair housing throughout the United States."[78] The act expressly prohibited racial or religious discrimination by governmental or most multifamily private market actors in the sale or rental of dwellings, or in their advertisement, financing, or commercial brokerage.[79]

The Fair Housing Act also required the Department of Housing and Urban Development (HUD) and other federal agencies to "administer their programs and activities relating to housing and urban development . . . affirmatively to further the purposes" of fair housing.[80] Yet the act provided very few federal tools to compel private compliance. Instead, it placed principal responsibility on the shoulders of aggrieved private litigants, who were authorized to file administrative complaints of housing discrimination with HUD and to initiate federal lawsuits if HUD failed to obtain "voluntary compliance" within thirty days.[81] Apart from their conciliation responsibilities,[82] however, federal authorities were given meaningful enforcement powers only if "the Attorney General ha[d] reasonable cause to believe that any person . . . is engaged in a pattern or practice of resistance," and if "such denial raise[d] an issue of general public importance."[83]

Congress enacted a second piece of responsive federal legislation, the Housing and Urban Development Act of 1968, in the wake of the urban riots.[84] This legislation created programs to spur low-income housing construction, including (1) new interest subsidies for low- and moderate-income homeownership,[85] (2) a new program to subsidize interest rates for developers who would agree to build and lease dwelling units for low-income persons,[86] (3) additional funding to increase public housing production by 375,000 units over the 1968–70 period,[87] and (4) numerous urban renewal modifications.

Three years later HUD promulgated regulations that were designed to channel low-income housing subsidies toward suburban jurisdictions,[88] and in 1974 Congress passed additional housing legislation that appeared on its face even more far reaching and directly responsive to the concerns of the Kerner Commission. The Housing and Community Development Act of 1974 (HCDA)[89] declared that it was aimed at "the elimination of slums and blight . . . and the deterioration of property and neighborhood and community facilities of importance to the welfare of the community, principally persons of low and moderate income."[90] The legislation promised to promote "the reduction of the isolation of income groups within communities and geographical areas and the promotion of an increase in the diversity and vitality of neighborhoods through the spatial deconcentration of housing opportunities for persons of lower income and the revitalization of deteriorating or deteriorated neighborhoods to attract persons of higher income."[91]

Yet the HCDA proved, in practice, to be unfaithful to the lofty assurances of its preamble, operating most often to undermine the real needs of the poor. The 1974 act abandoned narrowly tailored categorical grants in favor of broad, community development block grants that allowed local authorities to pursue locally developed priorities, subordinating the needs of the poor, who were usually politically powerless, to the desires of local political leaders. Although the HCDA formally required each community to develop a Housing Assistance Plan that would address likely future housing needs,[92] HUD was granted no substantive power to reject a local plan or to withhold block grant funds unless the locality's description of local needs and objectives was "plainly inconsistent" with available local data, or unless the proposed use of the block grant funds was deemed "plainly inappropriate" to meet the locality's announced goals.[93] Likewise, although the HCDA formally provided a mechanism for citizen input, the act required nothing more than provision of information and a public hearing to obtain community views. There was neither citizen veto power nor any other meaningful source of citizen resistance to a locality's decision.[94]

Thus, much like the Model Cities legislation that preceded it,[95] the HCDA's Kerner-Commission-inspired goals of racial and economic deconcentration were thwarted by powerful political opposition. Indeed, the HCDA's insistence on "spatial deconcentration" of low-income housing soon led to ironic consequences. As John Calmore noted at the time,

> In the name of expanding housing opportunities, the government has actually restricted [the development of] housing for poor inner-city residents and has adversely affected the social and political integrity of their communities. Because [the suburban dispersals of federally subsidized housing through] fair housing efforts, particularly on behalf of the non-white poor, have been and continue to be futile in other than tokenistic terms, the provision of low-income housing and community enrichment [in central cities] is being sacrificed without creating viable alternatives. Moreover, the occurrence of spatial deconcentration is too often merely a reconcentration of people in a different space. Finally, in light of extensive urban reinvestment, many so-called impacted areas are really transitional areas; absent more low-income housing in these areas, many poor will suffer displacement, being replaced by the return of the middle-class to the inner city.[96]

The Urban Crisis of the Early 1990s:
The Kerner Commission Report Revisited

The contributors to this volume have been invited to reassess the Kerner Commission's basic recommendations and to reflect on the present circumstances that confront African Americans and American cities, the principal objects of the Kerner Commission Report. As a prelude, I examine some measures of the contemporary status of African Americans in metropolitan areas—data on income and employment, educational attainment, health care, housing access, public welfare reliance, and political power. I offer the following observations and data to illuminate changes that have occurred since 1968 and to provide context for the broader discussion in which other contributors to this volume will be engaged.

Of course, few choices are more perilous than those among rival data. Not only do respected observers disagree over how to measure important phenomena; they differ even more on what is important. On subjects as controversial and emotionally charged as American racial relationships and urban problems, these choices can be especially difficult.

The data chosen here are summary statistics that highlight (1) unresolved racial disparities, (2) continuing urban challenges, and (3) unanswered questions (such as the effects of desegregation on black educational performance) with particular significance for the current policy debate.

Residential Patterns: Segregation by Race and Class

The commission contended in 1968 that changing urban residential patterns (most critically the growing concentration of blacks in the central cities and the departure of whites to the suburbs) would, if unchecked, contribute to the deterioration of every major aspect of urban life. In the decades since the report was issued, many of the underlying demographic trends forecast by the Kerner Commission have continued, although some have abated. The black migration from the rural South largely has ceased, and there is evidence that some African Americans are returning to the South from northern cities.[97] Overall, however, the United States in 1995 has become a significantly more urbanized society than it was in 1968,[98] and many of the nation's larger urban centers, especially in the northeastern and north-central states, have retained the urban characteristics sketched out in the Kerner Report: an older, central-city area surrounded by expanding, more affluent suburbs.[99] As predicted, the populations of America's central cities have become disproportionately black, Hispanic, and Asian, while suburban communities have remained disproportionately white.[100]

The 1989 report of the National Research Council's Committee on the Status of Black Americans (the Jaynes Committee) summarized the data as follows:

> Urban residential segregation of blacks is far greater than that of any other large racial or ethnic group, and there is extensive documentation of the purposeful development and maintenance of involuntary residential exclusion and segregation. . . . Black suburbanization rates remain low, and objective indicators of socioeconomic status that predict suburbanization for Hispanics and Asian-Americans do not do so for blacks. The social changes of the 1960s and 1970s that affected black status had

only slight effects on the residential segregation of blacks in large cities. Blacks are not free to live where they wish, whatever their economic status. Thus, black-white residential separation continues to be a fundamental cleavage in American society.[101]

Within cities, some researchers report that poor residents have become increasingly concentrated in certain black and Hispanic neighborhoods since 1960.[102] Yet there remains considerable dispute on how best to identify these "ghetto" or central-city areas, and whether the reported poverty concentration in these areas represents a general trend or is merely the experience of selected cities. William Julius Wilson has stimulated debate on this issue by theorizing that the urban black poor have found their plight worsened, ironically, by the antidiscrimination legislation of the 1960s, since that legislation allowed middle-class blacks to obtain better-paying jobs and to leave formerly segregated black neighborhoods for higher-income, suburban neighborhoods.[103]

> In the earlier years, the black middle and working classes were confined by restrictive covenants to communities also inhabited by the lower class; their very presence provided stability to inner-city neighborhoods and reinforced and perpetuated mainstream patterns of norms and behavior. . . .
> This is not the situation in the 1980s. Today's ghetto neighborhoods are populated almost exclusively by the most disadvantaged segments of the black urban community, that heterogeneous grouping of families and individuals who are outside the mainstream of the American occupational system.[104]

Reynolds Farley, by contrast, reports no increasing class stratification in the African American community due to outmigration by middle-income blacks. He agrees that more-prosperous blacks fled from inner-city neighborhoods to other, higher-income neighborhoods within cities during the 1970s, but he argues that this pattern is consistent with historical patterns of residential segregation by class among African Americans. Moreover, Farley has found that suburbanization by blacks during the 1970s was not limited to middle- or upper-income blacks. Instead, "blacks in all economic groups crossed city boundaries and moved into the suburban ring in large numbers," so that segregation by social class did not increase among blacks.[105] Farley explains the increased concentration of poverty in central cities largely as a function of increased poverty rates and persistent residential segregation: "If poverty rates increase substantially . . . and the residential segregation of social classes remains about the same, the population in poverty will increase and proportionally more of their neighbors will be poor. The demographic evidence for Chicago is unambiguous about these matters. The change that [William J.] Wilson describes in *The Truly Disadvantaged* is the rise in poverty among blacks, not an increase in residential segregation among social classes."[106]

Douglas Massey has reached a similar conclusion about the interactive effects of race and class segregation in American cities:

> When racial segregation occurs in the class-segregated environment of the typical American city, it concentrates income deprivation within a small number of poor black areas and generates social and economic conditions of intense disadvantage. These conditions are mutually reinforcing and cumulative, leading directly to the creation of underclass communities typified by high rates of family disruption, welfare, dependence, crime, mortality, and educational failure. Segregation creates the structural niche within which a self-perpetuating cycle of minority poverty and deprivation can survive and flourish.[107]

Paul A. Jargowsky and Mary Jo Bane have studied the extent to which "ghetto poverty" (defined to include all census tracts in which over 40 percent of the residents are poor) increased in the nation's standard metropolitan statistical areas (SMSAs) between 1970 and 1980. Jargowsky and Bane conclude that the growth of concentrated poverty in some ghetto areas is a complex process, involving interactions between general increases in the poverty rate and differential outmigration of poor and nonpoor persons from ghetto neighborhoods. "In none [of the four cities studied intensively] was the process a simple matter of the poor moving into ghetto areas or the nonpoor moving out. Nor can the situation in any city be described as one in which people basically stayed put but that changes in the poverty rate caused more areas to be pushed over the 40 percent line. Instead there was a general pattern of dispersion—probably part of a longer historical trend—interacting with changes in the poverty rate and continuing high levels of racial segregation."[108] Jargowsky and Bane note that while the absolute number of poor persons living in ghettos in metropolitan areas increased by 29.5 percent from 1970 to 1980, the increases were not spread uniformly among SMSAs. Instead, two-thirds of the increases came in only five eastern and north-central cities—New York, Chicago, Philadelphia, Newark, and Detroit—while southern and western cities, except Atlanta and Baltimore, saw decreases in their ghetto populations.[109]

Alarming increases, however, came between 1970 and 1990. While only 2.69 million persons were reported living in census tracts with poverty rates above 40 percent in 1970, the numbers increased to 3.83 million in 1980 and rose to 5.49 million in 1990. That high-poverty-concentration population in 1990 was 57 percent African American, 23.8 percent Latino, and 15.5 percent non-Latino white.[110] Viewed differently, by 1990 some 21 percent of the black poor and 16 percent of the Hispanic poor (but only

2 percent of non-Hispanic white poor) had come to live in the high-poverty, inner-city neighborhoods portrayed in the Kerner Commission Report.[111] John Kasarda has recently documented precisely how "the number and percent of poor blacks concentrated in poverty tracts, extreme poverty tracts, distressed tracts, and severely distressed tracts increased" during the 1980s.[112]

Moving contrary to these trends, a significant percentage of middle-class blacks left central cities for suburban areas.[113] For example, while only two percent of Cleveland's African American population lived in the suburbs in 1960, by 1990 one-third did.[114] By 1992 a majority of all blacks in the Washington, D.C., metropolitan area lived not in the District of Columbia but in its suburbs.[115] Indeed, as of 1989 over 27 percent of all black households lived in the suburbs, and 43 percent owned their own homes.[116]

Yet even these moves by African Americans to suburban locations most often have led them not to "white" or racially integrated communities but, instead, to older, near-city suburbs whose residents were predominantly black or that quickly underwent racial transition to majority-black status after racial integration began.[117] Thus, suburban blacks in 1993 typically find themselves, as in yesterday's cities, residentially segregated from the white majority.[118]

Employment and Income Patterns: Persistent Racial Disparities

Economically the years since 1968 have witnessed one decade of relative stagnation (the 1970s after 1973), seven years of vigorous economic expansion (1982–89), and three intervals marred by serious recessions (1974–75, 1980–82, and 1990–92).[119] During this quarter-century, employment prospects and average personal incomes have improved for many African Americans who have entered the black middle class.[120] Yet overall higher rates of poverty have continued to plague African American communities, unemployment rates among blacks have remained nearly twice as high as those among whites, and significant wage differentials have persisted.

Poverty Rates

In 1968 12.8 percent of Americans had incomes that placed them below the official poverty line. That percentage varied substantially by race; only 10.0 percent of whites but 33.5 percent of blacks were classified as officially poor.[121] The Census Bureau also reported that the poverty rate was substantially greater in central cities than in nonmetropolitan areas or the nation's suburbs.[122]

Progress toward the reduction of poverty between 1968 and 1995 has been slight. Poverty rates declined substantially between 1964 and 1973 but stagnated during the 1970s and rose again during the recessions of the early 1980s, failing to decline significantly even during the high-growth years of the middle 1980s.[123] With the onset of the recession of 1990, poverty rates began climbing again; in 1992 the rate was 14.5 percent, higher than at any time since 1996 (except 1983, when the rate briefly hit 15.2 percent).[124] Danziger and Weinberg have summarized recent data on poverty rates as follows:

> Poverty in America in the early 1990s remains high. It is high relative to what it was in the early 1970s; it is high relative to what analysts expected, given the economic recovery of the 1980s . . . ; it is high relative to what [it] is in other countries that have similar standards of living. . . . In addition, the poverty rates for some demographic groups—minorities, elderly widows, children living in mother-only families—are about as high today as was the poverty rate for all Americans in 1949! This lack of progress against poverty over the past two decades—the fact that poverty in 1992 is higher than it was in 1973—represents an American anomaly. For the first time in recent history, a generation of children has a higher poverty rate than the preceding generation, and a generation of adults has experienced only a modest increase in its standard of living.[125]

These overall statistics, furthermore, mask decidedly different experiences for some demographic subgroups. In 1993 only 9.9 percent of non-Hispanic white persons but 33.1 percent of blacks and 30.6 percent of Hispanics were below the official poverty line.[126] Thanks largely to the expansion of Social Security and Supplemental Security Income benefits during the past two decades, the poverty rate among the elderly, both blacks and whites, has fallen dramatically.[127] Poverty among the young, however, has remained very high: 46.1 percent of all black children under the age of eighteen lived in poverty in 1993, as did 13.6 percent of non-Hispanic white children and 40.9 percent of Hispanic children.[128] Moreover, among single-parent families headed by women—a growing percentage of all families during the past twenty-five years[129]—poverty rates remain very high: 38.5 percent in 1992.[130]

Recent observers have suggested that current poverty rates are a product of several convergent factors: the stagnation in overall wage growth during the past fifteen years, a growing income disparity between higher-wage and lower-wage jobs, a substantial decrease in real dollar terms in federal and state financial assistance to low-income families, and changes in demographic composition in American families.[131] One thing is clear: cities have been asked to bear the greatest burden of the new poverty. In central-city areas, poverty rates rose sharply, from 9.8 percent in 1970 to 15.4 percent in 1987, while suburban rates rose only slightly, from 5.3 percent to 6.5 percent during the same period. Nonmetropolitan poverty actually declined from 14.8 percent to 13.8 percent.[132]

Viewed from another angle, central cities, which had housed only 27 percent of the nation's poor in 1959, by 1985 had become home to 43 percent of the poverty population. This growing concentration of urban poverty was especially high for African Americans; the proportion of poor blacks living in central cities climbed from 38 percent in 1959 to 61 percent in 1985.[133]

Employment Rates

Professors Moss and Tilly have recently summarized the contemporary evidence on black male employment:

> Black men's fortunes in the United States labor market have taken a decided turn for the worse. Joblessness among black men has climbed through the 1960s, 1970s, and 1980s. Until the mid-1970s, growing joblessness was offset to some extent by the narrowing of racial wage differentials among men. But since the mid-1970s, the black/white wage gap has begun to widen anew. . . .
>
> Black men's employment/population ratios have been falling since the 1950s, and have dropped relative to those of white men since the mid-1960s. During the 1960s and early 1970s, the relative fall was driven primarily by black men's more rapid decrease in labor force participation; since then a widening gap in unemployment rates has accounted for most of black men's relative decline.[134]

Christopher Jencks also confirms that black male unemployment rates have remained more than twice as high as white rates throughout this period (see Table 1).

One prominent theory ties these lower African American employment rates directly to residential segregation, suggesting that most new job creation has been in predominantly white suburban areas that are relatively inaccessible to urban minorities.[135] James Rosenbaum and Susan Popkin have conducted research that seems to support the view that the "spatial mismatch" between the urban residences of low-income minorities and the developing suburban jobs, rather than individual attitudes or job skills, explains much black urban unemployment.[136] Rosenbaum and Popkin evaluated the labor market experiences of public housing residents in Chicago's inner city, nearly all of them African Americans, who were given subsidized housing in suburban communities as part of a court-ordered remedy in a massive housing segregation case.[137] In comparing the experience of

Table 1. Comparison of Unemployment Rates for Whites and Blacks

| | No Job during Week of the Survey | | | |
	1969	1975	1980	1987
Whites	4.4	10.0	8.8	10.2
Blacks	9.9	23.4	19.4	22.2

| | No Job during Calendar Year | | | |
	1968	1974	1979	1986
Whites	2.3	3.4	3.8	4.6
Blacks	4.7	11.6	10.4	13.6

Source: Christopher Jencks, "Is the American Underclass Growing?," in Jencks and Peterson, *Urban Underclass*, 44, tab. 3.

these new suburbanites with those of tenants who remained behind in private apartments, Rosenbaum and Popkin concluded,

> The Gautreaux participants responded to the improved employment opportunities in middle-class suburbs even though they came from low-income communities and had presumably been exposed to both negative attitudes about work and the work disincentives of the welfare system. . . . Most noteworthy, even after we controlled for training, education, and previous jobs, moving to the suburbs led to greater employment than moving within the city. That is, even respondents who were relatively disadvantaged did better in the suburbs than they did in the city.[138]

This is consistent with data that suggest that median household income varies not only by race but by residential location (see Table 2).

Other data suggest, however, that suburban versus urban residence is not the sole variable explaining racial employment differences. John Kasarda has recently reported that blacks experienced higher overall unemployment rates during the boom years of 1986–88, even when differences in urban/suburban residence are taken into account.[139]

Some have suggested that many central-city black males cannot find employment because they either have failed to develop sufficient skills to be marketable or have adopted cultural characteristics that render them unemployable.[140] Joleen Kirschenman and Kathryn M. Neckerman report the outcome of surveys of Chicago-area employers, who quite candidly confess such assumptions: "Employers view inner-city workers, especially black men, as unstable, uncooperative, dishonest, and uneducated. Race is an important factor in hiring decisions. But it is not race alone: rather it is race in a complex interaction with employers' perceptions of class and

Table 2. Average Median Household Income, 1992

	White	Black	Black/White
Suburbs			
Over 1 million	$41,363	$29,434	.7116
Under 1 million	33,150	20,289	.6120
City			
Over 1 million	$30,314	$17,704	.5840
Under 1 million	28,562	16,720	.5854

Source: Bureau of the Census, *Money Income of Households, Families, and Persons in the United States: 1992.*

space, or inner-city residence."[141] Other researchers report, however, that most inner-city residents are willing to work,[142] and in tight job markets, low-income, central-city blacks can and do find work, experiencing measurable gains in income.[143] If most African Americans in central cities are willing to work, what explains their very high rates of unemployment? Recent studies employing the "audit methodology"—sending "testers" of similar qualifications but different racial backgrounds to apply for the same job openings—have revealed substantial racial discrimination against blacks who seek entry positions in the Chicago and Washington, D.C., areas, especially for higher-level jobs.[144] Such discrimination is consistent with that reported by Kirschenman and Neckerman and with the long history of black exclusion from jobs in urban America.[145]

Income Levels

As noted, African American workers have not only continued to face higher unemployment rates, but those with steady employment have continued to receive salaries that are, on average, notably below those paid to white employees. The most recent data on average weekly earnings among full-time wage and salary workers, reflecting the gains from the economic expansion of the 1980s (although unadjusted for educational attainment and job qualifications) confirm the picture of significant wage differentials by race—and by sex as well (see Table 3).

The Kerner Commission suggested in 1968 that wage disparities between white and black workers could be explained in large part by the limited range of jobs open to most urban African Americans: "The concentration of male Negro employment at the lowest end of the occupational scale is greatly depressing the incomes of United States Negroes in general. In fact, this is the single most important source of poverty among Negroes. It is even more important than unemployment."[146]

Table 3. Median Weekly Earnings (current dollars)

	1983	1985	1990	1993
White				
Males	387	417	497	531
Females	254	282	355	403
Black				
Males	293	304	360	392
Females	231	252	308	349

Source: Bureau of the Census, *Statistical Abstract: 1994*, 429, tab. 665.

Since black educational attainment, measured by years of school completed, has largely overtaken that of whites, the racial wage gap should have closed if earlier wage differentials reflected no more than educational differences.[147] Instead, the wage differential between black and white workers continued to widen throughout the 1980s.[148]

Some respected scholars view the overall evidence on wages more positively. In summarizing black economic gains achieved during the forty years since Gunner Myrdal first issued his famous report in 1940, Smith and Welch wrote in 1986,

> The changes over the last forty years were dramatic. Fully 20 percent of working black men in 1980 were still part of the poor black underclass, a reminder than many blacks remained left out and left behind. But placed in historical perspective, such figures still represent enormous progress toward eradicating black poverty. Political rhetoric on the race issue must eventually balance two compelling truths. America has made considerable strides in reducing black poverty; but by the standards of a just society, black poverty remains at unacceptably high levels.

> However, the real story of the last forty years has been the emergence of the black middle class, whose income gains have been real and substantial. The growth in the size of the black middle class was so spectacular that as a group it outnumbers the black poor. Finally, for the first time in American history, a sizable number of black men are economically better off than white middle-class America. During the last twenty years alone, the odds of a black man penetrating the ranks of the economic elite increased tenfold.[149]

Yet Smith and Welch also acknowledged that, following 1979, black-to-white earnings ratios began to decline once again, and that this decline has continued throughout the 1980s.[150]

These continued racial disparities in income are related to the overall growth of income disparities that has become one of the most prominent features of the economic landscape in the 1980s.[151] However, growing income inequality has had a particularly adverse impact on African Americans, as Harrison and Gorham have reported:

> Between 1979 and 1987, whites experienced nearly a 31 percent increase in the number working under the poverty line, while for blacks, the increase was 44 percent. Whites, as a whole, suffered a decline in the number of high-wage workers [defined as those with incomes three times the poverty rate, or above $35,000] over this period of under 1 percent, while among blacks there were actually 7 percent fewer high-wage workers in 1987 than in 1979. Put another way, by 1987 there were two-and-a-half times as many whites earning high wages as blacks, and blacks were 33 percent more likely to be working below the poverty line than whites. . . . These trends—especially at the low end of the distributive spectrum—constitute a reversal of the pattern of the period 1963–1979, during which the proportion of jobs paying low wages was falling for all racial and demographic groups.[152]

One interesting comparison looks at median household incomes among young, two-parent couples where both spouses are working. Among those groups, black and white median household incomes converged toward parity by 1991. Indeed, in the average black two-parent family, aged twenty-five to thirty-four years, where both parents worked, incomes were 84.1 percent of the median incomes for similar white families.[153] In those families black working women had achieved 90.9 percent of the median weekly income of white women by 1989.[154] It was among black men, even in two-parent families, that incomes trailed substantially, amounting to only 70.4 percent of white male incomes.[155]

The other contributors to this volume will examine these and other data, assessing the extent to which residential segregation, employment discrimination, household composition, or other impersonal economic forces may have contributed to these racially disparate labor market patterns, which have persisted at every educational level, in good economic times and bad, throughout the past three decades.

Educational Changes: Narrowed Gaps in Attainment and Achievement

At the time the Kerner Commission Report was released in 1968, most African Americans, North and South, still attended public schools that were segregated by race. Although public school segregation had been declared unconstitutional in 1954,[156] hundreds of southern school districts had not adopted effective desegregation plans by 1968.[157] At that time, moreover, despite substantial improvement since the 1940s,[158] black pupils still lagged far behind whites on most educational measures: average number of years of school completed,[159] percentage of students obtaining high school and/or college degrees,[160] and average performance on national standardized achievement tests. Results of national testing during the academic year 1969–70, for example, revealed substantial gaps at all levels of schooling. Reading scores from the National Assessment of Educational Progress showed black 13-year olds with average scores of 45.4, versus 62.6 for white 13-year-olds, and black 17-year-olds with scores of 51.7, versus 71.2 for white 17-year-olds.[161]

Shortly before the Kerner Commission Report was issued in 1968, Professor James Coleman and colleagues had published a highly influential study strongly suggesting that a child's academic success was chiefly determined by his or her socioeconomic background, and that schools could do relatively little to affect educational outcomes.[162] The Coleman Report generated intense academic controversy;[163] it also tended to dampen hopes among some educational reformers that black educational performance could be improved significantly, either through desegregation or through other educational programs directed at poor and minority schoolchildren. "The common wisdom of the mid-1970s," Nathan Glazer recalled, was "that schooling did not improve achievement, achievement did not improve economic circumstances":

> Equality of Educational Opportunity had appeared in 1966, at a time of great ferment in programs addressed to poverty, but its impact on the academic community was expanded by the reanalyses of its data in Mosteller and Moynihan (1972). Also, Jencks's Inequality appeared in 1972. While it would be unfair to summarize the message of these major works as "nothing worked," that is certainly how the message came across. . . . The narrower evaluations of specific programs available during the first decade after the War on Poverty confirmed the verdict: nothing that one did in education worked.[164]

Contrary to those apprehensions, however, the black/white gap in academic achievement has narrowed significantly since 1968, as "both levels of schooling and rates of return to schooling [among black schoolchildren] have converged toward those of whites in recent years."[165] During the years 1969 through 1984, for example, the average performance of black children on national achievement tests improved more, at all grade levels, than did achievement among white children. Representative national data on reading performance illustrate the point (see Table 4).

The Jaynes Committee drew three conclusions from these and other relevant data:

Table 4. Correct Scores on National Achievement Tests (percent)

	9 Year Olds		13 Year Olds		17 Year Olds	
	White	Black	White	Black	White	Black
1969–70	66.4	49.7	62.6	45.4	71.2	51.7
1979–80	69.3	59.6	62.6	49.6	70.6	52.2
1983–84	69.1	57.4	64.4	52.4	72.5	60.0
Change, 1969–84	+2.7	+7.7	+1.8	+7.0	+1.3	+8.3

Source: Jaynes and Williams, *Common Destiny*, 349, tab. 7-1.

First, school achievement scores of blacks have increased at a faster rate than those of whites. Second, despite gains by blacks, substantial gaps in school achievement remain. Third, among the youngest age group and birth cohort, there is evidence of a possible decline in black performance relative to that of whites. . . .

. . . The math and verbal SAT performance of blacks has also improved in absolute terms and relative to whites in the past several years. . . . Overall, the SAT results are consistent with other data. There is a fairly clear record of improving achievement test performance by blacks.[166]

During this period of rising black student achievement and school attendance, a large percentage of black children entered desegregated public schools, especially in the southern states. According to Gary Orfield, southern schools had become more racially integrated than schools in any other region by 1986.[167]

One principal question in 1993 was whether the significant gains in academic achievement among black schoolchildren resulted from—or merely coincided with—the increase in desegregated schooling during those years. Many researchers concluded that desegregation substantially improves the educational achievement and the "life chances" of African American children.[168] Others, predictably, have disagreed.[169]

A reliable answer is made less certain by several factors. As Robert Crain and Rita Mahard have stressed, much depends on how desegregation is implemented and on the factors that accompany it:

Desegregation sometimes results in better curricula or facilities; it often results in blacks having better trained or more cognitively skilled teachers; it is frequently accompanied by a major effort to upgrade the quality of education; and it almost always results in socioeconomic desegregation. When desegregation is accompanied by all of these factors, it should not be surprising that there are immediate achievement gains half to two-thirds of the time. This suggests that desegregation is sufficient but not necessary to obtain these gains, since there are other ways to achieve curriculum reform or better teaching if the political will is present.[170]

In many officially desegregated schools, extensive racial isolation still exists at the classroom level.[171] Moreover, since other compensatory educational programs have been implemented in both segregated and desegregated settings since 1968—including preschool programs such as Head Start[172] and compensatory educational services for poor children funded through the Title I/Chapter 1 Program of the Elementary and Secondary Act of 1965[173]—difficult questions are posed about the relative educational impact of desegregation and these other compensatory programs.[174]

Whatever its educational value, school desegregation—a chief focus of black educational reform in 1968—became, by 1993, little more than a theoretical issue for many urban school districts. Supreme Court decisions in the 1970s severely limited the authority of federal courts to order school desegregation across school district lines.[175] Given the high degrees of governmental fragmentation and the severe residential segregation that characterize many northern and western metropolitan areas, the crucial educational issue for central cities in these areas has become how to educate a public school population that is disproportionately poor and overwhelmingly nonwhite.[176] Although numerous experiments with a variety of new educational approaches are under way in 1995,[177] no firm consensus has emerged on how best to address the needs of urban minority schoolchildren. Indeed, there is some mounting evidence that high concentrations of low-income children in a student body, of whatever racial composition, reduces the educational achievement of all children in the school, whether from low-income or middle-income families.[178] Such evidence, if substantiated, would suggest that no educational solution that fails to reduce the concentration of poor children in inner-city schools can be effective in providing meaningful educational opportunities.[179]

In confronting these educational trends, contributors to this volume face a formidable task: to assess the value of school desegregation and of "in-place" educational approaches, and to outline promising educational reforms for urban schoolchildren.

Health Care for Urban African Americans:
Largely Separate and Still Unequal

The Kerner Commission reported in 1968 that "the residents of the racial ghetto are significantly less healthy than most other Americans. They suffer from higher mortality rates, higher incidence of major diseases, and lower availability and utilization of medical services."[180] Even outside "racial ghetto" neighborhoods, the health of African Americans in 1968 was, on average, far poorer than that of whites, whether measured by infant mortality rates,[181] life expectancy rates,[182] or effective access to medical services.[183]

Nearly three decades later, despite generally improving health care for all Americans, racial disparities in health care persist on a wide scale.[184] While infant mortality has dropped sharply in absolute terms, black infants remain over twice as likely as whites to die within the first year of life.[185] Likewise, although both black and white life expectancies have improved significantly during this period, average black life expectancy is still years shorter than that of whites.[186]

During this period, efforts to achieve better access to health care for African Americans have been a mixed tale of success and failure.[187] The dramatic expansion of the Medicaid program has brought medical care to millions of low-income blacks, and the Medicare program similarly has had a positive effect on the elderly black population.[188] Nonetheless, Medicaid eligibility varies widely from state to state, and nearly 22 percent of all African Americans currently have neither private health care insurance nor access to Medicaid coverage.[189] Moreover, many hospitals and nursing homes presently limit the number of Medicaid and Medicare patients they treat, with a predictably adverse impact on black patients.[190] Recent studies also suggest that many doctors provide inferior treatment to African Americans for some medical conditions.[191]

Racial disparities in health care coverage have an important geographical dimension as well, with strongly adverse consequences for the minority poor in urban areas. While 15 percent of the overall nonelderly population lacked health insurance coverage in 1988, 34 percent of poor residents in urban areas are uncovered.[192] Even those minority residents who can pay for health care find that, for several reasons, health care providers are increasingly scarce or overburdened in urban areas. Problems include overcrowding of public hospitals that provide medical care for low-income urban residents,[193] clinic closures,[194] "runaway" hospitals that have eliminated or reduced medical services in central cities,[195] and a shortage of physicians and dentists willing to practice medicine in urban, minority neighborhoods.[196]

The other contributors assess the impact of race, geography, and economic status on the current health care crisis and identify the most promising strategies to provide adequate health care for urban and minority populations during the coming decades.

Housing in 1992: Scarce, Expensive, and Segregated

Chief among housing issues addressed by the Kerner Commission in 1968 was that of housing quality, primarily the prevalence of "substandard housing and general urban blight" in black residential areas.[197] The commission found that large percentages of urban nonwhites lived in "housing units classified as deteriorating, dilapidated, or lacking full plumbing in 1960."[198] The report noted greater overcrowding among nonwhite units,[199] and it offered evidence that a higher proportion of nonwhites paid at least 35 percent of their incomes for housing in many cities.[200]

Remedying these deficiencies, the commission proposed, would require a sharp increase in housing production for low-income citizens, with a target of 6 million new units in the 1968–73 period and a significant increase in antidiscrimination activities in order to assure urban minorities more housing options outside the central cities.[201]

The ensuing decades have seen a broad deterioration in the housing plight of many low-income residents, especially minority residents. Several trends are positive: overall housing quality arguably has improved,[202] and the percentage of poor renters receiving some form of housing assistance has grown substantially. William Apgar reports,

> According to the 1987 American Housing Survey, 4.3 million households resided in public housing or rental housing otherwise subsidized by federal, state or local governments. While growth in the number of subsidized households has slowed since the mid-1980s, the 1987 figure is up nearly 95 percent from the 2.2 million posted in 1974.
>
> Much of the increase in housing assistance in the last 15 years has gone to aid households at the lowest end of the income distribution. Among the very poor (incomes less than 50 percent of the poverty threshold), 919,000 (or 34 percent) received housing assistance in 1987, compared with only 225,000 (or 17 percent) in 1974. Among poor renters with incomes between 50 percent and 100 percent of the poverty threshold, the increase was more modest, rising from 681,000 (or 23 percent) in 1974 to 1,370,000 (or 33 percent) in 1987.[203]

Figures compiled for HUD tell a similar story. In 1989, 13,808,000 of America's 33,767,000 renter households (41 percent) were income-eligible for federally assisted housing. Among those 13.8 million eligible for federal assistance, only 4,070,000 renters (or 29 percent) received some form of federal housing assistance from HUD; 9,738,000 households, or over 70 percent, did not.[204] In addition to rental assistance, federal assistance was provided for approximately 1 million low-income homeowners, bringing the total number of low-income renters and homeowners assisted to 5.4 million in fiscal 1988.[205]

According to Apgar, over 3.2 million households below the poverty line in 1990 received neither federal housing assistance nor income assistance.[206] To compound the low-income housing problem, a shortage has developed in many low-income housing markets. The Center on Budget and Policy Priorities has put the shortage into stark numerical terms:

- In 1970, the number of low rent units was 9.7 million—approximately 2.4 million greater than the number of renter households with incomes of $10,000 a year or less.
- Between 1970 and 1978, there was a slight decline in the number of low cost units and a modest increase in the number of low income renter households. Despite these changes, *there were still 370,000 more low-cost units than low income households in 1978.*
- By 1985, however, there were *3.7 million fewer* low rent units than there were low income renter households—11.6 million renter households, but just 7.9 million low-rent units.[207]

This low-income housing crisis has been brought on by several combined trends. First, there has been a sharp slowdown in the production of new federally assisted housing, especially since the 1980s. The number of newly constructed units added to the federally assisted inventory never exceeded 10 percent of the annual total recommended by the Kerner Commission. In fact, the number of public housing units declined from 41,000 new units made available for occupancy during the average year between 1970 and 1979 to 7,181 public housing units started in 1988.[208] In total, while 412,490 new public housing units were developed in the 1970s, only 191,024, fewer than half that total, became available during the 1980s.[209]

Part of the explanation stems from the federal shift, after 1974, from the funding of public housing construction toward those production programs funded by Section 8 of the Housing and Community Development Act of 1974, which targeted funds to private developers who would build or refurbish existing but dilapidated dwelling units. During the 1980s approximately 383,531 of these Section 8 units were completed.[210]

An even greater part of the explanation for the decline in public housing stems from another major change in federal housing policy. During the Reagan years HUD shifted from reliance on the construction (or rehabilitation) of additional federally subsidized units—the principal housing strategy from 1937 through 1980—to the provision to low-income renters of HUD-financed certificates and vouchers, redeemable as cash rental assistance in the private housing market. As the Congressional Budget Office reported in 1988, "The production-oriented approach in rental programs has been sharply curtailed in recent years in favor of the less costly Section 8 existing-housing and voucher programs. Between 1977 and 1982, commitments through programs for new construction and substantial rehabilitation ranged annually from 53 percent to 73 percent of the total; since then, however, they have made up one-third or less of all additional rental commitments."[211] As Michael Stegman has reported, "Consistent with the [Reagan/Bush] administration's favoring of rental assistance over new construction programs, the number of subsidized housing starts per year dropped by more than 88 percent, from 175,000 [in 1979] to less than 21,000 [in 1989]."[212] Indeed, by 1989, 26 percent of all HUD-assisted units, or 1,060,000 households, were receiving not subsidized housing units but HUD certificates or vouchers.[213] Critics have charged that this strategy does not assist low-income renters in "tight" housing markets characterized by acute shortages where the fixed-limit certificates or vouchers cannot bring renters to the rental levels set by the private housing market.[214]

A second factor in the low-income housing crisis has been the disappearance of approximately 3.3 million older, low-income rental units from the private market.[215] Adding to the shortage has been a third factor, the widespread gentrification, or upward "recycling" of former lower- and moderate-income units, with resulting displacement of low-income tenants.[216] Finally, a fourth factor has been the accelerating loss of thousands of low-income units built with federal subsidies in the 1970s, some of which in the early 1990s began to be withdrawn by their owners from low-income use.[217]

Simultaneously, as low-income housing units have become more scarce, incomes among low-income and minority persons have stagnated or declined, and public welfare payments have lost approximately 40 percent of their 1977 value in real-dollar terms.[218] Thus, by the late-1980s low-income families, poorer in real-dollar terms than similar families had been in 1968, found themselves scrambling for shelter in markets characterized by a sharply diminished housing supply and sharply increased housing costs (see Table 5).

Among the consequences have been the emergence of a homeless population numbering in the hundreds of thousands in major cities,[219] unlike anything experienced in the United States since the depths of the Great Depression.[220] Homelessness, however, is only the most visible sign of the new housing crisis; the growth in the number of poor families, especially African Americans and Hispanics, who pay unsustainable fractions of their incomes for rent has been far more pervasive.[221] Overcrowding has also increased in many cities, as families struggle to avoid the streets,[222] and "shelter children," the denizens of huge, warehouselike facilities or dead-end welfare hotels, are now a common feature of many cities.[223]

The impact of these housing trends has been especially severe among the black and Hispanic urban poor. As one study noted, "In [1985], . . . half of all poor Hispanic and black households spent more than 57 percent of their income for housing. . . . Some 37 percent of poor black households— or 1.1 million households—paid at least 70 percent of their income for

Table 5. Housing Availability for Low-Income Renters

Year	Number of low-rent (under $250/mo.) units (in millions)	Number of low-income renters (in millions)
1970	6.8	6.4
1978	6.0	7.6
1983	5.9	9.7
1989	5.5	9.6

Sources: Lazere et al., *A Place to Call Home*, 5, fig. 1. See generally Schwartz et al., "The Need for a New National Housing Policy," 3–64 (summarizing the combined deleterious effects of national housing trends in the 1980s on lower-income residents).

housing costs."[224] Moreover, while the absolute number of households receiving federal housing assistance grew between 1979 and 1987,[225] as of 1987 more than 70 percent of all renters below the poverty line received no federal housing assistance at all, either through access to public housing or through federal housing subsidies.[226] During the Reagan years, furthermore, federal appropriations for low-income housing suffered the greatest cuts endured by any major federal program—a decline of over 80 percent.[227]

Beyond the problems of housing availability and affordability that have plagued urban African Americans, continued racial discrimination has remained a serious impediment even for urban African Americans who could afford to pay higher housing costs. George Galster reported in 1977,

> Despite 1968 federal civil rights law, housing discrimination clearly persisted in 1977, and was likely responsible for a significant portion of the extent and pattern of racial segregation observed in metropolitan areas where it was present. If, for example, housing discrimination were eliminated in SMSAs where it was present in both housing tenure markets, the results lead one to predict that . . . white exposure to blacks would increase by 45 percent, black exposure to whites would increase by 38 percent, and relative black centralization would decrease by 26 percent in these areas.[228]

Subsequent analyses in the 1980s and early 1990s continue to show very high levels of residential segregation.[229] The available evidence indicates that a substantial percentage of this segregation is not the product of private choice or income disparities between whites and blacks but, rather, of illegal discrimination against African American buyers or renters,[230] not only by sellers and landlords, but also by mortgage lenders and insurers.[231]

Discrimination has taken forms other than resistance to integration in the private sale and rental market. In many urban areas the public housing stock often is comprised of large, aging, racially segregated "housing projects." Public housing programs have long served African Americans in greater percentages than their proportion of the income-eligible population; currently blacks comprise 53 percent of public housing tenants, although they are only 28 percent of the income-eligible renters.[232] HUD and local public housing authorities have funded or operated these housing programs on a racially segregated basis in many areas of the country,[233] and many of these projects exemplify urban decay: dangerous, crime-ridden, squalid, and physically defaced.[234]

Yet despite such impressions, understandably seared into the public mind by crime-ridden, high-rise public housing projects such as Pruitt-Igoe in St. Louis or Robert Taylor Homes in Chicago, not all public housing projects share these horrific characteristics. Only one-third of the nation's 1,360,000 public housing units are in buildings of 50 units or more. Fully 18 percent are in single-family buildings; 30 percent are in buildings holding 2 to 9 families; and an additional 20 percent are in buildings comprised of 10 to 49 units.[235] Indeed, 73 percent of all those public housing tenants who had moved within one year prior to a major national survey undertaken in 1989 stated that public housing gave them a better home (and according to 44 percent, a better neighborhood) than the ones in which they previously had resided.[236]

Critics have nonetheless questioned sharply both the original rationale and current viability of the older, large projects and have urged the construction of far smaller and more spatially dispersed replacement units.[237] Yet when additional construction funds have been available, local housing authorities often encounter fierce resistance to plans for siting new housing projects outside traditional low-income and minority areas.[238] Thus tenants of urban public and assisted housing often find themselves tightly bottled within low-income, high-crime areas, unable to leave because of the absence of assisted housing options in the broader metropolitan areas in which they reside.

Our contributors, after assessing the current housing burdens faced by urban black families and urban dwellers generally, recommend housing strategies for the coming decades. Are massive new construction programs feasible, given the enormous federal deficit? If so, what kinds of housing should be funded, and where should it be built? If new construction programs are infeasible, what other kinds of housing assistance should be afforded, and who will pay for it? What should be the future role of community-based housing development corporations and community development corporations, which have assumed such an important role during the past decade of federal neglect?[239] If mobility is to be encouraged, is it feasible to expand the Gautreaux model to a national scale,[240] and if so, what kinds of governmental support should be provided to suburban apartment-seekers? Should housing assistance be tied to a coherent urban economic development policy? If so, what should it be?

Welfare in 1995: Still a Morass

The Kerner Commission undertook a broad examination of public welfare issues in 1968, explaining that "the burden of welfare—and the burden of the increases [in welfare recipient case rolls]—will fall principally on our central cities,"[241] and that "our present system of public assistance contributes materially to the tensions and social disorganization that have led to civil disorders. The failures of the system alienate the taxpayers who support it, the social workers who administer it, and the poor who depend on it."[242]

The commission identified several critical deficiencies in the welfare system of 1968: first, it excluded many who needed benefits; second, it provided "assistance well below the minimum necessary for a decent level of existence"; and third, it incorporated "restrictions that encourage continued dependency on welfare and undermine self-respect."[243]

The report observed that, under America's piecemeal approach to income assistance, only about a third of the 21.7 million nonelderly poor in 1966 received some form of major public welfare assistance; most of those recipients were children and mothers covered by the Aid to Families with Dependent Children (AFDC) program.[244] State AFDC programs in 1968 typically excluded two-parent families, regardless of whether the minimum incomes of those families were below the poverty line. Moreover, the total federal aid provided under the AFDC program was only $2 billion a year, or about $36 monthly for each recipient. AFDC payments were subject to wide state-by-state variations, from an average of $9.30 per month in Mississippi to $62.55 in New York.[245] Finally, the commission pointed to a number of harsh regulations adopted by most state programs—including a requirement of a year's residence prior to welfare eligibility, a deduction in welfare payments for any amounts earned by welfare recipients, and a precondition that at least one parent be absent from the home (the so-called absent father rule)—all of which tended to demean welfare recipients in their own, and the public's, eyes.[246]

To address these deficiencies the commission proposed a variety of responses, including (1) a commitment by the federal government to assume greater financial responsibility for AFDC, in order to provide "more adequate levels of assistance on the basis of uniform national standards";[247] (2) the extension of welfare payments to a far broader range of potential recipients—at a minimum, two-parent families with children;[248] and

(3) the development of job training, day care centers, and other programs to enhance the self-reliance of welfare recipients.[249]

The subsequent history of welfare policy is complex, since the nation has not adopted the Kerner Commission's recommendation to nationalize AFDC payments, and thus wide variations in state benefit levels and a welter of overlapping programs remain the rule. Nonetheless, some overall trends are discernible. Between the mid-1960s and early 1970s there was a substantial increase in the nation's AFDC population; one commentator, noting an expansion from 3.1 million recipients in 1960 to 10.8 million by 1974, described the increase as an "explosion."[250] By the mid-1980s this trend had prompted some to contend that AFDC was contributing to the perpetuation of a new welfare class, especially among the minority poor, who were being seriously deterred from entering the labor market by the receipt of welfare assistance.[251]

Nonetheless, the number of persons receiving AFDC payments remained virtually constant after 1975; indeed, the number actually declined slightly between 1975 through 1989, before rising again during the recession of 1990–92.[252] Furthermore, the expansion in AFDC caseloads was not accompanied by a similar increase in benefits:

> Since 1960, spending on cash assistance programs has gone through several distinct phases. . . . Between 1960 and 1973 federal, state, and local spending on AFDC rose more than 400 percent, as average benefit and participation in the program soared. Real spending surged again in 1975 and 1976 in response to the severe 1974–75 recession. But in the 1970s eligibility conditions were tightened and nominal benefit levels failed to keep pace with inflation; in the eight years after 1976 real outlays declined 15 percent. . . . At the end of the 1980s, participation in the program—and its cost—once again began to rise. Pushed up by the effects of the 1990–91 recession, AFDC caseloads and spending levels reached record highs in the early 1990s. Still, spending was only modestly higher than in the mid-1970s, when 2 million fewer people were collecting benefits.[253]

Thus while total AFDC payments, measured in absolute dollar terms, have increased substantially,[254] the per capita increases have been far less significant.[255] When adjusted for inflation, the maximum AFDC benefit for a family of three with no other income actually declined 42 percent between 1970 and 1991, and the average AFDC family of three currently receives an income no more than 42 percent of the poverty line.[256]

Of course, since the mid-1960s a number of important noncash programs have been created or expanded to help low-income recipients,[257] including the Food Stamp program,[258] the Women, Infants, and Children Supplemental Nutrition Program (WIC),[259] the National School Lunch

Program,[260] and the Medicaid program discussed earlier. There is debate over the net impact of these newer programs on the poor and on whether the traditional calculations of the poverty line, which exclude noncash benefits,[261] provide an accurate indicator of the actual plight of poor persons who receive such benefits.[262]

The most significant recent federal response to the "welfare problem" has been the Family Support Act of 1988.[263] This legislation was designed to encourage more AFDC recipients to obtain education or job training and eventually to become economically self-sufficient by entering the job market.[264] The actual impact of the act, however, has been far less revolutionary. The Job Opportunities and Basic Skills (JOBS) program that was central to the welfare-to-work approach of the Family Support Act is expected to move fewer than 1.3 percent of all AFDC families off public assistance and into full-time work by the end of 1995, embarrassingly short of the 20 percent goal originally envisioned by its sponsors.[265]

The Family Support Act has since been branded as inadequate by both Democrats and Republicans. The Clinton administration announced a new legislative reform proposal, The Work and Responsibility Act of 1994, on June 21, 1994; the legislation was formally introduced into Congress a week later.[266] Clinton's approach demands greater personal responsibility by AFDC recipients and requires that most AFDC parents find a private market job or accept a governmentally subsidized job after twenty-four months of AFDC payments.[267] Although substantially more strict than the Family Support Act, the Democratic proposal is far less draconian than its Republican counterpart, the Personal Responsibility Act, which was offered during the early days of the 104th Congress in 1995.[268] The Personal Responsibility Act would (1) end AFDC as an entitlement of all income-eligible families; (2) turn federal AFDC and related programs into a federal block grant given to each state, the amount to be frozen at fiscal year 1994 spending levels, with minor upward adjustments for population increases; (3) allow states almost unfettered control over reshaping or abandoning traditional public welfare programs; and (4) forbid even those states that would prefer to do so to grant federal AFDC payments to unmarried teenaged mothers under the age of eighteen, to their children, to children born while their mother is receiving cash benefits from the state, or to legal, resident aliens.[269]

While the legislative future of these alternative welfare proposals is uncertain at present, the public mood seems perceptibly to have shifted against the more generous approaches of the early 1970s. Indeed, under the Family Support Act of 1988, numerous states had obtained formal waivers from federal requirements to experiment with new ways of designing and delivering public benefits.[270] Most of these experimental state programs in the early 1990s were characterized by stricter requirements.[271]

Some critics of these developments have contended that public emphasis on "welfare" and anger over AFDC payments are misplaced, since most poor and minority families are *not* on AFDC but instead are struggling in minimum-wage or part-time jobs that simply do not pay enough to lift them from poverty.[272] President Clinton's legislative success in enlarging the Earned Income Tax Credit program during 1993 [273] plainly proceeds on the recognition of these realities, since it was designed affirmatively to reward low-income householders already in the labor market by providing them with substantial tax credits that, with food stamps, would lift a family of four with a full-time, minimum-wage worker to the poverty line.[274] As public policy appears poised to tilt against public welfare benefits, one conclusion is clear: none of the three major recommendations of the Kerner Commission has yet been adopted. Millions of poor Americans remain ineligible for public assistance. There are no minimum national standards for AFDC recipients, and no state provides benefits that lift recipients above the poverty line. Most states withdraw Medicaid coverage and AFDC payments to AFDC recipients who enter the workforce, perpetuating the financial disincentives to self-reliance that the Kerner Commission identified in 1968.

It falls to our contributors to assess the successes and failures of current public benefits programs, to chart their impact on the urban poor, especially on African Americans, and to evaluate the proposals for the future.

Black Political Power: Major Political Gains, Formidable Practical Challenges

In no area has black progress during the past three decades been more dramatic than in the attainment of political power in the nation's cities. Aided in the South by passage of the Voting Rights Act of 1965 [275] and in the North and West by the changing demographic composition of the urban electorate forecast by the Kerner Commission, African Americans have captured mayors' offices, school superintendents' offices, and other local power bases in dozens of major cities, including New York, Los Angeles, Chicago, Detroit, Philadelphia, Washington, Newark, Baltimore, Atlanta, Birmingham, New Orleans, and Denver.[276]

This greater political control has frequently led to significant tangible gains for black constituents, including an end to formal discrimination by city agencies, substantial minority hiring in city departments and agencies, city construction and purchasing contracts with minority business enterprises, and meaningful appointments to city administrative boards and agencies.[277] African American municipal leaders have thus been able to achieve benefits "much in the same way earlier ethnic groups, such as the Irish, took advantage of the benefits of office." [278] In some cities, employment opportunities have improved dramatically; by 1987, for example, 43 percent of all employees of the city of Cleveland were black, as were 47 percent of all employees of the greater Cleveland Regional Transit Authority, 73 percent of all employees of the Cuyahoga County Housing Authority, and 52 percent of the more than 10,000 people employed by the Cleveland Board of Education.[279] Such numbers were inconceivable twenty years earlier when, according to Norman Krumholz, "none of these agencies even had an affirmative action plan."[280]

Yet black political power, by and large, has done significantly less to bring major economic or social gains to the minority poor in these cities. Professors Gary Orfield and Carole Ashkinaze recently have offered a comprehensive look at Atlanta, Georgia, where two decades of exuberant metropolitan job growth and black political leadership might have been expected to lead to dramatic improvement for Atlanta's minority poor. Instead, Orfield and Ashkinaze report, the continued geographic segregation of Atlanta—a black central city surrounded by white suburbs and by separate and unequal black suburbs—has led instead to the development and expansion of a "dual market," in which most of the good jobs, the good schools, and the better neighborhoods continue to be reserved for suburban whites, with Atlanta's inner-city, predominantly black population left farther and farther behind.[281] Other political scientists who had studied Atlanta tell a similar story. Clarence Stone has concluded, "Benefit from the city's 'supply-side' development strategy has accrued to the black middle class, but there is not much evidence the lower class has gained. Atlanta is second only to Newark, New Jersey, among American cities in its poverty rate."[282]

Orfield and Ashkinaze attribute these failures in part to inaction by Atlanta's black political leadership, describing "a kind of celebratory politics, where black middle-class leaders took the evidence of their own success as proof of progress and many low-income blacks accepted that [success] as proof of the possibilities within the system."[283] Yet Clarence Stone observes that, very often, "democratic politics mirrors resource inequalities." While Atlanta's black middle class has been able to contribute substantial resources to Atlanta's governing coalition, lower-income groups have lacked both the organized voting strength and the economic resources necessary to prompt government to act meaningfully on their behalf.[284]

Moreover, even if city officials in Atlanta and elsewhere possessed the political determination to do so, they would lack power to overcome the root problems that afflict the urban poor:

Local government is not nearly so powerful as state government, federal government, or the private sector in affecting broad social, economic, and educational problems. Local government controls limited resources and struggles every year to maintain existing staff and services. Cutting city budgets means cutting into the black middle class since city government tends to hire much larger proportions of blacks than other large employers. Much of the discretionary money that used to fund new programs came from federal grants that fell sharply in the 1980s. Some critical programs, such as job training, were turned over to state government. Many of the programs cannot be solved, at any rate, within the boundaries of a single local government. . . .

The institutions and policies that most directly affect the mobility of young blacks are almost all outside the control of city leaders. City governments have no control of the suburbs, where most of the jobs are being created and almost all of the new housing is developed. The best opportunities for pre-college education are suburban. Educational funding, welfare policy, higher education, job training, and many other critical issues are decided largely at the state and federal levels, where suburban power is growing and city influence is shrinking as population disperses.[285]

Our contributors enter this critical debate, asking whether American municipalities, many of which are now under African American or Latino leadership, can find sufficient statutory authority, financial resources, and political will to make the changes needed by the urban minority poor.

American Cities: Still Central?

While African Americans were at the demographic center of the Kerner Commission's analysis, its geographical focus was on America's cities. The migration of blacks to cities since the 1920s, and their continued disproportionate presence there, has assured that the economic, social, and political destiny of many African Americans will, for the foreseeable future, be intertwined with the future of those cities. There are significant indications that the prospects for America's cities have grown dimmer during the past three decades.[286]

David Rusk, former mayor of Albuquerque, New Mexico, recently argued that the vitality of cities is directly correlated with their degree of economic and racial desegregation:

The "urban problem" at heart is the product of segregation—racial, ethnic, economic—not the result of inadequate overall resources and opportunities. . . . The crucial determinants are not overall growth or percentage of minorities but measures of disparity. . . . In [the booming] metro areas county governments tend to be the dominant local government, providing many public services and often controlling crucial development decisions. Many such areas also have very large, even county-wide, school systems. . . . The underlying dynamic is the same: the metro areas have avoided segregation by race and economic class better than others.[287]

Rusk offers statistics comparing the performance of 346 "growing cities," 71 "stagnant cities," and 101 "declining cities."[288] On average, Rusk notes, growing cities that are willing to incorporate their outlying areas grew in total physical area by 272 percent between 1960 and 1990, with an average 1990 size of 63 square miles, while declining cities (which had, on average, been 50 percent larger than growing cities in 1960) grew by only 16 percent, within an average size of 30 square miles in 1990.[289] Indexes of segregation in housing and public education were significantly lower in Rusk's growing cities, with fewer local school districts and municipalities in each metropolitan area, while metropolitan areas in declining cities were far more politically balkanized.[290]

The implication drawn by Rusk is that residential segregation declines in those metropolitan areas that are willing to share their governmental services widely. Rusk concludes that "to save the cities an effective urban policy must attempt more than to prop up decaying inner cities; it must address city and suburb together. It must be broad and visionary: directed toward integrating city and suburban economies (including tax bases), infrastructure, and educational systems as strategies for integrating communities."[291]

Other contributors address this proposed remedy and others that might affect the future economic viability of America's urban areas—areas plagued by declining industrial bases, mounting expenditures for social services and other municipal costs, and shrinking tax bases as better-paid workers depart for the suburbs.

Conclusion

There is some evidence that the conditions in which a substantial percentage of blacks live and work have improved in the last thirty years. Nonetheless, structural changes in the national and urban economies have, in the eyes of many observers, contributed to the apparent emergence, during the past three decades, of an "underclass"[292] concentrated in America's cities—a very poor, disproportionately African American population living in drug-plagued, inner-city areas bereft of adequate job opportunities and hampered by inadequate public services. The most striking facts about this poverty are its intense concentration within the nation's major cities and its overwhelmingly racial cast. Douglas Massey and Mitchell Eggers have developed the term "hypersegregation"[293] to underline the multidimensional urban trap in which these urban poor find themselves. Massey and Denton have recently explained: "In a racially segregated city, any increase in black poverty is confined to a small number of black neighborhoods; and the greater the segregation, the smaller the number of neighborhoods absorbing the shock and the more severe the resulting concentration of poverty. If neighborhoods are also segregated by class, not only is the additional poverty restricted to black neighborhoods, it is confined primarily to *poor* black neighborhoods." [294] Massey and Denton's work illustrates how race- and class-isolation extend their collective misery beyond individual households. During virtually any economic downturn such concentration quickly multiplies individual economic misfortune, producing a communitywide economic and social depression. [295]

Michael Katz adds that the injury to these inner-city neighborhoods is not merely economic: "Many institutions have deserted inner cities; the ones that remain are failing; along with city government, their legitimacy has collapsed. . . . Institutional withdrawal and collapse not only rob inner cities of the services they need, they knock out the props that sustain a viable public life and the possibility of community. They destroy the basis of civil society." [296]

Are Massey, Denton, and others correct in forecasting that economic policies designed to overcome African American poverty, if pursued alone, are doomed to failure unless they simultaneously overcome America's all-but-universal patterns of residential segregation, especially in its large, metropolitan areas? [297] This perennial question, at the heart of the Kerner Commission's 1968 report, was reopened in the late 1980s through the influential writings of William Julius Wilson and others. [298] It is surely the ultimate question that must be addressed by the contributors to this volume and, in the end, by the readers and the nation as well.

Notes

1. See, for example, Martin Luther King Jr., "Next Stop: The North," in *Testament of Hope: The Essential Writings of Martin Luther King, Jr.*, ed. James M. Washington (San Francisco: Harper and Row, 1986) 189–90, 192 ("The Negro freedom movement will be altering its course in the period to come. Conditions in the North will come into focus and sharpened conflict will unfold.").

Bayard Rustin, frequent strategist for the civil rights movement, explained the necessity for this redirection northward: "While school integration proceeds at a snail's pace in the South, the number of Northern schools with an excessive proportion of minority youth proliferates. And behind this is the continuing growth of racial slums, spreading over our central cities and trapping Negro youth in a milieu which, whatever its legal definition, sows an unimaginable demoralization" ("From Protest to Politics: The Future of the Civil Rights Movement," *Commentary* 39 [1965]: 25, 26). See generally Kenneth B. Clark, *Dark Ghetto: Dilemmas of Social Power* (New York: Harper and Row, 1965).

2. Michael Harrington, *The Other America: Poverty in the United States* (New York: Macmillan, 1962).

3. See Michael B. Katz, *In the Shadow of the Poorhouse: A Social History of Welfare in America* (New York: Basic Books, 1986), 251–73; James T. Patterson, *America's Struggle against Poverty, 1900–1985*, enl. ed. (New York: Basic Books, 1986), 99–114. Patterson noted, "During his campaign for the presidency, [Kennedy] had been shaken by the misery he witnessed first hand in West Virginia. In August of that year, speaking on the twenty-fifth anniversary of the passage of Social Security, he praised the law for undertaking a 'war on poverty.' His inaugural address five months later referred three times to poverty. 'If the free society cannot help the many who are poor,' he said, 'it cannot save the few who are rich'" (*America's Struggle against Poverty*, 127).

4. Harrington, *The Other America*, 151.

5. Katz, *In the Shadow of the Poorhouse*, 255–56.

6. Patterson, *America's Struggle against Poverty*, 101.

7. Professors Piven and Cloward have argued that President Kennedy's need to secure black political support was instrumental in his determination to develop a national urban policy:

> The Democratic presidential candidate in 1960 was keenly alert to [black-white tensions in urban areas]. Uncertain that he could resurrect Southern allegiance, Kennedy made a vigorous appeal to the black vote in the industrial states by campaigning on strong pledges to deal with civil rights and poverty. . . . The ghettos in a number of strategic Northern cities delivered overwhelming Democratic majorities, swinging several critical states to assure his election. . . . A way had to be found to prod the local Democratic party machinery to cultivate the allegiance of urban black voters by extending a greater share of municipal services to them, and to do this without alienating urban white voters. It was this political imperative that eventually led the Kennedy and Johnson Administrations to intervene in the cities. (Frances F. Piven and Richard A. Cloward, *Regulating the Poor: The Functions of Public Welfare* [New York: Pantheon, 1971], 255–56)

But see Patterson, *America's Struggle against Poverty*, 134–36 (arguing that Piven and Cloward misread the political motivations of the Kennedy administration); see also Hugo Heclo, "The Political Foundations of Antipoverty Politics," in *Fighting Poverty: What Works and What Doesn't*, ed. Sheldon H. Danziger and Daniel H. Weinberg (Cambridge, Mass.: Harvard University Press, 1986), 318–25 (offering an alternative account of the genesis of the War on Poverty); Nicholas Lemann, *The Promised Land: The Great Black Migration and How It Changed America* (New York: Knopf, 1991), 111–35 (offering yet a different account of the Kennedy administration's motivations).

8. Daniel P. Moynihan, "The Negro Family: The Case for National Action," in

The Moynihan Report and the Politics of Controversy, ed. Lee Rainwater and William L. Yancey (Cambridge, Mass.: MIT Press, 1967), 75.

9. Allen J. Matusow, "Origins of the War on Poverty," in *The Unraveling of America: A History of Liberalism in the 1960s* (New York: Harper and Row, 1984), 97–127; Patterson, *America's Struggle against Poverty*, 127–29, 138–41; James L. Sundquist, "Origins of the War on Poverty," in *On Fighting Poverty: Perspectives from Experience*, ed. James L. Sundquist (New York: Basic Books, 1969), 8–12; Adam Yarmolinsky, "The Beginnings of OEO," in Sundquist, *On Fighting Poverty*, 34–49. Several different groups within the White House were involved in this planning, including the President's Committee on Juvenile Delinquency and the chairman of the Council of Economic Advisors, Walter Heller. See, Lemann, *The Promised Land*, 124–55.

10. Johnson's War on Poverty was first announced in his state of the union address in January 1964 (Matusow, "Origins of the War on Poverty," 123–24). See generally Robert H. Haveman, ed., *A Decade of Federal Antipoverty Programs: Achievements, Failures, and Lessons* (New York: Academic Press, 1977) (describing the creation, aims, and accomplishments of the War on Poverty); Robert D. Plotnick and Felicity Skidmore, *Progress against Poverty: A Review of the 1964–1974 Decade* (New York: Academic Press, 1975) (providing the first detailed analysis of the achievements of the Great Society programs in reducing income poverty). For a far darker account of the forces that coalesced to create the War on Poverty, see Thomas F. Jackson, "The State, the Movement, and the Urban Poor: The War on Poverty and Political Mobilization in the 1960s," in *The "Underclass" Debate: Views from History*, ed. Michael B. Katz (Princeton: Princeton University Press, 1993), 403 (contending that the War on Poverty was not an economically transformative program and that its chief beneficiaries proved to be not the poor but the middle class, including social welfare professionals and recipients of governmental subsidies under Medicare and similar Great Society programs).

11. (1) The Equal Opportunity Act of 1964, Pub. L. No. 88-452, 78 Stat. 508 (codified as amended in scattered titles of the United States Code); (2) the Housing and Urban Development Act of 1965, Pub. L. No. 89-117, 79 Stat. 451 (codified as amended in scattered sections of 12 U.S.C. and 42 U.S.C.); (3) the "Model Cities" program, Pub. L. No. 89-754, 80 Stat. 1255 (codified as amended in scattered titles of the United States Code); and (4) the Elementary and Secondary Education Act of 1965, Pub. L. No. 89-10, 70 Stat. 27 (codified as amended in 20 U.S.C. § 236 et seq.).

12. Pub. L. No. 89-97, 79 Stat. 286, and the subsequent expansion of Social Security benefits. See Patterson, *America's Struggle against Poverty*, 157–70; Gary Burtless, "Public Spending on the Poor: Historical Trends and Economic Limits," in *Confronting Poverty: Prescriptions for Change*, ed. Sheldon H. Danziger, Gary D. Sandefur, and Daniel H. Weinberg (Cambridge, Mass.: Harvard University Press, 1994), 51, 58–63; Michael Katz, "Reframing the 'Underclass' Debate," in *"Underclass" Debate*, 440, 465 (observing that while "the War on Poverty's legacy emerges as much more impressive" than often acknowledged either by scholars or the general public, nonetheless, "it was programs outside the War on Poverty that did the most to reduce poverty and promote the health of disadvantaged Americans").

13. The Douglas Commission, chaired by Senator Paul Douglas of Illinois, drew its membership from the nation's leading political and academic ranks. President Johnson charged it with developing ideas and instruments for a revolutionary improvement in the quality of the American city (U.S. House Committee on Banking and Currency, *National Housing Goals: Hearings before the Subcommittee on Housing of the House Committee on Banking and Currency*, 91st Cong., 1st sess., 1968, H. Doc. 234).

14. The Kaiser Committee, headed by industrialist Edgar F. Kaiser, was appointed on June 2, 1967, and included a wide spectrum of business and labor leaders. It made interim suggestions to the Johnson administration during congressional consideration of what became the Housing and Urban Development Act of 1968, and it submitted a final report to the president on December 11, 1968. (*Report of the President's Committee on Urban Housing: A Decent Home* [Washington, D.C.: U.S. Government Printing Office, 1969], i).

15. *Report of the National Advisory Commission on Civil Disorders* (New York: Bantam Books, 1968) (hereafter cited as *Kerner Report*).

16. See generally James H. Johnson Jr., Cloyzelle K. Jones, Walter C. Farrell Jr., and Melvin L. Oliver, "The Los Angeles Rebellion: A Retrospective View," *Economic Development Quarterly* 6 (1992): 356.

17. See generally Gary D. Sandefur, "Blacks, Hispanics, American Indians, and Poverty—and What Worked," in *Quiet Riots: Race and Poverty in the United States: The Kerner Report Twenty Years Later*, ed. Fred R. Harris and Roger W. Wilkins (New York: Pantheon, 1988), 46 (surveying the economic, educational, and social status of whites, blacks, Hispanics, and Native Americans in light of the findings and recommendations of the *Kerner Report*); Marta Tienda and Zai Liang, "Poverty and Immigration in Policy Perspective," in Danziger et al., *Confronting Poverty*; Sheldon H. Danziger, Gary D. Sandefur, and Daniel H. Weinberg, eds., *Separate Societies: Poverty and Inequality in U.S. Cities* (Cambridge, Mass.: Harvard University Press, 1994), 331 (surveying the impact of the vast flow of immigration of the past two decades on America's poverty population and its social welfare programs); Marta Tienda and Leif Jensen, "Poverty and Minorities: A Quarter-Century Profile of Color and Socioeconomic Disadvantage," in *Divided Opportunities: Minorities, Poverty, and Social Policy*, ed. Gary D. Sandefur and Marta Tienda (New York: Plenum Press, 1988), 23 (examining changes in average income, employment status, and poverty among blacks, Mexican Americans, Puerto Ricans, other Native Americans, and non-Hispanic whites between 1959 and 1984); Nancy A. Denton and Douglas S. Massey, "Patterns of Neighborhood Transition in a Multiethnic World: U.S. Metropolitan Areas, 1970–1980," *Demography* 28 (1991): 41 (analyzing changes in the ethnic composition of urban neighborhoods inhabited by whites, blacks, Hispanics, and Asians).

18. Important recent studies that have reexamined the principal issues addressed by the Kerner Commission include Harris and Wilkins, *Quiet Riots*; Reynolds Farley and Walter R. Allen, *The Color Line and the Quality of Life in America* (New York: Russell Sage, 1987); Laurence E. Lynn Jr. and Michael G. H. McGeary, eds., *Inner-City Poverty in the United States* (Washington, D.C.: National Academy Press, 1990); Gerald David Jaynes and Robin M. Williams Jr., eds., *A*

Common Destiny: Blacks and American Society (Washington, D.C.: National Academy Press, 1989); William Julius Wilson, *The Truly Disadvantaged: The Inner City, the Underclass, and Public Policy* (Chicago: University of Chicago Press, 1987); Sandefur and Tienda, *Divided Opportunities*; Christopher Jencks and Paul E. Peterson, eds., *The Urban Underclass* (Washington, D.C.: Brookings Institution, 1991); George C. Galster and Edward W. Hill, eds., *The Metropolis in Black and White: Place, Power, and Polarization* (New Brunswick, N.J.: Rutgers Center for Urban Policy Research, 1992); William W. Goldsmith and Edward J. Blakely, eds., *Separate Societies: Poverty and Inequality in U.S. Cities* (Philadelphia: Temple University Press, 1992); Katz, *"Underclass" Debate*; Douglas S. Massey and Nancy A. Denton, *American Apartheid: Segregation and the Making of the Underclass* (Cambridge, Mass.: Harvard University Press, 1993); Anthony Downs, *New Visions for Metropolitan America* (Washington, D.C.: Brookings Institution, 1994); Danziger et al., *Confronting Poverty*; James A. Kushner, "Apartheid in America: An Historical and Legal Analysis of Contemporary Racial Residential Segregation in the United States," *Howard Law Journal* 22 (1979): 547; William L. Taylor, "*Brown*, Equal Protection, and the Isolation of the Poor," *Yale Law Journal* 95 (1986): 1700.

19. The Kerner Commission traced the inception of the disturbances to 1963, when urban disorders broke out in Birmingham, Savannah, Chicago, Philadelphia, and Cambridge, Maryland (*Kerner Report*, 35). The number and magnitude of racial disturbances increased in each succeeding year until 1967, when major rioting broke out in Newark, New Jersey; Detroit, Michigan; and 162 other American cities (ibid., 35–108).

20. See generally Southern Poverty Law Center, *Free at Last: A History of the Civil Rights Movement and Those Who Died in the Struggle* (1989). In 1963 and 1964 alone at least seventy black churches were burned or bombed. See John P. Davis, ed., *The American Negro Reference Book* (Englewood Cliffs, N.J.: Prentice-Hall, 1966), 451; Daniel S. Davis, *Struggle for Freedom: The History of Black Americans* (New York: Harcourt Brace Jovanovich, 1972), 224. See generally Taylor Branch, *Parting the Waters: America in the King Years, 1954–63* (New York: Simon and Schuster, 1988); Howell Raines, *My Soul Is Rested* (New York: Putnam, 1977); Juan Williams, *Eyes on the Prize: America's Civil Rights Years, 1954–1965* (New York: Viking Press, 1987).

The riots of the 1960s were far from the first interracial disturbances to rack American cities. Prior to the Civil War there were clashes in northern cities precipitated by various factors, including white resentment of African American workers and white desire to maintain economic and political dominance. In the decades following emancipation, outbreaks of interracial violence erupted episodically, many characterized by widespread white violence against black lives and property. See, for example, Leon F. Litwack, *North of Slavery: The Negro in the Free States, 1790–1860* (Chicago: University of Chicago Press, 1961), 100–102, 165–68. See generally Eric Foner, *Reconstruction: America's Unfinished Revolution, 1863–1877* (New York: Harper and Row, 1988), 425–44 (recounting Ku Klux Klan violence against African Americans during Reconstruction); John Hope Franklin and Alfred A. Moss Jr., *From Slavery to Freedom: A History of Negro Americans*

(New York: Knopf, 1967), 336 (Wilmington riot of 1898), 431–36 (riots by whites in the early twentieth century), 467 (lynchings and riots took 136 black lives in 1917–18, with 40 murdered by whites in East St. Louis), 472–75 (riots against blacks in 1919), 578 (Detroit riot of 1943); Gunner Myrdal, *An American Dilemma: The Negro Problem and Modern Democracy* (New York: Harper, 1944), 566–69 (summarizing the history of riots against African Americans); Arthur I. Waskow, *From Race Riot to Sit-In, 1919 and the 1960s: A Study in the Connections between Conflict and Violence* (Garden City, N.Y.: Doubleday, 1966) (examining riots of 1919).

21. Executive Order No. 11,365, 3 C.F.R. 674 (1966–70), reprinted in *Kerner Report*, 534.

22. Ibid.

23. *Kerner Report*, 1.

24. See generally A. Leon Higginbotham, *In the Matter of Color: Race and the American Legal Process: The Colonial Period* (New York: Oxford University Press, 1978) (assessing the legal status and treatment of blacks in colonial America); Winthrop D. Jordan, *White over Black: American Attitudes toward the Negro, 1550–1812* (Chapel Hill: University of North Carolina Press, 1968), 44–135 (discussing enslavement of blacks in America prior to 1700).

25. Don E. Fehrenbacher, *The Dred Scott Case: Its Significance in American Law and Politics* (New York: Oxford University Press, 1978), 26–27.

26. See generally Litwack, *North of Slavery*, vii–xi (describing how free blacks were often residentially segregated, denied access to schools, restricted to menial employments, denied the vote, and required to post bond for good behavior when entering many states).

27. See generally Foner, *Reconstruction*, 512–612; John Hope Franklin, *Reconstruction after the Civil War* (Chicago: University of Chicago Press, 1961), 152–227; C. Vann Woodward, *Reunion and Reaction: The Compromise of 1877 and the End of Reconstruction* (Boston: Little, Brown, 1951); W. E. B. Du Bois, *Black Reconstruction in America* (New York: Russell and Russell, 1962), 670–710. See also *Plessy v. Ferguson*, 163 U.S. 537 (1896) (establishing what became the "separate but equal" doctrine, condoning racial segregation); *Civil Rights Cases*, 109 U.S. 3 (1883) (declaring unconstitutional the Civil Rights Act of 1875, which protected blacks' right of access to public accommodations).

28. See generally C. Vann Woodward, *The Strange Career of Jim Crow*, 3d ed. (New York: Oxford University Press, 1974). See also Joel Williamson, *The Crucible of Race: Black-White Relations in the American South since Emancipation* (New York: Oxford University Press, 1984); Charles S. Mangum Jr., *The Legal Status of the Negro* (Chapel Hill: University of North Carolina Press, 1940).

29. *Kerner Report*, 206–35.

30. See generally Richard Kluger, *Simple Justice: The History of* Brown v. Board of Education *and Black America's Struggle for Equality* (New York: Knopf, 1976); Genna Rae McNeil, *Groundwork: Charles Hamilton Houston and the Struggle for Civil Rights* (Philadelphia: University of Pennsylvania Press, 1983); Mark V. Tushnet, *Making Civil Rights Law: Thurgood Marshall and the Supreme Court, 1936–1961*

(New York: Oxford University Press, 1994); Mark V. Tushnet, *The NAACP's Legal Strategy against Segregated Education, 1925–1950* (Chapel Hill: University of North Carolina Press, 1987).

31. 347 U.S. 483 (1954) (*Brown* I); see also *Brown v. Board of Education*, 349 U.S. 294 (1955) (*Brown* II) (outlining the remedial obligations of school boards and the responsibilities of lower federal courts).

32. See generally Branch, *Parting the Waters*; Clayborne Carson, *In Struggle: SNCC and the Black Awakening of the 1960s* (Cambridge, Mass.: Harvard University Press, 1981); Aldon D. Morris, *The Origins of the Civil Rights Movement: Black Communities Organizing for Change* (New York: Free Press, 1984).

33. Civil Rights Act of 1964, Pub. L. No. 88-352, 78 Stat. 241 (codified at 28 U.S.C. § 1447; 42 U.S.C. §§ 1971, 1975a–d, 2000a–h[6]).

34. Voting Rights Act of 1965, Pub. L. No. 89-110, 79 Stat. 437 (codified at 42 U.S.C. §§ 1973, 1973a–p, and 1973aa–dd6).

35. As Erol Ricketts has observed, the civil rights gains of the 1960s led many scholars, for a time, to discount the continuing significance of racial discrimination in American life (Ricketts, "The Underclass: Causes and Responses," in Galster and Hill, *Metropolis in Black and White*, 224–25). See generally William Julius Wilson, *The Declining Significance of Race: Blacks and Changing American Institutions*, 2d ed. (Chicago: University of Chicago Press, 1980).

36. *Kerner Report*, 234–36.

37. For a review of the earlier African American migrations from the rural South to the urban North and Midwest, see Jacqueline Jones, "Southern Diaspora: Origins of the Northern 'Underclass,'" in Katz, *"Underclass" Debate*, 27; Joe William Trotter Jr., "Blacks in the Urban North: The 'Underclass Question' in Historical Perspective," in ibid., 55.

38. *Kerner Report*, 12–13. In chap. 6 of the report, titled "The Formation of the Racial Ghettos," the commission set forth evidence of the changing urban demography since 1900 (ibid., 236–47).

39. Ibid., 2.

40. Ibid., 251–65 (chap. 7, "Unemployment, Family Structure, and Social Disorganization").

41. Ibid., 392.

42. Ibid., 255.

43. Ibid., 260.

44. See ibid., 266–69 (chap. 8, "Condition of Life in the Racial Ghetto I. 'Crime and Insecurity'").

45. See ibid., 269–73 ("Health and Sanitation Conditions").

46. Ibid.

47. Ibid., 274–77.

48. Ibid., 427 (citing James S. Coleman, Ernest Q. Campbell, Carol J. Hobson, James McPartland, Alexander Mood, Frederic D. Weinfeld, and Robert L. York, *Equality of Educational Opportunity* [Washington, D.C.: U.S. Government Printing Office, 1966], 23). Similar forecasts had been made by the United States Commission on Civil Rights in an important 1967 report. See "Racial Isolation and the

Outcomes of Education," in *Racial Isolation in the Public Schools* (Washington, D.C.: U.S. Government Printing Office, 1967), 73–114.

49. *Kerner Report*, 467–68. "Nationally, over 4 million of the nearly 6 million occupied substandard units in 1966 were occupied by whites" (ibid., 468).

50. Ibid., 473.

51. Ibid.

52. Ibid., 393.

53. Ibid., 399–400.

54. Ibid., 399.

55. Ibid., 400.

56. Chap. 15 was titled "The News Media and the Disorders" (ibid., 362–89).

57. Ibid., 363. The commission later elaborated on this criticism:

The news media have failed to analyze and report adequately on racial problems in the United States and, as a related matter, to meet the Negro's legitimate expectations in journalism. By and large, news organizations have failed to communicate to both their black and white audiences a sense of the problems America faces and the sources of potential solutions. The media report and write from the standpoint of a white man's world. The ills of the ghetto, the difficulties of life there, the Negro's burning sense of grievance, are seldom conveyed. Slights and indignities are part of the Negro's daily life, and many of them come from what he now calls "the white press"—a press that repeatedly, if unconsciously, reflects the biases, the paternalism, the indifference of white America. This may be understandable, but it is not excusable in an institution that has the mission to inform and educate the whole of our society. (Ibid., 366)

58. Ibid., 395.

59. Ibid.

60. Ibid., 396.

61. Ibid.

62. Ibid., 404.

63. Ibid., 397.

64. Ibid., 398.

65. Ibid., 401.

66. Ibid., 407.

67. Ibid., 24, 413–24.

68. Ibid., 25–26.

69. The commission's proposed approach relied on (1) voluntary desegregation, to be induced by offering federal financial and technical aid to all local school districts that would agree to undertake desegregation projects, and (2) strict enforcement of Title VI of the Civil Rights Act of 1964 against districts engaged in illegal discrimination (ibid., 438–44).

70. Ibid., 26, 445–55.

71. Ibid., 28. The commission reported that it had "canvassed the various alternatives, and ha[d] come to the firm opinion that there is no substitute for enactment of a federal fair housing law. The key to breaking down housing discrimina-

tion is universal and uniform coverage, and such coverage is obtainable only through federal legislation" (ibid., 481).

72. Ibid., 481.

73. Ibid., 474–82. This policy was echoed by the Kaiser Committee, which also called for the development of 6 million new, federally subsidized housing units by 1973 (*Report of the President's Committee on Urban Housing*, 216).

74. Tom Wicker, "President Steps Aside in Unity Bid—Says 'House' is Divided," *New York Times*, April 1, 1968; see also President Lyndon Johnson, "Address of March 31, 1968," in ibid.

75. Gary Orfield, "Separate Societies: Have the Kerner Warnings Come True?," in Harris and Wilkins, *Quiet Riots*, 101. For other accounts of policy currents during this period, see Henry J. Aaron, *Politics and the Professors: The Great Society in Perspective* (Washington, D.C.: Brookings Institution, 1978); Sar A. Levitan, *The Great Society's Poor Law: A New Approach to Poverty* (Baltimore: Johns Hopkins University Press, 1969); Daniel P. Moynihan, *Maximum Feasible Misunderstanding: Community Action in the War against Poverty* (New York: Free Press, 1969); Charles Murray, *Losing Ground: American Social Policy, 1950–1980* (New York: Basic Books, 1984); Piven and Cloward, *Regulating the Poor*, 248–348; Alexander Polikoff, *Housing the Poor: The Case for Heroism* (Cambridge, Mass.: Ballinger, 1978), 29–93.

76. Pub. L. No. 90-284, 82 Stat. 73 (codified as amended at 42 U.S.C. §§ 3601–19 [1992]).

77. See U.S. Senate Committee on Banking and Currency, 90th Cong., 1st sess., 1968, S. Rept. 721, 3–4. Richard H. Sander recounts the legislative history: "In 1965, President Johnson sent . . . [a comprehensive federal bill banning housing discrimination] to Congress, but after passing the House in 1966, the bill died in the Senate. Senate liberals introduced a still stronger bill in 1967; after a long filibuster battle and some concessions that won moderate votes, the Senate passed the bill in March 1968. The House approved the Senate version in the tense days following the assassination of Martin Luther King, Jr." (Richard H. Sander, "Comment: Individual Rights and Demographic Realities: The Problem of Fair Housing," *Northwestern University Law Review* 82 [1988]: 874, 880). See generally Jean Eberhart Dubofsky, "Fair Housing: A Legislative History and a Perspective," *Washburn Law Journal* 8 (1969): 149.

78. 42 U.S.C. § 3601 (1988).

79. 42 U.S.C. § 3604–13. The act provided an exemption for "any single-family house sold or rented by an owner," without benefit of brokerage services or advertisements, § 3603(b)(1), and for small, owner-occupied rooming houses, § 3603(b)(2). This exemption affected approximately 20 percent of the private housing market (Congressional Quarterly Inc., *Congress and the Nation, 1965–1968* [1970], 380, 386).

80. 42 U.S.C. § 3608(d).

81. 42 U.S.C. §§ 3610(a), 3613(a)(2).

82. 42 U.S.C. §§ 3608–9.

83. 42 U.S.C. § 3613.

84. Pub. L. No. 90-448, 82 Stat. 476 (codified as amended in various sections of

12 U.S.C., 40 U.S.C., and 42 U.S.C.). The House report on the bill began by under-scoring the relationship between poverty, urban unrest, and the proposed legislation: "A basic factor in the magnitude and urgency of our present housing problems has been the failure to include all parts of our population in the general rise in incomes and wealth. In fact this growth of prosperity has accentuated and may have even widened the gap between the poverty of the approximately 6 million families who still live in substandard housing and the affluent majority. Because of this contrast and the unrest it has created, the task of our housing and urban development programs is more critical than ever" (House Committee on Banking and Currency, *Housing and Urban Development Act of 1968*, 90th Cong., 2d sess., 1968, H. Rept. 1585, 1–2). This legislation borrowed heavily from the developing recommendations of the Kaiser Commission. See *Report of the President's Committee on Urban Housing*, 216–22.

85. H. Rept. 1585, 6–11.

86. Ibid., 21–25.

87. Ibid., 26.

88. 24 C.F.R. § 200.710; 24 C.F.R. § 880.112 (recodified at § 880.20).

89. Pub. L. No. 93-383, 88 Stat. 633 (codified as amended at 42 U.S.C. §§ 5301–20 [1983]).

90. 42 U.S.C. § 5301(c)(1) (1988 and Supp. II 1990).

91. 42 U.S.C. § 5301(c)(6).

92. See 42 U.S.C. § 5304(a)(1) and (c).

93. Ibid., § 5304(c).

94. Ibid., § 5304(a)(2–6)(1974). See Herbert Franklin, David Falk, and Arthur J. Levin, "Inclusionary Programs and the Larger Public Interest," in *After Mount Laurel: The New Suburban Zoning*, ed. Jerome G. Rose and Robert E. Rothman (New Brunswick, N.J.: Rutgers Center for Urban Policy Research, 1977), 297–300.

The HCDA formally required each locality to give "maximum feasible priority" to activities that would benefit low- or moderate-income persons (42 U.S.C. § 5304[b][2]). The requirement was widely ignored. Indeed, after 1981, localities no longer were required even to file their revised Housing Assistance Plans when applying for additional block grant funds (Pub. L. No. 97-35, 95 Stat. 384 [1981]). During the Reagan years the needs of lower-income persons were thus given even less consideration by many local communities.

95. The Demonstration Cities and Metropolitan Development Act of 1966 was designed as a national competition in which cities were invited to submit their most innovative proposals to provide low- and moderate-income housing as well as educational and social services to the urban poor. The winning submissions would receive federal grants to implement their proposals. As originally conceived, moreover, the act was more than an urban aid bill; it contained strong antidiscrimination and desegregation components, including provisions requiring the appointment of a federal coordinator for each funded city to ensure compliance with federal civil rights laws and to facilitate cooperation with federal antipoverty agencies. These provisions were stripped from the bill prior to passage because of stiff opposition from Republicans and southern Democrats.

Although the Model Cities program was meant to encourage cooperation between federal and municipal officials to achieve the ends of the legislation, once the strong antidiscrimination provisions were eliminated and once it became clear that most grant requirements would be generously interpreted, the program became pork barrel politics par excellence. Municipalities were granted virtually free reign in allocating the substantial amounts of federal largess provided by the program. See generally Phyllis A. Wallace, "A Decade of Policy Developments in Equal Opportunities in Employment and Housing," in Haveman, *Decade of Federal Antipoverty Programs*, 351–52 (emphasizing that the federally assisted housing programs of the 1960s were "extremely costly," benefited "only a small percentage of eligible low- and moderate-income families," and were plagued by "widely publicized scandals"); Margaret Weir, Ann Shola Orloff, and Theda Skocpol, *The Politics of Social Policy in the United States* (Princeton: Princeton University Press, 1988), 337–38.

96. John O. Calmore, "Fair Housing vs. Fair Housing: The Problems with Providing Increased Housing Opportunities through Spatial Deconcentration," *Clearinghouse Review* 14 (1980): 7, 8. A useful general chronological summary of antipoverty programs proposed and/or adopted by every presidential administration from that of John Kennedy in 1960 through that of George Bush in 1992 appears in James Jennings, *Understanding the Nature of Poverty in Urban America* (Westport, Conn.: Praeger, 1994), 25–50. Michael McGeary has recently analyzed all major federal programs of recent decades in terms of their impact on residential segregation and inner-city concentration of low-income persons (Michael G. H. McGeary, "Ghetto Poverty and Federal Policies and Programs," in Lynn and McGeary, *Inner-City Poverty in the United States*, 223, 224–40).

97. U.S. Department of Commerce, Bureau of the Census, *Statistical Abstract of the United States: 1981* (Washington, D.C.: U.S. Government Printing Office, 1981), 13, tab. 12 (showing net outmigration of blacks from the Northeast and Midwest, and net inmigration to the South and West, between 1970 and 1980).

98. In 1960 63 percent of the population of the United States, some 112,885,000 persons, were classified as residents of standard metropolitan statistical areas, or SMSAs. By 1992 the percentage classified as residents of the redefined "consolidated metropolitan statistical areas," or CMSAs, had grown to 79.7 percent, or 203,172,000 persons (U.S. Department of Commerce, Bureau of the Census, *Statistical Abstract of the United States: 1994* [Washington, D.C.: U.S. Government Printing Office, 1994], 37, no. 39).

99. John D. Kasarda, "Inner-City Concentrated Poverty and Neighborhood Distress: 1970 to 1990," *Housing Policy Debate* 4 (1993): 253; John C. Weicher, "How Poverty Neighborhoods Are Changing," in National Research Council, *Inner-City Poverty in the United States*, 68, 71–89; David Rusk, *Cities without Suburbs* (Washington, D.C.: Woodrow Wilson Center Press, 1993), 5–9.

100. Only 33.5 percent of white metropolitan residents in 1992 (or 54,115,000 residents) were classified as inhabitants of central cities, while 66.5 percent (or 107,280,000) were classified as "not central city" (U.S. Department of Commerce, Bureau of the Census, *Poverty in the United States: 1992, Current Population Reports*, series P-60, no. 185 [Washington, D.C: U.S. Government Printing Office, 1992], 61). Among black metropolitan residents the pattern is almost precisely the re-

verse: 66.7 percent (or 18,054,000) are central-city residents, while only 33.3 percent (or 9,022,000) reside outside central-city areas (ibid., 63).

101. Jaynes and Williams, *Common Destiny*, 49–50.

102. See, for example, Kasarda, "Inner-City Concentrated Poverty," 262–65 ("in 1990 non-Hispanic blacks still accounted for more than two-thirds of persons residing in distressed tracts in the 100 cities and 57 percent of those residing in extreme poverty tracts").

103. This is one of several interrelated hypotheses advanced by Wilson to account for the growth of poverty in urban minority communities. For a thoughtful introduction to the broader social scientific discussion stimulated by Wilson's hypotheses, see Ronald B. Mincy, "The Underclass: Concept, Controversy, and Evidence," in Danziger et al., *Confronting Poverty*, 109.

104. Wilson, *Truly Disadvantaged*, 8–9.

105. Reynolds Farley, "Residential Segregation of Social and Economic Groups among Blacks," in Jencks and Peterson, *Urban Underclass*, 282–93.

106. Ibid., 295.

107. Douglas S. Massey, "American Apartheid: Segregation and the Making of the Underclass," *American Journal of Sociology* 96 (1990): 329, 350. For a more comprehensive account of these phenomena, see Massey and Denton, *American Apartheid*.

108. Paul A. Jargowsky and Mary Jo Bane, "Ghetto Poverty in the United States, 1970–1980," in Jencks and Peterson, *Urban Underclass*, 239, 268–69.

109. Ibid., 255–56. John Kasarda has reported that, while the concentration of the urban poor in high-poverty neighborhoods continued to increase during the 1980s, some surprising regional variations occurred. Several major cities in the Northeast, for example, experienced notable declines in concentrated poverty, while large midwestern cities saw significant further deterioration (Kasarda, "Inner-City Concentrated Poverty," 281–82).

110. Kasarda, "Inner-City Concentrated Poverty," 263.

111. Jargowsky and Bane, "Ghetto Poverty in the United States," 252. William Julius Wilson and his colleagues have found "several significant trends" in their examination of changes in the nation's ten largest cities between 1970 and 1980: "a marked increase, in both relative and absolute terms, of urban poverty despite a net loss of population; an even sharper rise in the population living in poverty and extreme-poverty areas; an increasing concentration over time of the poor in the poorest sections of these cities; and widely divergent patterns of concentration between whites and minorities" (William Julius Wilson, Robert Aponte, Joleen Kirschenman, and Loïc J. D. Wacquant, "The Ghetto Underclass and the Changing Structure of Urban Poverty," in Harris and Wilkins, *Quiet Riots*, 123, 131).

112. Kasarda, "Inner-City Concentrated Poverty," 283. He added that "there was not only a greater growth in the number of black poor in the cities during the 1980s than the 1970s, but also a growth in the percentage of blacks who were poor during the 1980s, in contrast to the 1970s" (ibid., 266).

George Galster and Ronald Mincy have added to the complexity of the analysis through recent studies that suggest that some factors—especially the metropolitan-wide growth of employment and changes in the location of manufacturing enterprises—had similar effects on poverty rates in both African American and non-Hispanic white neighborhoods between 1980 and 1990, suggesting that "studies that focus exclusively on the idiosyncracies [sic] of so-called African-American ghetto poverty are unlikely to yield the kinds of insights policy makers need to mobilize more broadly based political support in the fight against universally increasing poverty in all sorts of neighborhoods" (George C. Galster and Ronald B. Mincy, "Understanding the Changing Fortunes of Metropolitan Neighborhoods: 1980 to 1990," *Housing Policy Debate* 4 [1993]: 303, 345).

113. See Larry Long and Diana DeAre, "The Suburbanization of Blacks," *American Demographics* 3 (1981): 16.

114. Norman Krumholz, "The Kerner Commission Twenty Years Later," in Galster and Hill, *Metropolis in Black and White*, 156. Nonetheless, an overwhelming percentage of all black suburbanites in Cleveland live in just one community, East Cleveland, which suggests that locational choices for blacks who have managed to move out of Cleveland's ghetto continue to be restricted. From 1960 to 1970 East Cleveland's population went from 2 to 51 percent black (ibid).

115. Joel Garreau, "Candidates Take Note: It's a Mall World after All," *Washington Post*, weekly ed., August 10–16, 1992.

116. According to the Census Bureau, 57.9 percent of all African Americans lived in central cities in 1992, while 27.5 percent lived in suburbs and 14.5 percent lived outside metropolitan areas (U.S. Department of Commerce, Bureau of the Census, *Money Income of Households, Families, and Persons in the United States: 1992*, series P-60, no. 184 [Washington, D.C.: U.S. Government Printing Office, 1993], 3). About 39 percent of all Hispanic households lived in suburbs in 1989 (ibid., 4).

117. See generally Phillip L. Clay, "The Process of Black Suburbanization," *Urban Affairs Quarterly* 14 (1979): 405; John R. Logan and Linda Brewster Stearns, "Suburban Racial Segregation as a Nonecological Process," *Social Forces* 60 (1981): 61; Douglas S. Massey and Nancy A. Denton, "Suburbanization and Segregation in U.S. Metropolitan Areas," *American Journal of Sociology* 94 (1988): 592.

118. In the early 1980s, Lake reported that

the suburbanization of blacks is being accompanied by the increasing territorial differentiation of suburbia along racial lines—and not by integration. Comparison of the experiences of black and white suburban homebuyers at the end of the 1970s provides strong evidence of a suburban housing market explicitly and implicitly organized along racial lines. . . . The mechanisms in place to enforce and reproduce a structural pattern based on race mean that at the individual level, suburbanization for blacks connotes constrained residential choice, a restricted and less efficient housing search process, and limited opportunities for housing equity and wealth accumulation. (Robert W. Lake, *The New Suburbanites: Race and Housing in the Suburbs* [New Brunswick, N.J.: Rutgers Center for Urban Policy Research, 1981], 239)

In a more recent study, Orfield and Ashkinaze have reached similar conclusions about black suburbanization in Atlanta during the 1980s: "In Atlanta, suburbanization for most [middle-income] blacks does not mean crossing the color line; it means the color line is moving out to incorporate parts of suburbia. Though they are still outside white society, blacks are now themselves divided by the city-suburban boundary" (Gary Orfield and Carole Ashkinaze, *The Closing Door: Conservative Policy and Black Opportunity* [Chicago: University of Chicago Press, 1991], 25–26; see also 101–2, 217–18, 223–24).

119. See Sheldon Danziger and Daniel Weinberg, "The Historical Record: Trends in Family Income, Inequality, and Poverty," in Danziger et al., *Confronting Poverty*, 21, 28.

120. In 1991, for example, 20.9 percent of all black households in the suburbs earned incomes of $50,000 or more, while 4.8 percent of all suburban blacks earned incomes in excess of $70,000 (U.S. Department of Commerce, Bureau of the Census, *Money Income of Households, Families, and Persons in the United States: 1991*, series P-60, no. 180 [Washington, D.C.: U.S. Government Printing Office, 1991], 9–10).

121. U.S. Department of Commerce, Bureau of the Census, *Poverty in the United States, 1959 to 1968*, series P-60, no. 68 (Washington, D.C.: U.S. Government Printing Office, 1969), 2–3.

122. In 1970 15.4 percent of the nation's central-city households had incomes below the poverty line, compared with 5.3 percent of the suburban households (Paul E. Peterson, "The Urban Underclass and the Poverty Paradox," in Jencks and Peterson, *Urban Underclass*, 3, 7, tab. 1).

123. Danziger and Weinberg, "Historical Record," 18–19, 25–38, tab. 2.2 (reporting the percentage of those in poverty every year from 1959 through 1992, calculated according to six alternative measures).

124. Ibid., 26–27, tab. 2.2.

125. Ibid., 18.

126. Center on Budget and Policy Priorities, *Despite Economic Recovery, Poverty and Income Trends Are Disappointing in 1993* (Washington, D.C.: Center on Budget and Policy Priorities, 1994), 5, tab. 1; see also Danziger and Weinberg, "Historical Record," 37, tab. 2.4 (reporting similar percentages for 1990).

127. In 1964 28.5 percent of all elderly persons lived below the poverty line (Sheldon H. Danziger, Robert H. Haveman, and Robert D. Plotnick, "Antipoverty Policy: Effects on the Poor and the Nonpoor," in Danziger and Weinberg, *Fighting Poverty*, 50, 556, tab. 3.2). By 1980 the percentage had fallen to 15.7 percent, and by 1993 to 12.2 percent (Danziger and Weinberg, "Historical Record," 37, tab. 2.4; Center on Budget and Policy Priorities, *Despite Economic Recovery*, 5, tab. 1).

128. Center on Budget and Policy Priorities, *Despite Economic Recovery*, 5, tab. 1.

129. Mary Jo Bane, "Household Composition and Poverty," in Danziger and Weinberg, *Fighting Poverty*, 213–14. According to Bane, "Family structure has changed dramatically over the past few decades, away from traditional married-couple families: in 1959, 85.8 percent of the population lived in male-headed families; in 1983, 74.4 percent did. . . . Household composition has changed much more dramatically among blacks over the two decades, with the percentage living in female-headed families rising from 19.0 percent in 1959 to 36.7 percent in 1983." See also Irwin Garfinkel and Sara McLanahan, "Single-Mother Families, Economic Insecurity, and Government Policy," in Danziger et al., *Confronting*

Poverty, 205, 210–11; Robert D. Mare and Christopher Winship, "Socioeconomic Change and the Decline of Marriage for Blacks and Whites," in Jencks and Peterson, *Urban Underclass*, 175; see generally Kathryn M. Neckerman, "The Emergence of 'Underclass' Family Patterns, 1900–1940," in Katz, *"Underclass" Debate*, 194; Mark J. Stern, "Poverty and Family Composition since 1940," in Katz, *"Underclass" Debate*, 220.

130. U.S. Department of Commerce, Bureau of the Census, *Poverty in the United States: 1992*, series P-60, no. 185 (Washington, D.C.: U.S. Government Printing Office, 1993), 14. According to Garfinkel and McLanahan, "Children who live in mother-only families are exposed to high levels of economic and social insecurity. About half of these children live in families with incomes below the poverty level, and nearly three-quarters live in families with incomes less than 1.75 times the poverty line. . . . Low income is only the most extreme form of economic insecurity. . . . Researchers have found that on average the postdivorce income of a single mother is about 60 percent of her predivorce income" (Garfinkel and McLanahan, "Single-Mother Families," 206).

131. See, for example, Danziger and Weinberg, "Historical Record," 50; Isaac Shapiro and Robert Greenstein, *Selective Prosperity: Increasing Income Disparities since 1977* (Washington, D.C.: Center on Budget and Policy Priorities, 1991), 11–15. The most significant change in family composition has been the growth in the percentage of female-headed, single-parent families, which experience a disproportionate share of income poverty and other economic difficulties. See, for example, Garfinkel and McLanahan, "Single-Mother Families," 205.

132. Peterson, "Urban Underclass and the Poverty Paradox," 7, tab. 1.

133. John D. Kasarda, "The Severely Distressed in Economically Transforming Cities," in *Drugs, Crime, and Social Isolation: Barriers to Urban Opportunity*, ed. Adele V. Harrell and George E. Peterson (Washington, D.C.: Urban Institute Press, 1992), 46.

134. Philip Moss and Chris Tilly, *Why Black Men Are Doing Worse in the Labor Market: A Review of Supply-Side and Demand-Side Explanations* (New York: Social Science Research Council, 1991), 3–4. See also John Bound and Richard B. Freeman, "What Went Wrong?: The Erosion of the Relative Earnings and Employment of Young Black Men in the 1980s" (unpublished paper, National Bureau of Economic Research, Cambridge, Mass., November 1990); Jaynes and Williams, *Common Destiny*, 302–6; Farley and Allen, *Color Line*, 250; Charles A. Hirschman, "Minorities in the Labor Market: Cyclical Patterns and Secular Trends in Joblessness," in Sandefur and Tienda, *Divided Opportunities*, 63–85.

135. See, for example, James H. Johnson Jr. and Melvin L. Oliver, "Economic Restructuring and Black Male Joblessness in U.S. Metropolitan Areas," *Urban Geography* 12 (1991): 542; John F. Kain, "The Spatial Mismatch Hypothesis: Three Decades Later," *Housing Policy Debate* 3 (1992): 371; John D. Kasarda, "Urban Industrial Transition and the Underclass," *Annals of the American Academy of Political and Social Science* 501 (1989): 26.

136. James E. Rosenbaum and Susan J. Popkin, "Employment and Earnings of Low-Income Blacks Who Move to Middle-Class Suburbs," in Jencks and Peterson, *Urban Underclass*, 342.

137. Ibid. See *Hills v. Gautreaux*, 425 U.S. 284, 305–6 (1976); see generally Florence Wagman Roisman and Philip Tegeler, "Improving and Expanding Housing Opportunities for Poor People of Color: Recent Developments in Federal and State Courts," *Clearinghouse Review* 24 (1990): 312, 329–31 (discussing *Gautreaux*).

138. Rosenbaum and Popkin, "Employment and Earnings of Low-Income Blacks," 353–54.

139. John D. Kasarda, "Structural Factors Affecting the Location and Timing of Urban Underclass Growth," *Urban Geography* 11 (1990): 234, 256–57.

140. See generally Lawrence M. Mead, *The New Politics of Poverty: The Nonworking Poor in America* (New York: Basic Books, 1992), 113 (asserting that while "much of the gap in earnings between blacks and whites may still be attributable to discrimination . . . it is less likely that bias can explain why so many lower-income blacks fail to work at all"). Mead suggests that negative work-related attitudes among many unskilled black men are a more plausible explanation for their high rates of unemployment: "Evidently, the worldview of blacks makes them uniquely prone to the attitudes contrary to work, and thus vulnerable to poverty and dependency" (ibid., 148).

141. Joleen Kirschenman and Kathryn M. Neckerman, "'We'd Love to Hire Them, But . . .': The Meaning of Race for Employers," in Jencks and Peterson, *Urban Underclass*, 203, 204.

142. In one recent study of the attachment of inner-city residents of Chicago to the labor market, researchers found that "willingness to work was the norm in Chicago's inner city" and that "at most, 6 percent of adults in Chicago's inner-city neighborhoods would meet our criteria for being shiftless" by being idle, able-bodied, and unwilling to work (Marta Tienda and Haya Stier, "Joblessness and Shiftlessness: Labor Force Activity in Chicago's Inner City," in Jencks and Peterson, *Urban Underclass*, 135, 151–54).

143. Richard B. Freeman, "Employment and Earnings of Disadvantaged Young Men in a Labor Shortage Economy," in Jencks and Peterson, *Urban Underclass*, 103, 119–20 (finding that labor market shortages significantly improve both the employment prospects and the wages of disadvantaged young men, "particularly blacks"); Paul Osterman, "Gains from Growth?: The Impact of Full Employment on Poverty in Boston," in Jencks and Peterson, *Urban Underclass*, 122, 131 (noting that while evidence exists of a "significant minority" with no attachment to the labor force, in general, lower-income "blacks have benefited a good deal from full employment in Boston [and] . . . given opportunity, they evidently responded in 'acceptable' ways").

144. See generally Michael Fix and Raymond J. Struyk, eds., *Clear and Convincing Evidence: Measurement of Discrimination in America* (Washington, D.C.: Urban Institute Press, 1993).

145. See generally Thomas J. Sugrue, "The Structures of Urban Poverty: The Reorganization of Space and Work in Three Periods of American History," in Katz, *"Underclass" Debate*, 85 (reviewing the extensive historical literature that examines employment difficulties faced by the nation's urban poor, especially African Americans, in labor markets from the nineteenth century through the 1960s).

146. *Kerner Report*, 254–55.

147. See n. 158 below.

148. According to Moss and Tilly, "Between 1973 and 1989, the earnings of young black males deteriorated relative to whites. The relative decline occurred within all educational groups and was most severe among college graduates and highs school dropouts. . . . Controlling for education does not substantially change the relative earnings decline for blacks. Blacks experienced declines in relative earnings in every education group" (Moss and Tilly, *Why Black Men Are Doing Worse*, 3). Bennett Harrison and Lucy Gorham have reported that "only a bit over 1 in 8 African-American college graduates were earning as much as $35,000 a year in 1987. White college graduates were twice as likely to be paid this much as were blacks with equivalent years of schooling (26.1 percent versus 13.1 percent)" (Bennett Harrison and Lucy Gorham, "What Happened to African-American Wages in the 1980s?," in Galster and Hill, *Metropolis in Black and White*, 56, 66).

149. James P. Smith and Finis R. Welch, *Closing the Gap: Forty Years of Economic Progress for Blacks* (Santa Monica, Calif.: Rand, 1986), viii–ix.

150. Ibid., xxii–xxix.

151. See generally Bennett Harrison and Barry Bluestone, *The Great U-Turn: Corporate Restructuring and the Polarizing of America* (New York: Basic Books, 1988); Danziger and Weinberg, "Historical Record," 21–25 (noting that "most of the net increase in inequality over the past two decades was concentrated in the 1980s. This decade stands out as a historical anomaly, a period of rising family incomes and rising [income] inequality"); see also Kevin Phillips, *The Politics of Rich and Poor: Wealth and the American Electorate in the Reagan Aftermath* (New York: Random House, 1990) (suggesting that growing income inequality between America's rich and its lower and working classes would prove to be a critical political issue in the 1990s).

152. Harrison and Gorham, "What Happened to African-American Wages?," 56.

153. Bureau of the Census, *Money Income: 1992*, 30–31. In 1992 the median annual income comparisons for white couples was $42,820, compared with $34,290 for black couples. The median income for two-parent Hispanic families was only $29,007—67.7 percent of the median white income (ibid).

154. Bureau of the Census, *Statistical Abstract: 1994*, 416, tab. 679.

155. Ibid.

156. *Brown v. Board of Education*, 347 U.S. 483, 495 (1954).

157. "The proportion of black pupils in desegregated schools in the South rose from 2 percent in 1964 to 15 percent in 1966, to 18 percent in 1968, and reached 46 percent in 1973. The proportions in the North and West, where the financial sanctions [under the Civil Rights Act of 1964] were not invoked, were constant at 28–29 percent" (Jaynes and Williams, *Common Destiny*, 75).

158. Between 1940 and 1970 the median number of years of schooling that had been completed by black males aged 25–29 nearly doubled from 6.5 years to nearly 12 years. The median average among white males rose much less sharply, from 10.5 years in 1940 to slightly over 12.5 years by 1970 (ibid., 334). The gap between black and white females aged 25–29 also converged toward parity during this same period, with black women moving from an average of 7.5 years of

schooling to nearly 12 years, while white women made less dramatic advances, from just below 11.9 years to 12.5 years (ibid., 335, fig. 7-3).

159. Ibid.

160. In the mid-1960s just over 70 percent of whites of both sexes had completed high school; among blacks, high school completion rates were approximately 50 percent (ibid., 338). The college completion rate among white males in 1970 was 20 percent; for white females, it was just under 15 percent. Among both black males and females, college completion rates in 1970 were no more than 6 percent (ibid., 337, fig. 7-4).

161. Ibid., 349, tab. 7-1.

162. Coleman et al., *Equality of Educational Opportunity*.

163. See, for example, Frederick Mosteller and Daniel P. Moynihan, eds., *On Equality of Educational Opportunity* (New York: Vintage Books, 1972); Christopher Jencks, Marshall Smith, Henry Acland, Mary Jo Bane, David Cohen, Herbert Gintis, Barbara Heyns, and Stephen Michelson, *Inequality: A Reassessment of the Effect of Family and Schooling in America* (New York: Basic Books, 1972), 16–17. But see Ronald Edmonds, Andrew Billingsley, James Comer, James M. Dyer, William Hall, Robert Hill, Nan McGehee, Lawrence Reddick, Howard Taylor, and Stephen Wright, "A Black Response to Christopher Jencks's *Inequality* and Certain Other Issues," *Harvard Education Review* 43 (1973): 76, 77 (strongly contesting Jencks's "methods, conclusions, and recommendations").

164. Nathan Glazer, "Education and Training Programs and Poverty," in Danziger and Weinberg, *Fighting Poverty*, 152–53.

165. Robert D. Mare and Christopher Winship, "Ethnic and Racial Patterns of Educational Attainment and School Enrollment," in Sandefur and Tienda, *Divided Opportunities*, 173, 174. See also Jaynes and Williams, *Common Destiny*, 335, fig. 7-3. Rates of high school completion among white youth climbed to just under 90 percent by 1980; for blacks, high school completion rates jumped from 50 percent in 1965 to nearly 80 percent in the early 1980s (Jaynes and Williams, *Common Destiny*, 338).

Rates of college completion during this period climbed from 20 to over 25 percent among white males and from 15 to 23 percent among white females. After increasing dramatically in the early 1970s, both black college enrollment and black completion rates languished and even declined during the mid-1970s, standing just above 11 percent for black females and over 10 percent for black males by 1980 (Jaynes and Williams, *Common Destiny*, 337, fig. 7-4).

166. Jaynes and Williams, *Common Destiny*, 348, 350.

167. Gary Orfield, Franklin Monfort, and Melissa Aaron, *Status of School Desegregation, 1968–1986* (Alexandria, Va.: National School Boards Association, 1989), 10, tab. 8. According to Orfield and his colleagues, however,

There [are] clear signs, . . . that the long-standing achievements in the South and in parts of the Border states [are] beginning to erode. This [is] particularly clear in the cases of Alabama and Mississippi which show major increases in segregation and have joined the list of the nation's most segregated states for black students. Other states, including Florida, are experiencing gradual declines in relatively high levels of integration, declines that may well reflect the failure of many districts in those states to update their desegregation plans in the past fifteen years as vast demographic changes have occurred. The evidence of a significant increase in integration in Missouri, on the other hand, shows the potential value of large-scale city-suburban voluntary exchanges of the sort developed in the metropolitan St. Louis consent agreement in the mid-1980s. (Ibid., 29)

168. See, for example, Jomills Henry Braddock II and James M. McPartland, "Social-Psychological Processes That Perpetuate Racial Segregation: The Relationship between School and Employment Desegregation," *Journal of Black Studies* 19 (1989): 267; Jomills Henry Braddock II, Robert L. Crain, and James M. McPartland, "A Long-Term View of School Desegregation: Some Recent Studies of Graduates as Adults," *Phi Delta Kappan* 66 (1984): 259; Robert L. Crain and Rita E. Mahard, "Desegregation and Black Achievement: A Review of the Research," *Law and Contemporary Problems* 42 (Summer 1978): 17 (reviewing approximately 100 studies of the effect of desegregation on black achievement). See also Christopher Jencks, "Comment," in Danziger and Weinberg, *Fighting Poverty*, 176 ("Such evidence as we have suggests that school desegregation has reduced the black-white [achievement] gap more than Title I [the federal compensatory education program]").

169. James S. Coleman, Sara D. Kelley, and John A. Moore, *Trends in School Segregation, 1968–1973* (Washington, D.C.: Urban Institute Press, 1975); David Armor, "The Evidence on Busing," *Public Interest* 28 (1972): 90.

170. Crain and Mahard, "Desegregation and Black Achievement," 49.

171. See Jeannie Oakes, *Keeping Track: How Schools Structure Inequality* (New Haven: Yale University Press, 1985); Janet Eyler, Valerie J. Cook, and Leslie W. Ward, "Resegregation: Segregation within Desegregated Schools," in *The Consequences of School Desegregation*, ed. Christine H. Rossell and Willis D. Hawley (Philadelphia: Temple University Press, 1983), 126.

172. Pub. L. No. 88-452, 78 Stat. 508 (1964) (repealed and replaced by 42 U.S.C. §§ 9831–52 [1988]).

173. Pub. L. No. 89-10, 79 Stat. 27 (codified as 20 U.S.C. § 2701 and various other sections of 20 U.S.C. [1988 and Supp. II 1990]).

174. A number of studies have reported positive educational effects among children who participate in Head Start programs; see, for example, Ruth Hubbell McKey, Larry Condelli, Hariet Ganson, Barbara J. Barrett, Catherine McConkey, and Margaret C. Plantz, *The Impact of Head Start on Children, Families, and Communities: Final Report of the Head Start Evaluation, Synthesis, and Utilization Project* (Washington, D.C.: U.S. Government Printing Office, 1988); Edward Zigler, "Assessing Head Start at Twenty: An Invited Commentary," *American Journal of Orthopsychiatry* 55 (1985): 603. Nonetheless, there is dispute about whether Head Start leads to permanent improvement in achievement test scores or whether its effects are limited to maintaining children at grade level and avoiding their placement in special education classes. See Nathan Glazer, "Education and Training Programs," 157; Richard B. Darlington, Jacqueline M. Royce, Ann Stanton Snipper,

Harry W. Murray, and Irving Lazar, "Preschool Programs and Later School Competence of Children of Low Income Families," *Science* 208 (1980): 202.

Other studies have found positive educational gains among children who have participated in Title I/Chapter 1 programs in earlier grades, but a declining impact as students progress to higher grades. See Launor F. Carter, "The Sustaining Effects Study of Compensatory and Elementary Education," *Education Researcher* 13 (1984): 4; T. W. Fagan and C. A. Heid, "Chapter 1 Program Improvement: Opportunity and Practice," *Phi Delta Kappan* 72 (1991): 582. The wide variety of permitted uses of these Title I/Chapter 1 funds prevents any broad generalizations about program effectiveness.

175. See *Pasadena City Bd. of Educ. v. Spangler*, 427 U.S. 424 (1976) (holding that "neither school authorities nor district courts are constitutionally required to make year-by-year adjustments of the racial composition of student bodies [to compensate for changing racial demographics] once the affirmative duty to desegregate has been accomplished"); *Milliken v. Bradley*, 418 U.S. 717 (1974) (holding that federal courts may not ordinarily order school desegregation across school district lines); *Keyes v. School Dist. No. 1*, Denver, Colo., 413 U.S. 189 (1972) (holding that the mere existence of de facto racial segregation in a school district's public schools cannot be remedied by courts, absent proof that the segregation is the product of intentional racial discrimination by state or local school officials). Gary Orfield views the Supreme Court's *Milliken* decision in 1974 as the effective end of national commitment to urban desegregation:

> There has been no progress in school desegregation on a national level since the Supreme Court's decision in the Detroit case [*Milliken v. Bradley*], which created an overwhelming barrier to city-suburban desegregation in the largest cities. None of the cities covered by the Kerner Report have succeeded in winning such a plan. . . . The Supreme Court's Detroit decision, together with the almost total failure of state and national leadership on the issue, has left the country without tools to deal with the vast disparity between minority central-city school districts and schools in white suburbs. (Orfield, "Separate Societies," 116–17)

For a comprehensive examination of the current status of desegregation efforts, finding more post-*Milliken* progress than does Orfield, see James S. Liebman, "Desegregating Politics: 'All-Out' School Desegregation Explained," *Columbia Law Review* 90 (1990): 1463, 1465–73.

176. See generally Farley and Allen, *Color Line*, 205, 207.

177. See, for example, James E. Comer, "Educating Poor Minority Children," *Scientific American*, November 1988, 42; Spencer H. Holland, "Positive Role Models for Primary-Grade Black Inner-City Males," *Equity and Excellence* 25 (1990): 40; "Note: Creating Space for Racial Difference: The Case for African-American Schools," *Harvard Civil Rights–Civil Liberties Law Review* 27 (1992): 186.

178. Susan E. Mayer, "How Much Does a High School's Racial and Socioeconomic Mix Affect Graduation and Teenage Fertility Rates?," in Jencks and Peterson, *Urban Underclass*, 321, 325; Judith Anderson, Debra Hollinger, and Joseph Conaty, *Poverty and Achievement: Re-examining the Relationship between School*

Poverty and Student Achievement (Washington, D.C.: U.S. Government Printing Office, 1992), 2–3, 5, tab. 1; Susan E. Mayer and Christopher Jencks, "Growing up in Poor Neighborhoods: How Much Does It Matter?," *Science* 243 (1989): 1441, 1442, and nn. 15–16; Mary Kennedy, Richard K. Jung, and Martin E. Orland, *Poverty, Achievement, and the Distribution of Compensatory Educational Services* (Washington, D.C.: U.S. Government Printing Office, 1986), 2:5–6; Coleman et al., *Equality of Educational Opportunity*, 22.

179. See generally Ira Katznelson and Margaret Weir, *Schooling for All: Race, Class, and the Democratic Ideal* (New York: Basic Books, 1985) (arguing that the balkanization of school boundaries within most metropolitan regions and the sharp racial and class divisions between city and suburban districts make equal educational opportunity all but impossible); Harvey Kantor and Barbara Brenzel, "Urban Education and the 'Truly Disadvantaged': The Historical Roots of the Contemporary Crisis, 1945–1990," in Katz, *"Underclass" Debate*, 366 (contending that the concentration and isolation of low-income, minority students in central-city schools as well as the unresponsiveness of city educational bureaucracies are central factors responsible for the poor educational achievement of students in central-city schools).

180. *Kerner Report*, 269.

181. The commission reported that infant mortality among white children was 21.5 per 1,000 live births in 1965; among nonwhites the rate nearly doubled, to 40.3 per 1,000 live births (ibid., 270).

182. In 1965 whites over age 25 had an average life expectancy of 73.6 years, while nonwhites had an average life expectancy of only 68.3 years (ibid., 270–71).

183. The poorer health of African Americans could be explained, in part, by the fact that "Negroes with incomes similar to those of whites spend less on medical services and visit medical specialists less often" (ibid., 271), a fact linked to the difficulty experienced by African Americans in obtaining access to doctors and medical facilities. This inaccessibility was due to both the "geographic concentration of doctors in higher income areas in large cities and . . . discrimination against Negroes by doctors and hospitals" (ibid., 272).

184. See, for example, Sylvia Drew Ivie, "Ending Discrimination in Health Care: A Dream Deferred," in *Civil Rights Issues in Health Care Delivery*, by U.S. Commission on Civil Rights (Washington, D.C.: U.S. Commission on Civil Rights, 1980), 282–92 (documenting health disparities between whites and nonwhites at all ages, over a wide range of diseases and conditions); Akwasi Osei, "The Persistence of Differing Trends in African-American Mortality and Morbidity Rates," in Galster and Hill, *Metropolis in Black and White*, 128. See generally David P. Willis, ed., *Health Policies and Black Americans* (New Brunswick, N.J.: Transaction, 1989).

185. Between 1960 and 1991 the infant mortality rate among white children declined from 22.9 to 7.3 deaths per 1,000 live births; among black children, infant mortality fell from 44.3 to 17.6 deaths per 1,000 during the same period (Bureau of the Census, *Statistical Abstract: 1994*, 91, no. 120). While the nationwide infant mortality rate was 11.5 deaths per 1,000 in 1982, in Washington, D.C., and Detroit—two cities with large minority populations—the rates were 21.2 and 21.8

per 1,000, respectively (Clay H. Wellborn, "Central City Population Characteristics," *Congressional Research Review* 9 [November–December, 1988]: 9).

186. Average life expectancy among white males in 1991 was 72.9 years; among white females the average was 79.6 years. The 1991 figures for black males and females were 64.6 years and 73.8 years, respectively (Bureau of the Census, *Statistical Abstract: 1994*, 87, no. 114). For a detailed discussion of this phenomenon, see Ronald M. Anderson, Ross M. Mulliner, and Llewellyn J. Cornelius, "Black-White Differences in Health Status: Methods or Substance?," *Milbank Quarterly* 65 (Supp. 1987): 72.

187. See generally Jaynes and Williams, *Common Destiny*, 393–428 (discussing health trends among African Americans); Woodrow Jones Jr. and Mitchell F. Rice, eds., *Health Care Issues in Black America: Policies, Problems, and Prospects* (New York: Greenwood Press, 1987), 3–56 (presenting an overview, "Black Health Care and Health Status").

188. "Since 1970, Medicaid has provided health coverage for about one of every five blacks under age 65. Approximately one-third of all Medicaid beneficiaries are black, and Medicare's coverage of the elderly has assured minimum benefits for blacks aged 65 or older" (Jaynes and Williams, *Common Destiny*, 430). See also Diane Rowland, "Medicaid: Financing Care for Low-Income Americans" (paper presented at conference, "An African American Health Care Agenda: Strategies for Reforming an Unjust System," Johns Hopkins University, Baltimore, October 31– November 2, 1991), 3–5 (discussing the role of Medicaid in meeting the health needs of African Americans).

189. Jaynes and Williams, *Common Destiny*, 430. See also Stephen H. Long, "Public versus Employment-related Health Insurance: Experience and Implications for Black and Nonblack Americans," *Milbank Quarterly* 65 (Supp. 1987): 200, 203, tab. 1. Other investigators have reported that the percentage of African Americans not covered by public or private health insurance rose during the decade from 1977 through 1987 (Pamela Farley Short, Llewellyn J. Cornelius, and Donald E. Goldstone, "Health Insurance of Minorities in the United States," *Journal of Health Care for the Poor and Underserved* 1 [1990]: 9).

190. See Geraldine Dallek, "Health Care for America's Poor: Separate and Unequal," *Clearinghouse Review* 20 (1986): 361, 365–71; Sidney D. Watson, "Reinvigorating Title VI: Defending Health Care Discrimination—It Shouldn't Be So Easy," *Fordham Law Review* 58 (1990): 939, 941–42 (citing Stan Dorn, Michael A. Dowell, and Jane Perkins, "Anti-Discrimination Provisions and Health Care Access: New Slants on Old Approaches," *Clearinghouse Review* 20 [1986]: 439, 441–51). See generally U.S. House Committee on Governmental Operations, *Equal Access to Health Care: Patient Dumping, Hearings before the Subcommittee on Human Resources and Intergovernmental Relations of the House Committee on Government Operations*, 100th Cong., 1st sess., 1987 (discussing potential Title VI violations, including segregation, both within and between health care facilities); Malcolm Gladwell, "HHS Criticized on Law Barring Patient 'Dumping'; Lack of Enforcement by Agency Denies Care to Uninsured Individuals, Consumer Group Says," *Washington Post*, April 24, 1991 (noting estimates suggesting that "dump-

ing," or denying delivery of care to indigent or uninsured individuals, occurs 250,000 times each year in United States hospitals, although the Department of Health and Human Services has identified only 140 hospitals in violation). See also *Linton v. Commissioner of Health and Env't*, 923 F.2d 855 (6th Cir. 1981).

191. Council on Ethical and Judicial Affairs, "Black-White Disparities in Health Care," *Journal of the American Medical Association* 263 (1990): 2344 (reporting that blacks are only one-half as likely as whites to receive angiography and one-third as likely to receive bypass surgery for anterior myocardial infarction, taking the severity of heart disease into account).

192. Deborah Chollet, Jill Foley, and Colleen Mages, *Uninsured in the United States: The Nonelderly Population without Health Insurance, 1988* (Washington, D.C.: Employee Benefit Research Institute, 1990).

193. Sylvia Drew Ivie noted in 1980 that "public hospitals are the primary providers of care for inner-city poor minorities. These facilities are grossly underfunded. A shrinking municipal tax base and the astronomical inflation in health care cost [sic] have left large urban public hospitals in financial crisis. Local governments have responded by cutbacks in dollars and full or partial closure of many public hospitals" (Ivie, "Ending Discrimination in Health Care," 305–6). See also American Public Health Association, "Report of the Task Force on Public General Hospitals," in U.S. Commission on Civil Rights, *Civil Rights Issues in Health Care Delivery*, 818–49.

194. See, for example, Institute of Medicine, *Homelessness, Health, and Human Needs* (Washington, D.C.: National Academy Press, 1988), 92 ("Under the Omnibus Budget Reconciliation Act of 1981 [P.L. 97-35], federal financial support both for community-based health and specialized maternal and child health care centers was substantially reduced. A number of localities closed or consolidated facilities. Many health centers, public and private, were forced to reduce their budgets and services.").

195. See, for example, Alan Sager, "The Closure of Hospitals That Serve the Poor: Implications for Health Planning," in U.S. House Committee on Energy and Commerce, *Extension of Health Planning Program: Hearings on Extension of HHS Aid before the Subcommittee on Health and the Environment of the House Committee on Energy and Commerce*, 97th Cong., 2d sess., 1982, H. Doc. 126, 530–44 (documenting a significant increase in the number of private hospitals that closed or relocated in fifty-two metropolitan areas, despite continuing need for medical services, and demonstrating a correlation between closures and the percentage of African Americans in the affected communities); Ivie, "Ending Discrimination in Health Care," 297–300. See generally Watson, "Reinvigorating Title VI," 173; "Note: Maintaining Health Care in the Inner City: Title VI and Hospital Relocations," *New York University Law Review* 55 (1980): 271, 273–79. See also *NAACP v. Medical Ctr., Inc.*, 657 F.2d 1322 (3d Cir. 1981); *Bryan v. Koch*, 627 F.2d 612 (2d Cir. 1980); *Jackson v. Conway*, 476 F. Supp. 896 (E.D. Mo. 1987).

196. As one leading advocate for African American health care has noted, "private physicians shun the practice of medicine in poor minority communities and, like hospitals, relocate as the proportion of minorities in an area increases. In the last few decades, ghettos and barrios have shown a steep decline in the number of

physicians available to treat inner-city residents" (Ivie, "Ending Discrimination in Health Care," 301, [citing House of Representatives report no. 266, 94th Cong., 2d sess., 1976, pp. 4966–67]). See also Cassandra Q. Butts, "The Color of Money: Barriers to Access to Private Health Care Facilities for African-Americans," *Clearinghouse Review* 26 (1992) (citing Mark Schlesinger, "Paying the Price: Medical Care, Minorities, and the Newly Competitive Health Care System," *Milbank Quarterly* 65 [Supp. 1987]: 270, 276), and David A. Kindig, Hormoz Movassaghi, Nancy Cross Dunham, Daniel I. Zwick, and Charles M. Taylor, "Trends in Physician Availability in Ten Urban Areas from 1963 to 1980," *Inquiry* 24 (1987): 136.

197. *Kerner Report*, 467.

198. Ibid., 468.

199. Ibid., 470.

200. Ibid., 471. The commission noted that African Americans actually experienced two different kinds of price discrimination. In some cities they paid rents that, on average, were similar to those of whites but obtained smaller, more deteriorated housing for their money (ibid., 470–71). In other cities they typically were required to pay more in rent to obtain similar housing, albeit in segregated neighborhoods (ibid., 471).

201. Ibid., 474–75.

202. See William Apgar, Denise DiPasquale, Jean Cummings, Nancy McArdle, and Marcia Fernald, *The State of the Nation's Housing, 1990* (Cambridge, Mass.: Joint Center for Housing Studies of Harvard University, 1990), 20.

203. Ibid., 21–22.

204. Connie H. Casey, *Characteristics of HUD-Assisted Renters and Their Units in 1989* (Washington, D.C.: U.S. Government Printing Office, 1992), tab. 1.

205. Congressional Budget Office, *Current Housing Problems and Possible Federal Responses* (Washington, D.C.: U.S. Government Printing Office, 1988), 36–37.

206. Apgar et al., *State of the Nation's Housing*, 22. In a more recent update, Apgar and his colleagues have noted the arbitrary distribution of federal housing assistance: "Some 1.5 million extremely low-income households (income less than 25% of area median) receive both housing assistance and income assistance; 2.5 million extremely low-income people receive neither" (Joint Center for Housing Studies, *The State of the Nation's Housing, 1993* [Cambridge, Mass.: Joint Center for Housing Studies of Harvard University, 1993], 15).

207. Paul A. Leonard, Cushing N. Dolbeare, and Edward B. Lazere, *A Place to Call Home: The Crisis in Housing for the Poor* (Washington, D.C.: Center on Budget and Policy Priorities, 1989), 8, (emphasis added). More recent studies have underlined that the shortages are not distributed uniformly among lower-income households. In many areas a surplus of housing units has developed affordable to those with incomes of 50 to 80 percent of median area incomes. Meanwhile, however, there continues to be a severe shortage of units that are affordable by those with incomes below 30 percent of area median incomes (Kathryn P. Nelson, "Whose Shortage of Affordable Housing?," *Housing Policy Debate* 5 [1994]: 401).

208. Michael A. Stegman, *The Role of Public Housing in a Revitalized National Housing Policy* (Cambridge, Mass.: MIT Center for Real Estate Development, 1988), 9.

209. Ibid.

210. Michael A. Stegman, *More Housing, More Fairly: Report of the Twentieth Century Fund Task Force on Affordable Housing* (New York: Twentieth Century Fund, 1991), 26, tab. 2.

211. Congressional Budget Office, *Current Housing Problems*, 37.

212. Stegman, *More Housing, More Fairly*, 25.

213. Connie H. Casey, *Characteristics of HUD-Assisted Renters*, 25, tab. 3.

214. See David C. Schwartz, Richard C. Ferlauto, and Daniel N. Hoffman, "The Need for a New National Housing Policy," in *A New Housing Policy for America: Recapturing the American Dream* (Philadelphia: Temple University Press, 1988), 57.

215. Phillip L. Clay, *At Risk of Loss: The Endangered Future of Low-Income Rental Housing Resources* (Washington, D.C.: Neighborhood Reinvestment Corp., 1987), 4, fig. 2.2. Harvard's Joint Center for Housing Studies reports that "although inventory removals slowed substantially by the mid-1980s, American Housing Survey data indicate that . . . 197,000 . . . rental units . . . were demolished each year from 1985 to 1989" (Joint Center for Housing Studies, *State of the Nation's Housing, 1993*, 14).

216. See generally Neil Smith and Peter Williams, eds., *Gentrification of the City* (Boston: Allen and Unwin, 1986); Richard LeGates and Chester Hartman, "Displacement," *Clearinghouse Review* 15 (1981): 207.

217. See U.S. House Committee on Housing and Urban Affairs, Subcommittee on Housing and Community Development, *Preventing the Disappearance of Low-Income Housing*, report prepared by the National Low Income Housing Preservation Commission, 100th Cong. 2d sess., 1988, committee print, 38–47; Clay, *At Risk of Loss*, 11.

218. Center on Budget and Policy Priorities and Center for the Study of the States, *The States and the Poor: How Budget Decisions in 1991 Affected Low Income People* (Washington, D.C.: Center on Budget and Policy Priorities, 1991), 8.

219. After evaluating data on homeless people in the 1980s, Peter H. Rossi suggested that "based on available information and reasonable assumptions, the most believable national estimate is that at least 300,000 people are homeless each night in this country, and possibly as many as 400,000 to 500,000 if one accepts growth rates in the past few years of between 10 percent and 20 percent" (Rossi, *Down and out in America: The Origins of Homelessness* [Chicago: University of Chicago Press, 1989], 70). See also Christopher Jencks, *The Homeless* (Cambridge, Mass.: Harvard University Press, 1994), 13 (estimating that about 350,000 Americans were homeless during March 1987).

220. Rossi notes that "although no definitive counts were made during the Great Depression, we can get some notion of the magnitude of homelessness from the activities of federal relief agencies: in 1933 the Federal Emergency Relief Administration housed 125,000 people in its transient camps, and a 1934 survey of social agencies in seven hundred towns and cities estimated 200,000 homeless" (Rossi, *Down and out in America*, 22).

221. "Some 18 percent of all Black and Hispanic households paid at least 50 percent of their income for housing in 1989, compared with nine percent of all white households" (Edward B. Lazere, Paul A. Leonard, Cushing N. Dolbeare, and Barry

Zigas, *A Place to Call Home: The Low Income Housing Crisis Continues* [Washington, D.C.: Center on Budget and Policy Priorities, 1991], 62). These figures are *down* from 1985, when 22 percent of black households, 20 percent of Hispanic households, and 10 percent of white households paid at least 50 percent of their incomes for housing (Leonard et al., *Place to Call Home*, 50).

222. "In 1989, eight percent of poor households—or approximately one million poor households—lived in overcrowded quarters" (Lazere et al., *Place to Call Home*, 24). Overcrowding is most common among poor renters and most severe among Hispanics: 26 percent of poor Hispanic households are overcrowded, compared with 9 percent of poor black households and 4 percent of poor white households (ibid.).

223. See generally Jonathan Kozol, *Rachel and Her Children: Homeless Families in America* (New York: Crown, 1988) (a harrowing account of homeless families with children); see also Alex Kotlowitz, *There Are No Children Here: The Story of Two Boys Growing up in the Other America* (New York: Doubleday, 1991) (account of children growing up in a large, high-rise, public housing project).

224. Edward B. Lazere and Paul Leonard, *The Crisis in Housing for the Poor: A Special Report on Hispanics and Blacks* (Washington, D.C.: Center on Budget and Policy Priorities, 1989), 1–2. Since some 35 percent of all black households were poor in 1985, this extremely heavy housing burden was shared widely in the African American community. Even taking into account both poor and nonpoor blacks, some 42 percent of *all* black households paid at least 30 percent of their income for housing. Among all white households, the comparable figure in 1985 was 27 percent (ibid., 4).

225. The total number of renter households receiving federal housing assistance grew from 2.7 million in 1979 to 4.3 million in 1988, representing an increase from 22 to 29 percent in the proportion of eligible renter households receiving such assistance. Since the number of poor families increased substantially during the 1980s, however, a larger number of eligible households (5.5 million) received no federal assistance in 1987 than in 1979 (4.0 million) (ibid., 24).

226. Ibid., 21–22.

227. See John O. Calmore, "To Make Wrong Right: The Necessary and Proper Aspirations of Fair Housing," in *The State of Black America, 1989*, ed. Janet Dewart (New York: National Urban League, 1989), 83 ("During the 1980s authorized funds for federal housing programs have plummeted almost 80 percent . . . from the $30 billion authorized for fiscal year 1981 to the $7.17 and $7.13 billion authorized respectively for fiscal years 1988 and 1989").

Between fiscal year 1977 and 1980 HUD made commitments to provide rental assistance to an average of 316,000 additional households per year. Between 1981 and 1988, the number of new commitments dropped from 316,000 to 82,000 per year (Leonard et al., *Place to Call Home*, 23).

228. George C. Galster, "More Than Skin Deep: The Effect of Housing Discrimination on the Extent and Pattern of Racial Residential Segregation in the United States," in *Housing Desegregation and Federal Policy*, ed. John M. Goering (Chapel Hill: University of North Carolina Press, 1986), 133–34.

229. See, for example, John E. Farley, "Segregation in 1980: How Segregated Are

America's Metropolitan Areas?," in *Divided Neighborhoods: Changing Patterns of Racial Segregation in the 1980s*, ed. Gary Tobin (Newbury Park, Calif.: Sage, 1989), 95; Nancy A. Denton and Douglas S. Massey, "Residential Segregation of Blacks, Hispanics, and Asians by Socioeconomic Status and Generation," *Social Science Quarterly* 69 (1988): 797; George C. Galster and W. Mark Keeney, "Race, Residence, Discrimination, and Economic Opportunity: Modeling the Nexus of Urban Racial Phenomena," *Urban Affairs Quarterly* 24 (1988): 87.

230. See generally Ronald E. Wienk, Clifford E. Reid, John C. Simonson, and Frederick J. Eggers, *Measuring Racial Discrimination in American Housing Markets: The Housing Market Practices Survey* (Washington, D.C.: U.S. Department of Housing and Urban Development, 1979); John Yinger, "Access Denied, Access Constrained: Results and Implications of the 1989 Housing Discrimination Study," in Fix and Struyk, *Clear and Convincing Evidence*, 69; George C. Galster, "Residential Segregation in American Cities: A Contrary Review," *Population Research and Policy Review* 7 (1988): 93.

231. See generally Ronald E. Wienk, "Discrimination in Urban Credit Markets: What We Don't Know and Why We Don't Know It," *Housing Policy Debate* 3 (1992): 217, 237 (reviewing methodological limitations of prior studies and concluding, "Does housing credit discrimination exist? Yes. Is the behavior of prospective buyers affected by discrimination? Yes. What do we know about credit discrimination and its effects? Very little."); William Dedman, "The Color of Money," *Atlanta Journal-Constitution*, May 1–4, 1988 (documenting racial disparities in credit and lending policies by Georgia banks); George Galster, "The Use of Testers in Investigating Discrimination in Mortgage Lending and Insurance," in Fix and Struyk, *Clear and Convincing Evidence*, 287 (reviewing various studies that found apparent lending and/or credit discrimination through the use of testers); but see Michael H. Schill and Susan M. Wachter, "A Tale of Two Cities: Racial and Ethnic Geographic Disparities in Home Mortgage Lending in Boston and Philadelphia," *Journal of Housing Research* 4 (1993): 245, 272 (reporting results of a study of Home Mortgage Disclosure Act data in Boston and Philadelphia and concluding tentatively that, once neighborhood financial risk is taken into account, the data "do not support the hypothesis that financial institutions redline neighborhoods" on racial and ethnic grounds).

232. Connie H. Casey, *Characteristics of HUD-Assisted Renters*, 4.

233. See, for example, *United States v. Yonkers*, 837 F.2d 1181 (2d Cir. 1987); *Jaimes v. Lucas Metropolitan Hous. Auth.*, 833 F.2d 1203 (6th Cir. 1987); *NAACP v. Secretary of HUD*, 817 F.2d 149 (1st Cir. 1987); *Gautreaux v. Romney*, 448 F.2d 731 (7th Cir. 1971); *Young v. Pierce*, 640 F. Supp. 1476 (E.D. Tex. 1986). See also *Walker v. HUD*, 734 F. Supp. 1231 (N.D. Tex. 1989) (violation of consent decree). See generally Mittie Olion Chandler, "Public Housing Desegregation: What Are the Options?," *Housing Policy Debate* 3 (1992): 509; Betsy Julian and Michael Daniel, "Separate and Unequal: The Root and Branch of Public Housing Segregation," *Clearinghouse Review* 23 (1989) 666–68; Roisman and Tegeler, "Improving and Expanding Housing Opportunities," 329–36 (discussing public housing cases in which racial discrimination was found); "Separate and Unequal: Illegal Segregation Pervades Nation's Subsidized Housing," *Dallas Morning News*, February 10–17,

1985, reprinted in *Discrimination in Federally Assisted Housing Programs: Hearings before the House Subcommittee on Housing and Community Development*, part 1, 99th Cong., 1st and 2d sess., 1985–86, pp. 20–66.

234. See generally Kotlowitz, *There Are No Children Here*, 21–26. According to a recent, comprehensive study of HUD-assisted renters, "Public housing units . . . were located more frequently than other [federally] assisted units or income-eligible, unassisted renters near buildings vandalized or with their interiors exposed (9 percent), near buildings with bars on windows (11 percent), and in neighborhoods with trash, litter, or junk on streets or properties (32 percent)" (Connie H. Casey, *Characteristics of HUD-Assisted Renters*, 18).

235. Connie H. Casey, *Characteristics of HUD-Assisted Renters*, 14.

236. Ibid., 20.

237. See National Commission on Severely Distressed Public Housing, *A Report to the Congress and the Secretary of Housing and Urban Development* (Washington, D.C.: U.S. Government Printing Office, 1992), 78–79, 83, 87.

238. See, for example, *United States v. Yonkers Board of Education*, 837 F.2d 1181 (2d Cir. 1987), cert. denied, 486 U.S. 1055 (1988) (upholding lower court decisions finding racial discrimination in city's prior public housing siting decisions and approving order requiring construction of subsidized housing units in racially integrated neighborhoods); *United States v. City of Yonkers*, 856 F.2d 444 (2d Cir. 1989) (discussing contempt proceedings against the city of Yonkers and white city council members who refused to authorize construction to go forward, despite federal court order, because of strong community opposition by white citizens) rev'd in part sub nom. *Spallone v. United States*, 493 U.S. 265, 110 S.Ct. 625 (1990).

239. See, for example, Charles Daye, Daniel R. Mandelker, Otto J. Hetzel, James A. Kushner, Henry W. McGee Jr., Robert M. Washburn, Peter W. Salsich Jr., and W. Dennis Keating, *Housing and Community Development* (Durham, N.C.: Carolina Academic Press, 1989), 179–87, 331–32.

240. For a discussion of the *Gautreaux* experiment, see nn. 136–38 above and accompanying text.

241. *Kerner Report*, 458.

242. Ibid., 457.

243. Ibid.

244. Ibid., 458–59. See Social Security Act of 1935, Pub. L. No. 74-271, §§ 401–6, 49 Stat. 620, 627–29 (codified as amended at 42 U.S.C. §§ 601–6 [1988]).

245. *Kerner Report*, 458.

246. Ibid., 459–60.

247. Ibid., 461–63.

248. Ibid., 462–63.

249. Ibid., 463–64.

250. Patterson, *America's Struggle against Poverty*, 171–84.

251. Lawrence M. Mead, *Beyond Entitlement: The Social Obligations of Citizenship* (New York: Free Press, 1986) (arguing that public welfare policy has been too permissive and that future policy should make benefits contingent on compliance with minimally acceptable standards of behavior, including a work requirement

for employable welfare recipients); Mead, *New Politics of Poverty* (contending that the underlying dispute over welfare is less about economics than about conduct and public order, with liberals willing to tolerate greater disorder and socially irresponsible, dependent behavior, especially in inner-cities, and conservatives insistent that the inner-city poor must alter their antisocial behavior and attempt to become self-reliant); Murray, *Losing Ground* (suggesting that AFDC has contributed to illegitimacy and dependence among the poor). A strong contrary view is offered by many social scientists, most prominently William Julius Wilson, Robert Aponte, and Kathryn Neckerman, "Joblessness versus Welfare Effects: A Further Reexamination," in Wilson, *Truly Disadvantaged*, 93–106 (maintaining that structural economic forces have led to the strongly unfavorable economic circumstances presently experienced by the inner-city poor, and that the behaviors and values Mead and Murray condemn are merely symptoms of, and not the causes of, these deteriorating economic circumstances).

252. The total number of AFDC recipients declined from 11,101,000 in 1980 to 10,924,000 in 1985, before shooting upward, during the recession of the early 1990s, to 14,035,000 in 1992 (Bureau of the Census, *Statistical Abstract: 1994*, 383, no. 597).

253. Burtless, "Public Spending on the Poor," 51, 55–58.

254. Total federal and state contributions grew from $4.85 billion in 1970 to $22.11 billion in 1992 (Bureau of the Census, *Statistical Abstract: 1994*, 383, no. 598).

255. Average monthly AFDC payments, unadjusted for inflation, rose from $229 to $383 during the fifteen years from 1975 through 1989, increasing by an average of just over $10 per year (ibid., 372, no. 612).

256. Center on Budget and Policy Priorities, *States and the Poor*, 8.

257. Federal dollars spent on Food Stamps rose from $550 million in 1970 to $22.91 billion in 1992. Expenditures on the school lunch program rose from $300 million to $3.86 billion between 1970 and 1992; on the school breakfast program, from $11 million to $787 million; and on the WIC program between 1980 and 1992, from $603 million to $1.96 billion (Bureau of the Census, *Statistical Abstract: 1994*, 386, no. 602).

258. Food Stamp Act of 1964, Pub. L. No. 88-525, 78 Stat. 703 (codified as amended at 7 U.S.C. §§ 2011–32 [1988 and Supp. II 1990]).

259. Pub. L. No. 89-642, as amended by Pub. L. No. 92-433, § 9, 86 Stat. 729 (codified as amended at 42 U.S.C. § 1786 [1988 and Supp. I 1989]).

260. National School Lunch Act of 1946, Pub. L. No. 396, 60 Stat. 230 (codified as amended at 42 U.S.C. §§ 1751–61, 1765–66, 1769 [1988 and Supp. I. 1989]).

261. See U.S. Department of Commerce, Bureau of the Census, *Current Population Reports, Measuring the Effect of Benefits and Taxes on Income and Poverty: 1979 to 1991*, series P-60, no. 182 (Washington, D.C.: U.S. Government Printing Office, 1992), A1–2, Appendix A (discussing the origin and development of various federal poverty formulas); see also Patricia Ruggles, *Drawing the Line: Alternative Poverty Measures and Their Implications for Public Policy* (Washington, D.C.: Urban Institute Press, 1990) (arguing that while the inclusion of noncash benefits will lower the reported poverty rate at any particular time, it will not alter the long-

term trends in poverty rates observed using a cash-only measure); Mollie Orshansky, "Counting the Poor," *Social Security Bulletin* 28 (1965): 3.

262. See, for example, Bureau of the Census, *Measuring the Effect*, vii–xxiv (discussing fifteen alternative formulas for measuring poverty); Danziger and Weinberg, "Historical Record," 25–31. Some have insisted that the percentage of households that are poor is currently overstated because of the omission of food stamps and other noncash benefits from the poverty calculation; see, for example, U.S. Senate Statement, "Data Collection and Poverty Level," reprinted in Bureau of the Census, *Measuring the Effect*, Appendix G. Isaac Shapiro and Robert Greenstein note that the reduction in the inflation-adjusted value of AFDC benefits has been so great during the 1970–91 period that "the average value of AFDC and food stamp benefits *combined* has now fallen to about the same level as the value of AFDC benefits *alone* in 1960, before the food stamp program was created" (Shapiro and Greenstein, *Selective Prosperity*, 13).

263. Pub. L. No. 100-485, 102 Stat. 2343 (1988) (codified in scattered sections of 42 U.S.C. and 26 U.S.C.).

264. One senator who led the legislative reform effort described its intentions as follows:

> Under the newly reformed welfare system, the presumption is that the family should and can be self-supporting. . . . To the maximum extent that resources can be found, . . . aid will be coupled with the tools—education, training, childcare and other services—needed to assure that dependence on public aid will be a temporary condition leading to restored self sufficiency. . . . The major elements of [the Family Support] Act were all designed to serve the same overall purpose—a redirection of our welfare system in ways that would help recipients attain self-sufficiency. (Lloyd Bentsen, "Reforming the Welfare System: The Family Support Act of 1988," *Journal of Legislation* 16 [1990]: 133, 134, 137)

Welfare rights advocates have taken a less charitable view. See, for example, Timothy J. Casey, "The Family Support Act of 1988: Molehill or Mountain, Retreat or Reform?," *Clearinghouse Review* 23 (1989): 930, 931 ("The FSA's basic aim is to reduce sharply the number of families receiving AFDC, although the measures adopted toward this end will almost certainly fail to achieve it and are even less likely to reduce childhood poverty rates significantly"). For a more comprehensive examination of the Family Support Act in historical context, see Joel F. Handler and Yeheskel Hasenfeld, *The Moral Construction of Poverty: Welfare Reform in America* (Newbury Park, Calif.: Sage, 1991); Michael B. Katz, *The Undeserving Poor: From the War on Poverty to the War on Welfare* (New York: Pantheon, 1989).

265. U.S. House Committee on Ways and Means, *Overview of Entitlement Programs* (Washington, D.C., U.S. Government Printing Office, 1992), 618. Mark Greenberg reports that in a typical month during fiscal year 1992 only 27,549 persons were working in any form of subsidized work activity under the JOBS program (Greenberg, *Understanding the Clinton Welfare Bill: Two Years and Work* [Washington, D.C.: Center for Law and Social Policy, 1994], iii).

266. The Work and Responsibility Act of 1994, H.R. 4605, 103d Cong., 2d sess.,

Congressional Record 140 (daily ed., June 21, 1994), H4755. See Center for Law and Social Policy, "Administration Announces Welfare Reform Bill," in *CLASP Update: A CLASP Report on Welfare Reform Developments* (Washington, D.C.: Center for Law and Social Policy, 1994), 1 (describing act).

267. See Greenberg, *Understanding the Clinton Welfare Bill*, 6–12.

268. H.R. 4, *Congressional Record* 141 (daily ed. January 4, 1995), H159.

269. The first form of this legislation was proposed by the newly elected Republican majority of the House of Representatives in November 1994. See Dan Bloom, Sharon Parrott, Isaac Shapiro, and David Super, *The Personal Responsibility Act* (Washington, D.C.: Center on Budget and Policy Priorities, 1994). A revised version is described in Mark Greenberg, *The Temporary Family Assistance Block Grant: Frozen Funding, Flawed Flexibility* (Washington, D.C.: Center for Law and Social Policy, 1995).

270. The states were given authority to seek such waivers for "demonstration programs" under Title V of the Family Support Act. See 42 U.S.C. § 1315.

271. See Mark Greenberg, *On Wisconsin?: The Case against the "Work Not Welfare" Waiver* (Washington, D.C.: Center for Law and Social Policy, 1993) (describing Wisconsin's "Work Not Welfare," or "learnfare," program, under which all AFDC mothers in two experimental counties were required to enroll in educational programs and/or obtain employment in order to qualify for cash assistance, and under which, after twenty-four months, they were automatically cut from assistance for at least three years); see also Lucy A. Williams, "The Ideology of Division: Behavior Modification Welfare Reform Proposals," *Yale Law Journal* 102 (1992): 719 (reviewing many of the state demonstration projects and experiments).

272. See, for example, David T. Ellwood, *Poor Support: Poverty in the American Family* (New York: Basic Books, 1988), 232; see also Theodore R. Marmor, Jerry L. Mashaw, and Philip L. Harvey, *America's Misunderstood Welfare State: Persistent Myths, Enduring Realities* (New York: Basic Books, 1990), 35–46, 96–104.

273. See Pub. L. No. 103-66, 107 Stat. 433, 312 (1993) (codified at 26 U.S.C. § 32). See Paul Leonard and Robert Greenstein, *The New Budget Reconciliation Law: Progressive Deficit Reduction and Critical Social Investments* (Washington, D.C.: Center on Budget and Policy Priorities, 1993), Appendix II, 15–19 (describing the "EITC provisions of the new law . . . as historic").

274. Leonard and Greenstein, *New Budget Reconciliation Law*, Appendix II.

275. 42 U.S.C. §§ 1973, 1973a–p, and 1973aa–dd6 (1989). For discussion of black electoral gains in the South, see Jaynes and Williams, *Common Destiny*, 230–36.

276. See Georgia A. Persons, "Racial Politics and Black Power in the Cities," in Galster and Hill, *Metropolis in Black and White*, 166, 173–76. In 1970 the nationwide total of black elected legislators at the federal and state level was only 179, with 715 more serving in elected city and county positions (Bureau of the Census, *Statistical Abstract: 1994*, 284, no. 443). By 1993 the number of black federal and state legislators had more than doubled, to 561, while the number of elected city and county officials had increased sixfold, to 4,819 (Bureau of the Census, *Statistical Abstract: 1994*, 284, no. 443). For an excellent collection of studies examining

the impact of black and Latino electoral power on urban political arrangements, see Rufus P. Browning, Dale Rogers Marshall, and David H. Tabb, eds., *Racial Politics in American Cities* (New York: Longman, 1994).

277. See Rufus P. Browning, Dale Rogers Marshall, and David H. Tabb, "Minority Mobilization in Ten Cities: Failures and Successes," in Browning et al., *Racial Politics in American Cities*, 8, 10 (describing the various expectations that minority electoral coalitions brought with them when they attained municipal power); see also Rufus P. Browning, Dale Rogers Marshall, and David H. Tabb, "Has Political Incorporation Been Achieved? Is It Enough?," in ibid., 212, 224–26 (surveying the gains achieved by minority city governments nationwide in city employment, appointment to boards and commissions, police-community relationships, and development of minority businesses).

278. Krumholz, "Kerner Commission Twenty Years Later," 28. In 1967, for example, 7.4 percent of Cleveland's police force was black, compared with 28.1 percent in 1990. The comparable gains for African Americans in Detroit are 5.2 to 53.7 percent; for Newark, 9.8 to 47.1 percent; for Oakland, 4.1 to 45.6 percent (Urban Institute, "Confronting the Nation's Urban Crisis: From Watts [1965] to South Central Los Angeles [1992]" [Washington, D.C., 1992, mimeographed], 9, tab. 1).

279. Krumholz, "Kerner Commission Twenty Years Later," 28–29.

280. Ibid., 29. See also Huey L. Perry, "The Evolution and Impact of Biracial Coalitions and Black Mayors in Birmingham and New Orleans," in Browning et al., *Racial Politics in American Cities*, 140 (offering detailed statistics on black gains in public employment and executive appointments in Birmingham and New Orleans between 1960 and 1985); Raphael J. Sonenshein, "Biracial Coalition Politics in Los Angeles," in Browning et al., *Racial Politics in American Cities*, 33, 41–42 (offering similar statistics on gains in Los Angeles under African American mayor Tom Bradley).

281. Orfield and Ashkinaze, *Closing Door*, 17–23.

282. Clarence N. Stone, "Race and Regime in Atlanta," in Browning et al., *Racial Politics in American Cities*, 125, 136; see generally Clarence N. Stone, *Economic Growth and Neighborhood Discontent: System Bias in the Urban Renewal Program of Atlanta* (Chapel Hill: University of North Carolina Press, 1976) (examining the systematic neglect of Atlanta's low-income, minority neighborhoods by Atlanta's moderate, pro-development mayoral regimes during the 1960s and early 1970s).

283. Orfield and Ashkinaze, *Closing Door*, 49–50 (quoting Robert C. Smith, "Recent Elections and Black Politics: The Maturation or Death of Black Politics?," *Political Science and Politics* 23 [1990]: 160–62).

284. Stone, "Race and Regime in Atlanta," 137. Elsewhere Stone and his colleagues have underscored, with unsentimental realism, the unattractive light in which the urban poor are often seen by municipal administrations:

1. There is a limited need for the cheap and unskilled labor they offer.
2. They do not vote in large numbers, and if they did, it would upset established political liens.
3. Their service demands exceed their revenue production—consequently they represent a revenue deficit.

4. Their problems are hard to solve and they are not a sought-after clientele by service agencies.

5. Their presence has a contagious effect, driving out the affluent and attracting more poor.

Local governments, for their part, are financially constrained; they have a limited tax base, limited borrowing power, and a restricted right to levy new taxes. They exist in economic competition, one metropolitan region with another and, within metropolitan regions, one jurisdiction with another. They are in open competition for enterprises that will add to the property tax and wage base, without adding unduly to the service costs. They are in covert competition to avoid accommodating the poor. (Clarence N. Stone, Robert K. Whelan, and William J. Murin, *Urban Policy and Politics in a Bureaucratic Age*, 2d ed. [Englewood Cliffs, N.J.: Prentice-Hall, 1986], 382)

285. Orfield and Ashkinaze, *Closing Door*, 24–25. Georgia Persons has observed,

The important thing to remember is that the plight of black-mayor cities and their citizenry is tied to larger economic forces over which African-Americans simply have no control. This is a profound economic reality that frequently drives the political path pursued by black mayors; and that path may offer only minimal, if any benefits to the African-American community. Indeed, the demands of governing are frequently very conflicting ones and frequently black mayors in their governing roles actually serve to reinforce the prevailing economic and social order that they were expected to aid in changing. (Persons, "Racial Politics and Black Power," 183)

See generally Paul E. Peterson, *City Limits* (Chicago: University of Chicago Press, 1981) (arguing that larger economic forces powerfully constrain and determine the course pursued by municipal officials).

286. See Peter Dreier, "America's Urban Crisis: Symptoms, Causes, and Solutions" (in this volume); see also Downs, *New Visions for Metropolitan America*, 45–94 (summarizing current data on the problems confronting American central cities and their suburbs); Helen F. Ladd and John Yinger, *America's Ailing Cities: Fiscal Health and the Design of Urban Policy* (Baltimore: Johns Hopkins University Press, 1991) (detailing the economic pressures on city governments); Thomas M. Stanback Jr., *The New Suburbanization: Challenge to the Central City* (Boulder, Colo.: Westview Press, 1991) (suggesting that the economic future of metropolitan areas lies in their suburbs, not their central cities); Joel Garreau, *Edge City: Life on the New Frontier* (New York: Doubleday, 1991).

287. David Rusk, "Cities without Suburbs," *New Democrat*, May 1992, 17, 19. See also Rusk, *Cities without Suburbs* (expanding on and elaborating his earlier analysis).

288. Rusk, "Cities without Suburbs," 19. Growing cities are defined as those that experienced a population growth rate greater than 10 percent between 1960

and 1990; stagnant cities grew 0 to 10 percent; declining cities lost 0 to 10 percent. See also Rusk, *Cities without Suburbs*, 51–84 (conducting an even more intensive analysis of 165 metropolitan areas).

289. Rusk, "Cities without Suburbs," 19.

290. For example, the growing cities averaged 25 local governments and 14 local school districts in 1987; the declining cities averaged 35 school districts and 78 local governments (ibid.).

291. Ibid., 17.

292. There is serious debate over whether a new "underclass" has really taken shape in America's cities. Compare, for example, Wilson, *Truly Disadvantaged*, 7–19 (contending that such a phenomenon is under way, prompted by economic and social forces), and Mincy, "The Underclass," 109, 133 (reviewing the research literature on the underclass issue and concluding that the debate "focuses on what may be a growing social policy challenge for which there are no well-known or agreed-upon solutions"), with Christopher Jencks, "Is the American Underclass Growing?," in Jencks and Peterson, *Urban Underclass*, 28, 96 (contending that the underclass notion is an oversimplification of more complex phenomena and that "the claim that America has a growing underclass does not help us to understand complex changes of the kind [he] . . . describes"), and Michael Katz, "The Urban 'Underclass' as a Metaphor of Social Transformation," in Katz, *"Underclass" Debate*, 3, 22 (arguing that "the word *underclass* . . . has little intellectual substance [and] lacks a consistent, defensible theoretical basis").

293. Douglas S. Massey and Mitchell L. Eggers, "The Ecology of Inequality: Minorities and the Concentration of Poverty, 1970–1980," *American Journal of Sociology* 95 (1990): 1153.

294. Massey and Denton, *American Apartheid*, 126.

295. Ibid., 130–47.

296. Katz, "Reframing the Debate," 477.

297. Ibid., 354.

298. Compare William Julius Wilson, "The Hidden Agenda," in Wilson, *Truly Disadvantaged*, 140–64 (arguing for a "fundamental shift from the traditional race-specific approach" toward universal economic programs that draw support from a wider spectrum of American society), and Theda Skocpol, "Targeting within Universalism: Politically Viable Policies to Combat Poverty in the United States," in Jencks and Peterson, *Urban Underclass*, 411, with George C. Galster, "The Case for Racial Integration," in Galster and Hill, *Metropolis in Black and White*, 270–82 (insisting that an integrated process is a crucial goal of urban policy); Gary Orfield, "Ghettoization and Its Alternatives," in Paul E. Peterson, ed., *The New Urban Reality* (Washington, D.C.: Brookings Institution, 1985), 161–93 (contending that residential integration is the only serious alternative to continued ghetto formation); and Robert Greenstein, "Universal and Targeted Approaches to Relieving Poverty: An Alternative View," in Jencks and Peterson, *Urban Underclass*, 437 (arguing that carefully tailored, class-specific, if not race-specific, economic and social policies are politically viable). See also Anthony Downs, *Opening Up the Suburbs: An Urban Strategy for America* (New Haven: Yale University Press, 1973) (offering a classic

argument in favor of policies that affirmatively promote residential desegregation); Anthony Downs, "Policy Directions Concerning Racial Discrimination in U.S. Housing Markets," *Housing Policy Debate* 3 (1992): 685 (reluctantly concluding that, in view of continuing, widespread public resistance to desegregation policies, principal policy efforts should be directed toward reduction of illegal acts of discrimination in housing sales and rental markets).

Part Two   An Urban Policy
for America

Is Such a Framework Feasible?

Peter Dreier # America's Urban Crisis

Symptoms, Causes, and Solutions

Introduction

Perhaps the biggest challenge facing America today is the crisis in its cities.
The obstacles to success are to some extent economic, given the federal
budget deficit. The end of the Cold War, however, offers an unprecedented
opportunity to reorder national priorities and address long-unmet domestic needs.

In reality the obstacles are primarily political and ideological. Federal
priorities are shaped by power politics, and cities have become increasingly
isolated in national politics. The nation's changing demographics, particularly the growth of the suburbs, also play an important part in shaping national priorities.

Even after the election of liberal Democrat Bill Clinton to the White
House, there emerged no national commitment to rebuild our cities. Many
Americans hoped that Clinton's victory in November 1992 would usher in
a new era of hope for the nation's cities. His victory was viewed as a mandate for a more activist government. But Clinton was elected without a majority mandate. He received only 43 percent of the overall vote. Equally important, his own party, while capturing a majority of the seats in Congress,
was deeply divided, with many members closely linked to big business interests who oppose progressive taxation, Keynesian pump-priming, and
social spending. They quickly rejected his economic stimulus plan, which
was based on a major federal investment in urban infrastructure.

In its first two years the Clinton administration's two major urban initiatives were relatively small-scale efforts: the enterprise/empowerment zone
program and the crime bill. Although not sold as an "urban" program, the
Earned Income Tax Credit probably had a bigger impact on cities than any
other Clinton initiative. The November 1994 elections exacerbated the political isolation of cities, as symbolized by Clinton's proposals a month later
to dramatically cut the budget of the United States Department of Housing
and Urban Development (HUD).

The barriers to developing a national urban policy go beyond the Clinton administration's strategic errors or lack of vision. Indeed, Clinton's

inability to enact even his moderate social and economic agenda reflects a much larger dilemma in our political economy.

Proponents of progressive urban policy face two major obstacles. First, for the past three decades social and economic conditions in our cities have deteriorated. As a result, many Americans believe that we have tried to save our cities, but that the cities resist being saved. Many Americans believe that even if there were ample money, we would not know what to do with it, or at least could not guarantee that it would be spent wisely or efficiently to solve the nation's urban problems. More than twenty-five years after the Kerner Commission Report, the condition of America's cities is in many ways worse than ever. From this reality, reinforced by an enormous corporate-sponsored ideological assault on government activism (particularly during the 1970s and 1980s),[1] many Americans have concluded that problems such as poverty and crime may be intractable. There is, at the very least, considerable public skepticism about the capacity of the federal government to solve the cities' social and economic problems.

Second, during that same period the political influence of cities has steadily waned. It is not simply that the 1992 election was the first with an absolute majority of suburban voters. The number of Congress members who represent cities is declining, while the number who represent suburbs is increasing. Members of Congress who represent suburban areas may have some personal sympathy, but less political motivation, to vote to spend their constituents' tax dollars to alleviate urban problems. Congressional redistricting (gerrymandering) and lower voter turnout among city voters also play a part in the declining political clout of cities. Congressional loyalties have shifted from urban political machines to national corporate campaign contributors. While the nation's major corporations have no single political agenda, powerful sectors within the business community influence government decisions regarding tax, spending, and regulatory policies in ways that undermine healthy cities. Thus, marshaling a congressional majority for an urban agenda has become increasingly difficult.

A New York Times/CBS national poll conducted the week following the Los Angeles riots in April 1992 found that 60 percent of Americans believed the nation was spending "too little" on cities—up from 46 percent in 1988.[2] Urban advocates realize, however, that this sentiment is unlikely to prevail—or translate into policy prescriptions—unless suburbanites believe that they, too, have a stake in revitalizing our cities, beyond short-term "riot insurance."

It is time to rethink the urban agenda—specifically, to find ways to overcome the political and policy obstacles needed to build an electoral and governing coalition at the national level that can address urban problems.

Federal policy should have two key criteria. First, does it address the social and economic problems concentrated in cities: poverty, unemployment, infant mortality, crime, and so on? Second, can it gain the support of a majority in Congress, including those who represent suburbs, especially working-class and lower middle-class areas?

Is such a policy possible? What arguments can be made to convince suburbanites that they have a stake in revitalizing the cities? How do we make the case for a federal urban agenda when the perception of (and news reporting about) cities is dominated by economic decline, social pathology, crime, and municipal mismanagement?[3]

In general, public opinion is more supportive of local government than of Washington. In fact, during the past decade many local governments have developed innovative ways to deliver basic services and improve management. They have also created partnerships with community-based organizations, increased citizen participation in decision making, and expanded the legal and regulatory tools for addressing issues such as housing, crime, and economic development. Many of the successful efforts to "reinvent" government have occurred at the local levels.[4] Efforts of this type are regularly reported in journals such as *Governing*, but they rarely find their way into the mainstream media.

The fact remains, however, that cities lack the resources to address the problems they confront. Until the nation's political climate is more hospitable to addressing these problems, cities will face continued isolation in national politics. That transformation will not be easy. Cities remain under attack as symbols of the failure of activist government and well-intentioned, but naive, liberalism. The conservative attack on cities is merely a part of a larger privatization agenda to reduce government and discredit public endeavors of economic uplift. In the 1980s the Reagan and Bush administrations slashed federal funds for urban aid. In 1980, federal dollars accounted for 14.3 percent of city budgets; by 1992, it was less than 5 percent.

Politically, cities suffer from voter backlashes against crime, drugs, illegitimacy, youth violence, minorities, the "undeserving" poor, and government itself. To the critics and cynics, programs such as public housing, Model Cities, Urban Development Action Grants, and welfare represent well-intentioned government gone awry. To an increasingly skeptical public, giving cities more money means handing tax dollars to politically connected developers (symbolized by the recent HUD scandal), big-city mayors who dole out patronage jobs to loyal constituents or incompetent bureaucrats, poor people who engage in destructive antisocial behavior, or well-meaning do-gooders who run social programs that seem neither to lift the poor out of poverty nor to teach them middle-class values.

This essay assumes that the political will *can* be mobilized to address the nation's urban crisis, but that it will require significant changes in political strategies. First, it examines the growing isolation of cities in national politics. It then reviews the symptoms and root causes of the urban crisis. Finally, it proposes a policy agenda for addressing these problems and confronting the political dilemmas.

The Political Landscape

In April 1992, while the largest civil disorder in American history was erupting in Los Angeles, staffers at *Atlantic* magazine were editing an article by political analyst William Schneider titled "The Dawn of the Suburban Era in American Politics."[5] The confluence of these two events reflects the dilemma of America's urban crisis; in ways not discussed in Schneider's article, however, it also suggests solutions.

For years, mayors and other urban advocates had warned that cities were ticking time bombs waiting to explode. When the Los Angeles riots erupted, many hoped that it would catalyze a major national commitment to revitalize the cities—an urban Marshall Plan. Unfortunately such pleas fell on deaf ears.

For example, at a meeting in August 1991 the nation's mayors discussed the idea for a "save our cities" march in Washington to be held in the midst of the presidential election. The mayors persuaded a variety of unions, public interest groups, church organizations, and other associations to agree to cosponsor the march, which they set for May 6. Only a few weeks before the scheduled event, the march was attracting little interest from presidential candidates or the media. The Los Angeles riots erupted a week before the scheduled march, which guaranteed a significant turnout—over 150,000 people—and reasonable media coverage, but the rally had little impact on the presidential campaign.[6] Although the 1992 Democratic and Republican conventions took place shortly after the Los Angeles riots and were held in two troubled cities—New York and Houston, respectively—the problem of urban decay was conspicuously absent from the speeches and the party platforms, as well as from the subsequent campaigns.

Indeed, for a few weeks following the Los Angeles riots, America's urban crisis was a hot topic. It was the subject of congressional debate and was discussed on television talk shows and featured in newsmagazine cover stories. Sociologists and other urban experts expounded about underlying causes and remedies. In the midst of a heated race for the White House, President Bush and his Democratic rivals visited Los Angeles and other cities to demonstrate their concern. Once the journalists left Los Angeles, however, Congress passed a meager quick-fix emergency urban aid pack-

age,[7] and the candidates for president turned their attention to other issues. The plight of America's cities returned to political obscurity. Why?

In their popular 1991 book, *Chain Reaction*,[8] Thomas and Mary Edsall
argued that "suburbanization has permitted whites to satisfy liberal ideals
revolving around activist government, while keeping to a minimum the
number of blacks and the poor who share in government largess."[9] They
concluded that "the nation is moving steadily toward a national politics
that will be dominated by the suburban vote" and that "a politics of suburban hegemony will come to characterize presidential elections."[10]

Schneider echoed this view in his *Atlantic* cover story, timed to coincide
with the two parties' nominating conventions. Schneider noted that the
1992 election would be the first in which suburbanites represented a majority of voters. He also argued that changing demographics are moving
American politics away from cities. We have begun a "suburban century"
in American politics, Schneider wrote, in which candidates for national
office and for a majority of congressional seats can ignore urban America
without paying a political price.[11]

Schneider noted that in 1960 the nation was divided about equally between urban, rural, and suburban residents. By 1990 the urban population
had declined to 31.3 percent, the rural population had fallen to 22.5 percent, and the suburban population had grown to 46.2 percent, nearly half
of the nation. Given suburbanites' higher rate of voter participation, they
now account for a majority of voters.

The Edsalls' book and Schneider's essay helped frame media coverage of
the 1992 elections, including the presidential campaign.[12] Reporters and
columnists spilled a lot of ink describing the race for the White House as a
contest for the "swing" suburban vote, especially the disaffected working-
class and middle-class "Reagan Democrats."

During the 1992 presidential campaign the candidates' basic strategy
was to focus on the suburban vote. Although Clinton campaigned in many
inner-city neighborhoods, and although the Democrats launched a small-
scale voter registration drive in inner cities, the Clinton campaign continued to define the key battleground as the suburbs.

Nonetheless, there were signs that Clinton was seeking to hold onto the
Democrats' urban base, even while reaching out to the suburban vote, by
finding a "common ground" message. Twice in May, with the Los Angeles
riot embers still smoldering, Bill Clinton campaigned in the Republican
California suburbs of Orange and San Diego counties, linking the problems
of suburbanites with those of the inner cities.[13]

Post-election analysts concurred that while Clinton won a majority of
the urban vote (in a three-way race that included independent candidate
Ross Perot, a Texas businessman who captured 19 percent of the popular
vote), including large margins in low-income and minority neighbor-

hoods, the key to Clinton's victory was his success in capturing (or making gains over earlier Democratic candidates) the suburban vote, particularly in the inner-ring suburbs.[14]

Schneider's view of a new "suburban century" has become the conventional wisdom among a growing number of political analysts, journalists, officeholders, and social scientists.

On September 1, 1991, following an interview with three big-city mayors on NBC's *Meet the Press*, panelist David Broder, the influential *Washington Post* political columnist, said, "I think it's very unlikely [that urban affairs will be a central issue in the presidential campaign]. There is nobody who is really city-based who is in the race at this point. And I think the focus will be on who can swing the suburban vote. Politically, that's where the numbers are now."[15] Bob Herbert of the *New York Daily News*, another panelist, agreed, observing, "Not only are the cities in trouble, the cities are in trouble for a long time to come. I think the fact that the urban agenda is not going to be a big campaign issue in '92 by either party is proof that the cities have been abandoned. Neither party sees any value in making that part of their campaign."[16]

Indeed, during the past three decades, cities have become increasingly isolated in national politics. The late 1940s represented the peak year of city electoral dominance. In the 1948 presidential election New York City had 50 percent of the total votes cast in New York state. Chicago had 46.5 percent of the Illinois turnout. Baltimore had 42.3 percent of Maryland's vote, and Detroit had 31.8 percent of Michigan's. Los Angeles and San Francisco combined for 51.3 percent of the California vote, while Philadelphia and Pittsburgh had 30.7 percent of Pennsylvania's electorate. Adding other cities to the electoral mix strengthened the urban vote even more. By 1992 New York City represented only 30.9 percent of the votes cast for president in New York state. The share of statewide voters in Chicago (22.3 percent), Baltimore (13 percent), Detroit (7.9 percent), Los Angeles and San Francisco (12.9 percent), and Philadelphia and Pittsburgh (16.1 percent) also showed dramatic declines.[17]

The strong political coalitions of the New Deal and the Great Society, including the labor movement and big-city mayors, have been shattered. Groups such as the United States Conference of Mayors (USCM) and the National League of Cities wield less clout in Washington lobbying circles today than in the past. The most recent effort to build an urban-centered electoral coalition, the National Rainbow Coalition, was marginalized after the Democrats' 1988 presidential defeat.

These demographic changes have significant political repercussions, as the Edsalls and Schneider point out,[18] but they should not be viewed as a major sea change in national politics but as part of an ongoing trend. The truth is that during the entire postwar period, cities have only had a major voice in national politics either when business leaders wanted to improve the commercial climate of downtowns or when disenfranchised people disrupted business as usual with protests or riots. When urban mayors and political machines helped deliver the vote for presidents and congressional candidates, they had greater access than they do now. But the proof of urban clout is in the way federal policies help or hurt cities, and, as described below, most federal policies during the entire postwar era—housing, transportation, defense, and others—have promoted the suburbanization of residents and business.

For many years political observers had opined that Americans fled to the suburbs to escape urban problems. In reality their move to the suburbs was subsidized by a host of federal policies. Federal aid to cities—whether to revitalize downtowns or to help low-income neighborhoods—has served, in effect, to "clean up" the problems created by federally assisted disinvestment.

The New Economics of Metropolitan Areas

What is relatively novel is the view that not only are cities *politically* weak, but that they are also *economically* obsolete.

During the early 1990s the bankruptcy or near-bankruptcy of several major cities led to a spate of news stories about the fiscal problems of America's cities and about the political implications of the widening gap between cities and suburbs. *USA Today* quoted the ubiquitous Schneider, who claimed that Americans no longer believe in the "myth" that cities are the engines of industry or centers of culture and that "they do not want to pay for them anymore."[19]

A week later *Newsweek* ran a story titled "Are Cities Obsolete?," arguing that with the decline of manufacturing and the suburbanization of people and jobs, cities no longer have a central function in American society. The newsmagazine's thesis was summarized by Daniel Mandelker, a Washington University law professor: "We do not need [cities] anymore."[20] In the *New Republic*, columnist Fred Barnes wrote that the idea of the federal government's aiding the cities is "no longer viable" because "suburban politicians make entire careers out of protecting their constituents from the spillover of urban social disorder. And there's another reason, familiar to any suburban parent, for the lack of concern for cities. Suburban kids scarcely go into the city anymore. Mine do not, anyway. When I was growing up in the suburbs (Arlington, Virginia) going into the city was a treat. My kids, third-generation suburbanites, regard it as an ordeal, they respond to the centrifugal pull of malls."[21]

Around the same time, *Washington Post* reporter Joel Garreau argued in a book titled *Edge City: Life on the New Frontier* that the growth of suburban office/retail/residential complexes, such as Tyson's Corner, Virginia—usually at the intersection of interstate highways—represents the wave of the future, rendering cities and central business districts increasingly obsolete. Rather than view this development as a product of federal policy decisions, Garreau viewed it primarily as the result of developers responding to consumer demand. Garreau's widely quoted book helped confirm the pessimistic analysis of America's cities.[22] *Edge City* paralleled a more academic work by economist Thomas Stanback, published the same year, *The New Suburbanization: Challenge to the Central City*, which identified the changing industrial and occupational composition of central cities and suburbs during the 1970s and 1980s.[23]

Following closely on the heels of *Edge City*, the *New York Times* sponsored a survey to analyze the changing role of New York City in the metropolitan area. Two headlines reflect its findings: "Region around New York Sees Ties to City Faltering" and "For Many in the New York Region, the City Is Ignored and Irrelevant."[24]

Cities and Suburbs: Common Ground?

The 1992 election confirmed the Edsalls' and Schneider's analysis of evolving trends. The changing political and economic landscape has put urban advocates at an unprecedented disadvantage. The dramatic decline in federal aid to cities during the Reagan/Bush years forced mayors and their urban allies to rethink how to put cities back on the nation's agenda.[25]

"We're tired of coming to Washington with a tin cup in our hands," said Boston mayor Ray Flynn when he assumed the presidency of the USCM in 1991. But the mayors recognized that moral appeals to social justice and human suffering are difficult to sustain, particularly during periods of economic distress among the middle class. This rethinking has led mayors and urban advocates to emphasize increasingly both the continuing economic importance of cities to metropolitan regions and to the nation in an effort to find common ground between cities and the rest of America.[26] Flynn emphasized this theme in his 1991 inaugural speech as president of the USCM: "As cities go, so goes America."

Initially, the mayors' calls for a "common ground" agenda met with some skepticism among journalists and Washington politicians. In the past few years, however, academic urban specialists, working closely with urban policymakers, have begun to challenge the view that cities are economic dinosaurs or are irrelevant to the lives of people who live and even work in the suburbs.

Political reality and academic research have now joined forces to examine whether, and what, arguments can be made to help convince suburbanites that they have a stake in revitalizing the cities. It began in the fall of 1990, when New York mayor David Dinkins, recognizing the growing political impotence of cities and the federal government's indifference to urban problems, invited the mayors of the nation's major cities to an urban summit to discuss their common concerns. At this meeting a number of mayors agreed to enlist the help of academics in their cities to develop an action plan—a policy agenda—for urban America.

Usually such meetings turn into a catalog of fiscal, economic, and social problems. At this meeting, however, the mayors agreed that it was important to emphasize the *value* of cities as well as their problems. But rather than simply emphasize their cities' pathologies and distress, they decided to focus as well on the important contributions urban America makes to the nation and its metropolitan areas. By this they did not mean to ignore the cities' plight or simply to portray cities as the cradles of civilization and culture. Rather, they wanted a hardheaded analysis of the role of cities in our nation's economic life and their "value added" contribution to making America competitive in the fast-changing global economy. The goal of the mayors was to change the way Americans view cities.

At the Urban Summit the mayors and academics established the Urban University Research Network, an unusual partnership between public universities and city halls. The mayors asked researchers to write reports on a variety of topics, including the changing demographics of urban regions, the way the media covers government, and the flight of industry from American cities. A year later, in November 1991, the Twentieth Century Fund published these reports. When the mayors issued their statement, they titled it *In the National Interest*.[27]

To make their case the mayors released the results of a national survey, conducted in October 1990, that sought to ascertain how city dwellers and suburbanites perceive cities by interviewing respondents who live in or around the nation's 100 largest cities. The survey found that people living farther from cities (broken down by those who live within twenty miles and those who live within twenty-one to sixty miles) have a positive attitude toward their central city. A vast majority of suburbanites are willing to pay higher taxes to provide programs such as housing for the poor (74 percent), AIDS treatment (72 percent), AIDS prevention (71 percent), and public schools (66 percent). In fact, of the thirteen programs identified in the survey, only two—middle-income housing (47 percent) and mass transit (40 percent)—received less than majority support. The survey also asked out-of-city residents how they use the city. Among those who live within twenty miles of the nearest big city, 46 percent of the households have at least one member who works in the city, 67 percent depend on that city for major medical services, and 43 percent have household members who attend or will soon attend an institution of higher education based in the city.[28]

The Urban Summit produced another significant study by H. V. Savitch and his colleagues at the University of Louisville's College of Urban Affairs. They looked at income, job, and population characteristics for cities and suburbs in twenty-two metropolitan areas and discovered that regions with narrow income disparities between cities and suburbs are the most prosperous, while regions with the widest gaps in city-suburb income have the weakest economic and population growth. This study, revised and then published in *Economic Development Quarterly* in 1993, concluded that "the blight of the inner city casts a long shadow. Companies will not grow or thrive in, or move to, a declining environment."[29]

About the same time that Mayor Dinkins convened the Urban Summit, two other groups—the National League of Cities (NLC) and the USCM— were thinking along parallel lines.

The NLC sponsored a series of studies by Larry Ledebur, an Ohio University economist, and William Barnes, NLC research director, examining the economic ties between cities and suburbs, on the one hand, and cities and the national economy, on the other. Their first report, published in 1992, looked at population and economic trends in seventy-eight metropolitan areas. Like Savitch, they found that those regions that had the widest gap between central-city income and suburban income had the most sluggish job growth. When central-city income was closer to the income of its surrounding suburbs, job growth was significantly better. Ledebur and Barnes also found that in the twenty-five regions where the suburbs experienced the most income growth, their central cities experienced income growth, too. When the incomes of central-city residents increased, the incomes of people living in that city's suburbs increased by an even higher percentage. In fact, for every dollar increase in central-city household incomes, suburban household incomes increased by $1.12. Conversely, where central-city incomes declined, so did suburban incomes.[30]

Another NLC report, released in August 1994, reconceptualized the nation's economy as a "common market of local economic regions," emphasizing the key connections between cities and suburbs. They argue that each metropolitan area is really one economy and one labor market, competing with other regions in the global economy.[31]

The USCM, in collaboration with the Economic Policy Institute, sponsored a study by economist Joseph Persky and sociologist Wim Wievel, both at the University of Illinois in Chicago, and Eliot Sklar, a Columbia University economist and urban planner. Their report, *Does America Need Cities?: An Urban Investment Strategy for National Prosperity*, published in 1991, refuted the notion that a majority of Americans can live in suburban and rural prosperity while the centers of our metropolitan areas decay.

Now that the United States no longer dominates the global economy and currently is engaged in fierce global competition, the report found, the nation as a whole cannot afford the burden of large numbers of unemployed and underemployed people in the inner cities. Further, urban decay will spread from inner cities to inner ring suburbs to outlying areas. Moreover, the study found, investment in cities yields the greatest return for improving the nation's economy. They argued that a federal plan to help rebuild the nation's crumbling urban infrastructure would be the most efficient way to jump start a national economic recovery.[32] (During his campaign, Clinton proposed a $30 billion economic stimulus plan based on the USCM's report.)[33]

In September 1992 economist Richard Voith published an article, "City and Suburban Growth: Substitutes or Complements?," in *Business Review*, sponsored by the Federal Reserve Bank of Philadelphia. Looking at employment and population trends in major metropolitan areas, Voith found that the economic bond between cities and their suburbs may not appear overnight. Some cities may be undergoing severe decay, while their suburbs experience some growth. Suburbanites may not recognize the connection because, relative to the central-city residents, they and their communities are still better off. What they fail to recognize is that "suburbs in metropolitan areas with declining cities are likely to be performing poorly when compared with other metropolitan areas with healthy cities." For example, even though suburban house values may be higher than house values in the city, suburban house values are still adversely affected by city decline. Eventually the cities' troubles drag down the suburbs. As Voith reported, "central city decline is likely to be a long-run, slow drain on the economic and social vitality of the region."[34]

These studies suggest that rethinking urban policy also requires rethinking our old notions of "city" and "suburb." The stereotype of the affluent, lily-white bedroom suburb no longer fits, if it ever did. Suburbs today no longer reflect the homogeneous affluent bedroom community depicted in the TV shows of the 1950s and 1960s, such as *Ozzie and Harriet* and *Leave It to Beaver*. Today the suburbs are much more diverse in terms of their income, employment, and racial composition as well as the mix of residential, commercial, industrial, and other land uses. Moreover, as economist Anthony Downs reports in *New Visions for Metropolitan America*, while most suburbanites now commute to work in other suburbs, not central cities, they still "use" the city in many ways—for work, culture, entertainment, sporting events, health care, education, and other functions.[35] As Alex Schwartz of the New School for Social Research found in a recent article in the *Journal of the American Planning Association*, many suburban jobs, especially professional and financial services employment, are functionally tied to the central city's economy.[36]

Many localities that the census and media term "suburbs"—such as Somerville, Massachusetts; Pomona, California; Parma, Ohio; and Harvey, Illinois—are themselves small or medium-sized cities, with considerable unemployment, poverty, crime, fiscal trauma, and related symptoms of decay. Many cities and their inner-ring suburbs have much in common.[37] For example, in 1990 19 percent of the central-city population and 8.7 percent of the suburban population lived below the poverty line. Overall, 42.4 percent of America's poverty population live in central cities, 30.5 percent live in suburbs, and 27 percent live in nonmetropolitan areas.[38] Studies by demographer William Frey of the University of Michigan found an increasing number of blacks, Latinos, and Asians live in suburbia, although African Americans tend to live in racially segregated areas.[39]

Similarly the newer, growing communities outside cities share many features and problems with larger, older cities. Although fewer suburbanites now commute to the central cities, their fates are still intertwined. Many bedroom suburbs may seek to quarantine themselves from the economic and social problems created by a troubled economy—widening income disparities, rising poverty, and the environmental and related problems created by sprawl—but they cannot do so successfully without reverting to a fortresslike, siege mentality that undermines the quality of life.

At the metropolitan level, political fragmentation, racism, and other obstacles have made it difficult for cities and suburbs to craft common solutions. Only a few cities are in a position to annex outlying areas. Efforts to forge metropolitan-wide government, with a few exceptions (such as Jacksonville and Indianapolis), have met with strong resistance, particularly by suburbanites. Special purpose districts or authorities—governing parks or transportation, for example—have made the most headway, but they deal with very specific issues.[40]

In making the case for the continued importance of cities, some social scientists, including sociologist Saskia Sassen of Columbia University, focus on the continued importance of America's "global cities"—New York, Los Angeles, Chicago, San Francisco, Boston, Seattle, and Atlanta—as corporate and administrative headquarters in the global information age. The vitality of these cities is thus typically identified with the economic activities of their central business districts.[41] But within blocks of their downtowns we find poverty and declining neighborhoods. As MIT's Bernard Frieden and Lynne Sagalyn demonstrate in *Downtown, Inc.*, there is little evidence that the prosperity of central business districts "trickles down" to poor and working-class neighborhoods, unless steered in that direction by public policy.[42]

Has this attempt to make the case for an urban-suburban common ground had any impact on public policy? In the short-term, not much.

Still, this research has played some role in shifting the public debate, reenergizing the academic analysis of cities, and reshaping the research agenda.

In April 1993 the American Assembly, Arden House, and HUD brought several dozen social scientists, government officials, foundations and businesses together for a four-day discussion of the role of cities in our national life. HUD secretary Henry Cisneros collected the major reports discussed at that gathering in a book, *Interwoven Destinies: Cities and the Nation*. In the volume's introduction, Cisneros, former mayor of San Antonio, wrote, "The strength of the nation's economy, the contact points for international economics, the health of our democracy, and the vitality of our humanistic endeavors, all are dependent on whether America's cities work." [43]

But the nation's urban crisis is still far from the top of the country's agenda. Until we engage in a serious rethinking of how to discuss the role of America's cities in our political discourse, the problems of urban America will continue to gnaw at our social fabric.

Symptoms

No other major industrial nation has allowed its cities to face the type of fiscal and social troubles—such as the concentration of poverty—confronting America's cities. Other nations do not permit the level of sheer destitution and decay found in America's cities. We see the consequences of inattention every day: growing poverty, homelessness, violent crime, and infant mortality; widening racial and economic segregation; crumbling infrastructure; and deepening fiscal traumas.

Poverty and Declining Living Standards

During the 1980s the rich got richer, the middle class saw their living standards decline, and more Americans suffered in poverty. The dramatic increase in poverty was concentrated in the cities. [44]

In that decade, junk-bond junkies, merger maniacs, and savings and loan speculators rode roughshod over the American economy. Corporate CEOs paid themselves large salaries and bonuses while laying off workers and busting unions. The Reagan-Bush White House cut taxes for the wealthy, theorizing that the wealthy would invest their money so that the benefit's would "trickle down" to the middle class and the poor. Federal funds available for domestic problem solving were significantly reduced.

While the wealthiest Americans prospered, most families did not benefit from the decade's growth. The richest 1 percent of the population received 60 percent of the economic growth. Their average pre-tax family income swelled from $315,000 in 1977 to $560,000 in 1989. By the end of the decade, according to the *Wall Street Journal*, the 2.5 million Americans at the top of the income scale were taking in as much each year as the 100 million people at the bottom.

Between 1980 and 1989, average hourly wages fell more than 9 percent. Hourly benefits—such as pensions, health insurance, and paid time off—fell by 13.8 percent. The vast majority of workers saw their wages and their spending power decline. American families worked more hours and weeks. For middle-class families, only the addition of another income—typically a working wife—kept their overall household income steady. At the same time, the bottom 40 percent of families had actual declines in household income.

The poverty rate was 11.6 percent in 1980, 12.8 percent in 1989, and 14.2 percent in 1991. By 1993 15.1 percent of all Americans—and 22.7 percent of all children—lived below the official poverty line. The number of poor Americans—39.3 million—represents the most poor people since 1964.[45] During the past three decades, thanks to federal social policies, poverty among the elderly has declined dramatically, while poverty among young families has increased.

But poverty is actually much worse than official figures show. According to Patricia Ruggles of the Urban Institute, the government's official poverty line ($13,924 for a family of four) is based on out-of-date standards (originally calculated in the early 1960s) and "does not reflect a realistic minimum level of living."[46] Using Ruggles's updated standards, the poverty rate would climb to over 23 percent, while more than 50 million Americans—and one of every three children—would be considered poor.

In addition to an increase in the overall number of poor Americans, the poor are now poorer, and they are poorer for a longer period of time, than a decade earlier. During the 1980s and early 1990s the poor also got a smaller share of the nation's income: in 1979 the poorest 20 percent of the population had 5.1 percent of the country's pre-tax income; by 1991 their share had fallen to 3.8 percent of the total.

Most poor Americans are white, but the 1993 poverty rate among blacks (33.1 percent) and Hispanics (30.6 percent) is higher than the rate among non-Hispanic whites (9.9 percent).[47] During 1989–91, however, poverty increased among every race and in every region of the country. More than 60 percent of poor blacks, 59 percent of poor Hispanics, and 34 percent of poor whites live in central cities.

In fact, the poor are increasingly concentrated in America's cities. Using the official poverty standards, the percentage of poor people living in cities increased from 30 percent in 1968 to 43.1 percent in 1989. Nationwide, about one-fifth (19 percent) of central-city residents are poor, but in some

cities the figures are much higher.[48] The poverty rates among children in
major cities are even more dramatic.[49]

During the past decade, much attention was paid to the so-called urban
underclass—poor people who live in "ghetto" neighborhoods.[50] According
to Kasarda, the number of "poverty" census tracts—where at least 20 percent of the population is poor—increased from 3,430 in 1970 to 4,713 in
1980 to 5,596 in 1990 in the nation's 100 largest cities. Poverty tracts as a
percentage of all central-city tracts increased from 27.3 percent to 34.2 percent to 39.4 percent. The number of "extreme" poverty tracts—where at
least 40 percent of the population is poor—jumped from 751 (6 percent of
all city tracts) to 1,330 (9.7 percent) to 1,954 (13.7 percent) during those
years. Some observers believe that this concentration of poverty exacerbates the problems associated with being poor, such as high rates of crime,
dependency on welfare, slum housing, drug use, and chronic unemployment. But while much attention was paid to ghetto neighborhoods, most of
the urban poor do not live in such areas. In 1990, for example, there were
6.4 million poor people living in poverty census tracts and ghettos and
2.6 million poor people in extreme poverty census tracks.[51]

Homelessness

During the 1980s a new element entered the landscape of America's cities:
homeless people sleeping in alleyways and subways, in cars, and on park
benches. A *New York Times* poll in 1990 reported that 68 percent of urban
Americans see the homeless in the course of their daily routine. Nationally
the figure was 54 percent, an 18 percent increase in four years.[52] Since
the early 1980s the USCM has conducted an annual survey of homelessness in major American cities. Despite the period's economic growth, each
year the study has found that the demands by people seeking emergency
housing increased substantially from the previous year. In 1993 alone requests for emergency shelter increased 10 percent on average in the cities
surveyed.[53]

The exact number of homeless people in America is unclear, and efforts
by the Census Bureau to count the homeless have failed. The most widely
cited report, conducted by the Urban Institute in 1987 (prior to the current
recession), estimated the number of homeless at 600,000 on any given
night and 1.2 million over the course of the year.[54] A random survey conducted in 1990 found that 3.1 percent of the adult population (5.7 million
Americans) reported having been "literally homeless" (sleeping in shelters,
abandoned buildings, bus and train stations, etc.) in the previous five
years; 7.4 percent of the population (13.5 million adults) reported being
"literally homeless" at some point in their lifetimes.[55]

As the decade began, the initial stereotype of a homeless person was of an alcoholic or mentally ill middle-aged man or "bag lady," many of whom were victims of deinstitutionalization resulting from the Community Mental Health Act of 1963. By mid-decade, however, surveys found that families and children were the fastest-growing subgroup among the homeless population. In the 1991 USCM survey, children comprised 24 percent of the homeless population in the survey cities. In its 1990 survey the USCM found that about one-quarter of the homeless worked at part-time or full-time jobs. Approximately one-third of homeless single men are veterans. A 1988 report by the United States General Accounting Office, reviewing nine research studies, provided estimates of the number of mentally ill among the homeless that varied from 10 to 47 percent. Substance abusers, some of whom may be considered mentally ill, comprise perhaps one-third of America's homeless. Clearly a significant number of homeless persons suffer some kind of personal pathology, but this focus can be misleading. It is unclear, for example, how much of their alcoholism, drug abuse, or mental illness is a result, rather than a cause, of their homelessness. More importantly, when more low-rent housing was available—including many rooming houses that were lost to gentrification—even people on the margins of society could afford a roof over their heads.

Between 1970 and 1989 the income of households at the bottom quartile dropped from $10,080 to $7,558 (in constant 1991 dollars). Meanwhile, the supply of low-rent apartments (affordable to bottom-quartile households paying no more than 30 percent of income for rent) declined from 5.8 million units to only 2.8 million units. By 1989 there were 4.1 million more poor households than low-rent apartments. More than 60 percent of poor renters pay at least 70 percent of their meager income for housing.[56] The number of poor households living in overcrowded apartments—doubling- or tripling-up—has increased. With no income cushion to fall back on, millions of families are one missed rent check from eviction—and on the brink of homelessness.[57]

Infant Mortality

In the shadow of some of the world's most sophisticated medical centers, infants in many urban neighborhoods die at rates comparable to those of Third World countries. The nation's infant mortality rate in 1989 was 10 infant deaths per 1,000 live births. Thus the United States ranks twentieth in the world, behind much poorer countries such as Singapore, Hong Kong, Spain, and Ireland. The rate of infant mortality in most American cities, however, is significantly higher than the national rate. In Washington, D.C., for example, in 1989 there were 22.9 infant deaths per 1,000 live births.[58] Among blacks the infant mortality rate is 18 deaths per 1,000 live births. This, too, compares unfavorably with many poorer countries; in fact, thirty nations—including Hungary, Poland, and Cuba—have lower rates. Black children in cities are even more vulnerable.[59] These dramatically high rates are linked to the results of poverty: poor prenatal nutrition among low-income mothers that leads to low-birth-weight babies and lack of access to nutritional and medical care, such as immunizations.

Violent Crime

In 1991 alone 26,250 people were murdered in the United States, an increase of 21 percent in five years, according to the National Center for Health Statistics.[60] This is the highest murder rate of any major nation. Many cities set new homicide records that year, but local officials expect that the trend will continue upward despite the fact that the demographic group with the most offenders (teenage males) is declining as a percentage of the population.

The rising murder rate reflects a growing epidemic of violence in the United States, particularly in its cities. According to the National Crime Survey, 5.8 million violent crime offenses occurred in the United States during 1989, including 135,410 rapes, 1.1 million robberies, and 4.63 million assaults. According to the survey, however, only 45 percent of violent crime offenses are reported to the police. Approximately 5 percent of all households nationwide had a member who experienced one or more violent crimes.

America has the highest crime rate in the industrialized world. A murder is committed every twenty-five minutes, a rape every six minutes, a burglary every ten seconds, and a larceny every four seconds. About three-quarters of Americans age twelve and over will be assaulted in their lifetime, and a third will be robbed. Two of every five Americans will be injured in an assault or robbery. Eight percent of American women will be raped. While these statistics are frightening, causing many Americans to live in fear, the likelihood that a person will be a victim of a crime varies dramatically depending on where he or she lives. Although the media and some politicians play to the fears of middle-class suburbanites (such as George Bush's "Willie Horton" advertisements in the 1988 campaign), the reality is that inner-city residents are the most frequent victims of violent crime.

People who live in cities, particularly large cities, are more likely to be victims of violent crime (40.6 offenses per 1,000 residents) than suburbanites (26 per 1,000) or rural dwellers (21.1 per 1,000). Poor people are at higher risk of experiencing violent crime than others. Blacks are more likely than whites to be victims of a violent crime. Overall, 4.4 percent of blacks, 3.9 percent of Hispanics, and 3.4 percent of whites were victims of violent crime in 1989. Violent crimes typically involve members of the same race. In 1990 72 percent of violent crimes committed against whites were committed by other whites, while 84 percent of violent crimes committed against blacks were committed by other blacks.

Murder is the nation's tenth leading killer. It is *the* leading cause of death among black teenagers. A study of eighty urban areas found that from 1987 to 1989, more than one of every thousand black males aged fifteen to nineteen was murdered. In some cities, including Washington, D.C., Los Angeles, Detroit, and Jacksonville, the rate was double the national average. Although blacks represent only 12 percent of the nation's population, they comprise half of all murder victims. In fact, blacks are six times more likely than whites to be murdered. The rate of homicide among teenagers in suburbs (5 per 100,000) is substantially lower than in large cities (28 per 100,000).

Almost two-thirds of all murders (64 percent) involve firearms, especially handguns. In a recent survey in five cities 28 percent of inner-city high school males said they had been threatened with a gun; 17 percent have actually been shot at. Emergency rooms at inner-city hospitals report a growing number of patients hurt by gunfire. A study at King Drew Medical Center in Los Angeles found that in 1985 only 19 percent of its patients suffered from gunshot wounds. By 1991 that figure had grown to 51 percent.

The rising violence in American society is linked to the epidemic of drugs. In Washington, D.C., for example, the rate of homicides identified as drug-related increased from 21 percent in 1985 to 80 percent in 1988. Many poor inner-city residents turn to crime to pay for their drug use. But some studies suggest that while much of the drug sales take place in America's ghettos, much of the drug *use* takes place elsewhere. A Rand Corporation survey in 1985 found that only 22.8 percent of cocaine users in the Washington, D.C., area actually lived in the city; most (77.2 percent) users live in the Virginia and Maryland suburbs. The inner city serves, in effect, as a drug supermarket—the wholesalers and consumers live elsewhere, but the "street traffic" among retail drug dealers takes place in cities, where competition for the market generates violent crime. Law enforcement officials focus their efforts on inner-city drug dealers rather than on white buyers in suburban communities.

The United States has the highest rate of incarceration in the world, with ten times more prisoners per capita than Japan or any western European nation. More than 1.2 million inmates were held in the nation's prisons in 1991—more than double the figure in 1980. Blacks, 12 percent of the nation's population, make up 44 percent of those in local, state, and federal prisons. A disproportionately high number of these blacks come from low-income backgrounds in inner cities.

The dramatic rise in the prison population is linked to the "war on drugs" and its long, mandatory sentences for drug offenders. In 1980 25 percent of federal prison inmates were incarcerated on drug charges. By 1992 drug offenders represented 58 percent of the federal prison population and are projected to fill 69 percent of prison beds by 1995. Since 1987 these prisoners have made up three-quarters of new inmates. About 70 percent of federal antidrug funding is directed toward law enforcement, while only 30 percent is tied to treatment and prevention. As a result, only a tiny proportion of prison inmates in need of drug treatment actually receive any therapy. Furthermore, the "get tough" policy, putting more Americans behind bars, has obviously not solved the crime problem, since the violent crime rate has grown dramatically during the 1980s. Despite the doubling of the prison population, few Americans feel safer than they did a decade ago.

In 1991 alone the United States spent $20.1 billion on building and operating prisons. Adding the costs of taking care of people on probation and parole, the total rose to $26.2 billion. These costs—plus the additional costs for police and courts—contribute to the fiscal crises facing state and local governments.

Segregation

America's metropolitan areas are racially segregated. Within metropolitan areas and within cities, whites, blacks, Hispanics, and other minorities are increasingly isolated from one another. Sociologists have coined the term *hypersegregation* to describe this pattern.[61] The 1990 United States census shows that 30 percent of black Americans live in virtually all-black (90 percent or more black) neighborhoods. Most other blacks live in neighborhoods that are still overwhelmingly black. Sixty-two percent of non-Hispanic blacks live in blocks that are 60 percent or more black. Forty percent of the Hispanic population live in blocks that are 60 percent or more Hispanic. At least two of every three white Americans live in essentially all-white neighborhoods. In the largest fifty metropolitan areas 37 percent of blacks live in all-black neighborhoods. In most major American cities more than 70 percent of the population would have to move to achieve proportional integration.

The 1980s witnessed a growing gap between the black poor and the black middle class. Many middle-class blacks moved out of urban ghettos. However, most did not relocate to integrated neighborhoods; instead they moved to segregated, middle-class neighborhoods within cities or in adjacent suburbs. Hispanics experienced the same trends, as did Asians, but to a lesser extent.

Crumbling Infrastructure

Periodically, when a major bridge collapses, a dam or sewer system bursts, or a train derails—causing death or costing huge sums—media attention and political debate are temporarily drawn to the problems of America's crumbling infrastructure.

America is sitting on a fragile foundation. Its roads, bridges, mass transit, airports, ports and waterways, sewers, wastewater treatment facilities, and solid waste disposal facilities are out of date and in disrepair. In most metropolitan areas, traffic is gridlocked. Congestion and flight delays at most airports are now the rule, not the exception. The United States also lags far behind other industrial nations in creating a modern, high-speed rail system. During the past decade several major reports examined the nation's capital investment needs; the estimates ranged from $37.8 billion to $140.5 billion per year.

Without a strong infrastructure neither people nor goods can be moved efficiently. Capital plants must be maintained and, over time, rebuilt. In older areas with deteriorating facilities and in newer areas with rapid population growth, new facilities must be built. Except for highways, most urban infrastructure systems—transit, water, and sewer—are a century old and have far exceeded their useful lives. Boston has lead in its pipes. New York City's century-old water mains regularly give out at key intersections. Los Angeles's old waste landfills are ruined by toxic wastes.[62] In New York State alone 68 percent of its bridges (11,808 of 17,313) are either structurally deficient or functionally obsolete—that is, inadequate for current traffic.[63]

America's 83,000 local governments are responsible for managing and maintaining over 70 percent of the nation's public works facilities. Three-quarters of the 250 million trips made by Americans each day are made in metropolitan areas; over 80 percent of these trips are made in private cars. The public transit systems in many cities—which millions of people, especially the poor, rely on—are physically deteriorating, but consumers cannot afford major fare increases to pay for repairs and replacement. Cities lack the resources to build and repair their crumbling infrastructure, undermining the economies of their regions and the country. Despite this problem, federal grants to state and local governments for public works projects have declined dramatically. In the 1980s, nonmilitary public investment in the United States fell to 2.4 percent of GNP—half of the 1970s rate, and one-quarter of that during the 1950s and 1960s.

According to the Economic Policy Institute, a major public works investment will boost the private economy and overall economic prosperity. The institute found that a dollar spent today on public infrastructure produces from two to five times more payoff in GNP growth than a dollar spent on tax cuts or deficit reduction.[64]

Fiscal Trauma

Cities, trapped by rising costs, shrinking resources, and borders they cannot expand, are now confronting fiscal calamity. Many cities face bankruptcy and are operating under severe austerity budgets. In the past few years Bridgeport, Connecticut; East St. Louis, Illinois; and Chelsea, Massachusetts plunged into bankruptcy. A number of other cities, including Philadelphia and New York, teeter on the edge of insolvency.

To avert fiscal collapse, many cities have closed schools, hospitals, health centers, police stations, and fire stations. They have laid off essential employees and reduced basic services, such as maintaining parks, repairing roads, and enforcing housing and health codes. A 1992 survey of 620 municipalities found that 53.9 percent were running deficits, 39.5 percent had cut workforces, and 61.2 percent had reduced their capital investments.[65] Fiscal conditions improved slightly in 1993 and 1994, but only because of the drastic measures—service cutbacks, work force reductions, and tax increases—taken in the previous few years.[66]

A number of factors contribute to this fiscal crisis. City residents, who are increasingly poor, cannot pay sufficient taxes, but they require more services. Further, most cities are responsible for providing services not only to residents but also to commuters and tourists, neither of whom pay taxes. Meanwhile the cost of providing public services has increased. Beginning in the 1980s three phenomena—homelessness, crack cocaine, and AIDS—placed additional burdens on city services. These trends were exacerbated by dramatic cuts in both federal and state fiscal assistance to local governments.

Many states impose restrictions on the ability of cities to raise revenues. Even if cities were allowed greater leeway, however, they would be caught in a fiscal catch-22. Poor residents cannot afford to pay higher taxes or fees, but city officials fear that imposing higher taxes on affluent residents or businesses would induce them to leave, aggravating the fiscal crisis.

In *America's Ailing Cities* Helen Ladd and John Yinger conclude that "although the financial difficulties of these cities may be exacerbated by politics or management practices . . . the policy tools available to city officials are weak compared to the impact on city finances of national economic, social, and fiscal trends."[67]

Root Causes

The plight of America's cities will not be solved without addressing the root causes of urban decline. These include five major trends and federal policies that have undermined the economic, social, and political health of cities.

Corporate Flight and Economic Restructuring

The electronics revolution has hastened the development of a global economy and footloose multinational corporations. Since the early 1970s there has been a tremendous flight of previously high-wage (primarily manufacturing) industries from United States cities to locations with more "favorable" business conditions—low wages, weak or nonexistent unions, and lax environmental laws—found mainly in suburbs, rural areas, and Third World countries.[68] The United States government promoted this flight with national tax policies that encouraged businesses to relocate to new sites (rather than modernizing and expanding their plants and equipment in cities) and with foreign policies that propped up Third World governments that suppress dissent.

According to demographer John Kasarda,

> The largest cities of the North spawned our industrial revolution in the late 19th and early 20th centuries, generating massive numbers of blue-collar jobs that served to attract and economically upgrade millions of disadvantaged migrants. More recently, these same cities were instrumental in transforming the United States economy from goods processing to basic services (during the 1950s and 1960s) and from a basic service economy to one of information processing and administrative control (during the 1970s and 1980s).[69]

In the process many blue-collar jobs that once constituted the economic backbone of cities and provided the employment opportunities for their poorly educated residents have either vanished or moved. These jobs have been replaced, at least in part, by knowledge-intensive, white-collar jobs with educational requirements that exclude many workers with substandard educations.[70] Since 1980 the Fortune 500 industrial companies have eliminated 3.9 million employees from their payrolls. Between 1978 and 1982 alone Los Angeles lost about 70,000 high-paying manufacturing jobs, most of which were concentrated in the predominantly black neighborhoods of South Central Los Angeles firms such as General Motors and Bethlehem Steel, which relocated or closed their plants. Textile sweatshops, employing undocumented immigrants at below-minimum wages, represent the only growth in Los Angeles's manufacturing sector. At the same time, in Los Angeles and other metropolitan areas, employment growth emerged in outlying suburban districts, especially in the light manufacturing, high technology, and retail services sectors.

In a global economy, cities have little control over local economic conditions, but in the absence of any federal effort to help cities, American cities have to compete with each other for tax revenue. This has led to an unhealthy bidding war to attract private capital investment, allowing multinational firms to pit cities against cities, states against states, and even the United States against other countries to bring jobs and tax-base revenue. In many cases local efforts to improve the "business climate" often mean lowering wages, health and safety standards, and environmental safeguards.[71]

During the 1970s and 1980s some cities sought to revitalize their downtowns with new office buildings, medical and educational complexes, hotels, urban shopping malls, convention centers, and sports complexes. For example, in 1970 only fifteen cities could have handled a trade show for 20,000; by the late 1980s some 150 cities could do so.[72]

To cope with disinvestment and fiscal crises, many city development officials became "entrepreneurs," competing with other cities for corporate investment. Some cities sought to lure businesses with tax breaks and other subsidies (such as the $100 million tax abatements granted Trump Tower in New York). Many economists claim that the bidding war has gone too far. They view these incentives and subsidies as unnecessary giveaways; this private investment, they argue, would have taken place anyway. One expert observed, "Corporations are playing cities like a piano. They understand the tune. But the cities don't."[73] But many city officials view these subsidies as important ammunition in the competitive war for new business and jobs. (This debate continues today over the effectiveness of urban "enterprise zones" for attracting jobs and businesses to inner cities.)

Of course, many cities could not compete on an equal footing, due to the lack of either good locations or adequate resources. Cities were not equally successful in making the economic transition from producing goods to producing information. Many cities tried, without much success, to retain existing blue-collar jobs or to lure new developers, tourists, and jobs. According to Bernard Frieden, "Most large northeastern and midwestern cities lost manufacturing jobs faster than they gained white-collar ones."[74] As a result, many American cities still have not recovered from the loss of blue-collar industry and jobs. As factories closed down and waterfronts were left vacant, downtown department stores went out of business.[75] Neighborhood business districts that had provided many retail stores and local jobs declined.[76] The tax bases of many cities suffered, making it more difficult for local governments to provide municipal services. The devastation of Youngstown, Detroit, Flint, Newark, Camden, Bridgeport, and Gary is perhaps the most visible symbol of the decline of American manufacturing in the global economy.

Sadly, even those cities that did successfully revitalize their downtown economies have not stemmed the growing tide of poverty only blocks from the glittering glass and steel. Not surprisingly, the percentage of America's poor living in cities grew from 30 percent in 1968 to 37 percent in 1979 to 43.1 percent in 1989.

Why? The service economy is predominantly a low-wage economy, and most of its jobs offer no career ladder or upward mobility. The "working poor" is the fastest-growing sector of the nation's poverty population. A recent Census Bureau study found that almost one-fifth of all full-time workers now earn poverty-level wages ($12,195 in 1990). In 1979 12.1 percent of all full-time year-round workers earned poverty-level wages. By 1990 the proportion grew to 18 percent, or 14.4 million workers. Among white workers 17.1 percent received poverty wages; among black workers, 25.3 percent; among Hispanic workers, 31.4 percent. One-fourth of women workers (24.3 percent) and one-seventh (13.9 percent) of male workers earned wages below the poverty line.[77] The percentage of full-time workers aged eighteen to twenty-four with poverty-level wages more than doubled—from 23 percent in 1979 to 47 percent in 1992.[78]

As William J. Wilson points out in *The Truly Disadvantaged*, the urban poor—disproportionately people of color and young people—face a widening mismatch between their skills and available jobs.[79] The exodus of many jobs, particularly entry-level jobs, to suburban locations exacerbated the problem, creating, according to Christopher Jencks, "the difficulty inner-city residents have finding a job many miles from home and the difficulty they have reaching such a job once they find it."[80]

Some argue that the key factor is not workers' inadequate skills or education but the overall labor market and, in the case of minorities, discrimination. Some suggest that in a tight job market with low unemployment, even unskilled workers have better job prospects. Between 1958–60 and 1968–70 the overall unemployment rate fell from 6 percent to 4 percent, and the unemployment rate among black high school dropouts fell from 16 percent to 9 percent. By 1978–80 overall unemployment rose to 6 percent; unemployment among black high school dropouts rose to 21 percent. Among white high school dropouts it increased from 5 percent to 11 percent.[81] During the mid 1980s the Boston area experienced an economic boom, with overall unemployment below 3 percent by 1985. Black unemployment that year was down to 5.6 percent.

But as the American economy restructures—in terms of the types, earnings, and locations of jobs—central-city residents without appropriate skills suffer, even when overall unemployment is relatively low. The educational requirements of most jobs are growing. Therefore, even though the number of young people completing high school is growing among all races,[82] the opportunities for those who do not complete high school (or who complete high school without acquiring the necessary skills) are declining. Between 1973 and 1989 the annual incomes of low-skilled white men in their twenties fell by 14 percent; for blacks, 24 percent. Incomes for white male high school dropouts in their twenties fell by 33 percent; for blacks, 50 percent.

Suburban Exodus

Since World War II the United States has witnessed one of the most dramatic population shifts in its history: the movement of Americans from cities to suburbs. Suburbanization is actually part of a larger trend, reflected in three interrelated demographic shifts: from the Snowbelt (the older industrial regions of the North and Midwest) to the Sunbelt (the South and Southwest), from rural to metropolitan areas, and, within metropolitan areas, from central cities to suburbs.

Some observers have concluded that America's postwar suburban migration in so short a period was a "natural" evolution, a result of millions of separate decisions by individual consumers seeking a single-family home, improved public schools, and a better life for their families. It is often described as the "white flight" or "suburban exodus" of consumers anxious to leave troubled neighborhoods for greener pastures.

In reality, the power brokers in America's corporate board rooms and developers' suites, and their allies in the White House and Congress, played a critical role in this suburbanization. As historian Kenneth Jackson describes in *Crabgrass Frontier*, these consumer choices were shaped (in fact, subsidized) by federal government policies that both pushed people out of cities and pulled them into suburbs. These included highway building policies that opened the hinterlands to speculation and development, housing policies that offered government-insured mortgages to whites in suburbia (but not in cities), and bulldozer urban renewal policies that destroyed working-class neighborhoods, scattering their residents to blue-collar suburbs, to make way for downtown business development.[83] Likewise, as described below, the population shift from the Snowbelt to the Sunbelt followed the move of business, subsidized by federal tax policy and antiunion laws and by the siting of Pentagon facilities and contracts.

This population shift, while not inevitable, is quite dramatic. During the first two-thirds of this century, immigrants from abroad (mostly Europe) and from rural parts of the United States (mostly the South) moved to the booming manufacturing cities of the North and Midwest. In the past few decades, immigration from abroad has stemmed primarily from Mexico, Latin America, and Asia, and the primary ports of entry are Los Angeles, San Francisco, San Diego, Miami, Houston, and other Sunbelt cities. Likewise, internal migration within the United States has shifted to the South and Southwest regions.

At the same time America's metropolitan areas grew significantly. The nation's 284 metropolitan areas now have a total of 192.7 million residents and account for 77.5 percent of the United States population. During the 1980s, metropolitan areas grew by 11.6 percent, while nonmetropolitan areas grew by only 3.9 percent. In that decade the largest metropolitan areas (those exceeding 1 million in population) grew the fastest (led by Sunbelt areas), while smaller metropolitan areas grew more slowly or, like Youngstown, Utica, Dubuque, Duluth, or Wheeling, declined. The thirty-nine metropolitan areas with a population of over 1 million comprise over half (50.1 percent) of the nation's population. (In 1950 there were only fourteen metropolitan areas with populations as large as 1 million, accounting for under 30 percent of the United States population). Of these thirty-nine largest metropolitan areas only five (Detroit, Cleveland, Pittsburgh, New Orleans, and Buffalo) experienced overall population decline during the 1980s.

Since the turn of the century, while metropolitan areas grew as a proportion of the nation's overall population, the suburban share of the metro population has grown steadily. This process accelerated beginning with the 1950s. In 1950 cities accounted for 32.8 percent of the nation's population; suburbs, 23.3 percent. By 1960 cities still had a small margin over the suburbs, 32.8 percent to 30.9 percent; but by 1970 the suburbs (37.6 percent) had surpassed the cities (31.4 percent). By 1980 cities had 30 percent, compared with 44.8 percent for suburbs. By 1990 the cities had 31.3 percent, while the suburbs had 46.1 percent.[84]

Since the 1960s and especially in the past decade, most older industrial cities lost population. During the past three decades St. Louis lost nearly half its population; Detroit lost more than one-third; Boston, Atlanta, Philadelphia, and New Orleans lost more than one-fifth. At the same time Sunbelt cities such as Houston, Miami, Phoenix, and Los Angeles increased in population.

In every region of the country—even where city populations are increasing—the fastest-growing parts of the metropolitan areas are the surrounding suburbs.[85] Los Angeles, for example, grew by 17.4 percent, while its suburbs grew by 29.5 percent; Baltimore lost 6.4 percent of its population, while its suburbs grew by 16.5 percent. During the 1980s only four of the thirty-nine metropolitan areas with a population of over 1 million experienced growth in the major central city at a rate more rapid than the metropolitan area as a whole. One of these was New York City; in the other three (Portland, Columbus, and Charlotte) the city's growth was aided by large annexations from the suburbs.

Two things, however, remain constant regardless of region or whether the metropolitan area is growing or declining. First, city populations have gotten poorer. Second, the percentage of minorities in cities has grown dramatically; in many cities people of color now comprise the majority of the population.

America's cities now face a shrinking tax base and fiscal traumas. In 1960 the per capita income of cities was 5 percent greater than that of their surrounding suburbs. In 1980 the ratio had fallen to 89 percent below the suburbs; by 1989, to 84 percent. In some metropolitan areas the economic disparities between city and suburbs are particularly acute. Newark's per capita income was only 43.1 percent of its suburbs; Paterson, New Jersey, 46.6 percent; Cleveland, 53.4 percent; Hartford, 53.6 percent; Detroit, 53.6 percent; Milwaukee, 62.9 percent; Gary, 63.4 percent; Baltimore, 64.3 percent; Philadelphia, 65.4 percent; Dayton, 66 percent; Chicago, 66.3 percent; Miami, 67.2 percent; and New York, 67.6 percent.[86] As noted earlier, however, these aggregate figures mask the variations among suburban communities.

Pentagon Drain

The Pentagon has played a critical role in the flight of business, jobs, and people from cities. During the postwar period military spending has accounted for the largest part of the federal budget. The Pentagon's decisions to locate military facilities and to grant defense contracts have greatly influenced the growth or decline of geographic areas. It has served as America's de facto "industrial policy," a form of government planning that has shaped dramatically the location of businesses and jobs.

During World War II the major sites of military manufacturing—shipyards, auto factories (which produced tanks and trucks for war), and aerospace facilities—were in major cities. After the war those sites began to change due to the influence of Cold War priorities and politics, including the influence of key congressmen in utilizing the "Pentagon pork barrel" to bring jobs to firms and workers in their districts. The multiplier (ripple) effects of Pentagon spending have dramatically changed the population and employment map of the entire country.

In reality, Pentagon spending is highly concentrated geographically. Most military installations are in rural (or once-rural) areas, while the vast majority of production and research dollars are concentrated in a few metropolitan locations. As Markusen and Yudken write, "Several major metropolitan areas in the nation are also highly dependent upon defense spending, particularly the Los Angeles and Boston areas, the Washington, D.C. area as a defense services center, San Diego as a naval center, and Seattle as a one-company military-industrial city."[87]

The production of weapons and the undertaking of military research and development have spawned new industries and new fields, but in doing so, much of the nation's resources and scientific expertise have been diverted from civilian production and research. Likewise, military production and research and the siting of facilities have helped some areas and drained others. Rather than employing research and development funds to help modernize the nation's basic manufacturing industries (for example, the steel and automobile industries) or developing new civilian industries to make the United States more competitive internationally (for example, high-speed railways), the Pentagon's priorities helped undermine key industrial sectors and the cities where they were located.

Even in those metropolitan areas that have won the Pentagon sweepstakes, however, the bulk of Pentagon dollars are located in suburbs, not central cities. In 1990 alone, for example, eighteen of the twenty-five largest cities suffered a total loss of $24 billion in their balance of payments with the Pentagon. In Los Angeles, for example, taxpayers sent $4.74 billion to the Pentagon and received only $1.47 billion back—a net loss of $3.27 billion, or $3,000 per family. That translates into almost 100,000 jobs.[88]

A study by Employment Research Associates for the Boston Redevelopment Authority analyzed all of the money coming into each city through military contracts and salaries. It then compared this sum to the amount drained out of the city by federal taxes going to the Pentagon. The sums lost are enormous. New York City loses $8.4 billion a year; Los Angeles, $3.3 billion; Chicago, $3.1 billion; Houston, $1.7 billion; Dallas, $731 million; and Detroit, over $900 million.[89]

The employment impact of this draining of funds is equally dramatic. Money going out means jobs lost. New York loses approximately 250,000 full-time jobs annually; Los Angeles and Chicago each lose about 100,000 jobs; Houston, over 50,000 jobs; Detroit, about 30,000 jobs; and Dallas, 22,000 jobs. The biggest losers have been the nation's industrial heartland, the areas surrounding the Great Lakes.

Even those cities gaining overall dollars and jobs from the Pentagon find that overdependence on military contracts has its downside, making them vulnerable to "downturns in the military spending cycle."[90] For example, both Seattle (dominated by Boeing, the nation's largest defense contractor) and St. Louis (where defense contractor McDonnell-Douglas is the largest employer) experienced severe economic hard times when the Pentagon reduced its funding for specific weapon systems or selected another contractor. Politics influences the rise and fall of regions and cities as a result of Pentagon spending.[91]

The $1.3 billion emergency urban aid program, passed by Congress after the Los Angeles riots and signed by President Bush in 1992, pales in comparison with what the Pentagon drains from America's cities. The Department of Defense saps that much just from New York City every six weeks.

Redlining

Redlining (discrimination in mortgage lending) by banks and insurance companies leads to a self-fulfilling prophecy of urban neighborhood decline.[92] Since its enactment in 1977, federal bank regulators have failed to enforce the Community Reinvestment Act, the nation's major antiredlining law. Under pressure by the banking industry, both the White House and Congress looked the other way while America's banks redlined cities, denying loans to homebuyers and small business entrepreneurs, while (thanks to deregulation) engaging in an orgy of speculation that led to the savings and loan crisis.[93]

Studies of local mortgage lending during the past decade have consistently shown that banks provide fewer loans to minority neighborhoods than to white neighborhoods with comparable socioeconomic characteristics.[94] This helps account for the low level of homeownership in minority neighborhoods. Residential redlining is compounded by commercial redlining, making it even more difficult for small businesses to open or expand in inner-city areas.[95] For example, Los Angeles County had 1,068 supermarkets in 1970, but only 694 in 1990; most of the boarded-up markets are in the city's minority areas. There is one supermarket for every 40,646 residents in South Central Los Angeles, compared with one supermarket for every 23,224 residents in the county.[96]

Prior to 1991, mortgage lending studies looked at disparities by geographic areas. Recent improvements in the federal Home Mortgage Disclosure Act, brought about through pressure from community activists, allowed researchers to look at disparities in mortgage loans to individuals by race, income, and gender. Using 1990 and 1991 data, the Federal Reserve Board analyzed the rates at which banks accept and reject mortgage applications from white, black, and Hispanic consumers. The first study examined 5.26 million home loan applications made in 1990 nationwide and also looked at the data for nineteen metropolitan areas. The study found that banks rejected blacks and Hispanics for home mortgages more than twice as often as whites with similar incomes. The second study, conducted a year later, found the disparities remained the same.[97] A study by the *Wall Street Journal*, using 1993 data, found that disparities between whites and blacks had not improved.[98]

In October 1992 the Federal Reserve Bank of Boston published the most conclusive study to date demonstrating lending discrimination. It looked at the creditworthiness of applicants in the Boston area to determine whether differences in rejection rates could be caused by differences in wealth, employment and credit histories, debt burdens, or other factors. It found substantial disparities between white and minority applications, even taking into account these factors.[99]

The absence of banks in inner-city neighborhoods compounds the problem of bank redlining. During the past few decades banks have disinvested physically as well as economically from America's cities. For example, the riot-torn areas of Los Angeles, home to more than 500,000 residents, have only nineteen bank branches.[100] Economic factors account for much but not all of this segregation. Because minorities are poorer than white Americans, they have fewer options in terms of renting or owning a home. Even those minority residents with the financial resources to provide such options, however, are often victims of discrimination by realtors and lenders. Recent studies by the Urban Institute and the Federal Reserve Bank document that blacks experience discrimination, regardless of income. Banks continue to redline minority neighborhoods and deny loans to black consumers at a rate much higher than that for whites with similar incomes. Realtors continue to steer into segregated areas black families seeking to rent an apartment or buy a home.[101]

Redlining by insurance companies, in terms of both residential and commercial policies, also exacerbates the problem of urban disinvestment. As the *New York Times* noted, "A lack of property insurance can strangle a neighborhood's economy. Banks usually refuse to give mortgages on uninsured property, and small businesses find it next to impossible to lease equipment or order goods on consignment if they are unprotected against fire, theft or civil disturbances."[102]

Insurance company policies—such as minimum policy requirements for homeowner or retail insurance—discriminate against cities and, in particular, minority areas. In addition, the location of insurance agents' offices (disproportionately in suburban areas) and the absence of agents who live in or are familiar with urban neighbors create a discriminatory effect.[103]

Federal Cutbacks

As noted above, federal government policies have encouraged, even subsidized, the flight of businesses, jobs, and people from America's cities. Then, to rub salt in these wounds, the federal government during the Reagan and Bush administrations slashed federal aid to cities, reversing five decades of steady growth in federal urban assistance.

The government cut three kinds of programs: direct grants to local governments, loans and grants to private and nonprofit groups for economic development and housing, and programs to help individuals cope with (or lift themselves out of) poverty. In addition, the federal government (and some states) imposed a large number of mandates on cities, costing these cities billions of dollars without providing additional funds, further exacerbating local fiscal crises.[104]

By withdrawing federal funds and increasing federal mandates, Washington was telling local governments to do more with less. Unfortunately, despite popular notions of local government corruption and mismanagement, there was little fat to trim. Washington's "fend-for-yourself federalism" simply meant that financially strapped localities had to cut programs and services during a time of growing needs.[105]

The combined impact of these cuts and mandates has been devastating to the ability of local governments to deliver services and to the capacity of urban residents to cope with poverty and the various health, housing, and other problems associated with poverty. Because the number of poor Americans grew significantly during the past decade while concentration of the poor in cities increased, cities experienced the most serious repercussions from the cutbacks in programs designed to serve individuals. The recession, which began in 1989, exacerbated the local fiscal crisis by undermining the capacity of local governments to raise revenues from property taxes.

During his administration President Reagan completely eliminated general revenue sharing, which in 1980 had provided $10.8 billion in direct funds to local governments ($1.75 billion to cities with a population of over 300,000).[106] In 1980, federal dollars accounted for 14.3 percent of city budgets. In 1992 it was less than 5 percent. During the 1980s some state governments provided funding to fill at least part of that gap, but in the late 1980s states began cutting local aid to the bone.[107] According to one expert, "If New York City had held on to the same percentage of its general expenditures funded by federal and state aid in 1989 as in 1980, it would have had some $4 billion more to spend and not had a budget crisis in 1990 and 1991, when it was forced to cut services and raise local taxes."[108] From the perspective of the states, Medicaid was by far the biggest budget-buster. Because states were required to allocate more of their own revenues to match federal dollars, they had less available to help cities.

Washington also slashed successful urban programs such as public works, economic development, job training, and transit by more than 70 percent. The federal government reduced funding for public service jobs and job training from $9.8 billion in 1980 to $3 billion in 1990. Community development block grants were cut from $6.2 billion to $2.8 billion. Local public works grants, $660 million in 1980, were eliminated entirely.

Federal housing assistance to the poor, budgeted at approximately $30 billion in 1980, also fell prey to Congress's sweeping budget cuts, suffering a reduction of over 70 percent. During the late 1970s, for example, the federal government added over 300,000 new subsidized housing units a year. By the end of the 1980s that number was under 30,000. These cuts parallel a dramatic rise in homelessness and a deepening housing crisis among poor and working-class Americans.

Programs targeted primarily to individuals—Medicaid; Aid to Families with Dependent Children (AFDC); Food Stamps; child nutrition; the Women, Infants, and Children Supplemental Nutrition Program; and housing vouchers—either increased slightly or remained about the same. The overall budget levels are misleading, however, because during the 1980s the number of poor people eligible for such programs increased significantly. As a result, fewer individuals actually received assistance; those who did received smaller benefits. For example, AFDC payments and Food Stamps benefits did not keep pace with inflation; as a result, families receiving AFDC were worse off at the end of the decade than they were at the beginning. Between 1980 and 1990 the average AFDC benefit per family dropped from $3,506 to $3,218 per family in 1990 constant dollars. Similarly, during the recession that began in 1989 a growing number of unemployed Americans were cut off from unemployment benefits because the time limit for eligibility had expired.

As local governments "downsize" their operations, the poor and working-class residents of America's cities are pitted against one another for these shrinking resources. This leads to heightened social and racial tensions. It also makes it more and more difficult for local officials to govern effectively.

Policy Solutions

Cities on their own cannot solve the problems of poverty or of urban decay. Cities are trapped by boundaries that will not expand and are subject to a national—and increasingly global—economy over which they have no control. For most of the period since World War II, and increasingly over the past twelve years, federal policies have contributed to the decline of the cities. It will require federal policies—with the help of state and local governments and community organizations—to bring cities back.

Thirty years ago Americans were confident that they could eradicate poverty and urban decay. Unfortunately many of the programs designed to achieve these goals proved unsuccessful. Many of today's opinion makers have learned the wrong lessons from the inadequate stop-and-go efforts of the past three decades. They argue that the government has tried and failed. This argument is unpersuasive, however, because most of these efforts were underfunded, misguided, and sought to serve too many goals. The War on Poverty, for example, was never really given a chance. Still, some of the programs that emerged from that period have demonstrated success, despite limited funding and commitment.[109] The magnitude of America's economic problems and its urban ills have grown, requiring new ideas and new approaches. Nonetheless, the view promoted by right-wing think tanks and pundits during the Reagan/Bush years—and accepted in part by many others—that the federal government can play no constructive role, or that "nothing can be done" because the problems are so intractable, contradicts much evidence and experience.

The key to revitalizing America's cities is to close the investment gap that lies at the root of America's economic troubles and competitive decline. There are three major components to a federal investment strategy to revitalize cities: First, the government must stimulate national economic growth and create jobs (with the goal of a full-employment economy), focusing major investment in the nation's physical infrastructure. Second, it must improve the nation's human infrastructure and the productivity of its current and future workforce. Third, it must invest in urban neighborhoods to improve the economic, physical, and social conditions of these communities.

While the first two components are not place-specific—not targeted directly to cities—they will have a disproportionate impact on cities because the nation's crumbling infrastructure, underutilized workforce, and most troubled populations are concentrated there. At the same time, federal policymakers must recognize that rebuilding urban neighborhoods requires direct investment to compensate for decades of disinvestment.

Without getting lost in details, it is possible to outline the broad principles and key elements of each investment strategy.

Jobs and Economic Growth

Most economists agree that investing in a jobs-creating program to rebuild the nation's crumbling infrastructure, including public transportation (highways, bridges, and aviation facilities), water, waste disposal, and sewer systems, is the most efficient way both to jump-start the economy and to promote long-term growth.[110] The United States, having fallen far behind Japan and Europe in investing in its infrastructure, does not have a first-class mass transit system; plans to build a high-speed rail line in the Boston-Washington corridor are still in the discussion stage.[111]

In early 1992 the USCM released a report, *Ready to Go*, identifying over

7,200 public works projects currently on hold across the country because cities lack the funds to implement them. Once started, these projects would create 418,400 construction jobs and, calculating the multiplier effects of such investment, over 1 million jobs within a year.

State and local governments own the bulk of the nation's public infrastructure—38 percent in the form of highways and streets, 16 percent as water and sewer systems, and 30 percent as schools, hospitals, and other buildings. Improvement in public infrastructure generates substantial returns to the private economy, including dramatic increases in GNP and productivity. Moreover, infrastructure located in cities provides substantial benefits throughout the entire metropolitan region. From a cost-benefit perspective, repairing and extending the existing infrastructure yields greater returns than building new facilities in outlying areas.[112]

Beyond infrastructure, there is a rationale for a broader public jobs initiative, targeted not only to public works but also to public service. Since the New Deal (with its Works Progress Administration, National Youth Administration, and Civilian Conservation Corps programs), other administrations have used public jobs creation as a countercyclical tool to combat the high unemployment accompanying a recessionary economy, although subsequent efforts paled in comparison with the scope of the New Deal program. But even in healthy economic times, some areas of the country and some sectors of the population (especially young people) suffer from high unemployment.

Opponents criticize such efforts as "make-work" jobs, but such initiatives can serve several goals: reducing unemployment, replacing welfare with work (thus reducing unemployment insurance and welfare expenditures while turning underutilized workers into taxpaying workers), and providing needed services. Some recent proposals include a public jobs program as a major component of any comprehensive welfare reform. For example, former senator David Boren (D-Okla.) proposed a Community Works Program Administration designed to create jobs for the unemployed and welfare recipients; a number of model work programs for youth, such as Public/Private Ventures in Pennsylvania and Youth Build (based in Boston, with affiliates in seven other cities), have shown success.[113]

Soon after taking office, the Clinton administration introduced an economic stimulus plan, focusing on creating jobs primarily through infrastructure improvements in urban areas. Attacking the proposal as a "budget buster," Congress killed the plan, forcing the president to retreat and to place greater emphasis on deficit reduction.[114] Ironically, many of the same business voices and congresspersons who opposed Clinton's plan lobbied strenuously for federal funds for public works when such expenditures were framed as "disaster relief" for the California earthquake, the Midwest floods, and other "acts of God."[115]

Although major investment in public infrastructure is a valuable first step toward sustained economic growth and job creation, additional steps are required. New sources of capital (particularly pension funds) must be tapped; research and development priorities must be changed to improve the productivity of the civilian economy, particularly in new growth sectors (such as telecommunications); trade, tax, and bank reform policies must encourage private enterprises to invest in productive jobs (as opposed to speculation and mergers) and to remain in the United States.

In the past, getting a job was the solution to poverty. But today at least one-fifth of all full-time workers receive poverty-level wages. If the poverty standard is updated, as many as 30 million Americans may be counted among the "working poor."[116] Clinton's success in expanding the earned income tax credit and his proposal to increase the minimum wage (which has fallen far behind inflation in the past twelve years) address this concern.[117]

Finally, a plan for economic renewal must confront the question of economic conversion. The end of the Cold War provides both an opportunity for and an obstacle to revitalizing America's cities. Current Pentagon spending levels can be cut by one-third to one-half over the next five years without endangering national security. These funds—over $150 billion a year—could be directed to both deficit reduction and new priorities, including cities.

Congressional debates on closing military facilities or cutting weapons systems no longer revolve primarily around national security concerns but around the short-term, adverse effects these cuts have on communities, workers, and firms that rely on military spending. But proponents of economic conversion face a cruel dilemma: even those lawmakers who favor cutting defense spending do not want cuts that will hurt workers, firms, and communities in their home districts. It is unreasonable to expect communities and companies to deal with their economic pain alone, but that is basically what is taking place. Although many in Congress have proposed comprehensive conversion bills, these initiatives have gone nowhere. America now needs a conversion plan to shift resources into improving the civilian economy and meeting social needs, including the improvement of the nation's cities. Such a plan would involve allocating funds for retooling plants and retraining workers as well as providing income maintenance and job relocation benefits and small business assistance to help subcontractors and supplier firms. The plan should also help local communities adjust to military base closures and major reductions at defense contracting firms and to change research and development priorities.

There is already considerable debate concerning how to carry out a post–Cold War conversion strategy that will minimize short-term pain and maximize the long-term benefits to the nation's economy.[118] An effective conversion plan by necessity involves elements of national planning and industrial strategy, but it must also incorporate local communities and businesses planning efforts. A federal agency to coordinate conversion planning should be located *outside* the Pentagon. This agency could coordinate a series of task forces and advisory committees, involving representatives of all parties with a stake in the peace dividend, including urban mayors and community leaders, to advise the president and Congress on a conversion plan.

Preparing the Workforce

There is growing recognition that America has fallen far behind its competitors in investing in "human capital"—its current and future workforce. A growing voice within American business is now joining more traditional liberal sectors in calling for expanding the nation's social programs. Both *Fortune* and *Business Week* featured post-riot articles calling for a major national investment in human capital—such as job training, health care, child care, and education (from Head Start through post–high school)—to improve the productivity of the workforce.[119] These business publications recognize that the social and economic costs of unemployment, welfare, and an unprepared workforce are a drain on America's competitiveness in the world economy. President Clinton echoed this view during his presidential campaign, constantly repeating the refrain, "We cannot afford to waste anyone."

Economists argue that the United States cannot (and should not) compete with Third World nations to attract low-skill, low-wage jobs. The future of the American economy, they suggest, lies in attracting high-wage, high-skill, high-productivity jobs. Thus, attention must focus on preparing the workforce for the twenty-first-century economy.[120] While there is some debate over this formulation—some economists argue that preparing the workforce will not guarantee that good jobs will be created, while others observe that the more immediate problem is finding jobs for today's low-skilled youth—there is no controversy over the need to invest more in America's youth and workforce.

Although the competency skills of American youth in reading, math, and science have steadily improved, they still lag far behind those of their counterparts in Europe and Japan. The overall high school graduation rate, as well as the rate among inner-city youth, has steadily increased. A high school diploma alone, however, does not guarantee that students have the required learning skills or competencies to succeed in the labor market. Among high school dropouts the problem of inability to compete is even worse.

New and expanded initiatives in education and training are needed. Some successful programs during the past decade suggest how this goal can be accomplished.[121] Preschool programs, such as Head Start, have demonstrated substantial success for disadvantaged youth; participants perform better in school and are more likely to graduate from high school. But Head Start, funded at $2.2 billion in 1992, currently reaches only one-fourth of the 2.5 million eligible children; a fully funded program would cost $7.7 billion by 1994.

Even the benefits of preschooling are sometimes undermined by students' school experiences and the other obstacles confronting inner-city youth. Most inner-city schools do not work for their students or the larger society. A school reform program should include the following key elements: changes in school governance (such as school-based management) and school funding (to narrow disparities between poor and wealthy localities); more parental involvement in active learning (including programs that teach parents to help teach their children); growing use of magnet schools; stronger integration between schools and after-school programs (such as recreation) and community health programs; changes in teacher training and retraining (to emphasize child development as well as pedagogy); changes in expectations toward student performance; and curriculum revisions to address the experiences of inner-city students (including immigrant children). Successful programs—such as those run by James Comer in New Haven and Deborah Meier in New York City—demonstrate that inner-city schools can be turned around. There is growing recognition, however, that mainstream schools cannot work for all students. At-risk youth—particularly adolescents and young teens from inner-city neighborhoods—need special help addressing questions of self-esteem and making positive "life-choices" in order to avoid falling into the subculture of gangs, drugs, teenage parenthood, and consequent poor school performance. A number of successful programs run primarily by community agencies—involving mentoring, streetworkers, community service (such as Boston's City Year program) and school-work linkages—have demonstrated some success. More intensive programs—such as urban prep schools—also have shown positive results.

The United States also must revise dramatically the way it prepares youth, particularly urban youth, for the job market. The current major job-training program, the Job Training Partnership Act, has not demonstrated much success. Mainstream vocational education programs are not tied to the labor market, especially for non-college-bound youth. They train youth either for jobs that no longer exist or for dead-end jobs with no potential for mobility. A growing number of companies support inner-city high school apprenticeship programs, but these ad hoc efforts do not add up to a comprehensive approach. America's European competitors place greater emphasis on ongoing training and retraining of noncollege students and adults. School-to-work transition programs must involve public schools, community colleges, and vocational/technical schools. The United States needs greater cooperation between educational institutions and private employers, more private sector involvement for worker education and training, training programs that focus on ready-to-work skills and that anticipate changes in the job market, and clearer performance standards, including a comprehensive system of certification for technical and professional skills.

More intensive residential "youth center" programs, such as the Job Corps and Youth Build, are needed to provide at-risk youth with an alternative to the regular school system. The Jobs Corps program (annual cost: $20,000 per participant) has proven very effective, particularly for at-risk youth, but there are long waiting lists. According to one study, every $1.00 spent on the Job Corps returns $1.46 in higher taxes and lower welfare, crime, and prison costs. Job Corps graduates have more employment and higher pay than similar youths who do not participate.[122] In the immersion approach of the Job Corps, for an average of eight months young people, especially high school dropouts, move out of their neighborhoods into special Job Corps centers, where they learn the discipline of high-performance work along with special skills instruction and ready-to-work socialization. The Job Corps, which now serves only 60,000 youth a year with a $920 million budget, should be dramatically expanded as part of a nationwide effort to provide at-risk youths with the necessary job skills. A similar program, called Youth Build (financed by several major foundations), has been successful in several cities, not only by providing inner-city young people (ages seventeen to twenty-five, mostly high school dropouts) with job skills but also by addressing issues of self-esteem and social skills. Several members of Congress have proposed a small, federally funded demonstration program based on Youth Build's success.[123]

Education and training efforts alone will not make America's workforce competitive in the world economy if the population's physical, social, and mental health remains in trouble. Investment in human capital also must involve a national health insurance plan and adequate child care allowances, to allow parents real choices about entering the labor force. School breakfast and lunch programs and expanded public health efforts through neighborhood-based community health centers (including immunization for all children) cost relatively little but have large payoffs.

Rebuilding Urban Neighborhoods

National policies that promote economic growth and that invest in people are necessary, but not sufficient, to improve America's cities and its most troubled neighborhoods. Just as a rising tide does not lift all boats, neither does a rising economy lift all troubled low-income neighborhoods, nor does it prevent stable neighborhoods from declining.

In the past, federal policies have done more to hurt urban neighborhoods than to help them, mostly by subsidizing the exodus of people and jobs. Even many policies specifically created to upgrade inner-city neighborhoods have had mixed results, in part because they were not well designed to achieve specific ends. For example, rebuilding cities requires more than changing a neighborhood's physical conditions—the mistake made by the urban renewal programs of the past.[124] It involves knitting together the economic and social fabric of urban neighborhoods.

People live in houses or apartments, but they also live in communities, which provide the economic and social supports that foster individual and family well-being and mitigate against antisocial behavior. People-oriented policies that help individuals lift themselves "up" may also give those individuals opportunities to move "out." Thus, place-specific policies designed to improve low-income neighborhoods require a careful balance. The programs must assist residents in upgrading physical, economic, and social conditions that make urban neighborhoods attractive to people with many choices, but without displacing or harming the people with few choices.

In the past decade we have learned a great deal about what works and what does not work. Turning these neighborhoods around requires policies that are place-specific. This includes several elements, discussed in turn below: providing jobs for neighborhood residents; creating a vital neighborhood business district with adequate retail services; creating decent affordable housing, especially homeownership, for residents; promoting public safety so that residents, entrepreneurs, and others feel free from crime and disorder; and fostering strong community institutions through which residents participate in improving their own neighborhoods.

Jobs for Neighborhood Residents

To bring jobs to inner-city neighborhoods, conservative policy analysts and former HUD secretary Jack Kemp have suggested some version of enterprise zones. The Clinton administration created its own version of this plan, called "empowerment zones," and, following a year-long competition, allocated the first grants in early 1995.

Empowerment or enterprise zones are essentially bribes (tax breaks and exemptions from regulations) to businesses to invest in urban neighborhoods troubled by high rates of poverty and unemployment. Experience so far suggests, however, that these zones simply intensify the bidding wars that already pit cities against one another to attract investment. Many studies also show that most businesses view tax incentives as only a marginal factor in deciding where to locate plants and offices. According to *Business*

Week, "A General Accounting Office study found that infrastructure, low crime rates, and access to labor markets were more important factors in site selection than tax rates."[125]

Thirty-seven states have sponsored more than 500 enterprise zones. This experience suggests that most of the jobs and businesses will be imported from another city or nearby neighborhood not quite devastated enough to fit the enterprise zone criteria. This zero-sum game—robbing St. Petersburg to pay St. Paul—offers no new jobs and does not reduce the overall unemployment rate. Moreover, the program offers no guarantee that the jobs will pay decent wages or go to inner-city residents.[126]

An effective enterprise zone program should provide businesses with incentives only if they create new jobs in the inner cities and hire inner-city residents for those jobs. Employers must also receive assistance for job-related training. In contrast, "programs that offer capital gains tax breaks dissipate their benefits. Owners tend to invest in capital rather than jobs, and shy away from the risks of local labor."[127]

In recent decades inner-city job creation has proved most successful when linked with local entrepreneurs, including community-based non-profit economic development organizations (typically called community development corporations or CDCs).[128] The problem is that for decades urban entrepreneurs have been swimming against the tide, facing unwilling lenders, few equity sources, and poor infrastructure. They also lack access to the technical expertise that large firms buy with ease. Without adequate access to capital, both debt and equity; adequate infrastructure and municipal services; and technical expertise, urban neighborhood businesses will remain small, struggling ventures.

The lessons of the success stories in neighborhood economic development are clear. Federal programs must provide seed capital, equity, and loans to community-based groups and small for-profit entrepreneurs to support neighborhood-based job creation projects. Senator Edward Kennedy has proposed a National Community Economic Partnership Act along these lines. The federal government could also assist start-up entrepreneurs by establishing small business development centers, modeled on several successful existing programs, to help provide basic capacities (auditing services, automated inventory control, business planning, and accounting control systems). Federal policies can also target specific fiscal assistance to local governments specifically for improving infrastructure and municipal services to inner-city business districts.

Many inner-city residents, however, are not likely to work in the neighborhoods where they live. In addition to people-oriented programs that provide residents with job skills, policies are also needed to overcome barriers to employment discrimination by race and to provide transportation to downtown and suburban employment. In one inner-city neighborhood in Chicago, for example, only 18 percent of residents had access to a car. Where public transportation from inner-city neighborhoods to jobs exists at all, it often involves lengthy commutes and transfers. Mark Hughes has recommended that the federal government create both job-information centers to help residents find jobs and "reverse commuting" carpooling systems necessary to get to them.[129]

Vital Neighborhood Business Districts

Strong neighborhoods provide most of the services that residents need on a day-to-day basis. Grocery stores, bank branches, clothing stores, pharmacies, and other retail services are critical. Not only are these services convenient for shoppers, but their presence guarantees that residents will meet in the course of their daily routines, reinforcing a sense of community. Such businesses also provide jobs and opportunities for entrepreneurship among local residents.

Many of the same policy tools described in the preceding section have been used to revitalize neighborhood business districts. CDCs and small entrepreneurs have played the major role in these efforts.[130] In addition, policies that encourage private capital and credit toward these geographic areas are essential. Despite lack of enforcement by federal regulators, the Community Reinvestment Act (CRA) has been a successful tool used by local governments and community organizations to attract bank financing, primarily for housing development and homeowner mortgages, and to pressure banks to open branches in inner cities.[131] Commercial loans are as important to neighborhood strength as home mortgages. Congress should expand the CRA to incorporate commercial loans as part of the regulators' evaluation of banks' lending performances. The Home Mortgage Disclosure Act should also add commercial loans to the data required on all bank reports, which identify where and to whom banks have made loans. Further, insurance companies should be added within the CRA's jurisdiction, given the important role that insurance plays in the success or failure of neighborhood business districts.

Affordable Housing[132]

In the past the federal government has depended primarily on market forces to provide housing to the poor—a strategy that has not worked. As noted above, only 29 percent of low-income households receive federal housing assistance: 1.36 million live in public housing, 1.65 million live in federally subsidized but privately owned developments, and 1.06 million receive rent certificates to help them find housing in the private marketplace.[133]

Rebuilding inner-city neighborhoods requires a variety of tested strategies. First, substandard housing must be upgraded, while new housing must be built to fill the vacant lots that scar inner-city neighborhoods. The major delivery system for carrying out this objective should be community-based housing development groups. Perhaps the silver lining in the dark cloud of the past decade's housing crisis has been the emergence of thousands of grassroots, neighborhood-based, nonprofit housing development organizations in inner cities across the nation.[134] Such organizations have patched together resources from local and state governments, foundations, corporations, churches, and other sources to build and rehabilitate housing against enormous odds. Through these increasingly sophisticated efforts, they have been able to leverage significant public and private investment in inner-city neighborhoods. In 1990 Congress passed a small program to encourage the expansion of the nonprofit housing sector. It required cities to set aside at least 15 percent of the $1.5 billion HOME (housing block grant) program for community-based nonprofit groups. To realize the full potential of this sector, comparable to the successful "third sector" housing program in Canada, this small program should be expanded. Moreover, as in Canada, federally assisted housing should promote economic and social diversity by encouraging mixed-income developments rather than ghettoizing the poor.[135] Single-family homeownership (such as New York's church-sponsored Nehemiah program, which builds low-cost homes and provides low-interest mortgages to low-income families) and limited equity cooperative housing developments sponsored by nonprofit agencies are preferable to rental projects. The federal government should also provide special mortgage subsidies to encourage working-class families to purchase and fix up homes in inner-city neighborhoods—a reversal of postwar subsidies that encouraged the middle class to move out of cities.

Second, the government should improve the nation's existing public housing and federally assisted privately owned developments. This involves giving residents a strong voice in management and, where tenants seek it, ownership. This should occur, however, only with adequate physical rehabilitation and ongoing financial assistance to avoid future foreclosures and physical decay. Megablock projects should be physically reconfigured to integrate them into surrounding neighborhoods, such as the successful efforts in Boston's Commonwealth and Alice Taylor projects. HUD should give residents a strong voice in reforming tenant selection and eviction policies. For example, tenants who "make it" should not be evicted but should be allowed to remain, to provide role models and contacts for job opportunities. Eviction policies should make it easier to rid developments of tenants engaged in criminal activities, including drug dealing and use. In addition, residents of subsidized developments should be linked to on-site community support services (job training, child care, health care, and substance abuse programs), such as the successful Family Development Center at Baltimore's Lafayette Court housing project.[136]

Third, HUD should provide all eligible low-income households with rental vouchers but require that the program be metropolitan-wide, so that residents can have greater choice and have opportunities to live outside inner cities. Chicago's successful Gautreaux Program, which provides housing counseling to low-income participants, should be replicated nationwide. Started in 1976, the program has allocated over 5,700 vouchers for low-income families, half of whom have found apartments in the suburbs. Gautreaux fosters racial and economic integration and deconcentrates poverty. Participants who find suburban apartments are more likely to find jobs, and their children are more likely to do well in school.[137] A universal rental allowance program would be the most effective strategy for dramatically reducing homelessness. In addition, some provision for community support services for homeless people with additional problems (for example, substance abuse) would be needed.

Public Safety

Community involvement in anticrime efforts is the most effective strategy for promoting public safety and reducing disorder. This, in turn, helps attract people and jobs to inner cities. Reducing the *fear* of crime and the perception of public disorder and chaos is as important as reducing the crime rate itself. Community-oriented policing—getting beat cops out of cars, onto neighborhood streets, and engaged in problem solving—has demonstrated success in several cities. Resident-sponsored "crime watch" efforts also help build trust between residents and law enforcement officials as well as fostering solidarity among neighbors. These efforts involve a range of activities, such as boarding up buildings, improving lighting, organizing "take back the streets" programs, setting up rape crisis hot lines, and creating computerized arson-prevention programs.

Violence fueled by drug abuse and trafficking comprises a major element of the urban crime problem. Interdiction policies have failed. Education and treatment programs are more effective, but drug treatment on demand must be a critical component of an urban anticrime strategy. Such programs save $11.50 for every dollar spent, much of it in reduced incarceration costs.[138] Programs to help at-risk youth are another key component of an urban anticrime policy.

Community Organizing

CDC-sponsored economic and housing development, resident management of subsidized housing, and neighborhood crime watches are all part of community self-help and empowerment strategies. Their success depends, at least in part, on strong resident involvement in neighborhood improvement efforts. Community organizing efforts have had their ups and downs, but even during the fallow 1980s, which saw dramatic cutbacks in the federal VISTA program, community organizations played an important role in successful, though small-scale, inner-city improvement.[139] National networks such as ACORN, the Industrial Areas Foundation, Citizen Action, and National Peoples Action, as well as more local initiatives, fostered citizen activism on a wide range of neighborhood and national issues. Many of the recent anti-redlining successes, for example, are a direct result of community organizing. A number of foundations and church groups helped fund these efforts. While historically skeptical of mainstream politics, these groups became increasingly engaged in electoral politics, helping to elect their own and other activists. Some of the nation's most progressive mayors, state legislators, and urban Congress members were catapulted to office by these organizing efforts.

Conclusion

Clearly, any effort to address the nation's urban crisis must result from serious rethinking about how these problems are framed and should build coalitions of mutual self-interest between cities and suburbs.

The major obstacle to carrying out some version of this urban policy agenda is not economic but political. The political influence of powerful business interests and the Pentagon and military contractors have distorted national priorities. Add to this equation the changing metropolitan demographics, congressional gerrymandering, and the impact of racism, and the prospects for building a national agenda that helps rebuild cities appear difficult. Overcoming these obstacles requires political reforms that will both level the playing field and give relatively powerless groups a strong voice in setting national priorities. From a political perspective the key question is whether it is possible to forge a national electoral and governing coalition that incorporates city dwellers and some segment of the suburban population. In fact, most urban policies provide little incentive for suburbanites (including residents of blue-collar suburbs) to have a stake in the condition of the cities.

Urban political strategy is still based on the outdated view that urban constituencies—mayors, African Americans, Latinos, the poor, and community-based organizations—can, on their own, mobilize sufficient political resources (through voting, protest, generating public sympathy for their plight, and other strategies) to get Congress to address urban needs. But in recent decades officials of the USCM, the NLC, and other groups have learned that cities are increasingly relegated to the status of yet another "special interest" group. The political dilemmas of American cities are also exacerbated by the fragmentation of urban constituencies and their organizations. On Capital Hill and in the news media the USCM and the NLC are typically defined as the "urban" lobby. To bolster their clout, they typically form ad hoc alliances with other constituencies—typically recipients of federal urban grants, such as community organizations, health care institutions, housing developers, civil rights groups, and others. These organizations have been losing influence over the past thirty years, reflecting demographic and fund-raising changes. Mayors can no longer "deliver the vote" as they could in the age of the urban political machine. Even if they could do so, the number of urban votes is shrinking.

The political equation is complicated by the reality that cities are not a monolithic interest in the same way that agribusiness or the aerospace industry is. Cities are quite diverse; the problems facing St. Paul may not be the problems facing St. Petersburg. Also, mayors, downtown business groups, community organizations, unions, and others do not always agree on public policy. In addition, the federal government is not organized to promote an urban agenda. In Congress, separate committees focus on banking and housing, health and welfare, transportation, and tax policy. In the executive branch, HUD is actually quite marginal to the overall well-being of cities, especially when compared with the impact on cities of Defense, Transportation, Health and Human Services, Environmental Protection, Justice, Commerce, and other agencies.

In light of these realities, existing political and policy strategies cannot be sustained if the goal is to create a congressional majority to address the problems of cities. What kind of political strategy and policy agenda will help build bridges between cities and suburbs and help create a congressional majority for helping cities?

Cities have long been off the policy agenda not because urban policy experts have lacked good ideas for programs and policies, but because cities—where most poor, working-class, and minority people live—lack political power. Their interests are overwhelmed by those of special interest and business groups who oppose Keynesian and redistributive policies. Reforms that would put cities back on the political agenda have little to do with urban policy per se. They are fundamentally political.

Here are some strategies to develop an electoral and governing majority to help America's cities:

Expanding the urban electorate. Unless urban residents vote, their concerns will be ignored. The United States has the lowest level of voter turnout of any major democracy. Typically only about half of the eligible electorate vote in a presidential election year and even less in off years.[140] Registration is the major barrier; more than two-thirds of those who are registered actually vote. Poor and minority voters, particularly those in large cities, are the groups least likely to register to vote. Once at the polls, urban voters—particularly the poor and minorities—tend to vote overwhelmingly for Democrats in national elections. The 55 percent turnout in the 1992 presidential election was the largest in almost thirty years. In the three-way 1992 presidential race, the Clinton-Gore ticket received 53 percent of the vote in central cities; the margin was higher in the larger cities.

In Canada, when an election is called, a complete national registration is carried out in a matter of weeks by a federal agency called Elections Canada. In national elections over 70 percent of eligible voters normally go to the polls. In the United States, by contrast, the onus is entirely on the individual to register. A major reason for the low rate of urban voting is the nation's complex, crazy-quilt voter registration laws. Rules differ from state to state and often from community to community. Cities generally have much lower voter participation than suburban counterparts. Urban interest groups were a key force in the successful campaign to pass the federal "motor voter" law, designed to remove obstacles to voter registration and to expand the electorate. Implementation by state governments started in January 1995.[141]

Since poor and minority (that is, urban) citizens have low levels of voter registration and turnout, motor voter advocates assume that increasing registration will expand political participation among these groups, thus helping tilt the political balance toward the poor and minorities and, thus, cities. The success of the motor voter law for urban concerns will depend on whether the mayors, community and labor organizations, and the Democratic Party mobilize potential voters around issues. These groups have shown little will or capacity for doing so. In recent presidential elections Republicans actually outspent Democrats in terms of registering new voters and mobilizing Republican registrants to get to the polls. In 1992 little effort was made to expand the urban electorate. In the 1994 midterm election low voter registration and turnout in cities played a key role in the Republican sweep in Congress.

Congressional redistricting. Civil rights groups have adopted a strategy based on congressional redistricting. The main thrust of these efforts has been to reshape congressional districts so that African-American, Asian, and Latino voters have a stronger voice, increasing the odds of electing persons of color to legislative bodies. Given the concentration of minority groups in cities, this typically means that more urban districts will be represented by minorities. But some critics argue that in doing so, these African American and Latino legislators and their caucuses will find themselves increasingly isolated. By carving out sure-thing minority districts, this approach also carves out a larger number of sure-thing all-suburban districts that are more likely to elect conservatives and Republicans, who have no urban constituency and little concern for urban problems.[142] Some observers believe this approach undermines potential coalition building between urban and working-class suburban constituencies in Congress. Instead the goal of "progressive gerrymandering" should be to create districts that straddle central cities and inner-ring suburbs, so that Congressmembers have a stake in building bridges among poor and working-class constituents.

Campaign finance reform. Political demographics and congressional redistricting alone do not explain the reluctance of our national leaders to push an urban agenda. Even those members of Congress who represent cities have weaker ties to organized voters. The skyrocketing costs of elections have profoundly shaped the way elected officials behave.

The demise of urban political machines is clearly linked to the emergence of big money in politics. During the first half of this century urban political machines played an important role in national political life, particularly as the electoral foundation of the Democratic Party. Big-city mayors traded jobs for votes, a formula that helped enfranchise several generations of immigrants. In the depression, Franklin D. Roosevelt catapulted to the White House on the urban vote. During the 1930s and 1940s the urban vote was the backbone of the New Deal coalition. Many scholars believe that John F. Kennedy owed his narrow margin of victory in the 1960 election to Mayor Richard Daley, who "delivered" Chicago's vote—and Illinois's key electoral votes. Through the 1960s even Democrats from suburban districts joined their urban colleagues in voting for many urban programs.

Starting in the 1970s, national corporate campaign contributors and national political action committees began to dominate campaign fundraising. Their financial backing increasingly influenced the priorities and votes of our elected officials in Washington. While big business has no single policy agenda, powerful sectors within the business community influence tax, spending, and regulatory policies that undermine healthy cities. We need to remove the legalized bribery system that currently makes it impossible to deal constructively with urban problems.

Even with a more activated electorate, the principle of "one person, one vote" is distorted by the power of big money in American politics. It distorts priorities on tax policy, defense spending, bank reform, and other issues, depriving cities and the poor of government assistance. Perhaps the most egregious example is the banking industry's influence over Congress, leading to industry deregulation during the early 1980s, the savings and loan crisis, and the massive taxpayer bailout, still under way.

The average race for a United States Senate seat now costs well over $1 million, House races cost well over $300,000, and presidential campaigns cost over $100 million. Most of these funds are spent on paid media, especially television advertising. Candidates for office and incumbents in office spend so much time raising funds, primarily from wealthy individuals and businesses, that they cannot spend enough time paying attention to other constituents. Big money shapes the kind of legislation Congress passes or does not pass. It even determines who can afford to run for office. At the local level, big money—particularly from real estate, banking, and related business sectors—plays a major role in local politics, where land-use issues are often paramount.

Reform of the nation's campaign finance laws should incorporate the following elements: public financing of elections, free broadcast time to political candidates, strict ceilings on the amounts that candidates for office can raise in an election season, strict ceilings on the amount individuals can donate to candidates, prohibition of campaign contributions from political action committees, and strict limits on "soft money" donations, which sidestep campaign finance limits.

An urban presidential primary. The way we elect our president undermines urban policy. The road to the White House begins in rural areas—Iowa, New Hampshire, and the "Super Tuesday" South. To be a contender in a presidential primary, candidates first have to appeal to voters in these early primaries, so they frame their message and policy agenda accordingly. By the time the winter primary season is over, cities are left out in the cold.

The USCM has proposed an intriguing way to address this imbalance: an urban presidential primary. Officially, party delegates are elected in statewide primaries, not by municipalities. But nothing can stop cities from adding presidential preferences to the ballots in municipal elections or—even better—a coalition of cities agreeing to hold a presidential preference ballot on the same day early in the campaign season in order to get a jump on candidates' attention. Organizers lined up eighteen cities—including Minneapolis, St. Paul, Baltimore, Boston, Tucson, Pasadena, Rochester, Spokane, and Olympia (Wash.)—to hold nonbinding (that is, no conventional delegates were to be selected) presidential preference ballots on November 7, 1995, simultaneously with municipal elections. The organizers invited declared presidential candidates to participate in a series of televised debates prior to what it is calling the CityVote primary. An expanded version of CityVote every four years would not only pressure presidential candidates and the media to focus attention on cities, but it would also help energize and mobilize urban voters, who are often turned off by presidential campaigns because candidates can ignore their concerns early in the campaign.

Labor law reform. When she fought for public housing in the 1930s, Catharine Bauer recognized that public housing was as much a jobs program as a social program. The backbone of the Public Housing Act of 1937 was the American labor movement, which at the time included about

35 percent of American workers. Since then, and especially during the last twelve years, the working people of the United States have been disenfranchised by the federal government's cold war against labor unions. As a result the United States has some of the most regressive labor laws among advanced democracies. Only 11 percent of the private sector workforce (and 16 percent of all workers) are union members.

Cities and inner-ring suburbs have increasingly become the location of low-wage service sector employment, the vast majority of which is not unionized. A key goal of urban policy should be to increase the incomes of the growing sector of the working poor concentrated in central cities and inner suburbs.

Labor law reform will help level the playing field between America's working people and business and help improve the political influence and standard of living of working people. Changes in the nation's unfair labor-management laws, which currently impede union organizing efforts, would help increase wages and benefits among poverty-level workers, particularly in the service and light-manufacturing sectors.[143]

Unless the political balance of power changes, all of those reforms that urban policy experts love to debate and recommend will be purely academic.

The end of the Cold War offers an unprecedented opportunity for America to reorder its priorities and devote its talent and resources to domestic matters, including the rebuilding of our cities. Whether the nation seizes the opportunity or wastes it, is a question of political will.

Notes

1. Kevin Phillips, *The Politics of Rich and Poor: Wealth and the American Electorate in the Reagan Aftermath* (New York: Random House, 1990), 59–66; Peter Dreier, "Capitalists vs. the Media: An Analysis of an Ideological Mobilization among Business Leaders," *Media, Culture and Society* 4 (1982): 111–32; Herbert Gans, "Deconstructing the Underclass," *Journal of the American Planning Association* 56 (1990): 271–77.

2. Robin Toner, "Los Angeles Riots Are a Warning, Americans Fear," *New York Times*, May 11, 1992.

3. See Jonathan Walters, "Cities on Their Own," *Governing*, April 1991, 27–32. For a discussion of media coverage of the Los Angeles riots, see Edwin Diamond, "It's Deja Vu All Over Again," *New York*, June 1, 1992, 40–43. For a discussion of media coverage of housing problems, see Peter Dreier and Alex Dubro, "Housing: The Invisible Crisis," *Washington Journalism Review*, May 1991, 20–24.

4. David E. Osborne and Ted Gaebler, *Reinventing Government: How the Entrepreneurial Spirit is Transforming the Public Sector* (Reading, Mass.: Addison-Wesley, 1992).

5. William Schneider, "The Suburban Century Begins," *Atlantic*, July 1992,

33–44. Perhaps to link Schneider's essay to the then-current national election, the title on the magazine's cover was "The Dawn of the Suburban Era in American Politics."

6. See, for example, Barbara Vobejda, "Mayors' Pleas Take on a New-Found Urgency," *Washington Post*, May 16, 1992.

7. After a month of political posturing and bargaining, the White House and Congress agreed on a $1.3 billion package, including a $500 million summer jobs program for youth and loans and grants to rebuild homes and businesses destroyed in the Los Angeles riot and the April flood in downtown Chicago. See Clifford Krauss, "Bush and Congress Reach an Accord on Aid for Cities," *New York Times*, June 18, 1992.

8. Thomas Byrne Edsall with Mary D. Edsall, *Chain Reaction: The Impact of Race, Rights, and Taxes on American Politics* (New York: Norton, 1991).

9. Ibid., 228.

10. Ibid., 229, 231.

11. Schneider, "Suburban Century," 33–44. Schneider had outlined his argument almost a year earlier in "Rule Suburbia," *National Journal*, September 28, 1991, 2335. Even earlier a *USA Today* reporter interviewed Schneider about the bankruptcy of Bridgeport, Connecticut. Anticipating what he would write a few months later, Schneider said, "It signifies the abandonment of the American city and the suburbanization of American politics. . . . Bridgeport could be the beginning of a problem that's going to spread all over the country" (Bruce Frankel, "Connecticut City's Bankruptcy May Be 'Dangerous' Precedent," *USA Today*, July 16, 1991).

A Bush administration official appeared to confirm Schneider's view when, soon after the Los Angeles riots, he told the *Boston Globe* that urban poverty and unemployment among black youth are "not our issue, not our constituency" (Michael Kranish and Peter G. Gosselin, "Aides Split over Bush Urban Plan," *Boston Globe*, May 17, 1992).

12. See Fred Barnes, "Up against the Mall," *New Republic*, October 21, 1991, 43; Robert Reinhold, "The Electorate: Chasing Votes from Big Cities to the Suburbs," *New York Times*, June 1, 1992. This view was reinforced following the 1994 elections, when Republicans captured the majority of seats in both houses of Congress. See Karen Dewitt, "Have Suburbs, Especially in the South, Become the Source of American Political Power?," *New York Times*, December 19, 1994.

13. Chris Black, "Clinton Links Suburbanites to Solutions for Urban Ills," *Boston Globe*, May 10, 1992; David Lauter, "Clinton Tells Orange County Not to Ignore Cities," *Los Angeles Times*, May 31, 1992.

14. See James A. Barnes, "Tainted Triumph?," *National Journal*, November 7, 1992, 2537–41.

15. *Meet the Press*, NBC, September 1, 1991.

16. Ibid.

17. These figures come from Richard Sauerzkopf and Todd Swanstrom, "The Urban Electorate in Presidential Elections, 1920–1992" (paper presented at the Urban Affairs Association meetings, Indianapolis, April 1993).

18. Edsall and Edsall, *Chain Reaction*, 228.

19. Frankel, "Connecticut City's Bankruptcy."

20. "Are Cities Obsolete?," *Newsweek*, September 9, 1991, 42.

21. Fred Barnes, "Up against the Mall," 43.

22. Joel Garreau, *Edge City: Life on the New Frontier* (New York: Doubleday, 1991). For critical reviews of *Edge City*, see Jane Holtz Kay, "No Place Like Home," *Nation*, October 14, 1991, 45, and Robert Wood, "The Developer as Folk Hero," *Boston Globe*, September 1, 1991.

23. Thomas M. Stanback Jr., *The New Suburbanization: Challenge to the Central City* (Boulder, Colo.: Westview Press, 1991).

24. William Glaberson, "For Many in the New York Region, the City Is Ignored and Irrelevant," *New York Times*, January 2, 1992; Elizabeth Kolbert, "Region around New York Sees Ties to City Faltering," *New York Times*, December 1, 1991.

25. See Alan Ehrenhalt, "The Mayors Need to Agree on a Message: Innovation or Desperation," *Governing*, September 1991, 11.

26. See, for example, Rob Gurwitt, "The Painful Truth about Cities and Suburbs: They Need Each Other," *Governing*, February 1992, 56–60; Mark K. Joseph, "Baltimore Makes the Suburbs Richer," *Baltimore Sun*, October 13, 1991; David Rusk, "America's Urban Apartheid," *New York Times*, May 21, 1992. Rusk is the former mayor of Albuquerque, New Mexico.

27. Ronald Berkman, Joyce F. Brown, Beverly Goldberg, and Tod Mijanovich, eds., *In The National Interest: The 1990 Urban Summit* (New York: Twentieth Century Fund, 1992).

28. Arthur S. Goldberg, "Americans and Their Cities: Solicitude and Support," in Berkman et al., *In the National Interest*, 37–45.

29. H. V. Savitch, David Collins, Daniel Sanders, and John P. Markham, "Ties That Bind: Central Cities, Suburbs, and the New Metropolitan Region," *Economic Development Quarterly* 7 (1993): 341–57.

30. Larry C. Ledebur and William R. Barnes, *Metropolitan Disparities and Economic Growth: City Distress, Metropolitan Disparities, and Economic Growth* (Washington, D.C.: National League of Cities, 1992); Larry C. Ledebur and William R. Barnes, *All in It Together: Cities, Suburbs, and Local Economic Regions* (Washington, D.C.: National League of Cities, 1994).

31. Larry C. Ledebur and William R. Barnes, *Local Economies: The U.S. Common Market of Local Economic Regions* (Washington, D.C.: National League of Cities, 1994).

32. Joseph Persky, Eliott Sclar, and Wim Wievel, with the assistance of Walter Hook, *Does America Need Cities?: An Urban Investment Strategy for National Prosperity* (Washington, D.C.: Economic Policy Institute, 1991).

33. B. Drummond Ayres Jr., "Mayors Applaud Clinton's Promise to Remake American Economy," *New York Times*, June 23, 1992.

34. Richard Voith, "City and Suburban Growth: Substitutes or Complements?," *Business Review*, September–October 1991, 21–33.

35. Anthony Downs, *New Visions for Metropolitan America* (Washington, D.C.: Brookings Institution, 1994).

36. Alex Schwartz, "Corporate Service Linkages in Large Metropolitan Areas," *Urban Affairs Quarterly* 28 (1992): 276–96; Alex Schwartz, "Subservient Suburbia:

The Reliance of Large Suburban Companies on Central City Firms for Financial and Professional Services," *Journal of the American Planning Association* 59 (1993): 288.

37. See, for example, Peggy McCarthy, "Cities on the Brink," *Boston Globe*, April 5, 1992 (discussing the bankruptcy of West Haven, Connecticut); Nicholas Lemann, "Naperville: Stressed out in Suburbia," *Atlantic*, November 1989, 34–38; John McCormick and Peter McKillop, "The Other Suburbia," *Newsweek*, June 26, 1989, 22–24; Karen De Witt, "Older Suburbs Struggle to Compete with New," *New York Times*, February 26, 1995.

38. Sheldon Danziger and Daniel Weinberg, "The Historical Record: Trends in Family Income, Inequality, and Poverty," in *Confronting Poverty: Prescriptions for Change*, ed. Sheldon H. Danziger, Gary D. Sandefur, and Daniel H. Weinberg (Cambridge, Mass.: Harvard University Press, 1994).

39. William H. Frey, "Minority Suburbanization and Continued 'White Flight' in U.S. Metropolitan Areas: Assessing Findings from the 1990 Census," *Research in Community Sociology* 4 (1994): 15–42.

40. Richard C. Hartman, "Academics Look at Regional Governance" (summary of discussion at seminar on metropolitan governance, John F. Kennedy School of Government, Harvard University, July 1991) (on file with author); Arnold Howitt, "Metropolitan Governance in the 1990s" (background memo prepared for seminar on metropolitan governance, John F. Kennedy School of Government, Harvard University, July 1991) (on file with author); see also Sarah Bartlett, "Cooperation Treaty Is Signed to Bolster Regional Economy," *New York Times*, October 8, 1991 (describing an agreement between New York, Connecticut, and New Jersey); Katherine Barrett and Richard Greene, "The Nutmeg Doughnut: Why America's Richest State Has Three of the Country's Poorest Cities," *Financial World*, February 18, 1992, 50–51 (explaining that Connecticut's tax structure has led to a polarization of the classes); David Rusk, *Cities without Suburbs* (Washington, D.C.: Woodrow Wilson Center Press, 1993).

41. Saskia Sassen, *The Global City: New York, London, Tokyo* (Princeton: Princeton University Press, 1991).

42. Bernard J. Frieden and Lynne Sagalyn, *Downtown, Inc.: How America Rebuilds Cities* (Cambridge, Mass.: MIT Press, 1989); Peter Dreier and Bruce Ehrlich, "Downtown Development and Urban Reform: The Politics of Boston's Linkage Policy," *Urban Affairs Quarterly* 26 (1991): 354–75.

43. Henry Cisneros, ed., *Interwoven Destinies: Cities and the Nation* (New York: Norton, 1993).

The question of the role of cities in national life has triggered a significant public debate in a variety of academic, policy, and business circles. For example, in May 1994 the American Sociological Association sponsored a three-day conference of twenty urban specialists and policy practitioners on the theme "Rethinking the Urban Agenda," which focused on the changing demographics, politics, and economics of urban regions. Theodore Hershberg, a University of Pennsylvania urban historian and director of its Center for Greater Philadelphia, described his efforts to bring city and suburban business, community, and political leaders together to forge a common legislative agenda in both Harrisburg and Washington. Political

scientist Margaret Weir of the Brookings Institution summarized her research on
the changing lobbying strategies of cities in state legislatures. Sociologist John Logan of SUNY-Albany explained that the federal policies with the most damaging
impact on cities are not "urban" programs but the siting of Pentagon facilities and
contracts, the mortgage interest deduction for homeowners, highways that bypass
urban neighborhoods, and the costs of Medicare to strained municipal budgets.
John Mollenkopf of the CUNY Graduate Center described the evolution of federal
urban policy and discussed the impact of congressional reapportionment and redistricting on urban-suburban and Democratic-Republican realignments.

Since Clinton took office, HUD, along with the Social Science Research Council,
has held several roundtable meetings on regional issues at which invited social scientists and policymakers debated the political and economic relations between
cities and suburbs, efforts at regional cooperation, and ways that federal policy can
improve regions by encouraging more collaborative planning. At the December
1994 meeting David Rusk described his theory of successful "elastic" cities that incorporate outlying suburban areas along with their middle-class population and
tax base. Recognizing that few cities and suburbs will agree to formal "metropolitan government" arrangements, Rusk described the efforts of business and civic
leaders to forge cooperative projects between cities and suburbs in a growing number of regions. Myron Orfield, a Minnesota state legislator, described his successful
strategy of convincing older blue-collar suburbs to join forces with Minneapolis
and St. Paul around tax, housing, transportation, and infrastructure policies.
Building on the theories of urbanist Jane Jacobs, economists Bennett Harrison of
Harvard, Maryellen Kelley of MIT, and Jon Gant of Carnegie-Mellon explained
why the most innovative firms (including global corporations) tend to "cluster" in
urban areas to reap the benefits of shared infrastructure, technology, and research.

Journalist Neal Peirce has drawn on many of these new studies in his syndicated
column and his recent book, *Citistates: How Urban America Can Prosper in a Competitive World*. As Peirce notes, global businesses look at entire regions when they
are deciding whether and where to expand, move, or invest. A successful region is
one that can "market" its strengths to firms in terms of the skills of the labor force;
the capacity of its airport, roads, and other infrastructure; the quality of its cultural
and recreational amenities; the quality and cost of its housing stock; and issues
such as public safety and the environment. In a recent interview Richard C. Levin,
Yale's new president, echoed these ideas: "It is very important to recognize that
metropolitan areas in the long run can only be as strong as their sources of employment, their economic hubs, are. If New Haven declines, eventually there will
be a ripple effect into the surrounding suburbs" (quoted in Nancy Polk, "On Town
and Gown at New Haven and Yale," *New York Times*, February 22, 1994).

"There are no moats around Hartford," Dennis Mullane, president of Connecticut Mutual Life, recently told the *Hartford Courant*. "The urban problems of today
are the suburban problems of tomorrow. As the city's economy goes down, so will
the suburbs."

44. Statistics in this section come from the following sources: U.S. Department
of Commerce, Bureau of the Census, *Slow Economic Growth Lowers Median Household Income and Increases Poverty Rate in 1991* (Washington, D.C.: U.S. Govern-

ment Printing Office, 1992); U.S. Department of Commerce, Bureau of the Census, *Money Income of Households, Families, and Persons in the United States: 1991*, series P-60, no. 180 (Washington, D.C.: U.S. Government Printing Office, 1992); U.S. Department of Commerce, Bureau of the Census, *Poverty in the United States: 1991*, series P-60, no. 181 (Washington, D.C.: U.S. Government Printing Office, 1992); U.S. Department of Commerce, Bureau of the Census, *Trends in Relative Income: 1964 to 1989*, series P-60, no. 177 (Washington, D.C.: U.S. Government Printing Office, 1991); Frank S. Levy and Richard C. Michel, *The Economic Future of American Families* (Washington, D.C.: Urban Institute Press, 1991), 1–132; Katherine McFate, *Poverty, Inequality, and the Crisis of Social Policy* (Washington, D.C.: Joint Center for Political and Economic Studies, 1991); Lawrence Mishel and David Frankel, *The State of Working America: 1990–1991* (Armonk, N.Y.: Sharpe, 1991); Isaac Shapiro and Robert Greenstein, *Selective Prosperity: Increasing Income Disparities since 1977* (Washington, D.C.: Center on Budget and Policy Priorities, 1991); Julie Kosterlitz, "Measuring Misery," *National Journal*, August 4, 1990, 1892; Paul Krugman, "The Rich, the Right, and the Facts," *American Prospect*, Fall 1992, 19–31; Patricia Ruggles, "Measuring Poverty," *Focus*, Spring 1992, 1–9; Jason DeParle, "House Data on U.S. Income Sets off Debate on Fairness," *New York Times*, May 22, 1992; Sylvia Nasar, "A Very Good Time for the Very Rich," *New York Times*, March 5, 1992; Robert Pear, "Ranks of U.S. Poor Reach 35.7 Million, the Most since '64," *New York Times*, September 4, 1992; David Wessel, "The Wealthy Watch Gains of 1980s Become Political Liabilities," *Wall Street Journal*, April 8, 1992; "Poverty Levels, Rates and Ranks: Places with Population Greater than 50,000" (unpublished information compiled for author by the Bureau of the Census, 1992); "Two Million More Americans Become Poor as Recession Hits and Wages and Incomes Decline" (background memo prepared by the Center on Budget and Policy Priorities, September 26, 1991); "New Census Report Shows Dramatic Rise since 1979 in Workers with Low Earnings" (background memo prepared by the Center on Budget and Policy Priorities, May 11, 1992); "Despite Economic Recovery, Poverty and Income Trends Are Disappointing in 1993" (background memo prepared by the Center on Budget and Policy Priorities, October 1994).

45. Center on Budget and Policy Priorities, *Despite Economic Recovery*.

46. Patricia Ruggles, *Drawing the Line: Alternative Poverty Measures and Their Implications for Public Policy* (Washington, D.C.: Urban Institute Press, 1990), 30.

47. Center on Budget and Policy Priorities, *Despite Economic Recovery*.

48. For example, about one-third of the entire population in Detroit, New Orleans, Camden, and Miami and over one-quarter of the population in Philadelphia, Chicago, Lawrence (Mass.), Hartford, Atlanta, Newark, Buffalo, Cleveland, St. Louis, Youngstown, El Paso, Provo, and New York live in poverty.

49. Poverty rates are given for children in the following cities: New Orleans, 38.7 percent; Baltimore, 32.5 percent; New York, 31.8 percent; Memphis, 31.6 percent; Detroit, 31.5 percent; Cleveland, 31.3 percent; Boston, 30.9 percent; Chicago, 30.8 percent; and Philadelphia, 30 percent.

50. For discussion of the term *underclass*, see William Julius Wilson, *The Truly Disadvantaged: The Inner City, the Underclass, and Public Policy* (Chicago: Univer-

sity of Chicago Press, 1987); Christopher Jencks and Paul E. Peterson, eds., *The Urban Underclass* (Washington, D.C.: Brookings Institution, 1991); Michael B. Katz, ed., *The "Underclass" Debate: Views from History* (Princeton: Princeton University Press, 1993); and Ronald B. Mincy, "The Underclass: Concept, Controversy, and Evidence," in Danziger et al., *Confronting Poverty*.

51. John D. Kasarda, "Inner-City Concentrated Poverty and Neighborhood Distress: 1970 to 1990," *Housing Policy Debate* 4 (1993): 253–302; Lawrence E. Lynn Jr. and Michael G. H. McGeary, eds., *Inner City Poverty in the United States* (Washington, D.C.: National Academy Press, 1990); see Mark Littman, "Poverty Areas and the Underclass: Untangling the Web," *Monthly Labor Review*, March 1991, 19–32.

52. See Joel Blau, *The Visible Poor: Homelessness in the United States* (New York: Oxford University Press, 1992), 3.

53. Laura DeKoven Waxman, *A Status Report on Hunger and Homelessness in America's Cities, 1993* (Washington, D.C.: United States Conference of Mayors, 1993).

54. Martha R. Burt, *Over the Edge: The Growth of Homelessness in the 1980s* (New York: Russell Sage, 1992), 13.

55. Bruce G. Link, Ezra Susser, Ann Stueve, Jo Phelan, Robert Moore, and Elmer Struening, "Lifetime and Five-Year Prevalence of Homelessness in the United States," *American Journal of Public Health* 84 (1994): 1907–12.

56. Edward B. Lazere, *San Francisco-Oakland, California, a Place to Call Home: The Crisis in Housing for the Poor* (Washington, D.C.: Center on Budget and Policy Priorities, 1990), xi.

57. See William Apgar, *The State of the Nation's Housing, 1994* (Cambridge, Mass.: Joint Center for Housing Studies of Harvard University, 1994).

58. Figures for other cities include the following: Detroit (21.1 per 1,000), Philadelphia (17.6 per 1,000), Chicago (17.0 per 1,000), Memphis (16.7 per 1,000), and Cleveland (16.3 per 1,000).

59. This is suggested by black infant mortality rates in the following cities: Washington (26.5 per 1,000), Detroit (23.9 per 1,000), Philadelphia (23.5 per 1,000), Los Angeles (22.9 per 1,000), Chicago (22.4 per 1,000), Indianapolis (21.8 per 1,000), Columbus (21.1 per 1,000), Phoenix (21.0 per 1,000), San Diego (20.3 per 1,000), and Cleveland (20.0 per 1,000).

60. Statistics in this section come from the following sources: Marc Mauer, *Americans behind Bars: One Year Later* (Washington, D.C.: Sentencing Project, 1992); U.S. Department of Justice, Bureau of Justice Statistics, *Violent Crime in the United States* (Washington, D.C.: U.S. Government Printing Office, 1991); W. John Moore, "Crime Pays," *National Journal*, May 25, 1991, 1218; Dennis Cauchon, "'Lock 'em up Policy' under Attack," *USA Today*, September 1, 1992; Dennis Cauchon and Desda Moss, "Doctors Vow to Wage War on Violence," *USA Today*, June 10, 1992; John Childs, "Partners in Crime," *Z*, June 1991, 84–86; Philip J. Hilts, "More Teenagers Being Slain by Guns," *New York Times*, June 10, 1992; Jonathan Marshall, "How Our War on Drugs Shattered the Cities," *Washington Post*, May 17, 1992; Michel McQueen, "People with the Least to Fear from Crime Drive the Crime Issue," *Wall Street Journal*, August 12, 1992; Barry Weisberg, "The Seduc-

tion of Violence," *National Bar Association Magazine*, April 1991, 17–18; "Around U.S., Cities Confront a Record Year for Homicides," *Boston Globe*, December 22, 1991; "Crime Peril Said Double in Cities," *Boston Globe*, June 8, 1992; "Violent Crime by Young Is up 25% in Ten Years," *New York Times*, August 30, 1992.

61. Data in this section draw on the following sources: Dan Gillmor and Stephen K. Doig, "Segregation Forever?," *American Demographics* 14 (1992): 48; Douglas S. Massey and Nancy K. Denton, "Hypersegregation in U.S. Metropolitan Areas," *Demography* 16 (1989): 373–91; Douglas S. Massey and Nancy A. Denton, "Suburbanization and Segregation in U.S. Metropolitan Areas," *American Journal of Society* 94 (1988): 592–626; William P. O'Hare and William H. Frey, "Booming, Suburban, and Black," *American Demographics* 14 (1992): 30; David J. Dent, "The New Black Suburbs," *New York Times Magazine*, June 14, 1992; David Judkins, "Patterns of Residential Concentrations by Race and Hispanic Origin," March 20, 1992 (unpublished manuscript on file with author).

62. Donna Shalala and Julia Vitullo-Martin, "Rethinking the Urban Crisis: Proposals for a National Urban Agenda," *Journal of American Planning Association* 55 (1989): 3, 6.

63. Statement of Richard P. Nathan, "The Case for a New State-Local Infrastructure Program" (1991), 6; see Marshall Kaplan, "Infrastructure Policy, Repetitive Studies, Uneven Response, Next Steps," *Urban Affairs Quarterly* 25 (1990): 371–88; Felix Rohatyn, "What the Government Should Do," *New York Review of Books*, June 25, 1992, 26–27.

64. David Alan Aschauer, *Public Investment and Private Sector Growth: The Economic Benefits of Reducing America's "Third Deficit"* (Washington, D.C.: Economic Policy Institute, 1990), 16.

65. Michael Pagano, *City Fiscal Conditions in 1992* (Washington, D.C.: National League of Cities, 1992), v–viii.

66. Michael Pagano, *City Fiscal Conditions in 1994* (Washington, D.C.: National League of Cities, 1994).

67. Helen F. Ladd and John Yinger, *America's Ailing Cities: Fiscal Health and the Design of Urban Policy* (Baltimore: Johns Hopkins University Press, 1991), 292.

68. For example, the percentage of overall employment in manufacturing in major cities declined dramatically between 1953 and 1970 and again between 1970 and 1986. Percentages are given for 1953, 1970, and 1986, respectively, in the following cities: New York City, 35.9, 25.8, 14.8; Philadelphia, 45.5, 33.3, 16.7; Boston, 28.4, 18.1, 9.0; Baltimore, 38.1, 28.6, 17.1; St. Louis, 44.9, 35.3, 23.0; Atlanta, 27.4, 19.4, 12.8; Houston, 26.8, 23.1, 14.0; Denver, 24.7, 19.0, 11.3; and San Francisco, 20.3, 14.7, 9.4. See John D. Kasarda, "Structural Factors Affecting the Location and Timing of Urban Underclass Growth," *Urban Geography* 11 (1990): 234–64 (discussing the demographic and economic conditions underlying the differential rise of urban poverty in northern cities).

69. John D. Kasarda, "City Jobs and Residents on a Collision Course: The Urban Underclass Dilemma," *Economic Development Quarterly* 4 (1990) 313; see John D. Kasarda, "Urban Industrial Transition and the Underclass," *Annals of the American Academy of Political and Social Science* 501 (1989): 26–47.

70. See Kasarda, "Collision Course," 313.

71. For a discussion of the potentials and limitations of progressive "redistributive" policies at the local level, see Susan Fainstein, Norman Einstein, Richard Hill, Dennis Judd, and Michael Smith, eds., *Restructuring the City* (New York: Longman, 1986); Gregory D. Squires, ed., *Unequal Partnerships: The Political Economy of Urban Redevelopment in Postwar America* (New Brunswick, N.J.: Rutgers University Press, 1989); Pierre Clavel and Nancy Kleniewski, "Space for Progressive Local Policy: Examples from the United States and the United Kingdom," in *Beyond the City Limits: Urban Policy and Economic Restructuring in Comparative Perspective*, ed. John Logan and Todd Swanstrom (Philadelphia: Temple University Press, 1990); Richard F. DeLeon, "The Urban Antiregime: Progressive Politics in San Francisco," *Urban Affairs Quarterly* 27 (1992): 555–79; Dreier and Ehrlich, "Downtown Development and Urban Reform," 354–75; Peter Dreier and W. Dennis Keating, "The Limits of Localism: Progressive Housing Policies in Boston, 1984–1989," *Urban Affairs Quarterly* 26 (1990): 191–216.

72. Frieden and Sagalyn, *Downtown, Inc.*, 270.

73. Robert Guskind, "Games Cities Play," *National Journal*, March 18, 1989, 634; see Peggy McCarthy, "City Wars," *Boston Globe*, November 23, 1992; John Schwartz et al., "Can You Top This?," *Newsweek*, February 17, 1992, 40 (describing the competition between Hartford, Connecticut, and nearby Springfield, Massachusetts, to attract businesses).

74. Bernard J. Frieden, "The Downtown Job Puzzle," *Public Interest* 97 (1989): 71, 73.

75. This trend continues. See Sarah Lyall, "In Downtown Syracuse, the Streets Get Emptier," *New York Times*, August 21, 1992; Stephanie Strom, "Macy Says It Will Close 8 Stores, Including 4 in the New York Area," *New York Times*, May 21, 1992; Charles Strum, "Newark Journal; No Miracle on Market Street for Final Retail Holdout," *New York Times*, May 21, 1992.

76. See Bill Turque, "Where the Food Isn't: Supermarkets Have Fled the Inner Cities, Leaving the Poor to Pay More for Less," *Newsweek*, February 24, 1992, 36.

77. See "New Census Report Shows Dramatic Rise since 1979."

78. Jason DeParle, "Sharp Increase along the Borders of Poverty," *New York Times*, March 31, 1994.

79. Wilson, *Truly Disadvantaged*, 39–46.

80. Christopher Jencks, *Rethinking Social Policy: Race, Poverty, and the Underclass* (Cambridge, Mass.: Harvard University Press, 1992), 123. For in-depth discussion of the effects of economic change on urban minorities, see James H. Johnson Jr. and Melvin L. Oliver, "Economic Restructuring and Black Male Joblessness in U.S. Metropolitan Areas," *Urban Geography* 12 (1991): 542; James Rosenbaum and Susan J. Popkin, "Why Don't Welfare Mothers Get Jobs? A Test of the Culture of Poverty and Spatial Mismatch Hypotheses" (unpublished manuscript, on file with author).

81. Jencks, *Rethinking Social Policy*, 125.

82. In 1970 44 percent of blacks and 22 percent of whites in their early twenties had not completed high school. By 1985 the figures were 19 percent for blacks and 13 percent for whites (ibid., 128).

83. Kenneth T. Jackson, *Crabgrass Frontier: The Suburbanization of the United*

States (New York: Oxford University Press, 1985), 190–218, 283–87; see Robert Fishman, "Megalopolis Unbound," *Wilson Quarterly* 14 (1990): 25–48.

84. These statistics are taken from William Frey and Alden Speare Jr., *U.S. Metropolitan Area Population Growth, 1960–1990: Census Trends and Explanations* (Ann Arbor: Population Studies Center, University of Michigan, 1991), and U.S. Bureau of the Census, *Metropolitan Areas and Cities: 1990 Census Profile No. 3* (Washington, D.C.: U.S. Government Printing Office, 1991).

85. See Wilson, *Truly Disadvantaged.*

86. These statistics are taken from Ledebur and Barnes, *Metropolitan Disparities and Economic Growth.*

87. Ann Markusen and Joel Yudken, *Dismantling the Cold War Economy* (New York: Basic Books, 1992), 171; see also Ann Markusen, Peter Hall, Scott Campbell, and Sabina Deitrick, *The Rise of the Gunbelt: The Military Remapping of Industrial America* (New York: Oxford University Press, 1991) (discussing the economic impact of the military-industrial complex).

88. Report to the Boston Redevelopment Authority by Employment Research Associates, Lansing, Michigan (1992) (unpublished manuscript on file with author); see Steven Greenhouse, "Study Says Big Cities Don't Get Fair Share of Military Spending," *New York Times*, May 12, 1992.

89. See n. 88, above.

90. Markusen and Yudken, *Dismantling the Cold War Economy*, 173.

91. For example, in September 1992 President Bush, far behind Governor Clinton in the Missouri polls, traveled to St. Louis to announce the sale to Saudi Arabia of F-15 jet fighters, which are manufactured by McDonnell-Douglas, the state's largest employer. The sale was highly questionable on defense and foreign policy grounds, but Bush made little pretense of discussing geopolitics. He emphasized the 7,000 local jobs generated by the weapon.

92. Paulette Thomas, "Small Businesses, Key to Urban Recovery, Are Starved for Capital," *Wall Street Journal*, June 11, 1992.

93. Peter Dreier, "Redlining Cities: How Banks Color Community Development," *Challenge*, November–December 1991, 15, 17–19; see Gregory D. Squires, ed., *From Redlining to Reinvestment: Community Responses to Urban Disinvestment* (Philadelphia: Temple University Press, 1992).

94. See Charles Finn, *Mortgage Lending in Boston's Neighborhoods, 1981–87: A Study of Bank Credit and Boston's Housing* (Minneapolis: Hubert Humphrey Institute of Public Affairs, University of Minnesota, 1989); Ann B. Shlay, "Financing Community: Methods for Assessing Residential Credit Disparities, Market Barriers, and Institutional Reinvestment Performance in the Metropolis," *Journal of Urban Affairs* 11 (1989) 201; William Dedman, "The Color of Money," *Atlanta Journal and Constitution*, May 1–4, 1988 (series of articles).

95. Thomas, "Key to Urban Recovery."

96. Richard W. Stevenson, "Riots Inflamed a Festering South-Central Economy," *New York Times*, May 6, 1992. Supermarkets have fled inner cities across the country. See Turque et al., "Where the Food Isn't," 36.

97. Glenn B. Canner and Dolores Smith, "Home Mortgage Disclosure Act: Ex-

panded Data on Residential Lending," *Federal Reserve Bulletin* 77, no. 11 (1991): 859; Mitchell Zuckoff, "Study: Denial Rate on Loans Still High for Minorities," *Boston Globe*, October 28, 1992.

98. Albert R. Karr, "Angry Lenders: Federal Drive to Curb Mortgage Loan Bias Stirs Strong Backlash," *Wall Street Journal*, February 7, 1995.

99. Alicia H. Munnell, Lynn E. Browne, James McEneaney, and Geoffrey Tootell, *Mortgage Lending in Boston: Interpreting HMDA Data* (Boston: Federal Reserve Bank, 1992).

100. Bill Montague, "Study: Many L.A. Lenders Fail Minorities," *USA Today*, May 12, 1992; see James Bates, "Large Banks Pressed to Hasten Rebuilding with Flow of Credit," *Los Angeles Times*, May 5, 1992.

101. For detailed discussion, see Margery Austin Turner, John G. Edwards, and Maris Mikelsons, *Housing Discrimination Study: Analyzing Racial and Ethnic Steering* (Washington, D.C.: U.S. Department of Housing and Urban Development, Office of Policy Development and Research, 1991); Margery Austin Turner, Raymond J. Struyk, and John Yinger, *Housing Discrimination Study: Synthesis* (Washington, D.C.: Urban Institute and Syracuse University, 1991), 25–33; Margery Austin Turner, "Discrimination in Urban Housing Markets: Lessons from Fair Housing Audits," *Housing Policy Debate* 3 (1992): 185–215.

102. Peter Kerr, "Riots Raise Concerns about Insurance Redlining," *New York Times*, May 4, 1992.

103. Gregory D. Squires, William Velez, and Karl Taeuber, "Insurance Redlining, Agency Location, and the Process of Urban Disinvestment," *Urban Affairs Quarterly* 26 (1991): 567–88; see Junda Woo, "Insurers May Not 'Redline' Appeals Court Says," *Wall Street Journal*, October 22, 1992; *A Policy of Discrimination? Homeowners Insurance Redlining in Fourteen Cities* (Washington, D.C.: Association of Community Organizations for Reform Now, 1993); U.S. House Subcommittee on Consumer Credit and Insurance, *Insurance Redlining: Still Fact, Not Fiction* (testimony presented before the Subcommittee on Consumer Credit and Insurance, U.S. House of Representatives, Washington, D.C., February 24, 1993); "Study Shows Discrimination by Insurers," *Los Angeles Times*, December 23, 1994.

104. U.S. Advisory Commission on Intergovernmental Relations, *Federal Statutory Preemption of State and Local Authority* (Washington, D.C.: U.S. Government Printing Office, 1992), 37; Joseph F. Zimmermann, "Regulating Intergovernmental Relations in the 1990s," *Annals of the American Academy of Political and Social Science* 509 (1990): 48–59; Joseph F. Zimmermann, "Federal Induced State and Local Government Costs" (paper delivered at the American Political Science Association meetings, Washington, D.C., September 1991).

105. See Richard Hill, "Federalism and Urban Policy: The Intergovernmental Dialectic," in *The Changing Face of Fiscal Federalism*, ed. Thomas R. Swartz and John E. Peck (Armonk, N.Y.: Sharpe, 1990).

106. Demetrios Caraley, "Washington Abandons the Cities," *Political Science Quarterly* 107 (1992): 1–30.

107. *Intergovernmental Relations: Changing Patterns in State-Local Finances* (Washington, D.C.: U.S. General Accounting Office, 1992); Michael deCourcy

Hinds, "States' Strained Finances Reveal Recession's Toll," *New York Times*, July 28, 1992; Michael deCourcy Hinds, "80's Legacy: States and Cities in Need," *New York Times*, December 30, 1990.

108. Caraley, "Washington Abandons the Cities," 9.

109. John E. Schwarz, *America's Hidden Success: A Reassessment of Twenty Years of Public Policy* (New York: Norton, 1983), 31–45.

110. See, for example, Aschauer, *Public Investment and Private Sector Growth.*

111. See Peter H. Stone, "The Faster Track: Should We Build a High-Speed Rail System?," *American Prospect*, Fall 1992, 99, 104.

112. Persky et al., *Does America Need Cities?*

113. Much of this material on job initiatives was drawn from Sar A. Levitan and Frank Gallo, *Spending to Save: Expanding Employment Opportunities* (Washington, D.C.: Center for Social Policy Studies, 1991); Peter T. Kilborn, "For the Urban Young, Carpentry Skills and Hope," *New York Times*, June 8, 1992; and Alan Murray, "New Deal's WPA and CCC Enjoy Renewed Vogue as Washington Tackles Poverty and Urban Decay," *Wall Street Journal*, June 1, 1992.

114. See Bob Woodward, *The Agenda: Inside the Clinton White House* (New York: Simon and Schuster, 1994), for a description of the political conflict over Clinton's economic plan.

115. Peter Dreier and Richard Rothstein, "Seismic Stimulus: The California Quake's Creative Destruction," *American Prospect*, Summer 1994, 40–46.

116. John E. Schwarz and Thomas J. Volgy, "Social Support for Self-Reliance," *American Prospect*, Spring 1992, 67, 69. Schwarz and Volgy present their work in detail in their book *The Forgotten Americans* (New York: Norton, 1992).

117. Clinton's budget raised taxes on the wealthy to help pay for his antipoverty strategy—primarily the Earned Income Tax Credit (EITC), expanded Food Stamps, and child immunization. Seeking to fulfill his campaign pledge to "make work pay," Clinton proposed a dramatic expansion of the EITC—a tax subsidy for the working poor, or a backdoor way of increasing the minimum wage. Under the EITC a family headed by a full-time worker earning the minimum wage ($8,840 a year), with two children, will get a subsidy of $2,528 (in 1994); by 1996 this subsidy will increase to $3,370, plus an inflation adjustment.

Clinton's original budget proposed extending EITC eligibility to families with incomes up to $30,000. With strong resistance in Congress, Clinton scaled back the EITC ceiling to $27,000. Despite the increase in jobs paying poverty-level wages, the EITC will help to reduce poverty for workers in low-wage jobs. Because the poor spend their money quickly (few have the luxury of putting it in savings), the EITC will have a stimulative effect on the economy.

In early 1995 Clinton proposed increasing the minimum wage from $4.25 an hour to $5.15 an hour over a two-year period. See Isaac Shapiro, *Four Years and Still Falling: The Decline in the Value of the Minimum Wage* (Washington, D.C.: Center on Budget and Policy Priorities, 1995). See also Michael W. Horrigan and Ronald B. Mincy, "The Minimum Wage and Earnings and Income Inequality," in *Uneven Tides: Rising Inequality in America*, ed. Sheldon Danziger and Petter Gottschalk (New York: Russell Sage, 1993).

118. See Markusen and Yudken, *Dismantling the Cold War Economy*; Marion An-

derson, *Converting the American Economy: The Economic Effects of an Alternative Security Policy* (Lansing, Mich.: Employment Research Associates, 1991); Marion Anderson, *A Shift in Military Spending to America's Cities* (Washington, D.C.: U.S. Conference of Mayors, 1988); Betty G. Lall and John Tepper Marlin, *Building a Peace Economy: Opportunities and Problems of Post–Cold War Defense Cuts* (Boulder, Colo.: Westview Press, 1992); Ann Markusen, "Dismantling the Cold War Economy," *World Political Journal* (Summer 1992): 389–99.

119. See "The Economic Crisis of Urban America," *Business Week*, May 18, 1992, 38; "What We Can Do Now," *Fortune*, June 1, 1992, 40, 41–48.

120. See Robert B. Reich, *The Work of Nations: Preparing Ourselves for Twenty-first Century Capitalism* (New York: Knopf, 1991); Robert B. Reich, "The Real Economy," *Atlantic*, February 1991, 35–52.

121. Some of the ideas in this discussion draw on the Urban Institute, *Confronting the Nation's Urban Crisis* (Washington, D.C.: Urban Institute, 1992); Billy J. Tidwell, *Playing to Win: A Marshall Plan for America* (New York: National Urban Leagues, 1991); Ford Foundation, *The Common Good: Social Welfare and the American Future* (New York: Ford Foundation, Project on Social Welfare and the American Future, 1989); Albert R. Karr, "Job Corps, Long Considered a Success, Gets Entangled in Political Tug-of-War," *Wall Street Journal*, June 1, 1992; and the final report of the National Commission on Children and several reports by the Children's Defense Fund.

122. Urban Institute, *Confronting the Nation's Urban Crisis*, 12; Karr, "Job Corps, Long Considered a Success."

123. Kilborn, "For the Urban Young."

124. See, for example, Marshall Kaplan, "American Neighborhood Policies: Mixed Results and Uneven Evaluations," in *The Future of National Urban Policy*, ed. Marshall Kaplan and Franklin James (Durham, N.C.: Duke University Press, 1990), 210–24.

125. "Situation Critical but Not Helpless," *Business Week*, May 18, 1992, 44–45. For reviews of the experience with enterprise zones, see Robert Guskind, "Enterprise Zones: Do They Work?," *Journal of Housing* 47 (1990): 47; Rochelle Stanfield, "Battle Zones," *National Journal*, June 6, 1992, 1348–52; Jill Zuckman, "All about Enterprise Zones," *American Caucus*, August 31–September 13, 1992, 1; Tom Furlong, "Enterprise Zone in L.A. Fraught with Problems," *Los Angeles Times*, May 19, 1992.

126. Phillip Kasinitz and Jan Rosenberg, "Why Enterprise Zones Will Not Work," *City Journal*, Autumn 1993, 63–69; William Fulton and Morris Newman, "The Strange Career of Enterprise Zones," *Governing*, March 1994, 32–34.

127. Urban Institute, *Confronting the Nation's Urban Crisis*, 17.

128. See Neal R. Peirce and Carol F. Steinbach, *Enterprising Communities: Community-Based Development in America* (Washington, D.C.: Council for Community-Based Development, 1990); Patrick Barry, "RX for Sick Cities," *Neighborhood Works*, August–September 1992, 16–23; Christopher Walker, "Nonprofit Housing Development: Status, Trends, and Prospects," *Housing Policy Debate* 4 (1993): 369–414; Peter Dreier and David Hulchanski, "The Role of Nonprofit Housing in Canada and the United States," *Housing Policy Debate* 4 (1993): 63–80.

129. Timothy Noah and David Wessel, "Urban Solutions: Inner City Remedies Offer Novel Plans—and Hope, Experts Say," *Wall Street Journal*, May 4, 1992.

130. See Peirce and Steinbach, *Enterprising Communities*; Barry, "RX for Sick Cities," 18–23.

131. Dreier, "Redlining Cities," 15–23.

132. This section draws on Peter Dreier and John Atlas, "Housing and Urban Development," in *Changing America: Blueprints for the Next Administration: The Citizens Transition Project*, ed. Mark Green (New York: New Market Press, 1992).

133. Connie H. Casey, *Characteristics of HUD-Assisted Renters and Their Units in 1989* (Washington, D.C.: U.S. Department of Housing and Urban Development, Office of Policy Development and Research, 1992), 4.

134. Peirce and Steinbach, *Enterprising Communities*; Neal R. Peirce and Carol F. Steinbach, *Corrective Capitalism: The Rise of America's Community Development Corporations* (New York: Ford Foundation, 1987); Avis Carlotta Vidal, *Rebuilding Communities: A National Study of Urban Community Development Corporations* (New York: Community Development Research Center, Graduate School of Management in Policy, New School of Social Research, 1991); *Expanding Horizons: A Research Report on Corporate and Foundation Grant Support of Community-Based Development* (Washington, D.C.: Publisher's Council for Community-Based Development, 1991); Alex Kotlowitz, "Community Groups Quietly Make Strides in Inner-City Housing," *Wall Street Journal*, September 17, 1992.

135. Peter Dreier and J. David Hulchanski, "Affordable Housing: Lessons from Canada," *American Prospect*, Spring 1990, 119–25; Dreier and Hulchanski, "Role of Nonprofit Housing," 43–80.

136. For a discussion of efforts to improve subsidized housing developments, see Langley Keyes, *Strategies and Saints* (Washington, D.C.: Urban Institute Press, 1992); John Atlas and Peter Dreier, "From 'Projects' to Communities: How to Redeem Public Housing," *American Prospect*, Summer 1992, 74–85.

137. James E. Rosenbaum and Susan J. Popkin, "Employment and Earnings of Low-Income Blacks Who Move to Middle-Class Suburbs," in Jencks and Peterson, *Urban Underclass*, 342–55.

138. Urban Institute, *Confronting the Nation's Urban Crisis*, 18.

139. See Harry C. Boyte, *CommonWealth: A Return to Citizen Politics* (New York: Free Press, 1989); Harry C. Boyte, Heather Booth, and Steve Max, *Citizen Action and the New American Populism* (Philadelphia: Temple University Press, 1986). Articles in a number of periodicals, such as *Social Policy* and *American Prospect*, have followed the recent history of community organizing efforts. For an overview, see Karen Paget, "Citizen Organizing: Many Movements, No Majority," *American Prospect*, Summer 1990, 115–28.

140. Frances Fox Piven and Richard E. Cloward, *Why Americans Don't Vote* (New York: Pantheon, 1988), 247; U.S. Bureau of the Census, *Voting and Registration in the Election of November 1988* (Washington, D.C.: U.S. Government Printing Office, 1989); U.S. General Accounting Office, *Voting: Some Procedural Changes and Informational Activities Could Increase Turnout* (Washington, D.C.: U.S. General Accounting Office, 1990); Clifford Krauss, "Senate Passes Bill to Force States to Make

Voter Registration Easier," *New York Times*, May 21, 1992; Richard M. Valelly, "Vanishing Voters," *American Prospect*, Spring 1990, 140–50.

141. A number of states are resisting implementation of this law on the grounds that it is an unfunded federal mandate. See Peter Dreier, "Fear of Franchise: Detouring the Motor Voter Law," *Nation*, October 31, 1994, 490.

142. Steven A. Holmes, "Experts Say Redistricting Added to the GOP Surge," *New York Times*, November 13, 1994; Carol Swain, "The Future of Black Representation," *American Prospect*, Fall 1995, 78–83.

143. Richard Freeman, ed., *Working under Different Rules* (New York: Russell Sage, 1994); Barry Bluestone and Irving Bluestone, *Negotiating the Future: A Labor Perspective on American Business* (New York: Basic Books, 1992); Frank Swoboda, "Labor Commission's Head Looks at Unshackling Cooperation on the Job," *Washington Post*, July 4, 1993.

Susan S. Fainstein

Ann Markusen

The Urban Policy Challenge

Integrating across Social and
Economic Development Policy

Introduction

Interest in urban policy has a cyclical nature. The uprisings that raged
through Los Angeles in April 1992 propelled the issue of urban policy onto
the national agenda. They left in their aftermath calls by community
groups and members of Congress alike for attention to the racial ghettos of
our distressed inner cities. Two years later, legislation to create urban empowerment zones and enterprise communities comprised the first major
federal attempt in nearly two decades to address urban issues. The Republican electoral victory of 1994, however, seemingly marked the end of renewed consideration of inner-city issues.

Efforts to deal with the situation of poor, inner-city residents seem
largely a response to civil unrest. When urban populations are quiescent,
attention turns elsewhere. The outcry following the Los Angeles uprising bore an uncanny resemblance to events in the late 1960s, as the subsequent turning away from cities resembled the retreat of the Nixon years.
During the 1960s, civil unrest in Watts and other American neighborhoods
prompted demands for national action, which led to the Kerner Commission Report. The situation described by the authors of that report continues today. Despite the repetition of the cycle of interest and neglect, the underlying dynamic that provoked demands for federal action goes on. We
therefore examine the recommendations of the Kerner Commission in order to evaluate their present utility, operating on the assumption that demands for an active urban policy will once again make themselves known.

Many of the Kerner Commission's concrete suggestions were implemented. But they tended to take the form of uncoordinated attacks on
poverty (through welfare and income maintenance), on unemployment
(through CETA), and on urban development (through block grants).
Eventually many of these programs were reduced or eliminated, but even

those that survived suffered in their isolation from a large, more powerful set of policies, mostly nonspatial in nature, that were simultaneously undermining the viability of the very communities that were targeted for aid. The failure to identify these larger forces made urban programs appear ineffectual and, worse, as money drains that became easy targets for budget cutters.

In this chapter we argue that the Kerner Commission got some things right and some things wrong. It got right the need for place-based policies to overcome poverty and disinvestment, a public policy principle abandoned during the twelve years of the Reagan and Bush administrations. What it missed was the need to integrate economic and social policy, at both the urban and the national levels. This blind spot led to the Kerner Commission champion policies that evolved into separate, piecemeal social services segregated from new local economic development policies. Together these independent social and economic policies had a perverse result: they failed to halt capital outmigration, deepened urban poverty in the inner city, and cut into the resources state and local governments had at their disposal to reverse these trends. This time around, an effective urban policy will have to blend social and economic policy if inner cities are to be revitalized and their residents reincorporated into a life of adequate employment and hope. We look first at the "place versus people" debate, then discuss the elements of integrated national policies oriented toward urban places.

Place-Based versus People-Based Policies

Since the 1960s, economists and policymakers have carried on a desultory intellectual debate over whether policies should be aimed at places, such as inner cities and depressed rural areas, or at people. In a seminal paper published in 1966, Louis Winnick argued against programs aimed at places and for those aimed at individuals.[1] He believed both that aiding places was an inefficient way of reaching worthy individuals, in that some unworthy (that is, higher-income) residents would receive some of the benefits, and that assisting some places at the expense of others imposed penalties on the worthy residents of places not targeted.[2] By and large, this view was adopted by most economists over the next two decades, even though the nature of politics in the American federal system, with its territorially based representation, ensured that some place-based policies would nevertheless be crafted.

The 1968 Kerner Commission Report, without explicitly tackling the rationale for them, argued for place-based policies. To combat unemployment, for instance, it endorsed the consolidation and spatial concentration of employment services in twenty select inner cities and two rural high-poverty areas, and it recommended tax credits for location and renovation of plants in a limited set of urban and rural impoverished areas.[3] But in 1980 the President's Commission for a National Agenda for the Eighties, which was established under Carter but reported on the eve of the Reagan administration, took a strong position in favor of assistance to individuals. It contended that place-oriented policies diluted the efficacy of funding directed at poverty alleviation and that some localities should be allowed to shrink and their residents encouraged to migrate to more promising locales.[4]

Dissenting scholars have written in defense of place-based policies, particularly those aimed at cities. Taking issue with the Commission for a National Agenda for the Eighties, Gordon Clark championed place and community as important national values that would be injured by policy-driven outmigration.[5] Ann Markusen argued against a national policy of neutrality toward the pace of change. She showed that rapid change, which decimated older, industrial inner cities, created underutilization of urban infrastructure and at the same time accelerated suburban and exurban growth, resulting in costly and unnecessary subsidies for erecting new infrastructure in the latter.[6] Roger Bolton has recently reviewed this literature. He pioneered a new conceptualization of the value of a "sense of place" and reissued the call for policy directed toward localities.[7]

Although Clark based his normative argument on equity grounds while Bolton and Markusen relied on efficiency criteria, both approaches agree on two basic phenomena: first, positive externalities not registered in the marketplace and not reducible to individual experience reside in places; second, preservation and enhancement of these externalities are in the national interest for both efficiency and equity reasons. Externalities, both positive and negative, result when the consequences of behavior are experienced not by the actor but by others in the environment, be they businesses, governments, or individuals. Espousing theoretical approaches that offer firms and workers the maximum flexibility in choosing where to live and do business does not guarantee that total social welfare will be maximized.

Several types of externalities are important for our analysis. First, there are impacts of firm and individual behavior on other individuals—the improvement or deterioration in social circumstances (the change in community, family, psychic satisfaction, recreational opportunities), in asset values (chiefly of owner-occupied housing), in job prospects, in the transfer of information, and in public services. Bolton's work is particularly acute in exploring the sense of place as an asset in which people are willing to invest and from which they gain returns.[8]

Second, a rich literature on urban agglomeration shows the value of place for firms;[9] the entry or exit of other firms in the environment may affect the cost structures and sales opportunities for existing firms. Central places such as cities offer important advantages due to economies of scale resulting from their status as major loci for information, goods, labor, and consumption. Disagglomeration—the deterioration of networks of firms and labor pools when capital outmigration occurs—is a dynamic process that can be set off by a rather mild but coincidental withdrawal of some subsegment of the economic community, causing a cumulative process[10] that can ultimately be quite destructive to the ensemble of income-generating activities characterizing an area economy.

Finally, rapid changes in neighborhoods affect subnational governments whose investments in infrastructure and public services presume a certain size and character of the locality. Both revenue concerns and scale economies shape the quality and level of public services and new investments in long-term infrastructure. Rapid rates of growth or unexpected rates of decline create negative externalities that make public service provision difficult and often inefficient. Underutilized public sector capacity is waste, while overutilized capacity diminishes the quality of services for residents. The allocation of federally funded infrastructure—highways and sewer and water projects—also may be inefficient and inequitable if it does not take place-based factors into account.

The justification for place-based policies is that benefits such as the sense of place, agglomeration economies, and public infrastructure are geographically fixed assets, with returns that are at least in part "public goods." Social service and employment policies aimed at individuals and economic development policies targeted at individual firms regardless of place can contribute to the deterioration of any or all of these place-based assets. For example, an investment tax credit that encourages firms to build new plants in suburban or exurban locations rather than maintaining or building them in existing communities has negative consequences for workers, firms, and city governments left behind.[11] A policy orientation that pays attention to these fixed assets leads inevitably, then, to advocacy for place-sensitive programs at the national level. Indeed, during the Carter years, it was recommended that all national policies be evaluated, via "urban impact statements," for their positive or negative impact on spatially fixed assets.[12]

In reality it is very difficult to measure agglomeration economies, public sector capacity utilization, and the value of an area's sense of place. Bolton explores the measurement problems for the latter at length, acknowledging the difficulties.[13] These externalities are indeed considerable; the size of our social services and economic development budgets are one indicator of just how substantial they may be. Place-based policies are a legitimate, if imprecise, way of preserving existing investment, economizing on the provision of public infrastructure, and eliminating some of the displacement that otherwise reappears as claims on the social services budget. Providing protection, stability, and continuity for existing communities and directing resources to those that, at any one point in time, are at risk can be a powerful way of increasing both standards of living and the viability of local economies. This has become a rather novel idea in the current era, in which we have developed national amnesia about the importance of place and the lessons of the 1960s. Yet, because racial concentration in inner cities has barely diminished in the last thirty years, the need for policies that take into account the coincidence of place and poverty has only become more obvious.

Place-based policies encompass both urban and rural locales. For historical reasons relating to both sectoral specialization and different cultural patterns of settlement, the two have been treated separately, with policy-making power delegated to different agencies. The problems of rural areas and their remedies have often been closely tied to agriculture and natural resource development and to the special problems of Native Americans (in the West), African Americans (in the cotton-belt South), and poor whites (in Appalachia). Urban areas, on the other hand, have problems associated with industrial decline, suburbanization of economic activity, and the mix of populations including poor black migrants from the rural South and immigrants from abroad. In this paper we confine our analysis to the urban case, although analogous arguments can be made for rural policies.

The Task: Integrating across Social and Economic Development Policy

When the Kerner Commission Report was published in 1968, the United States was at the peak of its post–World War II affluence. The massive restructuring of employment and space that loomed just beyond the horizon had not yet come into view.[14] The three overall policy choices set out in the commission's report—continuation of existing policies, ghetto enrichment, and racial integration[15]—assumed the existence of a healthy overall economic framework within which African Americans could achieve prosperity if their specific circumstances were altered. Consequently, it was possible to regard the situation of African Americans as an anomaly to be treated by overcoming economic and social barriers to their advancement. The commission attributed lack of access to jobs and low wages to blacks' inferior schooling, their exclusion from job referral networks, suburban decentralization of employment, and discrimination in hiring and promotion.[16] Proposed economic remedies boiled down to worker training (elimination of the skills mismatch), removing labor market frictions (bringing labor and jobs into proximity), and ending racial discrimination.[17]

Discussion of the characteristics now captured by the phrase "world economic restructuring" had not yet entered the policy discourse in 1968.[18] The effects of regional shift, internationalization of the United States economy, growth of the informal sector, downgrading of manufacturing,[19] flexible specialization of industry, decline of mass production industries, the hollowing out of the corporation, and the domination of central-city economies by financial and business services were just beginning to transform job markets in 1968.[20] The commission analyzed the spatial shift resulting from the movement of rural blacks to northern cities;[21] it lacked the foresight to predict the countermovement of manufacturing jobs from the industrial North to low-wage locations in the American South and West and around the world. Writing when the national unemployment rate was only 3.8 percent, the commission considered spatial mismatch only in terms of intrametropolitan rather than global location of industry and workers.[22] Similarly, it did not anticipate the massive increase in immigration that would heighten the competition for low-skilled jobs during the following two decades. National stagnation in employment, an increasingly polarized income distribution, and the resulting political strains had not yet simultaneously begun to produce increased poverty and greater public reluctance to assist the poor.

The commission made passing reference to stimulating industrial and commercial development in poverty areas through tax credits,[23] discussed the encouragement of small business in ghetto areas,[24] and stressed the importance of skills training and job placement.[25] It failed, however, to explore the relationship between the structure of the national economy and the position of black workers, and it did not propose strategies to affect the structure of industry through sectoral stimulus, development banking, employee or community ownership, or local development corporations. Furthermore, the dependence of households on female earnings had not yet been recognized;[26] therefore, the significance of the prevailing low wages in female-dominated occupations for the persistence of poverty was misinterpreted. The Kerner Commission saw the solution to the economic problems of black women in improving the employment situation of black men. After pressing for an "upgrading" of employment for black men, the report notes that "the fact that almost half of all adult Negro women work reflects the fact that so many Negro males have unsteady and low paying jobs."[27] The report does not suggest an upgrading of female employment.

With the hindsight of the 1990s, it is possible to see the economic position of African Americans as dependent on three factors: (1) the improvement in the aggregate performance of the United States economy; (2) the selection by the federal government of strategies for overall national economic development intended to have positive impacts on central-city populations as well as on the aggregate economy—that is, the choice of general policies for economic stimulus of the whole country that are also most likely to affect inner cities favorably; and (3) the formulation of programs targeted specifically at central-city economies that would stabilize the economic base and generate jobs accessible to local residents—that is, the design of programs that constitute what usually is labeled an urban policy. The principal thrust of the Kerner Commission's specific recommendations addressed social rather than economic policy. The commission did concern itself with the fragmentation of programs that affected low-income African American communities, commenting that "the typical ghetto resident has interrelated social and economic problems that require the services of several government and private agencies. At the same time, he may be unable to identify his problems to fit the complicated structure of government."[28] Nevertheless, the commission framed its concerns almost entirely in terms of social service provision rather than national economic programs or coordinating services to individuals with place-oriented economic development efforts.

Ironically, the preoccupation with social policy that characterized the Kerner Report was subsequently almost wholly reversed at both national[29] and local levels of government. The federal government cut back on social programs and especially on those grants-in-aid designed to assist localities in improving services.[30] City governments, forced to cope with this decline in federal assistance while they were experiencing population transformation and employment loss, moved strongly into the economic development arena, but with limited funds and few powerful planning tools. Without other sources of substantial financing at their disposal for supporting development, they entered Faustian bargains with the private sector, in which they traded away capital expenditures, land, and future revenues in order to attract development. The combination of impoverished populations and a constrained tax base then deprived them of the resources necessary for adequate social service programs.

The lion's share of local governmental effort and resources has been directed at property-led economic development based in downtown office projects.[31] Even so, municipalities have engaged in numerous experiments in community economic development.[32] These, however, have mainly lacked federal backing and have not been integrated into either national economic policy or local social policy. The many local economic development corporations have only very limited sources of financing, and much of the time and energy of their staffs is devoted to raising funds rather than operating programs. The extent to which they attempt to serve broad social purposes, such as providing needed neighborhood services or assisting the hard-core unemployed, varies considerably and depends on the orientations of the staffs. Although such groups deserve praise for their efforts to provide an indigenous economic base in inner-city neighborhoods, their total impact is quite small.[33]

Federal Policies

Currently, the problems of the national economy mean that, for political as well as economic reasons, the labor market disadvantages of the African American population can only be addressed by an overall urban economic policy that addresses issues of both place and poverty. This insight is fundamental to William Julius Wilson's argument developed in two influential books,[34] in which he attributes black poverty to economic restructuring and resulting changes in the labor market that have caused well-paying unskilled jobs to disappear.[35] He further contends that politically it is feasible to combat the predicament of the underclass only through universal policies aimed at redressing the inequalities being generated by the economy.[36]

Wilson's discussion raises the long-debated issue of the relative contribution of race and class to the disadvantaged position of minorities. His research incorporates not only the purely analytic question of the power of each variable in predicting lifetime earnings or educational achievement,[37] but also the political question of what emphasis likely produces the best policy response. Even if racial discrimination is the most important determinant of the status of African Americans, strong explicit policies aiming at redressing discrimination through affirmative action, hiring quotas, and forced residential integration provoke too much conflict to remain politically viable.

Such remedies are extremely divisive because they address the race problem without attempting to resolve class issues. If they worked, such policies would simply shift African Americans into slots now held by other members of the working class. In the 1990s the poor populations of the inner cities are more diverse than those of the 1960s, with substantial groups of Hispanics, Asians, and whites displaced from older industrial sectors competing for a shrinking number of jobs. African Americans still suffer the greatest discrimination and segregation, but unless affirmative action efforts are accompanied by economic policies that increase the aggregate number of jobs and raise wages at the lowest levels of the economy, they will simply alter the composition of the poor without diminishing their numbers.

Critics of Wilson justifiably have accused him of discounting racial factors in his analysis of the circumstances of black communities, of exaggerating the extent to which blacks ever lived in class-integrated communities, of overstating the geographic mobility of middle-class blacks,[38] and of disregarding the plight of low-wage female black workers. Such criticisms, however, do not contravene Wilson's thesis that general economic trends severely injure black workers who lack the educational qualifications, social connections, and spatial mobility to compete for the limited number of well-paying jobs in the modern economy. Economic policies through which the white, brown, and black working class can unite would command more political support than explicitly racialist programs. In addition, and of crucial importance for African Americans, who are disproportionately employed by governmental agencies, the surcease of attacks on the public sector, the restoration of federal revenue sharing with local governments, and a reversal of the thrust toward privatization would enormously enhance their economic prospects.

Effective policies for black, low-income, inner-city areas require federal programs with broad scope; they must foster economic enterprise, raise wage levels, train the workforce, place workers in jobs, and provide services such as health maintenance and day care that enable workers to keep their jobs. Such an ambitious mandate requires both instruments specifically designed to stimulate inner-city job growth and general programs of infrastructure investment, defense conversion, labor legislation, educational assistance, industrial and trade policies, and taxation that, at a minimum, do not harm central cities and that, when possible, disproportionately benefit them.[39]

During the 1970s a number of analysts pointed to urban policy as the unintended consequence of general legislation aimed at influencing the economy or building transportation infrastructure.[40] Cities, by and large, suffered from these policies; for example, the interstate highway program contributed strongly to middle-class flight from central cities, even though suburban development was not a goal of the program. During the Reagan-Bush years a variety of policies ostensibly intended to stimulate the economy, reduce inflation, cut the size of government, and free up the private sector had extremely negative effects on central cities. Tax reductions, the favored policy for encouraging investment, reduced the funds available for supporting social programs. Cuts in social service expenditures not only weakened programs but caused the physical withdrawal of agencies whose presence in low-income areas had provided a stable institutional framework. High interest rates combined with the strong dollar to decimate American manufacturing, particularly in the auto and steel industries, where well-paid minority workers were among the first fired. Privatization of governmental services destroyed public sector jobs that had offered career ladders for African Americans. Finally, the wave of mergers and acquisitions that thrived on deregulation exacerbated the plant closings and office consolidations that further shrank the economic bases of central cities.

A National Urban Policy

In addition to designing broad policies so that they channel benefits to low-income people, the federal government needs once again to endeavor to create an urban policy. As we argued at the beginning of this essay, spatially oriented programs are a necessary part of any effort to overcome urban poverty. During the Reagan and Bush administrations, enterprise zones (EZs) never attained congressional approval but were promoted as the Republicans' favored urban program. Within such zones, businesses would receive regulatory and tax relief. As eventually enacted under the Clinton administration, in the form of empowerment zones and enterprise communities, the program differs from the Republican version by incorporating a social service element.

The zones are touted as an effective remedy for the absence of business development in low-income neighborhoods. By 1990, EZs already existed in thirty-seven states, where they have received mixed reviews.[41] Despite their popularity, EZs are severely deficient in their capacity to rectify the income problems of the working poor, since their essence is to trade on the advantages of a low-wage workforce. Thus, in terms of the dual problems afflicting the African American community—unemployment and poverty-level wages—even at their most efficacious, EZs only address the first and may have a deleterious effect on the second.[42] Moreover, unless the zone's operators directed social services to potential workers and technical support to local businesses, EZ benefits would mainly go to corporations placing branch operations within the zones rather than to low-income residents.[43]

Not only did the Reagan and Bush administrations sharply cut funding for existing place-oriented programs, including the community development and social service block grants as well as the Economic Development Administration (EDA), they also showed little interest in improving the quality of program administration. For any place-based program to be successful, it must overcome the artificial boundaries imposed by the functional divisions among bureaucracies. The Kerner Commission accurately pointed out that "the system through which Federal programs are translated into services to people is a major problem in itself. . . . Federal programs often seem to be self-defeating and contradictory: field officials unable to make decisions on their own programs and unaware of related efforts; agencies unable or unwilling to work together; programs conceived and administered to achieve different and sometimes conflicting purposes."[44]

The commission noted that a number of attempts at coordination had been made during the 1960s and that the (both now defunct) Office of Economic Opportunity and the Model Cities program had been intended to bring together multiple agencies with the aim of reducing poverty.[45] The commission recommended formation of interagency task forces to achieve coordination at both the federal and municipal levels; it further suggested the establishment of multiservice centers and little city halls within urban neighborhoods.[46] The Nixon administration, which took office immediately following the publication of the Kerner Report, took little heed of its recommendations. Its principal policy innovation was the introduction of block grants, which had not figured into the commission's discussion, but which did partly overcome interagency conflicts at the federal level by removing many federal agencies altogether from poverty-related activities. The separation of social service from Community Development Block Grants (CDBG), however, sustained the fissure between social and economic policy, while the withdrawal of the federal government from its former interventionist role under the categorical grant system[47] did nothing to force coordination at the city level.[48]

Only in the area of "welfare reform" has there been a serious recent attempt to coordinate economic and social policy. The various plans adopted by the states in response to federal legislation authorizing experimentation in welfare programs have sought to move people from the welfare rolls into either training or jobs. These efforts have usually involved extensive social services and the identification of work opportunities. As economic programs, however, they have been restricted to job placement and have not been concerned with job creation.[49]

At the time of this writing the secretary of the Department of Housing and Urban Development (HUD), Henry Cisneros, is proposing the consolidation of all HUD housing and community development programs into three funds that will be distributed to states and localities on a block grant basis.[50] While potentially overcoming some of the blockages caused by divisions within HUD, this measure would still not deal with divisions between physical and social service bureaucracies. Moreover, it would depend on lower levels of government to achieve coordination, even though the quality of personnel, the will to deal with social problems, and the capacity to overcome bureaucratic obstacles are not clearly evident at those levels.

How to Do It Right

As the preceding discussion illustrates, broad policies to invigorate the economy have usually emphasized economic growth with little regard for social impacts. At the same time programs specifically designed to assist cities have been sharply curtailed. This section presents some examples of how economic and social concerns can be integrated within public policy;

we also give an illustration of how the federal government can support a local program aimed at stabilizing a city's economic base. We present first the case of defense conversion and then, more briefly, the examples of the construction of high-speed rail, the regulation of women's wages, and federal support of a local effort to sustain a vital industry.

Defense Conversion

In the 1990s, defense spending is targeted to be cut by 30 to 50 percent, reversing the enormous buildup of the 1980s and dramatically scaling back the facilities developed over forty years of Cold War.[51] While welcome for its ability to release resources for more productive uses in the economy, this transition is apt to worsen the circumstances of many minorities in selected United States communities, since defense spending is highly concentrated across the country.[52] The ironic consequence may be diversion of resources from inner cities, even though they have been the widely discussed targets for reinvesting of the peace dividend.

First, the cuts will disproportionately fall on staffing of the armed services rather than on procurement of equipment. Especially at the lower and less skilled levels, young urban blacks are overrepresented,[53] making them more vulnerable to cuts. For this group, a job in the volunteer army has offered a way out of urban poverty and a means for enhancing education and skills. The involuntary separation of soldiers and the evaporation of new positions for younger urban youth will worsen the current unemployment situation in inner cities and among blacks. Although Congress has passed a generous package of severance pay and job and educational transition assistance, there is no mechanism linking these benefits to new job creation. Second, a disproportionately high share of military facilities selected for closure are in urban areas, where they formed a major source of employment for inner-city residents. Examples are the Philadelphia Naval Shipyards and the Alameda (Oakland, California) Naval Air Station.[54] Civilian personnel at these facilities have few other attractive work options.

Third, a projected shift toward high-tech weaponry and away from older production lines in tanks, ordnance, fighter aircraft, and ships will concentrate associated unemployment in mature, working-class cities such as Groton, Connecticut; St. Louis, Missouri; and Long Beach, California. These are areas that recruited and absorbed black rural migrants as defense workers during the rapid expansion of weapons production during World War II and have since provided jobs for relatively skilled, high-paying blue-collar work. The closure of these plants and shipyards will deepen the unemployment in these centers, compounding poverty and economic decline. In contrast, design and manufacture of high-tech weaponry is concentrated heavily in suburban areas around Los Angeles, Boston, and Silicon Valley and in newly emerging agglomerations such as Orlando, Colorado Springs, and Huntsville, Alabama.[55]

Since 1989, when defense outlays first began to fall, a number of programs have been launched to facilitate adjustment. For the most part these have been piecemeal and ill coordinated, consisting of dozens of separate categorical programs spread over five agencies.[56] They treat firms, workers, and communities as separate, atomized candidates for services. Workers are individualized, offered little income support and only short-term training. Training of laid-off workers is not linked to better-funded industry programs for dual-use technology. Community economic diversification planning grants are available from the Department of Defense or the EDA in the Department of Commerce, where they are not tied to implementation funds, firm alternative use planning, or worker adjustment programs. As a result, little progress has been made in efficiently moving workers out of defense production into civilian activity.

The appropriate way to address the conversion problem would be to acknowledge its place specificity and to design programs that integrate firm assistance, worker assistance, and community economic development funds in a coherent way. For instance, economic development planning for a defense-dependent locale could be charged with producing a vision of the future of the area economy, complete with sectoral specializations that would build on the existing skills and expertise of the defense-dependent sectors in the area. This would be far better than recommending one more world trade center or biotechnology incubator, as is commonly done. Ways to ensure market creation through federal and state government procurement, standards, and regulations would be investigated, and each firm with worker involvement could be required to fashion alternative use plans that would be sensitive to the vision of the future area economy.

Workers, instead of becoming individualized recipients of unemployment insurance and retraining efforts, could be incorporated into alternative use planning and served at transition centers set up for counseling, entrepreneurship training, education and retraining programs, and even efforts at worker/management plant buyouts. By providing place-based rather than people-based assistance, these programs would preserve the communities' synergistic assets: a workforce with a long history of camaraderie and cooperation and the existing ensemble of physical and human capital. By keeping resources assembled, coordinated efforts can salvage much more than compensating programs that reduce former military bases and plants to real estate and displaced workers. Pursuing place-based policies would avoid the worst of the cumulative disinvestment process that might otherwise be set off by defense cuts.

National Programs with Spin-offs

The following two examples show how universal national programs could have significant inner-city benefits:

(1) In the early days of the Clinton administration, the president proposed the development of high-speed rail as an investment that would produce national economic growth.[57] In addition to its other spin-offs, it could affect the spatial distribution of commerce by bringing travelers directly into the center of cities. Unlike air travel, which carries passengers to peripheral points and stimulates nodes around the airport, high-speed rail could foster growth around centrally located train stations. Choices in the design of such systems, however, would determine whether or not benefits are actually targeted to central locations. If, in an effort to minimize initial expenses, rights-of-way were constructed to skirt cities rather than pass through them, the potential advantages would be lost. Even the construction of suburban stops in addition to central terminals would diminish positive externalities for core areas, as would the decentralization of depots for sorting of fast freight.

(2) Comparable-worth legislation, which would require equal pay for equivalent—even though not identical—work, would benefit all women; however, it would particularly enhance the living standards of African American families and add to the consumption fund within central cities. The wage discrepancy between white and black women is small compared with that between white and black men, but black women are far more likely than white women to be the sole source of support for their families. Although Wilson[58] and others have heavily emphasized unemployment among black men as the principal affliction of ghetto communities, the low income of African American women is the direct source of most poverty among ghetto children, since the majority of them live in households headed by single women.[59] Restructuring of central-city economies has increased the employment prospects for these women, who work disproportionately within the clerical, health service, and domestic service sectors that have expanded in the last fifteen years. Improvement in the relative compensation for these jobs would lift many African American families out of poverty.[60]

A general increase in the minimum wage would probably be politically more acceptable than comparable-worth legislation. Although less effective in diminishing black poverty, it would, to the extent that women disproportionately hold minimum-wage jobs, also serve to raise relative female wages. Although both comparable-worth legislation and an increase in the minimum wage are opposed by those who contend they would increase unemployment, many of the service jobs in which African Americans work are not exportable, and the effect of a uniformly imposed wage would prevent domestic competitive price cutting by creating a level playing field. The result then would more likely be inflation rather than unemployment,[61] as the pay increases are passed on to customers.

Federal Support of a Local Effort

In 1992 Macy's Department Store, already in Chapter XI bankruptcy, declared a loss of $1.25 billion.[62] Macy's is a national chain with its corporate headquarters and largest store in Manhattan. Although Macy's had stronger revenues per square foot of selling space than almost all competing department store chains, a mid-1980s leveraged buyout, in which its management took the store chain private, created a cost structure unsustainable during an economic downturn.[63] The impact of a total collapse of Macy's would fall heavily on New York's minority population, since Macy's employs many minority workers. Perhaps even more significantly, the store's purchases constitute a mainstay of the fragile New York garment industry, which is the city's largest manufacturing sector and a very important source of minority (especially Hispanic and Asian) employment.[64] It would also be a devastating loss to the segment of New York's financial industry that specializes in providing credit to retailers for purchase of stock.

The city of New York, in its various economic development programs, has offered huge tax subsidies for office construction and business retention;[65] it has also provided capital grants and technical assistance to small businesses and manufacturers and has provided large sums to keep the New York Yankees from departing. It has, however, never tried to rescue a bankrupt department store, even though a number of New York's most famous retailers have gone out of business. Many would argue that governmental intervention of this sort constitutes "lemon socialism,"[66] that bankruptcy disciplines businesses, and that the market will give rise to other suppliers that will fulfill Macy's function for New York's consumers. But the replacement of Macy's by branches of department stores with headquarters elsewhere—as is happening with the takeover of sites left vacant by Alexander's, a recently failed chain—would not produce the backward and forward linkages currently provided by Macy's. Rather than underwriting the construction costs of empty office buildings, New York City could affect its economy far more substantially by sustaining Macy's. To do so, however, it could not simply supply an off-budget tax break. Rather, it would have to provide capital up front, an expensive and politically risky undertaking. Only with the assistance of a federal development bank would such a venture be possible; the quid pro quo, however, would have to be a large equity share in the enterprise for the public. Such public participation in ownership of the corporation could assure that Macy's would maintain the full operation of its flagship store, that it would support New York business in its purchasing arrangements, and that it would hire New York residents and develop career ladders for the city's minority population.[67]

Restructuring Urban Policy: The Right Things at the Right Level

We recommend, then, a thorough revamping of urban policy that scales the barrier between economic and social policy while preserving a place-based orientation. Such a strategy offers the best route toward protection, stability, and continuity while encouraging economic revitalization. Contrary to the trade-off often assumed between the old and the new, preservation of existing assets and reticence in using public money to create new ones may not constitute a drag on economic development but rather a wise use of resources. This remains a hypothetical claim, since it is impossible to total up the sum of externalities and public costs that account for the difference between purely private cost and overall social cost. But at present, the continued deterioration of our cities and the worsening of rural poverty argue for steps toward policy integration and place-based policies.

Our recommendations present a major challenge, since simply reinvigorating place-based agencies such as HUD will not suffice. Many of the actions that affect the economic and social vigor of inner cities are currently lodged in agencies such as the Department of Health and Human Services, the Department of Labor, the Department of the Treasury, and various economic policymaking groups such as the Council of Economic Advisors and Clinton's new National Economic Council. Most of these have been relatively conservative and have focused on giveaways to business, but some refreshing new experiments have been undertaken in worker retraining, small business assistance (Michigan's Modernization Service), plant closing response (Massachusetts's Industrial Service Program), institution building (Pittsburgh's Steel Valley Authority), and sectorally oriented task forces (aerospace in Los Angeles, steel in Chicago, and polymers in Akron). A new national initiative would build on these experiments and replicate them elsewhere, rather than erecting unnecessary new layers of Washington bureaucracy.

What to Do in Washington

In Washington several things could be done to make urban policy more powerful and streamlined. First, an Office of Urban Policy could be set up in the White House which would oversee the packaging of urban programs in a way that would force coherence and amplify the effect of federal dollars. The director of the office would sit on the President's Economic Council, informing economic policymakers about the impacts of their proposed plans on cities and adding targeting criteria onto new initiatives such as the investment tax credit. The office should have the secretaries of Labor, Commerce, Energy, Health and Human Services, Housing and Urban Development, and Defense on its advisory board and should have discretion over pools of resources from each agency. Where state and local governments lacked institutional capacity to conduct cohesive economic development programs for inner cities, the office could help them build it. The office would have an ongoing monitoring function, collating relevant data and assessing differential urban performance.

A prototype for this kind of high-level coordination was created during the Bush administration in the Federal Coordinating Council on Science, Engineering and Technology structure for the coordination of science and technology policy. Chaired by the president's science advisor, the relevant secretaries (Defense, Energy, Transportation, Commerce, etc.) with significant technology programs began working together in this setting to rationalize federal technology policy. A similar Office of Economic Conversion, designed to be self-liquidating at the end of the decade, has been proposed to oversee the process of converting from a military to a civilian economy.[68] If established, such an office could ensure that conversion and urban policy might enhance rather than cancel out each other.

In designing new configurations for federal urban and industrial policies, the principle of federal funding with state and local implementation should be followed as closely as possible. In the conversion area, for instance, the director of the Massachusetts Industrial Services Program reported having to write seven grant applications to five different agencies in 1992 for conversion assistance. She would strongly prefer "one stop shopping"—an office to which she could apply for a package that covers worker retraining, community economic development, and firm assistance all in one bundle, with considerable flexibility in deploying it. New federal bureaucracies for administering programs should not be developed unless circumstances are exceptional. Each place to be targeted has its own unique circumstances that are best read and addressed at the local level.

What to Do at City Hall

By forcing states and cities to rely on their own resources, twelve years of Republican administrations succeeded in making lower levels of government far more capable of intervening in the local economic development process than previously. Officials have learned how to market their territories, how to negotiate with the private sector, and how to plan strategically rather than simply to generate master plans containing static conceptions of ideal land uses. Except in a few "progressive" cities,[69] however, governmental officials largely acceded to private interests and failed to retain a significant public benefit from the deals they made with business. In part this outcome was the consequence of their lack of significant bargaining resources.

Given the expertise that exists at the state and local level, the precedent of allowing subnational governments to carry out federally funded urban economic development and social programs ought to continue. The Kerner Commission's recommendation of a federal interagency task force to monitor programs and insure that they remain within broad federal guidelines indicates the appropriate degree of federal involvement. Backed by the federal government, local officials can extract better bargains from private business. Whether through an equity interest in private firms, contractual agreements, or the establishment of semiautonomous development corporations, an enriched local public sector can play an important role in assuring that local economic actors serve the needs of the local public.

State and local governments will have to tackle the problem of marrying social and economic policy, too. Several states have experimented with novel ways of doing so. In Washington, for instance, the state employment agency has permitted workers to take their unemployment compensation as a lump sum and invest it in a new business, thereby linking a social program (unemployment services) with job creation (economic development). Worker retraining programs in a number of cities and states have been linked to job commitments by firms and to first source hiring programs by government and business. Nevertheless, most state and city governments continue to run education, training, and social services programs separately from their economic development efforts. Bridging councils or offices like those we recommend for the federal government could play a comparable role at the subnational level.

In designing this federal system, some thought must be given to the possibility that patronage and corruption could destroy the effectiveness and legitimacy of new urban programs. Pass-throughs to the state and local level are good only if at those levels competent professionals manage the programs and if broad participation ensures that they are well crafted. Design principles that ensure such participation will help, as in the Model Cities program. Some federal monitoring of the use of funds would have to be done, and program evaluation should be well-funded at the national level to enable improvements in urban programs to be undertaken readily as we learn from new experiments.

Conclusion

The Kerner Commission Report offers a number of important insights that
could usefully be recycled as we approach the end of the century. On the
one hand, it argues for specific targeting of inner cities for revitalization.
Its depiction of the human potential and existing built environment of
cities makes a powerful case for place-based policies to preserve and restore the vitality of existing urban assets. The neglect of urban policy in the
decades following the report and the worsening of inner-city poverty and
deterioration since its publication suggest that its place-based prescription
was right. Right now the political tide has again turned against a meaningful urban policy. The withdrawal of public resources that is currently
threatening America's cities, however, will inevitably produce a reaction
and the demand for new approaches. An effective strategy will have to
blend place-based policies with general economic stimuli, social policy
with economic policy, and state and local with federal approaches. If this
can be accomplished, we may finally be able to consign the Kerner Commission Report to the historical archives, honoring it as a seminal document in the restoration of our great American inner cities.

Notes

1. See Louis Winnick, "Place Prosperity vs. People Prosperity: Welfare Considerations in the Geographic Redistribution of Economic Activity," in *Essays in Urban Land Economics in Honor of the Sixty-Fifth Birthday of Leo Grebler* (Los Angeles:
University of California, Center for Real Estate and Urban Economics, 1966), 273.

2. For a discussion of Winnick's contribution, see Roger Bolton, "Place Prosperity vs. People Prosperity' Revisited: An Old Issue with a New Angle," *Urban Studies*
29 (1992): 185–203. See also Matthew Edel, " 'People' versus 'Places' in Urban Impact Analysis," in Norman J. Glickman, ed., *The Urban Impacts of Federal Policies
for the U.S. Department of Housing and Urban Development* (Baltimore: Johns Hopkins University Press, 1980), 175–91.

3. See *Report of the National Advisory Commission on Civil Disorders* (Washington, D.C.: U.S. Government Printing Office, 1968), 233, 236 (hereafter cited as
Kerner Report).

4. See President's Commission for a National Agenda for the Eighties, *Urban
America in the Eighties* (Washington, D.C.: U.S. Government Printing Office,
1980). For a review of how urban policy lost its place-based focus and succumbed
to an economic developmentalist approach, see Ann Markusen and David Wil-
moth, "The Political Economy of National Urban Policy in the USA, 1976–1981,"
Canadian Journal of Regional Science 5 (1982): 125–44.

5. See Gordon L. Clark, *Interregional Migration, National Policy, and Social Justice*
(Totawa, N.J.: Rowman and Allanheld, 1983).

6. See Ann Markusen, "Federal Budget Simplification: Preventive Programs vs. Palliatives for Local Governments with Booming, Stable, and Declining Economies," *National Tax Journal* 30 (1977): 249.

7. See Roger Bolton, "An Economic Interpretation of 'A Sense of Place'" (Williams College Research Paper no. 130, 1989), 185–203.

8. Bolton, "'Sense of Place,'" 16.

9. For original works on agglomeration, see Wilbur R. Thompson, *A Preface to Urban Economics* (Baltimore: Johns Hopkins University Press, 1965); John Friedmann, *Urbanization, Planning, and National Development* (Beverly Hills, Calif.: Sage, 1973); Allan Pred, *City Systems in Advanced Economies: Past Growth, Present Processes, and Future Development Options* (New York: Wiley, 1977); and Harry W. Richardson, *Regional Economics: Location, Theory, Urban Structure, and Regional Change* (New York: Praeger, 1969).

10. See Nicholas Kaldor, "The Role of Increasing Returns, Technical Progress, and Cumulative Causation in the Theory of International Trade and Economic Growth," in F. Targetti and A. P. Thirwall, eds., *The Essential Kaldor* (New York: Holmes and Meier, 1989), 43–61.

11. See Michael Luger, "Some Micro-Consequences of Macro Policies: The Case of Business Tax Incentives," *Proceedings of the National Tax Association—Tax Institute of America* (1981).

12. See Glickman, *Urban Impacts of Federal Policies*, 3–19, esp. Ann Markusen, "Urban Impact Analysis in the U.S.: A Critical Review," 103–7, for a review of the urban impact statement proposal.

13. Bolton, "'Sense of Place,'" 32–37.

14. See Robert A. Beauregard, "Space, Time, and Economic Restructuring," in *Economic Restructuring and Political Response*, ed. Robert A. Beauregard (Beverly Hills, Calif.: Sage, 1989), 209, 210–15 (defining economic restructuring and providing an extensive series of references to the literature on the subject).

15. *Kerner Report*, 218–19.

16. Ibid., 91–93.

17. Ibid., 231–36.

18. For a sampling of the now vast literature, see generally David Harvey, *The Urbanization of Capital: Studies in the History and Theory of Capitalist Urbanization* (Baltimore: Johns Hopkins University Press, 1985) (examining capitalism as it relates to the urban process); Beauregard, *Economic Restructuring*, 209–40 (exploring the various conceptions of economic restructuring); Erica Schoenberger, "From Fordism to Flexible Accumulation: Technology, Competitive Strategies, and International Location," *Environment and Planning D: Society and Space* 6 (1988): 245, 250–54 (analyzing the shift from Fordism to flexible production); Allen J. Scott, "Flexible Production Systems and Regional Development: The Rise of New Industrial Spaces in North America and Western Europe," *International Journal of Urban and Regional Research* 12 (1988): 171, 178–82 (describing the emergence of flexible specialization in manufacturing systems); Manuel Castells, *The Informational City* (Cambridge, Mass.: Blackwell, 1991) (describing the role of technology in shaping economic restructuring).

19. Saskia Sassen describes the "downgrading of the manufacturing sector" as "a

process in which the share of unionized shops declines and wages deteriorate while sweatshops and industrial homework proliferate. This process includes the downgrading of jobs within existing industries and the job supply patterns of some of the new industries" (Sassen, *The Global City: New York, London, Tokyo,* [Princeton: Princeton University Press, 1991], 9).

20. See William W. Goldsmith and Edward J. Blakely, eds., *Separate Societies: Poverty and Inequality in U.S. Cities* (Philadelphia: Temple University Press, 1992) (providing an excellent recent discussion of the relationship between economic restructuring, race, poverty, and policy).

21. *Kerner Report*, 116–18.

22. Ibid., 217.

23. Ibid., 235–36.

24. Ibid., 236.

25. Ibid., 79, 232–33.

26. U.S. House Committee on Ways and Means, *Overview of Entitlement Programs*, 102d Cong., 1st Sess., 1991, committee print, 951.

27. *Kerner Report*, 125–26. The Kerner Commission's view of the greater importance of male than female wages is repeated by William Julius Wilson in his study of the underclass. See Adolph Reed Jr., "The Liberal Technocrat," *Nation* 246 (1988): 167, 168 (reviewing William Julius Wilson, *The Truly Disadvantaged: The Inner City, the Underclass, and Public Policy* [Chicago: University of Chicago Press, 1987]).

28. *Kerner Report*, 285.

29. The first national urban policy report prepared by the Reagan administration declared, "The basis of the Reagan Administration's Urban Policy is to place the highest priority on economic growth as the most important element of such policy" (U.S. Department of Housing and Urban Development, *The President's National Urban Policy Report* [Washington, D.C.: U.S. Department of Housing and Urban Development, 1982], 11).

30. Federal aid decreased from 23 percent to 15 percent of municipal own-source revenue between 1980 and 1984, and state aid (in turn dependent on federal transfers) declined similarly. Put another way, for every dollar the average city itself raised in 1980, it was able to spend $1.56, while for every dollar it raised in 1984, it could spend only $1.44. Curtailments of assistance for employment and training programs were especially severe; federal outlays under the Jobs Partnership Training Act were cut 69 percent in constant (1986) dollars between 1980 and 1986. See Susan S. Fainstein and Norman Fainstein, "The Ambivalent State: Economic Development Policy in the U.S. Federal System under the Reagan Administration," *Urban Affairs Quarterly* 25 (1989): 47–52.

31. See Marc V. Levine, "The Politics of Partnership: Urban Redevelopment since 1945," in *Unequal Partnerships: The Political Economy of Urban Redevelopment in Postwar America*, ed. Gregory D. Squires (New Brunswick, N.J.: Rutgers University Press, 1989), 12–13.

32. See Peter K. Eisinger, *The Rise of the Entrepreneurial State: State and Local Economic Development Policy in the United States* (Madison: University of Wisconsin Press, 1988).

33. See generally Michael B. Teitz, "Neighborhood Economics: Local Communities and Regional Markets," *Economic Development Quarterly* 3 (1989): 111–22. Professor Teitz argues that economic development policies at the local, neighborhood level "face great difficulties in raising incomes or bringing people into the economic mainstream" due to the "historic divorce of workplace from residence" (ibid., 112).

34. Wilson, *Truly Disadvantaged*; William Julius Wilson, *The Declining Significance of Race: Blacks and Changing American Institutions* (Chicago: University of Chicago Press, 1978).

35. Wilson, *Truly Disadvantaged*, 39–46; Wilson, *Declining Significance*, 88–121.

36. Wilson, *Truly Disadvantaged*, 140–64; Wilson, *Declining Significance*, 144–54.

37. For an extensive investigation of this question, see Andrew Hacker, *Two Nations: Black and White, Separate, Hostile, Unequal* (New York: Scribner's, 1992), 93–160.

38. See Reynolds Farley, *Blacks and Whites: Narrowing the Gap?* (Cambridge, Mass.: Harvard University Press, 1984); Norman Fainstein, "Race, Class, and Segregation: Discourses about African Americans," *International Journal of Urban and Regional Research* 17 (1993): 384–403; Norman Fainstein, "The Underclass/Mismatch Hypothesis as an Explanation for Black Economic Deprivation," *Politics and Society* 15 (1987): 403–51.

39. Theda Skocpol notes that United States policy has consistently lacked coordination between its economic and social components:

> Back during the founding period of its modern interventionist state, from 1930 through 1946, the United States originally opted *not* to closely coordinate "social" and "economic" interventions. . . . The technical and intellectual capacities of the federal government to devise and implement targeted industrial or labor market interventions were not improved during the era of commercial Keynesian dominance. Little intellectual or political legitimacy was built up for the notion that the federal government could—or should—pursue economic, employment, and social-welfare objectives through the same public policies or through deliberately coordinated public policies. (Skocpol, "The Limits of the New Deal System and the Roots of Contemporary Welfare Dilemmas," in *The Politics of Social Policy in the United States*, ed. Margaret Weir, Anna Shola Orloff, and Theda Skocpol [Princeton: Princeton University Press, 1988], 293, 301–2)

40. See Glickman, *Urban Impacts of Federal Policies* (containing a collection of articles by authors discussing the impacts of federal policies on urban areas).

41. See Roy E. Green, ed., *Enterprise Zones: New Directions in Economic Development* (Newbury Park, Calif.: Sage, 1991).

42. George C. Galster, "A Cumulative Causation Model of the Underclass: Implications for Urban Economic Development Policy," in *The Metropolis in Black and White: Place, Power, and Polarization*, ed. George C. Galster and Edward W. Hill (New Brunswick, N.J.: Rutgers Center for Urban Policy Research, 1992), 190, 204–5.

43. See Enid Beaumont, "Enterprise Zones and Federalism," in *Enterprise Zones: New Directions in Economic Development*, ed. Roy E. Green (Newbury Park, Calif.: Sage, 1991), 41–57.

44. *Kerner Report*, 230.

45. Ibid., 152.

46. Ibid., 150–55.

47. Categorical grants are directed to highly specified programs, usually on a discretionary basis (for example, water and sewer grants). Block grants are distributed on a formula basis to all eligible areas for broad purposes.

48. A portion of the CDBG may be used for social services at the choice of the recipient. See 42 U.S.C. § 9904(c)(1)(A) (1988). Many municipalities, however, do not exercise this option. A Department of Housing and Urban Development (HUD) official once commented to one of the authors that it was inappropriate that CDBG contain a social service component since HUD did not have the capability to monitor social programs. The concept of incorporating a social service component into a grant aimed primarily at physical redevelopment dated from the Model Cities program, which had been framed with the idea that residents affected by revitalization programs required supportive services. From the HUD official's point of view, however, the goal of coordinating development and social policy that had inspired the multipurpose intent of the grant did not outweigh bureaucratic logic.

49. Some local economic development programs that combine job creation with training and placement offer an example of the kinds of coordination that could be achieved. For example, the East Williamsburg Valley Industrial Development Corporation in Brooklyn, New York, offers technical assistance, marketing support, security, and sanitation services to manufacturers located in an old industrial area. It also refers job applicants (giving preference to ex-offenders and welfare recipients) to publicly supported training programs and offers a job placement program. It is currently seeking to develop a day care center for workers within the industrial area.

50. U.S. Department of Housing and Urban Development, *Reinvention Blueprint* (Washington, D.C.: HUD, 1994).

51. See Ann Markusen and Joel Yudken, *Dismantling the Cold War Economy* (New York: Basic Books, 1992), 1–8; Ann Markusen and Catherine Hill, *Converting the Cold War Economy: Investing in Industries, Workers, and Communities* (Washington, D.C.: Economic Policy Institute, 1992), 7–9.

52. See Ann Markusen, Peter Hall, Scott Campbell, and Sabina Deitrick, *The Rise of the Gunbelt: The Military Remapping of Industrial America* (New York: Oxford University Press, 1991), 8–25.

53. Paul Magnusson and Seth Payne, "Who Is Really Doing America's Fighting?," *Business Week*, February 25, 1991, 35.

54. Catherine Hill, "Base Closures in the 1990's: Lessons for Development" (working paper, National Commission on Economic Conversion and Disarmament, Washington, D.C., March 1993).

55. Markusen et al., *Rise of the Gunbelt*, 26–50.

56. Les Aspin, "Defense Conversion, Reinvestment and Transition Assistance Act of 1992 ($1.512 billion)" (memo to the National Conference of Mayors, Octo-

ber 12, 1992, U.S. House of Representatives, Committee on Armed Services).

57. See "The President's Address to a Joint Session of Congress," *New York Times*, February 18, 1993.

58. Wilson, *Truly Disadvantaged*, 46–62.

59. In 1990 56.2 percent of black children lived in single-parent households maintained by their mother. See U.S. House Committee on Ways and Means, *Overview of Entitlement Programs*, 951.

60. Of female-headed families with children whose mothers worked outside the home at least part time, 28 percent were classified as poor in 1989, and 12.7 percent were considered poor even when the parent worked full time (ibid., 1145, 1144). Since blacks are disproportionately represented among the poor, the figures for black families would likely be higher.

61. Rebecca M. Blank and Alan S. Blinder, "Macroeconomics, Income Distribution, and Poverty," in *Fighting Poverty: What Works and What Doesn't*, ed. Sheldon H. Danziger and Daniel H. Weinberg (Cambridge, Mass.: Harvard University Press, 1986), 180–208 (analyzing the effects of unemployment and inflation on the poor and concluding that unemployment has a far more negative impact).

62. Stephanie Strom, "Macy's Pins Hope for Rebound on 5-Year Plan," *New York Times*, November 6, 1992.

63. Ibid.

64. Roger Waldinger, "Race and Ethnicity," in *Setting Municipal Priorities, 1990*, ed. Charles Brecher and Raymond D. Horton (Montclair, N.J.: Allanheld, Osmun, 1989), 65.

65. See Susan S. Fainstein, *The City Builders* (Cambridge, Mass.: Blackwell, 1994) (concerning the use of incentives to real estate development and their impact in New York City).

66. See Staughton Lynd, "Towards a Not-for-Profit Economy: Public Development Authorities for Acquisition and Use of Industrial Property," *Harvard Civil Rights–Civil Liberties Law Review* 22 (1987): 13, 40.

67. Subsequent to the writing of this chapter, Macy's was taken over by Federated Department Stores, the country's largest department store chain, and removed from bankruptcy. At present it is committed to keeping management of the chain in New York, although it threatened to leave during an altercation with the state's attorney general. Because of antitrust problems and the desire not to compete with other stores that it owns, Federated will divest itself of some Macy's stores and close down the A&S chain, which it also owns. The ultimate impact of these moves on New York City remains unclear.

68. See Markusen and Hill, *Converting the Cold War Economy*, 56–59.

69. In his book *The Progressive City* (New Brunswick, N.J.: Rutgers University Press, 1986), Pierre Clavel examines Hartford, Cleveland, Berkeley, Santa Monica, and Burlington, Vermont. Chicago during the administration of Mayor Harold Washington and Boston under the Raymond Flynn regime are also often named as progressive cities.

James H. Johnson Jr.
Walter C. Farrell Jr.

The Fire This Time

The Genesis of the Los Angeles Rebellion of 1992

More than twenty-five years after the release of the Kerner Commission Report,[1] which assessed the conditions that sparked the civil disorders of the 1960s, the worst civil unrest of this century occurred in Los Angeles in the spring of 1992. Following the acquittal of four white police officers accused of the videotaped beating of black[2] motorist Rodney King, three days of burning, looting, and violence erupted that resulted in 58 deaths, 2,500 injuries, 16,000 arrests, and nearly $1 billion of property damage and loss. Quelling the civil unrest and reestablishing a sense of calm in the city required the deployment of the full forces of the Los Angeles Police Department (LAPD) and the Los Angeles County Sheriff's Department, as well as significant numbers of California Highway Patrol officers and military troops.[3]

In this essay we address the underlying causes of this civil disturbance. We begin with a critical evaluation of the Bush administration's account of the seeds of the uprising and then offer an alternative and, in our view, more realistic explanation anchored in the realities of life in the Los Angeles communities where the burning, looting, and violence were disproportionately concentrated.

We contend that the touchstones of the Los Angeles violence mirrored those that the 1968 Kerner Commission concluded had sparked the violent civil disorders of the 1960s[4] and that the 1988 Commission on the Cities found still existed as "quiet riots" in central-city ghetto communities twenty years later.[5] These factors included hopelessness and despair as a consequence of worsening economic deprivation, accelerating neighborhood decline and deterioration, and increasing spatial and social isolation from mainstream economic and educational opportunities—conditions aggravated by persistent incidences of police brutality and discriminatory treatment by the criminal justice system in general.

In addition to these "traditional" sparks, we note further that there was a unique trigger in this civil disturbance that was not a factor in inspiring the civil disorders of the 1960s: the presence of other nonwhite ethnic minority groups (for example, Asians and Hispanics) with whom blacks have found themselves in direct competition and conflict for jobs, housing, and other scarce resources.[6] Ethnic antagonisms among these minority groups figured heavily in the pattern of burning, looting, and violence.

Finally, we conclude with an assessment of selected strategies that have been proposed or implemented to revitalize South Central Los Angeles and other poor urban communities and to improve the life chances of their residents, and thereby to prevent recurrences of similar civil disturbances.

The Conservative Explanation

In the immediate aftermath of the recent Los Angeles civil unrest, the Bush administration accused South Central Los Angeles gangs of inciting and orchestrating the uprising.[7] The gangs were characterized as "opportunistic thugs" who used the verdict in the police brutality trial as an excuse to wreak havoc in the city.[8] The Bush administration also blamed the civil unrest on Democratic president Lyndon Johnson's War on Poverty programs of the 1960s.[9]

A careful analysis of the situation, however, reveals that neither of these contentions was true. South Central Los Angeles gang members constituted a slim minority of the participants, and there is no evidence to suggest that they were the leaders of the uprising, despite the arrest records of the involved gang members.[10] Moreover, the area affected by the civil unrest was far too extensive geographically for South Central Los Angeles area gangs to have orchestrated the violence. There were hot spots of rebellious activity throughout the Los Angeles metropolitan area. The civil unrest extended well beyond the boundaries of the Watts rebellion of 1965.[11]

Nor was the civil unrest related, in any significant way, to the War on Poverty programs of the 1960s. The Republicans were in control of the White House for all but four of the past twenty-five years. During this period, and especially during the Reagan administration, the Republicans waged a massive assault on War on Poverty programs, dismantling some and substantially reducing support for others.[12] As data from a fairly recent census report reveal, the national poverty rate was higher in 1992 than it was twenty-seven years ago, not because of the War on Poverty programs but, rather, as a consequence of Republican cuts in social welfare.[13] The recent civil unrest never would have occurred, in all probability, if President Johnson's War on Poverty had been allowed to run its course *as initially envisioned*.[14]

An Alternative Explanation

In response to the Bush administration's erroneous assertions, we argued in a recent paper that "the civil unrest was rooted in the high degree of frustration and alienation that had built up among the citizens of south central Los Angeles over the past quarter century as a consequence of poor relations between the LAPD and the minority community."[15] We argued further in another article that the unrest also reflected "a number of broader external forces that have increasingly isolated the south central Los Angeles community, geographically and economically, from the mainstream of Los Angeles society."[16] The real touchstones of the civil unrest, in our view, encompassed a wide range of triggers, including those discussed below.[17]

Perceived Abuses of Power

Repeated acts of what is widely perceived in the minority community to be a blatant abuse of power of the police and the criminal justice system in general fostered hostility. As we have argued elsewhere, "the verdict in the police brutality trial was merely the straw that 'broke the proverbial camel's back.'"[18] The videotaped beating of Rodney King was, in fact, only the most recent case in which serious concerns were raised about the possible use of excessive force by the LAPD to subdue or arrest a black citizen.[19] For several years the LAPD has paid millions of taxpayers' dollars in compensation to local citizens who were victims of abuse, illegal searches and seizures, and property damage.[20]

Moreover, the black citizens of the city of Los Angeles have been victimized disproportionately by the LAPD's use of the bar arm control and choke holds, outlawed tactics that formerly were employed to subdue suspects perceived to be uncooperative. Between 1975 and 1982 sixteen Los Angeles citizens died as a result of LAPD officers' use of these restraint tactics; of the sixteen, twelve were black.[21]

In a similar vein, the "not guilty" verdict rendered in the Rodney King police brutality trial was only the most recent in a series of decisions widely perceived in the black community to be grossly unjust. This decision followed closely on the heels of a controversial verdict in the Latasha Harlins case.[22] A videotape revealed that Ms. Harlins—an honor student at a local high school—was fatally shot in the back of the head by a Korean shopkeeper following an altercation over a bottle of orange juice. Although the jury found the shopkeeper guilty of felony manslaughter, the judge decided to place her on five years' probation and required her to perform only six months of community service.[23]

Demographic Changes

Recent changes have occurred in the composition of the Los Angeles population, and state and local elected officials have failed to implement human relations policies to mitigate the ethnic antagonisms that have accompanied this population change. Over the last thirty years the Los Angeles population has become more ethnically diverse.[24] In 1960 nearly two-thirds of the metropolitan Los Angeles population was non-Hispanic white. By 1990, largely as a consequence of heightened immigration (both legal and illegal) and the substantial exodus of non-Hispanic whites, non-white ethnic minority groups (such as Asians, blacks, and Hispanics) numerically had become the majority population of Los Angeles County, accounting for 58 percent of the total. Approximately one-third of the metropolitan population was Hispanic. Blacks and Asians each accounted for about 12 percent.[25]

Nowhere was this ethnic change more apparent than in South Central Los Angeles, where the civil unrest erupted and the burning, looting, and violence were most intensely concentrated.[26] Two types of ethnic transition have occurred in the formerly all-black South Central Los Angeles communities.[27]

The first was a black-to-brown population succession in the residential neighborhoods, which began in the 1960s and accelerated in the 1970s and the 1980s.[28] In 1970 an estimated 50,000 Hispanics were residing in South Central Los Angeles neighborhoods, representing 10 percent of the area's total population. That number had doubled to 100,000, or 21 percent of the total population, by 1980. Today roughly half of the population of South Central Los Angeles is Hispanic.[29]

Concurrent with this black-to-brown residential transition, an ethnic succession also was taking place in the South Central Los Angeles business community.[30] Prior to the Watts rebellion of 1965 most of the businesses in the area were owned and operated by Jewish shopkeepers. In the aftermath of those disturbances, the Jewish business owners fled the area and were replaced not by black entrepreneurs but, rather, by newly arriving Korean immigrants who opened small retail and service establishments in the area.[31]

These transitions in the residential and business communities of South Central Los Angeles have not been particularly smooth. The three ethnic minority groups—Asians, blacks, and Hispanics—have found themselves in fierce competition and conflict over access to jobs, housing, and other resources, including the political levers of power in the city.[32] The conflict has been most intense between black and Korean entrepreneurs.[33] Disadvantaged blacks in South Central Los Angeles view Korean merchants as "foreigners" who take advantage of them by charging high prices, refusing to hire local blacks, failing to reinvest any of their profits to otherwise aid the community, and being rude and discourteous in their treatment of black customers.[34] According to Edward Chang, an expert on black-Korean relations in Los Angeles, the disrespect that Korean merchants accord black customers is rooted in Korean stereotypes of blacks "as criminals, welfare recipients, drug addicts, and/or lazy."[35] Koreans acquire these stereotypes before they arrive in the United States, Chang contends, through American movies, television shows, and Armed Forces Korean Network programs.[36]

Prior to the jury's verdict in the Rodney King police brutality trial, Korean-black relations in Los Angeles had reached a state of near crisis. Blacks openly questioned how Koreans were able to generate the capital to start or take over businesses in their community when willing black entrepreneurs were unable to raise such funds. The *Los Angeles Sentinel*, the city's major black weekly newspaper, consistently derided Asian shopkeepers for their lack of courteousness to black customers and reported both the important and the trivial instances of conflict.[37] It was the previously described decision in the Latasha Harlins case, however, which preceded the verdict in the Rodney King case by only a few months, that escalated the conflict between black residents and Korean merchants in South Central Los Angeles to crisis proportions.[38]

Assessments of the 1992 civil unrest strongly support the contention that rapidly deteriorating relations between black residents and Korean merchants of South Central Los Angeles were also touchstones of the uprising. Korean businesses were strategically targeted in the burning and the looting. Roughly half of the buildings either severely damaged or destroyed during the civil unrest were either owned or operated by Koreans.[39]

The King verdict also brought to the fore what apparently was a brewing but previously hidden element of interethnic minority conflict in Los Angeles: antagonisms between Hispanics and Koreans in Koreatown.[40] While often viewed as an ethnic enclave demarcated by Korean control of businesses, Koreatown is actually a residentially mixed community with a large proportion of Hispanic residents (principally Central American immigrants) and Koreans. It was in this area that Hispanic involvement in the civil unrest was most intense. Post-disturbance surveys and focus group research indicate that Hispanics in this community come in contact with Koreans on multiple levels and apparently experience hostility at each level. First, on a residential level, Hispanics complain of discrimination by Korean landlords who rent houses and apartments according to racial background.[41] Second, Hispanic customers in Korean establishments complain of disrespectful treatment, similar to black customers.[42] Third, as employees in Korean business establishments, Hispanics express concern about exploitation by their Korean employers.[43] Apparently Hispanics vented their anger and frustration over such discriminatory treatment by looting and destroying a significant number of the Korean-owned businesses in Koreatown.[44]

Prior to the uprising, local elected officials were well aware that ethnic tensions were potentially explosive among nonwhite ethnic minority groups in Los Angeles. At both the city and the county levels of government, human relations commissions long have existed to deal with such problems. These agencies traditionally have been poorly funded, however, and they have been delegated little or no decision-making power or authority to develop policies to resolve the array of intergroup conflicts that are a part of life in the diverse communities of Los Angeles.

As a consequence, both the city and the county human relations commissions have limited their actions to convening hearings on racially, ethnically, and religiously motivated violence and to implementing educational programs that seek to change the stereotypical ways in which the diverse ethnic groups of Los Angeles view one another. For example, prior to the civil unrest the City of Los Angeles Human Relations Commission was instrumental in bringing black leaders and Korean entrepreneurs in South Central Los Angeles together for "prayer breakfasts."[45] These sessions were supposed to offer an opportunity for the two groups to iron out their differences and promote mutual understanding. Unfortunately neither this nor any of the other efforts sponsored by the human relations commissions have been very successful. In fact, realizing that little progress had been made in reducing the tensions between the two groups, black and Korean leaders recently agreed to stop holding such meetings.[46]

Changes in the Business Climate

The creation of a laissez-faire business climate has drastically altered the structure of economic opportunity in South Central Los Angeles and other inner-city communities. Over the past two decades the federal government has attempted to create a deregulated business environment to increase the competitiveness of U.S. firms in the global marketplace. Changes in antitrust laws and their enforcement have resulted in a growing concentration of large, vertically and horizontally integrated firms in key sectors of the economy. Due to their economic power and control of markets, these large conglomerates have been able to move capital quickly and efficiently to select national and international locations to take advantage of cheap labor.[47] There is growing evidence that the federal government, especially during the Bush administration, may in fact have used taxpayers' dollars to provide incentives for United States firms to relocate abroad, especially to Central American countries.[48]

Furthermore, to facilitate the competitiveness of firms remaining in the United States, the federal government, particularly during the Reagan years, relaxed environmental regulations and substantially cut both the budgets and the staffs of governmental agencies charged with the enforcement of laws governing workplace health, safety, and compensation as well as hiring, retention, and promotion practices.[49]

This shift toward a laissez-faire business climate is partially responsible for the wholesale exodus of manufacturing employment from urban communities. It also precipitated the emergence of new industrial spaces in the suburbs, exurbs, and nonmetropolitan areas in this country as well as the movement of manufacturing activities to Third World countries.[50] The new industrial spaces emerging on the U.S. landscape are, in fact, usually situated in places where there are few blacks in the local labor market and few blacks within reasonable commuting distances.[51]

Nowhere have the effects of these policies been more apparent than in South Central Los Angeles. Between 1978 and 1989 approximately 200,000 "good paying" manufacturing jobs disappeared from the Los Angeles economy.[52] South Central Los Angeles—the traditional industrial core of the city—bore the brunt of this deindustrialization.[53] For example, while well-paying and stable jobs were disappearing from South Central Los Angeles, local employers were seeking alternative sites for their manufacturing activities. These seemingly routine decisions stimulated the emergence of new employment growth nodes or "technopoles" in the San Fernando Valley, in the San Gabriel Valley, in El Segundo near the airport in Los Angeles County, and in nearby Orange County.[54] These communities have very small or nonexistent black and Hispanic populations and are geographically inaccessible to a majority of the residents of South Central Los Angeles.

At the same time, a number of Los Angeles-based employers also established production facilities in the Mexican border towns of Tijuana, Ensenada, and Tecate. Between 1978 and 1989 at least 215 Los Angeles-based firms participated in this deconcentration process, including Hughes Aircraft, Northrop, Rockwell, and many smaller firms.[55] Such capital flight, in conjunction with Los Angeles plant closings, essentially has denied the residents of South Central Los Angeles access to formerly well-paying, unionized jobs.[56]

New employment opportunities have emerged within or near the traditional industrial core in South Central Los Angeles.[57] Unlike the manufacturing jobs that disappeared from this area, however, the new jobs are in the competitive sector of the economy, including the hospitality services industry (hotels, motels, restaurants, and entertainment) and such craft specialty industries as clothing, jewelry, and furniture manufacturing.[58]

Competitive sector employers survive only to the extent that their prices remain nationally and internationally competitive. To remain competitive, they often hire undocumented workers, offer unattractive working conditions, and pay, at best, the minimum wage.[59] Research indicates that newly arriving illegal Hispanic immigrants, who have settled in South Central Los Angeles, often are preferred over blacks in the competitive sector employment market because of their undocumented status.[60]

In part as a consequence of these developments, and partly because of employers' openly negative attitudes toward black workers,[61] when the Rodney King police brutality verdict was handed down on April 29, 1992, South Central Los Angeles communities were characterized by high concentrations of two disadvantaged populations: the working poor, who were predominantly Hispanic, and the jobless poor, who were predominantly black.[62]

Most of the individuals inhabiting these communities thus had insufficient incomes to maintain a decent standard of living. Both groups—Hispanics and blacks—were isolated geographically from mainstream employment opportunities that pay livable wages. Intergroup tensions were high as poor blacks and Hispanics competed for competitive sector jobs and other scarce resources.[63]

Disinvestment by City Government and Local Institutions

In addition to the adverse impacts of a laissez-faire business policy on the structure of employment opportunities in South Central Los Angeles, the local government has failed to devise and implement a plan to redevelop and revitalize the community. Instead, the city has pursued avidly a policy of downtown and Westside redevelopment in an effort to lure international capital to Los Angeles.[64]

The "power of the pocketbook" appears to have driven this redevelopment strategy. Data compiled by Frank Clifford, Rich Connell, Stephen Braun, and Andrea Ford indicate that "since 1983, Los Angeles city officeholders and candidates have received $23 million in political contributions, mostly from the Westside, the San Fernando Valley, and Downtown businesses."[65] They note further that "political experts and City Hall critics say the contributions make elected officials more attuned to corporate interests and the suburbs than to the city's poorer areas."[66]

The transformation of the skylines of downtown and the so-called Wilshire corridor—the twenty-mile stretch extending along Wilshire Boulevard from downtown to the Pacific Ocean—is evidence of the success of this redevelopment strategy. A symbol of Los Angeles's emerging transactional economy, this area now houses the headquarters of a number of multinational corporations and other advanced service sector employers.[67]

This type of redevelopment, however, has done little to improve the quality of life of the residents of South Central Los Angeles. Jobs in the re-vitalized downtown area and along the Wilshire corridor typically require high levels of education and technical training—the ability to do "head" work as opposed to "hand" work—that most of the disadvantaged residents of South Central Los Angeles do not possess. The only low-skilled employment opportunities that exist in this area are low-level service and custodial jobs, which typically are filled by newly arrived immigrants.

Conservative Policymaking

More than two decades of conservative social policymaking, at both the federal and state levels of government, have adversely affected the quality of life of the residents of South Central Los Angeles and have accelerated the decline and deterioration of their neighborhoods.

Three examples of conservative social policymaking are provided here. The first involves the federal government's dismantling of the social safety net in poor communities such as South Central Los Angeles through massive cuts in federal aid to cities.[68] Preston Niblack and Peter Stan noted the impact on the city of Los Angeles: "The decline in federal aid is striking: in 1977 the city received federal aid worth $370 million; by 1990 these grants had dropped to $60 million—or from almost 18 percent of the city's operating budget to less than 2 percent."[69]

Perhaps most devastating for South Central Los Angeles has been the de-funding of community-based organizations (CBOs) due to this massive loss of federal assistance. Historically CBOs were part of the collective of social resources in the urban environment that encouraged the inner-city disadvantaged, especially disadvantaged youth, to pursue mainstream avenues of social and economic mobility and to avoid dysfunctional or anti-social behavior. In academic lingo, CBOs were effective "mediating institutions" in the inner city.[70]

In 1981, when President Reagan took office, CBOs received an estimated 41 percent of their funding from the federal government.[71] As a consequence of the Reagan administration's elimination of the revenue sharing program, Los Angeles and other cities have been forced to reduce substantially grant support for community-based programs that traditionally have benefited the most disadvantaged members of the community. In South Central Los Angeles and other inner-city communities, teenagers have been hurt most by this defunding of CBO initiatives and other safety net programs.

State governments' anticrime policy is the second area in which conservative attitudes have had a negative impact.[72] Paralleling the dismantling of social programs that discouraged disadvantaged youth from engaging in dysfunctional behavior and that rehabilitated those who did, states (with the encouragement and support of the federal government) have pursued for nearly three decades a policy of resolving the problems of the inner city through the criminal justice system.[73]

Once a leader in the rehabilitation of criminals, California epitomizes this shift in anticrime policy. In 1977 the California legislature enacted the Determinant Sentence Law, "which, among other things, embraced *punishment* (and, explicitly, *not* rehabilitation) as the purpose of prison, required mandatory prison sentences for many offenses formerly eligible for probation, and dramatically increased the rate at which probation and parole violators were returned to prison."[74] As a consequence of the passage of this law, the California prison population skyrocketed from 22,000 to 106,000 between 1980 and 1992, an increase of more than 500 percent.[75]

To accommodate this increase, California expanded the capacity of seven of its existing prisons and built thirteen new facilities to bring the current total to twenty-five; six additional correctional facilities currently are under construction or in the planning phase.[76] From 1987 to 1992 spending on the criminal justice system increased by 70 percent, approximately four times greater than total state spending. By comparison state spending on education increased by only 10 percent during this same five-year period.[77] Even more striking is that California moved from spending 2 percent of its budget on prisons in 1980 to spending 9 percent of its budget on prisons in 1994. If these expenditures continue at the present rate, it is estimated that "California prisons will consume 18% of the state's budget by the year 2002 if growth in prisoners continues at its current pace."[78] Moreover, a 1991 survey of inmates in 277 state prisons across the country revealed that more than one-third were unemployed prior to their arrest. Thus, we see a link between unemployment and incarceration.[79]

Minorities have been affected disproportionately by California's "get tough on crime" policies. Two-thirds of the prison population is black or Hispanic, with blacks constituting 35 percent of the total.[80] How have the minority residents of South Central Los Angeles fared under the current policy? Reliable statistics to answer this question are difficult to assemble, but the number of people arrested during the recent civil unrest who already had a criminal record is probably a fairly accurate barometer. Approximately 40 percent of those arrested had a prior brush with the law.[81] What are the prospects of landing a job if you have a criminal record? "Incarceration breeds despair, and hopelessness, and in the employment arena is the 'Scarlet Letter' of unemployability."[82]

Educational initiatives enacted at the state level during the late 1970s and the early 1980s, which were designed to address the "crisis" in American education, constitute the third affected policy domain.[83] Social science evidence indicates that policies such as tracking by ability group, grade retention, and the increasing reliance on standardized tests as the ultimate arbiter of educational success have, in fact, negatively affected large numbers of black and brown youths.[84] In urban school systems, they are placed disproportionately in special education classes and are more likely than their white counterparts to be subjected to extreme disciplinary sanctions.[85]

The effects of these policies in the Los Angeles Unified School District (LAUSD) are evident in the data on school-leaving behavior.[86] In the LAUSD as a whole, 39.3 percent of all students in the class of 1988 dropped out at some point during their high school years. For high schools in South Central Los Angeles, however, the dropout rates were substantially higher, between 63 percent and 79 percent. It is important to note that the dropout problem is not limited to the high school population. LAUSD data reveal that approximately 24 percent of the students in some South Central Los Angeles junior high schools also dropped out during the 1987–88 academic year.[87]

Twenty years ago it was possible to drop out of high school before graduation and find a good-paying job in heavy manufacturing in South Central Los Angeles. Today those types of jobs are no longer available. The result of the adverse effects of deindustrialization and the discriminatory aspects of educational reforms is a rather substantial pool of inner-city males of color who are neither at work nor in school. These individuals are, in effect, idle; previous research demonstrates that it is this population that is most likely to be involved in gang activity, drug trafficking, and a range of other criminal behaviors.[88] Moreover, it is idle minority males who experience the most difficulty maintaining stable families.[89] Together these phenomena account, at least in part, for the high percentage of female-headed families with incomes below the poverty level in South Central Los Angeles when the uprising began.[90]

Postscript

The Los Angeles civil unrest of 1992 differed, in several critical respects, from the civil disorders of the 1960s.

First, it required the deployment of a significantly greater number of emergency personnel, and it exacted a heavier toll on the local community than did the civil disorders of the 1960s.[91]

Second, although blacks were the main participants in most of the earlier civil disorders, a range of ethnic groups participated in the recent conflagration in Los Angeles. Some of the incidents, for example, included white as well as Hispanic participants.[92]

Third, whereas the geographical impact of the civil disorders of the 1960s was fairly localized, the Los Angeles civil unrest of 1992 affected a far more expansive area. Although much of the devastation was concentrated in South Central Los Angeles, numerous hot spots extended well beyond the boundaries of the Watts rebellion of 1965.[93]

Fourth, majority-owned businesses were the primary targets for destruction in past civil disorders, but the contemporary pattern revealed a more systematic focus on ethnic minority commercial establishments. Small, family-owned and operated, ethnic businesses (mainly Korean) were the primary targets in the burning and the looting.[94]

Finally, the verdict in the Los Angeles police brutality trial prompted acts of protest—violent and nonviolent—in many more cities than did the events precipitating the civil disorders of the 1960s. There was random property damage and looting in Atlanta, Las Vegas, Minneapolis, New York, Omaha, Seattle, and Washington, D.C., although the incidents were not on a scale comparable to those in Los Angeles.[95] In New York the type of civil unrest that paralyzed Los Angeles did not materialize, mainly because the mayor took specific steps to reduce tensions in the city.[96] Nonetheless, there was a literal "emptying out" of midtown Manhattan early Friday afternoon (May 1) as most businesses closed in anticipation of civil unrest.[97] However, the common thread among nearly all of the major urban uprisings from the 1960s to 1992 has been an incident of police brutality as a primary spark.

A wide array of initiatives has been proposed or launched by a range of public and private organizations to rebuild Los Angeles in the aftermath of this civil disturbance. Among the most visible and highly touted is Rebuild LA (now called RLA), initially headed by former baseball commissioner Peter Ueberroth, who was appointed by Mayor Tom Bradley with considerable fanfare.[98] The board of directors of RLA is comprised of representatives from government, business, community organizations, and a range of special interest groups, and the organization has a professional staff of lawyers, accountants, planners, and advertising and public relations experts to oversee the development of its strategies for rebuilding South Central Los Angeles.[99]

Ueberroth's goal was to create "thousands of permanent jobs and giv[e] new hope to residents who feel economically disenfranchised."[100] He proposed to achieve this goal not by attempting to lure a few large employers to the area but, rather, by encouraging a large number of companies to open small operations in South Central Los Angeles.[101]

However, a *Los Angeles Times* survey revealed that a significant number of the firms on the RLA list of private sector contributors denied ever pledging financial support to the rebuilding effort.[102] Several of the corporate heads indicated that they had never spoken to Mr. Ueberroth about the RLA initiative.[103] As a consequence of the misrepresentation of the level of corporate support, the hostility from diverse ethnic groups in South Central Los Angeles and other affected areas (for example, Korea-town), and RLA's lack of success in rebuilding the rebellion-torn communities in the year following the civil unrest, Peter Ueberroth resigned on May 21, 1993, as chairman. In the minds of many, his resignation confirmed the view that this private sector initiative was doomed from the outset.[104]

Ueberroth was replaced by Bernard Kinsey, a black corporate executive, who had previously served as one of his cochairs. But after only eight months on the job, Kinsey also resigned, citing the continuing problems and his need to return to his business-development consulting firm.[105] Kinsey was followed by Linda Griego, a Hispanic who served as deputy mayor for economic development in the Bradley administration. She has indicated that she would continue the job creation and corporate investment initiatives started under Ueberroth, feeling that they had not been given enough time to work.[106]

Undergirding most of the currently debated policy prescriptions for improving the quality of life in our nation's socially and economically depressed central cities is the notion that we can bring the poor into the mainstream of American society if we enhance their acceptance of personal responsibility and improve their personal values. Poor people, individually and through their community, civic, and religious institutions, have a responsibility to promote positive values and lifestyles in their communities and to socialize their youth into the mainstream.[107] But they cannot do it alone.

They cannot be held accountable for the massive plant closings, disinvestments, and exportation of jobs from our urban centers to Third World countries. There must be an equality of status in responsibility and authority across race and class lines if we are to resolve the poverty problem. Government, in a bipartisan fashion, must direct its resources to those programs determined to be successful with poor people; the poor must be permitted to participate in the design of programs for their benefit; and society at all levels must embrace personal responsibility and a commitment to race and gender equity. To effectively deal with poverty, it is imperative, in our view, that we adopt the following strategies:

First and foremost, we—all of us—must embrace the view that poverty and inequality are bad for business. As a recent article in *Business Week* magazine concluded, any jurisdiction that fails to develop fully its human capital potential and to deal effectively with the problems undergirding existing racial and gender disparities will find itself falling progressively further behind in the highly competitive global marketplace. Thus, taking steps to enhance the economic and sociocultural appeal of the nation's

concentrated poverty communities is a form of enlightened self-interest—
that is, it is good for business.[108]

Second, in our efforts to address the issues of concentrated and persistent poverty, we must not place all of our economic development eggs in
the microenterprise basket, which seems to be the "in vogue" economic development strategy of the moment. Microenterprise alone will neither revitalize our concentrated and persistently poor communities nor narrow the
economic gap between the "haves" and the "have-nots." The primary emphasis in economic development, we believe, must be on *macro*enterprise—pursuing major job generators—rather than on *micro*enterprise
initiatives. Without such anchors, or sets of anchors, the retail and service
establishments that seemingly dominate the economic landscape of persistently poor communities are likely to remain marginal enterprises. With a
stable supply of well-paying jobs, such establishments are more likely to
thrive, since workers will have discretionary income to purchase both
basic and nonbasic goods and services. RLA's initiative in that regard was
on the right track.

Third, and equally as important as the need for major job generators in
communities plagued by concentrated and persistent poverty, the recruitment and training of workers must be linked directly to specific job opportunities. Research shows that generic education and training programs—
those not connected to a specific job—have not worked in the past for
poor people of color, and they are unlikely to work in the future.[109]

Customized training programs, on the other hand, have proven to be
highly effective economic development tools, especially when they are offered at no cost to prospective employers as part of a locational incentive
package. Such programs have been instrumental in luring major job generators to formerly economically depressed regions of South Carolina and
Alabama. For individuals participating in these programs, job placement
rates are phenomenal—reportedly as high as 99 percent.[110]

Fourth, if we are to deal successfully with the nation's poverty problems,
the foregoing economic development strategies must not be pursued in
isolation. Rather, they must be undertaken in conjunction with efforts to
mend the social fabric of economically distressed communities. Midnight
Basketball Leagues are one example of a new generation of social resource
programs designed to enhance the social fabric of inner-city communities.

Recently we were members of a research team that conducted an evaluation of a Midnight Basketball League in Milwaukee, Wisconsin. Our findings revealed that the program (1) created a safe haven in which the participants and the fans could engage in positive social activities, (2) channeled
the energy of gang members in a positive direction, and (3) significantly
improved the educational and career aspirations of program participants.[111]
Additionally, according to Milwaukee Police Department statistics, crime

rates in the target area decreased by 30 percent during the program's first year of operation. Moreover, the program achieved these highly desirable outcomes with a modest investment of $70,000—roughly the same amount required to maintain two inner-city minority males in prison for one year. One does not have to be an investment banker to realize that programs like Midnight Basketball will contribute more to the revival of economically distressed communities than any or all of the enormously popular punitive and/or paternalistic policies currently advocated at all levels of government.

Finally, all of the nation's assets, including the resources of government, community-based organizations, the business sector, the philanthropic community, and especially our colleges and universities, must be mobilized if we are to deal effectively with poverty in the United States. What is the most effective and efficient way to go about doing this? It will require what we refer to as the four Cs: cooperation, collaboration, coordination, and capital. In our view, the philanthropic and corporate communities are most strategically positioned to mobilize the requisite financial resources. And we believe our system of colleges and universities—one of the nation's most underutilized resources—is best suited to establish the necessary institutional links.

There are outstanding scholars in our system of higher education who, with the proper incentives and direction from the philanthropic and corporate communities, are capable of designing a cooperative, collaborative, and coordinated strategy that draws upon and fully utilizes the complete range of the nation's assets to deal with the seemingly intractable problems that currently plague economically distressed communities. What is needed at this point is a bipartisan group of legislators who, like Michael Jordan in the final seconds when the game is on the line, are willing to take the final shot to score a victory for our nation. Our future competitiveness in the global marketplace hinges on such bipartisanship across the broad ideological and political spectrum.

Notes

1. The 1968 report of the National Advisory Commission on Civil Disorders, *The Kerner Report* (New York: Pantheon, 1988).

2. The terms *African American, black,* and *black American* will be used interchangeably to refer to persons of African descent living in the United States.

3. "Toll from the Riots," *USA Today,* May 5, 1992; "LA Aftermath at a Glance," *USA Today,* May 6, 1992.

4. *Kerner Report,* 236.

5. Fred R. Harris and Roger W. Wilkins, ed., *Quiet Riots: Race and Poverty in the*

United States: The Kerner Report Twenty Years Later (New York: Pantheon, 1988), iii.

6. James H. Johnson Jr. and Melvin L. Oliver, "Interethnic Minority Conflict in Urban America: The Effects of Economic and Social Dislocations," *Urban Geography* 10 (1989): 449–63; Melvin L. Oliver and James H. Johnson Jr., "Interethnic Conflict in an Urban Ghetto: The Case of Blacks and Latinos in Los Angeles," *Research in Social Movements, Conflicts and Change* 6 (1984): 57–94.

7. Jack Nelson, "Bush Reaction to Riots Splits Republicans," *Los Angeles Times*, May 8, 1992.

8. Ibid.

9. R. W. Apple Jr., "Bush Says Largess Won't Help Cities," *New York Times*, May 7, 1992; John Harwood, "Bush Reaffirms View That Federal Aid Isn't Solution to Cities' Problems," *Wall Street Journal*, May 7, 1992; Robert Pear, "Clinton Tours City's Damaged Areas and Chides Bush," *New York Times*, May 5, 1992; David E. Rosenbaum, "Decoding the Remarks by Fitzwater on Riots," *New York Times*, May 6, 1992; Andrew Rosenthal, "Quayle Says Riots Sprang from Lack of Family Values," *New York Times*, May 20, 1992; Michael Wines, "White House Links Riots to Welfare," *New York Times*, May 5, 1992.

10. Paul Lieberman, "40% of Riot Suspects Have Criminal Records," *Los Angeles Times*, May 19, 1992.

11. James H. Johnson Jr., Walter C. Farrell Jr., and Melvin L. Oliver, "Seeds of the Los Angeles Rebellion of 1992," *International Journal of Urban and Regional Research*, 17 (1993): 115–19.

12. Gary Orfield and Carol Ashkanize, *The Closing Door: Conservative Policy and Black Opportunity* (Chicago: University of Chicago Press, 1991); D. Lee Bawden, ed., *The Social Contract Revisited: Aims and Outcomes of President Reagan's Social Welfare Policy* (Washington, D.C.: Urban Institute Press, 1984); Ronald Walters, "The Reagan Revolution Sparked LA's Rebellion," *Wall Street Journal*, May 7, 1992.

13. "The War against the Poor," *New York Times*, May 6, 1992.

14. Bill Hendrick, "LBJ's War on Poverty Still Makes Sense Now," *Greensboro News and Record*, May 17, 1992.

15. Johnson, Farrell, and Oliver, "Seeds of Rebellion," 116.

16. James H. Johnson Jr., Cloyzelle K. Jones, Walter C. Farrell Jr., and Melvin L. Oliver, "The Los Angeles Rebellion: A Retrospective View," *Economic Development Quarterly* 6 (1992): 356–72.

17. Ibid.

18. Johnson, Jones, Farrell, and Oliver, "Retrospective View," 359.

19. Mike Davis, *City of Quartz: Excavating the Future in Los Angeles* (New York: Vintage, 1990), 267–322.

20. Ibid.

21. Johnson, Jones, Farrell, and Oliver, "Retrospective View," 359.

22. Seth Mydans, "Los Angeles Policemen Acquitted in Taped Beating," *New York Times*, April 20, 1992.

23. Ibid.

24. James H. Johnson Jr., Melvin Oliver, and Curtis Roseman, "Ethnic Dilemmas in Comparative Perspective," *Urban Geography* 10 (1989): 425–33.

25. Johnson, Jones, Farrell, and Oliver, "Retrospective View," 359.

26. Ibid.

27. Oliver and Johnson, "Interethnic Conflict in an Urban Ghetto."

28. Ibid.

29. Ibid.

30. Johnson and Oliver, "Interethnic Minority Conflict in Urban America."

31. Ibid.

32. Ibid.

33. Ibid.

34. Edward Chang, "Korean-Black Conflict in Los Angeles: Perceptions and Realities" (unpublished paper on file with authors, 1988), 20.

35. Ibid.

36. Ibid.

37. James H. Cleaver, "Asian Attitudes toward Blacks Cause Raised Eyebrows," *Los Angeles Sentinel*, August 18, 1983; James H. Cleaver, "Citizens Air Gripes about Asians," *Los Angeles Sentinel*, September 1, 1983; James H. Cleaver, "One Answer to an Outcry," *Los Angeles Sentinel*, March 19, 1987; James H. Cleaver, "Residents Complain about Alleged Asian 'Problem,'" *Los Angeles Sentinel*, August 25, 1983.

38. Mydans, "Los Angeles Policemen Acquitted."

39. *Report of the Ad Hoc Committee on Recovery and Revitalization to the Los Angeles City Council* (Los Angeles: Los Angeles City Council, 1992).

40. Lawrence Bobo, James H. Johnson Jr., and Melvin L. Oliver, *Public Opinion before and after a Spring of Discontent*, Occasional Working Paper Series, University of California at Los Angeles (Los Angeles: Center for the Study of Urban Poverty [CSUP], 1992).

41. Ibid.

42. Ibid.

43. Ibid.

44. Ibid.

45. Sophia Kim, "Seeking a Dialogue by Koreans, Blacks," *Los Angeles Times*, June 8, 1984.

46. "A Lament for the Loss of Some Dialogue," *Los Angeles Times*, December 29, 1992.

47. James H. Johnson Jr. and Melvin L. Oliver, "Structural Changes in the U.S. Economy and Black Male Joblessness: A Reassessment," in *Urban Labor Markets and Job Opportunity*, ed. George E. Peterson and Wayne Vroman (Washington, D.C.: Urban Institute Press, 1992), 113–47.

48. Michael deCourcy Hinds, "Survey Cited to Assail Bush on Overseas Jobs," *New York Times*, November 11, 1992.

49. John L. Palmer and Isabel V. Sawhill, ed., *The Reagan Record: An Assessment of America's Changing Priorities* (Washington, D.C.: Urban Institute Press, 1984).

50. Johnson and Oliver, "Black Male Joblessness."

51. Robert E. Cole and Donald R. Deskins Jr., "Racial Factors in Site Location and Employment Patterns of Japanese Auto Firms in America," *California Management Review* 31 (1988): 9–22.

52. Edward Soja, Rebecca Morales, and Goetz Wolff, "Urban Restructuring: An Analysis of Social and Spatial Change in Los Angeles," *Economic Geography* 58

(1983): 221–35; Data Center, *Plant Shutdowns Monitor Directory, 1982–1989* (Los Angeles: Data Center, 1990).

53. Johnson, Jones, Farrell, and Oliver, "Retrospective View."

54. Allen J. Scott, "Flexible Production Systems and Regional Development: The Rise of New Industrial Spaces in North America and Western Europe," *International Journal of Urban and Regional Research* 12 (1988): 171–86.

55. Soja et al., "Urban Restructuring," 200–202.

56. Barry Bluestone and Bennett Harrison, *The Deindustrialization of America: Plant Closings, Community Abandonment, and the Dismantling of Basic Industry* (New York: Basic Books, 1982); Gregory D. Squires, "'Run Away Plants,' Capital Mobility, and Black Economic Rights," in *Community and Capital in Conflict: Plant Closings and Job Loss,* ed. John C. Raines, L. E. Berson, and D. McI. Gracie (Philadelphia: Temple University Press), 62–97.

57. Johnson, Jones, Farrell, and Oliver, "Retrospective View."

58. Ibid.

59. Frank Levy, *Dollars and Dreams: The Changing American Income Distribution* (New York: Russell Sage, 1987).

60. Thomas Mueller and Thomas J. Espenshade, *The Fourth Wave: California's Newest Immigrants* (Washington, D.C.: Urban Institute Press, 1984).

61. Joleen Kirschenman and Katherine M. Neckerman, "'We'd Love to Hire Them, But . . .': The Meaning of Race for Employers," in *The Urban Underclass,* ed. Christopher Jencks and Paul E. Peterson (Washington, D.C.: Brookings Institution, 1991), 203–24.

62. At that time the black male jobless rate in some residential areas of South Central Los Angeles hovered around 50 percent (Johnson, Jones, Farrell, and Oliver, "Retrospective View").

63. Oliver and Johnson, "Interethnic Conflict in an Urban Ghetto"; Ed Luttwak, "The Riots: Underclass vs. Immigrants," *New York Times,* May 15, 1992.

64. H. Briavel Holcomb and Robert A. Beauregard, *Revitalizing Cities* (Washington, D.C.: Association of American Geographers, 1983); Frank Clifford, R. Connell, S. Baun, and A. Ford, "Leaders Lose Feel for L.A.," *Los Angeles Times,* August 30, 1992.

65. Clifford et al., "Leaders Lose Feel."

66. Ibid.

67. Holcomb and Beauregard, *Revitalizing Cities,* 25–26.

68. George E. Peterson, "Urban Policy and the Cyclical Behavior of Cities," in *Reagan and the Cities,* ed. George E. Peterson and Carol W. Lewis (Washington, D.C.: Urban Institute Press, 1986).

69. Preston Niblack and Peter J. E. Stan, "Financing Public Services in Los Angeles," in *Urban America: Policy Choices for Los Angeles and the Nation,* ed. J. Steinberg et al. (Santa Monica, Calif.: Rand Corporation), 255–80.

70. Melvin L. Oliver, "The Urban Black Community as Network: Towards a Social Network Perspective," *Sociological Quarterly* 19 (1988): 623–45.

71. Lester M. Salamon, "Nonprofit Organizations: The Lost Opportunity," in Palmer and Sawhill, *Reagan Record,* 261–85.

72. Joan Petersilia, "Crime and Punishment in California: Full Cells, Empty

Pockets, and Questionable Benefits," in Steinberg et al., *Urban America*, 175–206.

73. Ibid.

74. Ibid., 176.

75. Ibid., 177–79.

76. Ibid., 179.

77. Ibid., 181.

78. G. Pascal Zachary, "Economists Say Prison Boom Will Take Toll," *Wall Street Journal*, September 29, 1995, B6.

79. Ibid., B1.

80. Petersilia, "Crime and Punishment in California," 178.

81. Lieberman, "40% of Riot Suspects."

82. Johnson and Oliver, "Black Male Joblessness."

83. Gary Orfield, "Exclusion of the Majority: Shrinking College Access and Public Policy in Metropolitan Los Angeles," *Urban Review* 20 (1988): 147–63.

84. Ibid., 160–61.

85. Johnson and Oliver, "Black Male Joblessness."

86. *California Basic Educational Data System, Three Year Summary: Number of Dropouts in California Public High School Instruction* (Sacramento: California Department of Public Instruction, 1989).

87. Los Angeles Unified School District, *Dropout Rates in LAUSD Junior High Schools, 1987–88* (Los Angeles: Los Angeles Unified School District, 1989).

88. W. K. Viscusi, "Market Incentives for Criminal Behavior," in *The Black Youth Employment Crisis*, ed. Richard B. Freeman and Harry Holzer (Chicago: University of Chicago Press, 1986).

89. William Julius Wilson, *The Truly Disadvantaged: The Inner City, the Underclass, and Public Policy* (Chicago: University of Chicago Press, 1987).

90. Johnson, Jones, Farrell, and Oliver, "Retrospective View."

91. Ibid., 357.

92. Virginia Postrel, "The Real Story Goes beyond Black and White," *Los Angeles Times*, May 8, 1992.

93. Johnson, Farrell, and Oliver, "Seeds of Rebellion," 116.

94. Ibid.

95. B. Drummond Ayres Jr., "From Coast to Coast, Cities are Struggling to Control a Swell of Violence," *New York Times*, May 2, 1992; Dirk Johnson, "When Rumor Mixes with Racial Rage," *New York Times*, May 10, 1992; Alison Mitchell, "Fears and Rumors Roil a Nervous New York," *New York Times*, May 2, 1992.

96. David N. Dinkins, "Will Washington Heed the Marchers?," *New York Times*, May 5, 1992.

97. Ibid.

98. Richard W. Stevenson, "With Few Tools, Ueberroth Begins Mission in Riot Area," *New York Times*, May 7, 1992.

99. Ibid.

100. Ibid.

101. Ibid.

102. Nancy Rivera-Brooks and Henry Weinstein, "19 of 68 Firms Question Listing by Rebuild L.A.," *Los Angeles Times*, November 18, 1992.

103. Ibid.

104. Walter C. Farrell Jr. and James H. Johnson Jr., "Peter Ueberroth: A White Man Who Couldn't Jump," *Milwaukee Courier*, May 29, 1993; Calvin Sims, "Ueberroth, Amid Criticism, Quits Post at 'Rebuild L.A.,'" *New York Times*, May 22, 1993.

105. Calvin Sims, "Leader to Quit Post-Riot Panel in Los Angeles," *New York Times*, January 12, 1994.

106. Calvin Sims, "Who Said Los Angeles Could Be Rebuilt in a Day?," *New York Times*, May 22, 1994.

107. James Q. Wilson, "How to Teach Better Values in the Inner Cities," *Wall Street Journal*, June 1, 1992.

108. Aaron Bernstein, "Inequality: How the Gap between Rich and Poor Hurts the Economy," *Business Week*, 15 (1994): 78–83.

109. J. Fitzgerald and A. McGregor, "Labor-Community Initiatives in Work Training," *Economic Development Quarterly* 7 (1993): 160–71.

110. S. Overman, "Skilled States Lure New Business," *HR Magazine* 34 (1994): 61–62.

111. Walter C. Farrell Jr., James H. Johnson Jr., Marty Sapp, R. Mack Pumphrey, and Shirley Freeman, "Redirecting the Lives of Inner City Black Males: An Assessment of Milwaukee's Midnight Basketball League," *Journal of Community Practice* 2 (1995); Walter C. Farrell Jr. and James H. Johnson Jr., "Access to Social Resources Is Key to Problems in the Inner City," *Wisconsin Review*, October 1994, 23.

George C. Galster

Polarization, Place, and Race

Horatio Alger lies dead in the city. For millions of Americans the rags-to-riches fable has been reduced to ashes as surely as many neighborhoods in South Central Los Angeles.

For none has this been more true than racial-ethnic minority groups living in central cities of our larger metropolitan areas. Economic opportunity has increasingly become a myth for them because they have had to confront the massive industrial dislocations of the post–World War II era while bearing the twin burdens of place and race.

In a fundamental sense the success of the American experiment in democracy depends on widespread public belief in both the principle and the presence of equal opportunity. Opportunity provides an ethical justification for inequality of economic outcomes. It motivates diligence, investment, and perseverance. It provides a source of optimism about the efficacy of one's own efforts and the prospects for intergenerational social mobility. It legitimizes the entire social order.

Unfortunately, for too many of our inner-city residents, especially members of racial-ethnic minority groups, equal opportunity has become a sham in light of forces leading to intensifying and, apparently, permanent socioeconomic polarization. This essay examines aspects of urban polarization along racial-ethnic lines, why this polarization results from both place and race, and what can be done about it.

The essay begins by illustrating the extent and intransigence of racial polarization by reviewing data on education, employment, and earnings from the last two decades.[1] The source of this polarization is explored by positing a conceptual model of individual decision making about crucial life choices. Central to this model is the notion that choices are rationally made within the constraints perceived by the decision maker. Thus, observed behaviors that contribute to current and future socioeconomic status (educational attainment, labor force participation, etc.) are a product of the personal and contextual constraints within which decisions are made. Metropolitan areas are seen as complex webs of interrelated constraints: what I call the "opportunity structure." The impact of the opportunity structure on any individual is mediated by the "place-race lens": the severity of constraint depends on people's place of residence and their racial-ethnic status. Evidence on how both place and race affect opportunity is therefore presented. Finally, the essay outlines a policy approach that tries to respond seriously to the diagnosis of the problem as embodied in the concept of opportunity structure.

Racial Polarization in Education, Employment, and Earnings

Polarization among groups defined by racial and ethnic status can be measured along many dimensions. Here I focus on three crucial and interrelated dimensions of socioeconomic status: education, employment, and earnings. Each dimension reveals not only present wide interracial disparities, but also ones that typically have persisted or even grown over the last two decades. The disparities are particularly striking in metropolitan areas.

Education

Fundamental changes have taken place in the nation's economy in the postwar period, most dramatically the decline in high-wage manufacturing employment and the growth in both low- and high-wage service sector employment. The burgeoning service sector employment appears bifurcated: jobs either lack adequate pay, benefits, and chances for advancement or they require considerable skill or substantial educational credentials.[2] Considering the increasing importance of education, the statistics concerning interracial disparities in school attainment are sobering.

Table 1 shows percentages of whites, blacks, and Hispanics between the ages of eighteen and twenty-four not completing high school, during the last two decades. Although rates for blacks have declined, those for Hispanics have remained roughly the same. Interracial disparities in high school noncompletion rates can be seen either by taking ratios of figures or their differences; both are presented in this and subsequent tables. In both relative (ratio) and absolute (difference) terms, the black-versus-white gap in high school noncompletion rates narrowed from 1973 to 1991 but showed a widening in 1992. By both measures it has remained remarkably constant between Hispanics and whites, with the exception of the mid-1980s. In 1992 black youths were 30 percent more likely to not finish secondary school than whites; Hispanic youths were 170 percent more likely.

The situation is especially bleak for students in large, central-city school districts. As shown in Table 2, the dropout rates in such districts are well above the national average of 11 percent. Indeed, the dropout rate in the nation's forty-seven largest urban school districts combined is almost twice

Table 1. Percentage of Population Aged 18–24 Not Completing High
School and Not Enrolled by Racial-Ethnic Group, 1973–1992

Year	White	Black	Black/ White	Black– White	Hispanic[a]	Hispanic/ White	Hispanic– White
1973	14.2	26.5	1.9	12.3	38.9	2.7	24.7
1975	13.9	27.3	2.0	13.4	34.9	2.5	21.0
1980	14.4	23.5	1.6	9.1	40.9	2.8	26.5
1985	13.5	17.6	1.3	4.1	31.5	2.3	18.0
1990	13.6	15.1	1.1	1.5	37.3	2.7	23.7
1991	14.2	15.6	1.1	1.4	39.6	2.8	25.4
1992	12.7	16.3	1.3	3.6	33.9	2.7	21.2

Source: Bureau of the Census, *Statistical Abstract 1994*, tab. 260.

[a]Hispanic persons may be of any race.

Table 2. Secondary School Dropout Rates and Student Racial
Composition, by Selected Center-City School Districts

School District	Dropout Rate (1991) (%)	Racial-Ethnic Composition of Students (1980)		
		White (%)	Black (%)	Hispanic[a] (%)
Baltimore	22.8	21	78	0
Los Angeles	21.9	24	23	45
St. Louis	20.7	21	79	0
Dallas	20.0	30	49	19
Washington, D.C.	19.1	4	93	2
Detroit	18.8	12	86	2
Miami	18.5	32	30	38
Chicago	17.0	19	60	19
Denver	16.8	41	23	32
Philadelphia	15.7	29	63	7
New York	13.1	26	39	31

Source of school racial composition data: Orfield, *Public School Desegregation*,
tab. 20. Source of dropout data: U.S. Department of Education, "Dropout Rates in
the U.S.: 1991," cited by Sari Horwitz and Mary Jordan, "D.C. Dropout Rate
Among Worst in U.S.," *Washington Post*, September 17, 1992.

Note: Totals may not add to 100 due to rounding and other racial-ethnic categories
of students.

[a]Hispanic persons may be of any race.

Table 3. Percentage of Population 25 Years and Older Completing Four
or More Years of College, by Race-Ethnicity, 1970–1993

Year	White	Black	Black/ White	Black− White	Hispanic[a]	Hispanic/ White	Hispanic− White
1970	11.3	4.4	.39	−6.9	4.5	.40	−6.8
1980	17.1	8.4	.49	−8.7	7.6	.44	−9.5
1989	21.8	11.8	.54	−10.0	9.9	.45	−11.9
1993	22.6	12.2	.54	−10.4	9.0	.40	−13.6

Source: Bureau of the Census, *Statistical Abstract: 1991*, tab. 224, and *1994*, tab. 234.

[a]Hispanic persons may be of any race.

the national average.[3] Not surprisingly, all these districts enrolled large majorities of nonwhite students.[4]

College completion rates, as shown in Table 3, also evince wide, rigid
disparities. Higher fractions of all three racial-ethnic groups graduate from
college now than twenty years ago. The proportion has grown in absolute
terms more rapidly for whites, however, resulting in an ever growing absolute and relative difference in completion rates for higher education, especially between whites and Hispanics.[5] In 1993, college completion rates
for whites were 85 percent higher than those for blacks and 151 percent
higher than those for Hispanics. This gap is partially explained by the
aforementioned interracial differences in secondary school noncompletion
rates, but not completely. Even among high school graduates, college completion rates evince wide racial differentials. For illustration, by 1989 only
11.8 percent of black high school graduates had also graduated from college; the corresponding percentage for all persons was 21.1.[6]

Employment

As in the case of educational attainment, conventional indicators of labor
market activity have evinced significant and steadfast racial-ethnic disparities over the last two decades. Table 4, for example, shows that for all three
racial-ethnic groups, the percentage of their population sixteen years and
older who were gainfully employed gradually increased until the early
1990s but has declined since.[7] The gap between whites and Hispanics has
remained around 2 percentage points throughout the period; an even
larger 7 percentage point gap has persisted between whites and blacks.
Since 1990 both gaps have grown by a further percentage point.

Employment disparities appear even more dramatic when unemployment rates are examined. Table 5 shows, for example, that absolute unem-

Table 4. Employment Rates, by Race-Ethnicity, 1980–1993

Year	White (%)	Black (%)	Black/ White	Black− White	Hispanic[a] (%)	Hispanic/ White	Hispanic− White
1980	60.0	52.2	.87	−7.8	57.6	.96	−2.4
1986	61.5	54.1	.88	−7.4	58.5	.95	−3.0
1988	63.1	56.3	.89	−6.8	61.9	.98	−1.2
1990	63.6	56.2	.88	−7.4	61.6	.97	−2.0
1992	62.4	54.3	.87	−8.1	58.9	.94	−3.5
1993	62.7	54.4	.87	−8.3	58.9	.94	−3.8

Source: Bureau of Labor Statistics, *Employment and Earnings*, cited in Bureau of the Census, *Statistical Abstract: 1991*, tab. 635, *1994*, tab. 616.

Note: Employment rates are defined as civilian employed as percent of civilian noninstitutional population aged 16 years and older.

[a]Hispanic persons may be of any race.

Table 5. Unemployment Rates, by Race-Ethnicity, 1970–1993
(civilian noninstitutional population 16 years and older)

Year	White (%)	Black (%)	Black/ White	Black− White	Hispanic[a] (%)	Hispanic/ White	Hispanic− White
1970	3.6	6.3	1.75	2.7			
1980	6.3	14.3	2.27	8.0	10.1	1.60	3.8
1986	6.0	14.5	2.42	8.5	10.6	1.77	4.6
1988	4.7	11.7	2.49	7.0	8.2	1.74	3.5
1990	4.7	11.3	2.40	6.6	8.0	1.70	3.3
1992	6.5	14.2	2.18	7.7	11.2	1.72	4.7
1993	6.0	12.9	2.15	6.9	10.6	1.77	4.6

Source: Bureau of Labor Statistics, *Employment and Earnings*, cited in Bureau of the Census, *Statistical Abstract: 1991*, tab. 635, and *1994*, tab. 616.

[a]Hispanic persons may be of any race; data not available for 1970.

ployment rates for Hispanics have consistently remained at least 3 percentage points higher than rates for whites. This translates into a relative difference of over 70 percent. The gap for blacks has been twice as large in both absolute and relative terms.[8]

Some of these differences in labor market activity are, of course, related to the aforementioned gaps in educational attainment. But this is hardly the complete story, as Table 6 suggests. The upper panel of Table 6 shows that blacks and Hispanics of either gender have higher unemployment

Table 6. Ratios of Percentage Unemployed, by Race-Ethnicity,
Gender, Education, and Residence, 1980

	Black/White		Hispanic/White	
Educational Attainment	Men	Women	Men	Women
Not high school graduate	1.5	1.8	0.9	1.5
High school graduate	2.1	2.4	1.1	1.3
Some college	2.5	2.4	1.3	1.8
College graduate	3.4	1.3	2.4	1.2
	Black/White		Hispanic/White	
Residence	Men	Women	Men	Women
Central city	2.3	2.6	1.3	2.0
Suburb	1.9	2.2	1.4	1.6
Metropolitan area	2.0	2.0	1.3	2.5

Source: U.S. Commission on Civil Rights, *Unemployment among Blacks, Hispanics,
and Women, 1982*, tabs. 4.1 and 5.1.

rates than whites of the same educational attainment. For black and Hispanic men the gap in unemployment rates grows relatively higher as educational attainment increases. Place of residence also matters, as data in the
bottom panel of Table 6 indicate. For black men and women and Hispanic
women the unemployment gap with whites is substantially higher among
central-city residents than among individuals living in the suburbs.

Earnings

For many people, the socioeconomic bottom line is represented by the
third dimension of interracial polarization: earnings. Table 7 portrays the
severe and amazingly persistent pattern of income inequality between
whites, blacks, and Hispanics. Real median household income rose slightly
for whites and infinitesimally for Hispanics and blacks from 1975 to 1992.
Consistently throughout the last two decades the median household income (in inflation-adjusted terms) of blacks has remained about 59 percent of that earned by whites; the corresponding figure for Hispanics has
remained about 72 percent of that earned by whites. In absolute (1992)
dollar differences the black−white median income gap stands at over
$13,000; the Hispanic−white gap is over $9,000. Both gaps have grown by
at least $1,000 in real terms during the period.

A similar portrait is painted by statistics on poverty rates. Poverty rates
for all three groups have followed cyclical swings in macroeconomic per-

Table 7. Median Household Income in Constant (1992) Dollars, by Race-Ethnicity, 1970–1992

Year	White	Black	Black/ White	Black− White	Hispanic[a]	Hispanic/ White	Hispanic− White
1970	30,903	18,810	.61	−12,093			
1975	30,806	18,494	.60	−12,312	22,131	.72	−8,675
1980	31,851	18,350	.58	−13,501	23,271	.73	−8,580
1985	32,478	19,323	.59	−13,155	22,773	.70	−9,705
1990	33,525	20,048	.60	−13,477	23,970	.71	−9,555
1991	32,519	19,373	.60	−13,146	23,374	.72	−9,145
1992	32,368	18,660	.58	−13,708	22,848	.71	−9,520

Source: Bureau of the Census, *Statistical Abstract: 1994*, tab. 707.

[a]Hispanic persons may be of any race; data not available for 1970.

formance, with the latest upsurge occurring since 1989. As shown in Table 8, however, despite overall economic conditions, black families have maintained a poverty rate that is roughly three and a half times (20 or more percentage points higher than) the poverty rate of white families. By comparison, the Hispanic rate has remained roughly three times higher (16 to 17 percentage points more) than that of whites.

Once again, some of these interracial disparities can be traced to differences in educational attainment, but crucial gaps remain. In their path-breaking study of earnings changes over the last decade, Harrison and Gorham found that high-school-educated blacks experienced a 34 percent increase in their number who worked in jobs paying less than the poverty level; the figure for comparable whites was only 24 percent. As for college graduates, 20 percent of blacks in 1987 still worked under the poverty line, whereas 17 percent of such whites did so; 13 percent of blacks earned over $35,000 annually, whereas 26 percent of whites did so.[9]

Taken collectively, the foregoing statistics paint a sobering picture of severe and persistent racial-ethnic disparities in the key educational, employment, and earnings characteristics that embody socioeconomic status. The following sections explore the cause of this situation.

Life Choices: A Conceptual Framework
for Understanding Achieved Status

The central claim of this essay is that persistent racial-ethnic polarization in our metropolitan areas can be illuminated by positing a conceptual model of individual decision making about crucial issues affecting one's

Table 8. Percentage of Families below Poverty Level,
by Race-Ethnicity, 1970–1992

Year	White	Black	Black/ White	Black− White	Hispanic[a]	Hispanic/ White	Hispanic− White
1970	8.0	29.5	3.69	21.5			
1976	7.1	27.9	3.93	20.8	23.1	3.25	16.0
1978	6.9	27.5	3.99	20.6	20.4	2.96	13.5
1980	8.0	28.9	3.61	20.9	23.2	2.90	15.2
1982	9.6	33.0	3.44	23.4	27.0	2.81	17.4
1984	9.1	30.9	3.40	21.8	25.2	2.77	16.1
1986	8.6	28.0	3.26	19.4	24.7	2.87	16.1
1988	7.9	28.2	3.57	20.3	23.7	3.00	15.8
1990	8.1	29.3	3.62	21.2	25.0	3.09	16.9
1991	8.8	30.4	3.45	21.6	26.5	3.01	17.7
1992	8.9	30.9	3.47	22.0	26.2	2.94	17.3

Source: Bureau of the Census, *Current Population Reports*, cited in *Statistical Abstract: 1991*,
tab. 751, and *1994*, tab. 735.

[a]Hispanic persons may be of any race; data not available for 1970.

socioeconomic status, a model of what I call "life choices." Central to this
model is the notion that decisions are made rationally in the context of the
constraints perceived by the decision maker. Thus, observed behaviors
that contribute to current and future socioeconomic achievements (for example, labor force participation) are crucially shaped by the personal and
contextual constraints within which those decisions are made.

This section first sketches a model of life decisions in which place and
race form the primary constraints on individuals' feasible choices and on
the payoffs they can reap from these choices. It next provides introductory
descriptions of both place (the urban opportunity structure) and race (lingering racial-ethnic discrimination) dimensions of the urban scene. (More
detailed, quantitative analyses of place and race follow in the sections below.) The self-reinforcing aspects of the phenomenon are then considered.
And finally, the model is illustrated with a realistic scenario.

Overview of Conceptual Framework

To improve their socioeconomic status (and perhaps that of their children), individuals make many decisions relating to education, marriage,
fertility, labor force participation, illegal activities, residential location, and
sociopolitical participation. In making these life choices, individuals draw
on their values, aspirations, and preferences (arrow A in Figure 1). Factors

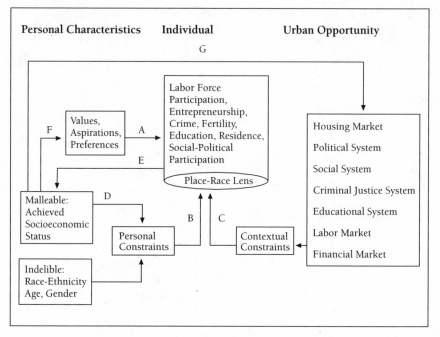

Figure 1. A Model of Life Decisions within Personal and Contextual Constraints

such as honesty, diligence, respect for authority and traditional institutions, risk aversion, and ability to plan and sacrifice for the future would be considered here.[10]

Personal and contextual constraints determine the feasibility of choosing certain options and the prospective benefits associated with each feasible option (arrows B and C in Figure 1). Some personal constraints, such as age, gender, immigrant status, and especially race and ethnicity, are indelible. Others are more malleable in that they are the product of previous choices (even though, once acquired, these attributes may no longer be malleable), such as employment, criminal activity, and education (arrow D in Figure 1).

Contextual constraints refer to various dimensions of the metropolitan structure, including local politics, social networks, criminal justice and social service systems, education, and labor, housing, and financial markets (arrow C in Figure 1). This structure operates in dramatically varied ways across and within metropolitan areas, enhancing or eroding opportunities for socioeconomic advancement depending on one's place of residence.

Given their values, aspirations, and preferences and a set of perceived personal and contextual constraints, individuals make a series of life choices during their lives. In combination with the possible payoffs from those choices permitted by the constraints, the particular combination of choices made will produce some level of achieved socioeconomic status (arrow E in Figure 1).

Past choices and achievements may, in turn, feed back to reshape individuals' current aspirations and preferences. For example, the choice to raise children may intensify one's aversion to risky entrepreneurial ventures or one's weighing of school quality when searching for a place to live. Similarly, if prior choices to seek legitimate employment have consistently been frustrated, one's ability to plan and invest for the future and respect for civil authority may wane (arrow F in Figure 1).

Finally, the urban opportunity structure itself is malleable over time. For example, the quality of the local public school system serving an individual's neighborhood constrains that individual's ability to gain skills. Yet, if many individuals decide to participate in a collective political process, the result may be a reallocation of fiscal resources to improve the local schools. The educational background of the parents of students living in the district also comprises an important element of constraint on school outcomes. Inasmuch as better-educated parents create more intellectually stimulating home environments, better monitor the completion of homework, and demonstrate more interest in what goes on in school, the quality of the classroom environment will be improved for all students. So if, in response to inferior public education, better-educated parents move out of the district or enroll their children in private schools, the constraint on all parents who remain in the public school system becomes tighter (arrow G in Figure 1).

An Illustration of the Framework

To render the model less abstract, consider the following illustration. Individuals derive income from three sources: earnings, transfers from household members, and government transfer payments. The amount and composition of income from these sources depend on life decisions about work, education, and family structure. Decisions about work are the first critical decisions that affect socioeconomic status. Most people who decide to participate in the labor force find jobs, but some enter unemployment, which usually lasts a few months.[11] Others suffer long spells of unemployment or drop out of the labor force entirely. Some of these people, as well as workers who earn very low wage rates, receive strong incentives to participate in criminal activities.

The particular labor force outcome will be influenced by the personal traits that the individual offers prospective employers. Those with less experience and fewer credentials are less likely to be hired for the better-paying positions and more likely to face unemployment. Moreover, women or racial minorities may have their experience and credentials subjectively downgraded in a discriminatory labor market.

Outcomes will also be influenced by residence.[12] An individual's neighborhood may be distant from job opportunities or may contain few role models of success achieved through diligent activities in the legal economy. Local social networks may be ineffective in transmitting information about potential jobs, and inferior local public services and schools may impair the health and education of potential workers.

A second set of life decisions that determine socioeconomic status are decisions about education. Success in finding high-paying, full-time employment depends on the attributes and educational credentials applicants bring to the labor market. Attainment of basic reading, writing, mathematical, communications, and critical thinking skills also significantly affects earnings. Recent studies not only illustrate increases in wage premiums for workers with college degrees and work experience but also show that earnings inequality has increased among workers with the same level of schooling and experience.[13] This suggests that employers are evaluating not just credentials but also the quality of the learning students obtain in school and the quality of the experience young workers obtain in their first jobs.

Of course, one's choice of educational level depends on a host of personal and contextual constraints. The perceived payoff from any educational credential will be less for those who believe that their only feasible educational institutions are of low quality or that they will face discrimination in the labor market once they graduate.[14] Moreover, the feasible choice set of postsecondary educational institutions will be determined by the investments in public higher education of the given state and locality, availability of scholarships from public and private sources, and parental wealth. Finally, peer effects seem especially potent in the case of educational attainment.[15]

Decisions about fertility are the third set of life decisions that directly or indirectly affect socioeconomic status. The direct effect occurs because fertility determines the number of dependents who rely on earnings and other sources of income (for example, government transfer payments). The indirect effect occurs because early fertility may reduce the mother's educational attainment and work experience.[16]

As with other life decisions, those regarding fertility are shaped by personal and contextual constraints. The individual's values and local cultural norms undoubtedly play a role. But the spatial context that specifies educational and employment opportunities also can be influential. A teenage girl may choose childbearing (coupled with welfare support) as the optimal course for personal fulfillment and socioeconomic stability if she believes there to be no legitimate, well-paying job opportunities even for those who complete high school.[17]

The Framework Applied to Racial-Ethnic Polarization

Given this overview of the conceptual framework, I return to the focus of this essay: place, race, and urban polarization. Members of racial-ethnic minority groups disproportionately face an urban opportunity structure that substantially constrains their mobility within socioeconomic strata. Given these constraints, minorities are more likely to make life choices that further impede their chances for social mobility and those of their children. Some of the most important place-based constraints are segregated housing; lack of positive role models as neighbors; limitations on capital; inferior public services; lower-quality public education; more violent, drug-infested neighborhoods; and impaired access to employment and job-related information networks.[18] As if these spatial penalties were not enough, racial-ethnic minorities face the additional burdens of personal discrimination in a variety of markets. Some forms of discrimination tend to lock minorities into particular spatial niches; others tend to erode the socioeconomic payoffs from certain choices and preclude other choices altogether. Put differently, minorities generally lag behind whites because the life choices they make and the socioeconomic payoffs that they gain from such choices are subjected to a more restrictive set of constraints. This phenomenon I call the "place-race lens" (see Figure 1). In order to substantiate this claim, I turn to a fuller development of the notions of place and race in the context of the conceptual framework.

Place: The Urban Opportunity Structure

As we have seen, "Opportunity Structure" means the geographically varying set of contextual constraints involving institutions, systems, and markets in a metropolitan area that limit personal and intergenerational socioeconomic advancement. I posit that the opportunity structure has seven key components: housing market, political system, social system, criminal justice system, educational system, labor market, and financial market (see Figure 1). Below I describe each of these components and the sorts of constraints they may present disproportionately to racial-ethnic minorities.

Housing Market

The housing market component of the opportunity structure involves the construction, maintenance, alteration, and pricing of housing, local land-use and building codes, and systems for the marketing and transfer of residential properties.

Where one lives is perhaps the most fundamental component of the opportunity structure because it significantly influences every other component. Unfortunately, the racial dimension of American metropolitan housing markets may be summarized with two words: segregation and centralization.

It is conventional to measure segregation with a "dissimilarity index," which shows how evenly various racial-ethnic groups are spread across neighborhoods within metropolitan areas. A score of 0 on this index indicates that the proportion of any particular group is the same across all neighborhoods (integration); a score of 100 indicates that every neighborhood has residents of only one particular group (complete segregation).[19] As Table 9 shows, virtually all of our major metropolitan areas where large numbers of minorities live are highly segregated. Although there have been modest reductions in white-black and white-Hispanic segregation since 1980, there has been little change since 1960.[20]

Moreover, minorities not only tend to live apart from whites, but their residences tend to cluster in or near the older, core municipality of the metropolitan area. Even though more minorities than ever live in suburbs, they remain relatively as clustered near the core as ever, because whites have increasingly moved out of the core and inner-ring suburbs and into metropolitan fringes.[21]

The causes of this phenomenon are complex. Suffice it to note here that interracial economic disparities, housing stocks increasingly separated into homogeneous value or rent groupings, the preference of most whites for predominantly white neighborhood racial composition, and illegal racial discrimination by public and private parties all contribute.[22]

More importantly, both segregation and centralization erect distinct obstacles to the socioeconomic advancement of minorities. Segregation can contribute to intergroup disparities in at least four ways.[23] First, separate informal networks and formal institutions serving the minority community, because they have a narrower scope and base of support, will have fewer financial, informational, and human resources to draw on. Therefore they will offer inferior options for the development of human capital and the discovery of alternative employment possibilities. Second, isolation can encourage and permit the development of distinct subcultural attitudes, behaviors, and speech patterns that may impede success in the mainstream world of work, either because they are counterproductive in some objective sense or because they are perceived to be so by prospective white employers. Third, an identifiable, spatial labor market may be formed in the minority community and attract employers offering only irregular, low-paying, dead-end jobs. Fourth, interracial competition and suspicions are abetted, encouraging the formation of discriminatory barriers in many markets, as we shall see below.

Table 9. Indexes of Residential Segregation for Selected Metropolitan
Areas with Large Minority Population, 1990

Metropolitan Area	% of Minority Population	Index of Segregation of Non-Hispanic Whites with	
		Blacks	Hispanics
Northern and Western Areas			
Boston	15	72	59
Buffalo	15	84	60
Chicago	38	87	65
Cincinnati	15	79	36
Cleveland	23	86	57
Columbus	15	71	34
Detroit	25	89	42
Gary-Hammond	28	91	53
Indianapolis	16	78	32
Kansas City	17	75	42
Los Angeles–Long Beach	59	74	63
Milwaukee	19	84	58
New York	52	83	68
Newark	36	84	67
Philadelphia	25	81	65
St. Louis	20	80	29
San Francisco	42	66	51
Southern Areas			
Atlanta	30	71	39
Baltimore	29	75	35
Birmingham	28	77	37
Dallas	33	68	54
Greensboro–Winston-Salem	21	66	35
Houston	44	71	53
Memphis	42	75	41
Miami	70	72	52
New Orleans	41	72	34
Norfolk–Virginia Beach	33	55	33
Tampa–St. Petersburg	17	74	47
Washington	37	67	43

Source: "By The Numbers, Tracking Segregation in 219 Metro Areas," *USA Today*,
November 11, 1991.

Dissimilarity Index: 100 = complete segregation, with no mixing of races in same
census tract.

The primary means by which the centralized pattern of minority residence affects minority well-being are twofold. First, minorities' employment opportunities will be restricted in light of progressive decentralization of jobs (especially those paying decent wages only with modest skill requirements) in metropolitan areas. The ability of minorities both to learn about and to commute to jobs declines as proximity to them declines.[24] Second, as we shall see below, location in central city more likely confronts a financially distressed municipality and public school system. This means that inferior public services and high tax rates may be the unenviable situation facing centralized minorities.

The statistical evidence makes it clear that minority households are significantly affected by the constraints imposed by segregation and centralization. One study estimated, for example, that racial segregation increases by as much as 33 percent the probability that a young black man does not work, and by as much as 43 percent the probability that a young black woman heads a single-parent family.[25] Other studies found that if we could cut segregation by 50 percent, the median income of black families would rise 24 percent,[26] the black homicide rate would fall by 30 percent,[27] the high school dropout rate would fall by over three-fourths, and poverty rates for black families would drop 17 percent.[28] Thus, it is clear that the constraints imposed by the segregated nature of metropolitan housing markets play a major role in explaining the persistent interracial disparities cited above.

Political System

The political system refers to the structure of local political jurisdictions, their fiscal capacities, and the types of power minority groups exert in them. A notable feature of most American metropolitan areas is their jurisdictional fragmentation: numerous municipalities, school districts, counties, and special-purpose districts subdivide the landscape into a complex, sometimes overlapping patchwork of jurisdictional boundaries.[29]

The primary way that this fragmentation raises constraints for minorities is by intensifying income class spatial segregation and attendant fiscal disparities among jurisdictions. Middle-income and upper-income suburbs limit the residential options of lower-income households by adopting restrictive land-use and housing policies. This residential segregation of income classes by jurisdiction leads to large disparities in fiscal capacity, especially when coupled with increasingly aggressive competition for employment between districts.[30] In turn, because of the economic polarization between whites and minorities, income class segregation in the context of jurisdictional fragmentation ultimately constrains the quality of education and other public services and the number of municipal employment options available to minorities. The coincidence of race-class segregation produces powerful racial effects as well, as we shall see below.

The political coalitions that control local governments can have significant influences on urban opportunities through their hiring practices, regulations, and contract awards. Minority power in urban governance varies dramatically from city to city. Further, the ability of minorities to convert power into avenues for economic advancement for large numbers of their constituents also varies widely across cities.[31]

Social Systems

Social systems consist of voluntary associations and social institutions at the neighborhood level, interpersonal networks, and community norms and values. An individual's neighborhood can provide a variety of institutional and interpersonal contacts that promote social mobility. Informally, neighbors can provide information about educational or employment opportunities and implicit support for norms and behaviors conducive to advancement. Formal associations within the community can play important roles in stabilizing and mobilizing economic, social, and psychological resources for advancement.

Quantification of local social systems is problematic. Nevertheless, numerous qualitative studies have concluded that, in many minority neighborhoods of many metropolitan areas, these social systems have become (or are rapidly becoming) dysfunctional.[32] In these areas, kin, friends, and community organizations are becoming less able to provide, in times of temporary financial distress, the material assistance needed to prevent more serious spells of poverty, or even hopelessness.[33] Some researchers see an exodus of middle-income minority residents from neighborhoods inhabited by lower-income residents, leaving the latter bereft of role models to raise aspirations and legitimize participation in the labor force.[34] Others see crack cocaine as debilitating many potential role models and overwhelming extended kinship support networks.[35]

In their pathbreaking investigation, Fernandez and Harris analyzed data on a variety of social contacts by African Americans living in Chicago census tracts where 20 percent or more of the residents were classified as poor.[36] They found that, independent of one's own economic status, the percentage of poor residents in one's neighborhood provided an important determinant of a variety of social contacts. African American women living amid concentrations of low-income people had fewer church contacts, less frequent and deep interpersonal contacts, and a smaller percentage of "mainstream" friends, those who were well-educated, employed, and not on public assistance. African American males evinced a similar relationship for contacts with political and social institutions and "mainstream" friends.[37] As an illustration of the magnitude of these powerful neighborhood effects, nonworking poor men and women who lived in a tract with no other poor individuals had roughly a quarter of their friends on public assistance. If they lived in a tract comprised completely of poor individuals, however, nearly two-thirds of their friends were on public assistance.[38]

The foregoing points to the importance of concentrations of low-income people—above and beyond an individual's low income itself—in shaping local social networks. Because of increasing spatial concentrations of lower-income minority populations, minorities bear a disproportionate share of socially isolated neighborhoods.[39] Put differently, urban minorities are much more likely to have more low-income neighbors than are urban whites, even when minorities and whites are of the same socioeconomic status. As noted above, this means a greater erosion of social networks for minorities and thus a more limiting set of constraints on their ability to use networks to achieve gains in socioeconomic status. But as we shall see below, there are also deleterious effects on the local school systems.

Criminal Justice System

The criminal justice component of the urban opportunity structure includes police and court procedures and resources, local legal sanctions, sentencing practices, and community-based security efforts. The criminal justice system in many urban neighborhoods seems to be caught in a dilemma, either branch of which constrains economic opportunities of some individuals. On the one hand, police and community efforts have failed to control rampant violence, most often associated with the drug trade. Such violence can erode social networks and discourage residents from working because of fear of leaving their homes. On the other hand, concentrated policing of such areas and subsequent stiff sentencing practices may have criminalized many (especially youthful) offenders who should have been treated less harshly. By exposing offenders to the brutality of the prison system and branding them with criminal records, the criminal justice system may severely limit the future life choices of these individuals. Consider more fully both sides of the dilemma.

African Americans and Hispanics have been disproportionately victimized by crimes against persons for at least the last two decades (see Table 10). In 1990 roughly 9 of 100,000 white males were victims of homicide, whereas 69 of 100,000 black males were victims. The comparable figures for white and black females were 3 and 13, respectively.[40]

The above statistics can be traced to a complex amalgam of deprivation, unraveling social networks, gang-related activities, and the use and trafficking of drugs, especially crack cocaine.[41] Indeed, the spatial coincidence of minority poverty concentrations, violent crimes, and criminal drug use

Table 10. Victimization Rates for Crimes against Persons, 1973–1992
(rates per 1,000 persons, 12 years and older)

Year	White	Black	Black/ White	Black− White	Hispanic[a]	Hispanic/ White	Hispanic− White
1973	32	42	1.31	10	36	1.13	4
1980–81	32.5	45.5	1.40	13	39.5	1.22	7
1982–83	31.5	42.5	1.35	11	39	1.24	7.5
1984–85	29.5	39.5	1.34	10	32.5	1.10	3
1986–87	28	37.5	1.34	9.5	33	1.18	5
1988	28	40	1.43	12	35	1.25	7
1992	29.9	50.4	1.69	20.5	38.2	1.28	8.3

Source: Bureau of the Census, *Current Population Reports*, cited in *Statistical Abstract: 1991*, tab. 751, and *1994*, tab. 311.

Note: Crimes include rape, robbery, and assault and exclude larceny and theft.

[a]Hispanic persons may be of any race.

and trafficking is notable. In Washington, D.C., for example, arrests for drug use or possession in 1980 were six times higher per capita in neighborhoods having more than 40 percent of their residents below the poverty line than in nonpoverty areas. From 1980 to 1988 the increase in per capita drug arrest rates was eight times greater in the former areas. Violent crime rates in these concentrated poverty neighborhoods were three times higher than those in nonpoverty locales in 1980; the increase in such crimes in the poverty areas was almost five times greater from 1980 to 1988.

The confluence of violence and drugs in certain minority-occupied neighborhoods creates a host of interlocking constraints on the ability of residents to enhance their socioeconomic status through legitimate means. As noted above, isolation from middle-class role models increases as "old heads" (middle-aged males formerly working full time in the legitimate economy) are siphoned off into the world of crack dependency while wealthy, glamorous drug lords come to the fore as new role models. Kin networks are shredded by prolonged exposure to the consequences of members who abuse drugs; perversely, some kin networks serve as conduits for teaching drug-culture norms to youths.[42] Other residents of these crime-ridden neighborhoods limit their social contacts and labor force participation out of fear of violent crime. Still others have their accumulated financial and human resources pillaged by property and personal crime, respectively. There thus appears to be an urgent need to fight crime and drugs. Unfortunately, the way we as a society have chosen to carry out the fight—selective neighborhood police sweeps coupled with stiff mandatory prison sentencing—has produced unintended consequences that impose almost insuperable constraints on many minority youths.

Several studies have documented the staggering racial differentials in arrest and incarceration rates. For example, in New York State in 1990 23 percent of African American males aged eighteen to thirty-five years were under criminal justice supervision (in jail, awaiting trial, being sought for arrest, or on probation or parole); the comparable figure for white males was 3 percent.[43] In major urban areas the figures are even more dramatic: 42 percent of the eighteen- to thirty-five-year-old African American men in the District of Columbia and 56 percent in Baltimore were under criminal justice supervision on an average day during 1991.[44] Seventy-three percent of those booked by the Cook County (Chicago) Department of Corrections in 1989 were black, and 9 percent were Hispanic. During 1989 29 percent of the county's black male population aged twenty to twenty-nine years were jailed at least once, compared with 6 percent of Hispanics and 4 percent of white males of similar age.[45]

The psychological consequences of prolonged incarceration and stigmatization are probably profound, though difficult to measure. More easily quantified is the employment effect. Freeman's analysis of 1980 National Youth Survey data revealed that 50 percent of those sampled who were in jail or on probation were employed in at least one month during the six months prior to incarceration, but only 10 percent were employed during any of the three months afterward.[46]

Educational System

The educational system includes public and private elementary and secondary schools and their associated bureaucracies and parent-teacher organizations. Education is a complicated channel for upward mobility. There are many schooling choices, and different subgroups of the urban population favor different paths. It appears that choices of public versus private schools, various public school districts, and courses of study within a particular school all affect academic achievement and the likelihood of labor market success.[47] However, the possibility of exercising choice (by migration to the suburbs, enrollment in a private school, or selection of a more academically oriented curriculum) often seems remote for urban minority groups.[48] The result is a set of educational constraints profoundly differentiated by race and ethnicity.

Racial differences in enrollment patterns reveal one dimension of this differentiation. Dissimilarity indexes of the degree of segregation between school districts for selected metropolitan areas for the 1989–90 school year are presented in Tables 11 and 12. They show that black students are

Table 11. White-Black Dissimilarity Indices of Interdistrict School
Segregation, 1989–1990, Selected Metropolitan Statistical Areas
(MSAs) with Large Percentages of Black Students

MSA	% of MSA Students Who Are Black	Dissimilarity Index
Baltimore, Md.	30	69
Charlotte, N.C.	28	33
Chicago, Ill.	30	77
Cleveland, Ohio	26	79
Dallas, Tex.	23	65
Detroit, Mich.	26	90
Ft. Lauderdale, Fla.[a]	26	49
Gary, Ind.	25	91
Houston, Tex.	23	59
Jacksonville, Fla.[a]	23	21
Los Angeles, Calif.	12	63
Louisville, Ky.[a]	19	37
Memphis, Tenn.	56	66
Miami, Fla.	33	56
Milwaukee, Wisc.	20	70
Mobile, Ala.	36	51
Montgomery, Ala.	43	34
Nashville, Tenn.[a]	20	47
Newark, N.J.	27	81
New Orleans, La.	50	64
New York, N.Y.	34	66
Philadelphia, Pa.	30	72
Washington, D.C.	25	65

Source: Unpublished calculations by Maris Mikelsons, Urban Institute, based on
U.S. Department of Education statistics; white persons are non-Hispanic whites.

[a] City-suburban desegregation orders in effect.

generally more unevenly distributed across districts than are Hispanic students, but that both minority groups are highly segregated from whites
across school districts, in rough correspondence to their degree of residential segregation.[49] But where are minority students preponderantly concentrated? Nationally, two-thirds of African American students and nearly
half of other minority students attend primary and secondary schools in
central-city districts; less than a quarter of white students do so.[50] In the
Chicago metropolitan area in 1990, three of every four black children and
two of every three Hispanic children attended the Chicago public schools;
only one in twenty white children did so.[51]

Table 12. White-Hispanic Dissimilarity Indices of Interdistrict School Segregation, 1989–1990, Selected Metropolitan Statistical Areas (MSAs) with Large Percentages of Hispanic Students

MSA	% of MSA Students Who are Black	Dissimilarity Index
Albuquerque, N.M.	40	44
Chicago, Ill.	14	69
Corpus Christi, Tex.	60	46
Dallas, Tex.	15	53
El Paso, Tex.	78	51
Fresno, Calif.	39	40
Houston, Tex.	22	50
Jersey City, N.J.	45	56
Los Angeles, Calif.	45	55
Miami, Fla.	46	48
Midland, Tex.	24	21
New York, N.Y.	15	54
Odessa, Tex.	36	23
Pueblo, Colo.	42	22
San Antonio, Tex.	56	59
San Diego, Calif.	25	44
Stockton, Calif.	23	33
Tucson, Ariz.	33	47

Source: Unpublished calculations by Maris Mikelsons, Urban Institute, based on U.S. Department of Education statistics.

Note: Hispanic persons may be of any race; white persons are non-Hispanic whites.

New research by Gary Orfield[52] demonstrates that the isolation of black and Hispanic students from white students has been increasing, especially in major metropolitan areas. Two of every three black students in 1992 attended schools in which more than half the student body was either black or Hispanic; the comparable figure for Hispanics was almost three or four. In Illinois, Michigan, New York, New Jersey, and Pennsylvania, over 40 percent of black students attended schools where more than 90 percent of students were minorities. In New York, New Jersey, and Texas, over 40 percent of Hispanic students had similar segregated situations.

Thus, the educational constraints facing the vast majority of white students are quite different from those facing African American and Hispanic students. Moreover, the educational opportunities of African American and Hispanic students are intimately connected to inner-city districts in the largest metropolitan areas. Unfortunately these districts tend to be racially, economically, and socially isolated and inferior providers of education on several counts.

Today in the forty-seven largest central-city school districts, whites comprise, on average, only 25 percent of the student population, while African Americans comprise 42 percent and Hispanics 27 percent. Although the student population in these districts accounts for only 13 percent of the nation's enrollment, it includes 25 percent of students from homes below the poverty level and 32 percent of those for whom English is a second language.[53] Across metropolitan Chicago high schools, there was a .92 correlation between the percentage of African American and Hispanic students and the percentage of students from low-income households in 1986. Although no predominantly white elementary schools in the area had as many as one-third low-income students, nine-tenths of elementary schools that were over 90 percent African American or Hispanic had a majority of low-income students.[54]

Thus, racial and economic segregation in the housing market is producing racial and economic segregation in the educational system and social systems. These systems place more limits on the educational achievement and attainment of poor children from African American and Hispanic families because these children have less contact with children from nonpoor families.[55] Racial segregation makes it more difficult for nonpoor minority children to build on their parents' progress toward upward social mobility, because the critical mass that influences their education and social systems is more heavily influenced by children from poor families.[56]

Finally, race and income segregation in housing markets and in the educational and social systems also can make it harder for minority children to acquire the "soft skills" valued in the labor market. These skills, especially styles of communication and interpersonal relationships, likely are derived from social patterns prevailing in white, middle-class culture. Children first may learn communication and interpersonal skills from family members and neighbors. Schools give children a second chance to learn these skills, however, because students interact with schoolmates from other families and neighborhoods. The opportunity structure appears to provide poor white children with opportunities for economic integration in the school and neighborhood but typically denies these opportunities to minority children. That is, minority children have little exposure at home or in school to patterns that set the standard for workplace communication and interpersonal relationships. These children may therefore develop alternative patterns that may serve them well on the streets but hinder them in the workplace.[57]

Inner-city schools manifest inferiority in other resource dimensions as well. Compared with suburban districts, the forty-seven largest urban districts spend $873 less per pupil;[58] fiscal disparities between individual districts can be even more dramatic.[59] Inner-city teachers are, on average, less well prepared, come from inferior colleges, and are fewer in number in several critical subject areas. The same is true of guidance counselors.[60]

In combination, the aforementioned limitations on social, financial, and human resources produce the expected inferior performance outcomes. For example, the "nonselective segregated high schools" serving about two-thirds of Chicago's students graduated only 8 percent of their students with reading ability at the national norm level.[61] Nine of ten Cleveland students (the vast majority of whom are minorities) failed the state proficiency exam in 1991.[62] Unsurprisingly, disproportionate numbers of minority students find dropping out to be a rational decision in light of such school quality, as demonstrated in Table 2. Perhaps most damning of all, many employers appear to be writing off graduates of inner-city school systems as prospective employees. Minority students who pursue college find the combination of inferior training and limited exposure to whites a deterrent to persisting in college. Thus, not only have the African American and Hispanic versus white gaps in college entrance rates been rising during the 1980s, but so have the gaps in college completion rates.[63]

Labor Market

The labor market component of the urban opportunity structure refers to the number of jobs and the distribution of employment by industrial and occupational category, location, skill requirements, advancement potential, on-the-job training, wages and benefits, and how job openings are filled. The contemporary metropolitan labor markets have been characterized by deindustrialization and decentralization.

Fundamental changes have taken place in the nation's economy in the last several decades, most dramatically represented by the decline in high-wage manufacturing jobs and the growth in both low- and high-wage service sector employment. From 1967 to 1987, for example, Chicago lost 60 percent of its manufacturing jobs; Detroit lost 51 percent; New York City, 58 percent; and Philadelphia, 64 percent. These four cities have the most severe concentrations of minority poverty. In these same central cities, moreover, service sector job growth was dramatic.[64] A concomitant shift raising the educational requirements of many jobs has reduced the demand for low-skilled labor. The same cities mentioned above experienced a similarly severe loss of jobs held by those with only a high school diploma or less.[65]

Given that African Americans and Hispanics are concentrated in the lower end of the educational distribution, the burdens of this industrial restructuring have fallen most heavily on them.[66] In large Northeast central cities in 1968–70 only 19 percent of black males aged sixteen to sixty-four years with no high school diploma were not working; by 1986–88 this had risen to 44 percent. The comparable figures for whites were 15 percent and 36 percent.[67] In large Midwest central cities the percentage of black males with no diploma who were not working rose from 24 percent to 58 percent; the comparable figures for whites were 12 percent and 39 percent.[68]

The decentralization aspect of the urban labor market refers to the fact that the remaining manufacturing jobs have progressively shifted to suburbs and small towns. These shifts, coupled with the continuing concentration of minorities near the urban cores, has created a spatial mismatch on top of the skills mismatch. Minority workers' opportunities both to learn about and to commute to jobs declines as their proximity to them declines, as noted above. Minorities living in the suburbs apparently have overcome this mismatch problem. As evidence, the rate of joblessness among black males with no diploma actually decreased from 1980 to 1986 in the suburbs of the same Northeast and Midwest metropolitan areas cited above.[69] Although the empirical significance of the mismatch hypothesis has been much debated,[70] there seems little doubt that labor market opportunities are becoming more strongly differentiated over space in ways that put African Americans and Hispanics in ever more disadvantageous positions.

Financial Market

The last component of the urban opportunity structure involves the institutions that make loans for starting, expanding, or acquiring businesses or buying, building, or renovating residential properties. One strategy for enhancing socioeconomic status that skirts the urban labor market is self-employment in small business. Successful pursuit of this route depends critically on the entrepreneur's education and personal financial resources, and therefore it is no surprise that rates of self-employment are much lower for minorities.[71] Capital constraints, however, remain the single largest obstacle to African Americans and Hispanics starting businesses; Asian entrepreneurs appear to have fewer capital constraints.[72]

Part of the limitation on capital is, of course, due to the aforementioned inferiority in education and personal assets. Yet, even controlling for those and other differences, it appears that bankers are less willing to lend if a borrower's business is located in a minority community.[73] Additional lending barriers have been created by the numerous recent bank mergers, because many smaller operators located in minority communities that used to be prime sponsors of new businesses have been eliminated. Banks remaining in these communities but owned by large conglomerates may have less sensitivity or commitment to local entrepreneurs.[74] In sum, it appears that the commercial finance market offers a different set of opportunities for entrepreneurs depending on the race of the owner and the location of the operation.

The ability to accumulate wealth in the form of home equity depends similarly on the availability of mortgage loans. The mortgage market (in combination, of course, with the housing market) will determine the degree to which renters can become homeowners and homeowners can make capital gains and move up to higher-priced homes. Access to such residential options not only influences the likelihood of acquiring an asset that will appreciate[75] but also influences access to neighborhoods possessing social networks, good public education, and job opportunities that promote upward social mobility.

Many studies have documented that African American and Hispanic neighborhoods receive a disproportionately small flow of mortgage loans, even controlling for a variety of factors that serve as proxies for the demand for residential financing.[76] There are multiple reasons for this observation.[77] Lenders may not be effective in developing loan products, marketing them, and locating branch offices in ways that attract minority applicants. Minority mortgage applicants tend to have smaller down payments and weaker employment and credit histories than their white counterparts, resulting in higher rates of denial.[78] Underwriting standards employed by lenders may disproportionately affect minority borrowers by discouraging loans in transitional neighborhoods and those with mixed land uses.[79] And, as we shall see below, there is mounting evidence of intentional racial-ethnic discrimination in the underwriting process. Again, these factors coalesce to present spatially differentiated opportunities to obtain financing.

Race: Discrimination in Multiple Market Contexts

In the previous section I demonstrated how each key component of the urban opportunity structure varied across space in the degree to which it presented constraints to socioeconomic achievement, and in such a pattern that African Americans and Hispanics were more severely hindered by their location. In this section I consider an additional factor: race itself. Independent of their metropolitan location, the racial-ethnic status of minorities defines a personal constraint that further impedes their chances for success because of discrimination in multiple market contexts. This section briefly considers evidence of discrimination in several components of the urban opportunity structure defined above: the housing market, the criminal justice system, the labor market, and the financial market.[80]

Housing Market

Incontrovertible evidence of the persistence, extent, and magnitude of racial-ethnic discrimination in metropolitan housing markets has been provided by dozens of studies employing paired testers who pose as home- or apartment-seekers. Gaining initial prominence during the Housing Market Practices Survey of forty metropolitan areas in 1977 sponsored by the Department of Housing and Urban Development (HUD), paired testing became a prosaic investigative tool during the 1980s, culminating in the HUD-sponsored Housing Discrimination Study of twenty-five metropolitan areas in 1989.[81]

This research has revealed (1) housing discrimination against both African American and Hispanic homeseekers and apartment-seekers occurs in roughly half of the instances when these persons interact with an agent; (2) typically this discrimination is subtle in nature and therefore difficult for the individual to detect; and (3) the frequency of housing discrimination appears not to have changed noticeably since 1977.[82]

As noted before, one of the most serious consequences of such discrimination is increased racial-ethnic segregation. A variety of econometric models suggest that if discrimination were to be eliminated from metropolitan areas where it now assumes its national average level, segregation would decline by at least one-fourth and perhaps by nearly one-half.[83]

Criminal Justice System

Although the evidence of racial bias is more circumstantial and qualitative than in the area of housing markets, a body of evidence suggests that the criminal justice system concentrates its police efforts disproportionately on minorities and treats minority offenders more harshly once they are apprehended. Much of the recent controversy has been spawned by the intensified "War on Drugs," an effort that, according to one commentator, is "biased on all fronts and has made young black men its enemy."[84]

The antidrug effort has focused on police sweeps in selected drug-trafficking neighborhoods. Typically these neighborhoods are heavily minority occupied, which, not surprisingly, nets a preponderance of minority offenders, especially African Americans. For example, in Baltimore during 1991 more than 11,000 of the approximately 13,000 people arrested on drug charges were African Americans; 1,304 African American youths were charged with drug sales, whereas only thirteen white youths were so charged.[85]

These differences cannot be attributed to greater drug use by African Americans. Whites make up 77 percent of all illegal drug users; African Americans, 15 percent; and Hispanics, 8 percent, roughly equal to their proportions in the population.[86] For males in high school, rates of marijuana or cocaine use have been higher for whites than for African Americans, consistently since 1976.[87]

Once arrested, African American offenders face an even tougher panoply of mandatory sentencing laws, instead of nonincarceration or treatment options. It has been estimated, for example, that 70 percent of Atlanta's antidrug resources are directed toward punishment, with only 30 percent for treatment.[88] The consequence, as noted above, is a generation of African American youths indelibly stamped by incarceration, with the concomitant distortion of their labor market opportunity structure.

Labor Market

Much evidence exists indicating that racist practices in the hiring, compensation, training, and promotion of minorities persist in metropolitan labor markets, reducing their chances of obtaining jobs and limiting their occupational options once they obtain employment.[89] In the conventional analysis of wage discrimination, the earnings of minority and white workers are compared when other factors serving as proxies for their productivity are controlled for statistically. Any unexplained residual between the groups constitutes evidence of such discrimination. Statistical evidence based on this methodology shows declines over time in unexplained wage gaps for both African Americans and Hispanics, although there remain significant variations across subgroups according to region and education.[90]

Of course, wage comparisons ignore intergroup variations in unemployment, underemployment, and characteristics of employment. As with wage disparities, employment disparities that cannot be accounted for by differences in productive characteristics provide statistical evidence of labor market discrimination. Here, the evidence for reduced discrimination is considerably weaker. For example, as shown in Table 6, with rare exception, black and Hispanic men and women experience higher unemployment than whites at all levels of schooling. Thus, black and Hispanic men who have graduated from college are more than twice as likely to be unemployed as white college graduates. Relative patterns of minority underemployment parallel those of unemployment.

In addition to higher unemployment and underemployment, minorities are more likely than whites to be in jobs offering fewer opportunities for career growth. Controlling for characteristics such as education and marital status, Boston finds that the probability of black men and women moving from secondary sector jobs (jobs characterized by low levels of training) to primary sector jobs offering more training is about one-half the corresponding probability for whites.[91]

Beyond the statistical record, controlled experiments using paired test-ers have investigated hiring discrimination. In these experiments, minority job applicants are paired with white applicants. The applicants are given similar backgrounds and are chosen and trained to be as similar as possible in job-related characteristics such as appearance, articulateness, and appar-ent energy level. How the minority applicants are treated in job applica-tions can then be observed and compared with the treatment received by their white "twins."

One study of entry-level jobs, involving 360 paired male applicants for randomly selected employers, found that foreign-looking/sounding His-panics were 30 percentage points less likely to receive interviews and job offers than their matched white counterparts.[92] Another study targeted at entry-level jobs concluded that in one of five paired tests, the white male applicant was able to advance further through the hiring process than his equally qualified African American counterpart.[93] Such experiments pro-vide irrefutable evidence of pervasive hiring discrimination.

The type of discrimination that hiring tests measure might be referred to as applicant discrimination: minority applicants for jobs are treated differ-ently than white applicants. Unfortunately, even if this type of discrimina-tion were eradicated, minorities would still continue to experience higher unemployment and underemployment than non-Hispanic whites. The rea-son is that employers hire using informal networks that are discriminating in effect.

The existence of network or word-of-mouth hiring has been docu-mented from jobs at the very highest levels of corporate employment to jobs requiring little or no training. Recent studies of the glass ceiling docu-ment network hiring for highly skilled corporate positions and unskilled employment.[94] Waldinger and Bailey describe how informal networks ex-clude minorities from work in construction.[95] Word-of-mouth hiring has the advantage that it is less costly in terms of time and money than adver-tising and it ensures a certain type of applicant who will mesh with other employers. By trying to replicate their current workforce through word-of-mouth hiring, many employers are simply following a common human trait of sticking with the tried and true. The societal problem with this type of hiring, however, is that it excludes applicants outside employers' famil-iar domains. As such, both overt hiring discrimination and seemingly be-nign hiring techniques contribute to the lower earnings, limited employ-ment, and occupational/industrial segregation of minorities.

Financial Market

Over a decade ago a handful of studies analyzed various unpublished data sources showing mortgage loan application dispositions by characteristics of the borrower. These studies showed that race had statistical significance in explaining high minority denial rates in most of the metropolitan areas investigated, even when other legitimate financial characteristics were controlled.[96] After a long hiatus the method recently was replicated by the Federal Reserve Bank of Boston in their analysis of over 3,000 mortgage loan underwriting decisions taken by 131 Boston-area banks, savings and loans, mortgage companies, and credit unions during 1991.[97] Their statistical analysis revealed that African Americans and Hispanics, in general, had more indebtedness, lower down payments, and weaker credit histories than typical white applicants, and that these factors did explain a substantial share of the observed 2.7-to-1 ratio of minority-to-white denial rates. Even controlling for all such differences, however, minorities were 60 percent more likely to be denied. This appeared to be the case for both large- and small-scale lenders equally.

This important study not only provides "conclusive evidence of *de facto* discrimination,"[98] but it also hints at the reasons for this outcome. Minorities with unblemished credentials were not denied. But the majority of borrowers of any group were not perfect, and thus lenders had considerable discretion about how seriously they would assess the imperfections and whether offsetting factors might be present. It was in this "gray area" that whites were favored systematically.

A dramatic illustration of systematic differential treatment of minorities by a mortgage lender is provided by the recently settled suit *U.S. Department of Justice v. Decatur (GA) Federal Savings and Loan Association*.[99] The Department of Justice concluded that at least forty-eight African Americans were discriminatorily denied mortgages between January 1988 and May 1992. The lender redefined its market service area to exclude large proportions of the African American population, rarely advertised its products in media oriented toward this community, and employed a virtually all-white staff of commissioned account executives who solicited business from real estate agents operating in white neighborhoods but rarely those operating in African American areas. As a result 95 percent of its loans were originated in white neighborhoods.[100]

Additional evidence has been culled from three experiments conducted between 1988 and 1991 that employed paired testers to probe behavior of lenders before formal applications were made. These experiments were conducted in Louisville, Kentucky; Chicago, Illinois; and New York City.[101] They revealed incidents when loan officers provided more information, assistance, and encouragement to the white tester and tended to direct the minority tester toward government-insured loans.

The foregoing discussion has dealt with discrimination in terms of illegal differences in treatment based on a protected classification such as color, race, or national origin. Yet, given precedents established in other contexts, such as housing and employment, discrimination can also be defined in terms of disparate impact: evenhanded treatment that results in adverse consequences for legally protected classes. A New York State Banking Department examination of ten savings banks found four promulgated standards (such as high minimum down payment ratios and loan sizes) that could adversely affect minority neighborhoods. The report was critical of the failure of all ten banks to offer mortgages insured by the Federal Housing Administration (FHA) and of inadequate outreach activities in local communities by six banks.[102]

Beyond mortgage lending, there also is some evidence that discrimination exists in the commercial lending market. Ando analyzed the experiences of minority and white owners who had been in business at least two years and who had applied for loans during a three-year period in the early 1980s.[103] White-owned firms had 90 percent of their applications approved; 87 percent of Hispanic-owned and only 62 percent of black-owned firms' applications were approved. Controlling for business experience, firm size, credit rating, industry, marital status, and collateral, black borrowers were still less likely to be approved.

Conclusion and Implications for an Urban Equal Opportunity Strategy

I have attempted to demonstrate that we have deep, multidimensional, and persistent polarization among whites, African Americans, and Hispanics in our metropolitan areas, and that this polarization can be traced to different constraints on socioeconomic advancement. Some of these constraints are associated with the racial-ethnic identity of the individual; others are associated with the place in which that individual resides, that person's "opportunity structure." I marshaled evidence to demonstrate that polarization is, indeed, a result of race and place.

Policy Implications

If we take this analysis seriously, clear policy implications emerge. In this chapter I can only provide an outline of these implications; I have, however, provided fleshed-out analyses elsewhere.[104] To combat constraints based on race, a toughening of antidiscrimination policy is required. This does not merely mean enhancing penalties for violators, increasing outreach to inform victims of their rights and means of redress, improving the speed of case adjudication, and expanding civil rights training of all those involved in the various urban market contexts where discrimination occurs, although all such efforts are to be applauded. Rather, it takes a completely different enforcement strategy, one based on matched testing investigations conducted by civil rights agencies, that creates a viable deterrent to discrimination.

The flaw in the current civil rights enforcement approach is that it relies on the victim to recognize and formally complain about suspected acts of discrimination. Given the subtlety of discrimination as typically practiced today, such reliance is misplaced. As a result, there is little chance of violators fearing detection or litigation; there thus is no chance of deterrence.

What is needed is a transfer of resources to empower private and governmental civil rights agencies to conduct ongoing enforcement testing programs, employing pairs of matched investigators who pose as housing, mortgage, or job seekers. These programs would not merely respond to complaints of alleged victims but would provide an ongoing presence in areas rendered "suspicious" by other evidence or, resources permitting, randomly throughout the market. Only through such a comprehensive enforcement testing policy can people be deterred from using race to constrain the opportunities of others.[105]

To combat constraints based on place is even more controversial and complex. Some analysts have suggested that residential locations can be continued if access to good jobs and schools is enhanced through, for example, new transportation schemes, enterprise empowerment zones, or school choice vouchers.[106] I argue that such schemes are inferior to those that aim directly at expanding the spatial extent of residential choices and desegregating communities by class and by racial-ethnic composition.[107] The gist of the argument is that unless the iron grip of residence is released, all other ameliorative efforts will necessitate inefficient subsidies and distortions of the market and will be blunted by elements of the opportunity structure that cannot easily be ruptured from the residential nexus: local social networks, political systems, and the criminal justice system.

What is needed is an intensified effort to expand geographically the housing choices for the less-well-off through voucherlike subsidies coupled with affirmative efforts to market residential areas that might be unfamiliar to subsidy recipients and, perhaps, ongoing supportive counseling services to smooth recipients' transition into new environments. Prototypical efforts associated with the Gautreaux Program in Chicago are representative of this strategy and have demonstrated their efficacy in enhancing opportunities for participants without deleterious side effects on their neighbors.[108]

More broadly, there should be comprehensive policies to encourage the movement of all households into neighborhoods where their racial-ethnic group is underrepresented. By developing strategies aimed both at lower levels of government and individuals, the federal government should take the lead in such policy development.

Federal programs should be designed to encourage lower levels of government to adopt coordinated pro-integration programs that fit their local contexts. Encouragement could be supplied through the careful tailoring of intergovernmental transfers. Federal bonus funds to states might, for instance, be provided for establishing and/or supporting regional fair housing organizations (either public or private) that enforce antidiscrimination laws and promote neighborhood racial integration in their metropolitan areas. Similarly, direct federal financial aid to municipalities for any number of activities might be awarded for formal cooperation with such a regional organization. Awards might be given to school districts progressing toward integration targets.

States and localities have at their disposal several examples of successful pro-integration efforts.[109] They could, for example, provide additional information to minority and white homeseekers about options in neighborhoods in which traditionally they would not have searched. Such affirmative marketing services have been successfully provided by the Leadership Council in the Chicago area, the East Suburban Council for Open Metropolitan Communities in the Cleveland area, and the Center for Integrated Living in the Milwaukee area, for example. In addition, state and local governments could provide a variety of financial incentives to encourage integration. Oak Park, Illinois, provides rehabilitation subsidies to landlords who have integrated apartment complexes. Southfield, Michigan, and Shaker Heights, Ohio, grant low-interest mortgages to house buyers making pro-integrative moves. The state of Ohio allocates a share of its revenue bond funds to provide below-market rate mortgages to first-time homebuyers making such moves.[110]

The other set of federal integration incentives could be directed toward individuals. Those who make moves that promote integration could be rewarded with a tax credit based on their moving expense deduction. Individuals receiving housing vouchers or Section 8 certificates might be encouraged to make pro-integrative moves by appending special bonus subsidies.

Recent Federal Policy Initiatives

Fortunately, recent federal efforts suggest movement in the policy directions suggested above. Especially noteworthy are intensified civil rights enforcement activities.

HUD and the Department of Justice (DOJ) have expanded significantly their fair housing enforcement activities under the Clinton administration.[111] Perhaps the centerpiece of these activities is stepped-up efforts involving testing. HUD's Fair Housing Initiatives Program (FHIP), initiated in 1987, has been expanded from $11 million in fiscal year (FY) 1993 to $26 million in FY95. In FY94 FHIP provided fifty-nine grants to private fair housing groups to support their efforts to test real estate practices and litigate suspicious findings. HUD itself has won several fair housing cases where it was plaintiff.[112] However, at this writing FHIP is slated to be terminated by Congress.

DOJ also expanded their fair housing enforcement testing investigations, an effort begun under the Bush administration. At this writing there are five groups of DOJ testing teams conducting unannounced pattern and practice investigations across the nation; they have thereby already won eighteen court cases against discriminating landlords, with settlements as high as $175,000. During FY94, DOJ also handled thirty-four housing cases based on race that were referred to it by HUD, with damage awards as high as $61,000.[113]

There also are numerous indicators of tangible intensification of fair lending enforcement efforts. For example, HUD sponsored paired testing of lenders by the National Fair Housing Alliance, which has produced litigation. The Office of Comptroller of the Currency has begun a pilot program to ascertain whether testing can be used effectively as part of the periodic lender examination process.[114] Finally, HUD is working to ascertain whether FHA lending regulations create illegal disparate impacts on minority borrowers.

Two important recent cases illustrate DOJ's increasingly aggressive fair lending posture. The Shawmut Mortgage Company (Boston) was sued by DOJ in December 1993, alleging discriminatory treatment in loan approvals. The settlement required the company to revise its underwriting procedures and compensate victims to the tune of almost $1 million.[115] In perhaps its most controversial initiative, DOJ in August 1994 accused Chevy Chase Federal Savings Bank (Washington) of violating fair lending laws by failing to extend services to predominantly black neighborhoods in the Washington, D.C., area. The settlement reached called for Chevy Chase to provide special mortgage packages to applicants in the neighborhoods adversely affected, open more loan offices in these areas, and hire more black loan officers; cost to the company has been estimated at $11 million.[116]

The Clinton administration has also taken strides to promote class and racial-ethnic diversity of neighborhoods. HUD secretary Henry Cisneros has made "promoting the geographic mobility of low-income households" a main priority of HUD.[117] HUD has continued to implement the Moving to Opportunity (MTO) demonstration, originally instituted in 1991, although with funding now more restricted by Congress. Now being tested in five cities—Baltimore, Boston, Chicago, Los Angeles, and New York—MTO provides Section 8 rental subsidies to residents of public and assisted housing, who are aided in moving to low-poverty neighborhoods throughout the metropolitan area by a nonprofit organization. Cisneros's HUD has also advanced two of its own initiatives.

The Choice in Residency Program (CIR) was designed to enhance the residential mobility of those using regular Section 8 certificates and vouchers. The proposed CIR would provide grants that will fund comprehensive tenant counseling services supplied by nonprofit organizations, such as housing search strategies, transportation assistance, and information to help assisted families move and rapidly adapt to nonpoverty neighborhoods. It would also attempt to reach out aggressively to recruit Section 8 landlords in such neighborhoods. At this writing, CIR has not been approved by Congress.

The Metropolitanwide Assisted Housing Strategies demonstration will fund a (governmental or nonprofit) clearinghouse to coordinate information about housing assistance on a regional basis. A key component would be a unified waiting list for assisted housing throughout the region so that eligible tenants would be offered the first available unit, regardless of location. CIR-like counseling could also be provided to facilitate moves, and other supportive services could also be centralized to create "one-stop shopping" for assisted households.

HUD under Cisneros has moved affirmatively to settle numerous desegregation suits that had been brought against it and local Public Housing Authorities (PHAs) during previous administrations. These suits alleged that defendant PHAs had practiced explicitly racially segregationist policies, such as maintaining separate waiting lists for projects on the basis of race. The current HUD strategy in settling these cases has been one of offering (among other things, such as public housing modernization funds) Section 8 subsidies to minority plaintiffs, in conjunction with the aforementioned CIR-like counseling services to encourage desegregative moves out of public housing and minority neighborhoods.[118] This strategy has carried over into more recent HUD "reinvention" proposals to provide all public housing tenants with vouchers that would allow them to search more widely for places of residence.[119]

Despite these aforementioned commendable efforts, HUD and the rest of the administration have done little to support the efforts of numerous communities and nonprofit groups aimed at achieving stable, racial integration of nonsubsidized households. One possible venue for addressing this gap is the new Fair Housing Planning requirements. HUD soon will issue regulations under this rubric that will require communities to analyze impediments to fair housing as part of their Community Development Block Grant application. Hopefully, these regulations will go beyond encouraging the fight against discrimination to encouraging pro-integration initiatives. Analogous potential exists when formulating standards for HUD's newly proposed consolidation of their programs into three, performance-based block grants.[120]

Conclusion

I recognize that enforcement testing, dispersal of low-income populations, and pro-integration schemes are not widely popular policy options. They are necessary nonetheless. This suggests that courageous national leadership will be required. Perhaps the key to political palatability is stressing that these policies are not about massive transfers of resources or "handouts." Rather, these policies are about creating preconditions for more equal opportunities, surely a bipartisan theme. Without such political will, place and race will continue to distort constraints in ways that maintain racial-ethnic polarization. The hallowed premise of an "equal opportunity society" will remain a hollow promise for many minority citizens of America.

Notes

1. When it is not awkward to do so, I refer to racial-ethnic differences, not merely racial ones, in recognition of the fact that Hispanics may be of any race. This essay focuses on differences among African Americans, Hispanics, and whites (non-Hispanic whites), as they are the predominant racial-ethnic groups in most American metropolitan areas. I employ the aforementioned language whenever possible. When citing governmental statistics, however, I employ their terminology: blacks, Hispanics, and whites. When the data so specify, I note whether whites are confined to non-Hispanics. Finally, I recognize that the term *Hispanic* encompasses a wide array of national origins and groups of varied socioeconomic success. Unfortunately, census and other readily available data rarely disaggregate the Hispanic category, so I have been forced to follow a similar convention.

2. For more on industrial restructuring and its effects on educational requirements, see John Kasarda, "Urban Industrial Transition and the Underclass," *Annals of the American Academy of Political and Social Science* 501 (1989): 26–47.

3. Mary Jordan, "Ills of Big-City Schools Tied to Lower Spending," *Washington Post*, September 23, 1992 (citing Educational Resource Service and Council of Great City Schools).

4. For a fuller analysis of contemporary conditions facing minorities in inner-city schools, see Edward Hill and Heidi Rock, "Race and Inner-City Education," in *The Metropolis in Black and White: Place, Power, and Polarization*, ed. George C. Galster and Edward W. Hill (New Brunswick, N.J.: Rutgers Center for Urban Policy Research, 1992), 108–27.

5. The apparent narrowing of the gap when expressed in relative terms is misleading here, because whites and Hispanics began with such a small base percentage in 1970.

6. U.S. Department of Commerce, Bureau of the Census, *Statistical Abstract of the United States: 1991* (Washington, D.C.: U.S. Government Printing Office, 1991), tab. 223.

7. Note that those not employed may be either unemployed (but looking for work) or not participating in the labor force.

8. John Blair and Rudy Fichtenbaum provide a fuller analysis of black-white differences in unemployment, underemployment, discouraged workers, and, especially, how they relate to the most disadvantaged subgroup of all: black male youth (John Blair and Rudy Fichtenbaum, "Changing Black Employment Patterns," in Galster and Hill, *Metropolis in Black and White*, 72–92).

9. Bennett Harrison and Lucy Gorham, "What Happened to African-American Wages in the 1980s?," in ibid., 56–71.

10. For a more detailed model of life choices, see George Galster and Sean Killen, "The Geography of Metropolitan Opportunity: A Reconnaissance and Conceptual Framework," *Housing Policy Debate* 6 (1995): 7–44.

11. U.S. Department of Commerce, Bureau of the Census, *Statistical Abstract of the United States: 1992* (Washington, D.C.: U.S. Government Printing Office, 1992), tab. 635.

12. For a review of the evidence, see Galster and Killen, "Geography of Metropolitan Opportunity."

13. Frank Levy and Richard Murnane, "U.S. Earnings Levels and Earnings Inequality: A Review of Recent Trends and Proposed Explanations," *Journal of Economic Literature* 30 (1992): 1333–81.

14. Even if expected earnings after discrimination would be higher with some particular educational credential, discrimination may so lower its marginal benefit that it appears inferior to its marginal cost, especially relative to other alternatives.

15. For a review of the evidence, see Galster and Killen, "Geography of Metropolitan Opportunity."

16. Dawn Upchurch and James McCarthy "The Timing of First Birth and High School Completion," *American Sociological Review* 55 (1990): 224–34.

17. For a review of the evidence, see Galster and Killen, "Geography of Metropolitan Opportunity."

18. For an empirical case study on the racial-ethnic disparities in the sorts of residential environments in which youth must make life decisions, see George Galster and Maris Mikelsons, "The Geography of Metropolitan Opportunity: A Case Study of Neighborhood Conditions Confronting Youth," *Housing Policy Debate* 6 (1995): 73–102.

19. For more on these indexes and additional data and history related to segregation, see Douglas S. Massey and Nancy A. Denton, *American Apartheid: Segregation and the Making of the Underclass* (Cambridge, Mass.: Harvard University Press, 1993).

20. Compare Table 9 with Gerald David Jaynes and Robin M. Williams Jr., eds.,

A Common Destiny: Blacks and American Society (Washington, D.C.: National Academy Press, 1989), tab. 2-5.

21. George C. Galster, "Black Suburbanization: Has It Changed the Relative Location of Races?," *Urban Affairs Quarterly* 26 (1991): 621–28.

22. For a fuller discussion of these causes and a review of the evidence, see George Galster, "Research on Discrimination in Housing and Mortgage Markets," *Housing Policy Debate* 3 (1992): 639–84, and Massey and Denton, *American Apartheid.*

23. For a fuller discussion of these four factors, including supporting empirical evidence, see George C. Galster, "A Cumulative Causation Model of the Underclass: Implications for Urban Economic Development Policy," in Galster and Hill, *Metropolis in Black and White*, 190–215.

24. For a recent review, see John F. Kain "The Spatial Mismatch Hypothesis: Three Decades Later," *Housing Policy Debate* 3 (1992): 371–462.

25. Douglas Massey, Andrew Gross, and Mitchell Eggers, "Segregation, the Concentration of Poverty, and the Life Chances of Individuals," *Social Science Research* 20 (1991): 397–420.

26. George C. Galster and W. Mark Keeney, "Race, Residence, Discrimination, and Economic Opportunity: Modeling the Nexus of Urban Racial Phenomena," *Urban Affairs Quarterly* 24 (1988): 87–117.

27. Ruth Peterson and Lauren Krivo, "Racial Segregation and Black Urban Homicide," *Social Forces* 71 (1993): 1001–26.

28. George Galster, "Housing Discrimination and Urban Poverty of African-Americans," *Journal of Housing Research* 2 (1991): 87–122. See also the estimates provided by Richard Price and Edwin Mills, "Race and Residence in Earnings Determination," *Journal of Urban Economics* 17 (1985): 1–18. Earlier studies have also identified correlations between segregation, centralization, and black-white occupational disparities; see George Galster, "Residential Segregation and Interracial Economic Disparities," *Journal of Urban Economics* 21 (1987): 22–44, and the literature review therein.

29. David Rusk, *Cities without Suburbs* (Washington, D.C.: Woodrow Wilson Center Press, 1993).

30. Daphne Kenyon, *Interjurisdictional Tax and Policy Competition: Good or Bad for the Federal Systems?* (Washington, D.C.: Urban Institute Press, 1988).

31. Rufus P. Browning, Dale Rogers Marshall, and David H. Tabb, *Protest Is Not Enough* (Berkeley: University of California Press, 1984); Georgia Persons, "Racial Politics and Black Power in the Cities," in Galster and Hill, *Metropolis in Black and White*, 166–89.

32. This appears most strongly to be the case in large central cities of the Northeast and Midwest and in African American areas. See George Peterson and Adele Harrell, "Introduction: Inner-City Isolation and Opportunity," in *Drugs, Crime, and Social Isolation: Barriers to Urban Opportunity*, ed. Adele V. Harrell and George E. Peterson (Washington, D.C.: Urban Institute Press, 1992), 1–26.

33. Robert J. Taylor, Linda Chatters, and Vickie Mays, "Parents, Children, Siblings, In-Laws, and Non-Kin as Sources of Emergency Assistance to Black Americans" *Family Relations* 37 (1988): 298–304.

34. William Julius Wilson, *The Truly Disadvantaged: The Inner City, the Underclass, and Public Policy* (Chicago: University of Chicago Press, 1987), chap. 1.

35. Eloise Dunlap, "Impact of Drugs on Family Life and Kin Networks in Inner-City African-American Single-Parent Households," in Harrell and Peterson, *Drugs*, 181–207; Ansley Hamid, "Drugs and Patterns of Opportunity in the Inner-City," in ibid., 109–39.

36. Roberto Fernandez and David Harris, "Social Isolation and the Underclass," in ibid., 257–93.

37. Ibid., tab. 9.16.

38. Ibid., tab. 9.11. Note that all classes had aspects of their social interaction diminished by increased neighborhood poverty concentrations.

39. Douglas S. Massey and Mitchell Eggers, "The Ecology of Inequality: Minorities and the Concentration of Poverty, 1970–1980," *American Journal of Sociology* 95 (1990): 1153–88; Harrell and Peterson, "Introduction," 1–26; John D. Kasarda, "The Severely Distressed in Economically Transforming Cities," in Harrell and Peterson, *Drugs*, 45–97.

40. U.S. Department of Commerce, Bureau of the Census, *Statistical Abstract of the United States: 1994* (Washington, D.C.: U.S. Government Printing Office, 1994), tab. 307, p. 201.

41. Jeffrey Fagan, "Drug Selling and Licit Income in Distressed Neighborhoods," in Harrell and Peterson, *Drugs*, 99–146.

42. Dunlap, "Impact of Drugs on Family Life," 181–207.

43. Study by Correctional Association of New York and New York State Coalition for Criminal Justice, cited by Jason DeParle, "DC's Black Men Swept up by Criminal Justice System," *Cleveland Plain Dealer*, April 19, 1992. See also Jaynes and Williams, *Common Destiny*, chap. 9.

44. DeParle, "DC's Black Men"; "Baltimore Report Lambastes US Drug War" *Washington Post*, September 2, 1992.

45. Gary Orfield, "Urban Schooling and the Perpetuation of Job Inequality in Metropolitan Chicago," in *Urban Labor Markets and Job Opportunity*, ed. George E. Peterson and Wayne Vroman (Washington, D.C.: Urban Institute Press, 1992), 161–99.

46. A control group had no change in employment during the period. See Richard Freeman, "Crime and the Employment of Disadvantaged Youths," in Peterson and Vroman, *Urban Labor Markets*, 201–34.

47. Eric Hanusheck, "The Economics of Schooling," *Journal of Economic Literature* 24 (1986): 114–77; Thomas Hoffer, "Achievement Growth and Catholic Schools," *Sociology of Education* 58 (1985): 74–87; Karl Alexander and Aaron Pallas, "School Sector and Cognitive Performance," *Sociology of Education* 58 (1985): 115–28.

48. Joe Darden, Harriett Duleep, and George Galster, "Civil Rights in Metropolitan America," *Journal of Urban Affairs* 14 (1992): 469–96; Hill and Rock, "Race and Inner-City Education," 108–27; Jaynes and Williams, *Common Destiny*, chap. 7.

49. The metropolitan areas with the two lowest levels of school segregation (Charlotte and Jacksonville) were subject to court-ordered, cross-district integra-

tion plans. See Gary Orfield, *Public School Desegregation in the U.S., 1968–1980* (Washington, D.C.: Joint Center for Political Studies, 1983), tab. 21.

50. Hill and Rock, "Race and Inner-City Education," tab. 7.3.

51. Orfield, "Urban Schooling," 163–64.

52. Gary Orfield, *The Growth of Segregation in American Schools* (Alexandria, Va.: National School Boards Association, 1994).

53. Jordan, "Ills of Big-City Schools" (citing data from Council of Great City Schools).

54. Orfield, "Urban Schooling," 165.

55. Christopher Jencks and Susan Mayer, "The Social Consequences of Growing up in a Poor Neighborhood," in *Inner-City Poverty in the United States*, ed. Laurence Lynn Jr. and Michael G. H. McGeary (Washington, D.C.: National Academy Press, 1990).

56. Wilson, *Truly Disadvantaged*, chap. 1 and 46–62, argues that, ironically, the involuntary confinement of middle-class minorities in the ghetto, while harming them, may aid their lower-income brethren. For an empirical test of this, see Galster, "Housing Discrimination."

57. Eileen Bleachman, "Mentors for High-Risk Minority Children" (paper presented at conference, "Mentoring Program Structures for Young Minority Males," Urban Institute, Washington, D.C., 1991); Katherine Neckerman, "What Getting Ahead Means to Employers and Disadvantaged Workers" (paper presented at Urban Poverty and Family Life Conference, University of Chicago, 1991).

58. Jordan, "Ills of Big-City Schools."

59. Jonathan Kozol, *Savage Inequalities: Children in America's Schools* (New York: Crown, 1991).

60. Orfield, "Urban Schooling," 166–70.

61. Ibid., 166.

62. Norman Krumholz, "Developing Nightmare," *Cleveland Plain Dealer*, June 3, 1992; in 1980 67 percent of Cleveland public school children were African American, and 4 percent were Hispanic; Orfield, *Public School Desegregation*, tab. 20.

63. Orfield, "Urban Schooling," 170–72. Orfield also notes that both the rates of entrance and completion for blacks and Hispanics fell during the 1960s while they were rising for whites.

64. Sunbelt cities had generally smaller losses in center-city manufacturing employment. See Kasarda, "Severely Distressed," 45–97; James H. Johnson Jr. and Melvin L. Oliver, "Structural Changes in the U.S. Economy and Black Male Joblessness: A Reassessment," in Peterson and Vroman, *Urban Labor Markets*, 113–49.

65. Kasarda, "Severely Distressed," tab. 3.13.

66. For a fuller review of the evidence, see Philip Moss and Chris Tilly, *Why Black Men Are Doing Worse in the Labor Market: A Review of Supply-Side and Demand-Side Explanations* (New York: Social Source Research Council, 1991).

67. The cities were Boston, Newark, New York, Philadelphia, and Pittsburgh (Kasarda, "Severely Distressed," tab. 3.14).

68. The cities were Cleveland, Chicago, Detroit, Milwaukee, and St. Louis (ibid.).

69. Ibid.

70. Harry Holzer and Wayne Vroman, "Mismatches and the Urban Labor Market," in Peterson and Vroman, *Urban Labor Markets*, 81–112; Johnson and Oliver, "Structural Changes in the U.S. Economy," 113–49; Kain, "Spatial Mismatch Hypothesis," 371–462.

71. See Timothy Bates, *Major Studies of Minority Business: A Bibliographic Review* (Washington, D.C.: Joint Center for Political and Economic Studies Press, 1990); Timothy Bates and Constance Dunham, "Facilitating Upward Mobility through Small Business Ownership," in Peterson and Vroman, *Urban Labor Markets*, 239–82.

72. Bates and Dunham, "Facilitating Upward Mobility," tabs. 7.8, 7.9.

73. Timothy Bates, "Small Business Viability in the Urban Ghetto," *Journal of Regional Science* 29 (1989): 625–43.

74. Joint Center for Political and Economic Studies, "Can America Solve Its Biggest Problems?," *Focus*, February–March 1992, 2–10 (citing Jennifer Henderson, Center for Community Change).

75. For evidence on differential home appreciation rates depending on neighborhood racial composition, see John Simonson and Barbara Lippman, "Home Price Appreciation in Central City Low-Income Neighborhood" (paper presented at Urban Institute conference, "Housing Markets and Residential Mobility," Airlie, Va., 1991).

76. Katharine Bradbury, Karl Case, and Constance Dunham, "Geographic Patterns of Mortgage Lending in Boston, 1982–87," *New England Economic Review* (1989): 3–30; Anne Shlay, "Not in That Neighborhood," *Social Science Research* 17 (1988): 137–63; Anne Shlay, Ira Goldstein, and David Bartelt, "Racial Barriers to Credit: Comment," *Urban Affairs Quarterly* 28 (1992): 126–40.

77. Ronald Wienk, "Discrimination in Urban Credit Markets: What We Don't Know and Why We Don't Know It," *Housing Policy Debate* 3 (1992): 217–40.

78. Alicia H. Munnell, Lynn E. Browne, James McEneaney, and Geoffrey Tootell, *Mortgage Lending in Boston: Interpreting HMDA Data* (Boston: Federal Reserve Bank, 1992).

79. Ann Schnare, "Secondary Market Business Practices and Mortgage Credit Availability" (paper presented at Fannie Mae Annual Housing Conference, Washington, D.C., 1992).

80. For a fuller analysis of discrimination in America, see Michael Fix and Raymond Struyk, eds., *Clear and Convincing Evidence: Measurement of Discrimination in America* (Washington, D.C.: Urban Institute Press, 1993).

81. For a fuller review of housing discrimination research, see Galster, "Research on Discrimination."

82. Margery Turner, "Discrimination in Urban Housing Markets: Lessons from Fair Housing Audits," *Housing Policy Debate* 3 (1992): 185–216. Discrimination in the marketing of homes has also been observed; see Galster, "Research on Discrimination," 659.

83. See Galster, "Research on Discrimination," for a fuller review of the evidence.

84. *Washington Post*, September 2, 1992 (quoting Jerome Milles, president of the National Center on Institutions and Alternatives).

85. Ibid.

86. Ibid.

87. Joint Center for Political and Economic Studies, "Can America Solve Its Biggest Problems?," 3–10.

88. Ibid., 7 (quoting Judge Thelma Cummings).

89. See, for example, Blair and Fichtenbaum, "Changing Black Employment Patterns"; George Peterson and Wayne Vroman, "Urban Labor Markets and Economic Opportunity," in Peterson and Vroman, *Urban Labor Markets*, 1–30; Darden et al., "Civil Rights in Metropolitan America."

90. Darden et al., "Civil Rights in Metropolitan America."

91. Thomas Boston, "Segmented Labor Markets," *Industrial and Labor Relations Review* 44 (1990): 99–115.

92. Harry Cross, Genevieve Kenney, Jane Mell, and Wendy Zimmermann, *Employer Hiring Practices* (Washington, D.C.: Urban Institute Press, 1990).

93. Margery Austin Turner, Michael Fix, and Raymond J. Struyk, *Opportunities Denied, Opportunities Diminished: Racial Discrimination in Hiring* (Washington, D.C.: Urban Institute Press 1991).

94. U.S. Department of Labor, *A Report on the Glass Ceiling Initiative* (Washington, D.C.: U.S. Department of Labor, 1991); Joleen Kirschenman and Kathryn M. Neckerman, "'We'd Love to Hire Them, But . . .': The Meaning of Race for Employers," in *The Urban Underclass*, ed. Christopher Jencks and Paul E. Peterson (Washington, D.C.: Brookings Institution, 1991).

95. R. Waldinger and T. Bailey, *The Continuing Significance of Race* (New York: Conservation of Human Resources, Columbia University, 1990).

96. For a fuller review, see Galster, "Research on Discrimination."

97. Munnell et al., *Mortgage Lending in Boston*.

98. Paul Wiseman, "Bankers Grumpy Despite Strong Profits," *USA Today*, October 19, 1992 (quoting Federal Reserve Governor John LaWare).

99. U.S. Department of Justice news release, "DOJ Settles First Race Discrimination Lawsuit against Major Home Mortgage Lender" (Washington, D.C., September 17, 1992).

100. For more citations of suits alleging lending discrimination, see Cathy Cloud and George Galster, "What Do We Know about Racial Discrimination in Mortgage Markets?," *Review of Black Political Economy* 22 (1993): 101–20.

101. For a complete review, see George Galster, "The Use of Testers in Investigating Discrimination in Mortgage Lending and Insurance Markets," in Fix and Struyk, *Clear and Convincing Evidence*, 287–334.

102. Ernest Kohn, Cyril Foster, Bernard Kaye, and Nancy Terris, *Are Mortgage Lending Policies Discriminating?* (Albany: New York State Banking Department Consumer Studies Division, 1992).

103. Faith Ando, "Capital Issues and Minority-Owned Business," *Review of Black Political Economy* 16 (1988): 77–109.

104. See Darden et al., "Civil Rights in Metropolitan America"; George Galster, "Federal Fair Housing Policy," in *Building Foundations: Housing and Federal Policy*, ed. Langley C. Keyes and Denise DiPasquale (Philadelphia: University of Pennsylvania Press, 1990), 137–57; Galster, "Cumulative Causation Model of the Underclass," 190–215; Don DeMarco and George Galster, "Pro-integrative Policy," *Journal of Urban Affairs* 15 (1993): 141–60.

105. DeMarco and Galster, "Pro-integrative Policy"; Galster, "Cumulative Causation Model of the Underclass," 142–52.

106. See generally G. Thomas Kingsley and Margery Austin Turner, eds., *Housing Markets and Residential Mobility* (Washington, D.C.: Urban Institute Press, 1993).

107. Galster, "Cumulative Causation Model of the Underclass," 202–8.

108. James Rosenbaum, "Changing the Geography of Metropolitan Opportunity by Expanding Residential Choice," *Housing Policy Debate* 6 (1995): 231–69.

109. Galster, "Cumulative Causation Model of the Underclass."

110. George C. Galster, "The Case for Racial Integration," in Galster and Hill, *Metropolis in Black and White*, 279–92; Mittie Olion Chandler, "Obstacles to Housing Integration Program Efforts," in ibid., 292–300.

111. The following section is based on Roberta Achtenberg, assistant secretary, Office of Fair Housing and Equal Opportunity, Department of Housing and Urban Development, "Statement before the House Committee on the Judiciary Subcommittee on Civil and Constitutional Rights, Oversight Hearings on Fair Housing," September 28, 1994.

112. For details, see ibid., 6–9.

113. Deval Patrick, assistant secretary for civil rights, Department of Justice, "Statement before the Subcommittee on Civil and Constitutional Rights, Committee on the Judiciary," U.S. House of Representatives, September 8, 1994.

114. Liz Spayd, "White House Targets Mortgage Loan Bias," *Washington Post*, May 6, 1993; "Agency to Step up Vigilance on Loan Discrimination," *Washington Post*, March 13, 1993.

115. Patrick, "Statement before the Subcommittee on Civil and Constitutional Rights."

116. Ibid.

117. Ibid.

118. Such was the case in the September 1994 settlement of *Sanders v. HUD* (Allegheny County, Pa.) and the May 1994 settlement proposed in *Young v. Cisneros* (East Texas); see Achtenberg, "Statement before the House Committee on the Judiciary Subcommittee on Civil and Constitutional Rights," 40–44.

119. U.S. Department of Housing and Urban Development, *Reinvention Blueprint* (Washington, D.C.: HUD, 1994).

120. Ibid.

Michael A. Stegman National Urban Policy
Revisited

Policy Options for the
Clinton Administration

Introduction

The United States first became a truly metropolitan nation in 1990 when
over half (50.2 percent) of its citizens lived in the thirty-nine metropolitan
areas with populations exceeding 1 million people or more.[1] The urbanization of America is not necessarily good news for cities; most metropolitan
growth has been suburban. As a result, less than a third of the population
now lives in cities.[2]

Despite a declining population base, cities continue to play a vital economic and cultural role in the nation's life: "They provide safe harbor and
a takeoff point for each generation's immigrants and for each region's in-
and out-migrants."[3] Nearly as many immigrants arrived on our shores in
the 1980s—600,000 a year—as came during the peak years of 1900 to
1910.[4] Most of these new arrivals head for the cities, adding "fresh entrepreneurial energy but also vast social service burdens" to their adopted
homelands.[5]

At the same time, however, dramatic shifts in the nationalities of immigrants have challenged the acculturation capacities of cities. During the
1980s, for example, only 11 percent of new arrivals to America were European, compared with the 1960s, when more than half were European.[6] Although the financial burdens that large-scale immigration places on cities
are hard to estimate, a recent report issued by Los Angeles County estimated that immigration-related costs are approaching a billion dollars, or
more than 30 percent of total expenditures.[7]

The combination of high rates of immigration and white flight to the
suburbs has contributed to the growth of racial-ethnic minorities into
the demographic majorities in many of our largest cities—57 percent of the
population in New York, 62 percent in Chicago, 63 percent in Los Angeles,
70 percent in Atlanta, 79 percent in Detroit, and 88 percent in Miami.[8]

Moreover, "to make good their escape from the city and its problems, the new suburbanites often passed laws prohibiting the city from expanding— condemning it to a future as an economic and racial ghetto."[9] These factors also have contributed to growing disparities between the incomes and re- sulting tax bases of cities and suburbs. Consider the contrast between Charlotte, North Carolina, and Cleveland, Ohio, two cities with similarly sized metropolitan populations but dramatically different future prospects:

> Charlotte's metropolitan area has gained 600,000 people in the past 40 years; Cleveland's 700,000. Both are roughly 20 percent black, metro- wide. But there the similarities end.
>
> Charlotte has grown, capturing nearly half of the growth of its metro- politan area. The population of Cleveland has shrunk, with most of the growth of its metropolitan area coming from people fleeing the city.
>
> Charlotte—with roughly the same size black population—is far more integrated than Cleveland. Charlotte's residents are prosperous; per cap- ita income in the city is 118 percent that of the suburbs. In Cleveland, per capita income is only 62 percent of that in the suburbs.
>
> The difference: Charlotte was allowed to expand, to follow its suburbs and keep the middle class—both white and black—within the city, pay- ing its taxes, running its government and solving its problems.[10]

Trapped by geographic boundaries that cannot expand and disadvan- taged by a labor force that is poorly prepared to compete in a global econ- omy that places a premium on advanced education, "cities on their own cannot solve the problems of the poor or of urban decay."[11] A prime ex- ample of such a severely distressed city today is Hartford, Connecticut, the former insurance capital of the nation that has become the poorest and one of the most crime-ridden cities in Connecticut.[12]

Sensitive to the national challenge posed by dramatic shifts in metropol- itan settlement patterns, and in partial response to the urban riots of the 1960s, Congress enacted legislation in 1970 requiring the president to pre- pare a biennial urban growth policy report. This essay traces the evolution of national urban policies from President Nixon through President Bush and concludes with recommendations for the Clinton administration. The second section summarizes how cities have fared since the 1960s, with particular emphasis on their fiscal condition and problems in their health, education, and criminal justice systems. The third section summarizes twenty-three years of national urban policies, and the fourth section ana- lyzes the principal reasons why these policies have been largely ineffective. The final section presents three national urban policy scenarios for consid- eration, with the preferred alternative combining an aggressive program of national investment in productivity-increasing human and infrastructure capital with community-based public-private partnerships.

How Cities Have Fared

With structural changes in the national economy[13] having contributed to the growth of an urban underclass,[14] and continuing problems with our educational, health care, housing, and welfare systems, one might conclude that all cities and most African Americans are worse off today than they were when the riots broke out in the late 1960s. While many cities are reeling from the recessions of the 1980s and more than a decade of relative federal neglect, they are not without hope. Despite their seemingly intractable problems, many cities are creating their own "macroeconomic" policies to make them more competitive in the "information age" global economy where "it's possible for millions of dollars to move in seconds from Miami to Milan, Dallas to Dhahran."[15] For example, "San Antonio is aggressively marketing itself as 'Telecity,'" and "New York City has a 'teleport'—an antenna farm on Staten Island linked to a regional fiber optic network—that permits the Big Apple's communications-hungry banks, brokerage houses and travel industries instant access to satellites and other global telecommunications media."[16]

Although conditions have worsened demonstrably for poor African Americans living in drug-plagued inner-city communities, there is some evidence that a substantial percentage of blacks have improved their lives and work in the last thirty years.[17] The income gap between affluent and poor blacks is greater today than the gap between blacks and whites.[18] "In the past 20 years, black families with incomes of $35,000 grew from 15.7 to 21.2 percent and black families with incomes of $50,000 increased 350 percent."[19]

Some economists, however, see these gains as illusory and short lived. Harrison and Gorham, among others, argue that the above-cited gains cannot be sustained for three reasons: most of the income gains reflected the increase in two-wage-earner families rather than higher real wage income for full-time workers;[20] the incidence of well-paid black workers, both men and women, fell during the 1980s;[21] and the increase in the number of black families headed by single women who are the sole breadwinners. Consequently, "in the absence of a truly major national policy effort to promote affirmative action in hiring and promotion, comparable worth, higher hourly wage rates for part-time workers, and extensive job training tied to well-paid stable employment opportunities, most black families, even more than white families, need two or more earners to attain a middle-class standard of living."[22]

Like their white counterparts, higher-income blacks are moving out of the cities. Forty-nine percent of all African Americans on Long Island make more money than does the typical white household in America. "The majority of all black people in the Washington area do *not* live in the District of Columbia. They live in the suburbs."[23] In 1989 26 percent of all black households lived in the suburbs, and 43 percent owned their own homes.[24] In 1960 about 2 percent of Cleveland's black population lived in the suburbs; by 1990 a third did.[25]

Fiscal Conditions

It is also difficult to generalize about the changing fiscal conditions of cities since the late 1960s. Local economies are subject to national business and growth cycles as well as regional swings that affect both revenues and expenditures. Even so, one thing is certain. During the past thirty years, America's cities have suffered severe declines in resident incomes and tax bases as a result of the flight of jobs and the middle class to the suburbs. In some metropolitan areas this flight has become so great as to have all but pauperized the central city.[26]

Although these trends suggest that cities are experiencing growing fiscal trauma, some measures of fiscal health actually show cities doing better today, while other measures paint a bleaker picture. Measured in terms of liquidity, cash balances, and deficit position, cities were in a better cash position in the mid-1980s than they were ten years earlier when New York was on the verge of bankruptcy.[27] Roy Bahl attributes this improved performance to a combination of more "conservative budgeting and fiscal planning" and the fact that "cities seem to have done a better job of expanding and contracting their budgets depending on the performance of their economies."[28]

When municipal performance is measured more broadly, however, there are indications that the fiscal health of large cities has generally deteriorated. According to Ladd and Yinger, "The average city experienced an eleven percentage point decline in its standardized fiscal health between 1972 and 1982, but the average fiscal health is markedly poorer in central cities with large populations than in those with small populations."[29] Bahl raises an interesting point about the fiscal responsibility debate. While conservative budgeting has helped cities balance their budgets, they have done so by "deferring their expenditures on certain activities to later years and allowing those public services to deteriorate."[30]

Public finance experts might disagree about this issue, but one thing is clear: today, cities must rely more heavily on their own devices for raising revenues.[31] Federal dollars have been sharply cut since the 1970s. This is especially true for large cities where direct federal aid as a percentage of locally raised revenues fell from 34 percent in 1977 to below 10 percent in 1987.[32] A 1992 report from the National League of Cities cites four reasons for increasing fiscal pressure: (1) the cost of unfunded state and federal mandates, (2) the depressed state of local economies, (3) high infrastructure needs, and (4) the rising cost of health benefits for municipal employees.[33] To deal with the general revenue shortfall, cities were forced, among other actions, to freeze budgets, raise taxes, and lay off municipal employees.[34]

For those who argue for state involvement in addressing the problems of cities by the Clinton administration, a cautionary note: as a result of the recession, in 1991 fifteen states reduced local grants-in-aid—some by as much as 25 percent.[35]

While the fiscal vitality of our cities is decidedly mixed, it is fair to say that many of the nation's largest cities have experienced fiscal deterioration since the 1960s. The transformation from a primarily goods-producing economy to a knowledge-based information economy caused a decrease in total manufacturing employment. Larger, older cities took the biggest hits: between 1967 and 1987, Detroit lost 51 percent of its manufacturing jobs; New York City, 58 percent; Chicago, 60 percent; and Philadelphia, 64 percent.[36]

Increasing Demands on Urban Services

Health Care

Deterioration is apparent in our health care system as well. The incidence of specific health problems is generally higher in central cities than in the nation as a whole, and higher still in big cities, especially those with large minority populations. A case in point is infant mortality. The infant mortality rate in the United States ranks twentieth in the world, primarily due to excessively high rates in major cities.[37] The 1989 national infant mortality rate was 10.0 infant deaths per 1,000 live births. In Washington, D.C., however, the 1989 infant mortality rate was 22.9; Detroit reached 21.1; Philadelphia, 17.6; and Chicago, 17.0.[38] Among black children the rates were drastically higher: 26.5 in Washington, D.C.; Detroit, 23.9; Philadelphia, 23.5; and Chicago, 22.4.[39]

Excess mortality is not only a problem among infants. "Nationally, black men in inner city neighborhoods are less likely to reach the age of 65 than men in Bangladesh, one of the poorest nations in the world."[40] The declining life expectancy of black males is not a function of elevated death rates among older males but the result of higher death rates for younger men due to a homicide epidemic in inner cities. A major inner-city hospital in Los Angeles reported in 1991 that 51 percent of its patients had gunshot wounds, compared with only 19 percent in 1985.[41] In addition, high levels of psychological stress in the form of depression, alcoholism, and substance abuse lead to excess mortality rates among urban minorities. "Cardiovascular disease, a stress-related condition, accounts for almost one quarter of the excess mortality cited in" a landmark study of black males in Harlem.[42] Finally, municipal hospitals in large cities have been stressed beyond the breaking point trying to cope with a growing AIDS epidemic. In New York City 83 percent of women with AIDS and 61 percent of all AIDS patients are Hispanic or black.[43]

Poverty and Homelessness

Between 1979 and 1989 the number of people living in poverty grew by 4.3 million to more than 31 million.[44] Poverty is not restricted to urban areas, but it is more concentrated there. In 1989 30 percent of all poor households lived in the suburbs[45] and were as likely to have housing problems as those living in cities. The percentage of the nation's poor living in central cities continues to grow: from 30 percent in 1968 to 37 percent in 1979 to 43.1 percent in 1989.[46] What is unique about urban poverty is its intense racial and spatial concentration.[47] While no municipality seems to be too small to have some homeless people, homelessness has reached epidemic proportions in major cities. Martha Burt found that

> During the recession of 1981–1982, emergency shelters and soup kitchens began reporting a greatly increased demand for their services, reflecting the effects of high unemployment, a rising cost of living, and a retrenchment in government programs that cushioned earlier economic downturns. Even when economic conditions improved after 1983, homelessness seemed to continue growing. The size of the homeless population was estimated at 250,000 to 350,000 for 1984 . . . and 500,000 to 600,000 for 1987. . . . A comparison of these estimates yields an annual rate of increase of about 22 percent for these three years. As the decade progressed, the homeless population increasingly included new groups of people, such as mothers with children, and more of certain types of individuals, such as the severely mentally ill and drug abusers.[48]

As Burt suggests, in New York and elsewhere the most rapidly growing segment of the homeless population is families with children. Throughout the 1970s the number of homeless families in New York City's emergency shelter system totaled just under 1,000. Most of these families were displaced by fire, illness, or other short-term crises.[49] Today there are more than 5,200 homeless families in New York City, with close to 1,000 new families entering the shelter system each month.[50] Moreover, today's homelessness is often not a result of an immediate crisis. Today more than 45 percent of all homeless families in New York have never had a place of their own to live; only 37 percent of homeless individuals have a high school degree; only 40 percent of all family heads have at least six months of work experience; and over 70 percent have varied levels of drug and alcohol abuse.[51]

In a study of homeless families in Los Angeles, a similar pattern was reported: "Homeless mothers reported more spousal abuse and drug abuse by their mates and were more likely to have had a child abuse report opened on the family and more likely to have personally required hospitalization for mental illness" than were a comparison group of poor housed families.[52] Also, "a history of substance abuse and family violence were more often reported for the homeless mothers' own family of origin."[53]

Education

As the earlier reference to Hartford's schools suggests,[54] no institution is in a greater state of crisis than the urban school system. "More people than ever graduate from high school. But in our big cities many of those who graduate are barely literate."[55] "The reading scores of black 17-year-olds from disadvantaged urban communities are no better than the reading scores of white 13-year-olds from more advantaged communities."[56] Today, "45 percent of black children and about three-quarters of immigrants are educated in or around 11 big cities."[57] And, while black males comprise about 6 percent of today's civilian labor force, they and other minorities are projected to comprise more than half of all new labor market entrants in the year 2000.[58] Thus, "a large fraction of these workers will enter the job market as products of urban schools or urban job training programs—preparatory mechanisms that are *failing minority groups*."[59] Financial returns from education are also lower for blacks and other minorities than they are for whites because of racial discrimination in the workplace.[60]

Crime

Finally, no assessment of the current state of urban America and future prospects can ignore crime and the role that the criminal justice system plays in contemporary America and in the lives of young African Americans and other minority young men. In America's urban areas there is a murder every twenty-two minutes, a forcible rape every five minutes, a robbery every forty-nine seconds, and an aggravated assault every thirty seconds.[61] To punctuate the seeming inability of our national government to stem the rise of urban violence, our nation's capital has become the murder capital of the nation.[62] But the incidence of lawlessness is more concentrated in some areas than others. This is illustrated by the fact that three-quarters of New York State's entire prison population comes from and preys upon just seven neighborhoods in New York City.[63]

Rising crime rates are not exclusive to our largest cities. Between 1985 and 1990 crimes against persons increased by more than 50 percent in eight of twenty-five surveyed cities with populations of 250,000 or more.[64] Fear of crime pervades cities of all sizes, adversely affects lifestyles, restricts the use of urban spaces, and fuels racial antagonisms. The rise of violent crimes during the 1980s has been linked to drug activities that have provided increased, albeit illegal, earnings opportunities for poorly educated, unemployed, minority young men. A recent study of incarcerated young offenders concluded that expected returns from illegal work exceeded those for legal work for both blacks and whites, but because of lower employment and earnings possibilities, the ratio of expected legal earnings to illegal earnings was much lower for blacks.[65] One result of these perverse economic incentives is frequent involvement with the local law enforcement system. Today, "one-quarter of black men ages 20 to 29 are in jail, in prison, or under a parole officer's supervision."[66] Because "run-ins with the law are so common among young males in inner-city areas that most of the stigma associated with being an offender is gone, and tensions between the community and the police are high."[67] In addition to forming a disproportionately large share of all prisoners, blacks are also more often the victims of crime.[68]

The cost of operating and expanding the criminal justice system is staggering. In 1988 direct expenditures on the criminal justice system by all levels of government totaled about $61 billion, including $14.9 billion for operating the state and federal prison systems.[69] Today the cost of building a single prison bed ($53,663)[70] is about the same as building a subsidized home for a low-income family. Interestingly, corrections spending is the second fastest growing item in state budgets—after Medicaid.[71] This suggests that without dramatic reform, the criminal justice system will continue to drain resources that could be used for investment in human capital and other more productive purposes for years to come.

Economic Decline and the Underclass

To conclude this section, it should be noted that analysis of the progress of cities since the late 1960s must also address the issue of the urban underclass. Whether used in an economic context as originally intended by Myrdal to describe people who have become technologically unemployable, or in a behavioral context to describe poor people who do not fit mainstream values, there is a consensus on two points: regardless of how cities as a whole have fared since the late 1960s, the underclass population has grown significantly, and its spatial concentration has intensified within the urban fabric.[72]

The most recent manifestation of these phenomena is the Los Angeles riots of April 1992, which one scholar sees as "the consequence of a lethal linkage of economic decline, cultural decay and political lethargy in American life."[73] To set the stage for the urban policy challenge confronting the Clinton administration and as a contemporary context for rethinking the Kerner Commission Report, consider the case of Los Angeles. Here is a summary of conditions that currently affect the quality of life in Los Angeles and South Central Los Angeles:

[1] Los Angeles is one of the most segregated communities in the United States. . . . [Sixty] percent of the census tracts in Los Angeles have almost no African American residents.

[2] Black families in Los Angeles bear a disproportionate share of the poverty there. Black people constitute only 13 percent of the city's population, but they comprise 18 percent of the low-income renter households. . . . Unemployment among black people in Los Angeles runs twice the rate for the county as a whole.

[3] In South Central itself, the median annual household income is $20,000, barely half the $38,000 median income for the county as a whole, and 17 percent of the households have incomes beneath $7,500, compared with the county-wide figure of 7.6 percent.

[4] There [are] only 11 supermarkets in South Central, one for every 40,000 people, whereas South Central would have had 22 supermarkets if it merely had the average for Los Angeles as a whole, and would have even more if it had as many as are in the white neighborhoods.

[5] There are only 53 bank branches in all of South Central, whereas there would be more than twice that number if South Central had as many banks per person as does the rest of Los Angeles. . . . The banks and SandLs [in L.A.] make fewer loans in the lower-income and minority neighborhoods than in the city as a whole, [even when differences in income are taken into account].

[6] There are fewer manufacturing jobs in South Central than in Los Angeles County as a whole: one for every 19 people, in contrast to one for every 14 county-wide. South Central lost 70,000 manufacturing jobs from 1978–1982 alone.

[7] The Los Angeles Unified School District is growing by 15,000 students a year, crowding the system so much it had been forced to bus children across town, resort to a year-round schedule, spill over into temporary trailers and jam classrooms with as many as 37 students per teacher. More than half of the students are from families with incomes low enough to qualify for free meals, and a third of the students—up from 7 percent a decade ago—have limited English.

[8] Only 20 percent of the residents could afford the median priced home, which sold for $210,850 in 1991. The average asking rent rose to $690 in 1990, an increase of 139 percent from 1980, during a decade in which median family income rose only 85 percent. . . . HUD's fair market rent for a two-bedroom unit is $804 in Los Angeles County and $900 in Orange County. . . . A mother with two children on welfare receives $663 a month.

[9] Forty-two thousand families live in garages illegally converted into living spaces. . . . Every night, 20,000 to 30,000 people are homeless [in Los Angeles], and over the course of a year 100,000 to 175,000 persons are homeless for some period.[74]

Twenty-three Years of National Urban Policies

The Nixon Years

National urban policy has been a concern of the executive and legislative branches of the federal government since 1969, when President Nixon created a National Goals Research Staff that would lead the executive branch's efforts to "project future trends—and thus to make the kind of informed choices which are necessary if we are to establish mastery over the process of change."[75] Appointing Daniel Patrick Moynihan, his chief urban advisor, as executive secretary to the Council for Urban Affairs "was a signal [to the nation's mayors] that central cities would be the focus of [a Nixon] urban policy."[76] The council's charge was to develop "coherent, consistent patterns" of activities that the national government should encourage or discourage in responding to the urbanization of American life.[77] Against a backdrop of urban riots, racial discrimination, a growing fiscal division between cities and suburbs, and a seeming inability of state and local political institutions to respond to these problems, Moynihan boiled down his analysis of the major urbanization issues confronting the nation to the following ten points that seem equally as relevant today as twenty-three years ago:

1. Poverty and social isolation of minority groups in central cities.
2. Enormous imbalances between urban areas in the programs that affect them.
3. Inadequate structure and capacity in local government.
4. Fiscal instability in urban government.
5. Lack of equality in public services among jurisdictions within metropolitan areas.
6. Migration of people displaced by technology, and from central cities to suburban areas.

7. Inadequate structure and capacity of states in their indispensable roles in managing urban affairs.
8. Ineffective incentive systems to encourage state and local governments and private interests to help implement the goals of federal policy.
9. Lack of adequate information as well as extensive and sustained research on urban problems.
10. An insufficient sense of the finite resources of the national environment and the fundamental importance of aesthetics in successful urban growth.[78]

President Nixon proposed a "national growth policy" in his 1970 state of the union message, and Title VII of the Housing and Urban Development Act of 1970[79] formalized the executive branch's responsibilities in this area by requiring the president to deliver a biennial report on urban growth. Stimulated by the previous decade's mass migrations from rural and small-town America to the nation's major metropolitan centers that were floundering in their ability to manage this growth, coupled with a belief that concerted national action could dramatically change the settlement patterns and the urban landscape, the Nixon urban growth policy featured the concept of "a national program of new city-building [that] would capture a good share of population growth and would also have strong symbolic value in recasting the image of what cities should be like."[80] A new communities-centered national urban growth policy was fostered by the work of a blue-ribbon panel that had enormous faith in the ability of the federal government to stimulate the private sector to create ten new towns that would become a blueprint for an entirely new urban fabric.[81] In retrospect, the new communities policy was poorly timed because people began leaving the cities in droves long before the building could begin.[82]

The Ford Urban Policy

Although it was never formally unveiled, in anticipation of an election victory in 1976 the Ford administration did prepare a draft urban policy that would "put the urban back into urban policy."[83] Organized around the concept of "targeted New Federalism," "the policy called for targeting more federal money to distressed areas by revising the distribution formulas for general revenue sharing and other block grant programs. Tax revision was also proposed which would encourage housing rehabilitation and central city redevelopment. Although the policy statement did not promise any new spending, it did advocate a countercyclical 'kicker' to the Community Development Block Grant program, which, if enacted, would have sent an additional $900 million to cities with high rates of un-employment." [84]

Shortly after the 1976 election the focus of national urban growth policy shifted permanently from a concern with broad patterns of urbanization to the growing problems of America's cities. Title VI of the Housing and Community Development Act of 1977 amended the 1970 legislation by dropping the word *growth* and requiring the president to issue a biennial report on urban policy in February of even-numbered years beginning in 1978 [85] and expanded the scope and content of the policy to include energy conservation, population distribution, and tax base considerations. [86] In that same legislation Congress declared that the national urban policy should be action and interventionist oriented, stimulate economic growth in communities of all sizes and regions, combat rural and urban poverty, and better orchestrate the delivery of federal programs. [87]

The Carter Urban Policy

Jimmy Carter took office midway into a decade that saw reversal of for-tunes in America's great cities. The index of "resident need" of the Depart-ment of Housing and Urban Development (HUD), which included data on poverty, unemployment, and income growth, confirmed the decline of large cities during the 1970–80 decade: "As of 1970, this index was signifi-cantly higher compared with the [U.S.] as a whole in only three of the fifty-six big cities: Newark, New Orleans, and El Paso. By 1980, twenty of the big cities showed such high levels of resident needs. If distressed cities are defined as those suffering both high resident need and rapid population loss, then no big U.S. city was distressed as of 1970, [but] fourteen of the fifty-six big cities met such standards for distress by 1980." [88]

In a speech to mayors during his 1976 campaign, Carter recognized the growing urban problem and made a commitment to doing something about it:

I think we stand at a turning point in history. If, a hundred years from now, this Nation's experiment in democracy has failed, I suspect that historians will trace that failure to our own era, when a process of decay began in our inner cities and was allowed to spread unchecked through-out our society.

But I do not believe that must happen. I believe that working together, we can turn the tide, stop the decay, and set in motion a process of growth that by the end of the century can give us cities worthy of the greatest Nation on earth. [89]

Carter repudiated the suburban-oriented Nixon growth policies that "subsidized the out-migration of middle income people and business from existing facilities in cities."[90] His administration's urban policies were premised on the belief that a growing number of America's cities were "finding it increasingly difficult to fulfill their historical roles as symbols of choice, hope and opportunity; places where millions of foreign immigrants and native-born Americans have sought to better their own lives and secure a brighter future for their children."[91] The thrust of this administration's policies was to aid people and cities in distress by

- expanding targeted job programs to create more jobs for the long-term unemployed;
- increasing housing assistance programs to provide improved housing for many low and moderate income households;
- restructuring the Community Development Block Grant program to focus on the most needy cities, neighborhoods and people;
- initiating the Urban Development Action Grant program (UDAG) to encourage public and private investment in the nation's distressed cities;
- strengthening the countercyclical public works program and extending anti-recession fiscal assistance;
- reforming and strengthening equal opportunity and affirmative action efforts.[92]

Recognizing that the federal government had neither the means nor the resources to tackle all the problems of the cities, the Carter administration declared its intent to foster a new partnership among the states, local governments, the private sector, and individuals. Carter's 1980 national urban policy report confirmed this commitment to work in partnership "to strengthen urban economies, improve job opportunities and job mobility for the long-term unemployed, promote fiscal stability, expand opportunity for those disadvantaged by discrimination and poverty, and encourage energy-efficient and environmentally-sound patterns of urban development."[93] In order to limit unnecessary federal activities that competed with the goals of the urban policy, an impact analysis of new or significantly changed nonurban programs of the federal government was also proposed.[94] The major legislative thrust of this wave of Carter urban policy was in the economic development area through programs that would make "grants, loan guarantees, and interest subsidies available to private firms investing in distressed communities."[95] This would have been carried out by the National Development Bank, had Congress approved its creation as proposed in 1978.[96]

In contrast to this ambitious inaugural urban policy report that was backed with an $8.3 billion package of budget proposals, the Carter administration's 1980 urban policy report was "heavy on administrative tinkering—interagency agreements, guideline revisions, improved criteria for measuring urban impact and the like—and light on actions that cost money."[97]

The President's Commission for a
National Agenda for the Eighties

Appointed by President Carter in October 1979, the President's Commission for a National Agenda for the Eighties was created to advise the next president and a new Congress on a wide range of policy issues, including national urban policy. In what Orlebeke refers to as a "painful footnote" to the Carter urban policy record,[98] the report of the urban panel on metropolitan and nonmetropolitan America forcefully rejected the Carter administration's place-oriented urban policies that "bond the underclass to locations of limited opportunity."[99] "In the oversimplified terms of the 'people vs. places' debate, it was people who mattered."[100]

The President's Commission favored policies to promote national economic growth without regard to their impacts on distressed cities, and programs to help the disadvantaged wherever they reside. It urged the American people to be "skeptical of narrowly defined, local economic development efforts, which have been associated with the promise of restoring vitality to a wide variety of local communities as if each were a self-contained entity."[101] Concluding that "the principal role of the federal government should be to assist communities in adjusting to redistributional trends,"[102] the panel urged the next president to balance urban policies so that "people-to-jobs strategies, whether by retraining or relocation or both, . . . receive the same degree of emphasis that is now reserved for jobs-to-people strategies."[103] A more place-neutral urban policy would focus on "upgrading the unskilled through manpower development efforts so that existing local job opportunities can be exploited, by removing barriers to mobility that prevent people from migrating to locations of economic opportunity, and by providing migration assistance to those who wish and need it."[104]

The Reagan Urban Policy

By essentially adopting the Carter commission's proposals, the Reagan administration's 1982 urban policy report repudiated the Carter administration's policies that targeted federal assistance to distressed cities. While its National Economic Recovery Program—featuring "tax cuts, reductions in the rate of federal spending, regulatory relief, and monetary restraint to restore economic vitality to American industry and create jobs for workers"—was largely consistent with the recommendation of the President's Commission for a National Agenda for the Eighties, the Reagan administration ignored the commission's call for programs that would implement the necessary "people-to-jobs" strategies of such a place-neutral urban policy.[105]

The first Reagan urban policy report also proposed a new kind of federalism that would shift decision-making responsibilities for urban-oriented programs from the federal to the state governments. Under this new arrangement, more than thirty grant-in-aid programs would be folded into a new state-administered block grant.[106] In a related theme that was not picked up in subsequent reports, it argued that central-city fiscal problems were caused by "arbitrary boundaries and inadequate state and metropolitan fiscal equalization policies" rather than by federal cutbacks, and called for cities and suburbs to consider forming a metropolitan government or adopting some form of revenue sharing.[107]

Subsequent Reagan administration urban policy reports steadfastly held to the belief that "'a healthy economy . . . is our most powerful tool for revitalizing our cities and improving their fiscal positions.'"[108] However, while the 1984 report noted that "our cities and urban areas are, in general, reaping the benefits of the nation's economic turnaround,"[109] by 1988 the administration acknowledged that economic recovery would not be enough for certain cities with long-term structural problems. The 1988 urban policy report identified a litany of urban problems that had worsened even while the national economy was growing: (1) high unemployment and skill deficiencies among youth and the disadvantaged, (2) illiteracy and high dropout rates from public schools, (3) alarming numbers of teenage pregnancies, (4) a high incidence of single-parent households headed by poor women, (5) neighborhoods with high concentrations of the poor and disadvantaged, (6) housing programs that lock the needy into neighborhoods without jobs or access to jobs, and (7) inadequate provision for occupational or geographic mobility for workers displaced by rapid structural change.[110] The administration's major response to these problems was its controversial proposal to create a series of Enterprise Zones in distressed cities to stimulate private investment.

The 1988 urban policy report also identified the primary cause of severe urban distress, namely, "the proliferation of single-parent families, ineffective schools, and drug addiction and crime."[111] The report also expressed the administration's frustration with the fact that these problems seemed "to resist simple economic and fiscal success."[112] The report repeated the administration's previous calls for an Enterprise Zone legislation and recognized the need for other refinements in urban policy that emphasize "measures to reinforce family stability, especially among those with low incomes, and increase family options to obtain jobs and educational opportunities." [113]

The Bush Urban Policy

The 1990 national urban policy report strongly critiques the Johnson administration's war on poverty and claims that the "Bush administration is making the boldest, most comprehensive effort of the last quarter century to address the problem of long-term poverty, by expanding opportunity, jobs, and homeownership, and increasing the quality of education for low income Americans." [114] According to HUD secretary Jack Kemp, "One major defect of the first war on poverty was its failure to make proper and effective use of the incentives on which private enterprise relies to reward work and achievement." [115] In contrast the Bush administration's new war on poverty would empower residents of distressed communities by eliminating "governmental and nongovernmental barriers to opportunity in America—to expand choices for the poor so that they can make their own decisions and control their own lives." [116] Empowerment, according to the 1990 report, "is neither wasteful extravagance nor austerity, neither increasing government dependency nor laissez-faire abandonment of those in need. Instead, empowerment and opportunity require that government build incentives to work, save, and to create enterprise in its strategy of waging war on poverty." [117]

The Bush administration's new war on poverty, which Jack Kemp has also referred to as America's second civil rights revolution, contains nine program elements:

1. Expanded refundable tax credits for child care.
2. Capital gains tax cut.
3. Enterprise Zones.
4. Assistance to low income tenants of public housing to manage and eventually own their own homes.
5. Job training improvement proposals.
6. Encouragement of state and local innovations in the design of assistance programs to promote self-reliance and transition from dependency to self-support.
7. Government construction opportunities for unemployed workers through relaxed Davis-Bacon provisions.
8. Reduction of de facto discrimination in the housing market by examining the effects of local rent control and zoning regulations, and challenging them where necessary.
9. Reduction of unfair taxation of senior citizens who want to stay in the

work force through a modest liberalization of the Social Security earnings test; and tax relief for low-income families through increases in child credits and wage credits for low income workers in Enterprise Zones.[118]

The Clinton Urban Agenda

It is still too early to determine the parameters of the Clinton administration's national urban policy. Nevertheless, the Clinton/Gore vision for America contained in their campaign publication *Putting People First* previews an ambitious urban agenda. In founding its urban program on a national economic recovery—"To rebuild America's cities, the most important thing we can do is to implement a national economic strategy that pulls us out of the recession"[119]—the Clinton/Gore urban strategy sounds similar to the initial Reagan urban policy. Unlike Reagan, however, Clinton/Gore would combine stimulative antirecessionary investments with substantial federal initiatives designed to expand inner-city investment and job opportunities. Under a Clinton urban policy,

> The federal government should create conditions conducive to economic recovery through a national economic strategy, targeted incentives and grants designed to revitalize the urban economy, and measures that empower city residents to take advantage of newly created opportunities through expanded education, job training, and child-care services. In return for federal assistance, the cities will adopt comprehensive strategies leading to revitalized urban centers; take advantage of opportunities created by the federal/municipal partnership to attract business and expand the urban economic base; and play a key role in the empowerment of urban residents as the primary provider of education, housing, and crime prevention.[120]

To put Americans back to work while enhancing productivity and economic competitiveness, Clinton would target federal funding and local Community Development Block Grant[121] spending to rebuild roads, bridges, and water and sewer treatment plants and to build low-income housing.[122] He would embellish the Reagan Enterprise Zone initiative with additional incentives for companies who hire inner-city residents.[123] To restore the flow of credit to urban areas, Clinton recommends more aggressive enforcement of the Community Reinvestment Act, which requires financial institutions to invest in their inner-city communities, and more rigorous training of federal bank regulators that will enable them to identify redlining and other prohibited lending practices.[124] To stimulate small business start-ups, cultivate the entrepreneurial spirit, and revive inner-city economies, Clinton would create a network of community development banks, which are community-based depository institutions that provide affordable credit along with technical assistance to low-income businesses.[125]

The Clinton program also emphasizes human capital development and rewards individual initiative and family responsibility: "No matter how hard we work to make the federal/municipal partnership a success, we will make no progress unless individuals take responsibility for their own lives, working tirelessly to overcome challenges and solve problems in their families and communities."[126] *Putting People First* calls for an expansion of job training programs funded in part by employers who would be required to spend 1.5 percent of their payroll for continuing education and training of their workforces.[127] Recipients of large federal contracts also would be required to create a mentorship, after-school employment, or summer employment programs for urban and rural disadvantaged youth.[128] By significantly expanding the Head Start and Women, Infants and Children (WIC) programs and increasing the Earned Income Tax Credit to ensure that no families that work full time remain in poverty, the Clinton administration would invest heavily in America's children, with stricter education and training requirements on people receiving public assistance, so that welfare is "a second chance, not a way of life."[129] Finally, in what may be the most significant departure from previous administrations' urban agendas, the Clinton/Gore plan also embraces education and health care reforms, without which neither the economies nor the livability of cities can possibly be restored.

National Urban Policy: A Flawed Content or Concept?

If the Carter countercyclical urban policies can be criticized for their view that our older cities' "decline in economic competitiveness is temporary, and therefore to be combated with temporary economic stimulus,"[130] the Reagan macroeconomic urban policies can be faulted for ignoring the unique problems of our large cities altogether, mistakenly assuming that a rising tide would lift all boats. The Bush/Kemp urban policies changed that approach with strategies to strengthen inner-city communities. The aim was to empower the poor through a kind of "opportunity capitalism" featuring the ownership transfer of public housing and other asset-building initiatives. The potential effectiveness of these narrow place-based policies, however, is limited by the absence of any larger domestic investment strategy to improve either America's competitiveness or its cities.

After almost a quarter-century of biennial national urban policy reports, there has been little serious analysis of the impacts of the various policies and even less consideration of the policy process itself and how reports are prepared and their recommendations translated into action agendas. The limited literature on the subject, however, confirms the pessimistic view of a former high-ranking HUD official that "although urban policymaking and report-writing should not be equated, the irrelevance of the President's Report is a fitting metaphor for the state of explicit urban policy." [131] Orlebeke and others attribute the failures of past comprehensive national urban policies to five factors: (1) the intractable nature of urban problems, (2) organizational disarray at HUD, (3) the problems coordinating programs across federal agencies, (4) the limits of federal authority, and (5) the lack of sustained presidential leadership. Each of these issues is discussed briefly below.

The Nature of Urban Problems

Evidence abounds that our nation is paying a heavy price for "cramming the poor into constricted center cities while suburbia maintains its walls of segregation." [132] Nevertheless, nearly twenty-five years of national urban policy efforts lead us to conclude that "the inescapable reality of urban problems is that they don't easily lend or commend themselves to the political attractions of national action." [133] Notwithstanding the unpopularity of an urban agenda, Ylvisaker believes that urban problems are nationally pervasive, threatening, and consequential and thus compel us to action. He argues that the price we will pay for ignoring the problems of cities and the education and training needs of central-city youth—a generation too precious to waste—is a permanent loss of economic competitiveness. [134] President Clinton's newly appointed economic policy czar, Robert Rubin, shares this sentiment. He has stated that the urban underclass represents "an enormous albatross around the economy" because it imposes such high costs on the rest of society and represents a loss of human potential and productivity. [135] And, pointing out that there "are things the private sector won't do that need to get done" and that "government must play an active role," [136] Rubin would seem to support some kind of national urban policy.

Another conclusion we can draw from our experiences is that, quite apart from its technical soundness, an urban policy that targets a disproportionate share of federal resources to a limited number of distressed cities and their residents cannot be politically sustained. In a retrospective analysis of the failure of the Carter urban policy that he helped craft, James concludes that the geographic targeting of urban aid "had the effect of virtually eliminating support for urban policy from the southern and western regions, . . . [and that] programs targeted to the disadvantaged are highly vulnerable in political terms." [137] "Targeted programs are more likely to be strong politically when they serve low-income and moderate-income

working families as well as the very poor. They are also more likely to succeed when they are regarded as providing an earned benefit or are otherwise linked to work, when they are entitlement programs with federally
prescribed and funded benefits, when they seem effective, and when they
are not provided in the form of cash welfare assistance for young, able-
bodied people who do not work."[138] Analysis also suggests that "'if there
is one lesson we have learned from all the evaluations and research that
has been conducted since the War on Poverty began, it is that service programs that provide limited benefits to many people, although politically
popular, are not effective in responding to the problems of the most seriously disadvantaged.'"[139]

James's analysis of the Carter urban policy suggests that the political vulnerability of targeted programs not only confronts voter opposition but
also faces reluctance by local politicians to concentrate assistance on the
severely disadvantaged, hard-core poor.

> Efforts by the Carter administration to target CETA benefits to highly
> disadvantaged persons, though initially supported by the Congress, may
> ultimately have backfired by weakening city support for the program.
> Cities benefitted from loose targeting in the early years of the CETA pro-
> gram because it enabled them to use much of the resources from the pro-
> gram for fiscal relief. Tighter targeting precluded them from hiring the
> kinds of workers needed for many civil service positions. The erosion of
> city support was one factor contributing to the demise of the CETA pro-
> gram during the early years of the Reagan administration.[140]

Issues Internal to HUD

Urbanists, including academics who have served at HUD, believe that national urban policies have failed largely because of issues relating to the
structure, mission, and effectiveness of HUD, the government agency that
historically has taken the lead in urban policy development. Three types of
failings have been identified. First, from its inception in 1965, HUD was
not given control over federal responsibilities and resources of vital urban
significance. Excluded from HUD's portfolio, for example, were poverty,
environment, and transportation programs and even the housing programs
administered by the Department of Agriculture and the Veterans Administration.[141] Moreover, from the beginning, HUD has been required to
pursue the incompatible goals of housing and cities. According to two
architects of the 1978 Carter urban policy, "The more powerful side of
HUD—the housing side—legitimately is concerned primarily with housing production, housing market trends, and housing developments in suburbia; the urban policy side of HUD, generally is concerned with restrain-

ing decentralization trends and its perceived corollary suburban housing production."[142] Unable to agree on its own mission, "consistency concerning urban policy or programs at any one point in time has been more the exception than the rule [at HUD]."[143] Lacking a consistent philosophy, HUD has been largely unable to marshal support from other agencies in pursuit of national urban policy objectives.

Political scientist and former high-ranking HUD official Robert Wood has identified seven traditional measures of federal organizational effectiveness: (1) prestige in the eyes of the Washington power community, (2) the extent of intradepartmental competitive or complementary behavior, (3) the comparative power of clienteles, (4) the relative complexity of programs, (5) the clarity of legal jurisdiction over assigned program responsibilities, (6) the degree of expertise acknowledged in the department's work, and (7) the relative frequency of presidential and congressional intervention in program management, in the department's work.[144] Wood also concluded that "by nearly all of these standards, HUD fares badly."[145] HUD lacks prestige, is plagued by intra-agency feuding, and lacks legal jurisdiction over important city/suburban fiscal and land-use, civil rights, and other important issues.[146] HUD's lack of clout and prestige is summed up in the words of a former local official who went on to a position at HUD: "I used to think the Secretary of HUD was equivalent to a Cardinal, guaranteeing an invitation to the Pope. Big deal! When you get over to Washington, you realize that the Secretary of HUD is the low person on the totem pole. It's the least important Cabinet position and no one really cares what they think about anything. They don't participate in any of the inner Cabinet Committees."[147]

Finally, Anthony Downs attributes much of HUD's ineffectiveness to an "'iron law of political dispersion'" that results in many programs receiving money in such small allocations as to insure that national program goals cannot be met.[148] Downs does not blame HUD for all of its limitations because he believes that the agency is "an ineffective symbolic gesture of concern" that was designed to fail. "'He contends that it was never meant to succeed—instead, it was intended to show concern, alleviate some problems, but not to change the tide of urban problems or alter the direction of underlying economic and social forces.'"[149]

Interagency Coordination

From the beginning of the national urban policy process in the Nixon administration and extending through the Carter years, it was recognized that the breadth and scope of federal policies with urban implications spilled beyond HUD's walls, and that some interagency entity would have to be created to formulate and implement these policies. For multiple reasons, including interagency competition, the lack of sustained backing from the White House, and the fact that agencies are more responsive to their own "iron triangles"—comprised of congressional committees, constituent groups, and agency bureaucrats—than to a loosely organized, ad hoc interagency organization, none of these vehicles worked.

In the Nixon administration the institutional vehicle for formulating and implementing urban policies was the Council for Urban Affairs, which was composed of cabinet secretaries from eight domestic agencies. Daniel Patrick Moynihan, the president's counselor on urban affairs, was appointed executive secretary of the council. Charles Orlebeke, a former HUD official in the Ford administration and chronicler of the national urban policy process, writes "how the search for broad policy can be quickly overwhelmed by the pressures of ad hoc decisionmaking, the unavoidable complexity of the policymaking machinery, and the competition among executive agencies" [150] so that the coordinating mechanism cannot maintain a disciplined focus on urban concerns. He asserts that "the frustration associated with these forces was part of the reason the Nixon administration, in effect, gave up on national urban policy at midterm and shifted to advocating a radical restructuring of domestic programs along New Federalism lines." [151]

While he never had a chance to implement his urban policy, President Ford created a Cabinet Committee on Urban Development and Neighborhood Revitalization that was chaired by HUD secretary Carla Hills in 1977, whose mandate was to "develop an urban policy to guide the hoped-for second term." [152] Jimmy Carter's approach to the coordination issue was similar to Ford's. "Upon taking office, Carter formed a cabinet-level Urban and Regional Policy Group (URPG) to formulate an urban policy." However, according to Franklin James, a participant in the process, "neither the President nor the White House staff provided effective leadership for the effort." [153] As a result, "the URPG process quickly became dominated by agency competition for ad hoc proposals rather than by thoughtful consideration of problems or policy." [154]

Formal interagency coordinating mechanisms were absent in the Reagan and Bush administrations, for different reasons. In Reagan's case, national urban policy was defined as the administration's national economic recovery program (that is, there was no explicit urban policy). The Bush administration's narrow urban policy featuring the privatization of public housing could be implemented exclusively by HUD.

The Limits of Federal Authority

In addition to the above limitations, there is a limit to executive branch authority. The federal government does not always have a grip on the policy levers necessary to effectuate desired changes. Despite massive income differentials between cities and suburbs, and resulting fiscal capacities, the president cannot impose a metropolitan form of government on these entities or force them to create tax-base sharing systems. Nor can he direct suburban communities to eliminate all land-use control and regulatory barriers to the production of affordable housing in their metropolitan areas. While Congress has the power to redistribute income through the tax system to ameliorate central-city income deficits and can use carrots and sticks to encourage states and localities to "do the right thing," the political will to do so has been lacking.

For the above reasons the Carter urban policy, the most aggressive of all national efforts to deal with urban problems, failed, in part. According to James,

> The Carter urban policy committed the federal government to solving fiscal and economic problems of cities, despite the fact that *states* had the principal powers shaping these dimensions of the well-being of cities. . . . States have the land use planning and regulatory powers needed to control urban sprawl or to limit undesirable suburban or nonmetropolitan competition with cities. . . . [As a result] the implementation of the urban policy repeatedly placed the federal government in the non-win position of intervening in bailiwicks such as highway planning where states had more power and where states did not share federal goals. . . . The Carter urban policy was developed without significant state participation and was implemented largely independent of the states. In part, as a result, significant state actions in support of the policy were few and far between.[155]

Accepting the limitations above, the federal government can still act more aggressively to enforce existing civil rights laws, including fair housing, and see to the provision of affordable mortgage financing and access to commercial credit. The Clinton administration already has committed to act in these areas.

The Lack of Sustained Presidential Leadership

When all else fails, presidential leadership can often save the day. Aside from presidential pronouncements on the importance of cities, however, no national urban policy has received the kind of sustained presidential support that is required to assure its implementation. Indeed, to the extent that the literature deals with this subject at all, it is replete with references to presidential indifference at best and, at worst, outright hostility to the ends and means of their administrations' urban policies. For example, Nixon tried to constrain HUD's activities, and "when it became apparent that [HUD secretary] George Romney was successfully implementing the Democratic program contained in the Housing and Urban Development Act of 1968, [Nixon] replaced him with James Lynn, whose job was reputed to be to shut down HUD."[156] Arguing that the high costs of federal housing assistance threatened to mortgage the nation's future, Nixon imposed a moratorium on all federal low-income housing programs and impounded nearly $13 billion of HUD appropriations.[157]

President Ford paid relatively little attention to HUD's urban agenda during his limited tenure, while Jimmy Carter enlarged the agency's portfolio considerably by significantly expanding the Section 8 housing program. Carter's administration was the first to fulfill the congressional mandate for a comprehensive national urban policy report, but he is reported to have kept such a careful eye on HUD's activities that it evoked "formal secretarial protests."[158] And while Carter's urban policy and the "accompanying budget proposals added up to an impressive rhetorical commitment to address the economic and fiscal problems of older central cities," he "telegraphed his ambivalence when at the last moment before the policy's public release, he nearly withdrew large parts of the budget proposals."[159]

Ronald Reagan's mistaking his own HUD secretary for a mayor is a metaphor for his administration's eight years of indifference to urban problems. And although the Bush administration's urban policy was directed by the HUD secretary, not until the Los Angeles riots in April 1992 did the president actively promote Jack Kemp's public housing conversion and empowerment policies.

Two questions emerge from the above analysis. First, does the rather dismal record detailed above support the continuation of the president's biennial urban policy report? Second, assuming that an important national purpose is served by paying special attention to urban problems, what part of the executive branch should be responsible? With respect to the former, those who have studied the subject concur with Paul Ylvisaker's comment that "the question is not so much whether we have a national urban policy . . . ; it's basically the challenge whether as a nation we're going to struggle explicitly with the problems the urban agenda represents."[160] "What is needed," says Ylvisaker, "is a national commitment and a readiness to consider all sorts of national policies (tax, employment, industrial development, education, training, etc.) in terms of their impact on the special problems of central cities."[161]

In reflecting on this issue at the end of Reagan's second term, which they saw as disastrous for central cities, Kaplan and James argued that the political climate would not support an explicit urban agenda and that "the best way to help cities could well be to encourage those fostering national domestic policy reforms to factor in city concerns."[162] In a "grab what you can" urban strategy, they urged city advocates to "try their best to gain the best possible deal they can from the new nonurban policies and programs likely to evolve through the Bush administration and Congress."[163]

With the election of Bill Clinton on an investment-oriented platform of "putting people first" that features an explicit urban agenda, it would be a mistake to call for the elimination of the president's biennial urban policy report. However, Glickman, Kaplan, and James, among others, are right that the totality of nonurban federal policies and programs have, and will probably continue to have, greater impact on cities than do explicitly urban policies.[164]

Because the Clinton agenda for the cities has been broadly drawn to include education and health care policies in addition to the traditional urban concerns, the placement of responsibility for urban policy is especially crucial in this administration. Clearly, as in previous administrations, the biennial urban policy report needs to be drafted under the auspices of some kind of interagency task force. Also, if we are to take James's criticism of the Carter process seriously, to the extent that implementation of the president's urban agenda will require the active cooperation of other governmental levels, states and localities should be invited to participate in the policy formulation process.[165] The same goes for the community sector.

The Clinton Putting People First plan clearly views urban policy as a subset of an expansive, investment-oriented domestic policy. Therefore, the logical chair of the urban policy task force is the president's assistant for economic policy. This is a new position created by President Clinton "to coordinate economic matters the way the President's national security adviser oversees foreign affairs."[166] Only by assigning the urban policy responsibility to a senior White House official who has the ear of the president on a day-to-day basis can interagency coordination be maximized, and the principles of opportunity, community, and responsibility—the building blocks of Clinton's urban agenda—be put into practice in our nation's cities.[167]

Alternatives for a New National Urban Policy

There are essentially three concepts for designing the next generation of national urban policy that have a firm footing in Clinton's ambitious Putting People First campaign that, if implemented, could significantly improve urban conditions. The first, which I refer to as the *competitive city strategy*, emphasizes macrolevel investment policies in the physical and human capital required to improve America's competitiveness, while conceding the importance that cities play in today's knowledge-based economy. This strategy anticipates significant new federal spending of at least

$80 billion over the next four years.[168] The second approach, which I refer to as a *community development strategy*, decouples national urban policy considerations from macroeconomic policies, anticipates few new major federal spending initiatives to improve productivity, and concentrates on finding ways to improve the quality of life in depressed cities and neighborhoods within existing resource constraints. This approach recognizes the considerable housing and economic development successes that community-based organizations have enjoyed in inner cities across the country during the 1980s, and recommends policies to accelerate their progress during the 1990s. The third approach, a *blended urban policy strategy*, appreciates the continuing importance of cities in today's global economy, takes specific account of the spatial implications of macroeconomic policies and productivity-enhancing capital investments, and utilizes the strengths of the community sector to rebuild the physical and human capital of urban America.

The Competitive City Strategy

Emphasizing macroeconomic and fiscal policies to improve national economic performance, this Clinton national urban policy will reach further than the President's Commission for a National Agenda for the Eighties by formally recognizing the importance of cities in today's knowledge-based economy. This strategy would attempt to close the investment gap between America and its global competitors who, throughout the 1980s, "invest[ed] more than twelve times what we spend on roads, bridges, sewers, and the information networks and technologies of the future."[169] The prizes in this knowledge-based economy are "the headquarter functions and the related clusters of producer services that finance and serve them. They will locate in the places that can provide them with the kinds of labor forces, services, facilities, and amenities they need to function most effectively."[170]

A national urban policy that focuses on improving America's global competitiveness cannot ignore the people and places left behind. At least two elements of the Clinton domestic agenda are relevant here. The first is an ambitious defense conversion program that would "ensure that the communities and millions of talented workers that won the Cold War don't get left out in the cold."[171] Second, without an adequately trained labor force, economic growth will grind to a halt, and demographics suggest that by the turn of the century a substantial portion of all new entrants into the labor force will be nonwhite, non-native-born residents of major cities. Economic policies that ignore the plight of our central cities also ignore the monumental costs that such benign neglect implies for both the public and the private sectors. Hanson summarizes these quite well:

Alongside the underclass, feeding on it, and sucking resources from the mainstream, there is in every considerable city a flourishing underground economy. The traffic in drugs, vice, stolen property, illegal gambling, and other crime can safely be estimated to exceed almost any other single industry in any city. The costs to the public for operation of the criminal justice system, other public services and facilities, and revenues not collected on illegal transactions represent a major part of a city's budget. The costs to the private sector in security, insurance rates, losses in goods and productivity, and the opportunity costs of billions of dollars invested in criminal enterprises rather than in the mainstream economy are monumental. To these financial costs, we should add the cost of lost public confidence in institutions resulting from corruption of public officials, police, and private firms and labor organizations.[172]

The urban component of a national growth strategy would be anchored in campaigns to improve the quality of tomorrow's labor force. This means heavy emphasis on education reform at all levels, including fully funding Head Start and the WIC program, and promoting other programs "which help disadvantaged parents work with their children to *build an ethic of learning at home* that benefits both."[173] It could also include new initiatives for community college, vocational and technical training of non-college-bound young people, and a youth conservation corps or other enterprises to prepare inner-city youth for future employment in the private labor market. It would certainly include welfare reform, since welfare does not cure poverty and the current system contains serious work disincentives. Decent-paying job opportunities must be available for welfare recipients who are willing and able to work, and since those who work their way off welfare lose Medicaid benefits, welfare reform must be accompanied by health care reform.[174] This strategy would also upgrade the importance of a host of recently enacted, but poorly funded, family self-sufficiency programs that were built into the 1990 National Affordable Housing Act.[175] These programs seek to tie the receipt of federal housing assistance to the recipient's willingness to improve his or her education and employability. Thus far, however, Congress has failed to appropriate funds for the crucial services components of these self-sufficiency programs.

A competitive cities strategy also would require the federal government to eliminate barriers to mobility, both within metropolitan areas and across states. Mobility-enhancing programs range all the way from the federal government standardizing Aid to Families with Dependent Children benefits—that currently range for a family of three from 16 percent of the poverty level in Alabama to 75 percent of the poverty level in Connecticut—

and assuming their full costs, to a more aggressive enforcement of fair housing laws, and to the creation of programs that assist black and other minority inner-city families to move to the suburbs where the jobs are.[176]

A Community Development Strategy

An alternative approach to national urban policy would examine ways to strengthen communities and improve life opportunities for poor and minority families in the worst sections of cities regardless of macroeconomic policies and the state of the national economy. This approach would take the position that, while national policies that succeed in fostering high rates of economic growth are better than those that do not, experience shows that the fruits of economic growth do not automatically benefit distressed cities, neighborhoods, or the poor. Moreover, ghetto communities have become poorer, more racially concentrated, and more isolated than they were a decade ago when policy analysts debated whether national urban policies should emphasize so-called ghetto enrichment or integration strategies.[177] In practical terms, the time for such a strategy may already have passed. For these reasons, even if the Congress were to emphasize deficit reduction over national investment to a much greater degree than Clinton preferred, Clinton's administration should still consider pursuing a national urban policy that works to improve the quality of life in poor communities, regardless of the specifics of national economic policies. This approach requires a community-development-based national urban policy.

I use the term *community development* to refer to "efforts to improve the overall quality of life in a low-income neighborhood through such initiatives as housing renovation, refurbishing of streets and public places, upgrading of public services, promotion of community identity and pride, job training and social services for community residents, and political advocacy."[178] This is consistent with the Clinton/Gore intent that "community groups and local citizen organizations will be the backbone of our urban improvement efforts."[179] A community-development-oriented national urban policy would give formal recognition to the growing network of nonprofit, community-based organizations that have worked tirelessly to improve the quality of life in depressed cities and sections of cities since the 1960s, and especially through the Reagan-era cutbacks in domestic programs. In the pre-Reagan days of the 1970s, it is estimated that fewer than 250 community-based nonprofit organizations were involved in development activities. By the late 1980s a national survey estimated the number of such entities to be in the range of 1,500 to 2,000.[180] According to one source, community-based organizations have built nearly 125,000 units of housing, most of it for low-income families; developed 16.4 million square feet of retail space, offices, industrial parks, and other industrial developments in economically distressed communities where for-profit developers would not venture; and accounted for the creation and retention of close to 90,000 jobs.[181]

This approach to national urban policy argues that when community-based institutions determine how to spend the billions of dollars of existing federal resources for housing, community development, economic development, and social welfare and participate in programs designed to help traditional social welfare agencies become more committed to "bottoms up" planning and program delivery, there would be significant positive impacts on the quality of life in distressed communities. One example is targeting the $2 billion a year in public housing modernization funds that Congress already appropriates to local public housing authorities to train inner-city youth in the construction trades. Another example would be to use federal laws such as the Community Reinvestment Act[182] and the Home Mortgage Disclosure Act[183] to stimulate a continual flow of financial capital into minority and other distressed communities, and to create a network of local community development banks in inner-city areas to support small business enterprise, microlending programs, and other initiatives. The administration's proposal to create a city assistance flexibility program to allow cities to redirect the use of 15 percent of the federal assistance they receive to meet their own community priorities and fund their local revitalization strategies would further strengthen a community-development-oriented national urban policy.

In short, the Clinton administration should propose such a policy direction in the absence of new multi-billion-dollar initiatives to improve our national economic performance. Without such capital-intensive policies, the most direct means of affecting positive change in depressed, resource-poor communities would be through expanding and strengthening the network of already existing indigenous, community-based organizations that "have the political and technical skills and the tenacity needed to pull together a complex array of resources needed to get projects done."[184] This approach is premised on the belief that "solutions to the economic and social problems of minority and low-income communities in the United States will continue to elude us as long as we ignore the reality that those who are experiencing the problems have little or no voice in designing solutions to those problems."[185]

Having argued for a community-development-oriented urban policy, there are two complementary approaches that the Clinton administration should pursue. The first would strengthen and expand the kinds of mainstream community-based development organizations that have partnered with traditional public agencies and the private business community to create housing and economic development projects. The second approach would support the nascent concept of opportunity capitalism in the inner city that is being promoted by former HUD secretary Jack Kemp and organizations such as the National Center for Neighborhood Enterprise. This concept emphasizes community self-help, homeownership, and asset accumulation, including resident management and ownership of public housing, entrepreneurialism, and the creation of economic opportunities that are largely independent of traditional social service agencies and government institutions, the mainstream economy, and traditional business institutions. Although it has been argued that no community or neighborhood is an independent entity, by emphasizing the creation and ownership of businesses by local residents to service their community, this approach to community development comes closest to endorsing that concept of community independence.

A Blended Strategy

A blended approach to national urban policy, and the approach I prefer, would recognize two links: those that exist between major national investment initiatives to improve America's competitiveness and their impacts on cities, and those between macro-investment policies and their implementation at the community level. In addition to being sensitive to the spatial impacts of national policies, a blended approach would emphasize the importance of the community sector in the design and implementation of local plans and projects to implement any large-scale national investment strategy. In practical terms, because the scale of national investment initiatives are likely to be modest, a blended approach would disproportionately emphasize the importance of the community sector in improving the quality of life in distressed communities. It would permit the administration to examine the potential benefits of extending the public/private partnership model—which it endorsed in 1982 as a means of reaching consensus on community goals, agreement on institutional roles, and sustained support for civic action—to accelerate the reform of traditional housing and social service agencies and programs to promote community revitalization, family development, and economic self-sufficiency.

Under a blended strategy, the Clinton administration would tackle what Hanson refers to as one of the greatest political challenges to the next generation of urban policymakers: "The invention of politically acceptable means of strategic targeting of available resources rather than allowing them to become subject to the iron law of political dispersion, which gives wealthy cities resources they do not need to support development that would likely occur without policy inducements and provides inadequate resources to those places least able to help themselves." [186]

To conclude, the worsening problems of our cities are both cause and consequence of our declining position in the world economy. In order to reverse that decline, we must revitalize our cities and their people. A coherent national urban policy is a necessary component of a larger domestic strategy of "Putting People First."

Although we have once again witnessed in South Central Los Angeles the explosive effects of the conditions that "'breed despair and violence . . . : ignorance, discrimination, slums, poverty, disease, not enough jobs'"[187]— the same deadly mix that ignited Watts, Hough, the Central Ward, and other inner cities more than twenty-five years ago—we are reminded of Lyndon Johnson's appeal to the higher moral purpose of our people. In his address to the nation on the riots of the 1960s, he argued that we should be motivated to action "'not because we are frightened by conflict, but because we are fired by conscience. We should attack them because there is simply no other way to achieve a decent and orderly society in America.'"[188]

Notes

This piece was originally published in a special edition of the *North Carolina Law Review*. Subsequent to that edition's publication and prior to the preparation of this volume, Mr. Stegman was appointed assistant secretary for policy and planning development at the U.S. Department of Housing and Urban Development. Due to the constraints imposed by his new role, Stegman's article is presented as it was originally published.

1. Neal R. Peirce, *Citistates: American Metropolises in the New World Economy* (Washington, D.C.: Seven Locks Press, 1993), 6.

2. "In 1950, cities accounted for 32.8 percent of the nation's population; suburbs, 23.3 percent. By 1960, cities still [had] a small margin over the suburbs, 32.8 percent to 30.9 percent. By 1970, the suburbs (37.6 percent) had surpassed the cities (31.4 percent). By 1980, cities had 30 percent, compared with 44.8 percent for suburbs. By 1990, the cities had 31.3 percent, while suburbs had 46.1 percent" (Raymond L. Flynn, *Rebuilding America's Cities Together* [Boston: Office of the Mayor, 1992], 26 [draft]).

3. Marshall Kaplan and Franklin James, "Urban Policy in the Nineties and Beyond: The Need for New Approaches," in *The Future of National Urban Policy*, ed. Marshall Kaplan and Franklin James (Durham, N.C.: Duke University Press, 1990), 351.

4. Peirce, *Citistates*, 6.

5. Ibid.

6. Just prior to 1965 over one-half of all immigrants entering the United States were Europeans, and over 30 percent were from North America. Relatively small percentages were from Asia, Africa, and Latin America. By the 1980s 46 percent of

the immigrants were from Asia as opposed to just 11 percent from Europe. Moreover, while the percentage from North America remained relatively unchanged, immigrants from this continent were much more likely to come from the Caribbean, Mexico, and Central America, compared with the 1950s, when Mexicans and Canadians predominated (New York Department of City Planning, *The Newest New Yorkers: An Analysis of Immigration into New York City during the 1980s* [New York: Department of City Planning, 1992], 1).

7. The report took an expansive view of the immigrant population: "Not only was the currently illegal [alien] included, but also the U.S. born children of those illegals (who are thus American citizens), those illegals granted amnesty under the 1986 immigration law, and the legal immigrants to the area since 1980. The four groups together accounted for about 25 percent of Los Angeles county's population in fiscal 1992" (Tim W. Ferguson, "California Feels Anti-Immigrant Tremors," *Wall Street Journal*, December 29, 1992).

The report found that this immigrant amalgam cost the county government $947 million in services for which it was not reimbursed by fees or subventions— or about 31 percent of that year's total county tab. Yet it was estimated (and this is more contentious arithmetic than the expense side of the ledger) that the same group accounted for only 10 percent of the county tax revenue (ibid.).

8. John D. Kasarda, "Urban Change and Ghetto Revitalization" (congressional testimony of John D. Kasarda, director of the Kenan Institute of Private Enterprise, University of North Carolina at Chapel Hill, May 27, 1992), 3.

9. Gene Marlowe, "Tale of Two Cities," *Atlanta Journal and Constitution*, December 12, 1992.

10. Ibid.

11. Flynn, *Rebuilding America's Cities*, 1.

12. The city's plight has been described thus:

[Hartford] must carry the baggage of poverty: crime, drugs, welfare dependency, teenage pregnancy, hunger and broken families. Hartford has the highest number of welfare recipients of any city or town in the state. . . . Teen pregnancy shackles city youngsters to the welfare system. . . . The city has so many halfway houses, group homes and social service agencies that some streets threaten to become social service malls. . . . Crime continues to suck the life out of the city. . . . Neighborhoods that drew middle-class homesteaders in the 1970s are losing them now because of crime, taxes and schools. . . . The public schools, more racially segregated than some in South Africa, are a disaster[, and t]he four-year dropout rate in the high schools is more than 50 percent. . . . City government is beset by bureaucratic inefficiency and expensive union contracts. (Peirce, *Citistates*, 21 [quoting Tom Condon, *Hartford Courant*, March 17–24, 1991])

13. See, for example, John D. Kasarda, "The Severely Distressed in Economically Transforming Cities," in *Drugs, Crime, and Social Isolation: Barriers to Urban Opportunity*, ed. Adele V. Harrell and George E. Peterson (Washington, D.C.: Urban Institute Press, 1992), 45, 65–82.

14. In 1959 only 27 percent of the poor resided in metropolitan central cities. By 1985 the central cities housed over half of the nation's population living in census tracts with high concentrations of poverty, up from just one-third in 1972. During the 1959–85 period the proportion of poor blacks living in central cities rose from 38 percent to 61 percent (ibid., 46).

15. Peirce, *Citistates*, 5.

16. Ibid., 4–5.

17. Linda Chavez, "The New Polemics of Race," *City Journal*, Summer 1992, 12 (reviewing Andrew Hacker, *Two Nations: Black and White, Separate, Hostile, Unequal* [New York: Scribner's, 1992]).

18. U.S. Senate Committee on Banking, Housing, and Urban Affairs, *The Plight of African-American Men in Urban America*, 102d Cong., 1st sess., 1991, p. 263 (hereafter cited as *Hearings*) (statement of Robert L. Woodson, president, National Center for Neighborhood Enterprise).

19. Ibid.

20. "Between 1979 and 1987, the proportion of white families with two or more wage-earners rose from 57 percent to 59 percent. But for black families, the change was in the opposite direction, from 50 percent in 1979 down to 46 percent in 1987" (Bennett Harrison and Lucy Gorham, "What Happened to African-American Wages in the 1980s?," in *The Metropolis in Black and White: Place, Power, and Polarization*, ed. George C. Galster and Edward W. Hill [New Brunswick, N.J.: Rutgers Center for Urban Policy Research, 1992], 56, 58).

21. Between 1979 and 1987, "whites, as a whole, suffered a decline in the number of high-wage workers over this period of under 1 percent, while among blacks there were actually 7 percent fewer high-wage workers in 1987 than in 1979" (ibid., 61).

22. Ibid., 57.

23. Joel Garreau, "Candidates Take Note: It's a Mall World after All," *Washington Post*, weekly ed., August 10–16, 1992.

24. Similarly, about 39 percent of all Hispanic households lived in suburbs in 1989 (F. John Devaney, *U.S. Bureau of the Census, Current Housing Reports, Series H123191–1, Housing in America: 1989/90* [Washington, D.C.: U.S. Government Printing Office, 1992], 10).

25. In the Cleveland metropolitan area an overwhelming percentage of all black suburbanites live in just one community, East Cleveland, which suggests that locational choices for blacks who have managed to move out of Cleveland's ghetto continue to be restricted in the suburbs. From 1960 to 1970, for example, East Cleveland's population went from 2 to 51 percent black (Norman Krumholz, "The Kerner Commission Twenty Years Later," in Galster and Hill, *Metropolis in Black and White*, 19, 25).

26. In 1960 the per capita income of cities was 5 percent greater than their surrounding suburbs. In 1980 per capita income of cities was 89 percent of that for the surrounding suburbs. By 1989 the ratio had fallen to 84 percent. In some metropolitan areas the economic disparities between city and suburbs are particularly acute. Newark's per capita income was only 43.1 percent of its suburbs; in Paterson, N.J., it was 46.6 percent; in Cleveland, 53.4 percent; in Hartford, 53.6 percent;

in Detroit, 53.6 percent; in Milwaukee, 62.9 percent; in Gary, Ind., 63.4 percent; in Baltimore, 64.3 percent; in Philadelphia, 65.4 percent; in Dayton, 66 percent; in Chicago, 66.3 percent; in Miami, 67.2 percent; and in New York, 67.6 percent (Flynn, *Rebuilding America's Cities*, 26).

27. "The experience of the 30 large cities surveyed over the period 1971–1984 shows that in the aggregate the governments (excluding New York) had an excess of revenues, as compared with expenditures, in 9 of those years and a deficiency of revenues in 5 of them" (Philip M. Dearborn, "Fiscal Conditions in Large American Cities, 1971–1984," in *Urban Change and Poverty*, ed. Michael G. H. McGeary and Laurence E. Lynn Jr. [Washington, D.C.: National Academy Press, 1988], 255, 266).

28. Roy W. Bahl, "States and the Financial Condition of Cities," in *Proceedings of the Eighty-Second Annual Conference, National Tax Association-Tax Institute of America*, ed. Frederick D. Stocker (Columbus, Ohio: National Tax Association, 1990), 81, 82.

29. The average actual fiscal health of cities with populations below 100,000 is 20 percentage points above the 1982 average, whereas the average fiscal health of the largest cities is 43 percentage points below the average (Helen F. Ladd and John Yinger, *America's Ailing Cities: Fiscal Health and the Design of Urban Policy* [Baltimore: Johns Hopkins University Press, 1989], 198).

30. Bahl, *Proceedings of the National Tax Association Conference*, 82.

31. The cities' predicament can be summarized in the following terms:

In 1959, local governments financed 28 cents of every dollar of expenditures from state and federal aid, whereas in 1975 the share was 43 cents and in 1978 it was 46 cents. The large urban aid programs—which went directly to cities—were an even more important story. For example, federal aid to cities as a percent of total revenues raised from own sources were as high as 70 percent in Cleveland, Buffalo and Detroit in 1978. This explains why local governments remained in a growth mode during much of the mid to late 1970s. The continuous increase in intergovernmental aid contributed to the attitude of local officials that external finances would pick up part of any shortfall due to recession. . . .

The fiscal restructuring of local governments began after the recession. Real levels of per capita spending, taxes and debt continued to rise between 1975 and 1978, but the line was held on state and local government employment levels and employee compensation. . . . The real cuts, however, started after 1978 when two important events occurred. Proposition 13 and 2-1/2 signaled the "official" unwillingness of voters to go along with further tax increases, and the election of Ronald Reagan in 1980 underlined this. The decline in federal aid to state and local governments began in 1978. (Roy W. Bahl, Jorge Martinez-Vasquez, and David L. Sjoquist, *Local Governments and the Current Recession* [1991], 14–15)

32. Bahl, *Proceedings of the National Tax Association Conference*, 82. For cities under a million, federal government revenues as a percent of government municipal revenue declined from 14.3 percent in 1979–80 to 4.8 percent in 1989–90 (Flynn, *Rebuilding America's Cities*, 21).

33. Michael A. Pagano, *City Fiscal Conditions in 1992: A Research Report of the National League of Cities* (Washington, D.C.: National League of Cities, 1992), vi.

34. Ibid., v. According to Pagano 73.4 percent of surveyed cities reduced the rate at which their operating spending increased; 71.5 percent raised taxes and fees or imposed new ones; 61.2 percent reduced their capital spending; 44.2 percent froze municipal hiring; 39.5 percent reduced their work forces; and 14 percent reduced service levels (ibid.).

35. "For example, New York cut revenue sharing by $343 million, including a 25 percent cut for New York City. Georgia cut aid to cities by at least $40 million. Governor Jim Edgar of Illinois proposed that the state keep the $237 million share of a temporary income tax surcharge that was to go to municipalities, but was overturned by the House. Boston lost $85 million in state aid during 1989–1991" (Roy W. Bahl, Jorge Martinez-Vasquez, and David L. Sjoquist, "City Finances and the National Economy," *Publius: The Journal of Federalism*, Summer 1992, 49, 61).

36. Kasarda, "Severely Distressed," 23.

37. Flynn, *Rebuilding America's Cities*, 16.

38. Ibid.

39. Ibid.

40. *Hearings*, 24 (statement of Douglas L. Wilder, Governor, Commonwealth of Virginia).

41. Flynn, *Rebuilding America's Cities*, 18. Nationally the "death rate from homicide . . . for Black males ages 25 to 34 is almost 5 times as high as for Black females . . . , 7.4 times as high as for white males . . . , and 24 times as high as the rate for white females" (Twenty-first Century Commission on African-American Males, "From Consternation to Conservation: Towards a National Policy for the Preservation of Black Males," reprinted in *Hearings*, 8 [submitted to the record by Senator Sanford]).

42. Urban Institute, "Confronting the Nation's Urban Crisis: From Watts (1965) to South Central Los Angeles (1992)" (Washington, D.C., 1992, mimeographed), 46 (prepared statement of Dr. Billy E. Jones, Commissioner, New York Mental Health). Also, while only 28 percent of the total population of New York City are black, one-third of the admissions to inpatient psychiatric units of municipal hospitals in New York City are black, as are 68 percent of the city's single, homeless, mentally ill population (ibid.).

43. Ibid., 3.

44. Felicity Barringer, "New Census Data Reveal Redistribution of Poverty," *New York Times*, May 29, 1992.

45. Forty-one percent of poor households were in central cities, and 29 percent were in nonmetropolitan areas (Devaney, *Housing in America*, 12).

46. Flynn, *Rebuilding America's Cities*, 23.

47. In 1985, for example, 54.6 percent of all families with a poverty-level income lived in central-city poverty areas that the Census Bureau defined as census tracts where 20 percent or more of the residents lived below the poverty line. The 1985 poverty rate among central-city blacks was 32.1 percent, compared with 14.9 percent among whites; in census tract poverty areas it was 41.2 percent and 34.2

percent, respectively, for blacks and whites (McGeary and Lynn, *Urban Change and Poverty*, 16).

48. Martha R. Burt, *Over the Edge: The Growth of Homelessness in the 1980s* (New York: Russell Sage, 1992), 3.

49. Homes for the Homeless, Inc., *The New Poverty: A Generation of Homeless Families* (1992), 1.

50. Ibid., 2.

51. Ibid., 3.

52. David Wood, R. Burciaga Valdez, Toshi Hayashi, and Albert Shen, "Homeless and Housed Families in Los Angeles: A Study Comparing Demographic, Economic, and Family Function Characteristics," *American Journal of Public Health* 80 (1990): 1049, 1050.

53. Ibid.

54. See n. 12, above, and accompanying text.

55. Urban Institute, "Confronting the Nation's Urban Crisis," 3.

56. Ibid.

57. Ibid., 13.

58. Twenty-first Century Commission, *From Consternation to Conservation*, 8.

59. Urban Institute, "Confronting the Nation's Urban Crisis," 8 (emphasis added).

60. In 1987 17.1 percent of whites with four or more years of college still worked under the poverty line. Among blacks the comparable proportion was 20 percent (Harrison and Gorham, "What Happened to African-American Wages?," 66). Just over one in eight African American college graduates was earning as much as $35,000 a year in 1987, while white college graduates with equivalent years of schooling were twice as likely to be paid that amount (26.1 percent versus 13.1 percent) (ibid.).

61. National Commission on Severely Distressed Public Housing, *Partnership in Crime Prevention, Final Summary* (Washington, D.C.: The Commission, 1992), 5.

62. "In 1988, . . . 372 people were murdered in [Washington, D.C., a] city of slightly fewer than 600,000 people. That was a record. So was the 1989 figure of 434. And the 1990 number of 483. And 1991's 489. So far this year, murders are off 10 percent from last year, but Washington still has the highest per capita murder rate in the country. . . . More people per capita are arrested in Washington[, D.C.,] than anywhere else, followed by South Africa" (Felicity Barringer, "Washington's Departing Police Chief Laments the Sleep of Murderers," *New York Times*, September 20, 1992). Violent crime rates are also very high in other large cities. For example, Miami and Atlanta each averaged more than four crimes against persons per 1,000 population in 1990, compared with a national average of less than one (John P. Vitella, *Security, Crime, and Drugs in Public Housing: A Review of Programs and Expenditures* [Washington, D.C.: Council of Large Public Housing Authorities, 1992], 35–36).

63. Francis X. Clines, "Ex-Inmates Urge Return to Areas of Crime to Help," *New York Times*, December 23, 1992.

64. Vitella, *Security, Crime, and Drugs in Public Housing*, 2.

65. *Hearings*, 62–63 (testimony of Samuel L. Myers Jr.).

66. Urban Institute, "Confronting the Nations's Urban Crisis," 3.

67. Ibid., 3–4.

68. *Hearings*, 12. In 1987 49.1 black males per 1,000 persons were victims of violence compared with 31.5 black females, 35 white males, and 20.1 white females. For younger black males these rates were even higher. Nearly 91 crimes of violence per 1,000 persons were committed against black males between 12 and 15 years of age. The rate for 16- to 19-year-old black males was even higher, 101 per 1,000 persons. In 1988 51.5 percent of all murders and homicides of black males were committed by other black males (ibid.).

69. Ibid., 13.

70. Ibid.

71. Urban Institute, "Confronting the Nation's Urban Crisis," 3.

72. At the same time, however, the scale of the underclass problem should not be overstated. According to the General Accounting Office,

> regardless of how they define the term, most experts agree that the urban underclass comprises a relatively small percentage of the population. . . . Size estimates range from less than 2 million, based on the able-bodied persistently poor in urban areas, to 5.6 million, based upon census tracts with high poverty concentrations. The number of residents in census tracts with high concentrations of families headed by women, school dropouts, welfare dependents, and jobless men is 2.5 million. The highest estimate of the U.S. urban underclass accounts for 13 percent of the nation's poverty population and 3 percent of its total population. (General Accounting Office, *The Urban Underclass: Disturbing Problems Demanding Attention* [Washington, D.C.: U.S. General Accounting Office, 1990], 6)

73. Cornel West, "L.A. Riots Spawned by Spiritual Poverty, Justifiable Rage," *New York Times*, August 2, 1992.

74. National Housing Law Project, Inc., "Racial Discrimination, Poverty, and Housing Policies: A Call for Justice in Los Angeles and Nationwide," *Housing Law Bulletin* 22 (1992): 45–48 (notes omitted).

75. Charles J. Orlebeke, "Chasing Urban Policy: A Critical Retrospect," in Kaplan and James, *Future of National Urban Policy*, 185, 189.

76. Ibid., 186.

77. Mary K. Nenno, "Urban Policy Revisited: Issues Resurface with a New Urgency," *Journal of Planning Literature* 3 (1988): 253.

78. Ibid., 254.

79. Pub. L. No. 91-609, 84 Stat. 1791 (1970).

80. Orlebeke, "Chasing Urban Policy," 189.

81. According to Orlebeke, "The rough arithmetic of the most enthusiastic new communities proponents went as follows: 'If we allocate one-half of the coming 100 million people to existing peripheral growth around existing cities and 10 percent to small towns and farms, the remaining 40 million would require the building of 20 cities of one million people each and 200 new towns of 100,000 each.'

More modestly, the National Committee on Urban Growth Policy, in making its own recommendations, simply sliced the goal in half to ten big new cities and one hundred smaller ones" (ibid. [quoting William E. Finley, "A Fresh Start," in *The New City* (New York: Praeger, 1969)]).

82. According to Franklin James,

1970 represented a watershed in U.S. patterns of population growth. Before that year, population migration was from rural areas to metropolitan areas, contributing to the congestion problems identified by the [C]ongress. Following 1970, a mounting number of people left the cities and suburbs for nonmetropolitan areas—as part of a process of demographic and economic decline that accelerated as the 1970s progressed. This shift was unanticipated and rendered the 1970 urban policy obsolete overnight. . . . Between 1970 and 1980, twenty of the fifty-six largest US cities experienced population declines of more than 10 percent. By contrast, only six US cities had such declines during the previous decade. (Franklin J. James, "President Carter's Comprehensive National Urban Policy: Achievements and Lessons Learned," *Environment and Planning C: Government and Policy* 8 [1990]: 29, 30–31)

83. Orlebeke, "Chasing Urban Policy," 197.

84. Ibid.

85. Pub. L. No. 95-128, 91 Stat. 1143–44 (1977).

86. Ibid., 1143.

87. Specifically, 42 U.S.C. § 4502(d) (1988) declares that the national urban policy should

(1) favor patterns of urbanization and economic development and stabilization which offer a range of alternative locations and encourage the wise and balanced use of physical and human resources in metropolitan and urban regions as well as in smaller urban places that have a potential for accelerated growth;

(2) foster the continued economic strength of all parts of the United States, including central cities, suburbs, smaller communities, local neighborhoods and rural areas;

(3) encourage patterns of development and redevelopment which minimize disparities among States, regions and cities;

(4) treat comprehensively the problems of poverty and employment (including the erosion of tax bases, and the need for better community services and job opportunities) which are associated with disorderly urbanization and rural decline;

(5) develop means to encourage good housing for all Americans without regard to race or creed;

(6) refine the role of the Federal Government in revitalizing existing communities and encouraging planned, large-scale urban and new community development;

(7) strengthen the capacity of general governmental institutions to contribute to balanced urban growth and stabilization; and

(8) facilitate increased coordination in the administration of Federal programs to encourage desirable patterns of urban development and redevelopment, encourage the prudent use of energy and other natural resources, and protect the physical environment.

88. James, "Carter's Comprehensive National Urban Policy," 31.

89. Ibid. (quoting President Carter).

90. Ibid., 32.

91. U.S. Department of Housing and Urban Development, *A New Partnership to Conserve America's Communities: A National Urban Policy: The President's Urban and Regional Policy Group Report* (Washington, D.C.: U.S. Department of Housing and Urban Development, 1978), P1–P2.

92. Ibid., P5–P6.

93. U.S. Department of Housing and Urban Development, *The President's National Urban Policy Report, Executive Summary* (Washington, D.C.: U.S. Department of Housing and Urban Development, 1980), 1.

94. James, "Carter's Comprehensive National Urban Policy," 33.

95. U.S. Department of Housing and Urban Development, *Executive Summary*, 4.

96. Ibid.

97. Orlebeke, "Chasing Urban Policy," 198.

98. Ibid.

99. John D. Kasarda, introduction to *Urban America in the Eighties: Perspectives and Prospects*, ed. Donald A. Hicks (Englewood Cliffs, N.J.: Prentice-Hall, 1982), vii.

100. Orlebeke, "Chasing Urban Policy," 198.

101. Hicks, *Urban America in the Eighties*, 5.

102. Ibid.

103. Ibid.

104. Ibid.

105. U.S. Department of Housing and Urban Development, *The President's National Urban Policy Report* (Washington, D.C.: U.S. Department of Housing and Urban Development, 1982), 3–4.

106. Potomac Institute, *Metropolitan Housing Memorandum 82-2* (Washington, D.C.: Potomac Metropolitan Housing Program, 1982), 1.

107. Ibid.

108. Congressional Research Service, *The President's National Urban Policy Report: A Critique* (Washington, D.C.: The Service, 1984), 2.

109. U.S. Department of Housing and Urban Development, *The President's National Urban Policy Report* (Washington, D.C.: U.S. Department of Housing and Urban Development, 1984) (transmittal letter).

110. U.S. Department of Housing and Urban Development, *The President's National Urban Policy Report* (Washington, D.C.: U.S. Department of Housing and Urban Development, 1988), 1.

111. Ibid.

112. Ibid.

113. Ibid.

114. U.S. Department of Housing and Urban Development, *The President's National Urban Policy Report* (Washington, D.C.: U.S. Department of Housing and Urban Development, 1990), 1-1.

115. Ibid.

116. Ibid.

117. Ibid., 1-2.

118. Ibid., 1-1.

119. Bill Clinton and Al Gore, *Putting People First: How We Can All Change America* (New York: Times Books, 1992), 52.

120. Ibid., 54.

121. Pub. L. No. 93-383, 88 Stat. 653 (1974).

122. Clinton and Gore, *Putting People First*, 55.

123. Ibid.

124. Ibid., 114; see 12 U.S.C. § 2901 (1988); see also Marion A. Cowell Jr. and Monty D. Hagler, "The Community Reinvestment Act in the Decade of Bank Consolidation," *Wake Forest Law Review* 27 (1992): 83, 87–94, 97–100 (discussing the development of the act and the need for strengthened enforcement).

125. Clinton and Gore, *Putting People First*, 55.

126. Ibid., 54.

127. Ibid., 56.

128. Ibid.

129. Ibid.

130. Urban Institute, "Confronting the Nation's Urban Crisis," 7.

131. Orlebeke, "Chasing Urban Policy," 185.

132. Peirce, *Citistates*, 22.

133. Paul Ylvisaker, "Eliciting an Effective and Necessary Policy Response," in Kaplan and James, *Future of National Urban Policy*, 346.

134. Ibid., 348.

135. Steven Mufson, "A Wall Street Whiz Takes a Gamble," *Washington Post*, weekly ed., December 21–27, 1992 (quoting Robert Rubin, Chairman of the White House National Economic Council).

136. Ibid.

137. James, "Carter's Comprehensive National Urban Policy," 35.

138. Christopher Jencks and Paul E. Peterson, eds., *The Urban Underclass* (Washington, D.C.: Brookings Institution, 1991), 438.

139. Ibid., 457 (quoting Isabel Sawhill).

140. James, "Carter's Comprehensive National Urban Policy," 35.

141. Robert Wood and Beverly M. Klimkowsky, "HUD in the Nineties: Doubtability and Do-ability," in Kaplan and James, *Future of National Urban Policy*, 254.

142. Kaplan and James, *Future of National Urban Policy*, 358–59.

143. Ibid., 358.

144. Wood and Klimkowsky, "HUD in the Nineties," 257.

145. Ibid.

146. Ibid., 256.

147. Ibid., 255 (quoting a former HUD assistant secretary of planning and community development during the Carter administration).

148. Ibid., 266 (quoting Anthony Downs).

149. Ibid. (citing Anthony Downs).

150. Orlebeke, "Chasing Urban Policy," 191.

151. Ibid.

152. Ibid., 197.

153. James, "Carter's Comprehensive National Urban Policy," 31.

154. Ibid., 32.

155. Ibid., 35.

156. Wood and Klimkowsky, "HUD in the Nineties," 264.

157. Ibid.

158. Ibid.

159. Orlebeke, "Chasing Urban Policy," 198.

160. Ylvisaker, "Eliciting an Effective and Necessary Policy Response," 348.

161. Ibid., 348–49.

162. Kaplan and James, "Urban Policy in the Nineties and Beyond," 356.

163. Ibid.

164. Norman J. Glickman, "Economic Policy and the Cities: In Search of Reagan's *Real* Urban Policy" (Lyndon B. Johnson School of Public Affairs Working Paper no. 26, 1984), 2; Kaplan and James, "Urban Policy in the Nineties and Beyond," 356.

165. James, "Carter's Comprehensive National Urban Policy," 34.

166. Mufson, "Wall Street Whiz Takes a Gamble," 12.

167. Clinton and Gore, *Putting People First*, 53–54.

168. Ibid., 144.

169. Ibid., 143.

170. Royce Hanson, *Urbanization and Development in the United States: The Policy Issues* (Washington, D.C.: The Congress, 1986), 22.

171. Clinton and Gore, *Putting People First*, 144.

172. Hanson, *Urbanization and Development in the United States*, 11–12.

173. Clinton and Gore, *Putting People First*, 60.

174. Laurie McGinley, "Clinton Faces Daunting Task in Turning Welfare Rhetoric into a Coherent Policy," *Wall Street Journal*, December 29, 1992.

175. 42 U.S.C. § 12701 (Supp. 1990) (originally enacted as Cranston-Gonzalez National Affordable Housing Act, Pub. L. No. 101-625, 104 Stat. 4079 [1990]).

176. See James E. Rosenbaum and Susan J. Popkin, "Black Pioneers: Do Their Moves to the Suburbs Increase Economic Opportunity for Mothers and Children?," *Housing Policy Debate* 2 (1991): 1179, 1183–91.

177. Anthony Downs, "Alternative Futures for the American Ghetto," *Appraisal Journal* 36 (October 1968): 486, 498–501.

178. Marc Bendick Jr. and Mary Lou Egan, *Business Development in the Inner-City: Enterprise with Community Links* (New York: Community Development Research Center, 1991), 1–2.

179. Clinton and Gore, *Putting People First*, 54.

180. National Congress for Community Economic Development, *Against All Odds: The Achievements of Community-Based Development Organizations* (Washington, D.C.: The Congress, 1989), 3.

181. Ibid., 1–2.

182. 12 U.S.C. § 2901 (1988).

183. 12 U.S.C. § 2801 (1988).

184. National Congress for Community Economic Development, *Against All Odds*, 4.

185. Robert L. Woodson, "Forward," in *Revitalizing Our Cities: New Approaches to Solving Urban Problems*, ed. Mark Libsitz (Washington, D.C.: Fund for an American Renaissance and the National Center for Neighborhood Enterprise, 1986), xix.

186. Hanson, *Urbanization and Development in the United States*, 24.

187. Lyndon B. Johnson, Address to the Nation (July 27, 1967), quoted in National Housing Law Project, "Racial Discrimination, Poverty, and Housing Policies," 45.

188. Ibid.

Part Three

Residential Mobility

Effects on Education, Employment, and Racial Integration

James E. Rosenbaum
Nancy Fishman
Alison Brett
Patricia Meaden

Can the Kerner Commission's Housing Strategy Improve Employment, Education, and Social Integration for Low-Income Blacks?

The Kerner Commission placed a heavy emphasis on racial integration, calling it "the only course which explicitly seeks to achieve a single nation rather than accepting the present movement toward a dual society."[1] And, as the introductory essay to this volume indicates, "only in the area of housing did the commission prescribe solutions tailored to address the urban/suburban racial segregation central to its analysis of the underlying problem."[2] Calling for the elimination of "the racial barrier in housing," the commission stated, "Residential segregation prevents equal access to employment opportunities and obstructs efforts to achieve integrated education. A single society cannot be achieved so long as this cornerstone of segregation stands."[3]

But were these hopes for integration, expressed twenty-five years ago, actually workable? Were they attainable? Does residential integration lead to employment gains, educational gains, and social integration? Given the persistence of de facto racial segregation in this country, our ability to address these questions and assess the Kerner Commission's aspirations for this strategy has been limited. In this essay, we attempt to overcome this limitation by examining evidence from ten years of research on a program that in many ways embodies the approach advocated by the commission: Chicago's Gautreaux Program. Gautreaux gives low-income blacks housing vouchers to move to many different kinds of communities including white middle-income suburbs and low-income black city neighborhoods. This essay reports the program's impact on the employment of participating adults and on the education, employment, and social integration of their children.

The Kerner Commission's Premises

In conducting its study of cities where civil disorder had broken out, the Kerner Commission found "widespread discontent with housing conditions and costs. In nearly every disorder city surveyed, grievances related to housing were important factors in the structure of Negro discontent."[4] Recommending that 6 million new low- and middle-income housing units be made available over the next five years, the Kerner Commission stated, "If the effort is not to be counter-productive, its main thrust must be in nonghetto areas, particularly those outside the central city."[5] Part of this wariness stemmed from the commission's belief that "future jobs are being created primarily in the suburbs."[6] This assumption has been borne out since the commission's report was issued. In recent decades large numbers of employers have left the central cities and relocated in the suburbs.[7] For example, between 1975 and 1978 2,380 firms in Chicago, Illinois, moved from the city to its suburban ring.[8] More recently, Cook County experienced a 1.5 percent decline in jobs over the 1980–88 period, while the surrounding counties gained from 7.6 percent to 59.5 percent.[9] "Chicago's share of metropolitan employment is also forecast to decline from 38.4 percent in 1986 to 32.8 percent in 1995. . . . This . . . pattern represents a serious labor market barrier for inner-city residents, especially those with minimal education and work skills."[10]

In spite of the stronger job market in the suburbs, low-income blacks have not followed jobs to the suburbs. Because of housing discrimination, housing costs, and personal preferences, low-skilled workers have not been leaving the cities as fast as low-skilled jobs have.[11] Long commutes between home and work impede employment for low-income blacks, who, because of existing patterns of residential segregation, are largely constrained to central cities.[12] This fact may also reduce the effectiveness of job training programs, most of which have only modest success at improving employment for low-income people, perhaps because job training cannot help people become employed if the employers have moved away.[13]

The commission's assertion that a failure to build new housing accessible to low-income blacks outside the central cities would be "counter-productive" seems to stem also from the commission's belief that "racial and social-class integration is the most effective way of improving the education of ghetto children."[14] That analysis has been supported empirically. A nationwide study found that blacks in predominantly black schools achieve at lower levels than blacks in integrated schools, and that socioeconomic segregation has similar effects.[15] Studies also indicate that desegregation has positive effects on black achievement.[16]

The Gautreaux Program

The Gautreaux Program is the result of a 1976 Supreme Court decision in a lawsuit against the Department of Housing and Urban Development (HUD) on behalf of public housing residents.[17] The suit charged "that these agencies had employed racially discriminatory policies in the administration of the Chicago low-rent public housing program."[18] Administered by the non-profit Leadership Council for Metropolitan Open Communities in Chicago, the Gautreaux Program allows public housing residents and those who had been on the waiting list for public housing as of 1981 to receive Section 8 housing certificates and move to private apartments either in mostly white suburbs or in the city of Chicago.[19] The agency finds landlords willing to participate in the program, notifies families as apartments become available, and counsels them about the advantages and disadvantages of the move; counselors accompany them to visit the units and communities. Since 1976 over 4,500 families have participated, and over half have moved to middle-income, predominantly white suburbs.

Because of its design, the Gautreaux Program presents a singular opportunity to test the effect of helping low-income people move to areas with better labor markets, better schools, and better neighborhoods. Racial and economic homogeneity remains the rule in most neighborhoods in the United States. It can be argued that those who break the residential barriers of race and class are themselves exceptional people, so their subsequent attainments may reflect more about themselves than about the effects of neighborhoods. Thus, when researchers study black employment in suburbs, they must assess whether the suburbs facilitated black employment or whether the blacks who happen to live in suburbs are different, perhaps moving to the suburbs after getting a job.[20] Similarly, most studies of black achievement in suburban schools cannot determine whether black children's achievement is due to the suburban environment or to some unmeasured family assets or values that may have drawn their families to the suburbs.

The Gautreaux Program circumvents racial and economic barriers to living in the suburbs. The program offers rent subsidies permitting participants to live in suburban apartments for the same cost to them as public housing. Moreover, unlike the usual case of black suburbanization— working-class blacks living in working-class suburbs—Gautreaux gives low-income blacks access to middle-income white suburbs.[21] Participants move to a wide variety of over 100 suburbs throughout the six counties surrounding Chicago. Predominantly black suburbs were excluded because of the desegregation goals, and very-high-rent suburbs were excluded by funding limitations of Section 8 certificates.

The program tries to avoid overcrowding, late rent payments, and building damage by not admitting families with more than four children, large debts, or unacceptable housekeeping.[22] But these criteria are only slightly selective, and all three only reduce the eligible pool by less than 30 percent.[23] Most participating families are very low income, are current or former welfare recipients, and have lived most of their lives in impoverished inner-city neighborhoods.

In any case, the program's procedures create a quasi-experimental design. While all participants come from the same low-income black city neighborhoods (usually public housing projects), some move to middle-income white suburbs, while others move to low-income black urban neighborhoods. In theory, participants have choices about where they move, but in practice, participants are assigned to city or suburban locations in a quasi-random manner. Apartment availability is determined by housing agents who do not deal with clients; counselors offer units as they become available according to the clients' position on the waiting list, not according to their locational preference. Although clients can refuse an offer, very few do because they are unlikely to be offered another in the six months that they are eligible. As a result, participants' preferences for city or suburbs have little to do with where they later move.

Suburban Obstacles: Four Questions

Despite the superior economic and educational opportunities in the suburbs, there may be obstacles to participants benefiting from these opportunities. Virtually all the mothers in Gautreaux have received public aid (most for five years or more), many have never had a job, and half grew up in families on public aid. They may lack the skills, motivation, or work experience necessary to obtain work. Moreover, they may face racial discrimination in the suburban labor market. Similarly, the children lack the home advantages of their suburban classmates, and their city schools may not have prepared them for the more demanding suburban schools. We must wonder if they will be able to compensate for these disadvantages. We must also wonder whether these low-income black youths face rejection and harassment or whether they interact with and receive support from their middle-income white classmates. The following sections explain in detail the questions that this paper will explore.

Will Low-Income Blacks Get Jobs in the Suburbs?

There are a number of reasons to expect that low-income blacks may not find jobs in the suburbs. After living in low-income environments for many years, these adults and children may have motivational problems that prevent them from doing well even after their opportunities improve. Some scholars contend that the primary problem of the urban underclass is a lack of motivation and social obligation among ghetto residents. In the 1960s much debate centered around Oscar Lewis's theory of the "culture of poverty."[24] Lewis argued that low-income children are socialized into a value system that reduces their motivation to succeed in the labor market: "By the time slum children are age six or seven, they have usually absorbed the basic values and attitudes of their subculture and are not psychologically geared to take full advantage of changing conditions or increased opportunities that may occur in their lifetime."[25] A variation of this view argues that current welfare policy encourages low-income people to feel no obligation to contribute to the larger society.[26]

Even those who subscribe to a structural, as opposed to cultural, approach to poverty might foresee employment difficulties for Gautreaux participants. Factors such as inadequate education due to the poor quality of Chicago ghetto schools, lack of skills and experience because of the diminished job market in the inner city, and racial bias among white suburban employers, individually or (more likely) in combination, might pose insurmountable obstacles to black job seekers in the suburbs.

Will Early Disadvantages Keep Children from Benefiting from Suburban Schools?

In the case of children's academic achievement, two conflicting outcomes seem possible. Low-income black youths might be permanently disadvantaged in the suburban schools, for various reasons: their economic backgrounds may make them less prepared or less motivated than middle-income suburban youths, they may have attitudes and habits deemed "undesirable" by suburban teachers and employers, or racial discrimination may deny them full access to suburban resources. For any or all of these reasons, the transplanted black youths may achieve at lower levels in the suburbs than, for instance, their city Gautreaux counterparts who do not face these barriers. Previous research has shown that school desegregation does not always have positive effects on black student achievement,[27] and it sometimes has negative effects.[28] In addition, suburban Gautreaux children face the added burden of having moved from familiar surroundings to a very different environment.

A contrary prediction is that instead of being hindered by these disadvantages, children who move to the suburbs will benefit from better educational resources and greater employment prospects, and that their fellow suburban students may serve as positive role models for achievement. Some research has found that school desegregation may have a beneficial influence on blacks' achievement.[29] Of course, we do not know which of these processes will operate or, if both do, which will dominate.

Will Harassment and Discrimination
Accompany Residential Integration?

Although large numbers of young, affluent blacks moved out of central
cities and into surrounding suburbs during the 1970s, blacks remained significantly more isolated in those suburbs than either Hispanics or Asians.[30]
Research also documents extensive antagonism to racial integration. While
the majority of whites have become increasingly supportive of racial integration in principle, they nevertheless remain opposed to any government
intervention to promote such integration.[31] Blacks moving into predominantly white areas have faced threats, physical attacks, and property damage.[32] A small-scale private effort to move black families from Chicago
housing projects to Valparaiso, Indiana, in the late 1960s was generally unsuccessful. The families encountered organized resistance from the town
government as well as verbal harassment and violence.[33] While some families stayed despite the hardship, most moved back to the city.[34] Throughout the past several decades, many black families who moved into white
neighborhoods of Chicago were driven from their homes by racial violence.[35] These incidents of harassment, while dramatic, may not reflect the
views of all residents, and other neighbors may welcome black newcomers.
This essay examines the harassment, threats, and fears that blacks face in
predominantly white schools as a racial and socioeconomic minority.

Will Residential Integration Lead to Social Integration?

Given the daily headlines about troubled race relations in American society, social integration may seem to be hopeless. But daily life is too mun-
dane to make the headlines, and daily life may tell a very different story.
This study looks at whether the black Gautreaux youths experience acceptance, establish friendships, and interact positively with white classmates,
and it assesses the relative frequency of positive and negative interactions.

The impact of school desegregation has been studied extensively.[36] Because blacks rarely live near whites, however, many of the school desegregation programs studied have entailed special busing efforts, and a busload
of students entering a white community may create high visibility for the
program, leading to backlash and stigma against participants. In addition,
the long periods of time children spend every day riding together on a bus
may reinforce a feeling of group separateness from those who live near the
school. Moreover, the logistics of commuting make after-school activities
difficult. Thus, busing as a method of desegregating creates its own limits
on racial interaction.

In contrast, this study examines a program that is distinctive because it
creates both residential and school integration. In the Gautreaux Program,
low-income black families receive housing subsidies allowing them to

move into private apartment buildings occupied largely by middle-income whites and located in middle-income, mostly white suburbs. As a result, children arrive in the suburban schools as community residents, not as outsiders in a busing program, and they come to school in the same buses as their white neighbors. Moreover, this program accomplishes residential integration with low visibility, reducing the likelihood of backlash and stigma.

Youths in this program, however, must face an additional barrier: socioeconomic differences. While researchers do not know much about social integration across racial groups, we know even less about social integration across socioeconomic groups. The participants in this program come from very-low-income families and face two kinds of barriers simultaneously—racial and socioeconomic. These low-income blacks enter schools and communities that are overwhelmingly white and middle-class. Students who have spent over six years in all-black urban housing projects, for example, may have different habits and tastes and have fewer economic resources than their classmates. Even the other black students they meet are different because their families are middle class. Given these barriers, observers have worried that youths in such a program would remain socially isolated.[37]

The Studies

Methods and Sample

The remainder of this essay summarizes studies of the Gautreaux Program, comparing participating families moving to white middle-income suburbs with participating families moving to low-income black city neighborhoods. These "city movers" are a strong comparison group for judging the effects of the suburban move because both groups meet the same selection criteria and receive better housing, varying significantly only on the destination of their moves. Thus we can have more confidence in attributing any observed effects to those destinations than we would through comparing suburban movers, for instance, with a group of Chicago housing project residents whose lives had not undergone any comparable systematic change. The effects of moving to the suburbs, judged in comparison to moving within the city, are, if anything, underestimated through this stringent comparison.

To examine adults' employment, we surveyed 332 women and conducted detailed interviews with another 95 women.[38] The first study of children interviewed one randomly selected school-age child (age eight to eighteen) from each of 114 families in 1982, as well as their mothers. The second study followed up the same children (and mothers) in 1989, when they were adolescents and young adults, and examined their educational and employment outcomes.[39] In both studies our adult respondents have been women because a large majority of our sample group—92 percent in the adult employment study and 87 percent in the mother and child study—were female-headed households with no male present. There were not enough men available in the sample for analysis.

Study of Adult Employment

The results of our study showed that those persons transplanted to the suburbs were more likely to be employed than city movers. Although both groups started from the same baseline, after moving the new suburbanites were at least 25 percent more likely to have had a job than city movers: while 50.9 percent of city movers had a job after moving, 63.8 percent of suburban movers did. Table 1 compares the pre- and post-move employment status of the city and suburban movers. Among respondents who were employed at some point before their moves, suburban movers were about 14 percent more likely than city movers to have a job after moving. In contrast, for those who had never been employed before their move, 46 percent found work after moving to the suburbs, while the figure for those in the city was only 30 percent. For this group of "hard-core unemployed," those who ended up in the suburbs were much more likely to have a job after moving than were the city movers.[40]

City and suburban movers did not differ in hourly wages or number of hours worked per week. Among those who had a job both before and after moving, both city and suburban movers reported gains in hourly wages and no change in hours worked.[41]

When asked how the suburban move helped them get jobs, all suburban participants mentioned the greater number of available jobs in the suburbs. Improved physical safety was the second most mentioned factor. Adults reported that they did not work in the city because they feared being attacked on their way home, or that their children would get hurt or get in trouble with gangs. The suburban move allowed mothers the freedom to go out and work. Many adults also mentioned that positive role models and social norms inspired them to work. This comment supports Wilson's contention about the importance of role models and social norms.[42] Upon seeing neighbors who worked, Gautreaux adults reported that they felt that they too could have jobs, and they wanted to try. In the city, adults had few such positive role models in their neighborhoods.

In sum, the employment rates of suburban movers surpassed those of city movers, particularly for those who had never had a job. The causes of unemployment in the past—lack of skills or lack of motivation—were not

Table 1. Percentage of Respondents Employed Post-Move as Compared with Pre-Move Employment, for City and Suburban Movers

	City		Suburb	
	group number	%	group number	%
Those employed pre-move and employed post-move	65	64.6	144	73.6
Those unemployed pre-move but employed post-move	43	30.2	80	46.2
Total employed post-move	108	50.9	224	63.8[a]

[a] Indicates Chi-square significant at the 0.05 level.

irreversible, and many held jobs after moving to suburbs. The Gautreaux Program apparently helped close the gap between low-income black adults and their white middle-income neighbors.

The Study of Children

Recognizing the Gautreaux children's initial poor preparation in city schools and their social disadvantages, we wondered how they would fare in suburban schools. In 1982 we studied how the Gautreaux Program affected children, comparing Gautreaux children who moved within the city with those who moved to the suburbs.[43] The two groups were similar in average age, proportion of female children to male children, and mothers' education. The families typically were headed by females in both the suburban and city groups.[44]

We found that suburban movers initially had difficulties adapting to the higher expectations in the suburban schools, and their grades suffered in their first years there. However, by the time of our study, after one to six years in the suburbs their grades and relative school performance were the same as those of city movers (according to their mothers' reports). In addition, compared to city movers, suburban movers had smaller classes, higher satisfaction with teachers and courses, and better attitudes about school. Although the mothers noted instances of teacher racial bias, the suburban movers were also more likely than city movers to say that teachers went out of their way to help their children, and to mention many instances of teachers giving extra help in classes and after school.

It is hard to measure academic success or improvement, and the first study had no systematic indicator. Yet the suburban movers clearly felt that the suburban schools had higher academic standards. They reported that the city teachers did not expect children to make up work when they were absent, to do homework, to know multiplication in third grade, or to write in cursive in fourth grade. "Passing grades" in the city did not indicate achievement at grade level, and even "honor roll" city students were sometimes two years behind grade level.

The Gautreaux mothers were in a good position to notice the changes in their children when they moved from the city to suburban schools. One mother commented, "[The suburban school] said it was like he didn't even go to school in Chicago for three years, that's how far behind he was. And he was going every day and he was getting report cards telling me he was doing fine."[45] Indeed, another mother related her own empirical test: "The move affected my child's education for the better. I even tested it out. . . . [I] let her go to summer school by my mother's house [in Chicago] for about a month . . . [and] she was in fourth grade at that time. . . . Over in the city they were doing third grade work; what they were supposed to be doing was fourth grade."[46] The city curriculum apparently was one to three years behind that of the suburban schools.[47]

While many suburban movers seemed to be catching up to the higher suburban standards by the time of the interviews, most had only been in the suburbs a few years and were still in elementary school, so it was hard to know how successful they later would be. Therefore, we were eager to do a follow-up study to see how things were turning out for these children.

The Follow-up Study of Youth

To document some of the Gautreaux Program's longitudinal results, we interviewed the children and their mothers in 1989.[48] By this time the children had achieved an average age of eighteen. To understand their responses, it is first necessary to understand a little about the schools that the youths attended. In 1990 the Illinois Department of Education collected average standardized test scores for all schools in the state. For the schools attended by the children in our sample, the suburban schools' average eleventh-grade reading test score (259) was just above the state average (250) but significantly higher than the city schools' average (198). Suburban schools' scores (21.5) on the ACT (the college admissions test most often taken in Illinois) were close to the state average (20.9) but significantly higher than the city schools' scores (16.1). Moreover, there was almost no overlap between the scores of city and suburban schools these children attended. While less than 6 percent of the city sample attended schools with ACT averages of 20 or better (that is, roughly the national average), over 80 percent of the suburban sample attended such schools. Just as the 1982 study suggested higher standards in suburban elementary

Table 2. Youths' Education and Job Outcomes,
City-Suburban Comparison

	City (%)	Suburb (%)
Drop out of school	20	5
College track	24	40
Attend college	21	54
Attend four-year college	4	27
Employed full-time (if not in college)	41	75
Pay under $3.50/hour	43	9
Pay over $6.50/hour	5	21
Job benefits	23	55

schools, these results indicate that the higher standards in the suburbs continued in high school.

Of course, higher standards create new challenges as well as new opportunities. The suburban movers must face much higher expectations than they had been prepared for in the city schools. The higher levels of achievement in suburban schools may be a barrier to students moving from city schools where they had been poorly prepared, and this may lead to a higher dropout rate, lower grades, lower tracks for those still in school, less college attendance, and less employment for those over age eighteen. The results of this study, shown in Table 2, contradict those expectations.

Dropping Out and School Grades

Although test scores were not available for individual respondents, grades provide a good indication of how students are achieving in the judgment of their teachers and relative to their peers. We found that suburban movers had virtually the same grades as city movers.[49] Since the national High School and Beyond (HSB) survey of high school sophomores indicates that suburban students get about a half-grade lower than city students with the same achievement test scores, the grade parity of the two samples implies a higher achievement level for suburban movers.[50]

In addition, more city movers (20 percent) dropped out of high school than did suburban movers (5 percent).

College Preparatory Curricula

Most high schools offer different curricula, through tracking systems, to college-bound and non-college-bound youth, and these different curricula can affect college opportunities.[51] Researchers find that blacks are underrepresented in the college tracks in racially integrated schools.[52] Indeed, after being desegregated, the Washington, D.C., public schools initiated a tracking system, which a federal district court subsequently ruled was undercutting integration.[53] Given the higher standards and greater competition in suburban schools, we might expect suburban movers to be less likely than city movers to be in college-track classes. The results showed the opposite. Suburban movers were more often in college tracks than city movers.[54]

College Attendance

Higher suburban standards might be expected to be a barrier to the Gautreaux youths' attending college. The results indicate the opposite. Suburban movers had significantly higher college enrollment than city movers.[55]

Four-year Colleges

The type of college is important. Four-year colleges lead to a bachelor's degree, two-year junior or community colleges lead to an associate's degree, and trade schools lead to a certificate. Moreover, while transfers to four-year colleges are theoretically possible, in fact trade schools almost never lead to four-year colleges, and two-year colleges rarely do. Only 12.5 percent of students in the Chicago city colleges, which are two-year programs, ultimately earn a four-year college degree—less than half the rate of some suburban community colleges in the area.[56]

Among the Gautreaux youth attending college, almost 50 percent of the suburban movers were in four-year institutions, whereas only 20 percent of the city movers were. Of those not attending four-year institutions, two-thirds of the suburban movers were working toward an associate's degree, while just half of the city movers were.

Clearly, the suburban students have not suffered from the challenging competition in the suburbs. Indeed, they have benefited from the higher academic standards found there.

Youths' Employment

For youths who were not attending college, a significantly higher proportion of those in the suburban area had full-time jobs than did their city counterparts.[57] Suburban youth also were four times as likely to earn over $6.50 an hour than were city youths.[58] In addition, the suburban jobs were significantly more likely to offer job benefits than city jobs.[59]

Youths' Social Integration

Suburban movers had increased opportunity for interacting with whites because there were many more whites in their schools than in the city schools. But that did not guarantee that interaction would take place or that the experience would not be problematic.

We expected that the suburban youths would experience more harassment than the city movers. The most common form of harassment was name-calling. In the suburbs, 51.9 percent of the Gautreaux youth reported at least one incident in which they were called names by white students, while only 13.3 percent of the city movers experienced name-calling by whites. This might be explained in part by the fact that there are simply fewer white students in the urban schools. Interestingly, however, 41.9 percent of the city movers experienced name-calling by other black students. As hypothesized, city movers do receive significantly less harassment than suburban movers; however, the city movers did also experience a great deal of verbal harassment.

A second, more severe form of harassment was measured by asking respondents how often they were threatened by other students. As expected, many suburban movers were threatened by whites: 15.4 percent of the suburban movers reported being threatened by whites a few times a year or more. However, 19.4 percent of city movers were threatened as frequently by blacks. Moreover, when we consider those who were threatened at least once a year (by blacks or whites), city movers are as likely to receive a threat as suburban movers.[60]

A third and serious form of harassment experienced by study youths was actual physical violence. When asked how often they were injured by other students at school, very few members of either group reported such incidents. A similar proportion of both city and suburban movers said they had never been hurt by other students.[61] In sum, the expected difference is not confirmed: suburban movers are not more likely than city movers to be threatened or hurt by others at school.

Social Acceptance

The second aspect of social integration we studied was whether youths moving to suburbs experience less social acceptance at school and develop fewer friendships than the city movers. Several questions in the interview were designed to discern how the children viewed themselves in the social context of the school and how they felt peers regarded them. Both city and suburban movers tended to agree somewhat with the statement, "I feel I am a real part of my school," and there were no statistically significant differences between the groups.[62] To the statement, "Other students treat me with respect," the suburban movers had more positive responses than the city movers, although the difference was not significant.[63] We asked the children how they believed others viewed them in a series of questions, including, "Are you considered a part of the 'in-group'?" "Do others think you do not fit in?" "Do others see you as popular?" and "Do others see you as socially active?" For each of these queries, no significant differences were found between city and suburban movers.[64] Both groups showed positive social integration for all questions. Contrary to our expectations, the suburban movers felt just as accepted by their peers as the city movers. The majority of the children in both groups felt that they fit into their schools socially and that they were regarded by others as at least somewhat socially active and popular.

We also expected that the suburban movers actually might have fewer friends than city movers. Given that the suburbs were overwhelmingly white, the suburban movers came in contact with fewer black peers than did city movers. Suburban movers, however, had almost as many black friends as did city movers. The mean number of black friends in the suburbs was 8.81, while the mean number of black friends in the city was 11.06, a statistically insignificant difference.

The suburban movers had significantly more white friends than did city movers. The mean number of white friends was 7.37 for suburban movers and 2.37 for city movers.[65] While only 17.3 percent of the suburban youths reported no white friends, 56.3 percent of the city sample did.[66] Only one of the city movers and one of the suburban movers reported having no friends at all.

Suburban Gautreaux youths spent significantly more time with white students outside class than did the city movers, as documented in Table 3a. Compared with city movers, the suburban movers more often did things outside school with white students, did homework with white students, and visited the homes of white students. When asked how friendly white students were, the suburban movers again were much more positive than the city movers.

When the same questions were asked about socializing with black students, no significant differences existed between city and suburban movers, as documented in Table 3b.

To get an overview, two index variables were computed based on the summed responses to each of the three items for interactions with whites and for interactions with blacks. The findings, set out in Table 4, suggest that the suburban movers divided their time almost equally between blacks and whites, while the city movers spent significantly more of their time with blacks than with whites. The experience of the suburban movers seems to reflect a more racially integrated peer network, despite the small numbers of blacks in suburban schools.

Are Harassment and Acceptance Inversely Related?

Our results indicate that negative behaviors are associated with each other: white name-calling correlates strongly with white threats. Positive behaviors also are correlated with each other: doing activities with whites is associated with visiting with whites in their homes.

Table 3a. Frequency of Activities Involving White Students,
by Percentage

How often do white students do things with you outside school?

Code	Suburb ($n = 52$)	City ($n = 30$)
Almost every day	44.2	6.7
About once a week	13.5	16.7
About once a month	1.9	16.7
A few times a year	23.1	10.0
Never	17.3	50.0
$t = 3.65$; $p < .001$		

How often do white students do schoolwork with you?

Code	Suburb ($n = 52$)	City ($n = 30$)
Almost every day	40.4	23.3
About once a week	21.1	16.7
About once a month	21.2	13.3
A few times a year	9.6	0.0
Never	7.7	46.7
$t = 2.92$; $p < .005$		

How often do white students visit your home or have you to
their home?

Code	Suburb ($n = 52$)	City ($n = 29$)
Almost every day	28.8	6.9
About once a week	25.0	10.3
About once a month	7.7	13.8
A few times a year	19.2	17.2
Never	19.2	51.7
$t = 3.75$; $p < .0001$		

We found, however, that negative behaviors do not predict an absence of
positive behaviors. In fact, the experiences of the suburban movers indicate that the two are not usually associated, and they are sometimes positively correlated. Suburban Gautreaux students who report being threatened by whites are slightly (but not significantly) more likely to participate
in school activities,[67] do activities with whites after school,[68] or visit with
whites in their homes.[69] Those reporting being called names by whites
are also slightly more likely to participate in activities with whites after
school[70] and to visit with whites in their homes.[71]
While these correlations are not statistically significant, they are sub-

Table 3b. Frequency of Activities Involving Black Students,
by Percentage

How often do black students do things with you outside school?

Code	Suburb ($n = 52$)	City ($n = 31$)
Almost every day	59.6	54.8
About once a week	19.2	32.3
About once a month	5.8	6.5
A few times a year	11.5	6.5
Never	3.8	–

$t = .70$ (statistically insignificant)

How often do black students do schoolwork with you?

Code	Suburb ($n = 52$)	City ($n = 31$)
Almost every day	46.2	64.5
About once a week	25.0	16.1
About once a month	7.7	9.7
A few times a year	11.5	–
Never	9.6	9.7

$t = 1.34$ (statistically insignificant)

How often do black students visit your home or have you to
their home?

Code	Suburb ($n = 52$)	City ($n = 31$)
Almost every day	50.0	25.8
About once a week	25.0	45.2
About once a month	3.8	22.6
A few times a year	15.4	3.2
Never	5.8	3.2

$t = 0.43$ (statistically insignificant)

stantively very important. They indicate that many of the same individuals
who are being threatened and harassed by whites are also being accepted
by whites, interacting with whites, going to each others' homes, and participating in school activities. That does not make the threats and name-
calling pleasant, but it does make it easier for these youths to feel as though
they are a part of these white suburban schools.

The statements of mothers and youths help us understand how these
youths handled the racial harassment they faced in the suburbs. Many
seemed to take harassment in stride as a minor annoyance that they ig-

Table 4. Comparisons of Index Variables Measuring Time Spent with
Black Friends vs. Time Spent with White Friends

	Suburb ($n = 60$)		City ($n = 38$)	
	mean	(std dev)	mean	(std dev)
Time with black friends	12.02	(3.09)	12.45	(2.17)
Time with white friends	10.41	(3.64)	6.89	(3.48)
	t = 3.05; p < .003		t = 9.04; p < .000	

nored.[72] Other suburban movers felt that the racial problems were likely to
exist anywhere or discounted the name-calling because they discounted
the people who were doing it.[73] Some youths said that the advantages of
living in the suburbs far outweighed the disadvantages. Although mothers
were unhappy that their children were being harassed in the suburbs, they
felt these incidents were relatively unimportant compared with the fear,
crime, and violence that had limited their lives in the inner city.[74] Both the
youths and their mothers felt they had overcome many of the problems
they faced in the suburbs with patience and endurance.[75]

In sum, although these Gautreaux youths experienced some harassment
and some difficulty gaining acceptance in the suburban schools, overall
they experienced great success in social integration. Despite some initial
difficulties, suburban movers have active social lives and feel they fit into
their new environments.

Individual Cases

Statistics provide the best indications of the program's effects, but statistics
cannot convey the personal experiences of the individuals involved. Indeed, in that respect, statistics can be misleading, for they can make the
process seem simpler and more mechanical than it is, and they can gloss
over people's struggles. It is a mistake to infer that educational and social
gains come easily and without great sacrifice. The very notion of "program
effects" conjures up an image of a simple causal process, like the push that
sets a pendulum in motion. But human actions are never so simply caused,
and holding onto a simple program-effects notion can, in fact, have serious
consequences. Participants and observers who expect this program to have
quick results and little pain would be greatly disappointed.

Unlike effects in physics, the Gautreaux Program's effects arise and outcomes result from what the program participants do with the opportunities
presented to them. The changes "caused" by this program occurred slowly

and were due only to the enormous efforts and sacrifices of the participants. We illustrate this with three case studies of individuals in the Gautreaux Program, participants in the children's study described above who
were interviewed with their mothers in 1982 and 1989. While the best
summary of the program's effects are contained in the statistical data reported above, the complexity of participants' experiences and their own efforts to overcome the obstacles they confronted are key elements to understanding the program effects of Gautreaux.

This analysis reveals participants' strengths and capabilities, qualities
that may have emerged because of their new opportunities. This analysis
also helps us really see characteristics of the suburban communities, both
positive ones that help new residents, and negative ones that they must
confront.

Laura

No one reflects the complexities of the Gautreaux experience more clearly
than Laura. Laura moved to the suburbs when she was eight. As her
mother, Noelle, said in 1982, almost four years after their move,

> For me it was getting her away from the city and all of the crime and . . .
> because, see, [my kids] grew up in the projects. . . . And I wanted them
> to see that there was more to life than what these people wanted. . . . And
> in order to let them see that, I had to get her out of the city and move her
> out here. She's twelve years old and some of her little friends back there
> are pregnant today. I feel that this would have happened to her. By her
> being out here she has a more open outlook on life. . . . Getting her out
> of the projects was the best thing I could have done for all of us.

Laura did not have a positive experience in the city schools. Her grades
were good, but both mother and daughter question how much she was actually learning. In 1982 Noelle commented that "Chicago schools are
raggedy. . . . The teachers complain that there wasn't enough room in the
classroom. It was so crowded . . . nobody is learning anything. She comes
home with headaches. . . . The whole attitude [of the teachers was] . . . 'I
don't care I've got mine. Either you learn it or you don't because I'm going
to give you a passing grade anyway.'"

Laura had many complaints about the city schools. She reported that
"they really didn't try to teach you anything," the teachers were "mean"
and did not listen, and broken glass covered the playground. In addition,
Laura was often afraid to go to school because of fights. Noelle also would
often have to walk Laura and her brothers to school because of their fears.

For eleven years Laura's family had lived in one of Chicago's housing
projects. Noelle says she did not trust any of the other kids in the neigh-

borhood; the area was dirty and very unsafe. The situation was difficult for both mother and child, as Noelle explained: "Every time I let her go downstairs or out to play, there was a fight. So it was just like, 'You just stay in the house and I'll let you come out when I come home,' or something like that. . . . She didn't like the attitudes of some kids. She would say, 'Why do they have to do this? Why do they fight?' and I'd just tell her to stay away from them and not be around that type of people."

One of the major reasons Noelle gave for moving to the suburbs was for "schools to better my children." In 1982 it seemed as though she believed she had been successful. Laura's grades actually went down a little, but as Noelle explained, "The work out here is much harder than what the kids are doing in the city. Yes her grades have changed because the work is harder now. Because the little math she was doing in the city, it counted for her to get that *A* in it. Now for her to come out here and just jump into geometry and trigonometry in sixth grade and still be getting *B*s and *C*s is good. The reason I feel she is doing better is because the teachers are different."

When they had first moved to the suburbs, Noelle said, Laura had to take a battery of tests to prove she was not "slow," that her problem was merely that she had not had the material that the suburban children had learned already. Laura passed these tests and did not have to repeat a grade, but the experience was difficult. And even though she passed, she still had to deal with the fact that the city schools had not taught her as much as the suburban schools expected of sixth-grade students.

But the suburban schools also offered an opportunity for Laura educationally. In addition to the more advanced curriculum, the schools provided the kind of extra attention that impressed both Noelle and Laura. Noelle mentioned this difference several times in the course of her 1982 interview:

The schools . . . are not overcrowded. They had time to give them the help they needed. The teachers out here, they seem to care more. . . . They will call you everyday to let you know how your child is doing in school. And send work home and tell you to help your child with this. Put them on special projects and different things.

It makes me happy because [the teacher] really doesn't have to call me and let me know these things. But she does. I just like talking to her. She calls me in the evenings. If you are not satisfied with your child's progress, you can always call the school and make a meeting.

Laura commented simply that her teachers "help you more." Her mother related several incidents where teachers went out of their way to help Laura. One teacher arranged for her to make up a missed exam; another, Laura's track coach, made a special effort to keep her from quitting the team.

Laura had a *B* average in high school and was in honors English and math classes. Planning a career in computers or word processing, Laura had finished high school by 1989 and was enrolled in, but not yet attending, the local community college for a two-year degree; she saw herself going on to a four-year program. She was working full time at her fifth job, at a clothing store, making $4.50 per hour with benefits. She said she liked the job but felt it was not teaching her any new skills.

In 1982 Laura had described herself as having four friends: one black and four white. She had not spent as much time with them as she would have liked, according to her mother, because they lived on the other side of town, and transportation was a problem. Noelle cited "living around whites" as being among the best things for Laura about the move to the suburbs. Part of the reason, in addition to the exposure itself, had to do with the types of amenities that such proximity brought. For example, Noelle appreciated the better-quality teachers in the suburban schools. Noelle also said, "The three years that I've been out here I've seen that white people want the best and they're going to get it."

With proximity, however, also came prejudice. While many of their neighbors were friendly, according to Noelle, "[Some people from the neighborhood] call [Laura] 'nigger' and say, 'Go back to the ghettos where you came from' or 'Go back to Africa.'" Laura mentioned in 1982 that the only thing she disliked about her school was the fact that "some kids are prejudiced." Similarly, Laura said that while she felt safer in the suburbs than in the city, she did not feel completely safe because she was black, and "some white people might not like that." She doubted that they would do anything physical to her, but they might verbally accost her. For both Laura and Noelle, the prejudice in the suburbs was much less threatening than the physical dangers they faced in the city. Noelle said specifically, "[In the city] I was worried about somebody breaking in. I was worried about somebody doing something to my children. I'm not scared about that now. The only thing I have out here is prejudice. There's nothing that can be done about making a person like you because you're you."

Laura is typical of our sample's suburban youths in reporting in 1989 that the majority of her friends were white.[76] There was no difference in the amount of time Laura spent with her white and black friends or in the types of activities in which they engaged. She strongly agreed that she was a real part of her school and that others saw her as popular, athletic, socially active, and at least somewhat part of the "in-group." Noelle also noted that her daughter's friends were a mixed group of white, black, and Hispanic kids.

Laura was able to attain some measure of academic achievement and social integration, but she did not avoid difficulties completely. There were teachers who helped and teachers who did not, as well as white friends and hostile white neighbors. Laura said that name-calling happened only a few times a year, and it was done by both whites and blacks.

Noelle's response to prejudice, in addition to going to the school to talk to school officials, was to emphasize, as other mothers did, the learning potential in these experiences: "And I don't care where you live, there's going to be somebody that doesn't like you regardless of what race, creed, or color they may be. . . . 'Cause you can live in Chicago and have blacks that don't like you or the person around the corner who doesn't even know you. It teaches you to be a strong person. It hurts sometimes to be called names, but I try to teach my kids not to be hurting from that, but to learn from that." In the end, the bottom line of the suburban experience for both Noelle and Laura was the comparison with life in the city. Laura explained, "I like a lot of the opportunities I have [in the suburbs]. Actually, I just don't like Chicago." When asked what life would have been like had she not moved, she replied, "I don't think I would have had a real good education. Probably would have had more fights than I ever dreamed of. Probably would have been robbed several times. Actually I probably wouldn't know half of the things that I know now if I had still lived in Chicago. Like I wouldn't know about white people and about being prejudiced."

Cheryl

For Cheryl the suburban move created greater educational gains, but it also created more serious social obstacles for her. Cheryl had lived in the suburbs for almost five years when we interviewed her in 1982 at age eleven. Cheryl had been exposed to Chicago public schools for only a short time before moving; she had attended kindergarten there. She did well and was quite advanced for her age. Problems, however, had already begun. According to her mother, Victoria,

> Where we used to live, there were fights all the time. She would come home from school—nervous, she wouldn't fight back, she would always get beat up.
>
> [The kids in the city] were fighting all the time, physically fighting machines. . . . I try to tell them why people act the way they act, or treat each other the way they treat each other. I try to use these other people as examples: "Don't be that way—God doesn't like that." But it was too much of a strain on me and a strain on the girls—they couldn't think, even in school, the pressures of getting kicked on the leg and things like this. Kids are mean to each other.

Cheryl often did not want to go to school because she was afraid of the fighting. Of their inner-city neighborhood, her mother said, "The drunk people that lay out on the street on Saturday night get so drunk they can't make it home and sleep on the streets. . . . I was burglarized twice while I was there and they took all of my most precious valuables, that's enough. The fact that my children didn't know self-defense, they all got beat up. It was difficult to keep the roaches under control."

At one level, Victoria was pleased with the change the suburbs provided for Cheryl, mentioning particularly the quality of the school system, extra activities such as sports and music, and the extra attention from the teachers, who will "walk that extra mile":

> I like the kinds of warmth and the kindness of most of the teachers there. They are concerned; if they feel as though there is a problem, they will call you. They will call you to ask if you have any suggestions on what they can do to help to improve the situation with the child. They want you to call any time, call their homes anytime if you feel that you have a problem or if you need some questions answered. It's like one big family. I like the principal, the way he has things set up there. He takes every child as his own, and whenever the school has activities, the teachers are involved in them.

Victoria said that she "wouldn't want to ever take [Cheryl] out of the school she attends," noting that "she's given a lot of responsibility by the instructors because she is excellent in class. . . . She likes all that, that's something she wouldn't have in Chicago." Cheryl had received mostly As and Bs on her last report card.

The 1989 follow-up interview revealed that Cheryl continued to do very well: she achieved mostly As and Bs her last year in high school, and she was in honors classes in English, math, and two languages, Spanish and French. She studied in South America her junior year in high school, and at the time of the interview was majoring in international marketing at the University of Illinois at Urbana, having received a scholarship. She felt fairly optimistic about her chances for working in international marketing because so far "everything has worked to my advantage." She has had five part-time jobs and was working at the time of the interview for Eastman Kodak as an intern doing research for the sales manager. She liked the job, which paid $7.75 per hour, and was learning new skills that she felt would help her get a better job. She says she preferred the suburbs overall because of the education she received and the relative safety. Asked how her life might have been different had they not moved, she responded, "I would be not as well educated, not as cultured, ignorant about whites. I would be hard, street-wise." Responding to the same question, her mother answered, "[Cheryl] probably would not have the drive, the challenge, you know, to want to advance, to get ahead, to compete. She wouldn't have that competitive, you know, that competitive attitude that's needed to get ahead in life. She probably would have just been absorbed with boys, and she wouldn't know as much. She wouldn't have had the job opportunities. You know, I think her life would have been pretty stagnant. She wouldn't have been prepared to attend the [University of Illinois]—that's for sure."

While Cheryl's academic experience was very positive, her social experience was more negative than that of most youths we spoke to. In 1982 her mother reported,

> Students occasionally call her "nigger." She's offended by that. They have a way of isolating her and that will make her feel bad. If they don't like something about the way she acts, they will stay away in groups and just leave her alone. And they will pass the word, . . . ignore her, call her names when they see her. . . . This doesn't occur often, but when it does occur, it's like, "Mom, do I have to go to [school] now, I'm the only black in my class—I have no one to go to"—the teacher is white. If she complains to the teacher about something like that, the teacher will say something like, "well." She isn't going to take it very seriously.

Racism among teachers was less a factor in high school than it was in elementary school. Victoria did mention one teacher whose own prejudice influenced the students in the class; they began calling Cheryl "nigger" and other names in class, knowing they would not be stopped. Cheryl's grades dropped precipitously as a result. Victoria complained to the school and reported to us that the teacher eventually resigned (though it is not clear if the two events were linked). According to her mother, Cheryl's grades improved considerably afterward.

In 1989 Cheryl stated that in general she did not fit into her school, which had a very affluent student body, and that the other students were unfriendly. Only 17.3 percent of suburban movers had no white friends, and Cheryl was in this group.[77] She did have friends, two black and one Indian; but "everybody was at the stage [where they were] caught up in cliques," and blacks "hung with themselves." This was a particular problem as far as dating was concerned; boys said they would not date her because she was black. While she did not say if this was the case with black as well as white boys, she did say that "I had no life as far as dating," and when asked what she did about it, she said she "got bitter against white guys." Unlike many other Gautreaux youths, Cheryl never visited white students at home or did things outside school with them, though she did occasionally do schoolwork with them. She felt like she was a real part of her school but did not think she was seen as part of the "in-group."

Both mother and daughter turned their encounters with white bigotry into lessons. As Victoria said in 1989, "It's something that you can adapt yourself to. And you know, you complain at first but then you say, 'Well, this is the way it is,' and you know, you accept it." Cheryl concluded that had she grown up in the city, she would have been "ignorant about whites." Instead of learning the city's lesson of being "hard" to the physical assaults of the streets, she learned the suburb's lesson of being hard to the insults of prejudice. This particular kind of education was probably not on the agenda of Dorothy Gautreaux and her fellow litigants, but it seems to have been inseparable from the other things Cheryl learned in the suburbs.

Because she had not yet entered school at the time of the move, Cheryl did not have to catch up in the suburban schools, and this worked to her advantage. Her academic accomplishments were considerable: she received high grades in honors courses at a very demanding suburban high school and attended a selective four-year university. Escaping the fighting and robberies she had experienced in the city was also a great relief to Cheryl.

Yet while Cheryl got more academic benefits than most of our suburban sample, she enjoyed much less social acceptance. She described more harassment and social barriers than most suburban movers. In some cases those barriers came down, as in the case of the prejudiced teacher, but for the most part they persisted. Both mother and child said they would again choose this mix of high academic and safety benefits and high social costs over the inner-city experience, but with serious reservations.

Kevin

For Kevin, the educational advantages were more modest, but the prejudice and social isolation were also much less severe. Kevin left the city when he was eight, five years prior to the 1982 interview. Describing where they had lived in the city, his mother, Alice, stated, "You know, we were just like in a prison." She compared their new location in the suburbs favorably to the city with regard to all aspects of the family's life. According to Alice, Kevin was in real trouble before they moved. His grades were mostly Fs, she said:

> He wasn't improving any in that school. And I think it was that the school was too crowded and they didn't have enough staff to detect [Kevin's] needs, his learning ability or anything. . . . So he was just going on and on and getting farther and farther behind. . . . He wasn't progressing any. He couldn't read. He couldn't write. The grade level that he was in, he couldn't even read the book. He couldn't do the math. So I don't think he was progressing at all in that school. And the kids, they would fight. When they get out of school, if you don't go down there and pick your child up, he's liable to come home with a black eye or a ball club hit him in the head or just anything.

In addition to being unable to function successfully in school, Kevin was also showing some other disturbing signs:

His behavior. It was kind of bad when we were in the city. He wouldn't mind. He had started picking up things in the house. Going in my wallet. Taking his sister's jewelry. He wouldn't fight. He wasn't that type of child that would get into fights or anything. But he just started picking up real bad habits. I would let him go outside and tell him to be home in two hours and he'd stay three or four. . . . My oldest daughter, she missed some rings. And he denied it, but we found it in his pocket before he went to school. And I missed two dollars out of my wallet one time.

Alice's response, a common strategy among the mothers in our sample, was to keep Kevin and his sisters inside because she did not trust the neighborhood or the other children who lived there. He had no friends during the last year before they moved to the suburbs.

For Alice the move to the suburbs meant a complete turn for the better for her son, both academically and behaviorally. He repeated a grade and was placed in a special program in which he received extra academic help. Both mother and son agreed that this program helped him: his grades went up afterward. In the seventh grade at the time of the 1982 interview, thirteen-year-old Kevin had received mostly Bs on his last report card and had much less trouble with his schoolwork than he had had in the city. He stated that he liked school and living in the suburbs; he remembered little about his life in the city. When asked if he would be someone else if he could, he responded that he would be "a smarter person," a response that seems to indicate both a knowledge of the problems he had had and a desire to improve. Such feelings could have led to the frustration and disruptive behavior Alice noticed in Chicago.

Alice raved about the changes she has seen in her son since their move:

He's a different boy now. He's considerate. He minds me. He does anything I say. He doesn't poke out his mouth. He doesn't give me any back talk. And he's very intelligent now. Before we moved out here, he was having difficulty with his speech. Now you can understand everything he says.

He understands the work now. He's good with what he's working on. He studies hard. He likes to go to school. He likes his teachers. And [Kevin] likes to impress his teachers, so he works very hard on his schoolwork. He's a charmer.

Alice attributed Kevin's changes primarily to the extra attention he was receiving from teachers and to changes in her own attitudes because of the move: "Now it seems like I've got more interest in things." She particularly praised the amount of information she gets from the teachers about Kevin's work and his behavior. They let her know right away—"It doesn't just go on and on."

Kevin maintained the momentum spurred by the move. According to Alice, he stayed in the special program through his junior year, for a few periods a day. Both mother and son spoke highly of his teachers, who often went out of their way for him and continued their regular contact with Alice about his progress. While schoolwork in high school was difficult for him, he received mostly Bs and Cs. As a member of the school's basketball team, he was required to maintain his grade point average, but Kevin stated that he also focused on grades because he wanted to go to college. Preparing to enter a two-year program at a local community college, he indicated that he planned to transfer eventually to a four-year school. At the time of the 1989 interview he was working full time as a truck driver. He said he liked the job, was learning new skills, and believed it would help him get a better job in the future.

In 1982 Alice mentioned that she had experienced racism from her neighbors at first, but that there had not been any problems recently. Her own attitudes, she found, changed as well: "At first I think I couldn't face the different nationalities. Now, I find that it's nice living with different nationalities." Their neighbors were friendly, although not as friendly as those in the city, and Kevin had both black and white friends in the neighborhood. He participated in Little League and used other local facilities such as the pool, the parks, and the YMCA—places he had not gone in the city because Alice thought many of them were dangerous. He also was able to play outside more often because of a difference Alice saw in the kids, as well as in the neighborhood: "They have good behavior [in the suburbs]. They don't fight and they don't talk bad. When they go outside, their mother knows exactly where they are. And before nightfall all kids are in the house."

Kevin did not mention any prejudiced behavior. Asked in 1989 what he liked about his school, he replied, "I got along with everyone. Everyone treated me nice." In high school the majority of his friends were white; he seemed to have divided his time fairly equally between his white and black friends, and he mentioned no incidents of name-calling, threats, or other problems. He agreed that he was "a real part of [his] school" and that other students treated him with respect and saw him as very much a part of the "in-group." Alice concurred that her son was a "likable boy" and that, in contrast to her earlier characterization of his behavior in the city, "he don't get in any trouble."

The suburban experience, then, appears to have been a very successful one for Kevin. The progress of what looked to be a downward trajectory in the city was turned around after the move. Alice, asked how life would have been different had they stayed, is confident, if brief, in her appraisal: "God, it would have been a disaster. The city's the pits." Kevin also answered that his life would have been different, that he would have joined a gang, sold drugs, and would not have finished high school. When asked why they stayed in the area from 1982 to 1989, he said he thought his mom wanted him to stay out of the city, away from the gangs.

It seems likely that the quality of education Kevin received, particularly the diagnosis of and attention to some kind of learning disability, played a key role in his overall social, academic, and perhaps even work achievements. He went from failing most of his classes to doing eventually average quality work and liking school. Its rewards—teacher attention and approval—appear to have become both attainable and desirable for Kevin. This was not the case during his early years in Chicago, which possibly had caused some of the discipline problems his mother mentioned. Kevin also did not experience much racial harassment. Alice mentioned some neighbors who were less than friendly, but overall the suburbs proved to be a hospitable environment for Kevin.

All three youths experienced dramatic changes in their lives because of the move to the suburbs. But their success in life was by no means assured by the program. Granted, the program did have some consistent effects on the environment for all three children. They, like many other suburban movers, reported that the suburbs offered a safer environment. They also reported that the suburban schools had higher standards and teachers who were more likely to go out of their way for students. These factors were also reported by most suburban movers who were interviewed.

Of course, the higher standards initially posed an obstacle to the students. Like many of the children who had moved after several years in city schools, Laura's and Kevin's performances were at first below those of their suburban peers. Laura passed the battery of tests she was given, but she still had to struggle to catch up with her classmates. Kevin did not pass the tests, and the results indicated that he needed to be placed in a special program. Both Kevin and his mother, however, felt that the program had helped Kevin by giving him additional attention and special resources. His mother's report that he understood, liked, and worked hard at his schoolwork certainly suggests that he responded well to the program. Both Kevin and his mother believed the suburban move prevented Kevin from becoming involved with gangs and drugs and from dropping out of school.

Not all the suburban teachers were supportive, and some were serious obstacles. One teacher was a serious problem for Cheryl, and this affected her performance in school. Fortunately, Cheryl's performance improved when she was taught by other teachers.

Anguish, isolation, and harassment were experienced by many individuals. Laura and Kevin experienced these problems mildly, but Cheryl had more difficulty. It is noteworthy that Cheryl was the most successful academically and was the most isolated socially. Both experiences may be a consequence of her attending an affluent school.

Conclusions and Policy Implications

The studies of the Gautreaux Program suggest that residential integration can contribute significantly to the Kerner Commission's aims of improving employment, education, and social integration of low-income blacks. The suburban move greatly improved adult employment, and many adults were employed for the first time in their lives. The suburban move also improved youths' education. Compared with city movers, the children who moved to the suburbs are more likely to be (1) in school, (2) in college-track classes, (3) in four-year colleges, (4) employed, and (5) employed in jobs with benefits and better pay. The suburban move led also to a considerable amount of social integration, friendships, and interaction with white neighbors in the suburbs.

Of course, the social integration was not complete; while harassment declined over time, some degree of prejudice remained. Similarly, the children's achievement gains were not immediate. Indeed, virtually all the children transplanted to the suburbs experienced great difficulties and lower grades in the first year or two. These difficulties, however, may have been an unavoidable part of adjusting to the higher suburban standards.

Some critics doubt that housing voucher programs can achieve the integration goals set by the Kerner Commission because low-income blacks will not choose to move to middle-income white suburbs. Indeed, a Detroit survey found that few blacks would choose all-white neighborhoods as their first choice.[78] Moreover, some previous efforts to use housing vouchers to encourage racial integration were unsuccessful. The national Experimental Housing Allowance Program had "little if any impact on locational choice, economic or racial concentrations, or neighborhood quality."[79] Similarly, Project Self-Sufficiency in Cook County resulted in very few black participants moving to white suburbs.[80] In both programs, participants were reluctant to make the moves because of strong personal ties to their neighbors, fear of discrimination, and unfamiliarity with the distant suburbs that possibly would have offered them better job prospects.

The results of the Gautreaux Program do not conclusively contradict these prior studies. Program design features—the lack of real choice about city or suburban locations—limit any conclusions about low-income blacks' preference about where to live. Still, the results are somewhat encouraging. They suggest that housing vouchers can result in low-income families moving to suburbs with better schools and better labor markets, and that adults and children can benefit from such moves. This program has been able to overcome the reluctance that these families might have felt, in part because the poor quality of life in the city limited the attractiveness of staying there. It is noteworthy that participation is voluntary and demand for the program slots is high.

The Gautreaux Program indicates that successful residential integration is possible, but that it requires extensive additional housing services. Real estate staff are needed to locate landlords willing to participate in the program, and placement counselors are needed to inform families about life in the suburbs, including addressing their concerns about such moves and taking them to visit the units and communities. Like participants in other voucher programs, Gautreaux participants were reluctant to move to distant suburbs, and few would have moved without the counselors' encouragement and visits to the suburban apartments. When contrasted with the failures of previous housing voucher programs, the success of this program indicates the value of having real estate staff and housing counselors.

The study also suggests some ways that the Gautreaux Program could be improved. Transportation was the greatest difficulty that people faced in the suburbs. The suburbs had little or no public transportation, so travel was extremely difficult. Minibus service is probably not practical because few families move to any one location, and a special minibus runs the risk of increasing visibility and labeling of participants. If the program could help people finance the purchase of a car, more people might get jobs, children would have an easier time participating in after-school activities, and participants would face fewer frustrations with daily tasks. Child care assistance would also have been extremely helpful, since suburban movers are unlikely to have friends or relatives nearby to assist. Finally, while this housing program improved employment more than most education or training programs, Gautreaux participants might have gotten better jobs if the program had also provided additional education or training.

Of course, voucher programs alone are not sufficient to move large numbers of families because of the limited number of housing units available. But if national policymakers made a long-term commitment to expanding the Section 8 program and increasing suburban moves, then builders and developers could make long-term investments in building apartments to respond to this program over the next decade. Such a program would not be cheap. The alternative, however, is to sink many billions of dollars into current housing projects that keep people in areas of the city that hinder their employment and educational opportunities. As we have seen, that has great human costs for the people living in the projects and great costs to society because adults have limited access to the labor market and children have limited access to good education.

This study supports the basic premises behind the Kerner Commission's proposals for creating housing options outside the ghetto: moving people to better areas can improve their opportunities. This should encourage Congress to fund housing voucher programs by supplying the resources and services needed for these programs to succeed. The Gautreaux Program demonstrated that moving to better neighborhoods can improve adult self-sufficiency and opportunities for their children. Certainly these results make housing vouchers a promising approach to housing poor families; it is worthwhile to invest more in programs that can produce similar results.

This study also has implications for nonvoucher programs. The results indicate three key factors that helped Gautreaux adults find employment in the suburbs: personal safety, role models, and access to jobs. If these factors were improved in the city, city residents could be helped without moving to the suburbs. In fact, the Chicago Housing Authority (CHA), at the initiative of its director, Vincent Lane, has recently made impressive efforts to improve safety, role models, and job access in public housing projects. To improve the safety of the housing projects, the CHA has taken security measures. To provide positive role models, the CHA has initiated a mixed-income housing development, Lake Parc Place, that includes working residents who are positive models for their unemployed neighbors. To improve access to suburban jobs, some housing projects have also provided minibus service to the suburbs. These are the same factors that Gautreaux adults noted as helping them, so the CHA measures represent promising efforts. However, it is not certain how thorough and successful these efforts will be or whether they will result in greater employment. Even improved security may not make the projects as safe as the suburbs, and one-hour commutes may limit the attractiveness of taking a minibus to low-paying jobs. It will be some time before we can assess the success of such programs.

The Gautreaux studies indicate clearly that the Kerner Commission's housing strategy can lead to gains in employment, education, and social integration for low-income blacks. Contrary to the pessimistic predictions of "culture of poverty" models discussed at the beginning of this essay,[81] the early experiences of low-income blacks do not prevent them from benefiting from suburban moves. The Gautreaux results also support a basic premise of the Kerner Commission report: geographic location has a substantial and significant effect on people's opportunities. Programs that help people escape areas of concentrated poverty can improve employment and educational opportunities for those people.

Notes

1. *Report of The National Advisory Commission on Civil Disorders* (New York: Bantam Books 1968), 407 (hereafter cited as *Kerner Report*).

2. See John Charles Boger, "Race and the American City: The Kerner Commission Report in Retrospect" (in this volume).

3. *Kerner Report*, 475.

4. Ibid., 472–73.

5. Ibid., 482.

6. Ibid., 406.

7. John D. Kasarda, "Urban Industrial Transition and the Underclass," *Annals of the American Academy of Political and Social Science* 501 (1989): 26–47; John D. Kasarda, "Urban Employment Change and Minority Skills Mismatch," in *Creating Jobs, Creating Workers: Economic Development and Employment in Metropolitan Chicago*, ed. Lawrence B. Joseph (Champaign: University of Illinois Press, 1990), 65, 82.

8. William Julius Wilson, *The Truly Disadvantaged: The Inner City, the Underclass, and Public Policy* (Chicago: University of Chicago Press, 1987), 135.

9. NCI Research, *Identifying Employment Opportunities for Inner City Residents* (1991), 5.

10. Ibid.

11. David T. Ellwood, "The Spatial Mismatch Hypothesis: Are There Teen-age Jobs Missing in the Ghetto?," in *The Black Youth Unemployment Crisis*, ed. Richard B. Freeman and Harry J. Holzer (Chicago: University of Chicago Press, 1986), 148.

12. John F. Kain, "Housing Segregation, Negro Employment, and Metropolitan Decentralization," *Quarterly Journal of Economics* 82 (1968): 175–97; Christopher Jencks and Susan E. Mayer, "Residential Segregation, Job Proximity, and Black Job Opportunities: The Empirical Status of the Spatial Mismatch Hypothesis" (Center for Urban Affairs and Policy Research, Northwestern University, working paper, 1989), 2.

13. Andrew Hahn and Robert Lerman, *What Works in Youth Employment Policy?* (Washington, D.C.: National Planning Association, Committee on New American Realities, 1985), 22–23.

14. *Kerner Report*, 407.

15. See James S. Coleman, Ernest Q. Campbell, Carol J. Hobson, James McPartland, Alexander Mood, Frederic D. Weinfeld, and Robert L. York, *Equality of Educational Opportunity* (Washington, D.C.: U.S. Government Printing Office, 1966), 330–31; Caroline Hodges Persell, *Education and Inequality* (New York: Free Press, 1977), 150–52.

16. See Willis D. Hawley, ed., *Effective School Desegregation: Equity, Quality, and Feasibility* (Beverly Hills, Calif.: Sage, 1981).

17. See *Hills v. Gautreaux*, 425 U.S. 284 (1976).

18. Kathleen A. Peroff et al., U.S. Department of Housing and Urban Development, *Gautreaux Housing Demonstration: An Evaluation of Its Impact on Participating Households* (Washington, D.C.: U.S. Government Printing Office, 1979), 1.

19. The Section 8 program is a federal program that subsidizes rents for low-

income people in private sector apartments, either by giving them a Section 8 certificate that allows them to rent apartments on the open market or by moving them into a new or rehabilitated building where the owner has taken a federal loan that requires some units to be set aside for low-income tenants.

20. Jencks and Mayer, "Residential Segregation," 26–41.

21. Ibid., 26.

22. On a scheduled day a Leadership Council housing counselor visits the apartment, looking primarily for serious property damage.

23. See James E. Rosenbaum and Susan J. Popkin, *Economic and Social Impacts of Housing Integration* (Chicago: Center for Urban Affairs and Policy Research, Northwestern University, 1990), 8 (report to the Charles Stewart Mott Foundation).

24. See Oscar Lewis, "The Culture of Poverty," in *On Understanding Poverty: Perspectives from the Social Sciences*, ed. Daniel P. Moynihan (New York: Basic Books, 1968), 187.

25. Ibid., 188.

26. Lawrence M. Mead, *Beyond Entitlement: The Social Obligations of Citizenship* (New York: Free Press, 1986), 1–17. See also Stephen Steinberg, *The Ethnic Myth: Race, Ethnicity, and Class in America* (New York: Atheneum, 1981), 106–27 (discussing the effect of current welfare policy on recipients' attitudes toward their productivity).

27. Martin Patchen, *Black-White Contact in Schools: Its Social and Academic Effects* (West Lafayette, Ind.: Purdue University Press, 1982), 257–94.

28. Donald R. Winkler, "Educational Achievement and School Peer Group Composition," *Journal of Human Resources* 10 (1975): 189–204.

29. Nancy H. St. John, *School Desegregation Outcomes for Children* (New York: Wiley, 1975), 36 ("Desegregation has rarely lowered academic achievement for either black or white children"); see also William L. Taylor, "The Continuing Struggle for Equal Educational Opportunity" (in this volume) (discussing this issue).

30. Douglas S. Massey and Nancy A. Denton, "Trends in the Residential Segregation of Blacks, Hispanics, and Asians: 1970–1980," *American Sociological Review* 52 (1987): 802, 803.

31. See Howard Schuman and Lawrence Bobo, "Survey-based Experiments on White Racial Attitudes toward Residential Integration," *American Journal of Sociology* 94 (1988): 273, 274–75.

32. See Brian J. L. Berry, *The Open Housing Question: Race and Housing in Chicago, 1966–1976* (Cambridge: Ballinger, 1979), 163, 190, 198–203.

33. See John Gehm, *Bringing It Home* (Chicago: Chicago Review Press, 1984), 83–109 (describing the Valparaiso experiment).

34. See ibid.

35. See Gregory D. Squires et al., *Chicago: Race, Class, and the Response to Urban Decline* (Philadelphia: Temple University Press, 1987), 127–51.

36. See Harold B. Gerard and Norman Miller, *School Desegregation: A Long Term Study* (New York: Plenum Press, 1975); See also Hawley, *Effective School Desegregation*; Patchen, *Black-White Contact in Schools*; St. John, *School Desegregation Outcomes for Children*.

37. See John Yinger, "Prejudice and Discrimination in the Urban Housing Mar-

ket," in *Current Issues in Urban Economics*, ed. Peter Mieszkowski and Mahlon Straszheim (Baltimore: Johns Hopkins University Press, 1979), 430.

38. Our refusal rate on the interviews was less than 7 percent. There are no systematic differences between the interview and survey respondents, but the interview sample is used only for qualitative analysis. Responses to the self-administered questionnaire were consistent with those from the in-person interviews. For a complete description of the sample, instrument, and other analyses, see Rosenbaum and Popkin, *Economic and Social Impacts of Housing Integration*, 6–8.

39. Low-income people move often and are difficult to locate over a seven-year period. We located 59.1 percent of our participants, a reasonably large percentage for such a sample. Of course, we must wonder what biases arise from this attrition, and whether we were more likely to lose the least successful people (because they were harder to find) or the most successful ones (because they got jobs in distant locations). We suspect both happen, but if one happened more often, then the 1989 sample could be quite different from the original 1982 sample.

The mothers from the program's early years are less educated than those in the above survey of adults because they are older and come from an earlier era when high school dropouts were more common.

40. The suburban advantage arises from a decline in employment for city movers. The 15.4 percent decline in employment by the city movers is virtually the same as the 16.3 percent decline found in the Current Population Surveys (CPS) between 1979 and 1989 among poorly educated central-city black adult males, while their noncentral-city CPS counterparts experienced little or no decline. Although selectivity concerns make the CPS data somewhat suspect, the quasi-random assignment makes selectivity less of a threat in our sample, and we find the same city/suburban differences as did the CPS. Apparently the suburban move permitted low-income blacks to escape declining employment rates in central cities during the 1980s.

Moreover, multivariate analyses find that suburban movers are significantly more likely to have a job than city movers, even after controlling for many other factors. That analysis finds that some of the following factors also influence employment: previous work experience, years since move, age (which is inversely related to employment), and young children (also inversely related to employment). The likelihood of employment is reduced by a low internal sense of control and being a long-term Aid to Families with Dependent Children (AFDC) recipient (five years or more), but not by being a second-generation AFDC recipient. Employment is barely influenced by education, and it is not affected at all by obtaining a high school equivalency diploma or attending college after the move. For details of these analyses, see Rosenbaum and Popkin, *Economic and Social Impacts of Housing Integration*, 60–65.

41. Multivariate analyses on post-move hourly wages and on hours worked per week (controlling for the same variables, plus months of employment and the pre-move measure of the dependent variable [wages or hours, respectively]) confirm the findings discussed above: suburbs have no effect on either dependent variable. Job tenure, pre-move pay, and the two "culture of poverty" variables (internal control and long-term AFDC) have significant effects on post-move wages. Job tenure,

pre-move hours worked, and post-move higher education have significant effects on post-move hours worked. None of the other factors had significant effects. For details of these analyses, see ibid.; see also nn. 25–26, above, and accompanying text (discussing Oscar Lewis's "culture of poverty" thesis).

42. See Wilson, *Truly Disadvantaged*, 63–92.

43. For a complete description of the sample, instrument, and other analyses, see James E. Rosenbaum et al., *Low-Income Black Children in White Suburban Schools* (Chicago: Center for Urban Affairs and Policy Research, Northwestern University) (report to the Spence Foundation of Chicago, 1986).

44. Women headed 86 percent of the suburban households and 88 percent of the city households.

45. James E. Rosenbaum, Marilynn J. Kulieke, and Leonard S. Rubinowitz, "White Suburban Schools' Responses to Low-Income Black Children: Sources of Successes and Problems," *Urban Review* 20 (1988): 28, 32.

46. Ibid., 30–31.

47. Ibid., 32.

48. For a complete description of the sample, instrument, and other analyses, see James E. Rosenbaum and Julie E. Kaufman, "Educational and Occupational Achievements of Low-Income Black Youth in White Suburbs" (paper presented to the annual meeting of the American Sociological Association, August 1991) (on file with James E. Rosenbaum).

49. Both city and suburban students had C+ averages.

50. See Rosenbaum and Kaufman, "Educational and Occupational Achievements."

51. James E. Rosenbaum, *Making Inequality: The Hidden Curriculum of High School Tracking* (New York: Wiley, 1976), 81. See generally James E. Rosenbaum, "Social Implications of Educational Grouping," in *Annual Review Research Education* (1980), 361 (describing academic tracking systems and their effects on student performance and socialization).

52. See Coleman et al., *Equality of Educational Opportunity*, 479–80; Jeannie Oakes, *Keeping Track: How Schools Structure Inequality* (New Haven: Yale University Press, 1985); James E. Rosenbaum and Stefan Presser, "Voluntary Racial Integration in a Magnet School," *School Review* 83 (1978): 156, 167–70.

53. *Hobson v. Hansen*, 269 F. Supp. 401, 443 (D.D.C. 1967), appeal dismissed, 393 U.S. 801 (1968) (holding that ability grouping as practiced in the Washington, D.C., public school system denied equal educational opportunity to the poor and to a majority of black students).

54. Of the suburban movers, 40.3 percent were in college-bound tracks, while 23.5 percent of the city movers were so situated.

55. Fifty-four percent of suburban movers were enrolled in college in 1989, as compared with 21 percent of the city movers.

56. Gary Orfield, Howard Mitzel, et al., *Chicago Study of Access and Choice in Higher Education* (Chicago: University of Chicago, Commission on Public Policy Studies, 1984).

57. Of the suburban youth, 75 percent had jobs, while only 41 percent of the city youths were employed.

58. Twenty-one percent of the employed suburban youths earned more than $6.50 an hour, while only 5 percent of the working city youths earned that much from their jobs.

59. Benefits (such as health insurance and paid leave) were offered by 55.2 percent of the suburban jobs but by only 23.1 percent of the city jobs in which sample youths were employed.

60. City movers received more threats than suburbanites: 22.7 percent of the city dwellers had been threatened, as compared with 21.2 percent of the suburban students.

61. The difference was less than 1 percent: 93.5 percent of city and 94.1 percent of suburban students reported that they had never been physically hurt.

62. Those surveyed were asked to choose from a five-point scale in which "strongly agree" earned five points and "strongly disagree" earned only one point. The mean answer to this question was a 3.55 for the city students; their suburban counterparts averaged 3.37 points. This difference is not statistically significant.

63. The mean for the city students was 3.93 points; suburban students averaged 4.00. The difference between these results is not statistically significant.

64. These responses were reported on a three-point scale where the response "not at all" earned zero points, "somewhat" earned one point, and "very" earned three points.

65. This result is statistically significant. All determinations of significance are made at the $p<.01$ level. Some of the statistics, however, were more strongly significant than others.

66. This result is statistically significant.

67. This result is statistically insignificant: $r=0.11$. The r is the Pearson product-moment correlation coefficient, a statistical indicator of the degree of association between two variables. The closer the r-coefficient is to 1.00, the stronger the observed correlation.

68. This result is statistically insignificant: $r=0.50$.

69. This result is statistically insignificant: $r=0.09$.

70. This result is statistically insignificant: $r=0.08$.

71. This result is statistically insignificant: $r=0.17$.

72. Said one respondent, "It's not awful like maybe what you see on TV. It's the kind of stuff where you ignore it. . . . You grow so accustomed to it until it doesn't even matter any more, but you know it's there."

Said another, "The name-calling could have been as often as once a week. That was just a regular thing, but it didn't bother me. . . . All you could do was just be yourself and let this person get to know you as the human being that you were."

73. Another two respondents commented: "When you live out here, you learn to relax and put up with [name-calling], because no matter where you go it would be there. Believe me."

"Sometimes a few [prejudices] came out, but it's only one or two incidents. I really couldn't count them because those were really ignorant people. I mean you're gonna find those anywhere you go."

74. Said one mother, "All I can really remember is the eleven years I stayed in the projects I never did let [my children] go out and play unless I was with

them. Every time I let [my daughter] go downstairs or out to play, there was a fight. So it was like, 'You just stay in the house and I'll let you come out when I come home.'"

Respondents also talked about the greater security in the suburbs: "This [suburban] neighborhood is better in 1,001 ways [than the city]. As far as peace of mind, it's not overcrowded, the mailboxes are not torn open. You don't have to use a key for the mailboxes out here. No bars on the windows. No bars on the doors. This is how free we are [in the suburbs]."

75. One mother put the issue very clearly: "Why would you live there [the projects] when you could move to the suburbs and pay the same kind of rent? . . . I only have to deal with people who don't like me, right? They're not doing anything to hurt me as far as I can see. They're not trying to break into my house. They're not trying to bust my child up the side of his head. They're not trying to lure him into [gangs and drugs]."

One youth related how her endurance had paid off: "When I first came out here, there wasn't hardly any black people. In my elementary school that I went to, there was about three black kids in the whole school, if that many. A lot of the white kids didn't understand what we're about 'cause we were different—most of us came from the projects or something like that. We were different—we were a lot more hard and rough around the edges. But eventually they got used to it and some of those people . . . are real good friends of mine now so they weren't bad."

76. See nn. 63–67, above, and accompanying text for the results of a survey of the youths about their friendships.

77. See nn. 63–67, above, and accompanying text for the results of a survey of the Gautreaux youths' friendships.

78. Reynolds Farley et al., "Barriers to the Racial Integration of Neighborhoods: The Detroit Case," *Annals of the American Academy of Political and Social Science* 411 (1979): 97, 109–13.

79. Francis J. Cronin and David W. Rasmussen, "Mobility," in *Housing Vouchers for the Poor: Lessons from a National Experiment*, ed. Raymond J. Struyk and Marc Bendick Jr. (Washington, D.C.: Urban Institute Press, 1981), 107, 108.

80. James E. Rosenbaum, "An Evaluation of Project Self-Sufficiency in Cook County" (unpublished manuscript on file with the Center for Urban Affairs and Policy Research, Northwestern University, 1988).

81. See nn. 24–26, above, and accompanying text.

John O. Calmore

Spatial Equality and the Kerner Commission Report

A Back-to-the-Future Essay

The goals and beliefs that Americans had about themselves are no longer tenable. And as a society, we are no longer prepared intellectually or spiritually for the world we actually live in. Our reaction is to want to go somewhere where we can hunker down and pretend we will find peace—somewhere the way we imagine things were, or should be.—Jim Dator, a futurist at the University of Hawaii, December 1992

Introduction

Eighty-six percent of white suburbanites live in residential neighborhoods where the percentage of black residents is less than 1 percent.[1] Indeed, the residential segregation of blacks and whites is now an accepted fact of life. It is taken for granted by most, seen as normal and unremarkable. Yet, as Douglas Massey and Nancy Denton have recently remarked,

> Although Americans have been quick to criticize the apartheid system of South Africa, they have been reluctant to acknowledge the consequences of their own institutionalized system of racial separation. The topic of segregation has virtually disappeared from public policy debates; it has vanished from the list of issues on the civil rights agenda; and it has been ignored by social scientists spinning endless theories of the underclass. Residential segregation has become the forgotten factor of American race relations, a minor footnote in the ongoing debate on the urban underclass. Until policymakers, social scientists, and private citizens recognize the crucial role of America's own apartheid in perpetuating urban poverty and racial injustice, the United States will remain a deeply divided and very troubled society.[2]

This observation is telling. It says to me that, as a nation, we have never really addressed the normative and practical shortcomings of integration as the answer to our own apartheid. At least in practical terms, one must begin to question integration's common sense understandings.

Since the Supreme Court's school desegregation decision in 1954, many unexpected complexities to integration have evolved. While a majority of blacks and whites indicate that they generally favor integration, many blacks now see that the process of integration as a means to equality of opportunity is more problematic than anticipated. As one commentator stated, "Among blacks who have worked, learned and lived in predominantly white settings, one theme occurs over and over again: such integration has not made many whites accept blacks as equals, and perhaps never will."[3] According to Lawrence Bobo, director of the Center for Research on Race and Politics and Society at UCLA, integration "is viewed with greater skepticism by blacks than it was in the past. That doesn't mean it's been repudiated. . . . But I think the benefits of it are more often questioned and the burdens that come with it are more prominent topics of discussion than they were in the past."[4]

In tracing the development of race consciousness, particularly during the period from the mid-1960s through the mid-1970s, Gary Peller observes that the national commitment to a centralized policy of integration virtually ignored the integrity and health of black institutions.[5] In his words, "Integration of dominant institutions, rather than reparations from one community to another, became the paradigm for racial enlightenment."[6] The demand for spatial equality calls for a paradigm shift in these terms and for a new day of racial enlightenment.[7]

Twenty-eight years ago the Kerner Commission Report concluded that the future of our cities would be enhanced only through the combination of enrichment programs designed to improve the quality of life in black communities and programs designed to encourage integration of substantial numbers of blacks into American society beyond the ghetto. The report warned us that integration would not quickly occur and that therefore enrichment had to be an important adjunct to any program of integration.[8] Spatial equality recognizes the continuing validity of this finding.[9] It therefore demands, as a matter of justice, that the enrichment program finally receive the policy attention and financial commitment necessary to compensate for decades of neglect and active exploitation.[10]

Dating back to Jamestown in the early 1600s, the African American housing situation has been problematic, almost intractably so. Today three mutually reinforcing conditions of that predicament cry out for redress: (1) extensive discrimination by government and private actors, as presently practiced and, more significantly, as a vestige of national history;

(2) housing and community deprivation and exploitation in multifaceted forms; and (3) persistent stigmatic segregative disadvantage, which is now largely an urban manifestation of restricted opportunity in the context of social and geographic isolation, containment, and expendability.

Karl Taeuber asserts that "the racial structure of housing in the United States is rooted in history."[11] The significance of this fact cannot be overstated. The harms associated with spatial inequality and diminished opportunity now plaguing so much of black America are primarily perpetuations of past discrimination by state and private actors who often operated in tandem. Spatial inequality's harms are reflected in persistent segregative disadvantage in education, employment, security, and residence. These harms are now increasingly superimposed on a rigid system of structural racial and economic inequality. Moreover, in a number of cities this condition is exacerbated by competition for community definition and for scarce resources, power, and opportunities. This competition is the result of urban disinvestment and demographic shifts over the last decade that have placed people of color in terrible intergroup conflicts—the multicultural nightmare of Los Angeles.[12]

Throughout African American history, the quest for affordable, decent, safe, and sanitary housing—for "fair housing"—has been black America's Sisyphean rock, even as we have progressed in areas of employment, cultural, educational, and political attainment. This quest is complicated because housing in America is conceptualized broadly. As Emily Achtenberg and Peter Marcuse state, "Housing, after all, is much more than shelter: it provides social status, access to jobs, education and other services, a framework for the conduct of household work, and a way of structuring economic, social and political relationships."[13] For most families, homeownership is not just the epitome of the American Dream; it is also the most important source of wealth one is likely to accumulate. Housing is really a "bundle" of disparate but inseparable components. According to Roger Montgomery and Daniel Mandelker, "Housing denotes an enormously complicated idea. It refers to a whole collection of things that come packaged together, not just four walls and a roof, but a specific location in relation to work and services, neighbors and neighborhood, property rights and privacy provisions, income and investment opportunities, and emotional or psychological symbols and supports."[14] Throughout this essay "housing" will denote this conception.

In considering the difficult issues of race and space twenty-eight years after the Kerner Commission Report, Professor Dator's observation, quoted in this essay's epigraph, is particularly insightful. The meaning of race in American society is not as straightforward as it was in 1968, and although racism remains at the center of so much, its form and expression are continually changing.[15] No matter how much America runs, it cannot hide from racism. We cannot, any of us, simply "hunker down and pretend we will find peace."[16]

The basic truth told in the Kerner Commission Report is more often than not denied now: "What white Americans have never fully understood—but what the Negro can never forget—is that white society is deeply implicated in the ghetto. White institutions created it, white institutions maintain it, and white society condones it."[17] Until dominant society rerecognizes, acknowledges, and takes responsibility for this situation, denial and neglect will continue to stand in the way of establishing a coherent urban policy that addresses not only matters of housing and community development but also the larger issues of social, economic, and racial justice. For now, the nation will continue to run scared, and time will continue to run out. Preventing this will be one of President Bill Clinton's principal domestic challenges.

The Kerner Commission stated that America was moving toward a deepening racial division, "two societies, one black, one white—separate and unequal."[18] The commission expressed great faith, however, and saw this trend as reversible. In lieu of either "blind repression or capitulation to lawlessness," it urged "the realization of common opportunities for all within a single society."[19] Today the nation's growing multicultural population displaces the propriety of continuing to view race relations as simply black and white,[20] but the required commitment described by the commission remains pertinent: "national action—compassionate, massive and sustained, backed by the resources of the most powerful and richest nation on this earth."[21] Accordingly, the commission called upon every American to approach the task with "new attitudes, new understandings, and, above all, new will."[22]

I had hoped that the election of Bill Clinton as President and his appointment of Henry Cisneros as secretary of the Department of Housing and Urban Development (HUD) would offer the opportunity for new attitudes, understanding, and will to reorient the nation away from the racial politics of division of the last twelve years. That hope, however, appears to be unrealistic.[23] We are left with the painful recognition that the Reagan-Bush years removed any illusion that the redress of spatial inequality and racial injustice would be directed by the Kerner Commission's finding that "there can be no higher priority for national action and no higher claim on the nation's conscience."[24] Instead, the response—really since the "benign neglect" days of Richard Nixon—has been to establish a situation in which "powerless conscience confronts conscienceless power."[25]

The second part of this essay discusses the concept of spatial equality and the need and propriety of realizing it. It urges black America to seek spatial equality even in the absence of integration. Too often integration, as an imperative, has simply displaced an orientation toward spatial equality, equating it with the separate-but-equal doctrine of another day. Thus, the third part, of necessity, offers a critique of residential integration as individualistic, tokenistic, gradualistic, and subordinating. The fourth part considers the intersecting impact of race and class factors on black community and cultural life. The fifth section assesses the federal government's historical involvement in endorsing, maintaining, and furthering spatial inequality by exploiting a black-white dual housing market, and therefore supports a claim that "territorial affirmative action" and reparations would be a proper result. In light of this, the final section offers some recommendations for legal advocacy and policy formulation.

The Meaning and Significance of Spatial Equality

Integrationists, black and white, have traditionally focused on an individualized equality of opportunity. In an ideal world, society would be race-neutral. Individuals could transcend the race-consciousness framework of our world, a framework that structures social stratification along race lines. This stratification, however, merges the race question with that of class. In most of our cities with a significant black population, the stratification has been spatialized. A unique, historical subjugation is perpetuated as race, class, and space intersect to compound the disadvantage that now determines the status of black society.[26] Blacks occupy an inferior position that is reflected in the quantitative and qualitative differences between the respective class structures of blacks and whites. Aside from spatial containment, the inferior status of blacks is constantly regenerated by economic forces, along with the legal, cultural, political, and social institutions that support them.[27]

Integrationists have never really accepted community enrichment as an appropriate prelude to broad-scale integration. Their early reaction to the terrible de jure segregation in the South extended itself to the de facto segregation in the urban North. They blurred the distinction between a compulsory ghetto and a voluntary black community and accepted as true the proposition that in all areas of life separate was inherently unequal. Civil rights advocates were thus simply "unable to argue simultaneously against Jim Crow and for the improvement of the Negro community."[28] This is a key but often overlooked failure of the civil rights movement. Moreover, influential white liberals argued that the ghetto enrichment strategy was politically infeasible because the strategy incorrectly assumed sufficient white goodwill and continued willingness to commit a great amount of resources.[29] Ghetto enrichment and integration were viewed as competing strategies, and the integrationists claimed consistently that "in a white dominated society, separate is inevitably unequal both in terms of the resources that go into a community and in terms of the way in which society values that community, its institutions, and its people."[30] As time has told, however, in a white-dominated society part of the domination has been to persist in blocking black entry into white residential areas or to flee from significant black entry.[31]

Title VIII of the Civil Rights Act of 1968 declared that it was national policy "to provide . . . for fair housing throughout the United States."[32] Although fair housing was not expressly defined in the act, its primary objective was initially interpreted to be "the replacement of ghettos by truly integrated and balanced living patterns."[33] This "integration imperative" legitimated the emphasis on desegregation rather than on simple nonsegregation[34] and the free choice as to where to live. This imperative has proven futile especially for those who live under the double bind of racial subordination and economic class subjugation. As it has turned out, integration presupposes relatively affluent black families effectively buying their way out of segregation. Even here success has been modest, however.[35]

This essay's demand for spatial equality extends a long-standing debate. In 1969, for example, John Kain and Joseph Persky authored an influential article that revived the unfortunate "gilded ghetto" metaphor, the imagery that set integration in a direction diametrically opposed to an enrichment strategy.[36] They argued that the ghetto was linked with the growing metropolis and stood in such an unfavorable position in comparison with the suburbs that it represented structural and "institutionalized pathology."[37] At best, enrichment and development of the black community under these circumstances would present only the deceptively attractive gloss, or gilding, of the community. Kain and Persky therefore called for the breakup of black communities and the dispersal of their inhabitants: "Although there are major benefits to be gained by both the Negro community and the metropolis at large through dispersal of the central ghetto, these benefits cannot be reached and are likely to be hindered by programs aimed at making the ghetto a more livable place."[38] Like other white and black liberals who believed ghetto enrichment to be politically infeasible, Kain and Persky failed to see any importance in maintaining a centralized black community.

A few years prior to the Kain and Persky article, Frances Fox Piven and Richard Cloward said what had to be said then and what must be said now: "The myth that integrationist measures are bringing better housing to the Negro poor comforts liberals; it placates (and victimizes) the Negro masses; and it antagonizes and arouses the bulk of white Americans."[39] Piven and Cloward correctly saw white backlash as a significant part of the desegregation legacy: "While turmoil rages over integration, housing conditions worsen. They worsen partly because . . . the energies and attention of reformers are diverted from attempts to ameliorate housing in the ghetto itself."[40]

Although history confirms the Piven-Cloward analysis, I am not arguing that integration be abandoned as a means of social mobility and betterment. I challenge, however, the integration imperative's tendency to sacrifice attention and reform directed toward ameliorating housing problems and furthering community development in black communities. Fair housing must be reconceptualized to mean not only increased opportunity for blacks to move beyond their socio-territorial disadvantage but also to mean enhanced choice to overcome opportunity-denying circumstances while continuing to live in black communities. Spatial equality is a group-based remedy that focuses on opportunity and circumstances within black communities and demands that both be improved, enriched, and equalized. Short of this, blacks as a group will be left with the inadequate "remedy" of individuals choosing, or being forced, to move to "better" space somewhere else.

Spatial equality compensates for past discrimination by legitimately combining the most effective features of affirmative action with expanded housing opportunity and choice. In many ways, it is analogous to educational equity advocacy.[41] If we really care about a more effective fair housing policy, we must expand its scope. Objectives limited to nondiscriminatory free access to housing and to desegregating the ghetto are insufficient given the intersectional features of race and class oppression, the extensive and persistent segregation we live with, and the historical legacy of denied opportunities associated with that oppression and segregation. Appropriate redefinition of fair housing policy would include locating and providing various types of housing "that address the special situation of oppressed groups, including the right to remain in place or to move to other neighborhoods of choice."[42] While we certainly must attempt to control and finally eliminate the housing market's pervasive discrimination and exclusion, we also certainly must target housing resources to revitalize existing communities of color "in order to protect and affirm the right of minority residents to enhance their social and political cohesiveness by remaining in place if they choose to do so."[43] The expansion of increased housing opportunity in other neighborhoods cannot diminish the prior commitment to neighborhood revitalization.[44]

A Critique of the Integration Imperative

In August 1963 Martin Luther King Jr. expressed a wonderful dream—"With this faith we will be able to transform the jangling discords of our nation into a beautiful symphony of brotherhood."[45] But King's hope for racial integration has died its hardest death in the area of housing. As one observer noted in July 1991, "Race fatigue grips America as the fight over a once-revered value [and] ideal has been overwhelmed by forces that either sharply slowed integration or are resegregating the land."[46] In June 1992 the *New York Times* reported that in a growing number of black suburbs, like Prince George's County, Maryland, even "affluent blacks are choosing to live among themselves."[47]

It is now time to rethink integration and examine its fundamental context-setting assumptions. In examining the progress of black-white integration since World War II, the National Research Council characterized "integration" as a broad term that refers to "the nature of intergroup relations, to the quality of group treatment or interaction that exists."[48] In an interracial or multiracial context, integration contemplates that each group is (1) significantly represented, (2) broadly distributed, and (3) sharing power and equality.[49]

After World War II, integration theory was influenced by a contact hypothesis that integration would be optimal when there was equal status between blacks and whites who pursued common, mutually supportive goals and there was authoritative sanction and support for this process.[50] This hypothesis was implicit in Dr. King's dream. In the early 1960s, integration was responsive to both political demands and moral claims. Today it is antagonistic to political demands, and its moral claims are rejected by whites who deny responsibility for segregation.

Because of the extent of exclusion of blacks from dominant institutions, integration packaged itself in a comprehensive way. Early integrationists assumed a linear, coherent, and symbiotic process whereby integrated schooling would provide children with a better education and training, which would in turn enable them to secure good jobs in an integrated labor market, which would in turn provide the sufficient economic resources to buy good housing in an integrated residential neighborhood. As the races got to know each other under these circumstances, they would come to appreciate one another as individuals who would be judged on the content of their character rather than the color of their skin. This process then would be enhanced and repeated for subsequent generations. What has occurred, however, is not coherent and packaged integration but, rather, segmental integration. By this I mean that fragments of integration in education, primarily at the college and graduate level; in politics and governance; in the employment and business sectors; and in social interaction have been attained in most cases without having been linked to residential integration.

Although it is frequently paid lip service, integration cannot be said to have been a broadly shared value within dominant America.[51] Integration has always been a tight, forced fit—too much so for the whole concept to work. For instance, when the school busing controversy raged during the 1970s, those advocating racially balanced public schools may have feared that to abandon busing would constrict the expanding civil rights movement.[52] To these people the debate over busing as a means to desegregate schools was viewed as a test of national commitment to continued civil rights progress. To sound a retreat on busing was deemed to be an abandonment of the whole-packaged commitment to integration and a re-embracing of the evils of segregation.[53] Under a kind of domino theory, establishment civil rights leaders feared that failure on the busing issue would trigger a string of defeats that would curtail the civil rights quest for integrated jobs, housing, public accommodations, and so on.[54]

Today, given the recognition of integration as a segmented rather than coherently packaged process, the domino theory should be rejected. Blacks of all socioeconomic classes still are forced to measure their progress in all areas of life primarily within the context of segregated housing and public education for our children. Each area of life must be analyzed separately to evaluate the connection between integration and concrete payoffs. We can no longer presume the linear progress that leads from an integrated neighborhood to integrated school to integrated workplace.

Although the meaning of integration and its value in various contexts are contested matters, most blacks remain committed to it as a pragmatic matter.[55] The integration imperative still drives many civil rights strategies, social and public policy deliberation and formulation, and moral and ethical discourse. It does so, however, primarily through wishful thinking and excessive loss of faith in black institutional and community capacity.[56] Spatial equality does not presume that benefits are automatically associated with integration, and it does not denigrate black capacity. It sees nonsegregation as an alternative to integration: "Nonsegregation implies both the right of people to remain indefinitely where they are, even if in ghetto areas, and the elimination of restrictions on moving into other areas. . . . Only white ethnocentrism could lead to the belief that all blacks would want to live in predominantly white areas."[57]

Integrationists too often see segregation as a result of mere discrimination; I see it as primarily a result of domination and exclusion. The evil of Jim Crow segregation began with the fact that whites chose to impose the separation on blacks. The invidious nature of the discrimination stemmed not simply from individual perpetrators engaged in the disparate treatment of individual blacks, but from a white group disposition of power to dominate and exclude blacks. The white desire to exercise this power remains strong today, especially when directed to poor, urban blacks. Hence, large gaps exist between black and white perceptions on the degree of integration that is acceptable. According to Reynolds Farley and Walter Allen, even when whites endorse the ideal of integrated housing, they would be uncomfortable if more than a token number of blacks were to enter their neighborhood.[58] In other words, whites accept integration only if black representation is minimal. Twenty-five percent of the whites surveyed by Farley in 1978 stated that they would feel uncomfortable if blacks constituted just 7 percent of the area population. Additionally, if the black percentage were 20, then over 40 percent of the whites would feel uncomfortable and 24 percent would try to move.[59] Blacks, by contrast, viewed integration as desirable only if they constituted a sizable percentage—"a number that [would] not only make whites uncomfortable, but [would] terminate white demand for housing in the neighborhood."[60]

Since Farley's 1978 study, racial polarization has greatly increased and the prospects for integration are less promising. Consider a 1985 study of white, working-class defectors from the Democratic Party.[61] The study's findings indicate the following:

> These . . . defectors express a profound distaste for blacks, a sentiment that pervades almost everything they think about government and politics. Blacks constitute the explanation for their vulnerability and for almost everything that has gone wrong in their lives; not being black is what constitutes being middle class; not living with blacks is what makes a neighborhood a decent place to live. . . . These sentiments have important implications, . . . as virtually all progressive symbols and themes have been redefined in racial and pejorative terms.[62]

Among liberal integrationists Gary Orfield is a consistently articulate voice. In 1988, however, two years after concluding that integration was the only real alternative to ghettoization, even he had harsh words for his own white liberal tradition.[63] Orfield claimed that white liberals failed to develop a coherent program of reform in response to the urban ghetto crisis that was brought into sharp focus during the mid-1960s.[64] By the beginning of the 1970s each branch of the federal government rejected efforts to make structural changes in the ghetto, and racial separation was accepted as natural. Anyone who suggested more than incremental changes was subjected to intense political and intellectual attack. Liberals thus focused on other issues.[65]

As liberals turned away from a structural analysis of urban inequality and racial oppression, the conservatives captured the policy agenda. They recharacterized compensatory programs as being based on the fact that the ghetto's inhabitants were in a subordinant position because of their own inherent personal behavior and group inferiority.[66] In the urban North during the early 1970s, and within a few years after the Kerner Commission Report found that white institutions were fundamentally responsible for urban racial inequality, there developed a totally different dominant understanding—the black community was responsible for its own problems and significant governmental action was no longer necessary: "The perception of the late 1960s that America faced a fundamental racial crisis was replaced by the belief that everything reasonable had been done and that, in fact, policies had often gone so far as to be unfair to whites."[67] Those who held these views included the officials who took charge of the principal social policy and civil rights agencies in the federal government.[68]

The acceptance of the ghetto system as natural was accompanied by the denunciation of policies aimed at challenging the color line, including aggressive fair housing enforcement and the dispersion of subsidized, low-income housing to the suburbs. The Nixon, Ford, and Reagan administrations adopted as a basic policy of the federal government the preservation of the racial status quo in metropolitan areas.[69] As the next section in this essay discusses, this preservation of the racial status quo has adversely affected blacks of varied socioeconomic classes.

Race and Class Intersection in the Quest for Community

Communities are based on things people hold in common. A community implies that its members' relationships are solidified by mutual ties that provide a feeling of collective identity, self-awareness, and affiliation. Because of persistently high levels of residential segregation, community cohesion is primarily based on racial homogeneity.[70] In the years following the Kerner Commission Report there has been a growing division within the black class structure that has raised questions about whether black inequality is attributable to race or class factors. Because of the growing concentration of ghetto poverty in areas from which the black middle class has moved, it is argued that black communities cannot really overcome class differences to build a community that incorporates the interests of the poor and the middle class.[71]

According to William Wilson, "Today the ghetto features a population, the underclass, whose primary predicament is joblessness reinforced by growing social isolation."[72] Wilson cites various economic and demographic factors as contributing to this situation, such as deindustrialization and the decline in manufacturing jobs, particularly in the Northeast and Midwest; the movement of blue-collar employment to the suburbs; and the growth of service jobs that eliminated jobs formerly held by unskilled but well-paid blacks. Additionally, these economic changes have reduced the pool of black men deemed to be marriageable, thereby contributing to the substantial number of poor, black, female-headed families who are largely dependent on welfare.[73]

Most relevant to this essay is Wilson's argument that, developing at the same time as the above-noted changes, there was a movement of black middle-class families from the ghetto, generated in part by the expansion of civil rights opportunities in housing and employment. The outmigration of middle-class blacks has concentrated the adverse effects of living in impoverished neighborhoods. Wilson enumerates such effects as "inadequate access to jobs and job networks, the lack of involvement in quality schools, . . . and the lack of exposure to informal mainstream social networks and conventional role models."[74]

Wilson's claim that black middle-class flight has caused the increased concentration of inner-city poverty is controversial. According to Douglas Massey and Mitchell Eggers, "Affluent and poor blacks are likely to live in the same neighborhoods, and only in communities with relatively low numbers of blacks has there been a trend toward segregation of blacks from each other according to income."[75] Farley also rebuts Wilson, arguing that poor blacks living in impoverished neighborhoods "occurred because of overall increases in black poverty rather than because of higher levels of residential segregation by social class or a new outmigration of prosperous blacks."[76]

Wilson focuses on ghetto poverty in neighborhoods where the poverty rate is over 40 percent.[77] I think Wilson is correct in seeing the poor as segregated from the middle class in such neighborhoods. I believe the ghetto poor are not as isolated as Wilson may argue, however, because the black middle class often resides close to the neighborhoods of ghetto poverty. Although upwardly mobile blacks, like whites, have sought to carve out neighborhood enclaves that contain only members of their own class, they have been relatively unsuccessful.[78] For example, Bart Landry found that in the Northeast the average percentage of middle-class blacks in a neighborhood was only 38 percent, as compared with 62 percent for whites.[79] He concluded that "the idea of a black middle class living in social isolation from the other classes is largely a myth."[80] Even though the black middle class may not live in ghetto neighborhoods, it often shares neighborhoods with the black working poor and near-poor.

It is important to keep in mind that black segregation is uniquely concentrated in cities.[81] Massey and Denton have characterized as "hypersegregation" that segregation which is multidimensional, or that exists in four of the following five ways: (1) uneven distribution of blacks in neighborhoods, (2) black isolation in neighborhoods, (3) concentration of blacks within small, physically compact areas, (4) black neighborhood clustering that forms one large ghetto, or (5) restriction of blacks to centralized neighborhoods close to the urban core.[82] In sixteen metropolitan areas blacks are highly segregated in this hypersegregated sense: Atlanta, Baltimore, Buffalo, Chicago, Cleveland, Dallas, Detroit, Gary, Indianapolis, Kansas City, Los Angeles, Milwaukee, New York, Newark, Philadelphia, and St. Louis.[83] According to Massey and Denton these sixteen metropolitan areas include six of the ten largest metropolitan areas in the United States. Residing there are 35 percent of the country's African American population and 41 percent of all African Americans who live in urban areas. Over one-third of the nation's blacks live under intense segregation.[84] Sadly ironic, "within a large, diverse, and highly mobile post-industrial society such as the United States, blacks living in the heart of the ghetto are among the most isolated people on earth."[85]

Another aspect unique to black residential segregation is the lack of significant change in its level as one climbs the socioeconomic ladder.[86] Regardless of occupational status, income, or educational achievement, blacks are highly segregated from similar whites.[87] According to the National Research Council, in 1980 the average segregation index for sixteen metropolitan areas was 75 for families with incomes of $10,000 to $14,999; 76 for those with incomes of $35,000 to $49,999; and 79 for those with incomes at $50,000 or more.[88] While the average segregation index for blacks is 80, it is only about 45 for Latinos and Asian Pacific Americans; indeed, it would take almost sixty years for the black-white index to reach current index figures for Latinos and Asian Pacific Americans.[89] Massey concludes that "as long as public policies ignore the impact of involuntary racial segregation and focus exclusively on class-related problems among blacks, they will fail because these problems are caused, in large part, by the persistence of racial segregation in American society."[90]

It is rare for blacks and whites to experience both integrated housing and a sense of community. Blacks demonstrate a history of integrating for a better housing package, not in quest of community. Integrated housing seldom represents "a path to belonging."[91] It is usually at the expense of community that blacks improve their housing package in integrated settings dominated by whites. The integration imperative is predicated on white dominance and virtual assimilation by blacks as preconditions to whites accepting blacks into their communities.[92] When these preconditions are not met, blacks who serve as the agents of integration risk living a life that lacks context and community. As Blair Stone indicates, "To be a part of a community one must feel 'at home' there. One must have a sense of attachment, both emotional and physical."[93] In the absence of these circumstances, affluent blacks who maximize the quality of their housing bundle do so at the expense of finding a home and community in the same space.

In light of the difficulty of linking home and community in the context of residential integration, there is evidence that even middle-class blacks are increasingly valuing black community attachment and affiliation at the expense of integration.[94] This is a controversial matter because opponents to fair housing have often cited voluntary segregation in denying the existence or extent of racial discrimination.[95] The theory that "blacks prefer to live among their own kind" is advanced to delay or prevent efforts toward decreasing black residential segregation. In turn, this rationale can support a community's efforts to "maintain the ethnic purity of its neighborhood without racist guilt."[96]

Nevertheless, I believe that a growing segment of the black middle class is voluntarily attaining housing that is in black areas. This may stem in part from the increase in black alienation from white society that has developed from the late 1960s and into the early 1980s among all segments of the black community. According to the National Research Council's survey, "Questions concerning white intentions or basic trust in whites elicit some of the most alienated responses."[97] Also, for the black middle class it has been possible to attain the benefits of socioeconomic mobility without living in integrated neighborhoods.[98]

Motivation aside, for the black middle class the existence of adequate housing alternatives to the most impoverished black areas has come within the context of persistent racial segregation from whites and the reduced push to move to all-white or integrated areas. The push to move to these areas was apparently more valued when they represented the only viable options to deplorable living conditions.[99] Moreover, given the past history of white resistance to residential integration—including acts of intimidation, harassment, and violence—the "voluntary" segregation may "simply reflect the judgment that entry into all-white communities is just not worth the risk or aggravation; and it is certainly no longer necessary to achieve a decent standard of living."[100]

Those who emphasize integration either as a value per se or as a pragmatic means of access to improved lifestyles and life chances often discount the growing importance of black cultural and community affinities. Take, for example, the black community of Los Angeles's View Park. To the outside observer it would probably appear ironic that this group of affluent and professional blacks, who have successfully integrated into various parts of mainstream society, choose to live in this mostly black neighborhood—"especially one that is situated a quick drive away from the gang-scarred neighborhoods east of Crenshaw."[101] Residents offer various explanations. According to a black airline pilot the presence of black role models for his two preadolescent children outweighed negative factors associated with living in an urban area: "In this community, they can see black doctors, writers, lawyers, artists, craftsmen, law-enforcement officials. They're all within a hundred yards of where we live."[102]

Many View Park residents reportedly experience relief upon returning home to a black environment after having endured the job stress of "competing on a white playing field all day."[103] Black parents, whose children attend predominantly white private schools, expressed a critical need to have their children come home to a black neighborhood where it is the norm to be black; otherwise the children could lose a social and cultural grounding that would militate against their growing up "lost, not knowing who they are." [104]

In spite of the growing class schism among blacks, spatial equality's group-based remedial orientation presents the potential to build black community and cultural life in ways that integration simply cannot. The integration imperative is a skimming off process that disperses from the community many of the very people who are needed as resources, often leaving behind in isolated circumstances those who are the most disabled and dislocated socially and economically. Spatial equality enables a relinking of black interests across class lines.

The Historical Linkage between Federal Policy and Spatial Inequality

The Kerner Commission awakened America to its national racism. As we examine the matters it addressed, we must recognize that racism changes through time as it takes on new forms and reflects various antagonisms in different contexts. [105] One view of contemporary racism is that blacks collectively personify a problem, or more precisely, a series of problems. Similarly, blacks are also characterized as perennial victims. Together, these perceptions remove from black life its historical dimension. Thus, Paul Gilroy states that "the oscillation between black as problem and black as victim has become, today, the principal mechanism through which 'race' is pushed outside of history and into the realm of natural, inevitable events." [106] In other words, "Racism rests on the ability to contain blacks in the present, to repress and to deny the past." [107] Opposition to racism must counter this by reclaiming and revealing to others the historical dimensions of black life.

A decade ago Eric Schnapper wrote that "the central discrimination issue of the 1980s will be to end the perpetuation of past discrimination." [108] In considering the remedy for black America's housing predicament, it is important to move beyond individual acts of racial discrimination and address "the government rules, policies, and practices that perennially reenforce the subordinate status of any group." [109] The urban oppression now experienced by so many blacks is neither natural nor inevitable. In assessing responsibility, little is gained by searching out individual perpetrators. A regime sustains subordination through generating "devices, institutions, and circumstances that impose burdens or constraints on the target group without resort to repeated or individualized discriminatory actions." [110] Through contextualizing the historical development of federal housing policies, we can look back to the future and see the nation's continuing responsibility for furthering the racist adventure that now plagues so many blacks in urban settings.[111]

In *Milliken v. Bradley*, the 1974 Detroit school desegregation case, Justice Potter Stewart concluded that the segregative disadvantages associated with spatial inequality had been caused "by unknown and perhaps unknowable factors."[112] This view badly misreads the historical role of the federal government since the 1930s. It is now clear that the dual housing market that undergirds racial demography and residential segregation has been preserved and expanded by the federal government's express endorsement of racism. As summarized by the Citizen's Commission on Civil Rights,

> During the period when FHA [Federal Housing Administration] mortgage assistance and other programs were operating full throttle, first to save the housing industry and then to finance suburban expansion, a "whites only" label was firmly affixed to these programs. Federal policymakers cooperated with state and local governments, real estate brokers, developers and financial institutions to assure that minorities were excluded from assistance designed to benefit the middle class and that low-income housing was provided only on a segregated basis. The federal government placed its imprimatur on the exclusionary and segregative practices of others and helped shape the current racial demography of the nation's cities. For [blacks], the government's housing policies meant that they were confined to ghettos, lacking choice and access to the jobs and services that would have afforded them the opportunity to become part of the mainstream.[113]

It is virtually impossible to overstate the significance of this involvement in creating, sponsoring, and perpetuating the racially segregated dual housing markets that divide America. The federal government should acknowledge its role and move to right these tragic wrongs. According to Dennis Judd, "The case for a policy of affirmative action to help blacks obtain access to housing can easily be made, not based on an abstract legacy of generations of discrimination but on the ground that within the past half-century the federal government itself helped to create the present patterns of residential segregation and therefore is obligated to enact policies of equal force to reverse the effects of its own racist policies."[114]

The legacy of the government's racist past is broad and far reaching. Consider the gap in black-white homeowner rates. In 1985, while 68 percent of all white households owned their homes, only 44 percent of all black households did.[115] Moreover, even the proportion of poor white households who owned their homes was 46 percent, thus exceeding all black homeowners.[116] Because homeownership represents the primary source of wealth in our society, these disparities explain in significant part the fact that in 1988 the net wealth of all white households was ten times greater than that of all black households.[117]

The racially discriminatory policies of the FHA and the Veterans' Administration (VA) that significantly transformed the nation's patterns of homeownership facilitated this huge discrepancy. Prior to World War II, banks and other lending institutions as a rule demanded a down payment of 50 percent and required repayment of the mortgage within ten years.[118] In contrast the FHA offered insured mortgages over thirty years, with only 5 to 10 percent down payments.[119] Aided by VA-insured mortgages, 3.75 million GIs were able to buy homes after the war with no more than a token $1 down payment.[120] The FHA and the VA were insuring 36 percent of all new nonfarm mortgages by 1950 and 41 percent by 1955.[121] As was said about FHA policy, however, it was essentially "separate for whites and nothing for blacks." Between 1934 and 1959 only 2 percent of the FHA units were made available to blacks.[122]

The new mortgage policies had their greatest effect in the suburbs, which could accommodate the new construction of single-family detached houses.[123] The FHA rated residential areas in terms of risks that might be associated with lending in a given area. Invariably, suburban areas received high ratings while urban areas were redlined as undesirable. According to historian Richard Polenberg, "It became virtually impossible to obtain a federally insured mortgage to buy an older home in the city. The deck was stacked in favor of those who wanted to buy a new home in the suburbs."[124] If blacks sought to buy in the suburbs, there was yet another deck stacked against them. Racially prejudiced local customs and exclusionary practices in the suburbs were federally endorsed by the FHA manuals that guided the agency underwriters issuing federal insurance. The manuals provided a blueprint to prevent blacks from entering neighborhoods where their mere presence would bring down property values.[125] One year after federal law established the federal mortgage insurance program, a 1935 manual stated that acceptable ratings would turn on neighborhoods that protected against "the occurrence or development of unfavorable influences" such as the "infiltration of inharmonious racial or nationality groups."[126]

In 1936 an agency underwriters' manual spelled out techniques for preventing this infiltration, recommending deed restrictions as preferable to zoning measures: "Where the same deed restrictions apply over a broad area and where these restrictions relate to types of structures, use to which improvements may be put, and *racial occupancy*, a favorable condition is apt to exist."[127] Finally, the manual explained that neighborhood stability was an important rating factor, and this too was coded in terms of race.

Neighborhood stability required properties to continue to be occupied by racially and socially homogeneous classes: "*A change in social or racial occupancy generally contributes to instability and a decline in values.*"[128]

These racist theories combined with other policies to establish rigid black-white segregation in public housing, to exclude blacks from white neighborhoods that received federal funds, and to deny mortgage assistance in black neighborhoods. These early policies continued after the war, and with the boom in suburbanization of the 1950s the federal government not only planted the seeds for today's persistent residential segregation; it joined hands with local government, realtors, and developers to nurture and extend lily-white suburban enclaves.[129] The urban civil disorders that prompted the Kerner Commission Report were just an unintended part of the harvest.

Recommendations

Litigation

The position articulated by National Housing Law Project attorney Florence Roisman presents the best balanced approach to assure affordable housing in communities of color as well as to provide integrated housing opportunities beyond those communities.[130] She argues that the conflict that I have raised between these two goals is a function of scarce housing supply, which she deems to be "an artificial constraint that is itself not acceptable."[131] Her central claim, with which I agree, is that integration must be achieved without disadvantaging people of color in the process.[132] She therefore advocates that constitutional and Title VIII legal principles and remedies be marshaled to produce increased housing and improved neighborhoods for people of color while also achieving integration.[133]

The fair housing bar is very small, however, and advocacy cannot adopt a "let's do it all" approach. Rather, it must set priorities in light of client need assessment and input, remedial feasibility, and the value orientations that advance fair housing and human development for the community of people who are represented as well as absentees from the litigation who would be affected. Until there is a universal entitlement to housing for poor people, the political reality, heavily dependent on privatization, simply does not hold out much promise for overcoming the scarcity issue that Roisman deems to be artificial.[134] I remain unconvinced that the push for integration—at least at this time—can move beyond the gradualism, tokenism, and cultural chauvinism that are the common expressions of white dominance.

While Roisman provides to the fair housing advocate an excellent litigation approach, the problems are primarily political. Any fair housing lawyer, however, should rely upon her constitutional and statutory arguments to establish liability and to provide remedy. Fair housing's antidiscrimination mandate requires an increase in the supply of housing so that whites and people of color can be treated equally. While I would press for *targeted* housing production, rehabilitation, and preservation in communities of color, Roisman would seek to enlarge the housing stock there and in proximate predominantly white developments so that both colored and white applicants would receive equal treatment "with respect to securing access to the enlarged stock."[135] Roisman presents an ambitious advocacy program that contemplates literally hundreds of systemic litigation cases.[136] These suits would require very complex, creative, and flexible remedy formulation whereby resources for housing would be expanded and redirected from white higher-income communities to support equalization.[137] Here is where I would stop. Roisman would go beyond this point and also seek remedies to require "previously closed communities to open up to poor people of color."[138]

Because of the Fair Housing Act's bias toward an integration imperative, and because fair housing advocacy has generally been directed by that bias, I fear that Roisman's two-pronged approach of mobility remedies and in-place remedies will not be adopted, but, rather, the access prong will be pressed at the expense of the equalization prong. Her strategy is really a luxury that contemplates both increased appropriations of federal financial resources for housing as well as increased lawyering capacity to litigate these cases. Her excellent discussion of case models presents an opportunity to direct effective advocacy efforts *if* opportunities are carefully selected and lawyering resources are not spread too thinly.

We must keep in mind that much litigation cost, time, and energy will necessarily be spent bringing defensive suits such as those that attempt to preserve public housing from demolition, prevent urban revitalization from causing racially impacted involuntary displacement, eliminate the effects of environmental racism, and prevent so-called benign quotas from limiting colored access to housing. To militate against resource diffusion, advocates should contemplate opportunities that would leverage quite heavily their efforts. One such move would be to search for cases that accommodate national class action lawsuits. For example, it is well documented that HUD-assisted, public, and subsidized housing programs reflect separate and unequal accommodations for blacks and whites.[139] A national class action against HUD could be filed to force HUD to equalize these housing accommodations across America. In this regard, for example, I believe there is tremendous untapped potential to further the goal of spatial equality through reliance on Title VIII's provision making it illegal "to discriminate against any person in the terms, conditions, or privileges of sales or rental of a dwelling, or in the provision of services or facilities in connection therewith, because of race, color, religion, sex, or national origin."[140] The provision protects not only the person seeking to secure housing on a nondiscriminatory basis, but also, and more importantly for this analysis, it provides a right to equal services and facilities once the person has actually secured the housing.[141] For example, the HUD fair housing regulations illustrate a violation of 42 U.S.C.A. § 3604(b) where a housing provider fails or delays proper maintenance or repairs of a dwelling because of the resident's race (or other protected status).[142] This is spatial equality.

National Urban Policy

Urban policy under the Clinton administration will not realistically be able to build on the preceding years of federal governance. Instead it must reorient and reestablish before it can advance a significantly new agenda. It must do no less than re-legitimate federal intervention in local matters of housing and urban development. As Peter Berger and Thomas Luckmann state, "Legitimation produces new meanings already attached to disparate institutional processes."[143] The process of legitimation both explains and justifies society's institutional order and arrangements. As a result, legitimation provides "a normative dignity" to the institutional order's "practical imperatives": "Legitimation not only tells the individual why he should perform one action and not another; it also tells him why things are what they are."[144] In legitimation, then, knowledge precedes value and therefore the nation must acquire a different knowledge about, and sense of responsibility for, urban-racial oppression in order to achieve a proper value reorientation to address it.

The national community—who we are and who we seek to become—must incorporate inner-city communities of color. In 1969 Daniel Moynihan proposed ten fundamental points of urban policy.[145] I would endorse the following five:

> The poverty and social isolation of minority groups in central cities is the single most serious problem of the American city today. It must be attacked with urgency, with a greater commitment of resources than has heretofore been the case, and with programs designed especially for this purpose. . . .
>
> A primary object of federal urban policy must be to restore the fiscal vitality of urban government, with the particular object of ensuring that

local governments normally have enough resources on hand or available to make local initiative in public affairs a reality. . . .

Federal urban policy should seek to equalize the provision of public services among different jurisdictions in metropolitan areas. . . .

The federal government must develop and put into practice far more effective incentive systems than now exist whereby state and local governments, and private interest too, can be led to achieve the goals of federal programs. . . .

The federal government must provide more and better information concerning urban affairs, and should sponsor extensive and sustained research into urban problems.[146]

While Senator Moynihan's policy recommendations are now twenty-seven years ignored, they are not really dated. Instead, at least as a point to begin conversation, they are more urgent today than they were then.

Conclusion

In the year the Kerner Commission Report was published, Martin Luther King Jr. was assassinated in Memphis. Shortly thereafter Congress passed the Fair Housing Act. When Dr. King died, it was said that the Dreamer could be slain, but not the Dream. I wish that were so, but I fear that it is not. Today, out of necessity black people are, as Patricia Williams might say, "regrouping in singular times."[147] Not only does spatial equality call for a compensatory policy that responds directly to a group history of racial subordination, but it also rebuts the contention that group-based social justice claims lack theoretical and moral foundation, that group affiliation is a mere "proxy" for individual claims not to be discriminated against.[148] We all have learned that for the most disadvantaged of our race, remedial strategies predicated on the enhancement of individual opportunities offer little real help or hope when they fail to improve group conditions.[149]

Gary Peller has written that "integrationists filter discussion of the wide disparities between African American and white communities through the nonracial language of poverty and class, and avoid altogether the racial implications of the institutional practices of 'integrated' arenas of social life."[150] The construction of race reform in integrationist terms has cost a great deal in terms of social resources and personal energy, resources and energy spent on integrating schools, neighborhoods, workplaces, government, and society. I cannot deny that the lives of many blacks, including myself, have been improved through integrationist efforts. Nor can I deny that the social climate of overt racist domination that America reflected forty years ago has been transformed. As Peller contends, however, the integrationist program "has been pursued to the exclusion of a commitment to the vitality of the black community as a whole and to the economic and cultural health of black neighborhoods, schools, economic enterprises, and individuals." [151] It is this neglected commitment that drives my call for spatial equality.

In 1979 I was a Legal Services attorney, attending a meeting of low-income housing advocates and clients in Washington, D.C. Some of the black clients questioned us as to why we were all so intent on trying to move them out of their communities instead of working to improve those communities. It was in response to representing their interests that I began to rethink integration. Since that time I have urged spatial equality as a moderating force to the pursuit of integration at all costs. Integration comes with a lot of freight for those such as the clients I have mentioned. We must awaken to its practical dysfunctions and conceptual shortcomings. When integration works, fine. When it does not work, we should not pretend that it will with just a little more time and understanding. Instead, we should move to something else; *"God gave Noah the rainbow sign / No more water, the fire next time."* [152]

Notes

1. Cornel West, *Race Matters* (Boston: Beacon, 1993), 4.

2. Douglas S. Massey and Nancy A. Denton, *American Apartheid: Segregation and the Making of the Underclass* (Cambridge, Mass.: Harvard University Press, 1993), 16.

3. Charisse Jones, "Years on Integration Road: New Views of an Old Goal," *New York Times*, April 10, 1994.

4. Ibid.

5. Gary Peller, "Race Consciousness," *Duke Law Journal*, 1990, no. 4 (1990): 758, 843.

6. Ibid.

7. Peller notes that the reappearance of race consciousness in critical race scholarship partly reflects an attempt "to reopen a political discourse that was closed off in the 1960s" (ibid., 847). This essay is a case in point. On other occasions my position has been vilified as "1960s retreaded black-nationalistic, black-power separatist rhetoric" (remarks of a white liberal speaker at the Conference on Homelessness, Twenty-fifth Anniversary of the *Villanova Law Review*, November 1990). His comments really were retreaded from the 1960s, when black power advocates were called "black neo-segregationists" and "advocates of apartheid." Then and now these charges are ridiculous. As Peller points out, black power troubled integrationists, in part, because one of its underlying assumptions was that power, rather than reason or merit, determined the distribution of social resources and opportu-

nities (Peller, "Race Consciousness," 790). I, too, think this is true. Peller further states, "Integrationists saw nationalists as regressive because, in the integrationist view, progress meant transcending race as a basis of social decisionmaking. . . . With the centering of integrationism as the mainstream ideology of American good sense, nationalism became marginalized as an extremist and backward worldview, as the irrational correlate to the never-say-die segregationists of the white community" (Peller, "Race Consciousness," 790). My orientation does draw on black nationalism, but I agree with Manning Marable "that the positive elements of integration be merged with the activist tradition of black nationalism" (Marable, *From the Grassroots: Social And Political Essays toward Afro-American Liberation* [Boston: South End Press, 1980], 15). See John O. Calmore, "Critical Race Theory, Archie Shepp, and Fire Music: Securing an Authentic Intellectual Life in a Multicultural World," *Southern California Law Review* 65 (1992): 2129, 2131 n. 5. This essay represents an attempt to practice what is preached in that article, especially parts V and VI (Calmore, "Critical Race Theory," 2206–28).

8. *Report of the National Advisory Commission on Civil Disorders* (New York: Bantam Books, 1968), 395–407 (hereafter cited as *Kerner Report*).

9. Today, although black movement to the suburbs has increased since the 1960s, the persistence of central-city poverty "is not likely to be substantially diminished in the foreseeable future through out-migration" (Thomas A. Clark, "The Suburbanization Process and Residential Segregation," in *Divided Neighborhoods: Changing Patterns of Racial Segregation*, ed. Gary A. Tobin [Newbury Park, Calif.: Sage, 1987], 115, 135).

10. See, for example, Gary Williams, "'The Wrong Side of the Tracks': Territorial Rating and the Setting of Automobile Liability Insurance Rates in California," *Hastings Constitutional Law Quarterly* 19 (1992): 845, 852–54, 856–59. Williams discusses the adverse racial impact of territorial rating in the context of housing segregation coupled with economic isolation and poverty concentration.

11. Karl Taeuber, "The Contemporary Context of Housing Discrimination," *Yale Law and Policy Review* 6 (1988): 339.

12. James H. Johnson Jr. and Melvin L. Oliver, "Interethnic Minority Conflict in Urban America: The Effects of Economic and Social Dislocations," *Urban Geography* 10 (1989): 449.

13. Rachel G. Bratt, Chester Hartman, and Ann Meyerson, eds., introduction to *Critical Perspectives on Housing* (Philadelphia: Temple University Press, 1986), xi, xviii.

14. Roger Montgomery and Daniel R. Mandelker, eds., *Housing in America: Problems and Perspectives*, 2d ed. (Indianapolis: Bobbs-Merrill, 1979), 3.

15. Michael Omi and Howard Winant, *Racial Formation in the United States: From the 1960s to the 1980s* (New York: Routledge, 1986), 61–69.

16. John Balzar, "California's Image: Fad to a Funk," *Los Angeles Times*, December 19, 1992 (quoting Jim Dator).

17. *Kerner Report*, 2.

18. Ibid., 1. In elaborating, the commission stated, "Reaction to last summer's disorders has quickened the movement and deepened the division. Discrimination and segregation have long permeated much of American life; they now threaten

the future of every American" (ibid.). This was implicitly echoed in Los Angeles in April 1992 when, amid cries of "No Justice, No Peace," that city experienced unprecedented civil disorder that caused over $775 million in damage and over fifty deaths. See "Special Report: Understanding the Riots," parts 1–5, *Los Angeles Times*, May 11–15, 1992.

19. *Kerner Report*, 1. After the 1992 civil disorder in Los Angeles, Marvin Fitzwater, White House press secretary under former president George Bush, attributed that disorder to the Great Society programs of the 1960s: "We are now paying the price" for the failure of these programs of the past in the big cities (editorial, "A Great Debate on the Legacy of the Great Society," *Washington Post*, 6 May 1992). The *Washington Post* editorialized, "The president's version of an urban policy is the warding off of a myth. Back to Orwell: 'And if all others accepted the lie which the Party imposed, . . . if all records told the same tale—then the lie passed into history and became truth'" ("Great Debate on the Legacy of the Great Society").

20. Barbara Vobejda, "Asian, Hispanic Population of U.S. Soared in 1980s, Census Reveals," *Washington Post*, March 11, 1991.

21. *Kerner Report*, 1–2.

22. Ibid.

23. See "A Critique of HUD's Reinvention Blueprint," *Housing Law Bulletin* 25 (1995): 29.

24. *Kerner Report*, 1–2.

25. "A Statement by the National Committee of Negro Churchmen," in *The Black Power Revolt*, ed. Floyd B. Barbour (Boston: Porter Sargent, 1968), 264.

26. See generally William W. Goldsmith and Edward J. Blakely, eds., *Separate Societies: Poverty and Inequality in U. S. Cities* (Philadelphia: Temple University Press, 1992).

27. Thomas D. Boston, *Race, Class, and Conservatism* (New York: Routledge, Chapman and Hall, 1988), 4.

28. Charles Silberman, "Beware the Day They Change Their Minds," *Fortune*, November 1965, 152 (emphasis omitted).

29. Gary Orfield, "The Movement for Housing Integration: Rationale and the Nature of the Challenge," in *Housing Desegregation and Federal Policy*, ed. John M. Goering (Chapel Hill: University of North Carolina Press, 1986), 18, 20.

30. Ibid., 21.

31. Gary Tobin, "Introduction: Housing Segregation in the 1980s," in Tobin, *Divided Neighborhoods*, 7, 11.

32. Fair Housing Act, 42 U.S.C. § 3601 (1968). The Fair Housing Act should combine with the national housing policy of the Civil Rights Act of 1866, which guarantees to blacks and other colored citizens the same housing rights as those enjoyed by whites (Civil Rights Act of 1866, 42 U.S.C. § 1982 [1866]). See *Jones v. Alfred H. Mayer Co.*, 392 U.S. 409 (1968). Fair housing should also incorporate the policy of the Housing Act of 1949 that "every American family" be provided "a decent home and a suitable living environment . . . as soon as feasible" (United States Housing Act, 42 U.S.C. § 1441 [1950]). This nation has never been fully

committed to any of these fair housing precepts. The nation should adopt what Paul Gewirtz characterizes as the "corrective ideal":

> The corrective conception does not tell us exactly what to do. Rather, it insists upon an imagery and locates a source of commitment. The images are rooted in the past—the awful, deliberate wrongs inflicted on black people for so long, the broad sweep of continuity between past deeds and present life. From that image of wrong comes the commitment to correction, the distinctive dynamic of racial justice. The corrective idea insists that racial justice not be assimilated to other distributive objectives. It affirms that, because of the past, the claims of black Americans are unique and uniquely just. It affirms, at the very least, a way of thinking about racial justice. (Gewirtz, "Choice in the Transition: School Desegregation and the Corrective Ideal," *Yale Law Journal* 86 [1986]: 728, 798)

33. U.S. Senate, remarks of Senator Walter Mondale, principal sponsor of the Fair Housing Act, *Congressional Record*, 90th Cong., 2d sess., 1968, 114:2276.

34. For a discussion of nonsegregation, see Michael R. Tein, "The Devaluation of Nonwhite Community in Remedies for Subsidized Housing Discrimination," *University of Pennsylvania Law Review* 140 (1992): 1463, 1492. Tein discusses how the emphasis on neighborhood integration stigmatizes the nonwhite community. See also Henry W. McGee Jr., "Afro-American Resistance to Gentrification and the Demise of Integrationist Ideology in the United States," *Urban Lawyer* 23 (1991): 25, 40. McGee discusses the attempt of the black community of Roxbury to separate from Boston and to incorporate itself.

35. Blacks of all income levels are highly segregated from similar whites, and in a 1980 study of sixteen metropolitan areas, the segregation index for families with incomes of $50,000 or more was equal to that of families in poverty (Gerald David Jaynes and Robin M. Williams Jr., eds., *A Common Destiny: Blacks and American Society* [Washington, D.C.: National Academy Press, 1989], 144).

36. John Kain and Joseph Persky, "Alternatives to the Gilded Ghetto," *Public Interest* 14 (1969): 74.

37. Ibid., 78.

38. Ibid., 82. A sample of responses to Kain and Persky includes Joel Bergsman, "Alternatives to the Non-gilded Ghetto: Notes on Different Goals and Strategies," *Public Policy* 19 (1971): 309; Peter Labrie, "Black Central Cities: Dispersal or Rebuilding," part 1, *Review of Black Political Economy* 1 (1970): 3; and Robert Browne, "Toward an Overall Assessment of our Alternatives," *Review of Black Political Economy* 1 (1970): 18.

39. Frances Fox Piven and Richard Cloward, "Desegregated Housing: Who Pays for the Reformer's Ideal?," *New Republic*, December 1966, 14.

40. Ibid. A similar critique has been made regarding education in Derrick Bell, "Serving Two Masters: Integration Ideals and Client Interests in School Desegregation Litigation," *Yale Law Journal* 85 (1976): 470.

41. John C. Brittain, "Educational and Racial Equity toward the Twenty-First Century—A Case Experiment in Connecticut," in *Race in America: The Struggle for Equity*, ed. Herbert Hill and James E. Jones Jr. (Madison: University of Wiscon-

sin Press, 1993), 167. According to Brittain, the concept of "educational equity" is used instead of "school desegregation" to offer "learning opportunities for the urban, poor nonwhite school children on an equal basis with those which the suburban, affluent, virtually all white children enjoy" (ibid., 170). Although racial balance is important, busing is deemphasized while improved educational opportunities within poor nonwhite schools are the goal.

42. Emily Paradise Achtenberg and Peter Marcuse, "Toward the Decommodification of Housing," in Bratt et al., *Critical Perspectives*, 474, 480.

43. Ibid.

44. Ibid.

45. "Black and White in America: The Integration Ideal of a Generation Ago is Vanishing," *U.S. News & World Report*, July 22, 1991, 18.

46. Ibid.

47. David J. Dent, "The New Black Suburbs," *New York Times Magazine*, June 14, 1992.

48. Jaynes and Williams, *Common Destiny*, 57.

49. Ibid. See also Rose Helper, "Success and Resistance Factors in the Maintenance of Racially Mixed Neighborhoods," in Goering, *Housing Desegregation*, 170, 171. Helper distinguishes between "integrated" and "racially mixed" neighborhoods.

50. Ankur J. Goel, "Maintaining Integration against Minority Interests: An Anti-Subjugation Theory for Equality in Housing," *Urban Lawyer* 22 (1990): 369, 387. The problem with the hypothesis is that blacks and whites seldom share equal status, which must precede white acceptance of integration (ibid., 388). This partly explains the phenomenon of "tipping" or "resegregation." See Bruce L. Ackerman, "Integration for Subsidized Housing and the Question of Racial Occupancy Controls," *Stanford Law Review* 26 (1974): 245, 254–55. Because of white flight, fueled by prejudice, and the resultant resegregation when blacks enter white apartments or neighborhoods, three negative results can occur: (1) entry quotas are imposed to limit blacks and to maintain stable integration; realtors are encouraged to indulge in (2) blockbusting or (3) steering. See, respectively, Rodney Smolla, "Integration Maintenance: The Unconstitutionality of Benign Programs that Discourage White Flight," *Duke Law Journal* 1981, no. 6 (1981): 891; *United States v. Starrett City Assoc.*, 660 F. Supp. 608 (E.D.N.Y. 1987), affirmed, 840 F.2d 1096 (2d Cir. 1988), cert. denied, 109 S. Ct. 376 (1988); Note, "Blockbusting," *Georgetown Law Journal* 59 (1970): 170; and Note, "Racial Steering: The Real Estate Broker and Title VIII," *Yale Law Journal* 85 (1976): 808, 809–12.

51. Probably, the shift from an emphasis on issues of principle to those of practical social policy "was the decisive change in racial issues in the 1970s" (Jaynes and Williams, *Common Destiny*, 124). Although blacks and whites share consensus on an abstract goal of achieving an integrated and equalitarian society, "their images of what constitute integrated, equalitarian, and racially harmonious conditions are often different or contradictory . . . and [their] perceptions of the genesis and reproduction of group inequality are sharply divergent" (ibid.). See Thomas Pettigrew, "New Patterns of Racism: The Different Worlds of 1984 and 1964," *Rut-*

gers Law Review 37 (1985): 673; David Benjamin Oppenheimer, "Negligent Discrimination," *University of Pennsylvania Law Review* 141 (1993): 899, 905–15.

52. Derrick Bell, *Race, Racism, and American Law,* 2d ed. (Boston: Little, Brown, 1980), 414.

53. Ibid.

54. Ibid.

55. Wilhelmina A. Leigh and James D. McGhee, "A Minority Perspective on Residential Racial Integration," in Goering, *Housing Desegregation,* 31, 39. The authors find that "the overriding issue here is better, more affordable housing for minorities, not housing integration."

56. Tein, "Devaluation of Nonwhite Community," 1463, 1492; McGee, "Afro-American Resistance to Gentrification," 25, 40.

57. Robert E. Forman, *Black Ghettos, White Ghettos, and Slums* (Englewood Cliffs, N.J.: Prentice-Hall, 1971), 46. See also John O. Calmore, "Fair Housing vs. Fair Housing: The Problems with Providing Increased Housing Opportunities through Spatial Deconcentration," *Clearinghouse Review* 14 (1980): 7, 12, and Comment, "Black Neighborhoods Becoming Black Cities: Group Empowerment, Local Control, and the Implications of Being Darker Than Brown," *Harvard Civil Rights–Civil Liberties Law Review* 24 (1988): 415, 428 (1988). In "Black Neighborhoods" the author discusses the attempt of the black community of Roxbury to separate from Boston and to incorporate itself.

58. Reynolds Farley and Walter R. Allen, *The Color Line and the Quality of Life in America* (New York: Oxford University Press, 1989), 154.

59. Jaynes and Williams, *Common Destiny,* 141.

60. Ibid.

61. The poll focused on suburban Detroit and was conducted by Stanley Greenberg. See Thomas Byrne Edsall and Mary D. Edsall, "Race," *Atlantic Monthly,* May 1991, 53, 56.

62. Ibid.

63. Gary Orfield, "Race and the Liberal Agenda: The Loss of the Integrationist Dream, 1965–1974," in *The Politics of Social Policy in the United States,* ed. Margaret Weir, Ann Shola Orloff, and Theda Skocpol (Princeton: Princeton University Press, 1988), 313.

64. Ibid., 315.

65. Gary Orfield and Carole Ashkinaze, *The Closing Door: Conservative Policy and Black Opportunity* (Chicago: University of Chicago Press, 1991), 206.

66. Ibid.

67. Ibid.

68. Ibid., 210. "A key assumption in the entire argument was that discrimination was no longer structural but only a secondary problem that could be dealt with by taking action against those few individuals who discriminated" (ibid., 207).

69. Ibid., 210.

70. Richard Briffault, "Our Localism: Part II, Localism and Legal Theory," *Columbia Law Review* 90 (1990): 346, 441. This is most clearly manifested in suburban communities where local politicians generally attempt to maintain class and

ethnic homogeneity. According to Briffault, "Local homogeneity is attained by separate incorporation, often followed by the adoption of exclusionary land-use policies." This exclusion is not merely practiced by affluent communities, since "less well-to-do communities are just as concerned about maintaining community status against the deterioration usually attributed to the influx of racial and ethnic minorities and poorer people." An important feature of suburban politics is "the protection of turf through the prevention of internal racial or income differentiation." Finally, the forces of homogeneity drive an insistence on separate suburban and city schools, which "reflects a determination to shield local children from exposure to economic, social and cultural differences that are perceived as a threat to family values." Integration becomes not merely infeasible, but impossible.

71. Richard Bernstein, "Twenty Years after the Kerner Report: Three Societies, All Separate," *New York Times*, February 29, 1988.

72. William Julius Wilson, "Public Policy Research and the Truly Disadvantaged," in *The Urban Underclass*, ed. Christopher Jencks and Paul E. Peterson (Washington, D.C.: Brookings Institution, 1991), 460, 462. The full thesis is set forth in William Julius Wilson, *The Truly Disadvantaged: The Inner City, the Underclass, and Public Policy* (Chicago: University of Chicago Press, 1987). Wilson focuses on the poor who live in metropolitan areas, or census tracts, where 40 percent of the population was poor according to 1980 data. As of that date, only 1 percent of the nation's population lived in these areas of concentrated poverty. While the percentage of poor people living in these neighborhoods was 9 percent, it was 21 percent for blacks, 16 percent for Latinos, and only 2 percent for whites (Paul A. Jargowsky and Mary Jo Bane, "Ghetto Poverty in the United States, 1970–1980," in Jencks and Peterson, *Urban Underclass*, 235, 252). Within metropolitan areas, approximately three in ten blacks lived in these areas of concentrated poverty. According to Jargowsky and Bane, "The 2.4 million ghetto poor were 65 percent black, 22 percent Hispanic, and 13 percent non-Hispanic white and other races. Thus ghettos are predominantly populated by blacks and Hispanics, and black and Hispanic poor are much more likely than white poor to live in a ghetto."

73. Wilson, "Public Policy Research," 462–63.

74. Ibid.

75. Douglas S. Massey and Mitchell L. Eggers, "The Ecology of Inequality: Minorities and the Concentration of Poverty, 1970–1980," *American Journal of Sociology* 95 (1990): 1153, 1171. Massey has authored or coauthored numerous instructive articles, not only on black segregation, but also on Latino and Asian segregation. See, for example, Douglas S. Massey and Eric Fong, "Segregation and Neighborhood Quality: Blacks, Hispanics, and Asians in the San Francisco Metropolitan Area," *Social Forces* 69 (1990): 15; Douglas S. Massey and Nancy A. Denton, "Trends in Residential Segregation of Blacks, Hispanics, and Asians," *American Sociological Review* 52 (1987): 94; Douglas S. Massey and Brendan Mullen, "Processes of Hispanic and Black Spatial Assimilation," *American Journal of Sociology* 89 (1984): 836; Douglas S. Massey and Nancy A. Denton, "Suburbanization and Segregation in U.S. Metropolitan Areas," *American Journal of Sociology* 94 (1988): 592; and Douglas S. Massey, Gretchen A. Condran, and Nancy A. Denton,

"The Effect of Residential Segregation on Black Social and Economic Well-Being," *Social Forces* 66 (1987): 29.

It would appear that Massey would focus on removing the barriers to residential integration rather than on striving for spatial equality. He says, "I think that a group that raises residential segregation to be an ideal is going to cut itself off from many of the benefits of society. You make it easier for the larger white population to eventually decapitalize it, and it basically becomes an easy target for racist attitudes. It becomes isolated politically" (quoted in Dent, "New Black Suburbs," 24).

76. Reynolds Farley, "Residential Segregation of Social and Economic Groups among Blacks, 1970–1980," in Jencks and Peterson, *Urban Underclass*, 274, 293.

77. See Wilson, "Public Policy Research," 61.

78. L. Bart Landry, *The New Black Middle Class* (Berkeley: University of California Press, 1987), 185. There is some evidence, however, that black yuppies, or "bubbies," are a demographic exception here. According to one report, over 65 percent of blacks with four or more years of college who moved during the 1970s moved to suburban census tracts that had less than 10 percent of black residents (William P. O'Hare et al., *Blacks on the Move: A Decade of Demographic Change* [Washington, D.C.: Joint Center for Political Studies, 1982], 88). The extent of black affluence, however, is small; only one of seven black households in 1989 had an income of $50,000 or more, whereas one of three white households had an income of $50,000 or more (William P. O'Hare, "African Americans in the 1990s," *Population Bulletin* 46 [1991]: 29).

79. Landry, *New Black Middle Class*, 185.

80. Ibid.

81. George C. Galster, "More Than Skin Deep: The Effect of Housing Discrimination on the Extent and Pattern of Racial Residential Segregation in the United States," in Goering, *Housing Desegregation*, 119. Galster finds that black segregation in metropolitan areas "is characterized both by the large extent of residential racial separation within and between neighborhoods and the pattern of black concentration in central city areas."

82. Massey and Denton, *American Apartheid*, 74.

83. Ibid., 75–77.

84. Ibid., 77.

85. Ibid.

86. Farley, "Residential Segregation," 286–89. See Nancy A. Denton and Douglas S. Massey, "Residential Segregation of Blacks, Hispanics, and Asians by Socioeconomic Status and Generation," *Social Science Quarterly* 69 (1988): 797, 805.

87. Massey and Denton, *American Apartheid*, 85–88.

88. Jaynes and Williams, *Common Destiny*, 144.

89. Ibid., 90.

90. Douglas S. Massey, "Racial Segregation Itself Remains a Corrosive Force," *Los Angeles Times*, August 13, 1989.

91. Kenneth Karst, "Paths to Belonging: The Constitution and Cultural Identity," *North Carolina Law Review* 64 (1986): 304.

92. Benjamin Ringer and Elinor Lawless, *Race-Ethnicity and Society* (New York:

Routledge, 1989), 134–36. By 1970 an increasing number of African Americans rejected integration as assimilation and opted to define it in terms of cultural pluralistic acculturation (Faustine C. Jones, "External Crosscurrents and Internal Diversity: An Assessment of Black Progress, 1960–1980," *Daedalus* 110 [1981]: 71, 79). Today that view is probably the prevalent view of black self-identity (Jaynes and Williams, *Common Destiny*, 200). Integration has come to mean something very different from the melting pot notion of the Kerner Commission's hope for a single society; now integration's social meaning refers to "a process whereby a group with a distinctive culture both adapts to and is accepted by a larger group without being forced to change its culture and associated practices in favor of those of the majority" (E. Ellis Cashmore, ed., *Dictionary of Race and Ethnic Relations*, 2d ed. [New York: Routledge, 1988], 146–47). Because cultural pluralism, in these terms, assumes mutually accepted coexistence of multiple cultures within American society, it is at war with the process of assimilation, "which refers to a process whereby a group changes its cultural beliefs and practices in favor of those of the group with which it comes into social contact" (Cashmore, *Dictionary*, 147). See Sharon O'Brien, "Cultural Rights in the United States: A Conflict of Values," *Law and Inequality Journal* 5 (1987): 267. In some ways "wild black power" and "nationalist nonsense" have come to be seen as common sense among many African Americans. For example, Malcolm X saw integration as "a manifestation of white supremacist ideology" (Peller, "Race Consciousness," 783). In 1968 Robert Browne said that "it was the black masses who first perceived that integration actually increases the white community's control over the black one by destroying institutions, and by absorbing black leadership and coinciding its interests with those of the white community. . . . Such injurious, if unintended, side effects of integration have been felt in almost every layer of the black community" (Peller, "Race Consciousness," 783, quoting Robert S. Browne, "A Case for Separation," in *Separation or Integration: Which Way for America—A Dialogue*, ed. Robert S. Browne and Bayard Rustin [1968], 7–15). Integrationists frequently extol the virtues of integration and present worst-case scenarios about black segregation. They offer no rebuttal, however, to references to integration's "injurious, if unintended, side effects" that disadvantage blacks. Spatial equality does recognize them. It does not, therefore, call for separation; it simply acknowledges the separate and unequal circumstances that already exist.

93. Blair Stone, "Community, Home, and the Residential Tenant," *University of Pennsylvania Law Review* 134 (1986): 627, 635.

94. Dent, "New Black Suburbs."

95. Joe T. Darden, "Choosing Neighbors and Neighborhoods: The Role of Race in Housing Preference," in Tobin, *Divided Neighborhoods*, 15.

96. Ibid., 37.

97. Jaynes and Williams, *Common Destiny*, 136.

98. Arnold R. Hirsch, *Making the Second Ghetto: Race and Housing in Chicago, 1940–1960* (New York: Cambridge University Press, 1983), 171–211; George C. Galster, "Black Suburbanization: Has It Changed the Relative Location of Races?," *Urban Affairs Quarterly* 26 (1991): 621; George C. Galster and Mark W. Keeney,

"Race, Residence, Discrimination, and Economic Opportunity: Modeling the Nexus of Urban Racial Phenomena," *Urban Affairs Quarterly* 24 (1988): 87.

99. Hirsch, *Second Ghetto*, 39.

100. Ibid.

101. Karen Grigsby Bates, "View Park: A Case Study of Racial Ironies," *Los Angeles Times*, September 18, 1989.

102. Ibid.

103. Ibid.

104. Ibid. See also Darlene Powell Hopson and Derek S. Hopson, *Different and Wonderful: Raising Black Children in a Race-Conscious Society* (New York: Prentice-Hall Press, 1990), 55.

105. Omi and Winant, *Racial Formation*.

106. Paul Gilroy, *Ain't No Black in the Union Jack* (Chicago: University of Chicago Press, 1991), 11.

107. Ibid.

108. Eric Schnapper, "Perpetuation of Past Discrimination," *Harvard Law Review* 96 (1983): 828, 864. See Jeremy Waldron, "Superseding Historic Injustice," *Ethics* 103 (1992): 4.

109. Laurence H. Tribe, *American Constitutional Law*, 2d ed. (Mineola, N.Y.: Foundation Press, 1988), 1516. See also Owen Fiss, "Groups and the Equal Protection Clause," *Philosophy and Public Affairs* 5 (1976): 108, 148–56. Fiss discusses the "group disadvantaging principle."

110. Schnapper, "Perpetuation of Discrimination," 834.

111. The first scholarly work to recognize this was Charles Abrams, *Forbidden Neighbors* (New York: Harper, 1955). See also Mark I. Gelfand, *A Nation of Cities: The Federal Government and Urban America, 1933–1965* (New York: Oxford University Press, 1975). The significance of federal involvement in creating the circumstances of spatial inequality, however, has been discounted by an emphasis on market factors in housing discrimination or by a belief that the private nature of housing prevents the government from redressing matters (Martha Mahoney, "Law and Racial Geography: Public Housing and the Economy in New Orleans," *Stanford Law Review* 42 [1990]: 1251, 1255–56). Mahoney presents a tandem causation analysis of federal policy combining with private practices to assess questions of cause and effect (Mahoney, "Law and Racial Geography," 1255–60).

112. *Milliken v. Bradley*, 418 U.S. 717, 756 n. 2 (1974) (Stewart, J., concurring).

113. Citizen's Commission on Civil Rights, *A Decent Home: A Report on the Continuing Failure of the Federal Government to Provide Equal Housing Opportunity* (Washington, D.C.: Citizen's Commission on Civil Rights, 1983), 81–82.

114. Dennis R. Judd, "Segregation Forever," *Nation*, December 9, 1991, 740, 742. See also James A. Kushner, "Apartheid in America: An Historical and Legal Analysis of Contemporary Racial Segregation in the United States," *Howard Law Journal* 22 (1979): 547.

115. Paul A. Leonard, Cushing N. Dolbeare, and Edward B. Lazere, *A Place to Call Home: The Crisis in Housing for the Poor* (Washington, D.C.: Center on Budget and Policy Priorities, 1989).

116. Ibid.

117. Lynne Duke, "Black Economic Disparity Deepens during 1980s," *Washington Post*, August 9, 1991. Additionally, in 1987 the median value of homes owned by blacks was $48,000, compared with $69,300 for whites (ibid.).

118. Richard Polenberg, *One Nation Dividable: Class, Race, and Ethnicity in the United States since 1938* (New York: Viking Press, 1980), 131.

119. Ibid.

120. Ibid.

121. Ibid.

122. Robert Chandler, "Fair Housing Laws: A Critique," *Hastings Law Journal* 24 (1973): 159, 161 n. 19.

123. Barry Checkoway, "Large Builders, Federal Housing Programs, and Postwar Suburbanization," in Bratt et al., *Critical Perspectives*, 119, 123. Checkoway writes, "Between 1950 and 1955 the total metropolitan population increased by 11.6 million people, 9.2 million of whom were suburban." Checkoway demonstrates how the federal government supported large builders, such as Levitt and Sons, as the federal government's suburban development stemmed directly from its effort to stimulate production in the housing sector and the national economy. Large builders accounted for only 5 percent of housing production in 1938 but 64 percent in 1959 (ibid., 122).

124. Polenberg, *One Nation Dividable*, 132.

125. Mahoney, "Law and Racial Geography," 1259. The author discusses "racialized appraisal policies based on their invention and institutionalization by the federal government."

126. Citizen's Commission, *Decent Home*, 7.

127. Ibid.

128. Ibid., 9 (emphasis in original).

129. During the 1970s, blacks moved significantly to the suburbs. Although blacks represented only 6 percent of the suburban population, one of five blacks resided in suburban areas in 1980. Generally, however, the move to the suburbs reveals a racialized demography, as blacks moved to spillover suburbs, close to the central city, or black enclaves in otherwise white suburbs. Integration as a result of black suburbanization has been minimal. The benefits of suburban life have been much less to blacks than to most whites. Blacks have gained less financially, as very few have been able to buy homes in the suburbs when the investments were the least and the gains the greatest (John O. Calmore, "To Make Wrong Right: The Necessary and Proper Aspirations of Fair Housing," in *The State of Black America, 1989*, ed. Janet Dewart [New York: National Urban League, 1989], 77, 92–93). With a majority of whites now living in the suburbs, racialized politics have negative consequences for the cities (Demetrios Caraley, "Washington Abandons the Cities," *Political Science Quarterly* 107 [1992]: 1), and for the poor (Helene Slessarev, "Racial Tensions and Institutional Support: Social Programs during a Period of Retrenchment," in Weir et al., *Politics of Social Policy*, 357).

130. Florence Wagnon Roisman and Philip Tegeler, "Improving and Expanding Housing Opportunities for Poor People of Color: Recent Developments in Federal and State Courts," *Clearinghouse Review* 24 (1990): 312.

131. Ibid., 314, 325.

132. Ibid., 314, 337–38.

133. Ibid., 314.

134. See, for example, Lawrence B. Simons, "Toward a New National Housing Policy," *Yale Law and Policy Review* 6 (1988): 259, 260. The author notes that during the 1980s, federal appropriations were cut almost 80 percent, more than any other item on the national budget. See also Chester Hartman, "Housing Policies under the Reagan Administration," in Bratt et al., *Critical Perspectives*, 362. According to Hartman the federal government has reversed fifty years of providing housing for those for whom the private market fails.

135. Roisman and Tegeler, "Improving and Expanding Housing Opportunities," 32.

136. Ibid.

137. Ibid. See also Yale Rabin, "The Roots of Segregation in the Eighties: The Role of Local Government Actions," in Tobin, *Divided Neighborhoods*, 208, 212–13. Rabin describes segregative local government actions that displaced black residential areas, created racial barriers to mobility, and promoted racial concentration. See also John M. Payne, "Title VIII and Mount Laurel: Is Affordable Housing Fair Housing?," *Yale Law and Policy Review* 7 (1988): 361, 373. Payne discusses the use of "regional contribution agreements," which permit cities to finance their fair share of affordable housing by providing cash transfers to "buy economic and racial exclusion."

138. Payne, "Fair Housing." There are demonstrations that mobility remedies may place poor people of color in positions to obtain better jobs (James E. Rosenbaum and Susan J. Popkin, "Employment and Earnings of Low-Income Blacks Who Move to Middle-Class Suburbs," in Jencks and Peterson, *Urban Underclass*, 342). But that access can be blocked by discrimination (Joleen Kirschenmann and Kathryn M. Neckerman, "'We'd Love to Hire Them, But .20.20.': The Meaning of Race for Employers," in Jencks and Peterson, *Urban Underclass*, 203).

139. See "Separate and Unequal: Illegal Segregation Pervades Nation's Subsidized Housing," *Dallas Morning News*, February 10–17, 1985, reprinted in *Discrimination in Federally Assisted Housing Programs: Hearings before the [House] Subcommittee on Housing and Community Development*, part 1, 99th Cong., 1st and 2d sess., 1985–86, pp. 22–60.

140. 42 U.S.C. § 3604(b).

141. 24 C.F.R. § 100.65(b)(2).

142. Ibid. See Richard G. Schweem, *Housing Discrimination Law and Litigation* (New York: Clark Boardman, 1990), sec.2014.3, pp. 14-6–14-10.

143. Peter Berger and Thomas Luckmann, *The Social Construction of Reality: A Treatise in the Sociology of Knowledge* (New York: Doubleday, 1966), 92.

144. Ibid., 93–94.

145. Daniel P. Moynihan, "Toward a National Urban Policy," *Public Interest* 17 (1969): 3.

146. Ibid., 8–18. I realize that incorporating Moynihan's views is ironic, given his subsequent proposal of a benign neglect policy for the cities. See David P. Moynihan, "Memorandum for the President," *New York Times*, March 1, 1970.

147. Patricia J. Williams, "Metro Broadcasting, Inc., v. FCC: Regrouping in Singular Times," *Harvard Law Review* 104 (1990): 525.

148. Paul Brest, "The Supreme Court, 1975 Term—Foreword: In Defense of the Antidiscrimination Principle," *Harvard Law Review* 90 (1976): 1, 48–52.

149. See Kimberle Williams Crenshaw, "Race, Reform, and Retrenchment: Transformation and Legitimation in Antidiscrimination Law," *Harvard Law Review* 101 (1988): 1331.

150. Peller, "Race Consciousness," 845.

151. Ibid.

152. James Baldwin, "Down at the Cross: Letter from a Region in My Mind," in *The Fire Next Time* (New York: Dell, 1964), 141.

Peter W. Salsich Jr. # A Decent Home for
Every American

Can the 1949 Goal Be Met?

Introduction

If one were looking for an image to dramatize the severity of the contemporary housing crisis in America, two stories in the Sunday, November 22, 1992, editions of the *New York Times* would be strong contenders. The news section reported that a state supreme court justice in Manhattan ordered New York City officials to spend the night on the waiting-room sofas and floors of city offices where homeless families have had to sleep because shelters were filled to capacity.[1] On the same day, the week-in-review section carried a feature describing the "shiver of alarm" experienced by local government officials around the country because of a federal judge's ruling the previous week that Miami must set aside two "safe zones" where 6,000 homeless people can live without fear of arrest. Housing advocates, while applauding the decision because of its vindication of constitutional rights of homeless people, expressed dismay at the combination of legislative inaction and public impatience that led to the judicial intervention, calling the remedy "a zone of sanctuary that is also a zone of discard."[2]

The courts in New York and Miami were filling a traditional role of American courts in protecting civil liberties and prodding governmental officials to act in the face of serious social problems. Nevertheless, the plight of the homeless in those cities is dramatic testimony to the prophetic warning by the Kerner Commission predicting a nation dividing into two societies, the haves and the have-nots, the whites and the blacks.[3]

In his keynote essay appearing in this volume, Professor Boger has crystallized in stark terms the extent of the housing crisis for low-income persons.[4] His characterization of housing in 1992 as "scarce, expensive, and segregated"[5] is a sobering reminder of how little of the Kerner Commission's housing strategy has been implemented and how far we have to go to achieve the goal of "a decent home and a suitable living environment for every American family," first articulated in the Housing Act of 1949[6] and reaffirmed in the Housing and Urban Development Act of 1968.[7] The record since 1968 is discouraging to say the least.

The Kerner Commission's key housing recommendations were (1) to expand massively the supply of housing suitable for low-income families and (2) to open areas outside ghetto neighborhoods to occupancy by minorities.[8] During the 1970s, federal housing policy sought to encourage the production of affordable housing units through the Section 236 mortgage interest subsidy program[9] and the Section 8 new construction/substantial rehabilitation rental assistance program.[10] During the 1980s, however, the Reagan and Bush administrations persuaded Congress to curtail sharply efforts to increase supply in favor of a limited program to increase effective demand for existing housing by providing certificates and vouchers to eligible, low-income persons.[11] As Professor Boger noted, the commission's goal to add 6 million units of low- and moderate-income housing to the market over a ten-year period was distinguished by a singular failure of the country to come close to, let alone achieve, that goal.[12]

As to the second goal, substantial progress has been made in establishing a national prohibition against discrimination in housing through the enactment of the Fair Housing Act of 1968[13] and the Fair Housing Amendments Act of 1988.[14] Successful implementation of an integrated housing policy, however, continues to be distressingly slow because of entrenched opposition to housing integration in many communities and the exclusionary impact of restrictive local zoning practices.

This essay will examine the shift of federal housing policy from an emphasis on production during the decade after the Kerner Commission Report to the current policy of limited support that enables a few low-income persons to choose their own housing. The growth of state and local housing support programs as well as the nonprofit community housing development movement will also be discussed. The essay will argue for a reaffirmation of the national housing goal of a decent home for every American, a redirection of policy toward decentralization, and a redistribution of housing subsidies so that more of the funds reach those who need them most.

A Review of Federal Housing Policy

Prior to the Kerner Commission Report there were two basic federal urban housing programs: (1) public housing that provided rental units to low-income households through local public housing authorities[15] and (2) mortgage insurance to encourage banks to make loans for single-family homes and apartments designed for moderate- and middle-income people.[16] Both programs were established in the 1930s and played major roles in the post–World War II migrations of low-income, mostly minority families from the rural South to the urban North and of middle-income families from the cities to the suburbs. During the period between World War II and 1968, Congress adopted a national housing goal,[17] incrementally adding a series of programs to attract private capital to housing development, such as mortgage insurance for housing for moderate-income and displaced families,[18] below-market interest rate loans,[19] direct loans to nonprofit developers of housing for the elderly,[20] and limited rent supplements.[21]

Housing and Urban Development Act of 1968

The Kerner Commission Report played a significant role in the enactment of the Housing and Urban Development Act of 1968 that established several major federal housing production programs. The programs of the 1968 act were designed to fill a widening gap in housing policy between the public housing and federal mortgage insurance programs. The primary federal subsidy added by the 1968 act was an interest subsidy by which the government made interest reduction payments to lenders who made loans to developers of housing for low- and moderate-income persons. The payments from the federal government were designed to reduce the cost of housing by reducing the effective interest rates of long-term mortgage loans to between 1 and 5 percent.[22]

The 1968 housing act programs resulted in the production of a substantial number of new housing units, both single-family and multifamily, during the brief period before the programs were effectively shut down by the Nixon administration in 1973. Reports of scandals in the administration of the programs in a number of cities, coupled with stories of low-income homeowners losing their homes because they were not able to afford the costs of operating them, provided impetus for the freeze.[23]

Housing and Community Development Act of 1974

Community Development Block Grants

In 1974 Congress enacted two major new programs. As an alternative to the categorical grants subject to more rigid national standards, the Community Development Block Grant (CDBG) program provides grants to cities and states to enable them to implement a variety of local public activities tailored to local conditions.[24] While the CDBG program has been extremely popular with local governments, tension among the legislative objectives of eliminating slums and blight, preventing blighting influences, providing decent housing and a suitable living environment, and expanding economic opportunities, "principally for persons of low and moderate income,"[25] has never been resolved satisfactorily. In recent years Congress has amended the CDBG program to impose an increasingly strict targeting requirement on the use of block grant funds.[26]

By 1993, CDBG funds could be used for twenty-six separate eligible activities, including support for efforts to provide affordable housing. The emphasis of CDBG support for housing traditionally has been on rehabilitation of existing units, but as federal support for housing production has declined, limitations on use of CDBG funds to support new construction have been relaxed.[27]

Section 8

The other major program enacted in 1974 was the Section 8 program.[28] The Section 8 program was designed to replace the interest subsidy programs of the 1968 act with a subsidy to the developer/owner patterned after the annual contributions contracts of public housing.[29] Section 8 subsidies are disbursed through an annual contributions contract between a developer/owner, the local public housing authority or state housing finance agency as administrator of the Section 8 funds, and the Department of Housing and Urban Development (HUD). The subsidy is the difference between a fair market rent established by HUD for the area in which the units or persons being supported are located and a rent paid by tenants that generally may not exceed 30 percent of their income.[30] At one time four types of housing were eligible for Section 8 support: new construction, substantial rehabilitation, moderate rehabilitation, and existing housing.

As a result of a policy shift during the 1980s from supply-side to demand-side subsidies,[31] along with disclosure of scandals in the administration of the Moderate Rehabilitation program,[32] the only active federal direct housing subsidy program at the beginning of the 1990s was the Section 8 Existing Housing program. Appropriations for this program have never permitted more than a small fraction of eligible persons to receive housing assistance. Under the Existing Housing program, rental assistance was provided in two ways: (1) certificates issued to property owners guaranteeing payments for fifteen years if the owner both rented to persons whose incomes were below 80 percent of the median income for the area and also maintained the property in accordance with local housing codes, and (2) vouchers issued to low-income persons guaranteeing payments for five years to owners renting acceptable units to them.[33] Scandalously long waiting lists for embarrassingly few vouchers illustrate the Existing Housing program's failure to make a measurable impact on urban housing needs.[34]

Low Income Housing Tax Credit (1986)

The Low Income Housing Tax Credit (LIHTC), enacted as part of the Tax Reform Act of 1986, offers an incentive for equity investment in low-income housing. Congress intended this credit to replace the real estate tax shelters largely eliminated by the Tax Reform Act.[35] Developers claim the credit annually for a period of ten years. The credit may amount to either (1) a present value of up to 70 percent of the depreciable basis in newly constructed or substantially rehabilitated housing units that do not receive other federal subsidies and are rented to low-income persons, or (2) the present value of up to 30 percent for the acquisition cost of housing that is rehabilitated, and for certain subsidized housing.[36] The credit percentages are adjusted annually for ten years. For January 1992 the annual percentages were 8.70 percent with a 70 percent present value credit and 3.73 percent with a 30 percent present value credit.[37]

Since 1986, the LIHTC has been the only active federal subsidy program designed to encourage private investment in the production of housing for low-income persons. Enacted as a temporary measure in 1986, it was extended past its expiration date three times before being made permanent in 1993.[38]

1990 Cranston-Gonzalez National Affordable Housing Act

Enactment of the 1990 Cranston-Gonzalez National Affordable Housing Act,[39] the first major renewal or revisitation of federal housing policy in sixteen years, introduced an additional range of programs. The centerpiece of the statute is the HOME program, a housing block grant program patterned after the CDBG program. The HOME program provides funds to enable states and local governments to support affordable housing initiatives such as construction loans, short-term gap and bridge loans, and tenant-based rental assistance.[40] A 1992 amendment to the HOME program eliminated a bias against new construction that existed in the 1990 act—a bias that represented a continuing drag on federal housing policy since 1982.[41] Three significant features of HOME both strengthen the program and make it more complex. First, local and state government recipients must prepare Comprehensive Housing Affordability Strategies (CHAS) that HUD must approve before HOME funds can be expended.[42] Second, 15 percent of local HOME funds must be set aside for eighteen months for qualified nonprofit organizations called Community Housing Development Organizations (CHDOs).[43] Finally, local communities provide matching funds through local tax revenues, bond proceeds, and contributions of land, labor, or materials equal to 25 percent of the total for rental assistance and rehabilitation, 33 percent of the total for substantial rehabilitation, and 50 percent of the total for new construction projects, subject to modification or waiver for communities in various stages of fiscal distress.[44]

The goal of the Bush administration's housing policy, homeownership, was added to the 1990 act in the forum of the Housing Opportunities for People Everywhere (HOPE) program.[45] Through HOPE, HUD can make planning and implementation grants to enable consortia of developers, nonprofit agencies, tenant organizations, and individuals to acquire existing units of public housing and privately owned subsidized housing. Acquisition may occur through a variety of ownership vehicles, including limited equity cooperatives, mutual housing associations, and scattered-site, single-family fee ownership. Funds can be used for acquisition, rehabilitation, and, in limited situations, operating of subsidies by cooperatives and other ownership vehicles. Funds may be utilized for down payment assistance for individual homebuyers as well as education and job training services. Nevertheless, CHAS and local match requirements described for the HOME program must still be met.[46]

Tax Subsidies for Middle- and Upper-Income Homeowners

Mortgage Interest Deduction and Other Tax Preferences

Congress has chosen to subsidize owner-occupied housing in a number of ways. Homeowners who itemize deductions on their tax returns can deduct the interest paid on residential mortgages of up to $1 million dollars, as well as the interest paid on home equity indebtedness of up to $100,000.[47] Homeowners may benefit from additional tax preferences in the form of favorable capital gains treatment, including nonrecognition of gain from the sale of a principal residence, if they reinvest the proceeds within two years.[48] Homeowners who are at least fifty-five also enjoy a one-time exclusion of $125,000 of capital gain from the sale of a principal residence.[49] Finally, homeowners benefit from no depreciation of basis used in calculating gain and the stepped-up basis at death.[50]

In addition to the mortgage interest deduction, homeowners receive a substantial subsidy in the form of tax-free, imputed income; that is, homeowners are not taxed on the stream of imputed rental income reflecting the "market value of the housing services produced by the property," even though they can deduct the mortgage interest and property tax costs of operation of the property.[51] Renters, by contrast, may not deduct their rental payments and must pay their rent with after-tax dollars.

Extent of Homeowner Tax Expenditures

Government spending for low-income housing has consistently been a fraction of the losses in revenues resulting from tax preferences to homeowners. A recent study calculated that in 1988, federal government subsidies to homeowners exceeded $81 billion. This figure takes into account the effects of the mortgage interest tax deduction, deduction for property taxes, and exclusion of imputed rental income.[52]

According to the president's budget for fiscal year (FY) 1993, the tax expenditures[53] for mortgage interest deduction, the deduction of property tax on owner-occupied homes, the deferral of capital gains on proceeds reinvested in another home within two years, and the one-time exclusion of capital gains for individuals over fifty-five years total approximately $74.7 billion.[54] In contrast, federal appropriations and tax expenditures for low-income housing assistance for FY 1993 amounted to approximately $18 billion.[55]

In 1988 only 29 percent of taxpayers claimed itemized deductions on their tax returns.[56] This figure is down from 40 percent in 1986.[57] In 1985 the number of homeowners claiming mortgage interest deductions[58] was 28.1 million. Despite an increase of several million in the number of homeowners, the Joint Committee on Taxation projected that the number of homeowners claiming the deduction would be only 24.1 million, 4 million less than the 1985 figure.[59]

The subsidies derived from the mortgage interest deduction heavily favor upper-income taxpayers. A study of 1988 tax receipts concluded that over half of the tax savings from this deduction accrued to people with incomes in the ninety-second percentile or higher.[60] Thus the majority of federal government tax expenditures and appropriations benefit those who least need assistance.

State and Local Housing Programs

One significant effect of the change in federal housing policy has been to engender truly creative thinking about housing in many states and municipalities. The first generation of state housing programs involved the sale of tax-exempt revenue bonds by state housing finance agencies in the 1960s and 1970s to stimulate housing production.[61] These activities were followed in the 1980s by a second generation of housing trust funds and related programs designed to respond to the curtailment of federal housing programs.[62]

Housing finance agencies administer more than 600 programs in all fifty states. Activities include down payment assistance and below-market-rate loans to first-time homebuyers, gap loans and grants to nonprofit community housing developers, and construction and permanent loans to for-profit and nonprofit developers.[63] While a relatively small number of states have appropriated state funds to supplement the traditional reliance on tax-exempt housing bond proceeds, all states have gained valuable experience in administering housing programs and determining how best to respond to local needs.

Connecticut has established an innovative program. It authorizes the state to provide housing grants and loans to municipalities that enter a regional housing compact, provided that the compact contains regional goals for the development of adequate, affordable housing and balances these developmental gains with environmental, economic, transportation and infrastructure concerns.[64] State grants and loans are available through a housing partnership program with municipalities that reduce regulatory barriers to, and provide support for, affordable housing. Connecticut has established a variety of funds, including a housing trust fund and a housing infrastructure fund, to provide both supply-side and demand-side housing assistance.[65]

New Jersey enacted a fair housing act in 1985.[66] The act was adopted in response to several state supreme court cases holding that every municipality in a growth area of the state has a constitutional obligation to provide, through its land use regulations, a realistic opportunity for the construction of a fair share of its region's present and prospective needs for housing for low- and moderate-income families.[67] The act established the state Affordable Housing Council to identify housing needs and adopt procedures for allocating municipal fair share housing needs.[68] The act also provides for state appropriations to be channeled through the State Department of Community Affairs and the New Jersey Mortgage and Housing Finance Agency to make grants and loans to municipalities to help them meet their low- and moderate-income housing needs.[69] An example of an innovative local program is a church-city coalition in Syracuse, New York, to develop and market affordable housing through a community land trust.[70]

A significant complement to state housing programs is the growing number of state requirements that local governments engage in formal analysis of local housing needs as a condition to exercising their zoning power. For example, prior to local zoning, Florida requires that six aspects of local housing be analyzed: (1) housing needs of current and expected future population, (2) elimination of substandard housing, (3) improvement of existing housing, (4) provision of adequate sites for future affordable housing with supporting infrastructure and public facilities, (5) provision for relocation housing, and (6) identification of housing to be conserved, rehabilitated, or replaced.[71]

Housing Policies since the Kerner Report

Federal housing policies since the Kerner Commission Report and, for that matter, since the first housing legislation of the depression era have been a mixed bag. Most Americans enjoy the best housing in the world. One of the true success stories of the past fifty years has been the increase in the standard of housing quality enjoyed by the vast majority of people in the United States.[72]

At the same time, however, an increasing number of persons at the lower end of the economic scale have not seen their housing conditions improve and, in many cases, have actually experienced a decline in housing quality. This is particularly true for the growing number of persons who fall into "service-dependent" categories such as single parents with small children, persons with disabilities, elderly persons who have become frail, and persons who have lost their homes through natural disasters.[73] Moreover, many Americans still experience segregation in housing despite comprehensive fair housing legislation in 1968 and again in 1988.

The federal role in housing began almost sixty years ago.[74] Since that time a variety of approaches has been tried, including direct loans and grants for acquisition and development, grants to reduce operating expenses, subsidies to lenders to reduce interest rates, and a number of tax credits and deductions. Despite billions of dollars and a mind-numbing range of programs, direct housing assistance to low-income persons does not appear to have been accepted by the American public. At the same time, the truly massive subsidies available to middle- and upper-income homeowners through the tax code are viewed by most recipients of those tax benefits as untouchable entitlements rather than subsidies.

Government programs have been characterized by a lack of direction and an ambivalence over the role of government. Programs have fluctuated continually between emphasis on producing new units and increasing effective demand for existing units, and between direct subsidies through appropriations and indirect subsidies through tax concessions. Congress, as well as the public, has been impatient. If a particular housing program did not solve housing problems within a few years, it was junked in favor of a new one. The twenty-five-year progression in programs featuring below-market rate loans; rent supplements; interest reduction payments; Section 8 housing assistance payments for newly constructed, rehabilitated, and existing housing; the low-income housing tax credit; and the new HOME block grant program is a case in point.

The debate continues about the most effective use of federal housing funds. The Congressional Budget Office (CBO) compared the cost effectiveness of housing tax credits and housing vouchers and concluded that vouchers will provide "assistance of equal value to tenants at a fraction of the cost of credits."[75] It remains a fact, however, that local public housing authorities report a scarcity of landlords willing to participate in the certificate and voucher programs, and many recipients return their certificates and vouchers unused because of an inability to locate decent units. This has led the National Housing Law Project to argue for converting the tax credit into a direct grant program, rather than simply substituting more vouchers for credits.[76] The direct grant program would be available to developers and owners who agree in advance to participate in the Section 8 programs.

Owners clearly have been favored over renters when the housing incentives in the tax laws are included in an assessment of national housing policy. This same favoritism is evident in the regulatory bias of local land-use laws, which favor single-family detached housing over rental housing.[77] A promising corollary of this favoritism is the growing interest in new forms of ownership and control of assisted housing such as CHDOs, cooperatives, community land trusts, and other forms of cohousing. Similarly, public housing resident management corporations may make it possible for more low-income persons to experience the benefits of homeownership.

A Program for Sharing the American Dream:
The Pieces Are in Place but Need to Be Tied Together

The housing block grant and homeownership components of the Cranston-Gonzalez National Affordable Housing Act of 1990[78] and the Housing and Community Development Act of 1992[79] have provided a legislative framework for an effective national housing policy designed to reach those persons without access to decent housing. A long-term, patient commitment to implement the national housing policy and reaffirm the 1949 housing goal by substantially increasing funding allocations is the missing ingredient.

The outline of a federal housing policy that includes a crucial role for the states is sketched in the remainder of this essay. Space constraints and the need for continued discussion of specifics require that the details be left for another day.

Restoring Housing to the National Domestic Agenda and
Renewing Commitment to Homes and Communities

The Kerner Commission concluded its report with the observation that it had "uncovered no startling truths, no unique insights, no simple solutions."[80] A perspective twenty-five years later yields the same conclusion. The Kerner Commission's main recommendation for national action remains as important in 1993 as it was in 1968: "The need is not so much for the government to design new programs as it is for the nation to generate new will."[81]

It is a truism that decent housing provides an essential foundation for stable families and revitalized neighborhoods. Housing was on the national "front burner" for a few years after the Kerner Commission Report spurred enactment of the 1968 Housing Act,[82] but national attention was diverted by Vietnam and Watergate and then dissipated through a perception that housing programs were doomed to failure because of the intractable nature of the problems of marginalized people and communities. The flurry of legislative activity since 1990 is evidence of a reawakening of interest in housing, but the paucity of appropriations indicates that a basic commitment has not yet been made.

Reallocating Housing Subsidies So That More of the Funds Reach the Impoverished

A concern of the Kerner Commission[83] that continues to frustrate housing advocates twenty-five years later is the large gap between need and resources for housing programs directed to low-income persons as compared with those serving middle- and upper-income groups. Studies published in 1991 and 1992 note that while a large number of families are receiving federal housing subsidies from HUD or Farmers Home Administration programs (5.5 million), an estimated additional 5.1 million families are eligible for but do not receive any aid.[84] This comes at a time when the main thrust of federal housing policy has been toward demand-side programs (Section 8 certificates and vouchers). When first proposed in the 1970s, these programs were considered "fairer" than the Section 236 and Section 8 New Construction supply-side programs because more people supposedly would be served by the certificates and vouchers. Frustration deteriorates into cynicism when urban areas have large waiting lists for public housing and subsidized units but receive only enough certificate or voucher allocations to provide assistance to a few hundred new families per year.[85] Not only has the supply of available units diminished,[86] but the certificate and voucher programs have not met the additional demand because of insufficient appropriations.

Some progress in closing the gap between need and availability will be made by reallocating funds for existing shallow subsidy programs, such as HOME, the LIHTC, and CDBG, to the deep-subsidy Section 8 certificate and voucher programs. Progress could also be made by requiring landlords who accept the benefits of the shallow subsidies also to accept the deep subsidies, as advocated by the National Housing Law Project.[87] Major improvement in the present housing crisis, however, will require addressing the basic imbalance between the tax subsidies available to middle- and upper-income homeowners and the rental subsidies available to low-income landlords and tenants.

Capping the Mortgage Interest Tax Deduction

One major difference between the national backdrop for the Kerner Commission Report and for this anniversary symposium is a huge federal deficit in 1993 that did not exist in 1968. The Kerner Commission emphasized that the "great productivity" of the economy and a "highly responsive" federal revenue system combined to "produce truly astounding automatic increases in Federal budget receipts," provided the economy continued to function at its capacity.[88] By contrast, the deficit hangover of the 1990s inhibits serious discussion of new social initiatives. Any proposal to increase spending for housing risks dismissal as frivolous, unless advocates of the proposal consider and account for its impact on the deficit.

Significant deficit reduction is not likely to occur until programs that benefit persons who can function effectively without the benefit are considered in the deficit reduction debate. One such program is the package of tax preferences available to homeowners. A serious, long-term commitment to housing for low-income persons could be funded by placing a cap on this benefit and earmarking the additional revenues generated by this cap to assist low-income families in meeting their housing needs.

Various caps on the mortgage interest deduction have been proposed.[89] During the 1992 campaign, presidential candidate H. Ross Perot called for a $250,000 cap.[90] The Joint Committee on Taxation estimated that $14.7 billion could be raised by a $300,000 cap between 1993 and 1997.[91] The CBO concluded that limiting the interest deduction to $20,000 per joint return, $10,000 per return for married couples filing separately, and $12,000 for individuals could generate $8.2 billion from 1991 to 1995.[92] According to the CBO, these limitations would allow full interest deduction on mortgages as large as $200,000 under 1990 interest rates, an amount almost double the average size of new mortgages closed in 1989.[93]

Another approach would be to require taxpayers to deduct the interest from the bottom of their income schedule.[94] A similar proposal examined by the CBO would limit the tax benefit of deductions to the lowest marginal rate, or a flat 15 percent. The CBO calculated that this would raise $52.9 billion from 1991 to 1995.[95]

Legitimate concerns about perceived unfairness as well as the economic consequences[96] of imposing such a cap could be addressed by phasing in the cap over a period of eight to ten years. Current homeowners could thereby amortize their "investment" in their mortgage interest tax deduction over a period corresponding roughly to the average time between moves by homeowners. For example, if Congress eliminated 12 percent of the deduction subject to the cap each year, the cap would be reached in slightly more than eight years. An alternative method of cushioning the impact would be to make the cap prospective in nature by imposing it after a home is purchased. Still another alternative would be to convert the deduction to a tax credit equal to the middle-class tax bracket percentage (28 percent), up to a maximum of $200. In addition to arguing that a credit would be available to or beneficial to more people, advocates estimate that it could generate at least $20 billion annually.[97]

The cap should be set at a level that would attempt to distinguish between use of the tax code to encourage homeownership and use of the tax code to accumulate wealth. While more money might be raised for assisted housing programs or deficit reduction efforts by eliminating the mortgage interest tax deduction entirely, that is not recommended because such a drastic measure has the potential of discouraging homeownership. It is worth noting, however, that Canada, which has achieved approximately the same percentage of homeownership as the United States, does not allow a deduction for mortgage interest, although it does provide some capital gains preference.[98] The Office of Management and Budget has estimated that an additional $12 billion in revenue would be recoverable if the property tax deduction were eliminated.[99] Tax reform advocates proposed elimination of the property tax deduction from 1985, but Congress deleted that feature from the Tax Reform Act of 1986 because of fears that high property tax states such as New York would be harmed disproportionately.[100]

Endowing a Low-Income Housing Investment Trust Fund

Funds derived from the cap on mortgage interest tax deductions should be split between deficit reduction efforts and endowment of a Low Income Housing Investment Trust Fund. This fund should be a dedicated fund similar to the Highway Trust Fund.[101] The seriousness of the current deficit problem requires that any new tax revenues be allocated at least partially for deficit reduction. A major portion of revenues generated by a cap on mortgage interest tax deductions, however, should be applied to benefit directly the people with the greatest housing needs.

As highways are a crucial part of the infrastructure of this nation, so decent homes are part of the infrastructure of stable families. The cap on mortgage interest deductions is premised on the philosophy that tax policy support for homeownership should be based on the opportunity that ownership gives people to control the environment in which they live, rather than as a means of generating wealth. Because of the great need that low-income persons have for assistance in obtaining decent housing, money generated by a cut in housing tax expenditures should either be used to reduce the deficit or for other types of housing programs.

Decentralizing Spending Decisions

One of the recurring criticisms of federal policies of the past fifty years is that the centralized control of the purse strings through HUD, coupled with the decentralized operation of the public housing program, has produced a situation of divided responsibility in which accountability and public support has been lost. The bureaucratic layers of HUD (area, regional, and national offices) interact with local public agencies (housing authorities) that depend on state and municipal governments for their legal existence but that, for the most part, are independent of these governments. The resulting top-down method of operation is inefficient, unresponsive, and inflexible and has led to a serious lack of public support for public housing and assisted housing programs, as well as isolation of public housing and its residents.[102]

While federal housing production programs have steadily declined in importance in the eyes of both national policymakers and the general public, the period since the Kerner Commission Report has been a time of innovation at the state and local levels. The growth and maturation of state housing finance agencies, coupled with twenty years' experience with the decentralized CDBG program and enactment of the HOME Investment Trust Fund block grant program,[103] have produced an environment in which a renewed commitment to housing for low-income persons could flourish.

Rather than channel money from a National Housing Trust Fund to HUD for distribution through the existing bureaucracy, Congress should establish a new form of distribution, through the states, patterned after the decentralized distribution system for the Highway Trust Fund. The distribution system should be "outside the beltway" so that it is closer to the problems than is Washington. It should also be capable of taking a broader view than that of the cities because of the extreme isolation that low-income persons have experienced and because of the need for more affluent suburban communities to share the burdens of the cities.[104] The states are the logical choice.

The states are in a position to distribute federal housing funds in much the same way that they distribute federal highway funds. They are closer, and thus more accountable, to people in the communities affected by federal assistance than is a federal bureaucracy.[105] They operate a range of sophisticated affordable housing programs from first-time homebuyer assistance to shelter for the homeless and are able to exert leverage on local governments to enter cooperative regional approaches to sharing the burdens of housing programs and reducing the isolation of beneficiaries of those programs.[106] In addition, they control the real culprit of segregated housing patterns—the zoning power.[107] Old patterns of neglecting urban issues have been replaced in many states by creative efforts of leaders forced to respond to the withdrawal of federal urban aid.

Decentralizing the distribution system does not mean that the federal government should get out of the housing business. Rather, as suggested by the trust fund and tax reform proposals, its role should be increased but changed to one of funding, and articulating and implementing national standards for use of federal housing funds. The national standards should include (1) a mandate to seek an end to housing segregation and the isolation of low-income households; (2) creation of true regional housing markets by removal of artificial barriers to affordable housing; (3) close attention to management issues, including balanced tenant selection policies that both emphasize tenant responsibility and recognize the stresses that accompany life on a limited or nonexistent budget, and provision of social services such as day care, family counseling, and locational education commensurate with the needs of the tenant population; and (4) opportunities for the development of tenant management and tenant ownership.

States should be free to permit a mix of new construction and rental assistance activities to be developed and adjusted to suit local housing conditions. State housing plans and local CHAS plans could play crucial roles in the development of flexible strategies.

Congress should require states to follow a targeted approach to assure that priorities for expenditures of National Housing Trust Funds are based on need. States should be free, however, to add flexibility to the targeting strategy by encouraging mixed-income and mixed-use developments to reduce the isolation of low-income households, and to permit the funds to be used in conjunction with efforts to provide integrated housing choices in suburban neighborhoods.

Establishing Permanently Affordable Housing

Despite a persistent belief that governmental support for housing can be temporary, several factors suggest that such a belief is unrealistic. Complex demographic changes in family structures, persistent segregation of housing patterns along racial and economic lines, increasing longevity, social policies favoring independence over institutionalization for disabled persons, and the large number of people who have lost jobs and ways of life because of the transformation from an industrial-based to a service-based economy indicate that an effective housing policy for the 1990s and beyond must include the assumption that a large stock of housing units should remain affordable to low-income persons for the foreseeable future.[108]

The failure to recognize the reality of long-term housing needs has been a major contributor to the impatient attitude with which most Americans view governmental housing programs. Recent federal housing policy has shown encouraging signs of changes in outlook. For example, amendments to the LIHTC legislation requiring tax credit applicants to enter revocable agreements with state housing agencies to retain the units for low-income use for at least thirty years;[109] enactment of the Low-Income Housing Preservation and Resident Homeownership Act of 1990,[110] with its mechanism for transferring ownership of assisted housing from profit-motivated to nonprofit entities in order to preserve the low-income status of the units; and the growing popularity of community land trusts as vehicles for preserving housing affordability illustrate the growing recognition of long-term needs.[111] These efforts should be supported and strengthened with three principles in mind:

1. Control of the quality and environment of housing, rather than investment opportunity, is the dominant motivation of stable householders.[112]
2. Long-term affordability programs must establish a reasonable market take-out mechanism for investors who are willing to put private capital into affordable housing efforts but who wish to realize a return on their investment over a far shorter time frame. One approach might be to waive any recapture penalties and perhaps even regular exit taxes if a profit-motivated owner transfers to a qualified nonprofit housing organization affordable housing units that have been maintained adequately so that the nonprofit organization does not have to expend funds to repair and renovate the units.[113]
3. A successful long-term affordability program should include a transfer mechanism to allow low-income families to retain their units as their income increases. A repeated flaw of federal housing programs has been the insistence that affordable housing units be physically occupied by low-income persons. What is needed instead is a constant inventory of affordable housing units in a setting that encourages diversity in housing and provides role models for others. For example, members of a welfare family renting a public or assisted housing unit who obtain jobs and begin to move up the economic ladder should be able to stay and purchase the dwelling unit, perhaps by first joining a limited equity cooperative and later by converting to a condominium or purchasing the fee simple if the unit is detached. The funds used to purchase the unit in this manner can then be used to add another unit to the affordable housing inventory. In effect, families would filter up rather than housing units trickle down.

Revitalizing Public Housing

Public housing is an enigma. While generally considered a failure by most Americans, it remains home for thousands of families who have little or no choice but to live in it.[114] It began as a noble experiment in federalism: states would authorize municipalities to borrow money to build public housing units, the federal government would reimburse cities for their production costs, and municipalities would manage the units with rental income received from tenants. Yet it was fatally flawed because most municipalities created independent housing authorities that operated outside the general purpose local government rather than becoming integral parts of those structures. As a result, many local housing authorities had to fend for themselves politically, instead of being able to function within the political shield of their constituent municipality.[115] Public housing became the refuge for millions of migrating families, but the demographic changes occasioned by that migration overwhelmed the basic structure of public housing in the center cities.[116]

Severely distressed public housing is a visible presence in many American cities. No housing policy can succeed without coming to grips with that fact. Simply pouring more money into the existing, flawed system will only add to the millions of dollars of housing funds that go underutilized or unspent.[117]

The maturing community-based housing movement offers a framework for revitalizing public housing. As a component of a decentralized housing delivery system, Congress should replace the centralized relationship between HUD and local public housing authorities with a new relationship in which states and local communities enter partnerships with public housing authorities. During a transition period, state and local governments would audit the public housing inventory through the CHAS process[118] and convene meetings of public housing tenants, neighboring residents, local government officials, and civic leaders to identify or organize community-based housing organizations capable of taking title to clusters of public housing units that can be renovated into livable communities. Public housing authorities would go out of business if all of their units could be absorbed by community-based housing organizations. Where governmental management of housing for people with special needs is necessary, public housing authorities could fulfill this role, but they should be brought into the local government structure as part of a housing and community development department responsible for integrating special-needs housing into overall community development planning. Those housing units, such as high-rise towers, that do not appear capable of being used effectively in a community-based housing program should be sold for other purposes or demolished.

Effective involvement of all elements of the community is a necessary ingredient for successful revitalization of public housing. While transfer of control to isolated public housing tenants without access to resources necessary for proper management is not the answer, transfer of control to nonprofit community development corporations that include public housing residents as well as neighborhood, church, and business leaders may provide the spark for success. Such organizations can supply three necessary ingredients for revitalizing public housing: (1) a framework through which public housing residents can take control over their environment, (2) access to necessary community resources and support services, and (3) removal of the barriers that dislocate public housing from the surrounding neighborhood and prevent it from becoming a community asset to which residents can point with pride.

Despite widespread publicity about homeownership alternatives for low-income persons, the lessons of previous federal and state efforts are that family stability and a predictable income of at least $17,000 to $20,000 are necessary for a successful homeownership program based on the fee simple concept, whether that be in scattered site or condominium configurations.[119] With the national median income for renters in 1989 at $18,192, but at only $6,571 for public housing tenants and $7,060 for Section 8 certificate and voucher holders,[120] it is apparent that programs encouraging traditional forms of homeownership for public housing tenants and recipients of Section 8 certificates and vouchers risk perpetuating a "cruel hoax if they are not coupled with substantial education, training and job opportunities."[121]

On the other hand, the limited equity cooperative may well be a workable ownership vehicle for very-low-income families. This is particularly true if cooperatives are subsidized adequately; coupled with social services, education, and job opportunities; and located in mixed-income settings to reduce the sense of isolation that often characterizes the public and subsidized housing experience.

Integrating Housing with Economic Development

There is little argument that jobs paying living wages would do more to improve housing opportunities for low-income persons than any housing program yet devised. For over fifty years federal housing policy has been driven by the impact that housing production can have on job development.[122] For a variety of reasons, housing policy generally has followed the filtering theory by intervening near the top of the market.

The goal of housing for low-income persons, where the housing crisis is, must be kept separate from the jobs goal. Otherwise the familiar shift in focus will take place, and tax dollars meant to improve housing quality for low-income persons will be racheted upward to people in the moderate- to middle-income levels. While there are good arguments for providing housing assistance for persons at the 80–140 percent of median range, that group is not in a housing crisis and that group is not homeless. While job development programs are an essential ingredient of a revitalized economy, housing policy for low-income households should not be driven by a desire to create jobs.

Two economic development movements that are particularly compatible with a decentralized, low-income-focused housing policy are the community development corporation (CDC) and the microenterprise movements. Nearly 2,000 community development corporations are in existence, with an increasing number using revolving loan funds to help small businesses finance start-up and expansion activities, along with their traditional housing and economic development activities. Following the lead of the South Shore Bank in Chicago, a number of banks have established bank CDCs or community investment corporations (CICs).[123] The Housing and Community Development Act of 1992 established a demonstration program to make grants and loans available to selected "community investment corporations" to "demonstrate the feasibility of facilitating the revitalization" of targeted areas by improving access to capital.[124] The financial community, along with government at all three levels, should encourage the CDC/CIC movement as a means of generating resources for a broad neighborhood reinvestment program that includes community-based housing activities.

Microenterprises, defined as commercial enterprises that have "five or fewer employees, one of which is the owner",[125] can be vehicles for low-income residents to use their talents to provide some of the essential support services for housing, such as day care, housecleaning, and groundskeeping. Legislation enacted in 1992 authorizes microenterprises to receive federal assistance through the CDBG and Small Business Administration programs.[126]

Removing Barriers of Race and Class

The most intractable aspect of the low-income housing crisis is the persistence of racial and class segregation despite decades of judicial and legislative pronouncements against it. The issue is both moral and legal and requires moral suasion as well as legal enforcement. A collaborative federal-state-local initiative focusing on two key elements of the housing development process—financing and land-use regulation—is an essential part of a renewed housing effort. Lenders can make or break local housing initiatives by their response to requests for credit. The Community Reinvestment Act of 1977[127] provides a framework for a major effort to persuade lenders to remove artificial barriers to financing low-income housing and neighborhood revitalization activities.[128] A similar collaborative effort to persuade municipalities to remove artificial zoning barriers should also be undertaken. The states are in a position to take the lead because, as repositories of the police power, they have ultimate control over local zoning decisions.

These efforts should be coordinated on a regional level by a coalition of neighborhood organizations, perhaps through the vehicle of the CHAS review process.[129] In addition, they must be accompanied by a sophisticated effort to involve churches and other community institutions in educational efforts to reduce the fear of "others" that underlies so much of the exclusionary mentality.

Conclusion

The 1949 goal of decent housing for every American family can be met if current housing subsidies are reallocated so that about 50 percent of the approximately $100 billion total benefits low-income households that are unable to afford homeownership, instead of the current 20 to 25 percent that they currently receive. An additional $20 billion per year reallocated to low-income housing programs by a revision of the tax code could make possible a combination of demand-side vouchers and supply-side grants for construction rehabilitation averaging $5,000 per year. This would enable an additional 4 million households to receive housing assistance, thus substantially closing the estimated gap between the total number of eligible low-income families who do not receive housing assistance and the number who actually receive housing assistance. If this amount were supplemented by state and local housing trust funds, the gap might be narrowed further still.

The phase-in contemplated for the recommended tax changes would necessitate incremental increases in the number of new households assisted. But even a 10 percent phase-in during the first year (400,000 households) would represent a tenfold increase over the number of households (35,400)[130] newly able to receive rental assistance in FY93.

Massive new top-down construction programs are not recommended, nor is continued withdrawal by the federal government. Rather, existing housing subsidies should be reallocated to increase the dollars allocated to programs for low-income households. Decisions on types of programs, location of housing, and methods of subsidy should be decentralized to the states, subject to broad national policies emphasizing the goals of ending housing segregation and isolation of low-income households, expanding housing locational choices to regional market levels, linking social services with other management objectives, and encouraging homeownership opportunities where feasible. State housing programs have matured to the point where a distribution system is in place that can respond effectively to local needs while confronting the reality that regional approaches are necessary to break down the barriers to full integration of housing.

The shifts in political power resulting from the 1994 elections have altered the landscape in which housing policy is being discussed. The new Republican-controlled Congress is paying greater attention to proposals to decentralize housing program decisions. HUD secretary Henry Cisneros has proposed a major reorganization that would fold sixty housing and community development programs into three large block grants to state and local governments, converting public housing operating subsidies into tenant-based housing vouchers and changing the Federal Housing Administration from a government bureaucracy to a "government-owned, streamlined, market-driven enterprise."[131]

A bill to create a federal housing trust fund seeded by a limit on mortgage interest and real property taxes of "3 percentage points for each $1,000 by which the modified adjusted gross income of the taxpayer exceeds $75,000" up to a maximum of 50 percent of allowable deductions[132] was introduced in the closing days of the 1994 congressional session by a Democratic congressman who survived the midterm Republican surge. Prospects for this bill are uncertain in the current antispending climate. But reorganization without a corresponding infusion of capital will not help the millions of low-income persons who seek opportunities for decent housing. Decentralization and flexibility without sufficient resources to respond to current housing needs may be a Pyrrhic victory.

The experiments have been conducted. The resources are available. Do we have the will to act?

Notes

The valuable research assistance of Mark Schulte, J.D., Saint Louis University School of Law, is acknowledged with gratitude. Special thanks are also due Lisa Pool Byrne, J.D., Saint Louis University School of Law, for her invaluable assistance in revising this essay for publication by the University of North Carolina Press. Particular thanks are extended to Richard Baron, Lynn Broeder, Thomas Costello, Michael Duffy, Maria Foscarinis, Michael Goeke, Robert Herleth, Walter Jones, Roberta Youmans, and Amy Ziegler for allowing me to pick their brains while preparing this essay.

1. Raymond Hernandez, "A Detour in the Search for Shelter," *New York Times*, November 22, 1992.

2. Larry Rohter, "Homelessness Defies Every City's 'Remedy,'" *New York Times*, November 22, 1992.

3. *Report of the National Advisory Commission on Civil Disorders* (Washington, D.C.: U.S. Government Printing Office, 1968) (hereafter cited as *Kerner Report*).

4. John Charles Boger, "Race and the American City: The Kerner Commission Report in Retrospect" (in this volume).

5. Ibid.

6. Housing Act of 1949, ch. 338, § 2, 63 Stat. 413, 413 (codified as amended at 42 U.S.C. § 1441 [1988]).

7. Housing and Urban Development Act of 1968, Pub. L. No. 90-448, § 1601, 82 Stat. 476, 601 (codified as amended at 42 U.S.C. § 1441a [1988]).

8. *Kerner Report*, n. 3, 27–29.

9. 12 U.S.C. § 1715z-1 (1988 and Supp. II 1990).

10. 42 U.S.C. § 1437f(b) (Supp. II 1990) (amended in 1983 to delete new construction and substantial rehabilitation in favor of existing housing).

11. Ibid. § 1437f(b) (1988 and Supp. II 1992).

12. Boger, "Race and the American City" (in this volume, text at n. 208) (noting that newly constructed federally assisted housing units never exceeded 10 percent of annual total recommended by the Kerner Commission).

13. Civil Rights Act of 1968, Pub. L. No. 90-284, tit. VIII, 82 Stat. 81 (codified as amended at 42 U.S.C. §§ 3601–19 [1988 and Supp. II 1990]).

14. Pub. L. No. 100-430, 102 Stat. 1619 (1988) (codified at 42 U.S.C. §§ 3610–14a, amending §§ 3602, 3604, 3605, 3607, 3608, 3615–19, and 3631 [1988 and Supp. II 1990]).

15. 42 U.S.C.A. §§ 1437–40 (West 1978 and Supp. 1992).

16. 12 U.S.C. § 1707 to 1715z-20 (1988 and Supp. II 1990).

17. Housing Act of 1949, ch. 338, § 2, 63 Stat. 413, 413 (codified as amended at 42 U.S.C.A. § 1441 [1988]).

18. Act of August 2, 1954, ch. 649, tit. I, § 123, 68 Stat. 599 (codified as amended at 12 U.S.C. § 1715l [1988 and Supp. II 1990]).

19. Housing Act of 1961, Pub. L. No. 87-70, tit. I, § 101(a), 75 Stat. 149 (codified as amended at 12 U.S.C. § 1715l[d][5] [1988 and Supp. II 1990]).

20. Act of September 23, 1959, Pub. L. No. 86-372, tit. II, § 202, 73 Stat. 667 (codified as amended at 12 U.S.C.A. § 1701q [West Supp. 1992]).

21. Act of August 10, 1965, Pub. L. No. 89-117, tit. I, § 101, 79 Stat. 451 (codified as amended at 12 U.S.C. § 1701s [1988]).

22. HUD Act of 1968, §§ 235–36 (codified as amended at 12 U.S.C. § 1715z to 1715z-1 [1988]).

23. *1973 HUD Annual Report*, 7; see National Center for Housing Management, Inc., *Report of the Task Force on Improving the Operation of Federally Insured or Financed Housing Programs* (Washington, D.C.: U.S. Government Printing Office, 1972), 3:1–2.

24. 42 U.S.C. § 5303 (Supp. II 1990).

25. Ibid., § 5301(c) (Supp. II. 1990).

26. Ibid., §§ 5301(c), 5304(b)(3) (Supp. II 1990) (requiring that at least 70 percent of the aggregate amount of CDBG funds received by a state or local government be used for "the support of activities that benefit persons of low or moderate income").

27. Ibid., § 5305(a) (1988 and Supp. V 1993).

28. Housing and Community Development Act of 1974, Pub. L. No. 93-383,

sec. 201, § 8, 88 Stat 633, 662 (codified at 42 U.S.C. §§ 1437[f] [1988 and Supp. II 1990]).

29. In an Annual Contributions Contract (ACC), HUD agrees to provide funds annually to pay particular costs: in public housing, the costs to amortize bonds sold to finance construction of housing units (42 U.S.C. § 1437 c[a][1] [1988]); in Section 8, the balance of an agreed-upon rent (contract rent) after tenants make their required payments (30 percent of income) (ibid., 42 § 1437f[3][A] [Supp. II 1990]). The maximum length of public housing ACCs is forty years (ibid., § 1437c[a][1] [1988]). The terms for Section 8 ACCs are fifteen years for the certificate program (ibid., § 1437f[d][2][A] [Supp. II 1990]), and five years for the voucher program (ibid., § 1437f[o][5] [1988 and Supp. II 1990]).

30. Ibid., § 1437a(a)(1) (1988). Rental payments are set at the greatest of the following: 30 percent of adjusted income, 10 percent of income, or welfare payments received that are designated for housing costs.

31. Supply-side subsidies seek to encourage production of more housing units by providing incentives to developers and lenders. Demand-side subsidies are designed to enable recipients to compete more effectively in the marketplace for existing housing units. See generally Henry Aaron, *Shelter and Subsidies: Who Benefits from Federal Housing Policies?* (Washington, D.C.: Brookings Institution, 1972), 44–52 (discussing economic effects of housing subsidies).

32. See Committee on Government Operations, *Abuse and Management at HUD: Twenty-fourth Report by the Committee on Government Operations Together with Additional Views*, 101st Cong., 2d sess., 1990, H. Doc 977, 3–4; Irving Welfeld, *HUD Scandals* (New Brunswick, N.J.: Transaction, 1992), 85–106; Michael A. Wolf, "HUD and Housing in the 1990s: Crisis in Affordability and Accountability," *Fordham Urban Law Journal* 18 (1991): 545, 553–67.

33. 42 U.S.C.A. §§ 1437a(b)(2), 1437f(a), (c), (d)(2)(A), (o)(3)(A), (o)(5) (West 1978 and 1992).

34. The 1993 HUD appropriation provided funds for approximately 35,000 units and/or families to be assisted under Section 8, split about equally between the certificate and the voucher programs. In fairness it should be noted that the administration request of 82,000 units of assistance was more than double the amount actually appropriated in 1993 (Winners and Losers in HUD's FY93 Budget, Roundup [Low Income Hous. Info. Ser., October, 1992], 1, 3) (unpublished newsletter). As Professor Boger notes, a 4.1 million gap existed in 1989 between the number of low-rent units and the number of low-income renters (Boger, "Race and the American City" [in this volume, text at n. 204]).

35. Tax Reform Act of 1986, Pub. L. No. 99-514, § 252, 100 Stat. 2085, 2189–2208 (codified at I.R.C. § 42 [1988 and Supp. II 1990]); House Conference Report No. 99-841, September 18, 1986 [To accompany H.R. 3838], II-85, 1986 U.S. Code Congressional and Administrative News, 4173; Janet Stearns, "The Low-Income Housing Tax Credit: A Poor Solution to the Housing Crisis," *Yale Law and Policy Review* 6 (1988): 203, 209 (critiquing the effectiveness of the LIHTC and proposing alternative ways to encourage private sector development of low-income housing).

36. I.R.C. § 42, 469 (i)(3) (1988 and Supp. II 1992.

37. Congressional Budget Office, "The Cost-Effectiveness of the Low-Income Housing Tax Credit Compared with Housing Vouchers" (staff memorandum, 1992), 4. A two-part, fifteen-year targeting requirement is imposed: (1) building rentals must meet a 40:60 or 20:50 ratio of percentage of units rented and percentage of median income; (2) rents may not exceed 30 percent of the applicable qualifying income standard (I.R.C. § 42[g], [i][1] [1988 and Supp. II 1990]).

38. Pub. L. No. 103-66, § 13142(a)(1), 107 Stat. 438 (1993) (repealing 26 U.S.C. § 42(o). At press time, an effort to end the tax credit was under way. "Finance Committee Members, Others Pressure Roth to Save Low-Income Housing Tax Credit" [Current Developments], *Housing and Development Reporter* (BNA) 23 (October 9, 1995): 324.

39. Pub. L. No. 101-625, 104 Stat. 4079 (codified as 42 U.S.C. §§ 12701–898 [Supp. II 1990]). Since the repeal of the Section 8 New Construction and Substantial Rehabilitation programs in 1983, federal housing policy has supported efforts to use the existing housing stock rather than building new units. See 42 U.S.C. § 12741(a) (Supp. II 1990).

40. 42 U.S.C. § 12741–42 (Supp. II 1990).

41. Housing and Community Development Act of 1992, Pub. L. No. 102-550, § 203, 106 Stat. 3672, 3752 (October 28, 1992).

42. 42 U.S.C. § 12705 (Supp. II 1990). In 1995 HUD folded the CHAS planning requirement into a new consolidated plan and consolidated report process designed to replace twelve documents. Department of Housing and Urban Development, Consolidated Submissions for Community Planning and Development Programs, 24 CFR Part 91, 60 FR 1896, January 5, 1995.

43. Ibid., § 12771; see also, 42 U.S.C.A. § 12704 (6) (West Supp. 1992) (definition of CHDO).

44. 42 U.S.C. § 12750 (Supp. II 1990).

45. Cranston-Gonzalez National Affordable Housing Act of 1990, Pub. L. No. 101-625, §§ 421–48, 104 Stat. 4079, 4162–80 (codified at 42 U.S.C. §§ 12871–98 [Supp. II 1990]).

46. See 42 U.S.C. §§ 12871–98 (Supp. II 1990).

47. I.R.C. § 163(a), (h)(1–3) (1988).

48. Ibid., § 1034.

49. Ibid., § 121.

50. Ibid., § 1014.

51. James R. Follain and David C. Ling, "The Federal Tax Subsidy to Housing and the Reduced Value of the Mortgage Interest Deduction," *National Tax Journal* 44 (1991): 147, 148; see Joseph Isenbergh, "The End of Income Taxation," *Taxation Law Review* 45 (1990): 283, 288–89.

It is interesting to note that in one of the precursors to the modern tax code, rent paid for a dwelling was deductible (Act of Mar. 3, 1863, ch. 74, § 11, 12 Stat. 713, 723). Certain types of interest were deductible as early as 1864, with all interest being deductible in 1870 (Act of July 14, 1870, ch. 255, § 9, 16 Stat. 256, 258).

52. Follain and Ling, "Federal Tax Subsidy," 157.

53. A tax expenditure is the amount of tax revenue foregone by the Treasury because a deduction or exclusion of income is allowed. See Stanley S. Surrey and

Paul R. McDaniel, *Tax Expenditures* (Cambridge, Mass.: Harvard University Press, 1985), 3.

54. Budget of the United States, Fiscal Year 1993, tab. 24-3, part 2, 39.

55. Allen D. Manvel, "Upside-Down Housing 'Aid'?," *Tax Notes* 53 (1991): 743.

56. Ibid., 746.

57. Ibid. This is largely due to the increase in the standard deduction, capturing many homeowners at the low end of the income scale and lowering the marginal tax rates.

58. This does not assume that only these taxpayers benefited from the deduction preferences. Some of the individuals not itemizing may have used the subsidies in the past but may no longer have the volume of deductions necessary to move out of the category for standard deductions. Retirees would be expected to be in this category.

59. James M. Poterba, "Taxation and Housing: Old Questions, New Answers," *Empirical Public Finance* 82 (1992): 237, 239.

60. Ibid.

61. See Peter W. Salsich Jr., "Housing Finance Agencies: Instruments of State Housing Policy or Confused Hybrids?," *Saint Louis University Law Journal* 21 (1978): 595, 597–98.

62. See, for example, National Council of State Housing Agencies, *State HFA Program Catalogue* (Washington, D.C.: National Council of State Housing Agencies, 1992) (a five-volume reference cataloging more than 600 programs).

63. Ibid.

64. Conn. Gen. Stat. Ann. §§ 8-336 f, 8-336 l, 8-384 to 387, 8-395 (1989 and West Supp. 1992).

65. Ibid.; see also § 8-395 (West Supp. 1992) (providing tax credit for businesses that contribute to nonprofit housing programs).

66. N.J. Stat. Ann. §§ 52:27D-301 to 329 (West 1986), upheld in *Hills Development Co. v. Bernards Township*, 103 N.J. 1, 40, 510 A.2d 621, 642 (1986).

67. *Southern Burlington County NAACP v. Mount Laurel*, 92 N.J. 158, 199, 456 A.2d 390, 410, 413 (1983); *Southern Burlington County NAACP v. Mount Laurel*, 67 N.J. 151, 174, 336 A.2d 713, 724–25, app. dis. and cert. den. 423 U.S. 808 (1975).

68. N.J. Stat. Ann. 52:27D-305 to 307 (West 1986).

69. Ibid., §§ 52:27D-320 to 321 (West 1986).

70. "Syracuse Church-City Coalition Links Housing, Land Trust," [Current Developments] *Housing and Development Report* (BNA) 20 (December 7, 1992): 622.

71. Fla. Stat. Ann. § 163.3177(2–7) (West 1987); see also Cal. Govt. Code § 65302 (West 1983 and Supp. 1993) (requiring zoning ordinances to be in accordance with land-use and housing elements of master plan); N.J. Stat. Ann. § 40:55D-62 (West 1991); Or. Rev. Stat. § 197.175(2)(a) (1991) (requiring cities and counties to prepare comprehensive plans in compliance with goals approved by the Land Conservation and Development Commission).

72. See James W. Rouse and David O. Maxwell, foreword to *Building Foundations: Housing and Federal Policy*, ed. Langley C. Keyes and Denise D. Pasquale (Philadelphia: University of Pennsylvania Press, 1990), vii.

73. See Edward B. Lazere, Paul A. Leonard, Cushing N. Dolbeare, and Barry Zigas, *A Place to Call Home: The Low Income Housing Crisis Continues* (Washington, D.C.: Center on Budget and Policy Priorities, 1991), 39.

74. United States Housing Act of 1937, ch. 896, 50 Stat. 888 (codified as amended at 42 U.S.C.A. §§ 1437–1437ee [West 1978 and 1992]).

75. Congressional Budget Office, "Cost-Effectiveness of the Low-Income Housing Tax Credit," 2.

76. National Housing Law Project, "Changing Federal Housing Policy" (November 1992), 11; see also National Housing Law Project, "A Suggested Framework for National Housing Programs" (1987), 17–21 (statement submitted to the Senate Committee on Banking, Housing, and Urban Affairs and the House Committee on Banking, Finance, and Urban Affairs) (suggesting "shift[ing] . . . from a system of subsidizing long-term financing to one of capital grants," avoiding limited capital subsidies, and eliminating tax shelter subsidies).

77. See, for example, Edward H. Ziegler, "The Twilight of Single Family Zoning," *UCLA Journal of Environmental Law Policy* 3 (1983): 161.

78. Pub. L. No. 101-625, 104 Stat. 4079 (codified at 42 U.S.C. §§ 12701–898 [Supp. II 1990]).

79. Housing and Community Development Act of 1992, Pub. L. No. 102-550, 106 Stat. 3672 (codified at 42 U.S.C. § 5301).

80. *Kerner Report*, 483.

81. Ibid., 412–13.

82. HUD Act of 1968, Pub. L. No. 90-448, 82 Stat. 476 (August 1, 1968); see text accompanying n. 22, above.

83. *Kerner Report*, 28 (contrasting the performance of the public housing program over a thirty-one-year period—800,000 units produced—with the performance of the FHA mortgage insurance program over a similar thirty-four-year period—insured mortgages for 10 million new housing units for middle- and upper-income persons).

84. National Housing Law Project, "Changing Federal Housing Policy," 9 (citing Lazere et al., *A Place to Call Home*, 32).

85. See, for example, Carri Allen and Edward B. Lazere, *A Place to Call Home: The Crisis in Housing for the Poor, St. Louis, Missouri* (Washington, D.C.: Center on Budget and Policy Priorities, 1992): 22–23 (reporting that in 1992 more than 29,000 households were on waiting lists maintained by the city of St. Louis and the five counties in the St. Louis metropolitan area, which currently administer federal housing assistance through public housing and rental assistance programs to approximately 21,500 households).

86. Boger, "Race and the American City" (in this volume, text at nn. 206–12).

87. National Housing Law Project, "Changing Federal Housing Policy," 9. Shallow subsidies, such as tax credits to investors and below-market-rate loans to developers, reduce the cost of housing but only to a level that is affordable by persons in the sixty-eighth percentile of median-income range. Deep subsidies, such as Section 8 rental assistance payments, enable persons whose incomes are well below the fiftieth percentile of median income range to afford decent housing.

88. *Kerner Report*, 411.

89. All of the following proposals were offered in the context of deficit reduction, not subsidy redistribution.

90. H. Jane Lehman, "Where Candidates Stand on Housing," *Chicago Tribune*, November 1, 1992.

91. Joint Committee on Taxation, "Issues Involved in Possible Revenue Options to Reduce the Federal Deficit" (staff memorandum, JCX-20-92, June 4, 1992).

92. Congressional Budget Office, *Reducing the Deficit: Spending and Revenue Options* (Washington, D.C.: U.S. Government Printing Office, 1990), 357.

93. Ibid., 358.

94. Interest payments of less than $32,450 would be deducted at a 15 percent rate (for married individuals filing joint returns), then at a 28 percent rate for amounts up to $78,400, and finally at a rate of 31 percent for amounts up to the $1 million plus $100,000 limit.

95. Congressional Budget Office, *Reducing the Deficit*, 357.

96. Compare Follain and Ling, "Federal Tax Subsidy," 157 ("If discounted at 10 percent, the present value of the subsidy to owner-occupants is over a quarter of the value of the average house"); see also Gene Steuerle, "Limits on the Home Mortgage Interest Deduction," *Tax Notes* 58 (1993): 787 (arguing mortgage interest payments are deductible "mainly because the real tax expenditure toward housing cannot be measured easily"); and Joseph A. Snow, "My Home, My Debt: Remodeling the Home Mortgage Interest Deduction," *Kentucky Law Journal* 80 (1992): 431 (analyzing proposals for modifying or eliminating the mortgage interest tax deduction and arguing for its retention with respect to principal residences).

97. Arlene Zarembka, *The Urban Housing Crisis* (New York: Greenwood Press, 1990), 155. Zarembka notes that the tax loss from mortgage interest reduction would be reduced by $20 billion annually.

98. Congressional Budget Office, *Reducing the Deficit*, 357.

99. Budget of the United States, Fiscal Year 1993, tab. 24-3, part 2, 39.

100. Paul Houston, "Major Fight Likely over Killing Deductions for State, Local Taxes," *Los Angeles Times*, May 30, 1985; Susan Kellam, "Congressmen Join Tax Fight," *New York Times*, June 23, 1985.

101. Surface Transportation Revenue Act of 1991, Pub. L. No. 102-240, 105 Stat. 2203 (codified at 23 U.S.C., 26 U.S.C., and 49 U.S.C.) (extending highway-related taxes and trust fund).

102. See, for example, "Subsidy Reductions, HUD Restructuring Proposed by Progressive Policy Institute," [Current Developments] *Housing and Development Report* (BNA) 20 (December 21, 1992): 644–45; *The Final Report of the National Commission on Severely Distressed Public Housing* (Washington, D.C.: U.S. Government Printing Office, 1992), 10–31, 108–19.

103. Cranston-Gonzalez National Affordable Housing Act of 1990, Pub. L. No. 101-625, § 218, 104 Stat. 4079, 4109–10 (codified at 42 U.S.C. § 12748 [Supp. II 1990]).

104. I am indebted to Thomas P. Costello, a former executive director of the St. Louis Housing Authority, for helping crystallize the idea of shifting the decision-making authority to the states.

105. An eloquent argument for "dividing the job" between the federal government and the states by devolving a host of "productivity" programs, including housing and community development, to the states was made by Alice M. Rivlin, deputy director of the Office of Management and Budget in the Clinton administration (Alice M. Rivlin, *Reviving the American Dream* [Washington, D.C., Brookings Institution, 1992], 110–25). See also John R. Nolon, "Reexamining Federal Housing Problems in a Time of Fiscal Austerity: The Trend toward Block Grants and Housing Allowances," *Urban Law* 14 (1982): 249, 265–70 (explaining impact on state and local governments of block grant programs).

106. For example, Connecticut has established a state housing fund for distribution to local communities that enter regional fair housing compacts (Conn. Gen. Stat. § 8-387 [West Supp. 1992]); see n. 31, above, and accompanying text.

107. See, for example, *Britton v. Town of Chester*, 595 A.2d 492, 496 (N.H. 1991) (holding that the state zoning enabling act did not permit municipalities to zone out forms of housing, such as apartments and smaller houses that would be affordable to low- and moderate-income persons).

108. The term *permanently affordable* often is used to mean that subsidies, price restrictions, or both will remain in effect for the expected useful life of the building. See, for example, 12 U.S.C. § 4112(c) (Supp. II 1990) (defining "remaining useful life" of a low-income housing project to be a minimum of fifty years).

109. 26 U.S.C.A. § 42(h)(6)(D), (E) (West Supp. 1992).

110. Pub. L. No. 101-625, 104 Stat. 4249 (codified at 12 U.S.C. §§ 4101–25 [Supp. II 1990]).

111. In community land trusts, the ownership of housing is split between the land and the buildings, with nonprofit organizations dedicated to long-term affordability holding title to the land and entering long-term ground leases with the building owners (David M. Abromowitz, "Community Land Trusts and Ground Leases," *American Bar Association Journal of Affordable Housing and Community Development Law*, no. 2 [Spring 1992]: 5).

112. A survey of housing attitudes by the Federal National Mortgage Association (Fannie Mae) noted that control and security issues outweighed economic advantages as reasons for desiring to own a home. "Barely half of adults consider the tax advantage of homeownership an important argument for owning a home" (*Fannie Mae National Housing Survey*, [Washington, D.C.: Fannie Mae, 1992], 7).

113. A creative example of the possibilities for using state resources is the sale of taxable bonds to finance the purchase of a fifteen-year-old apartment complex for the elderly in Rhode Island. In return for the bond financing, the new owners pledged to put a portion of annual gross rents into an affordability preservation fund, to be used for rental assistance in the event a Section 8 subsidy contract is not renewed when it expires (NAHRO, "State Reports," *Journal of Housing* 49 [1992]: 308).

114. In calling attention to the magnitude of the problems of the estimated 86,000 units of public housing that are "severely distressed," the National Commission on Severely Distressed Public Housing noted that 94 percent of the approximately 1.4 million public housing units "continue to provide an important

rental housing resource for many low-income families and others" (*Final Report of the National Commission on Severely Distressed Public Housing*, 2).

115. The story of the compromises struck in the public housing legislation to overcome doubts about the legality of direct federal intervention in housing and vociferous opposition from the real estate industry is told in Lawrence M. Friedman, *Government and Slum Housing: A Century of Frustration* (New York: Rand McNally, 1968; reprint, New York: Arno, 1978), 94–113.

116. Public housing residents in the 1940s and 1950s were characterized as "poor, but [generally] employed and accustomed to urban living," but by the 1960s the population had shifted to "a very high proportion (over 50 percent) of female headed households of one kind or another on public assistance" (Robert M. Moroney, *Housing Policy in Social Policy and Social Work: Critical Essays on the Welfare State* [New York: Aldine de Gruyter, 1991], 91–92 [quoting from studies conducted in 1966 and 1971]).

117. See, for example, Lindsey Gruson, "Billions in U.S. Housing Aid Are Unspent by Poor Cities," *New York Times*, June 15, 1992 (reporting that an informal HUD review of two major housing and community development programs found $7.2 billion in unspent federal funds through the end of 1991).

118. While not recommending the type of change proposed here, the National Commission on Severely Distressed Public Housing declared, "The Federal Government cannot expect to apply the same laws, regulations, and administrative practices effectively to more than 3,000 different PHAs and approximately 1.4 million units of public housing nationwide" (*Final Report of the National Commission on Severely Distressed Public Housing*, 5).

119. See, for example, "Results of Programs to Sell Units to Public Housing Residents Examined," [Current Developments] *Housing and Development Report* (BNA) 16 (March 6, 1989): 896–97 (discussing report prepared by the Council of Large Public Housing Authorities and research reports submitted to HUD by Dr. Michael Stegman).

120. "Study Finds Assisted Rents Often Exceed 40 Percent of Income," [Current Developments] *Housing and Development Report* (BNA) 20 (September 28, 1992): 390; U.S. Department of Commerce, Bureau of the Census, *Current Population Survey* (Washington, D.C.: U.S. Government Printing Office, 1991).

121. Compare Michael Stegman, "The New Mythology of Housing," *TransAction*, January 1970, 55, 61 (arguing that encouraging homeownership "without moving toward reducing levels of unemployment and underemployment might be the cruelest hoax yet perpetuated on the low-income population").

122. See, for example, Moroney, *Housing Policy in Social Policy and Social Work*, 88–89 (citing studies that 22,000 to 25,000 jobs will be created by each $1 billion spent on housing construction and that an additional 276,000 jobs per $1 billion expenditure will result from the multiplier effect).

123. See, for example, "CDCs Begin to Focus on Business Development Finance," [Current Developments] *Housing and Development Report* (BNA) 20 (September 28, 1992): 392–93, and "Two Southern Banks Establish Bank CDCs," [Current Developments] *Housing and Development Report* (BNA) 20 (August 31, 1992): 315.

124. Community Investment Corporation Demonstration Act, Pub. L. No. 102-550, § 853, 106 Stat. 859, 3864 (1991) (codified at 42 U.S.C.A. § 5305 [West Supp. 1991]).

125. Housing and Community Development Act of 1992, Pub. L. No. 102-550, § 807, 106 Stat. 3672, 3849.

126. Ibid., 3847–50 (amending 42 U.S.C. §§ 5302, 5305); Microlending Expansion Act of 1992, Pub. L. No. 102-366, 106 Stat. 989 (amending 15 U.S.C. § 636[m]).

127. 12 U.S.C. §§ 2901–5 (1988 and Supp. II 1990).

128. See also Marion A. Cowell Jr. and Monty D. Hagler, "The Community Reinvestment Act in the Decade of Bank Consolidation," *Wake Forest Law Review* 27 (1992): 83, 87–94, 97–100.

129. 42 U.S.C. § 12705 (Supp. II 1990).

130. See n. 28, above.

131. U.S. Department of Housing and Urban Development, *Reinvention Blueprint* (Washington, D.C.: HUD, 1994), 14.

132. H. Rept. 5275, §§ 101, 103. Representative Major Owens (D-N.Y.) introduced the Housing Trust Fund Act, H.R. 5275, on October 7, 1994, during the closing days of the 1994 congressional session.

Chester Hartman

A Universal Solution to the Housing Problems of Minorities

Undeniably, the nation's housing problems are severe and are deteriorating for all racial groups and for middle- and lower-income households. Still, the most alarming problems afflict poor racial minorities. The housing crisis ranges from the inability of middle-income households to afford to buy homes or to keep their homes to the obscenity of outright homelessness for up to 3 million Americans.[1]

The Nature of the Housing Crisis

A June 1994 report to Congress by the Office of Policy Development and Research of the Department of Housing and Urban Development (HUD)[2] reported that, according to the Census Bureau's American Housing Survey, "there were 13.2 million very low-income renters [i.e., renter households] eligible for federal rental assistance programs"[3] and "another 8.5 million very low-income households faced crowded or physically inadequate housing or paid a significant portion of their income for rent and utilities." The special category of needy households with "worst case" housing needs[4] totaled 5.3 million households, an increase of 385,000 over the previous two years. Homeowners as a group face less serious quality, space, and affordability problems, although substantial numbers (along the order of millions) of households in this larger tenure category face one or more of these difficulties.[5]

As a general observation, it is likely that the nation's housing quality problems are considerably more serious than Census data reveal. There have always been issues of data quality and reliability, as Census enumerators rarely have the training required to identify structural and technical problems in the homes they survey, and residents may also, for different as well as similar reasons, be poor judges of deficiencies. In this context, it is important to note a largely unheeded critique of housing data, described in a background report prepared for the National Commission on Urban Problems (the Douglas Commission):

> It is readily apparent that even the most conscientious user of Census data . . . would arrive at a total "substandard" ["deficient," using more recent federal nomenclature] housing figure which grossly underestimated the number of dwelling units having serious local housing code violations. To use a total thus arrived at as a figure for substandard housing is grossly inaccurate and misleading, because it flies in the face of extensive consideration given by health experts, building officials, model code drafting organizations, and the local, state and federal court system to what have [sic] become over a period of many years, the socially, politically and legally accepted minimum standard for housing of human beings in the United States. . . . Even if public and private efforts eliminate all housing which is substandard under most federal definitions, there will still be millions of dwelling units below code standard.[6]

This array of problems affects all racial groups. In most ways, Hispanic and African American households are disproportionately represented among these various housing deficiencies, although for African Americans (but not for Hispanics) their disproportionately higher use of government housing subsidy programs (most notably, public housing) somewhat offsets this general observation. Neighborhood conditions, as well as extreme degrees of spatial isolation and the disadvantages this imposes,[7] clearly are worse for minority households. The most serious problem for minority households—as is true for whites, although proportionately less so than for Hispanics and African Americans—is affordability. The condition of shelter poverty (see below) is twice as high among African Americans and Latinos as it is among whites.[8]

There is no consensus as to what percentage of income families "should" spend on housing.[9] The extant standard under federal housing programs— the percent above which subsidies kick in for households fortunate enough to be served under one of the federal housing subsidy programs—is 30 percent.[10] Until 1981 that standard was 25 percent, but the standard was raised after President Reagan was elected in order to reduce the amount of federal subsidy required.[11] A more stringent and realistic approach, known as the "shelter poverty" or "market basket" approach, suggests that such fixed standards should not be used at all. Instead, the percentage of income devoted to housing should be a function of household income and size, with lower-income and larger families being required to pay lower, and in some cases far lower, percentages for housing. This lower percentage would be based on their needs for other basics, such as food, clothing, transportation, and medical care, which cost proportionately more for large households and very poor households.

Michael Stone, in his seminal research on shelter poverty,[12] employs the U.S. Bureau of Labor Statistics' detailed model budgets[13] to derive what households of various sizes need for nonshelter basics. He then computes what is left for housing if all such basics, as estimated by the federal government, are to be met. Not surprisingly, Stone's calculations reveal that vast numbers of households in the United States cannot "afford" 30 percent, 25 percent, or even 10 percent of their income for housing. Stone calculates that in 1991, 29 million U.S. households—30 percent of all households—were shelter poor, and half of these households cannot afford a single penny for housing if they are to meet basic nonshelter costs.

The implications of the shelter poverty concept and the figures generated by this approach are enormous. Stone calculates that in order to cover the gap between housing costs and incomes—a fundamental structural gap inherent in the current U.S. economy and housing system—some $100 billion would be required.[14]

When comparing the nation's health crisis with the nation's housing crisis, it is important to recognize that for lower-income families, the staggering and out-of-control health costs are borne largely by the government under the Medicaid and Medicare programs. The housing costs of lower-income Americans, however, are borne primarily by the households themselves. Nearly two-thirds of poor renters do not receive a rent subsidy under any federal, state, or local programs, nor do they live in public housing. Virtually no poor homeowners receive any direct government housing subsidies. The vast majority of the nation's poor pay their housing costs solely out of the family's budget.[15]

In other words, solving the nation's housing problem—attaining the National Housing Goal (promulgated by Congress in its preamble to the 1949 Housing Act and then reiterated in the 1968 Housing and Urban Development Act) of "a decent [affordable][16] home and suitable living environment for every American family"—would require more government subsidies than the society seems at present willing to acknowledge or consider.

The Implications of a Real Solution

Costs aside, a serious effort to attain the National Housing Goal by some future date (say, the year 2005) would have to address profound social and political issues. A disproportionate number of people needing housing aid are minorities. Consequently, whatever programs are devised would provide disproportionate benefits to such groups.[17] And since housing is a special social good that involves location and the various implications of location, profound social policy issues would have to be met head-on.

A major schism within the civil rights community exists between proponents of dispersion remedies and proponents of "in-place" remedies.[18] Advocates of dispersion remedies favor using housing vouchers or certificates to allow minority inner-city residents to move in order to improve their housing conditions, achieve affordable rents (defined by the 30 percent of income standard), and attain the communitywide benefits of non-inner-city locations. These benefits include improved schools, better access to jobs, less neighborhood crime, less concentration of families with a range of social problems, and greater racial and class heterogeneity. A body of evidence exists from the Gautreaux experiment[19] indicating that use of housing vouchers or certificates in this fashion can have positive results, particularly with respect to increasing employment rates, parent satisfaction, and social integration. Many questions arise, however, even among supporters of the program: How much "creaming" exists in selection of beneficiaries? In other words, are only those most likely to "succeed" selected, making the program of only limited applicability to central-city minority households? How much available and appropriate housing (considering size, cost, and location) exists for use by certificate or voucher holders? What is the possible inflationary impact of this added demand on the local housing market? Will access to jobs raise people out of poverty if wages are so low as to produce below-poverty incomes? Can the necessary counseling and support services available under the Gautreaux Program be replicated on a broad scale? Will an influx of central-city minority households trigger "white flight" or even flight of higher-income minority households? Would a broad-scale, locally well publicized (unlike the Gautreaux experiment) use of the program trigger racist political opposition?[20]

Those who advocate in-place remedies, or as it often has been labeled, "gilding the ghetto," express resentment that dispersion programs send the message that only by "going white" or breaking up inner-city neighborhoods can minority households improve. Why not, they ask, provide a real choice by creating improved education, community facilities, housing conditions, and neighborhood environments where people currently live? A single mother living in Chicago's Robert Taylor Homes offered the opportunity to escape with a "Gautreaux ticket" would be foolish not to take it. But she should have the option via substantial investment and creative programs tied to her own neighborhood, say the in-placers, of an improved neighborhood without having to give up existing friendship, extended family, and community ties. At this time, existing studies largely support the dispersionists' approach, due to the well-designed and -publicized research in Chicago and Cincinnati.[21] To make a fair comparison, it would be important to assemble similar data concerning employment, schooling, safety, and satisfaction regarding local attempts to improve housing and neighborhood conditions in the inner city.

In reality, both strategies are necessary to solve the nation's housing and neighborhood problems. The real question is how the two strategies should be combined—an issue involving resource allocation decisions, national and community politics, expressed preferences, and housing market and neighborhood realities.

The Major Low-Income Housing Programs

The principal low-income housing programs have been public housing and the Section 8 vouchers or certificates. The public housing program has taken a considerable public relations beating in recent years, to an extent because of valid criticisms but also because of exaggerations, distortions, and unwarranted implications put forth by those ideologically opposed to substitution of government programs for the free market. It would be foolish to deny that a substantial part of the public housing stock is in deep trouble, in no small part due to faulty program design, defective local administration, and intentional subversion by hostile federal administrations. But it would be equally foolish to ignore the considerable success of this approach. Public housing options are frequently superior to private market alternatives in cost, physical conditions, and management practices, evidenced by the sound shape of most of the nation's 1.3 million public housing units, residents' satisfaction with their conditions, and the long waiting lists of even the most troubled housing authorities.[22]

The notion of extensive government subsidies to create, via construction, rehabilitation, or purchase of existing buildings, housing specifically for households the market does not serve is sound. As is argued below, government subsidies can and must form the core of a serious approach to attain the National Housing Goal within a decade, so long as we also learn well the lessons of why some parts of the public housing program have failed. The architectural, siting, locational, and social mistakes embodied in much big-city public housing must not be replicated. Operating subsidies must be sufficient. Adequate maintenance and modernization funds must be provided. More responsive and competent management must exist, including, where possible and appropriate, tenant self-management. More emphasis must be placed on mixed-use and mixed-income developments. The full range of needed supportive services must be as much a part of housing programs as the bricks and mortar.

The second major, and newer, government approach to providing housing subsidies for low-income households is Section 8 rent subsidies, which allow families to live in privately owned units. The advantages of this approach, in the certificate or voucher form, are flexibility, economy (in other words, ability to take advantage of slack in the existing housing stock), maximization of individual choice, and portability. But this program has its limitations as well, and these were clearly revealed in the Experimental Housing Allowance Program (EHAP), one of the largest social science experiments ever undertaken in this country. EHAP involved giving housing allowances to 30,000 households over a period of years and under a variety of conditions in order to test demand effects, supply effects, and administrative variations. The experiment results showed that when certificates were available to all who met eligibility criteria, less than half of all eligible households used them; that participation rates were lowest for minority, poor, and large households and those living in poor-quality dwellings; that participation rates rose sharply when (as in some of the subexperiments) no housing quality standard had to be met—that is, when recipients could rent substandard quarters, which actually occurred in about two-thirds of the cases; and that participation triggered little geographic mobility by recipients and resulted in few housing repairs by landlords.[23]

Although housing allowances are not a panacea, under certain conditions—when there is market slack and when the program is accompanied by effective quality and rent controls—they can be an important component of the government's overall housing program.

Needed: A Comprehensive Program

The disproportionately severe housing problems of minorities must and should be solved as an integral part of a general solution to the nation's housing problems. And a serious program to attain the National Housing Goal within a decade necessarily will involve a mixture of both dominant past approaches: (1) creating permanently affordable housing and (2) providing subsidies for families to move to or continue living in decent existing units.

What might the first approach—a revised public housing program—look like?[24] There are three key elements of such an approach:

1. Structural changes in the financing of housing in order to minimize the amount of government subsidies needed and to provide the basis for the assurance of permanent affordability;
2. Assuring an ownership and subsidy structure that guarantees permanent affordability for those who cannot afford the going market costs of housing;
3. A commitment to provide sufficient government subsidies to close the gap between income and housing costs, as long as there are people with incomes insufficient to meet existing market costs of housing.

Structural Changes in the Financing of Housing

The central housing cost in our economy is the cost of the capital needed to construct or purchase the dwelling—a capital good with a value usually several times the annual income of the occupants. Almost invariably, credit is used for the initial transaction, and the cumulative cost of repaying the principal, with interest, typically is several times the actual amount of the capital borrowed. For the consumer with a mortgage debt, the cost of servicing that loan in most cases overwhelms the sum of all other housing costs. For example, data from the 1990 Housing Census show that the median monthly housing cost for owner-occupied units bearing a mortgage was $737, while the comparable figure for owner-occupied units without mortgage indebtedness was only $209.[25] For a tenant, the proportion of rent payment similarly routed, albeit indirectly, to the lender will vary with the landlord's actual financing situation. Use of second, and even third, mortgages by building owners to extract cash from properties rapidly and frequently can raise the percentage for renters higher than for the average homeowner.

An essential element of a strategy to reduce housing costs and keep government subsidies to a minimum will therefore logically aim at the element of housing costs that dwarfs all others. Were housing to be treated as social infrastructure, we might socialize the provision of capital and require users to pay only the ongoing costs of occupancy: utilities, property taxes, insurance, maintenance, and repairs. A fundamental restructuring of the housing finance system would reduce housing costs for the average consumer by more than two-thirds in some cases, thereby making housing more affordable for a vast portion of the present population experiencing housing problems.

This government-provided capital could be raised either through the tax system or by government borrowing, but in either case there would be a one-time payment of the capital costs (up front in the former case, over the life of the bonds in the latter case), rather than the present system of reborrowing and refinancing each time a house is sold, incurring new and usually higher debt, so that monthly debt-service costs in effect become a permanent occupancy cost.

An Ownership and Subsidy Structure That Assures Affordability

A massive structural change in the housing finance system would necessitate changes in the traditional concept and workings of homeownership: specifically, housing financed under this reformed system would not be bought and sold under existing market arrangements. No individual would own housing in the traditional sense of being able to sell it for profit. Ownership of housing would be a multilayered concept. Essentially, it boils down to three somewhat distinct attributes: the right to sell for whatever the market will bear; security of tenure; and the right to alter living space to suit one's needs and preferences. These last two attributes arguably are more important to resident satisfaction and community stability than the economic rights inherent in traditional forms of housing ownership.[26] Under a system of social provision of capital, both security of tenure and the right to modify one's living space would survive and, in fact, would be enhanced. With substantially lower monthly costs, the huge number of households evicted for nonpayment of rent or mortgage foreclosure would be reduced considerably.[27] The ability to live in decent housing for one-half to one-third of present costs, plus the greater security of tenure, would, for most lower-income people, substantially outweigh the speculative value of being able to reap a capital gain from the possibly increased value of one's house when selling it—one of the traditional attractions of conventional homeownership.[28]

Housing financed in this manner therefore would be owned by nonprofit social entities, within or independent from government. The "public housing" built under this drastically reformed subsidy system would be developed and owned by a range of nonprofit organizations: government agencies, neighborhood groups, tenant cooperatives, community development corporations, community land trusts, and religious and labor organizations. A more appropriate label would be "social housing," a term and concept widely used in Europe. The motivation for such groups to involve themselves in housing development and management would be to provide the best housing, with supportive community facilities and social services, at the lowest cost to the consumer. The motivation is not, as under the dominant present system, profit maximization by all the key actors: lenders, land speculators, developers, realtors, landlords, and property managers. Such a system also represents the most efficient use of government tax dollars. The dominant current federal low-income housing program, Section 8, provides virtually no controls over the cost elements of private financing, ownership, and management, and it merely throws into this uncontrolled market as many dollars per unit as are needed to close the gap between what a recipient can afford and what the market is charging for that unit.[29] The defects so often associated with bureaucracies like local housing authorities would largely be avoided, because community-based entities would be directly responsible and accountable to the residents and communities in which they operate.

Even with a government "gift" of capital costs, there nevertheless will be families with incomes too low to afford ongoing operating costs and to have sufficient income for nonshelter basics. Further subsidies, therefore, will be needed for such persons, in the form of operating funds to be paid to the owner or manager, or rent vouchers or certificates to be used by the resident.[30] These supplementary funds must be available for however long they are needed.

In addition to programs creating additional units of affordable housing, programs are needed to remedy unacceptable conditions prevalent in the existing housing stock, such as overcrowding, physical deterioration, or unaffordability. Three additional elements, therefore, would be needed:

1. *Conversion of privately owned subsidized units to permanently affordable nonprofit status.* Some 350,000 low- to moderate-income rental units, built under various federal mortgage subsidy programs, are owned privately (by for-profit as well as nonprofit entities), and after twenty years the owners can opt out of the subsidy arrangements and disengage from any restrictions on rent levels or occupancy.[31] Many owners are in the process of or are planning to do just that, and a subsidy program is needed to retain these units in the affordable housing stock and avert massive displacement.

2. *Giving low- and moderate-income homeowners the option of converting their residences to social ownership (through a social housing entity) and simultaneously being relieved of debt obligations.* Homeowners are virtually shut out from existing government subsidy programs (save those who can take advantage of the indirect subsidy provided by the homeowner deduction of mortgage interest and property tax payments from their taxable income base). A great many, however, are living in substandard conditions and/or paying unaffordable homeownership costs. Of these homeowners, many are losing their homes due to mortgage foreclosure. Under a variation of the basic social provision of capital described above, such owners would be given the ability to remain in their homes. Federal funds would be used to retire the debt (over time or all at once), and the home would forever remain debt-free, for permanent use by other income-eligible households whenever the existing residents departed. Such an arrangement could be expanded to allow any low- or moderate-income homeowner, regardless of his or her mortgage delinquency or foreclosure status, to engineer such a conversion, in effect trading the possibility of profiting from eventual resale of the home for security of tenure and drastically reduced monthly housing costs.

3. *Transferring ownership of buildings to nonprofit entities and providing the operators with sufficient subsidies to repair and continuously maintain the units, while requiring the residents to pay no more than an affordable*

portion of their income. The largest single group of families with housing problems, including substandard housing, overcrowding, and unaffordable housing costs, are lower-income renters. According to the American Housing Survey, 6.3 million renter households are paying 50 percent or more of their income for housing, of whom 3.6 million are paying 70 percent or more. The combination of long-term undermaintenance, profit-maximizing behavior by landlords, rising costs of operation (property taxes, utilities, insurance, and repairs), and low tenant incomes offers little hope for improvement absent radical measures. Thus, a major element of a comprehensive program to attain the National Housing Goal involves giving nonprofit entities control over low-income housing units and sufficient resources to maintain them.

Commitment to Sufficient Government Subsidies

Such reforms are ambitious and problematic, which emphasizes why the housing problem largely has been avoided in most discussions of antipoverty strategies. The costs of such a program will depend in part on how rapidly it is implemented and which parts are implemented first, as some are inherently more expensive than others. The first-year cost estimates of this comprehensive program, as put forward by the Institute for Policy Studies Working Group on Housing, ranged from $29.5 billion a year to $87.8 billion a year; the medium cost figure was $54.9 billion.[32] That figure is several times what the federal government now spends on low-income housing subsidies. But the largest federal housing subsidy of all—the homeowner tax deduction—is now some $89 billion a year. That indirect subsidy goes primarily to middle- and upper-income taxpayers, and it generally is regarded as a matter of right and not a subsidy at all. The political difference between providing benefits to individuals by allowing them to pay lower taxes and keep more of their income for personal consumption, and providing direct consumption assistance via money raised through the tax system, seems weighty.

The medium-level cost figure noted above would provide a massive influx of housing benefits compared with recent and current levels. Six and a half million households alone would be aided by a system of operating subsidies for housing in the social sector; another 1.5 million households would receive benefits from other elements of the program such as construction of new social housing units, conversion of homeownership units to social ownership in exchange for debt relief, conversion to social ownership and modernization of existing privately owned subsidized units, and conversion to social ownership and rehabilitation of existing privately owned nonsubsidized units.

Conclusion

Will the nation adopt this or a similar program? Will we spend the tens of billions of dollars needed to meet the National Housing Goal? It would be foolish to offer a positive, or even mildly optimistic, answer given current political and fiscal realities. The federal deficit dominates all discussions of domestic spending programs.

Given the current (mid-1995) climate—with massive rescissions in HUD's budget, serious congressional proposals to eliminate the agency altogether, rejection of the entitlement concept in various safety-net programs, and the general antipoor, antiminority sentiment in much of the nation, it is highly unlikely that there will be any substantial new housing programs or increased expenditures in the next few years. And it is even less likely that the major structural reforms in the U.S. housing system needed to ensure attainment of the National Housing Goal will be carried out. Nevertheless, it is important and useful to report the unvarnished truth about the magnitude and dimensions of the nation's housing needs, the impossibility of meeting that need without vastly increased government subsidies, and the limitations of even major increases in commitment without a corresponding restructuring of the way in which housing is financed, developed, owned, and managed in the United States.

Notes

1. Estimates are used because hard data are impossible to generate. No one disputes, however, that the numbers are rising and that employed persons and households with children are found in increasing numbers among shelter residents. A recent study reported that at some time during the 1985–90 period, 5.7 million people in the United States had been literally homeless (sleeping in shelters, bus/train stations, abandoned buildings, etc.), while 8.5 million people reported some type of homelessness (such as sleeping in a friend's or relative's house because the respondent had no home of his or her own) during that period. Lifetime homelessness figures showed 13.5 million people reporting literal homelessness and 26 million reporting some type of homelessness. These figures are far higher than any previous estimates of homelessness, which typically refer to a given point of time. See Bruce G. Link, Ezra Susser, Ann Stueve, Jo Phelan, Robert Moore, and Elmer Struening, "Lifetime and Five-Year Prevalence of Homelessness in the United States," *American Journal of Public Health* 84 (1994): 1907–12.

2. "Worst Case Needs for Housing Assistance in 1990 and 1991: A Report to Congress" (prepared for U.S. Department of Housing and Urban Development by Division of Policy Development, Office of Policy Development and Research, June 1994). See also Joint Center for Housing Studies, *The State of the Nation's Housing,*

1994 (Cambridge: Joint Center for Housing Studies of Harvard University, 1994).

3. Only one-quarter of these low-income renters actually live in public or assisted housing.

4. This term is defined by Congress as those unassisted renters whose incomes do not exceed 50 percent of area median income and who also have priority housing problems. They pay more than half their income for rent and utilities, live in severely substandard housing or are homeless, and/or were involuntarily displaced.

5. Homeowners' expenses and their relationship to income are far more complex to calculate, as they vary enormously with credit status (whether there is a mortgage or not—about one-third of all homeowners have no mortgage); the down payment/mortgage split; opportunity cost of the down payment; historical differences in mortgage rates depending on when the loan was assumed; whether the mortgage is fixed or variable rate; widely differential individual tax savings attributable to the homeowner deduction; whether and how value appreciation is taken into account; and other factors.

6. Oscar Sutermeister, "Inadequacies and Inconsistencies in the Definition of Substandard Housing," in *Housing Code Standards: Three Critical Studies*, Research Report no. 19 (Washington, D.C.: National Commission on Urban Problems, 1969), 83, 102.

7. See Douglas S. Massey and Nancy A. Denton, *American Apartheid: Segregation and the Making of the Underclass* (Cambridge, Mass.: Harvard University Press, 1993); John F. Kain, "The Cumulative Impacts of Slavery, Jim Crow, and Housing Market Discrimination on Black Welfare" (unpublished paper, n.d.).

8. Michael Stone, *Shelter Poverty: New Ideas on Housing Affordability* (Philadelphia: Temple University Press, 1993), 33.

9. For a general discussion of the affordability issue and shifting standards, see Chester Hartman, "Affordability of Housing," in *Handbook of Housing and the Built Environment in the United States*, ed. Elizabeth Huttman and Willem van Vliet (New York: Greenwood Press, 1988), 111–20.

10. Various adjustments of the base income to account for expenses, such as excessive child care, medical costs, or dependent children, can yield a slightly lower true percentage of total income.

11. For a discussion of this history, see Chester Hartman, "Housing Policies under the Reagan Administration," in *Critical Perspectives on Housing*, ed. Rachel G. Bratt, Chester Hartman, and Ann Meyerson (Philadelphia: Temple University Press, 1986), 362–76.

12. Stone, *Shelter Poverty*.

13. The government stopped publishing these figures in 1981 with the onset of the Reagan administration, but Stone has updated them using published Bureau of Labor Statistics data on annual consumer price changes.

14. Stone, *Shelter Poverty*, 57.

15. The average consumer unit in the lowest 20 percent income percentile spent $4,032 in 1991 on shelter (including fuel and utilities but not household operations and furnishings or housekeeping supplies) and $1,041 for health care. See U.S. Department of Commerce, Bureau of the Census, *Statistical Abstract of the*

United States: 1993 (Washington, D.C.: U.S. Government Printing Office, 1993), 454–55, tab. 705.

16. Congress did not cite affordability as a goal, largely because in 1949 the prevailing issues were slum clearance (the 1949 act introduced the urban renewal program) and increasing the stock of decent low-cost housing (the same legislation authorized 810,000 units of public housing over six years). Out-of-reach rents in the private sector were not a salient concern at that time. Obviously, however, a national housing goal is not terribly meaningful if the cost of obtaining housing leaves a family unable either to afford life's other basics or to achieve a minimum decent standard of living. The issue of a "suitable living environment" has never been defined or even considered. Were we to attempt to achieve truly decent, safe neighborhoods and communities, the figures that refer solely to housing costs would have to be increased greatly.

17. A useful summary of the targeting versus universal strategies debate can be found in Theda Skocpol, "Targeting within Universalism: Politically Viable Policies to Combat Poverty in the United States," in *The Urban Underclass*, ed. Christopher Jencks and Paul E. Peterson (Washington, D.C.: Brookings Institution, 1991), 411–36, and Robert Greenstein, "Universal and Targeted Approaches to Relieving Poverty: An Alternative View," in ibid., 437–59.

18. For a statement of the in-place position, see John O. Calmore, "To Make Wrong Right: The Necessary and Proper Aspirations of Fair Housing," in *The State of Black America, 1989*, ed. Janet Dewart (New York: National Urban League, 1989), 77. A good statement of the dispersionist position may be found in Donald L. DeMarco and George C. Galster, "Pro-Integration Policy: Theory and Practice," *Journal of Urban Affairs* 15 (1993): 141–60.

19. This refers to a complex and lengthy lawsuit, originating in 1966, that alleged racial discrimination in tenant selection and assignment in Chicago's public housing and led to a pilot program making a large number of Section 8 housing subsidies available to the city's public housing residents and those on public housing waiting lists. Detailed follow-up studies have been undertaken by researchers at Northwestern University. See James E. Rosenbaum and Susan J. Popkin, *Economic and Social Impacts of Housing Integration* (Chicago: Center for Urban Affairs and Policy Research, Northwestern University, 1990); James E. Rosenbaum, Marilynn J. Kulieke, and Leonard S. Rubinowitz, "White Suburban Schools' Responses to Low-Income Black Children: Sources of Success and Problems," *Urban Review* 20 (1988): 28–41; James E. Rosenbaum and Susan J. Popkin, "Black Pioneers: Do Their Moves to Suburbs Increase Economic Opportunity for Mothers and Children?," *Housing Policy Debate* 2 (1991): 1179–1214; Guy Gugliotta, "Lottery Offers Chicago's Black Welfare Families a Ticket out of Town," *Washington Post*, February 24, 1993.

20. A protest in two white Baltimore neighborhoods over a rumored plan (called Moving to Opportunity) to move inner-city public housing families into their areas, in a replication of the Gautreaux strategy, caused such an uproar that Maryland senator Barbara Mikulski, chair of the Senate Appropriations Committee for HUD, killed second-year funding for the entire program. See Ann Mariano, "Hill Panel Halts Plan to Move Poor Families," *Washington Post*, September 3, 1994.

21. Paul Fisher, "Is Housing Mobility an Effective Anti-Poverty Strategy? An Examination of the Cincinnati Experience" (report to the Steven H. Wilder Foundation, 1991).

22. For an overall evaluation of the accomplishments and defects of the public housing program, see Rachel Bratt, "Public Housing: The Controversy and the Contribution," in Bratt et al., *Critical Perspectives on Housing*, 335–61; Paul Leonard and Edward Lazere, *The Low Income Housing Crisis in Forty-four Major Metropolitan Areas* (Washington, D.C.: Center on Budget and Policy Priorities, 1992), xviii–xix. A survey by the National Association of Housing and Redevelopment Officials reported a nationwide aggregate of 1.1 million households on local housing authorities' waiting lists (in addition to 1.2 million households on waiting lists for subsidized privately owned housing). A more general evaluation of the full range of federal housing programs may be found in Chester Hartman and Barry Zigas, "What Is Wrong with Our Housing Programs," in *Homeless Children and Youth: A New American Dilemma*, ed. Julee H. Kryder-Coe, Lester M. Salamon, and Janice M. Mulnar (New Brunswick, N.J.: Transaction, 1991), 197–224. See also the author's interview with HUD assistant secretary for public housing Joseph Shuldiner, in *Shelterforce*, September/October 1994, 6–14, 26–27.

23. See Katharine L. Bradbury and Anthony Downs, eds., *Do Housing Allowances Work?* (Washington, D.C.: Brookings Institution, 1981) (presenting the findings and implications of the EHAP at a conference held by HUD at the Brookings Institution in November 1979); Raymond J. Struyk and Marc Bendick Jr., eds., *Housing Vouchers for the Poor: Lessons from a National Experiment* (Washington, D.C.: Urban Institute Press, 1981) (analyzing the design, operation, findings, and policy implications of the EHAP); Chester Hartman, "Housing Allowances: A Critical Look," *Journal of Urban Affairs* 5 (1983): 41–55 (concluding that EHAP is an ineffective housing program); Chester Hartman, "Rejoinder to 'Another Look at Housing Allowances,'" *Journal of Urban Affairs* 5 (1983): 159–70 (responding to HUD assistant secretary Philip Abrams's defense of housing allowances in "Another Look at Housing Allowances: A Response to Chester Hartman," *Journal of Urban Affairs* 5 [1983]: 151–58).

24. Elements of the program description that follows are based on Institute for Policy Studies Working Group on Housing, *The Right to Housing: A Blueprint for Housing the Nation* (Washington, D.C.: Institute for Policy Studies, 1989), 24–60.

25. U.S. Department of Commerce, Bureau of the Census, *1990 Census of Population and Housing, Summary: Social, Economic, and Housing Characteristics* (Washington, D.C.: U.S. Government Printing Office, 1992), 375, tab. 8. Nonmortgage costs include real estate taxes; fire, hazard, and flood insurance; utilities; and fuels.

26. Extensive studies of Boston's West End, bulldozed away in the late 1950s under the urban renewal program, showed dramatically how residents, under tenancy conditions characterized by low rents and ostensible total security of tenure, behaved like homeowners. Duration of residence in the neighborhood was extraordinarily long, and until the onset of the urban renewal program, the prevailing belief was that people could remain as long as they wished in their small tenement buildings, which in most cases were owned by neighbors, relatives, or former neighbors, the vast majority of whom were first- and second-generation Italian

Americans. One consequence of these conditions was a very high degree of the same kind of investment of family funds and self-help labor in apartment improvements that one normally associates only with homeowners. See Herbert J. Gans, *The Urban Villagers* (New York: Free Press, 1982) (reporting study and observation of the West End neighborhood from October 1957 to May 1958); Marc Fried, "Grieving for a Lost Home," in *The Urban Condition*, ed. Leonard J. Duhl (New York: Basic Books, 1963), 151, 169 (concluding that spatial and group identity were the "critical foci of the sense of community" for those relocated from the West End and arguing that lessons from the West End can be used to "create a housing system that retains and strengthens the noneconomic value of traditional home ownership while eliminating the economic dimension"); Chester Hartman, "Homeownership: Whose [sic] Got to Have It," *City Limits*, May 1990, 19–20; Chester Hartman, "Social Values and Housing Orientations," *Journal of Social Issues* 19 (1963): 113–31 (studying effects on mental health of forced relocation from the West End and suggesting alternative considerations for conceptions of slums).

An analogous instance of treating rental apartments as "one's own," under conditions of secure tenure and below-market rents, occurs with faculty living in university-owned (and -subsidized) units; such persons often will undertake, with their own funds, extensive kitchen remodeling, installation of built-in bookshelves, and other costly and nonmovable improvements.

27. Nearly 5 percent of all home mortgages in the United States were past due in late 1992, that is, thirty or sixty days behind in payment (Mortgage Bankers Association of America, *National Delinquency Survey, 3rd Quarter 1992* [Washington, D.C.: Mortgage Bankers Association, 1992]). No national data are available on tenant evictions, which are carried out by state and local courts. Moreover, definitional problems are involved: Is a tenant evicted only when a court order is enforced? Or is it more meaningful to describe as eviction a "voluntary" move in response to a court order and before the sheriff or marshal arrives to enforce the order? Or is an eviction a move in response to the landlord's notice to vacate, absent any court proceedings or official communication? Depending on what definition is used, most experts estimate the annual number of evictions to be in at least the six-figure range, and likely well into the millions.

28. For a comparison of the implications for household economics of the present mortgage system with the system described here (resident-savers), see Stone, *Shelter Poverty*, 197, tab. 7.1.

29. HUD does establish Fair Market Rents (FMRs) for each local housing market and will not provide Section 8 subsidies above that level. But these FMRs are established and periodically updated based on the realities of the local housing market and thus are designed to avoid paying more than prevailing market prices. They do nothing to lower or control market costs; in fact, a large amount of Section 8 subsidy funding introduced into a housing market will cause price and rent inflation and, consequently, an increase in the FMR.

30. In the current public housing program, capital costs similarly are excluded from the local housing authority's operating budget, and there is no need for tenant rents to cover repayment of these costs. Most commonly, local housing author-

ities issue long-term tax-exempt bonds and then enter an annual contributions contract with the federal government, which calls for annual federal payments equal to the costs of servicing those bonds. More recently, for the trickle of new public housing still being built, the federal government has been using the cheaper method of supplying a capital grant up front. Yet the poverty of public housing tenants and the increasing cost of maintaining public housing have created a severe gap between what it costs to operate public housing and the income generated by tenants' rents, which are set, as noted above, at 30 percent of income. A variety of supplementary federal subsidies has been introduced to cover this shortfall, and tenant rents in many large cities cover only about half of the actual operating costs. This shortfall illustrates the inadequacy of capital cost subsidies alone to make housing affordable, absent additional subsidies.

31. See Emily Achtenberg, *Preserving Expiring Use Restriction Projects in Massachusetts: A Handbook for Tenant Advocates, Community Groups, and Public Officials* (Boston: Citizens Housing and Planning Association, 1992).

32. Institute for Policy Studies, *Right to Housing*, 63. These figures are in 1989 dollars. The report estimated costs at three levels, depending on the mix of different program elements and the rapidity of progress in meeting the National Housing Goal.

John Charles Boger Toward Ending
Residential Segregation

A Fair Share Proposal for the
Next Reconstruction

Introduction

The finest scholars who have written on residential segregation in the post–Kerner Commission era agree on two things: segregation has devastating social consequences, and it is apparently intractable. Their deep pessimism stems in part from doubt that Americans will ever summon the political will to end segregation. Beyond the question of will, however, lies an uncertainty about means: whether effective governmental policies can ever be fashioned to overcome metropolitan racial divisions in a nation unwilling to dictate housing choices to the private market. All governmental policies to promote racial or economic integration, they observe, must ultimately confront the harsh judgments of the marketplace, where housing consumers are free to leave, or refuse to enter, any integrating community, thereby assuring its resegregation.

This essay proposes a policy tool, a National Fair Share Act that would create market incentives to support integrative housing choices and simultaneously would provide market disincentives to discourage segregative choices.[1] The act would have three features:

1. Drawing on lessons learned from the nation's attempt to end racial segregation in voting, public education and employment, and from New Jersey's experience with "fair share" housing legislation, the act would require the calculation of specific housing goals for every municipality that has not yet assumed its fair share of racially and economically integrated housing.

2. As an incentive to meet these goals, the act would authorize federal housing funds to all municipalities that chose to shoulder their fair share housing obligations. As a disincentive, this legislation would modify the federal tax code so that property holders in municipalities that chose to ignore their prescribed housing goals would progressively

lose their mortgage interest and property tax deductions. These tax code modifications would prompt citizens to encourage municipal leaders to comply with federal law, thereby hastening metropolitan integration. They would also reverse the economic advantages that currently flow toward property holders in segregated communities.

3. Mindful that local participation is crucial to success, the act would grant local municipalities flexibility in devising plans to meet their fair share obligations. Moreover, as amplified below, the legislation would permit each municipality to opt either for a racial integration emphasis or for a low-income housing emphasis.

Before examining the specifics of the National Fair Share proposal, I briefly contrast the remedial strategy of the Fair Housing Act of 1968 (the principal federal statute presently available to combat housing segregation) with strategies embodied in three other civil rights statutes (the Voting Rights Act of 1965, and Titles VI and VII of the Civil Rights Act of 1964), each of which has proven more effective at achieving compliance. Next I examine the fair share housing legislation developed in New Jersey during the 1980s—a housing strategy that could be refashioned to approach the remedial success of the federal voting, public education, and employment statutes. After noting several weaknesses in the New Jersey legislation, I introduce a strengthened federal alternative, the National Fair Share Act.

The Persistence of Residential Segregation

In 1968 the Kerner Commission warned that America's residential areas were drifting toward racial polarization: the nation's central cities were disproportionately becoming home to an impoverished, African American minority, while the growing suburbs increasingly were populated by a more prosperous white majority.[2] The commission cautioned that this growing residential isolation would inflict grave economic disadvantage on African Americans[3] and simultaneously would spell social and economic decline for many American cities.

Subsequent developments have largely confirmed the Kerner prognosis. Metropolitan geography has contributed substantially to the maintenance, if not the intensification, of racial subordination.[4] Although the starkness of the present residential apartheid is obscured by the visible progress of that minority of African Americans who have attained an uneasy middle-class economic status,[5] even the black middle class has not experienced the degree of residential mobility that should have accompanied their economic success.[6] Moreover, residential segregation continues to confine urban blacks to employment and housing markets that are economically inferior;[7] they live in segregated neighborhoods that are debilitated by private disinvestment[8] and are underserved by grossly inadequate educational, health care, public safety, and other municipal services.[9]

Residential Segregation: An "Inevitable Consequence?"

One of the most striking features of racial segregation in the 1990s is the national sense that it is inescapable. Despite legal successes in combating other forms of racial discrimination in public and private life, residential segregation is often viewed as an "inevitable consequence"—of economic inequality between blacks and whites, of the private preferences of black renters and homeowners, and of inexorable sociological and economic forces.

Those who explain residential segregation as a product of income differences between blacks and whites, or as a reflection of black neighborhood preferences, rarely find it morally problematic. For these observers, segregation is a by-product of the American commitment to free markets and private choices.[10] A careful review of the evidence demonstrates, however, that neither income inequality nor African American preferences can, in fact, explain current patterns of housing segregation.[11] While black citizens, on average, have lower incomes (and thus less residential mobility) than whites, blacks *at all income levels* continue to face widespread exclusion from neighborhoods they can afford.[12] Blacks confront housing discrimination far more pronounced than that experienced by other ethnic groups, including non-black Hispanics and Asians in similar economic circumstances.[13] Nor do black citizens' neighborhood preferences—the "birds of a feather" explanation—adequately explain America's segregated living patterns. Numerous studies confirm that a substantial majority of African Americans would prefer to live in racially integrated residential neighborhoods if they could move without threats of violence or hostility from their new neighbors.[14]

Two other theories, less benign than income differences or black neighborhood preferences, provide more plausible explanations for America's continuing housing segregation: (1) that illegal acts of housing discrimination are perpetuated against African American homeseekers nationwide, and (2) that most white homeseekers refuse to buy or rent in racially integrated communities. Strong evidence exists to support the first theory, that America's housing sales and rental markets, and perhaps its mortgage lending markets as well, are rife with illegal, discriminatory behavior.[15] The Department of Housing and Urban Development (HUD) has sponsored two national studies of housing discrimination, completed in 1979 and 1989, respectively.[16] The more recent HUD study found that African Americans can expect to experience discrimination in 59 percent of their home sales encounters and 53 percent of their leasing encounters.[17] This pervasive pattern of illegal conduct, which persists in defiance of federal statutes that were adopted over a generation ago, has denied millions of black citizens access to municipalities and neighborhoods in which whites have invested their housing dollars.

Additionally, there is strong evidence that whites regularly refuse to seek housing in integrated communities where blacks currently reside or are likely to move in great numbers.[18] While some whites doubtless act out of racial prejudice, others claim that they act out of economic self-interest, since racial integration inevitably leads to a decline in property values and an increase in local taxation.[19] Whether or not empirically correct,[20] these beliefs tend to become self-fulfilling prophecies, for when potential white homebuyers shun communities that welcome integration, the market demand for housing in those communities, and perforce, the market value of those homes and apartments, tends to decline.[21]

This market explanation for the dynamics behind residential segregation is particularly sobering, for it suggests that, even if every illegal act of discrimination could somehow be ended, economic incentives would continue to prompt whites to make perfectly legal housing choices that, cumulatively, would lead to segregated neighborhoods. In a country firmly committed to private markets and to freedom of movement (for those with sufficient capital), no governmental remedy can succeed in ending segregation without sufficiently altering housing market forces to induce millions of blacks and whites to change their behavior and choose racially desegregated communities.[22]

It is thus little wonder that many students of residential segregation concur in the gloomy belief that segregated living patterns are all but inevitable in the foreseeable future.[23] Not only do political forces seem aligned against effective reform, but the law appears relatively powerless to combat residential segregation directly. Thus, Anthony Downs notes,

> Residential segregation by race can and does arise because of factors that are not illegal, but voluntary (though illegal behavior may contribute to it). Such segregation is relatively easy to detect, but it cannot be attacked *per se*, as can racially discriminatory behavior. Such segregation arises because of the collective results of many individual actions that are not illegal and, hence, cannot be directly discouraged through fines and punishment. Moreover, public support for antisegregation actions is not nearly as strong or widespread as public support for antidiscrimination actions. . . . This analysis indicates that *policies designed to reduce residential segregation by race are not likely to be nearly as effective in achieving their goal—at least in the near future—as those designed to reduce racially discriminatory behavior in housing market transactions.*[24]

Downs's analysis leads him and other commentators to advocate more of the same—vigorous enforcement of fair housing laws, in the hope that enforcement might somehow deter market actors from discriminating against minority citizens who seek integrated housing opportunities.[25]

The National Fair Share proposal put forward in this essay aims to accomplish what Downs says cannot be done: to "attack segregation *per se*." [26] While it neither outlaws segregation entirely nor dictates private housing choices, it does place upon local municipalities an affirmative burden to end segregation. It also imposes sharp economic costs on residents in municipalities that do not comply, thereby changing the economic calculus for potential renters and homebuyers. This proposal is not modest in scope, for it would require combined action by the federal government, each of the states, and thousands of municipalities. Nor would it be cost free; the federal government would be required to increase the national investment in subsidized housing, which dwindled under the Reagan and Bush administrations, and which appears in jeopardy under the Clinton administration as well. Yet, at bottom, the Fair Share Act would eschew a massive, federal housing production program in favor of a more manageable redirection of the nation's ongoing residential growth in directions that would eventually bridge the racial chasm that currently divides us. Moreover, the act borrows key elements from proven legislative strategies that have succeeded in other civil rights contexts.

Federal Fair Share Strategy

The Deficiency of a Case-by-Case Approach

The Fair Housing Act of 1968[27] is the principal federal statute designed to combat residential discrimination. Enacted in the wake of the Kerner Commission Report and the assassination of Dr. Martin Luther King Jr. in 1968,[28] the act prohibits acts of racial (or religious) discrimination by governmental and most private actors in the sale or rental of multifamily dwellings.[29] The Fair Housing Act also requires HUD and other federal agencies to "administer their programs and activities relating to housing and urban development . . . affirmatively to further the purposes of" fair housing.[30]

By most accounts, the Fair Housing Act has been a disappointing failure.[31] Until 1988, when substantial legislative revisions were adopted,[32] the act provided aggrieved private parties with only trivial economic incentives to initiate corrective lawsuits.[33] Moreover, federal agencies were given very limited authority to pursue independent enforcement actions.[34]

Although amendments to the Fair Housing Act in 1988 have addressed these deficiencies,[35] other problems remain.[36]

The Fair Housing Act's central flaw is its reliance on a tort or criminal liability model that requires the identification of a violation, the detection of a perpetrator, and proof at trial that the perpetrator's act has violated the federal housing statutes. Since realtors, lenders, or sellers rarely decline outright to service black customers or otherwise reveal their intent to discriminate, injured parties often remain unaware that the law has been violated.[37] Various steps could (and should) be taken to improve the efficacy of the Fair Housing Act—more aggressive use of "testing" or housing audit methods to detect misconduct,[38] more vigorous enforcement by federal authorities, a larger enforcement budget,[39] and increased financial assistance to private fair housing organizations.[40] Still, none of these steps, even viewed collectively, seem likely to detect or deter most of the estimated 2 million acts of housing discrimination committed every year, or to counter the powerful economic incentives that prompt this illegal behavior.[41]

The Efficacy of Systemic Approaches

Widespread resistance to civil rights laws is nothing new. Decades of experience in other areas have proven that effective compliance strategies do not rely on the punishment of individual acts of misconduct. Affirmative, systemwide remedies are indispensable.[42] The fifty-year battle in the South to restore the effectiveness of the Fifteenth Amendment and end racially motivated voting discrimination against African Americans offers a useful example.[43] Each legal step forward in the campaign to secure the vote was countered by white official and private resistance no less determined than that which today confronts the proponents of residential desegregation— a veritable dance of sallies, sidesteps, and false assurances that produced little measurable progress toward genuine enfranchisement.[44] Only when Congress enacted the Voting Rights Act of 1965[45] did blacks begin to register to vote in great numbers.[46]

The structure of the Voting Rights Act merits our consideration. It abandoned a case-by-case search for identifiable misconduct in favor of a wholesale suspension of all state voting "tests or devices," such as literacy tests or character tests,[47] in every jurisdiction where noncompliance was deemed likely.[48] In those jurisdictions, without further proof of fault, the act delegated broad remedial powers to the federal Department of Justice to appoint federal voting registrars who would supplement (if not replace) local registrars.[49] The act made illegal not only those voting devices that had been enacted "for the purpose" of abridging the voting rights of racial minorities, but also all devices that, in practice, had such an effect.[50] Finally, the act authorized the Department of Justice to "preclear" all proposed changes in local voting procedures in order to intercept and forestall any changes that would violate the ends of the act.[51]

A similar congressionally initiated change of strategy proved necessary to end school segregation in the face of determined southern resistance. In 1954 the Supreme Court's unanimous decision in *Brown v. Board of Education*[52] declared that de jure public school segregation violated the Fourteenth Amendment and ordered desegregation "with all deliberate speed."[53] Despite hundreds of lawsuits brought to compel compliance, however, the Court's mandate yielded little actual desegregation during the decade that followed.[54]

A meaningful breakthrough came only with passage of the Civil Rights Act of 1964,[55] which authorized the Department of Health, Education, and Welfare (HEW) to issue administrative guidelines demanding measurable desegregation.[56] The HEW regulations required every formerly de jure school district hoping to receive federal aid either to submit an effective desegregation plan for certification by HEW or to demonstrate that it was operating under a judicial decree requiring school desegregation.[57] To create an economic incentive for compliance, Congress soon enacted the Elementary and Secondary Education Act of 1965,[58] which appropriated billions of federal dollars for states that would agree to comply with federal civil rights statutes.[59] By vesting HEW with the authority both to prescribe Title VI regulations and to withhold appropriations from school boards whose plans were judged inadequate, Congress created extremely powerful tools to speed meaningful public school desegregation throughout the South. Once those tools had been forged, progress toward desegregation was remarkable.[60]

Likewise, widespread racial desegregation in private employment came only after Congress empowered an administrative agency, the Equal Employment Opportunity Commission (EEOC), to investigate and remedy charges of unlawful employment discrimination[61] and to issue regulations to enforce Title VII of the Civil Rights Act of 1964.[62] The EEOC[63] and the Supreme Court[64] interpreted Title VII to prohibit not only individual acts of discrimination[65] but also an employer's use of employment criteria that underrepresented blacks in the workforce, unless those criteria could be shown to be required as a matter of business necessity.[66] Moreover, both the EEOC[67] and, ultimately, the Supreme Court[68] read Title VII to approve race-conscious hiring and/or promotional goals and timetables that required employers to hire a specific number of minority workers within a fixed time as a remedy for past discrimination, and to authorize damage awards including back pay for employees wrongfully discharged or denied promotions.[69] The effects of Title VII on the composition of the American workforce has been significant.[70]

The cumulative lessons of the voting, public education, and employment statutes are that serious civil rights remedies (1) must rely on objective, systemwide goals; (2) must demand concrete progress toward those goals from the chief institutional actors who implement them; and (3) must offer powerful financial incentives, both positive and negative, to promote compliance.

The "Fair Share" Approach

No federal housing statute has ever met with systemwide success in combating residential segregation, because none, neither the Fair Housing Act of 1968 nor the Housing and Community Development Act of 1974, was ever designed to demand systemwide results. One such housing strategy did emerge at the state level during the 1970s and 1980s, however: the fair share statutes associated most prominently with New Jersey's *Mount Laurel* decisions[71] and its 1985 Fair Housing Act.[72]

The New Jersey approach was prompted by a decade-long litigation effort, originally filed on behalf of poor and minority citizens, to challenge the exclusionary zoning laws of Mount Laurel, New Jersey, a suburban municipality whose zoning ordinances effectively barred construction of low-income, multifamily housing. Although the plaintiffs initially alleged that Mount Laurel's ordinances were racially motivated,[73] the New Jersey Supreme Court ultimately declined to decide that issue,[74] instead adopting a different approach. The court held that New Jersey's state zoning enabling laws (empowering local municipalities to promulgate zoning ordinances)[75] were subject to a provision of New Jersey's constitution that required all legislation to be enacted "for the general welfare." Any zoning ordinance that denied housing opportunities to a "fair share" of a region's low- and moderate-income citizens, the court reasoned, contravened both the enabling statute and the New Jersey constitution's "general welfare" requirements.[76]

Mount Laurel radically reinterpreted traditional zoning concepts by conditioning the legality of a municipality's ordinances upon its prior consideration of regional and statewide housing needs. Many perceived *Mount Laurel* as a decision that would permit New Jersey's urban poor some meaningful access to the state's growing suburban areas.[77] Predictably, the decision provoked widespread criticism and substantial resistance.[78] Because the original decision announced a new municipal responsibility without specifying effective, complementary remedies—indeed, without even offering clarity on its key terms[79]—it became the object of complicated, lengthy litigation that delayed actual implementation for a decade.[80] Only after further judicial elaboration in 1983[81] and then after New Jersey's legislature passed a statutory scheme in 1985 to provide administrative enforcement[82] did the full contours of the fair share doctrine take shape.

As presently interpreted, the New Jersey approach requires municipalities to do more than modify exclusionary zoning laws that expressly deny housing opportunities to a region's low- and moderate-income population.[83] Local municipalities must take affirmative steps to meet each region's documented low- and moderate-income housing need. To supervise these efforts, New Jersey's 1985 statute created a statewide administrative body, the Council on Affordable Housing (COAH),[84] which is required to divide the state into housing regions[85] and calculate the present and foreseeable housing need within each region.[86] It then must allocate a fair share of low- and moderate-income housing to each municipality within the region.[87] Municipalities subsequently are invited to submit specific fair share plans to COAH, explaining how they intend to supply their designated housing need.[88] Until COAH has certified a municipality's fair share plan, the municipality remains open to so-called builders remedies—lawsuits, first recognized in *Mount Laurel II*, that permit private developers to demand that local zoning boards open sites to low- or moderate-income development.[89]

Mount Laurel and the 1985 statute stop somewhere short of requiring municipalities to use their own funds to build needed low-income housing.[90]

Instead, the statute contemplates that many municipalities will rely on "density bonuses," mandatory "set-asides," or other zoning devices that allow developers to build more housing units per acre than would otherwise be permitted if they include some low- and moderate-income units among their market-level developments.[91] To date, New Jersey's fair share approach has generated a substantial flow of new low- and moderate-income housing.[92]

Despite its virtues, the New Jersey approach has five serious deficiencies in design and in implementation that render it insufficient as a federal remedy for residential racial segregation.[93] First, because the statute omits express racial goals and fails to require monitoring of low-income participants to ensure racial diversity, suburban municipalities may act subject only to the weak antidiscrimination requirements of the federal and state fair housing laws. Not surprisingly, recent surveys reveal that virtually all of the housing units built under New Jersey's fair share program have been filled by white applicants.[94]

Second, the statute has effectively permitted municipalities to meet their fair share obligations by serving only the relatively better-off among New Jersey's needy households. This is true for several reasons. The New Jersey approach links eligibility for *Mount Laurel* housing to the state's median income. An applicant can qualify for a "moderate income" unit with an annual income that is 80 percent of the statewide median, and for a "low income" unit with an annual income that is 50 percent of the statewide median.[95] Because New Jersey has a relatively high median income (roughly $38,000 in 1990), *Mount Laurel* units are available to applicants with incomes of $19,000 to $30,400.[96] While persons at these income levels undoubtedly experience difficulty in purchasing or renting housing in markets such as those of the 1980s, they are not the urban poor whose housing plight prompted the Kerner Commission Report or the initial *Mount Laurel* opinion.[97]

Moreover, by tying *Mount Laurel* eligibility to current income, the statute allows municipalities to provide below-market housing to many persons who are income poor only because of predictable, short-term, life-cycle circumstances (for example, students or young married couples) or because of sudden, temporary economic changes (for example, recently divorced persons). In fact, a significant proportion of *Mount Laurel* beneficiaries appear to fall into these relatively less needy categories.[98]

Additionally, the New Jersey statutes and regulations do not mandate the bedroom size of housing units. Since many municipalities correctly calculate that smaller families place fewer demands on local fiscal resources than do large families with school-aged children, there is a strong tendency to favor one-bedroom townhouses or other smaller units that are inappropriate for larger families.[99] No serious attempt is made to require a proportionate number of larger units to meet the family needs of the state's low- and moderate-income families.

A third principal flaw is that neither the New Jersey statute nor COAH's implementing regulations have obligated municipalities to engage in any affirmative marketing of their units to low-income residents of urban areas, nor have they forbidden municipalities from filling their fair share housing with their own long-term, low-income residents.[100] While this deficiency might not have been problematic if COAH had calculated fair share obligations in a manner that accounted fully both for each municipality's internal low-income needs and for its share of the regional need, many critics have argued that COAH's calculation of regional need has been far too low. As a consequence, many municipalities can fulfill their fair share requirements without ever venturing beyond municipal boundaries to find low-income applicants, thereby defeating one major objective of the original plan.[101]

Fourth, because of the scarcity of substantial state or federal housing subsidies, New Jersey's approach has relied very heavily on the private market for the creation of affordable housing.[102] Since for-profit developers approach their *Mount Laurel* obligations with the natural desire to maximize their profits, not with a commitment to satisfy the state's most compelling housing needs, and since economic conditions in the mid-1980s promised greater potential profits from new homes than from rental apartments, most New Jersey developers used their density bonuses and mandatory set-asides to build new homes, even though these "affordable" units entailed far higher consumer costs (such as substantial down payments and closing costs) than would rental or rehabilitated units, and even though these new *Mount Laurel* homes proved far beyond the financial reach of many low-income persons.[103]

Finally, the statutes do not contain any absolute requirement that municipalities participate, and many have not done so, apparently unconcerned by the prospect of facing builders remedy litigation.[104] Thus, municipal responsibilities for fair share are not distributed fairly, and New Jersey, perhaps exhausted by its twenty-year struggle for a statewide statute, has taken no meaningful affirmative steps to enforce the law against noncomplying jurisdictions.

The Federal Fair Share Plan

Basic Features of the Program

Drawing on both the positive and the negative experiences in New Jersey, this essay proposes a National Fair Share Act to implement the positive features of New Jersey's important state-level experience. That act should take the form of a traditional federal grant-in-aid statute[105] that would require all states and localities wishing to receive federal benefits to comply with its terms. The structure for implementing such an act can already be found in the Cranston-Gonzalez National Affordable Housing Act of 1990.[106] Some may question why Congress must act at all if a number of states already have begun to address the issue. The answer is clear: without congressional prodding, most states are unlikely to initiate meaningful reform. Indeed, the present highly decentralized distribution of responsibility for subsidized housing virtually assures that meaningful action against residential segregation will not occur absent federal intervention.[107]

At the federal level, the Fair Share Act should authorize a substantial sum of monies over a substantial period, perhaps $5 billion a year for ten years, to assist states and municipalities in implementing the act. It should also designate a lead agency to administer the act, granting it authority to promulgate implementing regulations. The lead agency, probably HUD, should have the technical capacity to offer active assistance to states and municipalities in their planning efforts, as well as the power to enforce compliance with the statute.

The statute should require each state participating in the fair share program to designate a central planning or development agency, like COAH in New Jersey, to coordinate and oversee implementation of the statute at the state level. Why is state-level oversight necessary? There are two reasons. First, most local municipalities operate under the influence of strong parochial interests that prevent them from addressing regionwide housing needs with impartiality:

> The spatial fragmentation of land-use controls . . . means that no public body represents the interest of the metropolitan area as a whole. All governments with powers over land use have parochial interests and focus their policies on serving only the welfare of their own relatively narrow group of residents. In this governmental system . . . no entities exist that are motivated to formulate [metropolitanwide] policies, and none have the legal power to adopt them. . . .
>
> This inherent parochialism is a crucial attribute of the U.S. policy environment concerning land-use matters. Policies that require metropolitan area-wide perspectives or behavior remain largely theoretical in most such areas because no real-world organizations with much power will adopt them or can execute them. This is true even though many of society's most pressing problems could only be effectively ameliorated by actions designed and carried out from a metropolitan-area-wide perspective.[108]

Once the need for oversight is clarified, the choice of overseers quickly narrows either to HUD or to a state agency. The task is too large, however, for HUD or any other federal agency to do well. Indeed, one contributing reason for the failure of the Housing Assistance Plan program under the Housing and Community Development Act of 1974 was its dependence on HUD to review thousands of local plans, an administratively unrealistic burden.

State agencies would thus be charged with the responsibility (1) to identify housing regions throughout the state, (2) to calculate both the low-income housing need and the extent of residential segregation in each region,[109] (3) to assign to each municipality its fair share of the ascertained regional need, (4) to assist those municipalities that have not created municipal fair share plans, (5) to monitor municipal compliance with their fair share plans, (6) to supervise selection of tenants and potential homeowners,[110] and (7) to assure adequate re-rental and resale restrictions.[111]

To carry out these activities, each state should receive federal financial assistance for the additional staff and technical assistance necessary to assist willing municipalities.[112] States also should receive substantial funds to disperse to municipalities, local housing authorities, private nonprofit housing corporations, fair housing groups, housing trust funds, or others acting in furtherance of state and local fair share objectives.[113]

Many municipalities, perhaps a majority, would not have any new housing obligations under this legislation since they already contain a substantial number of low- and moderate-income housing units or are already racially diverse. Research suggests that municipalities and regions vary widely in their extent of residential segregation, with the Midwest and Northeast the most segregated, and the South and the West the least so.[114]

Each municipality found to have an unmet fair share responsibility, however, should be obligated to (1) choose a low-income goal or an integration goal, (2) develop concrete plans for meeting the goal, (3) submit these plans to the designated state agency for certification (subject to ultimate federal agency review), and (4) once certified, take necessary steps to implement the plan.

The act should be framed to avoid the deficiencies of the New Jersey fair share legislation. First, subject to the election options set forth below, the act should require states and municipalities to take explicit account of the racial composition of their fair share households. Second, the act should require municipal plans to address the needs of a broader income distribution among low-income applicants, with a substantially greater percentage of very-low-income applicants. States should also prescribe housing goals by bedroom sizes, so that municipalities will be able to accommodate the housing needs of large low-income families as well as smaller families and single persons. These goals are already reflected in the Affordable Housing Act of 1990, although they are not set forth as indispensable requirements there. The exact targets under the new act should reflect the proportionate income distributions, the family-size variations, and other pertinent characteristics of the low-income population of each metropolitan area. For example, in areas where the income distribution is skewed toward very-low-income citizens and large families, the proportion of very-low-income citizens and large families targeted as participants in the program should be greater than in metropolitan areas with different income characteristics. States should also be required expressly to disaggregate each category by race and ethnic origin and to assign overall housing goals in a manner that does not inadvertently disadvantage African Americans or other ethnic minorities with different income or family-size characteristics from other low-income participants in the program.

Third, the act should require municipalities to select a substantial fraction of recipients from beyond their municipal borders, drawn from lists to be established in conjunction with social service agencies and administered by the state agency. The New Jersey experience demonstrates the need to require affirmative outreach beyond the municipality's borders. However, the experience under HUD's Affirmative Fair Housing Marketing Program strongly suggests that merely requiring developers of low-income housing to market their units affirmatively to those "least likely to apply" is an insufficient approach.[115] Instead, drafters of this legislation should require either an expansion of the Gautreaux Program, including the development of metropolitan-wide housing counseling and placement services, or the development of low-income housing eligibility rules in coordination with state and local agencies that administer the Family Support Act.

Fourth, states and municipalities should be encouraged to provide many more subsidized rental apartments via the rehabilitation of existing units, Section 8 certificate placements, or public housing. This encouragement would come through the act's expansion of federal housing subsidies, in addition to the stimulation of private, for-sale units through density bonuses and other market-driven strategies.[116]

Finally, as we shall explore in the next section, it is critical for the act to have unmistakable, strong incentives to stimulate state and municipal cooperation.

Incentives for Compliance

The fair share framework outlined above creates myriad possibilities for delay and evasion by municipalities motivated to resist the act. To ensure its success, therefore, strong federal incentives must be created to induce municipal compliance. History teaches that positive financial incentives, although necessary, will not alone induce many suburban communities to participate in federal programs that might lead to racial or economic dispersal.[117]

Some policy analysts have suggested that noncomplying jurisdictions be threatened with loss of all federal community development funds.[118] Yet numerous municipalities, especially in upper-income areas, receive little direct federal funding; for those communities, at least, the threat would be hollow.[119] Moreover, extending the cutoff to other locally received federal funds might prove counterproductive. Many federal dollars that currently flow into municipalities are targeted for programs that disproportionately serve lower-income residents (for example, Title I educational grants). To deprive municipalities of these funds would impose a disproportionately heavy burden on the municipality's lower-income citizens. Indeed, municipalities that are deeply resistant to further economic and racial integration might well forgo these federal benefits and allow their indigenous low-income population to suffer rather than assume their fair share obligations.

There is, however, another possible approach. Most suburban officials plausibly explain their resistance to low-income and fair housing proposals as a reflection of "the will of their constituents."[120] Constituents, in turn, understandably (even if erroneously) explain their resistance as self-protective economics.[121] How can this link between residential integration and potential economic loss be broken? My suggestion is to adjust two current features of the income tax system: the homeowner mortgage interest deduction[122] and the local property tax deduction.[123] Together, these deductions provide indirect federal housing subsidies or "tax expenditures" to American property holders totaling some $81 billion each year.[124] In municipalities refusing to establish and meet fair share goals, the National Fair Share Act would progressively withdraw these two tax deductions from property owners. The withdrawal would occur in increments, over a period of years—perhaps 10 percent during the first year of noncompliance, 20 percent the second year, and so on until a complete withdrawal of the deductions would be in place after ten years.[125]

Let me emphasize at once: the act's objective would be neither to end federal support for this important social policy nor to deprive any taxpayer of these deductions.[126] No withdrawal should ever occur in the vast majority of American municipalities—for the good reason that most municipalities would comply with the terms of the act. Furthermore, the graduated phase-in of withdrawals would allow taxpayers in noncomplying municipalities ample time, before any significant financial penalties have been felt, to press reluctant public officials to cooperate with the fair share approach.

As an added incentive to prompt cooperation, tax receipts generated by any loss of deductions should not be returned to the general treasury, but instead should be segregated by the Internal Revenue Service for eventual use in the noncompliant municipality to support low-income or fair housing initiatives that would further the objectives of the act.[127] In other words, municipalities engaged in noncompliance should be forewarned that they ultimately could not succeed in avoiding racial or economic integration. If a municipality were to resist the act, the tax subsidies formerly enjoyed by the municipality's citizens under national tax policy would be recaptured and redirected to their own communities in furtherance of more paramount housing policy—to foster racial and economic integration.

Beyond its deterrent value, this tax approach would have a second, greater function: it would transform the market incentives that currently work against desegregation. Because buyers or renters of homes in fair share municipalities would continue to receive considerable federal tax advantages, equivalent housing in resisting municipalities would become less financially attractive to many purchasers in a metropolitan housing market. Property values in racially and economically segregated communities would begin to fall, even as overall federal tax burdens borne by municipal residents began to rise. As a result, market advantages would shift toward those communities choosing actively to pursue integration.

This approach has one additional attraction. In the coming decades, when federal budget deficits are likely to make new federal revenues difficult to find,[128] it would "create" new dollars for low-income and minority housing by redirecting the flow of federal subsidies that are currently received by property holders in communities determined to resist integration toward low-income and minority housing needs.

In addition to the powerful individual, tax-based incentives for compliance outlined above, the act also should contain municipal sanctions by denying federal dollars for community infrastructure, community development, or housing purposes that would otherwise be destined for noncompliant jurisdictions.[129] Municipalities in active noncompliance also should be declared ineligible to issue municipal bonds free of federal taxation.[130] Although, as we have noted earlier, these sanctions alone would not likely prompt compliance with the fair share proposal, they would surely provide useful additional motivation beyond the losses faced by resident taxpayers.

Finally, if an entire state were to refuse to cooperate with the fair share program, the act would require the forfeiture not only of the state's fair share funds but also of other federal funds for the development or improvement of municipal infrastructure[131] and for state infrastructure improvements, such as highways or bridges, that would otherwise assist segregated states in maintaining their racial or economic exclusivity.

Let me end this section by reemphasizing that the objective of these proposed sanctions would not be punitive. Instead, the sanctions would be designed to prompt meaningful compliance and to alter the views of market actors about the relative attractiveness of segregated and integrated communities. Yet they would convey federal determination that no federal funds should be expended in furtherance of residential living patterns that have proved to be destructive to the social, economic, and educational prospects of millions of citizens of the United States.

Local Fair Share Options

Since racial discrimination has both racial and economic dimensions,[132] and since both must be addressed simultaneously to make meaningful progress on either, municipalities should be given a choice of pursuing racial or low-income housing objectives under a Fair Share Act. Some commentators have advocated attacking residential segregation merely by providing (or permitting) more suburban low-income housing units, often with the expectation that African Americans, because of their disproportionate poverty, would be the chief beneficiaries of such programs.[133] In effect, both *Mount Laurel* and New Jersey's fair housing legislation have followed such an approach. Because of the nation's widespread, unmet need for affordable housing, however, municipalities operating under such plans can and, as New Jersey's experience confirms, often do meet their low-income housing goals without any benefit to minority citizens.

On the other hand, analysts who propose to confront residential segregation directly by establishing race-specific goals[134] face several difficult questions. William Julius Wilson and other researchers have argued that race-conscious remedies that ignore economic differences rarely reach lower-income blacks with the greatest need and, indeed, almost invariably benefit those African Americans who already possess the highest incomes, the most assets, and the greatest mobility.[135]

The adoption of race-conscious residential goals also raises serious constitutional and statutory questions. Scholars and courts have long wrestled with whether public housing authorities and residential communities may constitutionally engage in "integration maintenance"—the self-conscious monitoring of, and interference with, housing markets to assure racial and ethnic stability in a community. Many commentators have emphasized a distinction, however, between minimum, or "floor," quotas for racial minorities, which guarantee some minority presence, and maximum, or "ceiling," quotas, which limit minority presence in the ostensible interests of maintaining integration.[136] The Supreme Court has not addressed these issues in a housing context, and the lower courts are divided on their constitutionality.[137] The Fair Share Act would avoid the problems of racial ceiling quotas by relying on carefully crafted floor goals in municipalities throughout each metropolitan region.

Finally, a policy limited exclusively to race-specific housing goals would ignore the substantial evidence that not all African Americans or other racial and ethnic minorities would choose to live in predominantly white communities, even if discrimination and housing affordability no longer presented barriers to their entry into white communities.[138]

The Fair Share Act should require state planning agencies to calculate both (1) low-income housing need and (2) the racial and ethnic composition of each region. It would then calculate each municipality's low-income obligation and its racial goal, dependent on various demographic factors, including the extent to which the racial and economic makeup of the municipality's residents varied from that of the metropolitan region as a whole. The act would then allow each municipality an option to meet the state-designated low-income goal, its racial goal, or perhaps a "mixed goal" comprised of both low-income units and racially integrated units. Such a provision would require a sliding scale, with a proportionally smaller low-income housing goal for municipalities that agree to seek a greater percentage of minority residents, and vice versa.

Different communities could choose to pursue one of these options after assessing factors such as their present demographics; their rate of new housing growth (and, therefore, the likelihood of achieving low-income housing goals through market-driven density bonuses or set-asides); and the funds available from federal, state, and local sources to build subsidized rental housing or assist nonprofit housing development. Older municipalities without undeveloped land for new development might be drawn toward racial integration goals, and such municipalities might establish and support local fair housing groups or engage in affirmative marketing or conduct real estate seminars for local realtors on how best to comply with fair housing laws.[139] These communities might reason that middle- to upper-income black professionals and managers ultimately would be more desirable neighbors and more reliable taxpayers than lower-income residents of any race.

By contrast, younger communities that are undergoing strong private residential development might decide to meet their fair share goals by relying on market forces and thus concentrate on low-income housing production. In either case, the act would draw on the resourcefulness and common sense that local municipalities always bring to those problems they want to solve, rather than those they want to avoid.

Lower-income housing goals typically would be more expensive to implement, since they would involve some form of subsidized housing. Racial integration goals could be met in many communities without municipal housing subsidies simply through affirmative market programs designed to induce black homebuyers or renters to choose housing there. The overall bias of the act would thus tend to favor racial integration goals. Indeed, if the program worked ideally, many municipalities within each region might well find themselves in an informal competition to offer more attractive housing options to minority homeseekers throughout the region.

Presumably, if the program worked as hoped, the need for integration maintenance would diminish substantially. At present, suburban municipalities that openly welcome minority residents risk resegregation, since minority homeseekers and renters, frustrated by discrimination in other municipalities, often turn to any racially "open" community.[140] Yet, when African American homeseekers are afforded a wide variety of neighborhood options, it is likely that their residential choices will become less skewed toward a handful of compliant communities and instead will be distributed more widely throughout each metropolitan region, based on individual employment choices, school choices, or other community characteristics.[141]

The act possibly could provide for a third option not fully explored in this essay. In some metropolitan regions, chiefly in the South and the West, metro-wide government is the rule. Schools, housing authorities, municipal hospitals, and other public services are shared throughout geographically extensive areas.[142] Under these governmental patterns, low-income residents and racial minorities are not invariably deprived of high-quality public goods and services because of balkanized local government patterns so prevalent in the Midwest and Northeast.[143] Since the proposed legislation will assure its beneficiaries access only to a municipality itself, not to any particular neighborhood, there is some merit to the argument that urban areas choosing to govern themselves regionally, and to distribute their public goods and services to all within the region, already have achieved most of what the act aims to accomplish.[144]

Yet it is possible to imagine metro-governments, unitary in formal terms, that remain subdivided into segregated units for the provision of educational, health care, and other services so effectively as to deny low-income and minority citizens equal access to public goods. If so, formal citizenship in the overall metro-government would not suffice to meet the integrative goals of this act.[145]

Moreover, both the proposed low-income goals and racial integration goals implicitly promise new or rehabilitated low-income housing resources, an outcome that would not necessarily follow from the metro-government option. In a nation still deeply in need of additional low-income housing resources,[146] this might prove a decisive factor in assessing whether to include a metro-government option in National Fair Share legislation.[147]

Conclusion

This essay's National Fair Share proposal would not directly provide jobs, health care, preschool education, increased welfare benefits, or other needed social services to those who need them most. Nor would it directly address the desperate need of our beleaguered cities and their residents for aid with their immediate problems. Yet pilot programs such as the Gautreaux experiment demonstrate that a successful fair share program would afford multiple, substantial benefits to most fair share participants. Moreover, by creating housing options for low-income and minority citizens in suburban areas, the act would diminish the demand for, and thereby lower the market price of, urban housing units. It should also widen the employment choices of urban residents, reduce pressures on overcrowded urban school systems, and spread the local costs of social services among municipalities throughout each metropolitan region.

Apart from these more concrete gains, a fair share program would gradually, over the course of a decade, begin to redirect America's current drift toward economically homogeneous, racially segregated, mutually antagonistic geographical areas. One of the most important achievements of American society has been its ability to provide meaningful social mobility for millions of lower-income citizens. This social fluidity, though failing millions who find themselves locked into almost insurmountable poverty, nonetheless has lifted millions more into middle-class status, forestalling the crystallization of deep, destabilizing interclass antagonisms like those that plague less mobile societies. The National Fair Share legislation should serve these basic American social goals.

Some have worried that "dispersal" strategies might undermine hard-won minority political control of many cities throughout the country.[148] Such concerns overestimate the likely dispersal effect of even the most successful fair share program, whose purpose would not be to depopulate cities or scatter their entire low-income and minority populations, but instead (1) to ensure that some fraction of the poor and middle-income minorities now trapped in central cities have the choice of suburban living, and (2) to guarantee that suburban communities do not become so economically homogeneous that their residents lose all political and economic motivation to support national policies that benefit poor and minority citizens.[149] The population of America's largest cities will remain disproportionately African American, Latino, and Asian even if some fraction of its current population relocates in suburban municipalities, and even if some repopulation of cities by whites were to accompany the end of the current segregation.

Since 1968 the nation has lost nearly an entire generation of poor and minority children, who have grown up deprived of adequate medical care, assigned to hopelessly inadequate schools, consigned to inferior housing, and cut off from mainstream labor markets.[150] It is no idle charge that segregative forces presently are contributing to the perpetuation of a social and economic underclass.[151] While at this writing there is no sign of any political will to reverse these devastating trends, our national experience provides remarkable examples of transformative political moments—when genuine, far-reaching reforms, previously considered unthinkable, have been implemented with broad popular support.[152] The fair share legislation proposed in this essay is designed for such a period of national reconstruction, with the hope that it might one day help to combat the forces that work to maintain a nationwide system of residential segregation.

Notes

1. The central features of the Fair Share legislation have several predecessors. In a magisterial article, James A. Kushner, "Apartheid in America: An Historical and Legal Analysis of Contemporary Racial Residential Segregation in the United States," *Howard Law Journal* 22 (1979): 547, Professor Kushner suggested a variant of this proposal, though without exploring its potential for redirecting market incentives (ibid., 671–75). Professor Derrick Bell recently has mused about a "Racial Preference Licensing Act," under which governments would redirect market forces by licensing racially discriminatory conduct in exchange for payment of a fee that would be used to underwrite black economic development (Bell, *Faces at the Bottom of the Well: The Permanence of Racism* [New York: Basic Books, 1992]). See also Michelle J. White, "Suburban Growth Controls: Liability Rules and Pigovian

Taxes," *Journal of Legal Studies* 8 (1979): 207, 225–30 (suggesting that suburban exclusionary zoning regulations should be taxed to offset their external social and economic costs).

2. *Report of the National Advisory Commission on Civil Disorders* (New York: Bantam Books, 1968), 1–2, 10.

3. Ibid., 23–29.

4. See generally John Charles Boger, "Race and the American City: The Kerner Commission Report in Retrospect" (in this volume) (suggesting that despite significant achievements, urban blacks still lag far behind suburban whites in employment rates, average income, access to quality education, health care, housing, and other social services).

5. See Reynolds Farley and Walter R. Allen, *The Color Line and the Quality of Life in America* (New York: Russell Sage, 1987), 289–90. Farley and Allen note that middle-income blacks in the mid-1980s were far less secure in their overall economic circumstances than were equivalent middle-income whites, in part because of significantly lower levels of total wealth: "Racial differences in wealth are very much greater than racial differences in current income. . . . Black households in late 1984 had monthly incomes which were 62 percent of those of white households, but their median assets were only 9 percent of those of whites."

6. Robert W. Lake, *The New Suburbanites: Race and Housing in the Suburbs* (New Brunswick, N.J.: Rutgers Center for Urban Policy Research, 1981), 239 (asserting that "the suburbanization of blacks is being accompanied by the increasing territorial differentiation of suburbia along racial lines—and not by integration"); see also Phillip L. Clay, "The Process of Black Suburbanization," *Urban Affairs Quarterly* 14 (1979): 405, 416–19 (describing the persistence in suburban communities, at all but the highest income levels, of a "racially segmented housing market"); Gary Orfield and Carole Ashkinaze, *The Closing Door: Conservative Policy and Black Opportunity* (Chicago: University of Chicago Press, 1991), 69–102 (reporting that Atlanta's housing market is racially segregated at all income levels).

7. See, for example, Margery Austin Turner, "Discrimination in Urban Housing Markets: Lessons from Fair Housing Audits," *Housing Policy Debate* 3 (1992): 185, 210.

8. Douglas S. Massey and Nancy A. Denton, *American Apartheid: Segregation and the Making of the Underclass* (Cambridge, Mass.: Harvard University Press, 1993), 136 (noting that racially and economically segregated neighborhoods are often so fragile that normal economic downturns "rapidly cause the failure of most nonessential businesses and eliminate many services that depend on the ability of clients to pay").

9. In their careful study of residential mobility in Philadelphia, Douglas Massey and his colleagues report that middle-class blacks "have a difficult time achieving a spatial outcome commensurate with their [socioeconomic status]" (Douglas Massey, Gretchen A. Condran, and Nancy A. Denton, "The Effect of Residential Segregation on Black Social and Economic Well-Being," *Social Forces* 66 [1987]: 29, 42). "Patterns of residential segregation have separated blacks and whites [in Philadelphia] into two vastly different environments: one that is poor, crime-

ridden, unhealthy, unsafe, and educationally inferior, and another that is markedly richer, safer, healthier, and educationally superior" (ibid.).

10. Of course, any justification of residential segregation based on present differences in the economic status of blacks and whites must respond to evidence that residential location itself is a crucial factor in determining a resident's economic success. See, for example, George C. Galster and Mark Keeney, "Race, Residence, Discrimination, and Economic Opportunity: Modeling the Nexus of Urban Racial Phenomena," *Urban Affairs Quarterly* 24 (1988): 87; John F. Kain, "The Spatial Mismatch Hypothesis: Three Decades Later," *Housing Policy Debate* 3 (1992): 371.

11. Richard H. Sander, "Comment: Individual Rights and Demographic Realities: The Problem of Fair Housing," *Northwestern University Law Review* 82 (1988): 874, 885–88.

12. John O. Calmore, "To Make Wrong Right: The Necessary and Proper Aspirations of Fair Housing," in *The State of Black America, 1989*, ed. Janet Dewart (Washington: National Urban League, 1989), 77, 90–95 (pointing out that levels of black residential segregation remain high irrespective of education or income); George C. Galster, "Residential Segregation in American Cities: A Contrary Review," *Population Research and Policy Review* 7 (1988): 93, 95 (noting "a clear-cut consensus" in the research that "interracial differences in *income* [i.e., the affordability of housing] *alone* explain relatively little of the observed segregation").

13. See, for example, Nancy A. Denton and Douglas S. Massey, "Residential Segregation of Blacks, Hispanics, and Asians by Socioeconomic Status and Generation," *Social Science Quarterly* 69 (1988): 797, 807 (noting that Hispanics and Asians, unlike African Americans, have experienced decreases in residential segregation as their socioeconomic status has risen; indeed, residential segregation from whites remains higher among college-educated blacks than among Hispanics with zero to four years of education); John E. Farley, "Segregation in 1980: How Segregated Are America's Metropolitan Areas?," in *Divided Neighborhoods: Changing Patterns of Racial Segregation*, ed. Gary A. Tobin (Newbury Park, Calif.: Sage, 1987) 95, 104–7 (observing that Hispanics in general are significantly less segregated than blacks and that Hispanic segregation levels have declined more over time).

14. See, for example, Reynolds Farley, Charlotte Steeh, Tara Jackson, Maria Krysan, and Keith Reeves, "Continued Racial Residential Segregation in Detroit: 'Chocolate City, Vanilla Suburbs' Revisited," *Journal of Housing Research* 4 (1993): 1, 32–33 (finding that "even in a metropolis as riven by race as Detroit," most whites in 1992 "would be comfortable living in an area that had the racial composition of the [broader] metropolis and would even consider buying a home in such a neighborhood"); Mittie Olion Chandler, "Obstacles to Housing Integration Program Efforts," in *The Metropolis in Black and White: Place, Power, and Polarization*, ed. George C. Galster and Edward W. Hill (New Brunswick, N.J.: Rutgers Center for Urban Policy Research, 1992), 286, 287 (reporting that 65 percent of black respondents in a 1985 Cleveland survey indicated that neighborhoods with an even distribution of blacks and whites were ideal); Joe T. Darden, "Choosing Neighbors and Neighborhoods: The Role of Race in Housing Preference," in Tobin, *Divided Neighborhoods*, 15, 26 (finding "a black preference for mixed or half-black half-white neighborhoods and the rejection of all black and all white ones"); Reynolds

Farley, Howard Schuman, Suzanne Bianchi, Diane Colasanto, and Shirley Hatchett, "'Chocolate City, Vanilla Suburbs': Will the Trend toward Racially Separate Communities Continue?," *Social Science Research* 7 (1978): 319, 328–31 (reporting on a Detroit study that found a majority of blacks favor integrated neighborhoods).

15. See, for example, George C. Galster, "Racial Discrimination in Housing Markets during the 1980s: A Review of the Audit Evidence," *Journal of Planning Education and Research* 9 (1990): 165 (reviewing over seventy housing discrimination studies, most of which find racial discrimination); Turner, "Discrimination in Urban Housing Markets," 201–10 (describing widespread discrimination against blacks and Hispanics by real estate sales and rental agents); Ronald E. Wienk, "Discrimination in Urban Credit Markets: What We Don't Know and Why We Don't Know It," *Housing Policy Debate* 3 (1992): 217 (acknowledging the existence, though not the extent, of mortgage and other credit discrimination); James H. Carr and Isaac F. Megbolugbe, "The Federal Reserve Bank of Boston Study on Mortgage Lending Revisited," *Journal of Housing Research* 4 (1993): 277, 311 (concluding, after a thorough reanalysis of 1992 Federal Bank data that found disparate treatment of mortgage applications on racial grounds, that "a close examination . . . reveals an even stronger statistical case for discrimination than was originally reported").

16. See Margery Austin Turner, Raymond J. Struyk, and John Yinger, *Housing Discrimination Study: Synthesis* (Washington, D.C.: Urban Institute and Syracuse University, 1991); Ronald E. Wienk, Clifford E. Reid, John C. Simonson, and Frederick J. Eggers, *Measuring Racial Discrimination in American Housing Markets: The Housing Market Practices Survey* (Washington, D.C.: U.S. Department of Housing and Urban Development, 1979).

17. Turner et al., *Housing Discrimination Study*, vii.

18. Farley et al., "'Chocolate City, Vanilla Suburbs,'" 336.

19. Anthony Downs, *Opening Up the Suburbs: An Urban Strategy for America* (New Haven: Yale University Press, 1973), 68–70 (cataloging eight principal white objections to residential integration, the first three of which are a likely rise in property taxes, a likely increase in federal taxes, and a fear of falling property values).

20. John Stahura, "Rapid Black Suburbanization of the 1970s: Some Policy Considerations," *Policy Studies Journal* 18 (1989–90): 279, 288 (noting 1980 census data that suggest that black municipal population growth does not lead to tax increases and, in fact, has a positive effect on housing values).

21. See George C. Galster, "The Case for Racial Integration," in Galster and Hill, *Metropolis in Black and White*, 270, 278–79. Thomas Schelling's much-debated "tipping" model suggests that even if both whites and blacks are willing to live in racially integrated communities, eventual resegregation is inevitable so long as there are any systematic differences in the percentage of integration that whites and blacks will accept (Schelling, "Dynamic Models of Segregation," *Journal of the Mathematic Society* 1 [1971]: 143, 181–86). Although the assumptions of Schelling's model have been strongly challenged (see Galster, "Residential Segregation," 100–102), the real-world difficulties experienced by communities that are committed to maintaining a multiracial population suggest that some variant of Schelling's phenomenon is at work in many communities that undergo racial tran-

sition. See, for example, Alexander Polikoff, "Sustainable Integration or Inevitable Resegregation," in *Housing Desegregation and Federal Policy*, ed. John M. Goering (Chapel Hill: University of North Carolina Press, 1986), 43–56 (describing problems with racial stabilization programs); Chandler, "Obstacles to Housing Integration," 291–302.

22. See Sander, "Comment: Individual Rights," 902–3.

23. Anthony Downs's 1973 classic, *Opening Up the Suburbs*, remains the most powerful argument for residential desegregation. Recently, as the twentieth anniversary of his work approached, Downs observed, "I am skeptical that truly equal racial housing outcomes can be achieved as long as residential areas remain segregated by race. Nevertheless, the obvious, persistent, and widespread white antipathy to racial residential integration makes it unlikely that this condition will be attained on any really large scale in my lifetime" (Downs, "Policy Directions Concerning Racial Discrimination in U.S. Housing Markets," *Housing Policy Debate* 3 [1992]: 685, 688 n. 1). See also John Goering, "Concluding Remarks," in Goering, *Housing Desegregation*, 327, 333; Gary A. Tobin, "Introduction: Housing Segregation in the 1980s," in Tobin, *Divided Neighborhoods*, 8, 14 (voicing a similar expectation); John Yinger, "On the Possibility of Achieving Racial Integration through Subsidized Housing," in Goering, *Housing Desegregation*, 290, 306–7.

24. Downs, "Policy Directions," 725.

25. Ibid., 739–42. Downs is joined in this emphasis by George Galster, who has urged a redirection of fair housing toward "collective modes of enforcement," including more aggressive and well-funded "testing" to be conducted by public agencies and fair housing organizations (Galster, *Federal Fair Housing Policy in the 1980s: The Great Misapprehension*, Working Paper no. HP-5 [Cambridge, Mass.: MIT Center for Real Estate Development, 1988], 17–23).

26. An effective legal response cannot rely directly on constitutional remedies. The Supreme Court has repeatedly held that private choices that are not the product of government action, even if they lead to segregated residential communities, do not directly violate the Equal Protection Clause of the Fourteenth Amendment: "Where resegregation [of public schools] is a product not of state action but of private [residential] choices, it does not have constitutional implications. It is beyond the authority and beyond the practical ability of the federal courts to try to counteract these kinds of continuous and massive demographic shifts. . . . Residential housing choices . . . present an ever-changing pattern, one difficult to address through judicial remedies" (*Freeman v. Pitts*, 112 S. Ct. 1430, 1448 [1992]).

Congress, however, has broad authority under § 2 of the Thirteenth Amendment and § 5 of the Fourteenth Amendment to legislate against racial ills (*Katzenbach v. Morgan*, 384 U.S. 641 [1966]).

27. Pub. L. No. 90-284, 82 Stat. 73 (codified as amended at 42 U.S.C. §§ 3601–31 [1988 and Supp. II 1990]).

28. Jean Eberhart Dubofsky, "Fair Housing: A Legislative History and a Perspective," *Washburn Law Journal* 8 (1969): 149, 160.

29. 42 U.S.C. § 3604(a) and (b) (1988). The act also prohibits discrimination in the advertisement, financing, or commercial brokerage of housing units (§§ 3604[c], 3605–6).

30. 42 U.S.C. § 3608(d).

31. See, for example, Galster, *Federal Fair Housing Policy*, 14–17; James A. Kushner, "An Unfinished Agenda: The Federal Fair Housing Enforcement Effort," *Yale Law and Policy Review* 6 (1988): 348, 351–55; see also U.S. House of Representatives Report No. 711, 100th Cong., 2d sess., 1988, 13–17 ("Twenty years after the passage of the Fair Housing Act, discrimination and segregation in housing continue to be pervasive").

32. Fair Housing Amendments Act of 1988, Pub. L. No. 100-430, 102 Stat. 1619 (codified at 42 U.S.C. §§ 3602–8, 3615–19, 3631 [1988] and 28 U.S.C. §§ 2341–42 [1988]). See James A. Kushner, "Federal Enforcement and Judicial Review of the Fair Housing Amendments Act of 1988," *Housing Policy Debate* 3 (1992): 537, 548–59.

33. Prior to 1988 the Fair Housing Act limited successful parties to the recovery of their actual damages and a maximum of $1,000 in punitive damages (Pub. L. No. 90-284, § 812[c], 82 Stat. 73, 88 [amended by Fair Housing Amendments Act of 1988, Pub. L. No. 100-430, 102 Stat. 1619 (codified at 42 U.S.C. §§ 3602–8, 3615–19, 3631 [1988] and 28 U.S.C. § 2341–42 [1988])]). Since the principal damages in such cases are often dignitary injuries, not out-of-pocket losses, this provision served as a severe financial disincentive to parties trying to decide whether to undergo the expense and uncertainties of litigation. Moreover, even though Title VIII cases often are difficult to litigate and large recoveries are rare, the statute formerly provided that attorneys' fees would be awarded only to prevailing parties who could demonstrate that they were "not financially able to assume said attorney's fees." The pre-litigation conciliation provisions of the 1968 act, §§ 810(d), 812(a), 88 Stat. 86, 88, were often ineffective as well (Kushner, "Federal Enforcement and Judicial Review," 538 n. 7).

34. Apart from conciliation responsibilities under §§ 808–10, the 1968 act gave HUD independent enforcement powers only if HUD found "reasonable cause to believe that any person . . . is engaged in a pattern or practice of resistance," and only if "such denial raise[d] an issue of general public importance" (Pub. L. No. 90-284, § 813[a], 82 Stat. 73, 78).

35. James A. Kushner, "The Fair Housing Amendments Act of 1988: The Second Generation of Fair Housing," *Vanderbilt Law Review* 42 (1989), 1049, 1087–92. The 1988 amendments have lifted the cap on punitive damages (42 U.S.C. § 3613[c][1] [1988]) and made attorneys' fees more readily available (§ 3613[c][2]). The amendment now contemplates the option of court-appointed attorneys for plaintiffs in their litigation against offenders under the act (§ 3613[b][1]).

36. Professor Kushner reports that, by broadening the scope of the Fair Housing Act in 1988 to forbid discrimination based on sex or familial status, Congress has provoked a flood of non-race-based housing claims that now swamp the HUD resources previously available for the investigation of claims of racial discrimination (Kushner, "Federal Enforcement and Judicial Review," 565–66).

37. Robert G. Schwemm, "Private Enforcement and the Fair Housing Act," *Yale Law and Policy Review* 6 (1988): 375, 379–80. Discrimination can occur at any of multiple stages in the process that leads to a real estate purchase or lease. See

Turner, "Discrimination in Urban Housing Markets," 189–91 (detailing the steps at which housing discrimination may occur). It is especially difficult to detect methods of housing discrimination that involve the withholding of information about the full range of housing options (Darden, "Choosing Neighbors," 8).

38. Galster, *Federal Fair Housing Policy*, 17–18.

39. See, for example, Kushner, "Federal Enforcement and Judicial Review," 585–86; John Yinger, "The Racial Dimension of Urban Housing Markets in the 1980s," in Tobin, *Divided Neighborhoods*, 43, 63–64. For an interesting account of the possibilities, and the inevitable limitations, of a vigorous federal enforcement campaign, see Joel L. Selig, "The Justice Department and Racially Exclusionary Municipal Practices: Creative Ventures in Fair Housing Act Enforcement," *University of California at Davis Law Review* 17 (1984): 445, 475–504 (describing a special two-year initiative to enforce the Fair Housing Act undertaken by the U.S. Department of Justice during the latter years of the Carter administration).

40. Roderic V. O. Boggs, Joseph M. Sellers, and Marc Bendick Jr., "Use of Testing in Civil Rights Enforcement," in *Clear and Convincing Evidence: Measurement of Discrimination in America*, ed. Michael Fix and Raymond J. Struyk (Washington, D.C.: Urban Institute Press, 1993), 317, 340 (urging the establishment and funding of a national center to provide training and coordination on audit methods); Downs, "Policy Directions," 739–40.

41. George Galster, pointing to some successes reported in Cleveland Heights, Ohio, and in Kentucky, has argued from the limited evidence presently available that aggressive use of audit methods "can create a potent deterrent" (Galster, *Federal Fair Housing Policy*, 18).

Yet a housing discrimination strategy founded on interdiction and deterrence—largely directed against the "suppliers" of the illegal product—may have little greater success than the similar approach adopted in the nation's campaign against the sale of illegal drugs. In that arena, neither a sharp increase in criminal penalties levied against convicted suppliers of drugs nor an increased financial commitment for federal and state drug law enforcement has proved successful. Many authorities now concede that, unless consumer demand for the illegal product is reduced, the success of an interdiction effort is unlikely (John J. DiIulio Jr., "Crime," in *Setting Domestic Priorities: What Can Government Do?*, ed. Henry J. Aaron and Charles L. Schultze [Washington, D.C.: Brookings Institution, 1992], 101, 125–27) (noting that major, costly law enforcement efforts to identify and incarcerate drug dealers in New York and Florida have done almost nothing to diminish drug traffic).

42. William L. Taylor makes this argument effectively in his "*Brown*, Equal Protection, and the Isolation of the Poor," *Yale Law Journal* 95 (1986): 1700, 1717–25.

43. See Derrick Bell, *Race, Racism, and American Law*, 3d ed. (Boston: Little, Brown, 1992), 190–212, §§ 4.4–4.7 (chronicling the campaign for enfranchisement).

44. The Supreme Court emphasized the ineffectiveness of more moderate legislative remedies in *South Carolina v. Katzenbach*, 383 U.S. 301 (1966), which upheld the more radical legislative solution embodied in the Voting Rights Act of 1965:

In recent years, Congress has repeatedly tried to cope with the problem [of voting discrimination] by facilitating case-by-case litigation. . . . Despite the earnest efforts of the Justice Department and of many federal judges, these new laws have done little to cure the problem. . . . The previous legislation has proved ineffective for a number of reasons. Voting suits are unusually onerous to prepare, sometimes requiring as many as 6,000 man-hours spent . . . in preparation for trial. . . . Even when favorable decisions have finally been obtained, some of the States affected have merely switched to discriminatory devices not covered by the federal decrees or have enacted difficult new tests designed to prolong the existing disparity between white and Negro registration. (Ibid., 313–14)

See, for example, *United States v. Mississippi*, 380 U.S. 128, 143–44 (1965) (reviewing the seventy-five-year legal campaign by Mississippi officials to deny African Americans the franchise).

45. Pub. L. No. 89-110, 79 Stat. 437–45 (codified as amended at 42 U.S.C. §§ 1971, 1973–1973b[b] [1988]).

46. See Cynthia Wright, "Comment: The Effects of Sections 2 and 5 of the Voting Rights Act on Minority Voting Practices," *Howard Law Journal* 28 (1985): 589, 592 (noting that over 1 million blacks registered to vote between 1965 and 1972) and 600 (reporting that black voter registration doubled between 1960 and 1980 in eleven southern states, with almost 2 million blacks added to registration rolls by 1975).

47. 42 U.S.C. § 1973b(c) (1988).

48. The act was designed to apply to every district that used a "voting test or device" where fewer than 50 percent of eligible voters had registered to vote in that district as of November 1, 1964, or where fewer than 50 percent of those registered had actually voted in the 1964 presidential election. Together these criteria targeted the southern states and a few random jurisdictions in other parts of the country. See U.S. House of Representatives Report No. 439, 89th Cong., 1st sess., 1965, 13–16.

49. 42 U.S.C. § 1973(d), (e) (1988). The act did grant a narrow "escape clause" to a state or jurisdiction able to demonstrate that incidents of racial discrimination in the application of its tests or device were "few in number and have been promptly and effectively corrected," if it could also be proven that "the continuing effect of such incidents has been eliminated" with "no reasonable probability of their recurrence in the future" (§ 1973a[a]).

50. 42 U.S.C. § 1973a(b).

51. 42 U.S.C. § 1973c.

52. *Brown v. Board of Education (Brown II)*, 349 U.S. 294 (1955); *Brown v. Board of Education (Brown I)*, 347 U.S. 483 (1954).

53. *Brown II*, 349 U.S., 301.

54. By 1964, a decade after *Brown*, only 2 percent of all black children in the South were attending desegregated public schools (Gerald David Jaynes and Robin M. Williams Jr. eds., *A Common Destiny: Blacks and American Society* [Washington, D.C.: National Academy Press, 1989], 75); see *United States v. Jefferson County*

Board of Education, 372 F.2d 836, 853–56, 860–61 (5th Cir. 1966) (summarizing judicial efforts), modified per curium en banc, 380 F.2d 385, cert. denied, 389 U.S. 840 (1967).

55. Pub. L. No. 88-352, § 401, 601–2 78 Stat. 246, 252–53 (1964) (codified as amended at 42 U.S.C. § 2000c and 200d-1 [1988]).

56. Congress declared in Title VI of the Civil Rights Act of 1964 that "no person . . . may be excluded from participation in, be denied the benefits of, or be subjected to discrimination under any program or activity receiving Federal financial assistance" (42 U.S.C. § 2000d [1988]). Congress empowered the Department of Education, among other federal departments, to issue rules and regulations to enforce the prohibitions of § 2000d (§ 2000d-1).

57. 34 C.F.R. § 100.1–100.13 (1992). The HEW regulations included detailed guidelines spelling out the administrative steps necessary to bring a school district into compliance with Title VI (§ 100.4[a–c]). See *Green v. County School Board*, 391 U.S. 430, 433–34 n. 2 (1968) (describing the promulgation of HEW guidelines).

58. Pub. L. No. 89-10, 70 Stat. 27 (codified as amended at 20 U.S.C. § 236–46 [1988]).

59. The Senate report that accompanied the act indicated an intention to provide $1.06 billion to local school districts for educational assistance to disadvantaged children (U.S. Senate Report No. 146, 89th Cong., 1st sess., 1965, 5–6).

60. See Gary Orfield, *Public School Desegregation in the United States, 1968–1980* (Washington, D.C.: Joint Center for Political Studies, 1983), 5 (reporting that the percentage of southern black children in all-black schools dropped from 98 in 1963 to 25 in 1968 as a result of enforcement of the Civil Rights Act of 1964 by HEW and federal courts) and 4, tab. 2 (reporting that the percentage of black children in "predominantly minority" schools in the South declined from 80.9 in 1968 to 57.1 in 1980).

61. 42 U.S.C. § 2000e-5 (1988).

62. 42 U.S.C. §§ 2000e-4–12.

63. See 29 C.F.R. § 1607.3, 35 Fed. Reg. 12333 (Aug. 1, 1970) ("The use of any selection procedure which has an adverse impact on the hiring, promotion, or other employment or membership opportunities of members of any race . . . will be considered to be discriminatory . . . unless the procedure has been validated in accordance with these guidelines").

64. See, for example, *Griggs v. Duke Power Co.*, 401 U.S. 424, 431 (1971).

65. See *McDonnell Douglas Corporation v. Green*, 411 U.S. 792, 801–6 (1973) (prescribing burdens of production and proof in "disparate treatment" cases).

66. In *Griggs*, a "disparate impact" case, the Supreme Court interpreted Title VII to invalidate the Duke Power Company's use of intelligence tests or the requirement of a high school diploma as employment criteria. Both policies had a sharply adverse impact on potential black employees and were held improper, absent proof by the employer that "the high school completion requirement . . . [or] the general intelligence test . . . bears a demonstrable relationship to successful performance of the jobs for which it was used" (*Griggs*, 401 U.S. at 431). The Court reasoned,

"[Title VII] proscribes not only overt discrimination but also practices that are fair in form, but discriminatory in operation. The touchstone is business necessity. If an employment practice which operates to exclude Negroes cannot be shown to be related to job performance, the practice is prohibited."

67. See *EEOC's Guidelines on Affirmative Action*, 44 Fed. Reg. 4422 (1979) (codified at 29 C.F.R. §§ 1608.1–12 [1992]).

68. In *Local 28, Sheet Metal Workers' International Association v. EEOC*, 478 U.S. 421 (1986), the Court held that a district court, as a remedy for violations of Title VII, may order an employer to engage in preferential hiring or promotion of African Americans who were not themselves the identifiable victims of the employers' previous acts of discrimination (478 U.S. at 482–83).

69. Affirmative action plans have generated intense scholarly and judicial controversy because they place in conflict two important goals: the remediation of prior acts of discrimination that have denied equal employment opportunities to African Americans, and the constitutional desire to treat all persons without regard to their race. A deeply divided majority of the Court suggested in *Wygant v. Jackson Board of Education*, 476 U.S. 267 (1986), that an employer could not justify the layoff of more senior, nonminority teachers while retaining less senior, minority teachers, solely to overcome prior *societal* discrimination against minorities absent a court determination that the defendant employer had engaged in specific acts of discrimination against identifiable victims (ibid., 274–76).

The Supreme Court nonetheless has recognized broad power in Congress under § 5 of the Fourteenth Amendment to enact race-conscious federal legislation to overcome the effects of past societal discrimination against African Americans. See, for example, *Fullilove v. Klutznick*, 448 U.S. 448, 483–87 (1980); compare *City of Richmond v. J. A. Croson Co.*, 488 U.S. 469, 486–91 (1989) (invalidating a municipal minority business set-aside program because it was not justified by evidence identifying past discrimination in the city's construction industry that would warrant "race-based relief").

70. Taylor, "*Brown*, Equal Protection," 1712–13 (noting several studies that have documented the positive effects of Title VII on minority employment opportunities).

71. *South Burlington County NAACP v. Township of Mount Laurel (Mount Laurel I)*, 67 N.J. 151, 336 A.2d 713 (1975), cert. denied and appeal dismissed, 423 U.S. 808 (1975); *South Burlington County NAACP v. Township of Mount Laurel (Mount Laurel II)*, 92 N.J. 158, 456 A.2d 390 (1983). Some commentators have described *Hills Development Co. v. Township of Bernards*, 103 N.J. 1, 21, 510 A.2d 621, 634 (1986), in which the New Jersey Supreme Court upheld the constitutionality of the New Jersey Fair Housing Act of 1985, as *Mount Laurel III*. See, for example, Harold McDougall, "From Litigation to Legislation in Exclusionary Zoning Law," *Harvard Civil Rights–Civil Liberties Law Review* 22 (1987): 623. As John M. Payne explained in another context, "'Mount Laurel' is both an idea and a case. The *idea* is . . . that land development is a quasi-public utility and should be regulated in the public interest" (Payne, "Rethinking Fair Share: The Judicial Enforcement of Affordable Housing Policies," *Real Estate Law Journal* 16 [1987]: 20, 44).

72. N. J. Stat. Ann. §§ 52:27D-301–29 (West 1986 and Supp. 1992).

73. See John M. Payne, "Title VIII and Mount Laurel: Is Affordable Housing Fair Housing?," *Yale Law and Policy Review* 6 (1988): 361–62.

74. "We accept the representation of the municipality's counsel at oral argument that the regulatory scheme was not adopted with any desire or intent to exclude prospective residents on the obviously illegal basis of race, origin or believed social incompatibility" (*Mount Laurel I*, 67 N.J. at 159, 336 A.2d at 717).

75. Act of April 3, 1928, ch. 274, 1928 N.J. Laws 696 (zoning enabling statute) (repealed by Act of January 14, 1976, ch. 291, 1976 N.J. Laws 1107).

76. The New Jersey Supreme Court reasoned,

It is plain beyond dispute that proper provision for adequate housing of all categories of people is certainly an absolute essential in promotion of the general welfare required in all local land use regulation. Further, the universal and constant need for such housing is so important and of such broad public interest that the general welfare which developing municipalities like Mount Laurel must consider extends beyond their boundaries and cannot be parochially confined to the claimed good of the particular municipality. It has to follow that, broadly speaking, the presumptive obligation arises for each such municipality affirmatively to plan and provide, by its land use regulations, the reasonable opportunity for an appropriate variety and choice of housing, including, of course, low and moderate cost housing, to meet the needs, desires and resources of all categories of people who may desire to live within its boundaries. (*Mount Laurel I*, 67 N.J. at 179, 336 A.2d at 727–28).

77. See, for example, Jerome G. Rose, "Is There a Fair Share Housing Allocation Plan That Is Acceptable to Suburban Municipalities?," in *After Mount Laurel: The New Suburban Zoning*, ed. Jerome G. Rose and Robert E. Rothman (New Brunswick, N.J.: Rutgers Center for Urban Policy Research, 1977), n. 32, 114, 116 (observing that "it should be clear that the purpose of a fair share housing allocation plan is to provide an opportunity for low- and moderate-income families to escape from the older central cities to the newer developing suburbs"); James A. Kushner, "Land Use Litigation and Low Income Housing: Mandating Regional Fair Share Plans," *Clearinghouse Review* 9 (1975): 10, 12 (noting that "*Mount Laurel* adds new life to the hope that land use litigation may successfully break down metropolitan racial and economic segregation").

78. See, for example, Harold A. McDougall, "*Mount Laurel II* and the Revitalizing City," *Rutgers Law Journal* 15 (1984): 667 (describing the "blistering academic criticism, municipal intransigence and legislative inaction" that followed *Mount Laurel I*); see also Payne, "Rethinking Fair Share," 22 ("It is difficult to convey adequately the intensity of the public reaction to the *Mount Laurel* process since 1983. Where *Mount Laurel I* could be ignored because it was ineffective, *Mount Laurel II* worked and it stirred up a firestorm."). In addition to criticism directed against the wisdom of its policies, the New Jersey Supreme Court also was condemned strongly for intruding into what many contended was the legislative sphere. See, for example, Lawrence Berger, "Inclusionary Zoning Devices as Takings: The Legacy of the Mount Laurel Cases," *Nebraska Law Review* 70 (1991):

186–200; Jerome G. Rose, "Waning Judicial Legitimacy: The Price of Judicial Promulgation of Urban Policy," *Urban Lawyer* 20 (1988): 801, 818–39.

79. See, for example, Jerome G. Rose, "Is the Decision Based on Wishful Thinking?," in Rose and Rothman, *After Mount Laurel*, 184–85 (noting that there are at least four basic alternative ways to measure fair share); Norman Williams Jr., "On from *Mount Laurel*: Guidelines on the 'Regional General Welfare,'" in ibid., 79, 85–96 (discussing unresolved issues raised by *Mount Laurel I*).

As the New Jersey Supreme Court itself acknowledged in *Mount Laurel II*, "Although the Court [in *Mount Laurel I*] set forth important guidelines for implementing the doctrine, their application to particular cases was complex, and the resolution of many questions left uncertain. What was a 'developing' municipality? What was the 'region,' and how was it to be determined? How was the 'fair share' to be calculated within that region? Precisely what must that municipality do to 'affirmatively afford' an opportunity for the construction of lower income housing? Other questions were similarly troublesome" (*Mount Laurel II*, 92 N.J. 158, 205, 456 A.2d 390, 413 [1983]).

80. As Professor McDougall observed, "The *Mount Laurel I* decision was a pathbreaking departure from previous approaches. Nonetheless, it could only tentatively sketch practical remedies for the rights it established. Consequently, the suburbs did not change their behavior and built little low and moderate income housing after the decision. Moreover, the uncertainty of standards for municipal compliance emboldened the suburbs to tie matters up in court with extensive argument over details" (Harold A. McDougall, "Regional Contribution Agreements: Compensation for Exclusionary Zoning," *Temple Law Quarterly* 60 [1987]: 676); see also Daniel E. Chall, "Housing Reform in New Jersey: The Mount Laurel Decision," *Federal Reserve Bank of New York Quarterly Review* 10 (1985–86): 19 n. 2 (noting that as of June 1985 over 135 *Mount Laurel* cases were in various stages of litigation).

81. The New Jersey Supreme Court made it clear in *Mount Laurel II* that municipalities were obligated to do more than remove exclusionary zoning statutes that denied low- and moderate-income housing opportunities; municipalities had affirmative obligations to bring about meaningful access to their communities (*Mount Laurel II*, 92 N.J. at 214–17, 258–78, 456 A.2d at 418–19, 442–52). The court also held that the obligation applied not only to "developing communities" that were undergoing rapid expansion, but to all communities, even older, more stable, "developed" communities, so long as they were designated as "growth areas" in New Jersey's State Development Guide Plan (ibid., 214–15, 456 A.2d at 418). Finally, the court explicitly authorized "builders remedies," under which developers could sue noncompliant municipalities to obtain density bonuses that would permit them to build more housing units than a municipality's zoning ordinance would otherwise permit, so long as they agreed to designate a percentage of the units for low- or moderate-income sale (ibid., 218, 279–81, 456 A.2d at 420, 452–53).

82. N.J. Stat. Ann. §§ 52:27D-300–29 (West 1986 and Supp. 1992).

83. Daniel Chall has underlined this new obligation: "[*Mount Laurel II*] calls for affirmative measures when simply removing restrictions on multi-unit structures

would result in the construction of only high-priced middle-income housing. . . .
Nowhere does the opinion suggest that these social goals approximate the outcomes that would have prevailed in the absence of past exclusion. The Court's rul-
ings instead seem to aim for specific land-use allocations that might never have
otherwise occurred, even in a non-exclusionary housing market" (Chall, "Housing
Reform in New Jersey," 24–25).

Professors Hughes and VanDoren have described the new obligation in even
more dramatic terms: "The court not only ruled that there are severe limits on the
right of suburban communities to restrict the entry of lower-income households
but also set in motion the most fundamental redistribution of property rights ever
attempted by a state government in the United States. The court insisted that
the state's municipalities have an affirmative obligation to redistribute low- and
moderate-income households more evenly across the state" (Mark Alan Hughes
and Peter M. VanDoren, "Social Policy through Land Reform: New Jersey's Mount
Laurel Controversy," *Political Science Quarterly* 105 [1990]: 97).

84. N.J. Stat. Ann. § 52:27D-305 (West 1986).

85. N.J. Stat. Ann. § 52:27D-307.a, .e.

86. N.J. Stat. Ann. § 52:27D-307.b.

87. N.J. Stat. Ann. § 52:27D-307.c. The statute instructs COAH in calculating a
municipality's fair share, to credit each municipality "on a one-to-one basis [for]
each current unit of low and moderate income housing of adequate standard"
(§ 52:27D-307.c[1]), and to take into account such factors as "available vacant
and developable land, infrastructure considerations or environmental or historic
preservation factors" (§ 52:27D-307.c[2]).

88. N.J. Stat. Ann. § 52:27D-309, -310.

89. *Mount Laurel II*, 92 N.J. 158, 267–74, 456 A.2d 390, 446–50 (1983). According to New Jersey commentators, it was largely the desire for a "safe harbor"
from "builders remedies" that prompted many municipalities to support the adoption of the 1985 act. See Jerome G. Rose, "New Jersey Enacts a Fair Housing Law,"
Real Estate Law Journal 14 (1985): 195, 209–10.

COAH has authority to certify a municipal fair share plan (N.J. Stat. Ann.
§ 52:27D-313 [West Supp. 1992]). Certification by COAH entitles the municipality to a six-year period of repose, allowing it to transfer any builder's lawsuit during this period to COAH; certification also provides a strong, statutorily created
"presumption of validity" to a municipality's housing plan (§ 52:27D-317 [West
1986]). See generally McDougall, "Regional Contribution Agreements," 680–81.

90. Professor Jerome Rose describes the requirements of the act as follows: "The
[1985] legislation reduces, but does not eliminate, the ambiguity of the extent of
the municipal obligation to help finance affordable housing. The legislation declares in several places that the obligation imposed . . . relates to *regulation of land
use* with the implication that it does not include *funding*. However, in the preparation of a municipal housing element, the Act requires every municipality to 'consider' several techniques that involve municipal expenditures" (Rose, "New Jersey
Enacts," 207; see N.J. Stat. Ann. § 52:27D-311.a [West 1986] [detailing the tech-
nique to be considered]).

91. N.J. Stat. Ann. § 52:26D-312.a (West 1986). In a controversial modification of the original judicial approach, the 1985 statute also has allowed any municipality to "transfer" up to 50 percent of its fair share obligation to a "receiving jurisdiction" (usually a central city) by offering to pay for the construction of Mount Laurel units in the receiving jurisdiction (§§ 52:27D-311.c, -312).

This provision has stirred theoretical debate. See generally McDougall, "Regional Contribution Agreements," 681–95 (contending that New Jersey cities' weak financial position makes them unable to bargain with suburban "sending" municipalities for payments that will cover the full municipal costs of the transferred housing and that will protect the housing needs of urban dwellers); Hughes and VanDoren, "Social Policy through Land Reform," 108–10 (urging that each region include not only a receiving municipality but several potential sending municipalities, so that receiving municipalities can bargain for the best deal). The provision, however, appears to have had little practical impact; according to one recent survey, only 813 regional contribution units were identified among the 23,516 on which the surveyors had information (Martha Lamar, Alan Mallach, and John M. Payne, "Mount Laurel at Work: Affordable Housing in New Jersey, 1983–1988," *Rutgers Law Review* 41 [1989]: 1210, tab. I). Professor Stegman, quoting the executive director of COAH, suggests that barely 1,000 units—fewer than 10 percent of the 11,451 completed units in his survey—were the product of regional agreement units (Michael A. Stegman, *A Review of Production under New Jersey's Mount Laurel Inclusionary Housing Process: A Comparison of States and Localities* [Trenton: Council on Affordable Housing, 1990], 24).

92. Lamar et al., "Mount Laurel at Work," 1209 (noting that 54 municipalities surveyed in 1988 reported that 2,803 affordable units had been completed, that 11,133 more were pending or under construction, and that 8,740 were proposed by 1993, for a total of 22,703 units) and 1258 ("This is far and away the principal source of affordable housing being constructed for lower-income households in New Jersey"); see also Stegman, *Review of Production*, 24–25 (reporting that a total of 32,000 fair share units have been completed or are under construction—ten times the recent production rate for federally assisted housing in New Jersey).

93. See generally Payne, "Rethinking Fair Share," 30–32 (noting that COAH has defined New Jersey's housing regions in ways that "wall off" those areas with the greatest housing need from those areas with the greatest source of supply, and that COAH has grossly underestimated actual housing need).

94. The available data, while incomplete, show minority underrepresentation to be a very serious problem: "Many developments have very small minority populations and, within that minority population, even smaller numbers of black residents. At least three *Mount Laurel* developments appear to have no black residents; in some other developments the percentage of black homebuyers varies from 1% to 3%" (Lamar et al., "Mount Laurel at Work," 1256). This was not an unforeseen development. Norman William, one of the lawyers for the original *Mount Laurel I* plaintiffs, warned in 1975 that the predominant beneficiaries of the decision would likely be white ethnic citizens. See Norman Williams Jr., "On from *Mount Laurel*," 79, 95.

95. Lamar et al., "Mount Laurel at Work," 1232–33.

96. Ibid., 1237 (discussing maximum incomes and different-sized families and providing a table showing income eligibilities from $10,621 [for a single-person family at 40 percent of median] to $32,128 [for a nine-person family at 80 percent of median]).

97. The New Jersey public advocate has charged that COAH regulations on income exclude more than half of New Jersey's moderate-income families and almost 75 percent of New Jersey's low-income families from the effective reach of the fair share program (Initial Comments by the Dep't of the Public Advocate upon the Proposed Substantive Regulations of the Council on Affordable Housing, Stephen Eisdorfer, Ass't Deputy Public Advocate, June 30, 1980, 4–6, cited in McDougall, "From Litigation to Legislation," 640–41 n. 111). This, too, is not an unexpected development. See George Sternlieb, "Mount Laurel, Economics, Morality, and the Law," in Rose and Rothman, *After Mount Laurel*, 291, 296 ("Without deep and widespread subsidies, *Mount Laurel* will enrich many landholders while making it possible to accommodate more of the middle class").

One recent analysis has suggested that a similar failure to target the needs of very-low-income renters seriously mars the National Affordable Housing Act of 1990 (the HOME program) and the low-income housing tax credit (LIHTC), two recent federal legislative initiatives designed to increase the low-income housing supply (Kathryn P. Nelson, "*Whose* Shortage of Affordable Housing?," *Housing Policy Debate* 5 [1994]: 401, 436–37 [arguing that a shortage of housing units exists only for renters with incomes at 30 percent or less of the area median income, well under the income level served by HOME and LIHTC programs]).

98. See, for example, Hughes and VanDoren, "Social Policy through Land Reform," 105; see also Lamar et al., "Mount Laurel at Work," 1254 (observing that the occupations of *Mount Laurel* participants "are very close to the national distribution of occupations by general category," with the largest single category being "professional, technical, [and] managerial administrative workers") and 1259 (finding that *Mount Laurel* beneficiaries typically come from three groups, "the temporarily poor . . . mostly young people, some just out of college and in their first jobs, and some recently-divorced women").

99. The public advocate has faulted COAH regulations for failing to prescribe a minimum number of multibedroom units (McDougall, "Regional Contribution Agreements," 685 n. 151) and for permitting developers to sell larger-bedroom units to single-person households, thwarting the social end in having such larger units (Lamar et al., "Mount Laurel at Work," 1236).

100. Lamar et al., "Mount Laurel at Work," 1222–23 (discovering that among ten COAH-certified municipalities that were studied intensively, most had formal criteria favoring applicants already connected with the municipality, such as municipal residents, employees in the community, etc.). Once again, this pattern was forecast by earlier commentators.

101. See, for example, McDougall, "Regional Contribution Agreements," 684–85.

102. According to the 1983–88 study of *Mount Laurel* programs, some 75 percent of all housing units completed were the products of market-driven, set-aside

development (Lamar et al., "Mount Laurel at Work," 1210–11). In their recommendations, these analysts urged a far greater financial commitment from the state of New Jersey (ibid., 1268–69).

103. See, for example, McDougall, "Regional Contribution Agreements," 685 n. 151 (noting that the New Jersey public advocate has criticized initial COAH regulations for their failure to require a focus on rental housing); Lamar et al., "Mount Laurel at Work," 1261 ("Rental housing is the only possible option for many low-income households who are unable to get financing or do not have enough cash for down payments and closing costs. . . . [Yet] rental housing for non-elderly low-income households is almost non-existent in the *Mount Laurel* plans surveyed.").

104. Lamar et al., "Mount Laurel at Work," 1266–67.

105. To avoid constitutional issues that might emerge if Congress directly imposed the obligations of this act (see *New York v. United States*, 112 S.Ct. 2408 [1993]), the statute should be structured as grant-in-aid legislation, under which states and municipalities that choose not to meet the requirement of the act will be excluded from participating in the financial benefits of the federal program. Grant-in-aid programs have been routinely employed by Congress since the 1930s to further nationwide compliance with important policy objectives while simultaneously honoring state sovereignty and federalism concerns reflected in the Tenth Amendment and the structure of the federal Constitution. See, for example, *Steward Machine Co. v. Davis*, 301 U.S. 548, 585–98 (1937). Modern constitutional conceptions of federal-state relations permit federal statutes such as the National Fair Share Act to "attach conditions on the receipt of federal funds, and . . . employ the [spending] power 'to further broad policy objectives by conditioning receipt of federal moneys upon compliance by the recipient with federal statutory and administrative directives'" (*South Dakota v. Dole*, 483 U.S. 203, 206 [1987] [quoting *Fullilove v. Klutznick*, 448 U.S. 448, 474 (1980) (opinion of Burger, C.J.)]).

106. Pub. L. No. 101-625, 104 Stat. 4079 (codified at 42 U.S.C. §§ 12701 et seq. [1990]). That act presently requires all localities wishing to receive HUD funds to submit a Comprehensive Housing Affordability Strategy (CHAS) (42 U.S.C. § 12705[a][1–2] [1990]). The act contemplates that CHAS will address, among other issues, "the jurisdiction's need for assistance for very low-income, low-income, and moderate-income families, specifying such needs for different types of tenure and for different categories of residents, such as very low-income, low-income, and moderate-income families, the elderly, single persons, large families, residents of nonmetropolitan areas . . . and other categories of persons residing in or expected to reside in the jurisdiction that the Secretary [of HUD] determines to be appropriate" (§ 12705[b][1]). A local CHAS also must address the issue of local "tax policies affecting land and other property, land use controls, zoning ordinances, building codes, fees and charges, growth limits" and "describe the jurisdiction's strategy to remove or ameliorate negative effects, if any" (§ 12705[b][4]). Additionally, the CHAS must discuss the local private, nonprofit, and public housing institutions available to assist the municipality to meet its housing needs (§ 12705[b][5]), as well as the expected nonfederal sources of revenue on which it will rely to meet those needs (§ 12705[b][6]).

107. See Philip D. Tegeler, "Housing Segregation and Local Discretion," *Journal*

of Law and Policy 3 (1994): 209 (examining the constraints posed by decentralization of responsibility for governmentally assisted housing programs); see generally Richard Briffault, "Our Localism: Part I, The Structure of Local Government Law," *Columbia Law Review* 90 (1990): 1; Richard Briffault, "Our Localism: Part II, Localism and Legal Theory," *Columbia Law Review* 90 (1990): 346 (offering a comprehensive view of how modern suburban jurisdictions have used law and political power to avoid assuming fiscal and social responsibility for low-income metropolitan residents).

108. Downs, "Policy Directions," 715.

109. Various measures might be developed to determine racial segregation, from the simplest (a gross calculation of the disparity between the racial composition in the municipality and in the wider metropolitan region) to very complex measures taking dozens of nonracial factors into account. This proposal does contemplate, however, that a municipality's fair share for racial purposes would approach some significant fraction of the overall metropolitan racial percentage.

Of course, it would be crucially important in drafting the act and its implementing regulations to adopt clear standards to guide states in this allocation process, ensuring a meaningful degree of actual desegregation. At this stage of the analysis, however, a precise determination of the acceptable minimum percentages is a secondary consideration.

110. Each state should designate state or regional entities to take applications from low-income persons in various urban areas who are willing to relocate in municipalities that have fair share obligations. At present, the Affordable Housing Act already requires each locality receiving HUD funds to "make reasonable efforts to confer with appropriate social service agencies regarding the housing needs of children, elderly persons, persons with disabilities, homeless persons, and other persons served by such agencies" (42 U.S.C. § 12705[e] [Supp. II 1990]). This requirement, however, does not establish any affirmative obligation to provide housing for such persons, or to look beyond municipal borders.

The act should draw on the successes of the Gautreaux demonstration experiment, which was first established under a settlement between HUD and plaintiffs in a Chicago lawsuit (*Hills v. Gautreaux*, 425 U.S. 284, 286 [1976]). Under the settlement reached in that case, HUD agreed to provide housing certificates that would supplement the rental payments of inner-city residents and support an office that counsels residents who sought to relocate to rental housing throughout the metropolitan Chicago area. The program has been in operation for over fifteen years and has placed over 3,900 families. See James E. Rosenbaum, Nancy Fishman, Alison Brett, and Patricia Meaden, "Can the Kerner Commission's Housing Strategy Improve Employment, Education, and Social Integration for Low-Income Blacks?" (in this volume); James E. Rosenbaum and Susan J. Popkin, "Employment and Earnings of Low-Income Blacks Who Move to Middle-Class Suburbs," in *The Urban Underclass*, ed. Christopher Jencks and Peter E. Peterson (Washington, D.C.: Brookings Institution, 1991), 342.

Alternatively perhaps, very-low-income applicants could be selected from volunteers among those who had successfully completed the education or employment training components of the Family Support Act (42 U.S.C. §§ 602[a][19], 607[b][1][A][ii], 681–87 [1988]). Such an approach would provide an additional incentive for families with children in the Aid to Families with Dependent Children program to complete their Support Act obligations, and it would assure a steady stream of very-low-income applicants to be placed in fair share communities.

Under either alternative, the provision of well-supervised prescreening and counseling services should help alleviate suburban fears that the urban participants in such programs would bring crime or antisocial values to their new communities. See Downs, *Opening Up the Suburbs*, 73–77 (noting that the fear of crime and aberrant social behavior by inmigrants are two major white objections to racial integration).

111. As under the New Jersey Fair Housing Act, it would be necessary to provide resale or re-leasing constraints in order to preserve the low-income character of housing units created by market-related programs. Otherwise a participant could simply resell a below-market unit at the market price to a bona fide market purchaser, pocket the profit, and defeat the essential purpose of the legislation. See N.J. Stat. Ann. §§ 52:27D-321f, -324 (West 1986).

112. The Affordable Housing Act already empowers HUD to provide federal funds and other assistance to create state and local technical and administrative capacity (42 U.S.C. §§ 12781–83 [Supp. II 1990]).

113. 42 U.S.C. § 12747(a)(1) (Supp. II 1990).

114. See, for example, Reynolds Farley, "Residential Segregation of Social and Economic Groups among Blacks, 1970–80," in Jencks and Peterson, *Urban Underclass*, 274, 281–82.

115. See John M. Goering, introduction to Goering, *Housing Desegregation*, 202–5.

116. This goal is currently reflected both in the graduated level of local matching contributions in the Affordable Housing Act of 1990—which requires only a 25 percent local contribution of local funds to receive federal funds for rental assistance and housing rehabilitation projects, but a 50 percent local contribution to receive federal funds for new construction projects (42 U.S.C. § 12750[a] [Supp. II 1990])—and in the act's provisions for federal targeting of funds (§ 12747[b][1]).

117. See, for example, Chandler, "Obstacles to Housing Integration," 519 (observing that "suburban opposition to public housing is evident in the relative absence of public housing authorities and units within suburbs") and 523–24 (describing middle-income neighborhood resistance); Goering, introduction to Goering, *Housing Desegregation*, 206 (reporting that "some local jurisdictions have consistently evaded any responsibility to rehouse blacks in better quality, less segregated areas by simply not applying for federal funds"). See also Phillip L. Clay, "The (Un)Housed City: Racial Patterns of Segregation, Housing Quality, and Affordability," in Galster and Hill, *Metropolis in Black and White*, 93, 99–100 (noting the failure of federal rental voucher and certificate programs alone to disperse black families). George Galster's proposal to provide tax credits for those willing to make housing moves that would promote racial integration is a variant of this idea, targeted to higher-income citizens (Galster, *Federal Fair Housing Policy*, 24). His

program would be a welcome additional approach, but because of acute federal budget constraints, it should not be the centerpiece of federal desegregation and low-income housing efforts.

118. See Downs, "Policy Directions," 721–22. Michael Vernarelli has described how HUD secretary George Romney attempted to induce more suburban communities to participate in federal housing programs during the early 1970s by "mak[ing] the deconcentration of assisted housing within a metropolitan area a condition for local communities' receipt of HUD housing and community development funds" (Vernarelli, "Where Should HUD Locate Assisted Housing?: The Evolution of Fair Housing Policy," in Goering, *Housing Desegregation*, 214, 216–17). Vernarelli reports that "the get-tough strategy did not succeed, mainly because HUD could not offer most communities enough of an economic reward to justify a local political confrontation over racial integration. The most conspicuous failures were in suburban communities" (Vernarelli, "Where Should HUD Locate?," 217); see also Alexander Polikoff, *Housing the Poor: The Case for Heroism* (Cambridge, Mass.: Ballinger, 1978), 31–41 (describing Romney's unsuccessful efforts during the early Nixon administration).

119. Helen F. Ladd and John Yinger, *America's Ailing Cities: Fiscal Health and the Design of Urban Policy* (Baltimore: Johns Hopkins University Press, 1989).

120. See *Spallone v. United States*, 110 S. Ct. 625, 628, 634–35 (1990) (vacating contempt fines imposed on city council members who refused to comply with federal housing desegregation orders and argued that they had both First Amendment rights and absolute legislative immunity when discharging their legislative responsibilities to constituents who opposed desegregation).

121. See Farley et al., "'Chocolate City, Vanilla Suburbs,'" 336 (reporting that 40 percent among the more than 400 whites in a Detroit survey who said they would move out of a neighborhood if it became one-third black cited concern about declining property values).

122. See 26 U.S.C. § 163(h)(3) (1988).

123. See 26 U.S.C. § 164(a)(1).

124. James R. Follain and David C. Ling, "The Federal Tax Subsidy to Housing and the Reduced Value of the Mortgage Interest Deduction," *National Tax Journal* 44 (1991): 147, 157.

125. This feature of the National Fair Share Act is a variant of a proposal for a "Pigovian tax" put forward by Michelle White in 1979 (White, "Suburban Growth Controls," 210). Professor White proposed to require local communities that wished to adopt exclusionary zoning regulations to pay a tax to a regional governmental body. Such a tax would reflect the external costs, to nonresidents of the community, of the exclusionary zoning (ibid., 225–30). As Professor White explained, "A standard economic remedy for nuisances is the Pigovian tax, which gives nuisance creators a choice between paying a tax per unit of nuisance or ceasing to create the nuisance. The tax . . . is intended to discourage zoning by forcing the community to pay a positive price for it" (ibid., 210).

126. In this sense the National Fair Share proposal is less radical than the proposal put forward by Peter Salsich, who suggests an absolute cap on mortgage interest deductibility and who also appears to muse about the elimination of the

property tax deduction (Salsich, "A Decent Home for Every American: Can the 1949 Goal Be Met?" [in this volume]).

127. This idea bears some resemblance to Salsich's proposal for a Low Income Housing Investment Trust Fund, since it would create a stream of revenue dedicated to low-income housing construction (ibid.). The principal difference is that the revenue here would be redirected toward housing resources in the very communities whose residents had forfeited their deductions because of municipal noncompliance with the Fair Share Act.

128. See Robert Greenstein, "Universal and Targeted Approaches to Relieving Poverty: An Alternative View," in Jencks and Peterson, *Urban Underclass*, 437, 453–55 (noting that federal budget constraints during the 1990s are likely to be fierce due to the projected annual deficits and the large national debt).

129. See, for example, Downs, *Opening Up the Suburbs*, 161–62 (advocating establishment of effective local low-income housing programs as a prerequisite to receipt of various types of federal financial assistance); Downs, "Policy Directions," 741–42 (advocating establishment of effective local anti-racial-discrimination programs as a prerequisite to receipt of federal community development block grants).

130. See 26 U.S.C. §§ 103(a), 141–50 (1988 and Supp. II 1990).

131. See, for example, 42 U.S.C. § 5306(d) (1988 and Supp. II 1990) (allocating 30 percent of federal Community Development Block Grant funds to the states for redistribution to localities selected by the states).

132. See Martha Mahoney, "Law and Racial Geography: Public Housing and the Economy in New Orleans," *Stanford Law Review* 42 (1990): 1251 (emphasizing "the necessity of considering both race and access to economic opportunity," not race or class issues alone, when formulating public policy).

133. See, for example, Paul Davidoff and Linda Davidoff, "Opening the Suburbs: Toward Inclusionary Land Use Controls," *Syracuse Law Review* 22 (1971): 509, 528–32; Thomas Kleven, "Inclusionary Ordinances: Policy and Legal Issues in Requiring Private Developers to Build Low Cost Housing," *University of California at Los Angeles Law Review* 21 (1974): 1432, 1438.

134. See, for example, Michael F. Potter, "Racial Diversity in Residential Communities: Societal Housing Patterns and a Proposal for a 'Racial Inclusionary Ordinance,'" *Southern California Law Review* 63 (1990): 1151, 1196 (advocating the adoption in California of a mandatory set-aside statute that would require developers of new residential housing projects to reserve 25 percent of all sale or rental units for racial and ethnic minority group members).

135. William Julius Wilson, *The Truly Disadvantaged: The Inner City, the Underclass, and Public Policy* (Chicago: University of Chicago Press, 1987), 109–24.

136. See, for example, Bruce S. Gelber, "Race-Conscious Approaches to Ending Segregation in Housing: Some Pitfalls on the Road to Integration," *Rutgers Law Review* 37 (1985): 921, 950–60 (arguing that floor quotas and affirmative marketing may be constitutionally permissible, but that ceiling quotas are unconstitutional and violate the Fair Housing Act); Polikoff, "Sustainable Integration," 47–56 (supporting the constitutionality of race-conscious, affirmative counseling programs for homeseekers); Sander, "Comment: Individual Rights," 926–28 (arguing that floor quotas, but not ceiling quotas or race-conscious assignments in a public

housing context, might be constitutional if they are temporary); "Note: Benign Steering and Benign Quotas: The Validity of Race-Conscious Government Policies to Promote Residential Integration," *Harvard Law Review* 93 (1980): 938, 947 (arguing that benign steering of white homeseekers, but not benign ceiling quotas, would be constitutional); "Note: Tipping the Scales of Justice: A Race-Conscious Remedy for Neighborhood Transition," *Yale Law Journal* 90 (1980) 377, 380–99 (noting that benign steering of white homeseekers would be constitutional); compare Bruce L. Ackerman, "Integration for Subsidized Housing and the Question of Racial Occupancy Controls," *Stanford Law Review* 26 (1974): 245, 270–309 (defending both floor and ceiling quotas, albeit on different constitutional grounds); Dorn Bishop, "Fair Housing and the Constitutionality of Governmental Measures Affecting Community Ethnicity," *University of Chicago Law Review* 55 (1988): 1229, 1246–65 (arguing that all forms of integration maintenance devices, including floor and ceiling quotas and affirmative marketing, can survive constitutional and statutory scrutiny if they are narrowly tailored so that their integrative benefits outweigh their costs); Rodney A. Smolla, "In Pursuit of Racial Utopias: Fair Housing, Quotas, and Goals in the 1980's," *Southern California Law Review* 58 (1985): 947, 980–99 (arguing that all integration maintenance devices are unconstitutional and violate the Fair Housing Act).

137. Compare *Otero v. New York City Housing Auth.*, 484 F.2d 1122, 1125 (2d Cir. 1973) (upholding a plan to maintain racial integration in a public housing project by limiting minority participation to 40 percent of the units) with *United States v. Starrett City Assoc.*, 840 F.2d 1096, 1100 (2d Cir.), cert. denied, 488 U.S. 946 (1988) (condemning use of racial ceiling quotas for minority applicants to federally subsidized housing project that had been approved as part of a court-supervised settlement), and *Burney v. Housing Auth. of Beaver Co.*, 551 F. Supp. 746, 753 (W.D. Pa. 1982) (striking a race-conscious tenant assignment plan that had the effect of preferring white applicants).

138. See generally John O. Calmore, "Fair Housing vs. Fair Housing: The Problems with Providing Increased Housing Opportunities through Spatial Deconcentration," *Clearinghouse Review* 14 (1980): 7, 12; Michael R. Tein, "The Devaluation of Nonwhite Community in Remedies for Subsidized Housing Discrimination," *University of Pennsylvania Law Review* 140 (1992): 1463.

139. These are among the activities proposed by George Galster and others as prerequisites for community receipt of federal funds. See Galster, *Federal Fair Housing Policy*, 25. One intended virtue of the National Fair Share approach is its clear placement of responsibility to identify effective desegregation methods on municipal decision makers themselves; unless the methods they adopt actually work to meet the municipality's fair share goal, serious adverse consequences will automatically follow. Thus, municipalities will be strongly motivated to select effective remedies, rather than to delay or make remedial choices that, while formally adequate, will not achieve meaningful results.

140. Ibid., 11–12.

141. "If blacks begin to appear in all or most neighborhoods—even if in small numbers—the widely accepted notion that the entry of a few black households

into a neighborhood or community signals the start of a certain process that must end in that neighborhood or community becoming an all-black slum will become less credible" (John F. Kain, "Housing Market Discrimination and Black Suburbanization in the 1980s," in Tobin, *Divided Neighborhoods*, 68, 82; see also Sander, "Comment: Individual Rights," 901).

142. See Advisory Commission on Intergovernmental Relations, *Fiscal Disparities: Central Cities and Suburbs, 1981* (Washington, D.C.: Advisory Commission on Intergovernmental Affairs, 1984), 11 (noting the difference between "Eastern" metropolitan areas, characterized by stark contrasts between central cities and suburbs, and "newer" cities of the South and West, which have used aggressive annexation to create cities with "substantial suburban characteristics"); David Rusk, *Cities without Suburbs* (Washington, D.C.: Woodrow Wilson Center Press, 1993) (contrasting the positive economic, social, and political experience of those "elastic" metropolitan areas in the United States that have expanded to incorporate their suburbs between 1940 and 1990 with the less satisfactory experience of those relatively "inelastic" cities that have allowed separate suburban jurisdictions to develop outside their central-city limits).

143. David Rusk reports that cities that have aggressively annexed their surrounding suburbs "have avoided segregation by race and economic class better than others," and that "creating a more open society also seems related to maintaining broad public institutions, such as the dominant city or county governments, or county-wide school systems, which link 'city' and 'suburb'" (Rusk, *Cities without Suburbs*, 19).

144. Anthony Downs anticipated this possible solution in 1973: "Admittedly, opening up the suburbs is not the only way to counteract existing fiscal disparities. One much simpler remedy would be dissolving the political boundaries that fragment each metropolitan area and creating a single metropolitan government. This has been done in Indianapolis, Nashville, and Jacksonville" (Downs, *Opening Up the Suburbs*, 40).

145. David Rusk observes that while aggressive annexation to create metropolitan-wide government is the "surest way to avoid or reverse patterns of racial and economic segregation" in small and medium-sized areas, "for larger, more complex metro areas, metro government may be neither politically feasible nor administratively desirable" so long as fair share housing policies and relatively equitable public services are guaranteed (Rusk, *Cities without Suburbs*, 123).

146. Edward B. Lazere, Paul A. Leonard, Cushing N. Dolbeare, and Barry Zigas, *A Place to Call Home: The Low Income Housing Crisis Continues* (Washington, D.C.: Center on Budget and Policy Priorities, 1991), 3–4 (reporting that in 1989 the difference between the number of low-income households and the number of available units was 4.1 million, a much wider gap than at any point during the 1970s).

147. Furthermore, since a major purpose of the National Fair Share legislation is to overcome residential segregation's role in creating a "spatial mismatch" that prevents urban racial minorities from reaching areas of suburban job growth, a metrowide government could meet this objective of the act adequately only if it provided a mass transit system to city residents that would afford ready access to major met-

ropolitan employers. See Kain, "Spatial Mismatch Hypothesis," 450 (evaluating the research findings in support of the spatial mismatch hypothesis).

148. See, for example, Wilhelmina A. Leigh and James D. McGhee, "A Minority Perspective on Residential Racial Integration," in Goering, *Housing Desegregation*, 31, 36 (contending that "to the extent that the movement of blacks from cities to suburban areas reduces their numbers in inner-city voting jurisdictions, they are reducing their power as the plurality or majority of voters in certain wards"); Georgia A. Persons, "Racial Politics and Black Power in the Cities," in Galster and Hill, *Metropolis in Black and White*, 166, 185–87 (arguing that "the politics of suburbia is both strongly anti-city and heavily racially tinged," putting suburban blacks at a decided political disadvantage); compare Norman Krumholz, "The Kerner Commission Twenty Years Later," in Galster and Hill, *Metropolis in Black and White*, 19, 25–31 (arguing that black urban power is a "prize of substantial value to the African American citizens of a city, and a prize worth fighting for").

149. Anthony Downs long ago observed that there might be some political advantages to increasing the black political presence in suburban communities: "The presence of at least some black residents in most suburban areas would greatly reduce the probability that white suburbanites would define suburban interests in ways that are antiblack as well as anti-central-city. Black suburbanites would be able to exercise at least some beneficial influence that would not arise if nearly all blacks remained in central cities" (Downs, *Opening Up the Suburbs*, 82). See generally Robert Reinhold, "The Electorate: Chasing Votes from Big Cities to the Suburbs," *New York Times*, June 1, 1992 (examining the demographic realignments following the 1990 census and their implications for the political and racial loyalties of suburban politicians).

150. See generally Alex Kotlowitz, *There Are No Children Here: The Story of Two Boys Growing up in the Other America* (New York: Doubleday, 1991) (chronicling two years in the lives of two "underclass youths" growing up in inner-city Chicago); Children's Defense Fund, *S.O.S. America! A Children's Defense Budget* (Washington, D.C.: Children's Defense Fund, 1990) (advocating a "peaceful transformation" to an America that ensures no child will grow up without health care, food, shelter, or education).

151. See generally Erol Ricketts, "The Underclass: Causes and Responses," in Galster and Hill, *Metropolis in Black and White*, 216 (focusing "on some of the major agreed on causes of the underclass and the expected direction that the responses motivated by subscription to these causes would take"); Wilson, *Truly Disadvantaged*, 6–8 (noting the causes of the social and economic dislocation of the "ghetto underclass").

152. See generally W. E. B. Du Bois, *Black Reconstruction in America, 1860-1880* (Cleveland: World Publishing, 1964) (describing the legislative and social achievements of the post–Civil War Reconstruction era); Eric Foner, *Reconstruction: America's Unfinished Revolution, 1863–1877* (New York: Harper and Row, 1988); Arthur M. Schlesinger Jr., *The Coming of the New Deal 1933–1934* (Boston: Houghton Mifflin, 1958) (describing the legislative achievements of President Franklin Roosevelt's New Deal); Michael B. Katz, "Reorganizing the Nation," in *In*

the Shadow of the Poorhouse: A Social History of Welfare in America (New York: Basic Books, 1986), 206–47 (describing the broad social welfare reforms adopted during the New Deal of the 1930s); Taylor, "*Brown*, Equal Protection," 1701–17 (describing the significant legislative achievements of the civil rights era of the 1960s); Robert D. Plotnick and Felicity Skidmore, eds., *Progress against Poverty: A Review of the 1964–1974 Decade* (New York: Academic Press, 1975), 47–188 (describing the legislative achievements of President Lyndon Johnson's War on Poverty programs).

Part Four   America's Social Policy

How Race Matters in Developing
Health, Education, and Welfare
Policies

Sidney D. Watson   Health Care in the
Inner City

Asking the Right Question

MIAMI—June Kirchik, fifty-eight years old, discovered a large lump in her breast. When she went to a private hospital, she was denied treatment because she was indigent and her case was not considered an emergency. A public hospital performed a biopsy, which was positive, and gave her an appointment for treatment three weeks later. When Mrs. Kirchik arrived for treatment, however, the public hospital turned her away because she had not yet applied for Medicaid. Mrs. Kirchik tried another public hospital but was turned away because she was not a resident of the hospital's service area. When Mrs. Kirchik's story appeared in the newspaper, the first public hospital admitted her—to a private room—four months after she had first discovered the lump. Two weeks later, Mrs. Kirchik died.[1]

The June Kirchiks of this country seem forgotten in the current debate about health care reform. Americans keep asking, How do we contain the ever increasing costs of health care? How do we pay for health care? We are so focused on these questions that we have narrowed our vision too much and lost sight of the real questions and the real issues.

The real question for American health care reform ought to be How do we improve the health of Americans? Especially, how do we improve the health of those, like June Kirchik, who live in the inner city, are poor and overwhelmingly minority, and are systematically underserved by our health care establishment? This is the question we should be asking. Sadly, we are not.

Race and Health Care

Race, poverty, and geographic inaccessibility to health care interact. As a result, an urban black[2] typically is sicker and in greater need of health care than a suburban white, but is less likely to be able to afford or obtain health care. Given the greater poverty among minorities, health care discrimination based on race is virtually inevitable in a system in which one must purchase health care.[3]

Simple statistics tell a good part of the story and highlight what happens when we ask the wrong question. The poverty rate for black families is three times that of white families.[4] A third of all black households, and almost half of all black children, live in poverty.[5] Nearly 30 percent of black households report having no assets, and more than 50 percent have assets of $5,000 or less.[6]

In a 1986 survey 9 percent of black Americans reported they could not get health care for "economic reasons."[7] Only about half of all blacks have private health insurance; one in five have Medicaid or Medicare; and one in five have no health coverage.[8] Blacks are twice as likely as whites to have no health insurance and five times more likely to be covered by Medicaid.[9] Forty percent of those on Medicaid are black.[10]

The problem is exacerbated by the story the statistics do not relate. Blacks, particularly poor, inner-city blacks, have greater health care needs than whites. Inner-city residents are exposed to twice the environmental health hazards that suburban dwellers face—bad air, polluted water, crime, and drugs.[11] Inner-city residents suffer from hypertension, heart disease, chronic bronchitis, emphysema, sight and hearing impairments, cancer, and congenital anomalies at a rate 50 percent higher than that of suburbanites.[12] The rate of neurological and mental disorders in inner-city residents is nearly twice that of suburbanites.[13]

The problem begins at birth. In this country, black infants are twice as likely to die in their first year of life as are white infants. Babies born in America's inner cities are more likely to die than babies in Costa Rica and Jamaica. In fact, nineteen developed countries have lower infant mortality rates than the United States.[14]

The problem is exacerbated by the dual epidemics of AIDS and tuberculosis. Both diseases disproportionately affect blacks and Hispanics, particularly those in the inner city.[15] Together blacks and Hispanics account for almost half of all people diagnosed with AIDS in the United States.[16] A primary reason for the high rate of AIDS in these groups is that minority life in the inner city is identified with poverty, massive unemployment, and rampant intravenous drug use.[17] Blacks and Hispanics have higher rates of tuberculosis than whites because life in the inner city is more likely to create the conditions in which tuberculosis spreads—overcrowded housing, homeless shelters, and prisons.[18]

Although minority inner-city residents have more illness and need more medical care than other Americans, they have less access to health care. A study of ten U.S. cities found that the number of office-based primary care physicians in poor, inner-city areas declined 45 percent from 1963 to 1980.[19]

Historically, inner-city blacks, like other poor inner-city residents, have relied on hospital emergency rooms and, where available, public outpatient clinics for care.[20] Federal budget cuts have forced many inner-city primary care clinics to close,[21] however, and private hospitals, once a major source of emergency primary care, have abandoned the inner city.[22]

ATLANTA—Grady Memorial Hospital in downtown Atlanta turned away ambulances twenty-three times in 1990 because it had no beds available.[23]

The waiting time for an appointment to receive treatment for AIDS is six months.[24]

Between 1937 and 1977, 210 private hospitals with 30,000 hospital beds in fifty-two of the largest cites in the country either closed or relocated.[25] A disproportionate number of these hospitals were located in neighborhoods where blacks constituted at least 60 percent of the population. The hospitals that closed served the patients whom other hospitals were reluctant to serve, in areas where few doctors were willing to practice.[26] The facilities that closed served twice as many minority patients and twice as many Medicaid patients as the hospitals that remained open.[27] The private hospitals that remained behind often limited the number of Medicaid and Medicare patients treated, disproportionately excluding black patients, who, as noted earlier, are five times as likely as whites to be covered by Medicaid.[28]

NEW YORK—New York City's six public hospitals have a 97 percent occupancy rate, and many private hospitals have closed their emergency rooms to keep out uninsured patients. The results are witnessed at public Bellevue Hospital, where patients wait as long as two days to be treated in the emergency room.[29]

At New York City's public hospitals, it takes six weeks to get a first appointment at an AIDS clinic and two months for an appointment at City Hospital's general medicine clinic. Women wait up to three months for prenatal care and four months for gynecological care.[30]

Most public hospitals in urban areas are located in the inner city and are the primary care providers for inner-city, poor minorities.[31] These public facilities are grossly underfunded[32] and suffer from rapidly deteriorating conditions, overcrowding, long waits for emergency treatment, staff shortages, and outdated equipment.[33] Patients with private insurance avoid these decaying inner-city public hospitals and choose newer, less crowded, more patient-friendly private facilities—the same ones that are more likely to limit the number of Medicaid and Medicare patients they treat.

The result is America's segregated health care system. The black, poor, inner-city resident receives treatment at overcrowded, underfunded, disproportionately black public hospitals. Those with private insurance, who are disproportionately white, receive care at more modern, better-equipped, and better-staffed private hospitals.

NEW ORLEANS—"When 64 year old Marie Barnett arrived at Charity Hospital suffering from piercing pains in her arm and chest, she needed the constant medical care and high-tech attention of an intensive care unit. Unfortunately, the . . . intensive unit . . . was full." Half of its beds had been converted to storage closets because of a lack of money to pay for nurses to staff the unit. Mrs. Barnett was put on a regular ward, "without special equipment to monitor her condition or extra staff to respond quickly to problems. A few hours later, she had a second heart attack"—finally earning a place in one of Charity's six intensive-care beds. At Charity, New Orleans's only public hospital, the sick and poor, who are overwhelmingly black, wait six months for a routine outpatient clinic appointment, pipe leaks are left unattended, and nearly half of its 920 beds have been taken out of service since 1986 because of a budget stalled at 1985 levels.[34]

Compounding the problem, few urban blacks who need care receive it because the care provided by public hospitals is effectively rationed by the inconvenience and waiting time inherent in these overcrowded and understaffed facilities.[35] A worker employed at an hourly-wage job forgoes a hypertension checkup because the wait to be seen in a crowded public clinic would cost her a day's pay; three months later she dies of a heart attack. A teenage mother assumes that prenatal care is not particularly important when she is informed that she must wait eight weeks for her first appointment; the baby she delivers is twice as likely to die.[36]

The care that public hospitals provide, moreover, is generally the more expensive, inpatient variety because overcrowding and underfunding prevent patients from obtaining preventive and primary care. A vicious circle results: overcrowding and long waits cause patients to delay necessary care, which causes health conditions to worsen; more serious conditions, in turn, require more intensive and more expensive treatment, which, to close the circle, increases demand on the limited resources of the public hospitals. The consequences are needless suffering and death as many poor patients do not receive any medical care until they are beyond help.

NEW ORLEANS—Manuela Chacon is a retired hotel maid who was diagnosed with diabetes. Soon after, she felt dizzy, so she went to Charity's one outpatient clinic early one Monday morning. After waiting more than ten hours and taking a battery of tests, Ms. Chacon was told to return the next day. On Tuesday, after a six-hour wait and more tests, she was told to return on Friday. On Friday she got her test results: her diabetes was under control, but she needed further tests and possible treatment because her liver enzyme levels were suspiciously low. Ms. Chacon was told to come back in six weeks—the first available date when a doctor could examine her.[37]

What Gunnar Myrdal concluded in 1944 in his seminal study of blacks in America remains true today:

It is hard to separate the effects of discrimination from those of concentration of Negroes in those areas where medical facilities are not easily available and in those income brackets which do not permit the purchase of medical facilities in the competitive market. Discrimination increases Negro sickness and death both directly and indirectly and manifests itself both consciously and unconsciously. . . . Ill health reduces the chance of economic advancement, which in turn operates to reduce the chance of getting adequate medical facilities or the knowledge necessary for personal care.[38]

In 1968 the Kerner Commission agreed with Myrdal's conclusions[39] but made no recommendations directed specifically at health care reform. The commission's strategy of integrating inner-city blacks into the suburbs was designed to increase employment opportunities for blacks, and with better jobs would come employer-provided health care. Those left behind in the inner city would be able to obtain medical care through the new federal programs—Medicaid for the poor and Medicare for the elderly. But urban blacks have not been able to escape to the suburbs. The inner city is still a ghetto bereft of health care providers and populated predominately by poor blacks unable to purchase health care in a competitive market. Many urban blacks have not entered the job force; those who are employed often hold low-paying, nonunionized jobs that do not provide health insurance. While Medicare has provided virtually universal coverage to the elderly population, Medicaid provides insurance to only 42 percent of the nonelderly poor. The details of the health care crisis for inner-city minorities may have changed, but the broad outlines remain the same: few providers of health care and little money with which to purchase care from even those few.

The best way to improve the health of minority inner-city residents is still to provide jobs, increase incomes, improve socioeconomic status, and encourage relocation outside the inner city. Good health correlates primarily with higher socioeconomic status; poor health correlates directly with poverty.[40] Those who live in crowded conditions run a higher risk of disease. In the inner city, this risk is aggravated "by low wages and high unemployment, inferior education systems, unstable sources of health care, substandard housing, violence, and high transportation and food costs."[41] To improve the health of inner-city minorities, we not only need to reduce the risk of disease but also to increase access to jobs, better schools, adequate sources of health care, good housing, less crime, and more affordable transportation and food.

Until these socioeconomic goals, which will have a profound, long-term effect on minority health, are accomplished, any strategy to provide adequate health care for minority urban populations must expand beyond the narrow financing questions that predominate the political debate. Reformers need to address the larger question of how to improve American health generally and, specifically, the health of minorities in the inner city. Achieving real improvement requires us to address four issues: (1) financing health care, (2) attracting sufficient health care providers to the inner city, (3) combating discrimination in the delivery of health care, and (4) developing new health care delivery systems responsive to the needs of inner-city residents.

My point is not that the present national debate focused on health care financing—providing the means to purchase health care—is wrong; it is, however, only the beginning. If we are serious about improving the health of inner-city blacks and assuring that health care providers are available in the inner city, we must focus attention equally on dismantling the race discrimination that pervades health care delivery and on developing new health care delivery systems that meet the needs of poor, inner-city, minority patients.

Health Care Financing

Today's front-burner issue—health care financing—is the place to begin. Middle-class and upper-middle-class Americans justifiably worry about the spiraling cost of health care and insurance underwriting practices that limit their access to private health insurance.[42] American businesses today pay drastically higher premiums than they once did and, ironically, provide less health care for their employees. State governments appropriate ever increasing amounts of money for what is now their first or second largest expenditure, the Medicaid program.[43] More and more Americans are uninsured, and hospitals complain that they can no longer bear the cost of treating increasing numbers of uninsured patients. Meanwhile, insurance companies are increasingly reluctant to underwrite the costs of care for the indigent.

While Congress seems unable to enact major health care legislation, states are taking the lead in health care financing reform. Six states have initiated major Medicaid reform and expansion initiatives, and another seven states have requested federal approval to overhaul their Medicaid programs.[44] In the midst of this activity, two types of financing reforms have taken center stage: market reform plans and single payer programs.[45]

Market reform proposals, while differing in their details, share four key ingredients. First, they rely on a pluralist approach to health care financing. Employers provide insurance for workers and their dependents as the primary means of providing health care,[46] and state and federal programs cover persons not insured by an employer. Second, they require health insurance policies to provide a set, minimum package of health care benefits. Third, most contain provisions prohibiting exclusions for preexisting conditions and other barriers to insurability. Fourth, all rely on a variety of measures to reduce unnecessary health care expenditures and contain health care costs.[47]

In contrast, single payer proposals make the government directly responsible for financing and administering health insurance by divorcing health insurance from employment and covering everyone under a unitary public insurance program. Financing is achieved primarily through the tax system rather than through premiums paid by individuals and employers to insurance companies. Levels of care, patient cost-sharing and rates of provider reimbursement are determined through the political process rather than through individual or employer contracts with insurance companies.[48]

As states and Congress debate health care financing reform, my fear is that the debate, and any resulting legislation, will focus too narrowly on one issue: containing rising health care spending. If it does, poor people—particularly poor urban minorities—may lose for another twenty-five years their chance to gain access to health care.

In reforming health care financing, we should not focus solely on narrow issues framed from the limited vantage point of consumer, provider, or employer. We need to reform health care finance and delivery as part of our response to a broader, more fundamental question: How can we best improve the health of Americans?

To improve the health of America's inner-city blacks and poor, any health care financing reform package must contain certain crucial characteristics: universal coverage for all residents, comprehensive coverage of preventive and primary health care, no serious financial barriers to participation, and provider reimbursement rates for any public system comparable to those of privately provided insurance.

Universal Coverage

The most basic strategy to improve the health of poor, urban minorities requires universal health care financing for all Americans—black and white, young and old, urban and rural, sick and well. Nearly 32 percent of Hispanics and 21 percent of African Americans have no health insurance.[49] In 1991 726,000 additional Americans went without health insurance; 57 percent of the newly uninsured were African Americans.[50]

Our present system of health care financing disproportionately excludes minority, inner-city residents from the primary source of coverage: employer-provided health insurance. First, inner-city minorities are more likely than suburbanites to be unemployed and, therefore, uninsured. Second, even when inner-city minorities are employed, they are more likely to be working in service jobs or nonunionized jobs and trades that traditionally do not provide their workers with health insurance. Even for those inner-city minorities with employer-provided insurance, the promise of health insurance is often illusory because of limitations on coverage for preexisting conditions. As noted earlier, low-income blacks suffer a disproportionate rate of chronic illnesses such as heart disease and high blood pressure.[51] Private insurance's exclusion of coverage for preexisting illnesses means that even blacks who have private insurance may not have coverage for the very condition that most demands treatment.

Not surprisingly, a disproportionate number of minorities do not qualify for Medicare. Since minorities are less likely to be employed than whites, they are also less likely to be eligible to receive those Medicare benefits that are conditioned on a sufficient work record.

Moreover, a disproportionate percentage of those ineligible for the Medicaid program are minorities.[52] Even though a greater percentage of minorities are poor, not all poor people are eligible for Medicaid—only those who fit within certain categories defined by federal law.[53] Medicaid does not cover those who are temporarily or partially disabled, young adults, childless couples, unemployable people below age sixty-five, undocumented aliens, or anyone else who does not fit within the federal statutory categories.[54] In addition, income eligibility levels vary drastically from state to state. Many states, faced with declining revenues, ever increasing health care costs, and expanding federal categories of people eligible for Medicaid, have attempted to limit the number of people on Medicaid by holding down their Medicaid financial eligibility levels. Currently only 42 percent of people living at or below the federal poverty level receive Medicaid.[55] Seventy-five percent of those ineligible are workers or their dependents, most of whom are newly employed or employed at jobs that pay enough to disqualify them for Medicaid but do not provide private health insurance.[56]

Popular opinion assumes that inner-city residents without private insurance, Medicaid, or Medicare nonetheless find health care. We assume they may be inconvenienced by the form and location of the services, but that they still have access. Sadly, this assumption is wrong.[57] While emergency rooms in hospitals that accept Medicare are legally obliged to provide emergency services,[58] other private health care providers have no such obligation. Long waiting lists for the few public services available to the uninsured poor mean that many either never obtain medical care or obtain care only when their condition is beyond treatment.[59]

To improve Americans' health, America needs true universal health care coverage. Single payer proposals explicitly provide universal coverage. While many market reform proposals also purport to create universal coverage, the details of how they will provide coverage are not always clear. With market reform proposals, the question remains: Will the proposal, in fact, provide insurance coverage for the poor and minority in the inner city? Market reform plans that encourage or require employers to provide health insurance for their workers and dependents provide little help in inner cities plagued by staggering unemployment. Proposals that encourage or require individuals to purchase their own health insurance are irrelevant to the one-third of black households that live at or below the federal poverty level.[60]

To accomplish real universal health care coverage, market reform plans must expand government health insurance programs to include all low-income people without regard to their welfare or categorical status. Income eligibility guidelines need to be set at levels that realistically reflect the cost of buying private health insurance and the income levels at which households can afford to purchase private insurance.

Such universal health care coverage will be expensive, but compassion compels America to fund care for all its people—the United States and South Africa are the only industrialized countries that do not have a national system to finance health care for all citizens.[61] While universal health coverage is costly, it is not prohibitively expensive.[62] In fact, in terms of broad, societal costs, universal health insurance is a more cost-effective method of providing health care than our present system. When the uninsured delay needed treatment, not only does treatment become more expensive, but other costs also are incurred as more time is lost from work and more short- and long-term disabilities occur.[63]

How do we improve the health of inner-city minorities? We begin by providing them with health insurance. This insurance coverage should include a federally mandated minimum benefit package that includes preventive and primary care as well as physician and hospital services.

Preventive and Primary Health Care Coverage

The skewed structure of health care delivery in this country favors high-tech, hospital-based, end-stage cures rather than basic, primary care.[64] Historically, American health insurance has not paid for preventive or "well" care such as regular checkups, Pap smears, and mammograms. Rather, coverage generally reimburses for medical treatment only after a disease or illness develops. For example, in 1990 the Medicaid programs of only three southeastern states—Kentucky, Mississippi, and North Carolina—paid for yearly checkups, routine mammograms, and other disease screenings and preventive care. The other states in the region waited until patients became acutely ill before paying for treatment.[65] Medicare only began covering mammograms for women over age sixty-five in 1991.[66] Until recently,

Medicare, Medicaid, and private insurers used provider reimbursement systems that encouraged more expensive hospitalization rather than office-based treatment.[67]

Health care for the urban uninsured also focuses on acute, hospital-based care. Underfunded, understaffed public hospitals necessarily have had to conduct triage, treating the most seriously ill and placing those in need of nonemergency care on long waiting lists. Those on the waiting lists often end up in emergency rooms and hospital beds because they do not receive the routine, preventive care that could have cured or forestalled their illnesses.[68]

This problem is particularly acute among, and well illustrated by, inner-city women's need for routine prenatal care. Because of the lack of prenatal care in the inner city, a high number of low-weight babies are born to poor, minority residents.[69] These children subsequently have a greater number of long-term illnesses and disabilities. This sequence eventually exacts a far greater price than providing preventive care from the start.

When short shrift is given to basic and preventive care, everyone suffers, and the overall costs of providing health care rise. We need to abandon our historical emphasis on coverage limited to hospitalization, end-stage cures, and triage in favor of an outlook that emphasizes prevention. Any health care financing proposal should focus on providing preventive and primary care.

No Deductibles or Copayments

Private insurance and Medicare generally require patients to pay deductibles and copayments as health care cost-containment mechanisms.[70] The theory is that if a third-party insurer fully reimburses, creating "free" medical care, people will request expensive, perhaps unnecessary, services and thereby increase the overall costs of medical care. These arguments, while plausible in theory, fail in fact. It is usually the physician—not the insured—who decides which tests will be run, which procedures will be performed, and when a patient will be hospitalized.[71] Studies indicate that copayments and deductibles do not discourage the use or reduce the cost of acute or inpatient care. They do, however, discourage the use of routine preventive services[72] and increase the administrative costs of delivering health care.[73]

Copayments may actually increase the overall cost of medical care for the poor. Poor people lack sufficient disposable income to afford deductibles and copayments. After paying for food and shelter, even those whose incomes are 200 percent to 250 percent of the federal poverty level have little or no income left to pay for health care.[74] Copayments and deductibles cause the poor to delay getting needed medical care. In the long run, medical costs increase when care is delayed until conditions become emergencies that require more extensive and expensive treatment.[75]

Any reformulated financing system that seeks to improve America's health must recognize the long-term health benefits and cost savings that result from treating people early and preventing disease from progressing. Instead of cost-sharing programs, we need to create incentives to encourage people to use preventive care programs and to obtain early medical care.

Cost Containment

The present debate on health care financing focuses on the need to contain costs. Appropriate cost containment is, of course, essential. Without it, we will squander the financial resources to provide universal health care coverage. Many forms of cost containment—elimination of unnecessary or ineffective treatments, health care planning, coordination of capital expenditures, and bulk purchasing arrangements, for example—facilitate cost-effective delivery of medical care. However, other cost-containment mechanisms—restrictive eligibility levels, unrealistic cost-sharing requirements, low provider reimbursement levels, and some managed care systems—can limit minority, and particularly poor minority, access to necessary health care.[76]

Two popular cost-containment strategies—managed competition and managed care—present particular risks for low-income, minority patients. Managed competition encourages providers to deliver care through managed care organizations similar to health maintenance organizations.[77] Case management systems require patients to obtain care from a case manager, usually a primary care physician, who contracts with the insurer to deliver primary care services and to make referrals to specialists and hospitals. Both managed care organizations and case management plans attempt to save costs by paying providers prospectively on a per-patient basis, regardless of the actual cost of care. Under traditional fee-for-service medical payment, the provider is paid for each service provided and has no financial incentive to forgo additional, expensive treatment, since each additional service is reimbursed. Prospective payment systems, by paying a set amount for each patient treated regardless of the type or number of services provided, create a financial incentive for physicians to minimize costs and to use services more efficiently.[78]

However, prospective payment systems can also reduce health care access for minorities. Prospective payment systems can create physician incentives to treat only those patients likely to be profitable, given the prospective reimbursement rate, and patients who need less medical treatment are more profitable patients under a prospective payment system. Since blacks have more health problems than whites and the poor are sicker than the middle class, poor, minority, inner-city residents need more health services than do white, middle-class residents. A prospective payment system that pays the same prospective rate for all patients may cause providers to exclude those who are sicker—people of color and those who are poor.

Even when providers treat poor, minority patients, prospective reimbursement systems still may limit access to necessary medical care. Unrealistically low per capita reimbursement levels can create incentives for doctors to minimize costs by forgoing necessary as well as unnecessary treatment. Rather than totally excluding minority patients, providers simply may provide them with less medical care than their conditions require. The effect on minorities and poor patients can be devastating.[79]

While case management systems and managed competition plans offer promise for both controlling costs and improving the delivery of health care, any system that seeks to insure the poor and minorities through a prospective payment strategy must take into account variations in health status and index provider reimbursement to health status. Payments must reflect accurately the costs of treating high-risk groups like urban minorities. Otherwise, these cost-containment strategies will further reduce access to health care for poor minority urban dwellers.

Universal health care financing alone, even a plan that provides routine and preventive health care at competitive reimbursement rates with no co-payments or deductibles, will not solve the inner city's health care crisis or improve the health of inner-city blacks. Inner-city dwellers have greater and special health care needs: higher rates of environmental diseases, mental illness, and alcohol and drug abuse. AIDS and tuberculosis are epidemic in the inner city. The infant mortality rate in America's inner cities is higher than that in most Third-world countries. At the same time, there is a dearth of providers in the inner city. Private hospitals have "run away" to the suburbs; private doctors have chosen to practice in the suburbs. Universal health care financing, without other structural changes, simply will freeze the present inequities into America's health care system without improving the health of urban minorities. Improving America's health requires programs to attract providers to the inner city, to enforce vigorously existing civil rights laws to combat discrimination in providing health care services, and to develop new health care delivery systems that meet the needs of those who continue to dwell in the inner city.

Attracting Providers

The inner city needs hospitals, outpatient facilities, and primary care physicians, dentists, and other health care professionals. Health policy needs not only new strategies for financing health care, but also to attract providers back into the inner city. Private hospitals abandoned the inner city because their base of insured patients left before them, but universal health care financing, even with competitive reimbursement policies, will improve only marginally the shortage of inner-city health care providers. Comparable and competitive health care reimbursement for services provided to inner-city residents might create a financial incentive that slows the outward migration of hospitals from the inner city, but equal reimbursement alone will not be enough to attract *new* institutional providers.

Health planning is needed to complement competitive financing. Health planning programs assess the need for capital expenditures. As a prerequisite to building or expanding, health care facilities must obtain a certificate of need from the appropriate state agency. Health planning agencies can deny certificates of need to hospitals that seek to leave the city, where facilities are needed, and relocate in suburban areas that have sufficient medical services. Planning agencies can also encourage new hospitals and outpatient clinics to locate in the inner city and other areas that need providers.

In the late 1980s the federal government ended its financial support for state health planning activities. Although strapped for money to continue their programs, most states have maintained some sort of state planning programs, often on a reduced basis.[80] Federal support for health planning activities should be reestablished.

Doctors and other health care professionals need incentives to locate in the inner city. Currently, doctors have no economic incentive to practice in cities. It is impossible, in any practical sense, to produce so many physicians that a given area becomes super-saturated with care so that physicians will relocate elsewhere for economic reasons. A doctor can maintain a thriving practice almost anywhere;[81] so when faced with a choice, most doctors, like other middle- and upper-middle-class Americans, choose to live in suburban and smaller urban areas. Like others, they are drawn by good housing and schools, easy access to shopping, and cultural attractions.[82]

From the average doctor's perspective, inner-city minority patients are less desirable patients to treat. Because they lack education, such patients may not understand the need for, or be able to afford, preventive care. They may not know how or appreciate the need to follow their doctor's instructions. Because of their socioeconomic status, they are sicker when they seek care and thus more difficult to cure. Cultural differences often make communication difficult.

Because of these factors, strategies in addition to universal health care financing are necessary to attract health care professionals into the inner city.[83] Medical education scholarship and loan forgiveness programs have shown some success in attracting health care providers into medically underserved areas; such programs need to be reinstituted and generously funded. From 1972 to 1987 the National Health Service Corps Program provided grants and scholarships to medical students who agreed to work in medically underserved areas following completion of their training.[84] The program attracted 13,600 young doctors as well as many dentists, nurses, and other health professionals into rural and inner-city areas. In 1985 alone the program placed 1,500 doctors in community health centers in poor communities. When the federal government abolished the program in the late 1980s, poor communities were unable to replace the National Health Service Corps doctors they lost.[85]

Yet incentives to practice in the inner city need to be structured carefully to assure that the health professionals they attract are sensitive to their patients' cultures. Unwilling, hostile doctors on a short, one-year tour of duty in the ghetto will not help. In fact, such doctors can inflict tremendous harm. Medical school admissions policies should seek explicitly to attract and train doctors sensitive to the needs of minorities and poor people.

One way to do this is to recruit minority health professionals. Black doctors are more likely to practice in poor, urban areas with high minority populations than are white doctors, and consequently more often treat minority and poor patients.[86] Sadly, while African-Americans make up 12 percent of our population, they represent only 3 percent of our doctors.[87]

A concerted effort to attract and train African American and other minority doctors is therefore needed. Additional programs, such as the Disadvantaged Minority Health Improvement Act of 1990, aimed specifically at increasing the number of minority health care professionals, would help.[88] Minority health care providers are likely not only to be sensitive to the needs of minority patients but also to educate their fellow doctors about minorities' needs.

Civil Rights Enforcement

Even when blacks are able to find geographically accessible private health services, lingering discrimination limits available medical services.[89] Prior to the passage of the 1964 Civil Rights Act, health care providers openly discriminated against blacks. Most hospitals excluded black patients and black physicians altogether.[90] Health care discrimination is no longer illuminated by WHITE ONLY signs, but apparently race-neutral policies often operate disproportionately against minorities, setting up barriers that exclude them from health care.

For example, many hospitals admit only patients who have a treating physician with admitting privileges.[91] Other hospitals require substantial deposits before a patient will be treated in the emergency room or admitted for inpatient care.[92] Increasingly, hospitals and doctors refuse to deliver babies for mothers who have not received a minimum amount of prenatal care.[93] Many doctors refuse to treat Medicaid patients. While most hospitals participate in the Medicaid program, many explicitly cap the number of Medicaid patients they will treat. Others use a variety of mechanisms to exclude Medicaid patients.[94] Each of these policies operates to exclude a disproportionately large number of minorities. Each may foreclose access to health care in inner cities.

Even when poor minorities find a hospital that will treat them, they often receive segregated treatment. Prior to the passage of the 1964 Civil Rights Act, hospitals that admitted blacks segregated them in separate wards with black physicians and support staff.[95] Although this blatant discrimination has ended, many hospitals continue to separate poor blacks by assigning Medicaid and uninsured patients, who are disproportionately black, to one area of the facility while assigning privately insured patients, who are disproportionately white, to other areas.

America also operates a dual system of long-term care. Licensed nursing homes, primarily funded by the Medicaid program, serve whites. Substandard boarding homes, for which Medicaid does not pay, serve blacks.[96] Nursing homes are the most segregated publicly licensed health care facilities in America.[97] Elderly blacks have more health problems and are more likely to be disabled than elderly whites, with a correspondingly greater need for nursing home care.[98] Yet, even after controlling for income, elderly blacks have considerably lower rates of nursing home use.[99] Indeed, blacks make up 23 percent of the elderly population and 29 percent of the Medicaid-eligible population but comprise only 10 percent of the Medicaid intermediate care nursing home patients and only 9 percent of Medicaid skilled nursing facility patients.[100]

Much of the discrepancy in black and white use of nursing homes results from the ability of nursing homes to control the number of beds certified for Medicaid payment. Many nursing homes will not accept Medicaid patients, other than continuing care for private-pay residents who exhaust their resources and become eligible for Medicaid. Such patients are generally white rather than black, because blacks are more likely to be poor and without the private resources initially to finance nursing home care.[101]

In the language of civil rights laws, much racial discrimination in health care results from facially neutral policies that have a disproportionate adverse impact. The policies are "facially neutral" because they do not mention race specifically. Indeed, they may not have been enacted with the subjective intent of discriminating on the basis of race. Nevertheless, their impact is disproportionate because they hit poor minorities harder than whites. Their effect is especially adverse in the health care context because such exclusionary policies can be deadly.

Congress passed Title VI of the 1964 Civil Rights Act[102] to ensure that federal money could not be used to support segregated health care facilities.[103] Title VI prohibits programs and activities receiving federal financial assistance, including hospitals and nursing homes, from discriminating on the basis of race.[104] Title VI's implementing regulations prohibit facially neutral policies and practices that have a disproportionate adverse impact on minorities, even in the absence of intentional discrimination.[105] They also require recipients of federal funds to take affirmative action to overcome the effects of prior discrimination,[106] prohibit recipients from subjecting individuals to separate or segregated treatment on the basis of race,[107] and prohibit recipient hospitals and other institutions from establishing facility locations with discriminatory effects.[108]

Nevertheless, Title VI so far has proved fairly ineffective in ending the health care discrimination caused by the myriad of policies that disproportionately exclude minorities. Almost from the enactment of Title VI, the health care enforcement efforts of the Office of Civil Rights (OCR) of the Department of Health and Human Services[109] have been criticized as inadequate.[110] Under the Reagan and Bush administrations, OCR almost completely abdicated its Title VI health care monitoring and enforcement responsibilities. Little has changed under the Clinton administration.

The most fundamental shortcoming of OCR's Title VI enforcement effort is that it has produced no data for evaluating Title VI compliance. Although underutilization of health services by minorities has been documented repeatedly,[111] the only study analyzing Title VI compliance by health facilities was conducted by the General Accounting Office in 1971 and 1972.[112] Although required by federal law to collect data necessary to effective enforcement, OCR has never attempted to compile this data on a regular basis.[113]

Data compilation and analysis are necessary for OCR to identify patterns of discrimination. OCR has relied for too long on individual complaints as a means of enforcement. More far-reaching results and more economical enforcement can be achieved through systematic compliance reviews than from investigation of isolated individual complaints.

Specific definitions of prohibited discrimination and acceptable remedial action are also needed. The Title VI regulations specifying prohibited practices are quite vague.[114] While they identify broad categories of prohibited activities, these regulations do not identify specific health care provider policies and practices that impermissibly exclude and segregate minorities.[115]

Although federal law requires the Department of Health and Human Services to supplement the general Title VI regulations with more specific guidelines for each program to which it extends assistance,[116] the agency

has not issued guidelines for health care providers. These guidelines are intended to provide the specificity lacking in the general Title VI regulations,
to give examples of prohibited practices in the context of particular programs, to outline required or suggested remedial action, and to provide
data collection requirements for health care providers.[117] Guidelines are
needed for hospitals, nursing homes, and state Medicaid agencies, as well
as managed care organizations.[118] They would give providers better notice
of specific activities that violate Title VI, thereby streamlining OCR enforcement activities.

Race discrimination in American health care remains a silent, pervasive
problem. OCR must begin collecting and examining data so that the nature
of the problem can be better understood and appropriate corrective measures identified. The health of poor minorities will not be improved until
we fully identify their problems.

Alternative Providers

Since the American health care system is market driven, it generally delivers care in a manner that meets the needs of those with money and insurance to purchase care—middle-class, white patients with education,
motivation, and time.[119] The inner-city minority poor have different needs
and different health problems. Many of the health problems that disproportionately affect black central-city dwellers, such as high infant mortality, tuberculosis, and drug and alcohol abuse, result from a combination
of problems: substandard housing, bad sanitation, poor diet, the lack of
health care providers, and the lack of transportation, money, and the motivation to seek help. To improve health, delivery systems must make care
accessible despite the realities of life in the inner city. This requires education, outreach, and coordination.

Preventive health care begins with education. Sex education can help
teach teenagers to avoid unwanted pregnancies and sexually transmitted
diseases. Community- and school-based health education can assist in reducing drug, tobacco, and alcohol use—all of which play a role in illness.
These and other reeducation efforts must form an integral part of any reformed health care delivery program to teach avoidance of sexually transmitted diseases and unwanted pregnancies.[120]

Outreach programs have demonstrated their effectiveness in improving
prenatal and infant health. Norfolk, Virginia, for example, has a Perinatal
Lay Home Visitor program in which women from low-income communities are trained to provide information and referrals to their neighbors and
friends.[121] The program has strengthened the community by creating a

source of information within it, and after four years the number of low-birth-weight babies relative to all births in Norfolk was halved.[122] Other effective prenatal care programs send nurses and social workers into poor areas to seek out pregnant women and provide on-the-scene prenatal care and other services ranging from transportation to food stamps.[123]

These same outreach concepts should be applied to other health problems, such as teenage pregnancy, hypertension, AIDS, and tuberculosis.[124] Nurses and other providers who go into the community can provide information and care to community members who might otherwise never see a health care provider.

Similarly, health care can be delivered in new locations if it is provided where people gather, rather than requiring people to come to care. Travel time and expense create barriers to access for inner-city minorities who are more likely than whites to be dependent on public transportation.[125] Transportation problems can be alleviated by taking care to people rather than expecting people to get to the sources of care. A few schools are already providing children a full range of preventive and primary health services through school-based clinics.[126] This same concept of taking health care to people can work in other settings. Adults can be seen at their workplaces. Both children and adults can be treated at their churches, historically important gathering places for African Americans.

Unfortunately, targeting the poor with unique providers runs the risk that these providers will become separate and, by definition, unequal providers. Most doctors and hospitals who serve only the poor do, in fact, provide unequal care.[127] In some cases the differences may be only cosmetic or accommodational, such as no decorator-designed offices, or longer waiting times. In other instances the differences mean less than optimal service—fewer prescription drugs, less staff, and less care. Under our present system, inequality results from inadequate financing. Even with financing reforms, however, the poor do not have the political clout to demand better services, and programs designed specifically for their needs may slip inexorably into providing substandard care.

Some separate, specialized providers, however, have a long tradition of providing high-quality care to the poor. Migrant health centers and Indian health services, in rural areas, and community health centers, in more urban areas, provide models for health care programs to meet the needs of poor, inner-city blacks.[128] More than 90 percent of the patients served by community health centers have family incomes less than twice the poverty level, 42.7 percent of the patients are uninsured, and 42.9 percent are publicly insured by Medicaid or Medicare.[129] Sixty percent of all community health center patients are minorities, and the patients served by urban centers are 37 percent black and 27.2 percent Hispanic.[130] On the whole, community health centers operating in urban areas provide better health care at lower cost than do private physicians or public hospitals.[131]

The superior health care provided by community health centers reflects a philosophy broader than that of most health care providers. Community health centers operate on the belief that many of the most serious medical problems of the poor have multiple underpinnings, all of which must be treated if medical care is to be effective. Health center services at community health centers are offered by multidisciplinary teams and extend beyond traditional medical care to include environmental, preventive, and social services.[132]

To meet the health care needs of minority inner-city residents more adequately, we must confront and accept the realities of life in the inner city. We need to develop systems that deliver comprehensive services and primary care—systems that focus on preventing illness, early intervention, continuity of care, and coordinated service delivery, as well as better integration of medical and social services.

Conclusion

Even with all these changes in place—universal financing, an adequate number of providers, the elimination of discrimination, and the creation of new delivery systems—access to health care probably can increase the health status of inner-city minorities only slightly. Race, geography, and economic status all play a role in the poor health status of disadvantaged minorities.

How can we best improve the health of inner-city minorities? We must not only provide better access to health care, we also need jobs that pay a living wage and programs that deliver decent housing, adequate sanitation, and good education. Only when all of these strategies coalesce will we make real headway in the fight to improve the health of poor minorities in the inner city.

Notes

1. See Ellen Bilofsky, "Mammography for the Poor: The Deadly Waiting Game," *Health/PAC Bulletin*, Summer 1991, 31.

2. I use the terms *African American* and *black* interchangeably because both terms currently are used, particularly in the African American community. I use *black* because the term does not designate merely a skin color but a specific cultural group.

3. See Mark Schlesinger, "Paying the Price: Medical Care, Minorities, and the Newly Competitive Health Care System," *Milbank Quarterly* 65 (Supp. 1987): 270, 275–77.

4. Schlesinger, "Paying the Price," 270, citing Woodrow Jones Jr. and Mitchell F. Rice, "Black Health Care: An Overview," in *Health Care Issues in Black America: Policies, Problems, and Prospects*, ed. Woodrow Jones Jr. and Mitchell F. Rice (New York: Greenwood Press, 1987), 3, 7.

5. Schlesinger, "Paying the Price," 275.

6. Cassandra Q. Butts, "The Color of Money: Barriers to Access to Private Health Care Facilities for African-Americans," *Clearinghouse Review* 26 (1992): 159, 160, citing Population Reference Bureau, *African Americans in the 1990s* (Washington, D.C.: Population Reference Bureau, 1991), 443.

7. Schlesinger, "Paying the Price," 276, citing Howard E. Freeman et al., "Americans Report on Their Access to Health Care," *Health Affairs* 6 (1987): 13–14.

8. John Charles Boger and Michael A. Stegman, "Race and the American City: The Kerner Commission in Retrospect, an Introduction," *North Carolina Law Review* 71 (1993): 1289, 1329.

9. Schlesinger, "Paying the Price," 276.

10. Ibid.

11. See prepared statement by Sylvia Drew Ivie, "Ending Discrimination in Health Care: A Dream Deferred," in *Civil Rights Issues in Health Care Delivery*, by U.S. Commission on Civil Rights (Washington, D.C.: U.S. Commission on Civil Rights, 1980): 282, 295.

12. Ibid.

13. Ibid.

14. *Nightline*, "America's Infant Mortality Crisis" (American Broadcasting Company broadcast, April 12, 1990), available in LEXIS, Nexis Library, transcripts file.

15. U.S. National Commission on Acquired Immune Deficiency Syndrome, *The Challenge of HIV/AIDS in Communities of Color* (Washington, D.C.: U.S. National Commission on Acquired Immune Deficiency Syndrome, 1992), 3–11.

16. See ibid., 4. As of September 1992, African Americans and Hispanics accounted for 46.4 percent of AIDS cases in the United States. While African Americans compose only 11.8 percent of the U.S. population, they comprise 29.7 percent of AIDS cases. Hispanics constitute only 9 percent of the population, but they account for 16.7 percent of AIDS cases.

17. Ibid., 9–10.

18. Ibid., 8–9.

19. David A. Kindig, Hormoz Movassaghi, Nancy Cross Dunham, Daniel I. Zwick, and Charles M. Taylor, "Trends in Physician Availability in Ten Urban Areas from 1963 to 1980," *Inquiry* 24 (1987): 136, 140. This compares with a 27 percent decline in nonpoverty areas of the cities.

20. Henry T. Greely, "The Future of the American Health Care System: An Introduction to the Health Symposium," *Stanford Law and Policy Review* 3 (1991): 16, 17.

21. See Boger and Stegman, "Race and the American City," 1330.

22. Ibid.

23. See Hal Straus and Mike King, "In Sickness and in Wealth, Urban Decay, Rural Waste," *Atlanta Constitution*, September 30, 1990.

24. See Kathleen Brockel and Stephanie J. Morrison, "The Age of AIDS: Will Zell Miller Supply the Funds to Save Lives?," *Atlanta Constitution*, December 1, 1992.

25. Butts, "Color of Money," 161, citing U.S. Congress, House or Senate, Committee on Energy and Commerce, Subcommittee on Health and the Environment, *The Closure of Hospitals That Serve the Poor: Implications for Health Planning*, 97th Cong., 2d sess., 1982 (statement of Alan Sager, Ph.D.).

26. Ivie, "Ending Discrimination in Health Care," 297–300.

27. Butts, "Color of Money," 161.

28. Schlesinger, "Paying the Price," 276.

29. Straus and King, "In Sickness and in Wealth."

30. See Curtis Rist, "Cuts Force Long Waits," *Newsday*, October 14, 1992, 31.

31. Ivie, "Ending Discrimination in Health Care," 305–6.

32. Ibid.

33. Butts, "Color of Money," 160.

34. See Straus and King, "In Sickness and in Wealth," A11.

35. Greely, "Future of the American Health Care System," 17.

36. In Detroit, a city with an infant mortality rate twice the national average, it takes eight weeks to get a prenatal care appointment at public Hutzel Hospital (*Nightline*).

37. See Straus and King, "In Sickness and in Wealth."

38. Gunnar Myrdal, *An American Dilemma: The Negro Problem and Modern Democracy* (New York: Harper, 1944), 174.

39. "From the standpoint of health, poverty means deficient diets, lack of medical care, inadequate shelter and clothing, and often lack of awareness of potential health needs. . . . Negro households generally are larger, requiring greater non-medical expenses for each household, and leaving less money for meeting medical expenses. . . . In addition, fewer doctors, dentists, and medical facilities are conveniently available to Negroes—especially to poor families—than to most whites. This is a result both of geographic concentration of doctors in higher income areas in large cities and of discrimination against Negroes by doctors and hospitals" (Kerner Commission, *Report of the National Advisory Commission on Civil Disorders* [New York: Bantam Books, 1968], 271–72).

40. Marianne Foley and Glen R. Johnson, "Health Care of Blacks in American Inner Cities," in Jones and Rice, *Health Care Issues in Black America*, 211, 212.

41. Ibid., 214.

42. Celinda Lake, "Health Care: The Issue of the Nineties," *Yale Law and Policy Review* 10 (1993): 211, 213.

43. See Robert L. Schwartz, "Medicaid Reform through Setting Health Care Priorities," *St. Louis University Law Journal* 35 (1991): 837, 840. Schwartz notes that Medicaid generally receives the largest or the second largest appropriation in a state.

44. *BNA Medicare Report*, December 16, 1994, 48.

45. Madison Powers, "Efficiency, Autonomy, and Communal Value in Health Care," *Yale Law and Policy Review* 10 (1992): 316.

46. "Employer mandate" proposals require businesses to provide private health insurance benefits to their employees. "Play-or-pay" proposals give employers an option. They either have to provide private insurance to their employees or pay a payroll tax for the government to use in setting up a public program to cover uninsured employees. Employers receive a tax credit for the amount they spend on health insurance benefits up to the limits of the health insurance payroll tax level.

47. See Powers, "Efficiency, Autonomy, and Communal Value," 317.

48. Ibid., 318.

49. *Medicare & Medicaid Guide* (CCH), no. 728, December 30, 1992, 3.

50. Ibid.

51. See nn. 12–13, above, and accompanying text.

52. Michele Melden, Michael Parks, and Laura Rosenthal, "Health-Care Rights of the Poor: An Introduction," *District of Columbia Law Review* 1 (1992): 181, 189.

53. Historically the federal categories were limited to those individuals receiving cash welfare payments—parents and children who, because one parent is absent, disabled, or unemployed, receive Aid to Families with Dependent Children, and the aged, blind, and disabled who receive Supplemental Security Income. In the 1980s, federal law extended Medicaid coverage to pregnant women, infants, and children through age five whose incomes are less than 133 percent of the federal poverty level, and to children age six and older born after September 30, 1983, whose family income does not exceed the federal poverty level. While federal law requires states to provide Medicaid to these groups, states may also provide Medicaid to people who fit these categories—the disabled, pregnant women, children, and one-parent families—but who have incomes somewhat higher than required by welfare eligibility guidelines. See Melden et al., "Health-Care Rights of the Poor," 181–84.

Medicaid is a joint federal-state program. It is state administered and state designed, but each state's program must conform to numerous federal statutory and regulatory requirements in order for the state to receive federal matching funds. See 42 U.S.C. § 1396 et seq. (1988). In 1989 Medicaid spent $62.4 billion, with $35.5 billion coming from the federal government and $26.9 billion from the states (Rand E. Rosenblatt, "Statutory Interpretation and Distributive Justice: Medicaid Hospital Reimbursement and the Debate over Public Choice," *St. Louis University Law Journal* 35 [1991]: 793, n. 1, citing Katherine R. Levit and Mark S. Freeland, "National Medical Care Spending," *Health Affairs* 7 [1988]: 124, 131 [Exhibit 5]).

54. Melden et al., "Health-Care Rights of the Poor," 188–89.

55. Ibid., 188.

56. Geraldine Dallek, "Health Care for America's Poor: Separate and Unequal," *Clearinghouse Review* 20 (1986): 361, 363.

57. Schwartz, "Medicaid Reform through Setting Health Care Priorities," 841.

58. 2 U.S.C. § 1395dd (1988).

59. See nn. 20–38, above, and accompanying text.

60. See n. 6, above, and accompanying text.

61. George J. Annas, Sylvia A. Law, Rand E. Rosenblatt, and Kenneth R. Wing, *American Health Law* (Boston: Little, Brown, 1990), 44.

62. The Congressional Budget Office estimated the costs of universal health in-

surance under both a market reform plan and a single-payer plan. It concluded that under either plan, persons presently uninsured could be insured without a dramatic increase in national spending on health care. Using 1989 statistics with the market reform plan, the change in national health care spending would range from a decrease of $17.3 billion to an increase of $30 billion, depending on the assumptions used. Under the single-payer model, the change in spending would range from a decrease of $58.1 billion to an increase of $7.4 billion (*Medicare & Medicaid Guide* [CCH], no. 682, January 17, 1992, 1–2).

63. See text accompanying n. 69 (discussing prenatal care).

64. See Jane Perkins, "The Effects of Health Care Cost Containment on the Poor: An Overview," *Clearinghouse Review* 19 (1985): 831, 833 (discussing a recent Medicare program and noting that the program "represents an important departure from the previous, cost-based, 'fee-for-service' system").

65. Hal Straus and Mike King, "Holes in the Safety Net," *Atlanta Constitution*, October 2, 1990.

66. Bilofsky, "Mammography for the Poor,". 31.

67. Stuart Guterman and Allen Dobson, "Impact of the Medicare Prospective Payment System for Hospitals," *Health Care Financing Review* 7 (1986): 97, 103–12.

68. In a Washington, D.C., study, one-fourth of the hospital admissions of indigent patients arriving at emergency rooms could have been avoided had the patient previously had access to primary care. For those with chronic diseases, the percentage of avoidable admissions rose to 45 percent (Stephan G. Lynn, "National Alert: Gridlock in the Emergency Department," *Health/PAC Bulletin*, Spring 1991, 5, 7).

69. Pregnant women who do not receive prenatal care are three times more likely to have low-weight babies (Gerald David Jaynes and Robin M. Williams Jr., eds., *A Common Destiny: Blacks and American Society* [Washington, D.C.: National Academy Press, 1989], 402).

70. Deductibles are a set amount the patient must pay for medical care before insurers will begin paying. Copayments are either a set amount or a percentage of each charge the patient must pay even when insurance pays the remainder of the cost.

71. William Hsiao and Nancy L. Kelly, "Restructuring Medicare Benefits," in *Conference on the Future of Medicare, Subcommittee on Health of the House Committee on Ways and Means*, 98th Cong., 1st sess., 1983, 35, 37.

72. Annas et al., *American Health Law*, 795; Alan Sager, "Health Care for All and Not a Penny More: A Proposal," *Health/PAC Bulletin*, Spring 1988, 21, 22.

73. Sager, "Health Care for All," 22.

74. Melden et al., "Health-Care Rights of the Poor," 188.

75. See Perkins, "Effects of Health Care Cost Containment on the Poor," 841.

76. See Laura M. Rosenthal, "Health Coverage for the Uninsured: A Primer for Legal Services Advocates," *Clearinghouse Review* 24 (1991): 1250, 1259.

77. *Managed care* is a term originally coined by Stanford economist Alain Enthoven. The phrase now represents a variety of approaches, all of which basically rely on health care providers and insurance companies to contain increases in

health care costs. For example, one aspect of managed competition assists small purchasers of health care, such as small businesses, to join together in larger purchasing units to negotiate lower insurance premiums.

78. Medicare employs such a system, paying hospitals a set amount based on the patient's primary and secondary diagnosis, regardless of the actual cost of providing care to the individual patients.

79. Medicaid case management plans, while varying in their organizational designs and locations, have encountered remarkably similar problems regarding access to necessary specialized medical services. In Louisville, Kentucky, there was a 40 percent drop in the number of specialty visits by patients during the first nine months of the program (Perkins, "Effects of Health Care Cost Containment on the Poor," 840).

80. James B. Simpson, "State Certificate-of-Need Programs: The Current Status," *American Journal of Public Health* 75 (1985): 1225–27.

81. U.S. House of Representatives, 94th Cong., 1st sess., 1976, H. Rept. 266.

82. Ibid.

83. We need to do more than just create incentives for city practices. Inner cities need doctors trained in primary care—family practice, obstetrics/gynecology, internal medicine, and general pediatrics. Federal and state loan forgiveness programs, grants, and scholarship programs should be developed and expanded to encourage doctors to enter primary care practice in lieu of more specialized areas of care. Physician reimbursement also needs to be reformed so that primary care physicians are reimbursed at levels comparable to those of paid specialists. See Physician Payment Review Commission, *Annual Report to Congress*, April 29, 1989, reprinted in *Medicare & Medicaid Guide* (CHH), par. 37,830 (1989-2 Transfer Binder), 19,832.

84. Annas et al., *American Health Law*, 721.

85. Ibid., 722.

86. Jaynes and Williams, *Common Destiny*, 436–37.

87. Christina Kent, "Minority Medical Schools: Rough Sailing Ahead," *Medicine & Health*, June 17, 1991.

88. See Disadvantaged Minority Health Improvement Act of 1990, Pub. L. No. 101-527, § 782(b)(2), 104 Stat. 2311, 2318.

89. See also Butts, "Color of Money," 160 n. 4 (noting that African Americans comprised only 3 percent of the physicians in the United States in 1991).

90. See U.S. Congress, House, 88th Cong., 2d sess., 1964, H. Rept. 914, pt. 1, 25–26, pt. 2, 24, reprinted in 1964 U.S.C.C.A.N. 2391, 2511.

91. See Stan Dorn, Michael A. Dowell, and Jane Perkins, "Anti-Discrimination Provisions and Health Care Access: New Slants on Old Approaches," *Clearinghouse Review* 20 (1986): 439, 441. Since blacks and other minorities often do not have private physicians (see Jaynes and Williams, *Common Destiny*, 431), this policy tends to exclude minority patients.

92. See Dorn et al., "Anti-Discrimination Provisions," 441. Thirty-four percent of blacks, Hispanics, and Native Americans have incomes below the poverty line, compared with only 11 percent of whites. Because minorities are more likely to be

poor, they are also more likely to be turned away by hospitals because they cannot pay in advance. See U.S. Department of Health and Human Services, *Report of the Secretary's Task Force on Black and Minority Health* (Executive Summary) (Washington, D.C.: U.S. Department of Health and Human Services, 1985), 189.

93. See Dorn et al., "Anti-Discrimination Provisions," 441. While 80 percent of white women receive prenatal care during the first trimester of pregnancy, only 60 percent of black women receive such care. The percentages for Hispanic and Native American women are even lower. See U.S. Department of Health and Human Services, *Report of the Secretary's Task Force,* 188.

94. For example, a requirement that all patients have a treating physician with admitting privileges excludes most Medicaid patients when the only physicians with admitting privileges take few, if any, Medicaid patients. See Dorn et al., "Anti-Discrimination Provisions," 441. Because Medicaid patients include a disproportionate number of minorities, anti-Medicaid policies effectively block minority access. See Dallek, "Health Care for America's Poor," 365–71. Still other hospital business policies create language and cultural barriers. These include a lack of interpreters, inadequate translations of signs and forms, and preadmission inquiries into a patient's citizenship, national origin, or immigration status. See Dorn et al., "Anti-Discrimination Provisions," 441.

95. See U.S. Congress, House, 88th Cong., 2d sess., 1964, H. Rept. 914, pt. 1, 25–26, pt. 2, 24, reprinted in 1964 U.S.C.C.A.N. 2391, 2511.

96. See *Linton v. Tennessee Commissioner of Health and Environment,* 779 F. Supp. 925, 932 (M.D. Tenn., 1990), aff'd, 923 F.2d 855 (6th Cir. 1990); David B. Smith, "Population Ecology and the Racial Integration of Hospitals and Nursing Homes in the United States," *Milbank Quarterly* 68 (1990): 561; "HCFA Statistics Demonstrate Racial Disparities in Medicaid Coverage for Nursing Home Care," *National Senior Citizens Law Center,* October 11, 1991, 1.

97. Butts, "Color of Money," 163–64 (citing David B. Smith, "Discrimination in Access to Nursing Homes in Pennsylvania" [unpublished manuscript, 1991], 5–7). Private nursing homes are more segregated than state-run homes, and when blacks do manage to gain access to nursing homes, they are more likely to reside in nursing homes that have been cited as substandard. See Ibid., 164.

98. Ibid.

99. Ibid.

100. See Vernellia R. Randall, "Racist Health Care: Reforming an Unjust Health Care System to Meet the Needs of African Americans," *Health Matrix* 3 (1994): 155–56 (citing NAACP Legal Defense and Education Fund, Inc., "An African American Health Care Agenda: Strategies for Reforming an Unjust System, Racial Disparities in Medicaid Coverage for Nursing Home Care" [1991]). See also David Barton Smith "The Racial Integration of Health Facilities," *Journal of Health Politics, Policy and Law* 18 (1993): 850.

101. Other nursing home discrimination is more blatant, such as racial steering—social workers identify certain facilities by race and then make referrals based on race. Since nursing homes control the number of beds certified for Medicaid payment, if a home wishes to accept a white Medicaid patient, another Med-

icaid bed can be certified; if the home does not wish to accept a black Medicaid patient, the home simply may refuse to certify another bed for Medicaid payment even though it has bed space available.

102. Pub. L. No. 88-352, 78 Stat. 252 (codified at 42 U.S.C. §§ 2000d–2000d-4 [1982]).

103. See *Congressional Record*, 110:1658 (1964).

104. See 42 U.S.C. §§ 2000d–2000d-4 (1988). The operative section of Title VI provides, "No person in the United States shall, on the ground of race, color, or national origin, be excluded from participation in, be denied the benefits of, or be subjected to discrimination under any program or activity receiving Federal financial assistance" (ibid., § 2000d).

Both Medicaid and Medicare are considered federal financial assistance for purposes of Title VI. See *Frazier v. Board of Trustee of North West Mississippi Regional Medical Center*, 765 F.2d 1278, 1289 (5th Cir. 1985), cert. denied, 476 U.S. 1142 (1986); *United States v. Baylor University Medical Center*, 736 F.2d 1039, 1046 (5th Cir. 1984), cert. denied, 469 U.S. 1189 (1985). The Title VI regulations list a number of other health grant programs that also provide federal financial assistance, including health planning grants, loans and loan guarantees for hospitals and other medical facilities, Maternal and Child Health grants, and Crippled Children's Services grants. See 45 C.F.R. § 80 app. A (1983).

105. These regulations prohibit "criteria or methods of administration which have the effect of subjecting individuals to discrimination because of their race, color, or national origin, or have the effect of defeating or substantially impairing accomplishment of the objectives of the program as respect individuals of a particular race, color, or national origin" (45 C.F.R. § 80.3[b][1][vii][2] [1989]). For a discussion of case law upholding the validity of this regulation, see Sidney D. Watson, "Reinvigorating Title VI: Defending Health Care Discrimination—It Shouldn't Be So Easy," *Fordham Law Review* 58 (1990): 939, 948–55.

106. 5 C.F.R. § 80.3(b)(6)(i) (1989).

107. Ibid., §§ 80.3(b)(1)(iii), 80.5(a).

108. Ibid., § 80.3(b)(3).

109. Prior to the establishment of the Department of Health and Human Services, health care civil rights enforcement was the responsibility of the Department of Health, Education, and Welfare.

110. See Ken Wing, "Title VI and Health Facilities: Forms without Substance," *Hastings Law Journal* 30 (1978): 137, 138.

111. See Institute of Medicine, *Health Care in a Context of Civil Rights* (Washington, D.C.: National Academy Press, 1981), 36–39 (documenting racial disparities in those seeking professional health care); Jaynes and Williams, *Common Destiny*, 431 (reporting that "blacks are twice as likely as whites to be without a regular source of medical care"); U.S. Department of Health and Human Services, *Report of the Secretary's Task Force* (comparing use of health professionals by black, Hispanic, and white populations); Paula Diehr, Diane P. Martin, Kurt F. Price, Linda Friedlander, William C. Richardson, and Donald C. Riedel, "Use of Ambulatory Care Services in Three Provider Plans: Interaction between Patient Characteristics

and Plans," *American Journal of Public Health* 74 (1984): 47, 49 (noting that differences in rate of physician visitation cannot be attributed to differences in ability to pay, because when middle-class whites and blacks are compared, blacks still use doctors significantly less than whites); Freeman et al., "Americans Report on Their Access to Health Care," 12–18 (recognizing that although blacks are generally in worse health than whites, they receive fewer services from doctors and hospitals).

112. See Wing, "Title VI and Health Facilities," 176–79. OCR also conducted a limited survey of hospital compliance in 1981.

113. Federal regulations require OCR to "provide for the collection of data and information from applicants for and recipients of federal assistance sufficient to permit effective enforcement of title VI" (28 C.F.R. § 42.406[a] [1992]) and also require "timely, complete and accurate compliance reports at such times, and in such form and containing such information, as the responsible Department official or his designee may determine to be necessary to enable him to ascertain whether the recipient has complied or is complying with this part. For example, recipients should have available for the Department racial and ethnic data showing the extent to which members of minority groups are beneficiaries of and participants in federally assisted programs" (45 C.F.R. § 80.6[b] [1991]).

114. See 45 C.F.R. § 80.3(b) (1991). For example, the regulations prohibit "criteria or methods of administration which have the effect of subjecting individuals to discrimination because of their race, color, or national origin, or have the effect of defeating or substantially impairing accomplishment of the objectives of the program as respect individuals of a particular race, color, or national origin" (ibid., § 80.3[b][1][vii][2]); see also nn. 96–101, above, and accompanying text (discussing the segregated system of health care in the United States).

The Title VI regulations are purposely broad and general. Soon after passage of Title VI, a task force was created to develop consistent, enforceable Title VI regulations for all federal agencies charged with enforcing the act. Ultimately the task force drafted twenty-two sets of regulations, all of which follow the same basic pattern and describe prohibited discrimination in the same general terms (Linda R. Singer, Janet R. Altman, John W. Blouch, Robert A. W. Boraks, Richard O. Cunningham, Gordon W. Hatheway Jr., Carol P. Kelley, Robert Lewis, and Daniel C. Schwartz, "Comment: Title VI of the Civil Rights Act of 1964: Implementation and Impact," *George Washington Law Review* 36 [1968]: 824, 846).

115. Wing, "Title VI and Health Facilities," 185–86.

116. 8 C.F.R. § 42.404–.405 (1992).

117. OCR issued guidelines for hospitals and nursing homes in 1966, prior to promulgation of the federal regulation. These guidelines, however, unlike other Title VI guidelines, were written in letter form by a former director of OCR and were merely circulated by OCR staff. They have never been issued through a formal administrative rulemaking process and are not published in the Code of Federal Regulations. Their legal status is difficult to define. See Wing, "Title VI and Health Facilities," 155 n. 68.

118. Ivie, "Ending Discrimination in Health Care," 312–13.

119. The market has been responsive to changes in middle-class lifestyle. Al-

though the house call has gone the way of the carrier pigeon, "urgent care centers" now provide evening and weekend primary care for those with money or insurance to pay for care.

120. See Jaynes and Williams, *Common Destiny*, 413–15.

121. *Nightline* (interviewing Margaret Konefal, Resource Mothers Program).

122. Ibid.

123. See Mike King and Hal Straus, "Whitney Kelly: Roadside Birth, Burial," *Atlanta Constitution*, October 1, 1990.

124. See Jaynes and Williams, *Common Destiny*, 440.

125. See Ivie, "Ending Discrimination in Health Care," 298.

126. See, for example, Gail Hagans, "Adding Health to Education," *Atlanta Constitution*, January 10, 1995.

127. Dallek, "Health Care for America's Poor," 369.

128. Sara Rosenbaum and Anne Dievler, "A Literature Review of the Community and Migrant Health Center Programs" (unpublished report, George Washington University Center for Health Policy Research, 1992), 2–13, 35. Community Health Centers operate as community-based providers. Each center is controlled by a local board of directors, a majority of whom are low-income patients of the center. The centers seek to train and hire low-income people from their service area in clerical and paraprofessional health care positions (ibid., 9).

129. Ibid., 14.

130. Ibid.

131. Gary D. Sandefur, "Blacks, Hispanics, American Indians, and Poverty—and What Worked," in *Quiet Riots: Race and Poverty in the United States: The Kerner Report Twenty Years Later*, ed. Fred R. Harris and Roger W. Wilkins (New York: Pantheon, 1988): 46, 68; Rosenbaum and Dievler, "Community and Migrant Health Center Programs," 17. Rosenbaum and Dievler reviewed fifty-five studies of the effectiveness of community and migrant health centers. Measured in terms of program outcomes, outputs, or contributions to the community, they found health centers to have a positive effect on patients, the appropriate utilization of health care services, the contribution of health centers to the community, and the efficiency of services delivered by health centers.

132. Rosenbaum and Dievler, "Community and Migrant Health Center Programs," 8.

William L. Taylor

The Continuing Struggle for Equal Educational Opportunity

Introduction

In March 1968 the Kerner Commission issued its report warning of the dangers of a nation divided into two societies, separate and unequal.[1] Less than a month later Dr. Martin Luther King Jr., the most eloquent and persuasive voice in the effort to break down walls of segregation and establish racial and social justice, was dead, struck down by an assassin.

Ever since, those who have sought to keep Dr. King's dream alive have had to wage a difficult battle to overcome new rationalizations for the existence of inequality and increasing calls for separatism. It is striking, in reviewing the quarter-century since the Kerner Commission Report and King's death, to realize that almost all of the major legislative and judicial initiatives that have sustained the effort for equal opportunity—the Supreme Court's decision in *Brown v. Board of Education*,[2] the Civil Rights Act of 1964,[3] the Head Start program,[4] the Elementary and Secondary Education Act of 1965,[5] and other elements of the War on Poverty—were in place *before* the events of 1968. Several other important policy events occurred in the five years that followed. The Civil Rights Act of 1968 barred discriminatory practices in housing.[6] In the *Green*, *Swann* and *Keyes* cases, the Supreme Court prescribed effective school desegregation remedies in the South and set forth rules against intentional segregation in the school districts of the North and West.[7] Further, the Court's unanimous decision in *Griggs v. Duke Power Co.* broadly interpreted fair employment law to bar unintentional job discrimination practices that harmed minorities and could not be justified by business necessity.[8]

Over the last two decades the most notable positive developments have been the extensions of civil rights guarantees to members of other groups that have been victims of systemic discrimination, particularly women, Hispanic Americans, and people with disabilities,[9] and the legislative restoration of rights and remedies that had been limited by the restrictive interpretation of civil rights laws on the part of an increasingly conservative

Supreme Court.[10] Only in rare instances did statutes or court decisions seek to remove barriers to equal opportunity faced by the minority poor.

In a sense then, the drive for equality has been running on empty for almost twenty years, sustained by laws and moral authority whose origins are remembered only dimly by millions of Americans. Although the officially sanctioned caste system that replaced slavery in the South and the sanction of racism throughout the nation are gone, racial animosity and fear still lie just beneath the surface and have erupted in recent years with frightening regularity in places such as Miami, Florida; Forsythe County, Georgia; and Howard Beach, Bensonhurst, and Crown Heights in New York City. The 1992 uprisings in Los Angeles, spurred by the acquittal of police officers accused of beating Rodney King, had a far more devastating impact in the minority community than the counterpart events in the 1960s that gave rise to the Kerner Commission.[11]

More daunting still are the combination of race and poverty and the seemingly impersonal structures and institutions that deprive the minority poor of opportunities for advancement. When the Kerner Commission wrote its report in 1968, many cities were still great centers of employment and economic activity. Now, employment and economic wealth have shifted to suburbs and to "new cities," while the movement of middle-class citizens (including the minority middle class) out of cities has intensified.[12] The growing wealth of suburbs has brought superior education and other public services, often financed without great difficulty out of local property and income taxes. For the minority poor in cities, services have declined. Today, cities face a form of triage in seeking to meet a host of health, social, housing, and education needs.[13]

In the face of these difficulties, what is surprising is not that the movement for equality has faltered but that it persists, and that people continue to move out of the shadows of deprivation and discrimination to lead productive lives. The longevity of the movement is a tribute to the power of the idea of equality embodied in the Fourteenth Amendment and to a recognition during the 1960s that implementation required affirmative effort to undo the effects of past wrongs. The staying power of the movement is due also to the ability of so many black citizens to use *Brown* and other decisions as a means of empowering themselves through education, employment, and political and community action, and to the fact that race continues to be the central dilemma of our society and to gnaw at the American psyche.

This essay focuses almost exclusively on developments in the area of public education as they have affected the life chances of minority children born into poverty. Such an emphasis risks a justified charge of oversimplification, since the interconnectedness of policies in employment, economic development, housing, education, health, and nutrition is beyond dispute. Moreover, it may be said that a narrow focus on education ignores the ghetto's "institutionalized pathology"—the phrase used by Kenneth Clark to describe symptoms of social disorder and disease associated with isolated low-income minority areas.[14]

Without underestimating the difficulty of the challenge of providing opportunity for those who are most deprived in this society and the need for multifaceted approaches to removing barriers to opportunity, this essay suggests that part of the problem in confronting contemporary issues of inequality is our tendency to immobilize ourselves by making the issues excessively complex. This essay demonstrates that intervening early in a child's life through child development and public education has been shown to be a highly promising initiative even if taken independently of other efforts. What is most needed in the lives of many children is the caring and sustained attention of adults in a setting conducive to learning, with enough outside support to assure that the child is healthy and that there will be some positive reinforcement for the education effort outside the school.

Educational Progress since the
Kerner Commission Report

If the major educational initiatives of the 1960s—school desegregation, Head Start, and federal aid to economically disadvantaged students in elementary schools—had not resulted in progress, either because they were not implemented widely or because they were not effective, there would be true cause for despair and for an active search for other approaches. This does not appear to be the case, however.

Striking evidence of progress is found in the performance of black children over the years on reading tests conducted by the National Assessment of Educational Progress (NAEP).[15] As analyzed by Marshall Smith and Jennifer O'Day, black children born in 1971 scored an average of 189 on NAEP reading tests when they were nine years old, 236 when they were thirteen, and 274 when they reached age seventeen in 1988; white children born in 1971 scored 221, 263, and 295 at the same junctures.[16] The authors conclude, "These are extraordinary data. By conservative estimate, they indicate a reduction in the gap between African American and White students over the past 20 years of roughly 50 percent when the students are 17 years old."[17]

Likewise, a 1994 study by the Rand Corporation analyzing and comparing standardized test scores and demographic statistics for teenagers in

1970 and 1990 concludes that American students made solid academic gains during the last twenty years and that, while white students' gains were about as great as the researchers had expected, the scores of black and Latino students increased by about two-thirds more than predicted. While the study notes that a significant gap remains, it asserts that "the dramatically rising test scores of minorities have resulted in a significant closing of the achievement gap between minority and nonminority youth and less inequality in educational outcomes." [18]

While social scientists and educators are cautious in ascribing causes for these trends, there is evidence that school desegregation has played an important role. Black elementary students in the Southeast recorded the greatest gains in reading on the NAEP assessments during the 1970s. [19] These gains occurred during the period when school desegregation was occurring all across the region for the first time. The Rand researchers hypothesized that the greater test score increases they found for minority youth were the result of social programs beginning with the Great Society, and "changing public policies in the area of equal educational opportunity and increased public investment in schools." [20]

This strong indication of a link between desegregation and academic achievement is reinforced by case studies of particular communities that have undergone desegregation. The studies reveal that in most cases where courts have ordered desegregation and the process is begun early in a child's school career, the achievement levels of minority students have risen modestly or significantly while those of white students have remained unchanged or have risen slightly. [21]

Apart from results on achievement tests, in the longer term black children attending desegregated schools are more likely to complete high school, to enroll in and graduate from four-year desegregated colleges, and to major in subjects nontraditional for minority students—subjects that lead to more remunerative jobs and professions. [22] In addition, low-income black children who receive a desegregated education have a good chance to avoid situations and behavior (such as teenage pregnancy or hostile encounters with the police) that blight the prospects of many of their peers. [23]

As with school desegregation, studies have shown positive results stemming from the availability of preschool child development programs for young children. [24] The most widely noted study tracked the lives of disadvantaged children who had participated in the Perry program for three- and four-year-olds in the 1960s in Ypsilanti, Michigan. [25] The children were matched with a demographically similar group of disadvantaged children who did not participate in the program. By age nineteen, the children displayed striking differences. Those who had participated scored higher on standardized tests, were more likely to graduate from high school, to be enrolled in college, or to be employed, and were more likely to have avoided various forms of pathology.[26] Similar conclusions have emerged from a longitudinal evaluation of a New York State program and from evaluations of other early childhood initiatives.[27]

Certainly there are caveats about preschool education, and continuing areas of debate. Experts such as Sharon Kagan and Edward Zigler caution that dangers exist in subjecting young children to rigid academics before they are ready to learn and that preschool programs must be developmentally appropriate for each age group.[28] Others note that many of the early gains for children can be dissipated through inattention to their needs as they move through public school.[29] On the central point, however—that where investments are made in preschool programs for economically disadvantaged children, many more children are likely to succeed in school—there is little, if any, disagreement.

Positive results emerge also from evaluations of the effectiveness of Chapter 1, the federal program established in 1965 to assist economically disadvantaged students, which was restored in the 1994 reauthorization of the Elementary and Secondary Education Act to its original designation, "Title I."[30] Here, too, there are caveats. While Chapter 1 assistance has helped many minority and disadvantaged youngsters master basic skills, the program has had far less success in equipping them with the higher-order skills of reasoning and analysis that are needed in today's job market.[31]

Nevertheless, a general consensus has developed concerning the important initiatives to be taken on behalf of disadvantaged children. For example, commentators have recognized the need to focus intensively on developing the reading skills of children in the primary grades.[32] Examinations of reading programs that have proved successful have identified a number of common elements: instruction of children in small groups; tutoring by teachers, aides, parent volunteers, or older children; a systematic plan for instruction; frequent assessments of student progress; and modifications of groupings or instructional content to meet the needs identified.[33]

Barriers to Educational Progress

If the picture painted in the preceding section is accurate—if significant numbers of minority and economically disadvantaged students have indeed made progress in the public schools over the past two decades, and if educators can identify the initiatives (desegregation, preschool programs, specific education services) that have helped produce this progress—then why does the outlook appear so grim? Why are we confronted with evidence of dysfunctional public schools and massive educational failure, particularly in the nation's largest cities? If particular initiatives have worked elsewhere, why can they not be employed in the largest population centers of the nation?

The answers have to do with structural barriers that have intensified racial and socioeconomic isolation and that have produced self-perpetuating engines of inequality, and also with an apparent lack of national will to remove these barriers.

Desegregation and Concentrations of Poverty

The research on desegregation shows that black children achieve the most substantial gains when they participate in metropolitan or countywide plans, plans that often entail substantial busing.[34] These plans ordinarily achieve substantial desegregation across socioeconomic status as well as racial lines. The findings, consistent with research going back to the 1960s, demonstrate that disadvantaged children fare better in schools and classrooms comprised largely of advantaged students rather than in classroom settings isolated with others of the same background.[35]

Desegregation across socioeconomic class lines is beneficial to disadvantaged children for many reasons, including the fact that in schools consisting largely of advantaged children, the norms set by the parents and teachers, and by students themselves, ordinarily are high. Academic success and advancement to college are expected or demanded of advantaged children. When schools fall short on teacher quality or resources, middle-class parents are practiced in wielding influence to bring about change. Youngsters from low-income families in these schools also may acquire the practical know-how and contacts they can use to enter middle-class society.[36]

The great barrier to implementing desegregation plans that combine racial and socioeconomic diversity is that school districts in the metropolitan areas of the North and West increasingly have become divided by race and economic status, and the Supreme Court has treated school district lines as almost impenetrable borders.[37]

In most of the South, school districts are countywide and encompass both central cities and suburbs. Thus, systemwide desegregation plans in places such as Charlotte-Mecklenburg, North Carolina, and Tampa-Hillsborough, Florida, have achieved diversity that has led to educational gains, and the South has become far more desegregated than the North.[38]

The trouble is that the big cities where the barriers exist contain a very substantial proportion of the minority population of the nation. Gary Orfield and Sean Reardon report that the nation's twenty-five largest urban school districts served 27 percent of all African American students in the nation, 30 percent of all Hispanic students, but only 3 percent of white students.[39]

While many central cities became more diverse ethnically with new Latino and Asian American arrivals, the cities also grew poorer. As the Kerner Commission Report predicted, middle-class whites continued to move to the suburbs, and in several metropolitan areas—Washington, D.C., and Cleveland, Ohio, among them—there was substantial suburbanization of black middle-class families as well.[40]

The result has been a tremendous intensification of poverty in inner cities. At the end of the 1980s, in the 100 largest cities in the country, nearly three children in ten were poor.[41] In 31 of these cities at least half the black children were poor; in 19 at least half of the Native American children were poor; and in 10, at least half the Hispanic children were poor.[42] Between 1970 and 1980, at a time when the overall population of the largest cities was declining, the number of poor people living in census tracts defined as poverty areas (more than 20 percent poor residents) rose from 3.4 million to 4.4 million, and those living in high-poverty areas (more than 40 percent poor residents) increased by 66 percent.[43] These trends continued throughout the 1980s.[44]

With this background, consider the implications of Figure 1, which shows the link between concentrations of poverty in public schools and performance on tests of basic reading skills.[45]

As Figure 1 indicates, 30 percent of poor children in schools with a high proportion of students living in poverty score in the lowest tenth percentile, three times the percentage of those who are in schools with a low proportion of students living in poverty. In contrast, 30 percent of poor children who are in low-poverty schools score in the top half, compared with only 16 percent who are in high-poverty schools.[46]

This is not to say that it is impossible for children to do well in minority schools with high concentrations of poor children. In Cincinnati, where the author serves as counsel for black students in a school desegregation case, one school, the Hoffman school, in which almost 100 percent of the children are black and eligible for free or reduced-priced lunches, has made remarkable progress in reading, math, and science over the last eight years, moving from one of the lowest-scoring elementary schools in the city to the middle range. The key appears to lie in a remarkable principal who has been able to assemble a talented, hard-working group of teachers and to involve parents in their children's education.

The odds are stacked against schools with high concentrations of poverty, however. The reasons are not hard to discern. In the words of Orfield and Reardon, "These schools have to cope with homelessness, severe health and nutrition problems, an atmosphere of gangs and violence threatening children and few jobs for high school graduates."[47]

In fact, Smith and O'Day report that *nonpoor* students attending schools

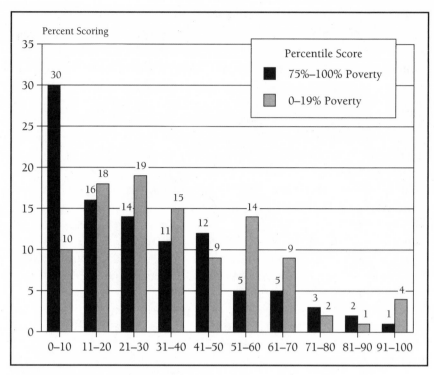

Source: Abt Associates, Prospects.

Figure 1. Distribution of CTBS Reading Scores of Chapter 1 Participants in Poor and Nonpoor Schools (defined by free/reduced-price lunch eligibility)

with high concentrations of poverty perform less well on the average than poor children attending nonpoor schools.[48] In light of these facts and considering that it is the minority poor, not the white poor, who find themselves in schools with high concentrations of poverty, the surprise is not that the gap between black and white students' school performance has not closed more, but that it has closed as much as it has.

The Growth of Educational Resource Inequality

The odds against poor minority students achieving success in high-poverty schools might be decreased if these schools had adequate funds to invest in the services that are calculated best to improve student performance.[49] As noted, over the past fifteen years, researchers have become increasingly confident about which services and initiatives make a difference in the education of poor and minority students. They have stressed the importance of preschool child development programs, reading programs in the early grades, reducing class sizes to pupil-to-teacher ratios of fifteen to one or better, providing counseling and identifying needs for health and social services, working to involve parents in the education of their children, finding and retaining teachers who are experienced and teaching in their fields of certification, and having a broad and challenging curriculum.

All of this requires money. Yet, throughout the nation, the ability of localities to finance schools depends to a great extent on their property wealth, the main source of funding for many schools. The inequities that this system creates—largely between cities and rural areas, on the one hand, and suburbs on the other—were serious enough to spawn a great deal of litigation beginning in the late 1960s and 1970s. The Supreme Court's five-to-four decision in *San Antonio Independent School District v. Rodriguez* rejected claims of a denial of equal protection and brought such federal suits to an end.[50]

Over the past twenty years many large central cities have lost substantial numbers of manufacturing jobs. At the same time they have faced growing demands for health and social services as well as education. Suburbs, meanwhile, have become major centers of employment, and the personal and property wealth of their inhabitants has increased greatly.

What this has meant in practice is well illustrated by the situation in the Texas districts that gave rise to *Rodriguez*. The prototype districts cited by the Court in *Rodriguez* were the property-poor Edgewood district with a 96 percent minority population and property with an assessed valuation of $5,960 per pupil, and the property-rich Alamo district with a 19 percent minority population and an assessed valuation of $49,000 per pupil.[51] When state and federal contributions, which had an equalizing effect, were included, Edgewood spent $356 per child with a much greater tax effort than Alamo, which spent $594.[52]

By the end of the 1980s, when a second challenge to the Texas school finance system was litigated in state court, Edgewood had increased from $5,960 per student in property wealth to $38,854, while Alamo had gone from $49,000 per child to $570,000.[53] The 100 wealthiest districts in the state expended an average of $7,233 per child, while the 100 poorest, with a much greater tax effort, managed to spend $2,978 per child.[54] The Texas experience was replicated in many other states—even in those such as Illinois, where the state had made efforts to reduce inequity by contributing a larger share of the educational budget of local school districts.[55]

In practice this means that many of the property-poor districts with the largest numbers of minority and poor children simply cannot afford to furnish the services that educators now consider vital. For example, Texas funds a highly regarded preschool program, but participation by local districts has required matching funds and adequate facilities, requirements that have operated to exclude a number of the poorest districts.[56] Similarly, when the property-poor city of Baltimore, Maryland, is compared with wealthier districts, particularly suburban Baltimore County and Montgomery County, the city suffers in its ability to provide reading programs in the early grades, small class sizes, counselors, school psychologists, and nurses.[57]

Most important, property-poor central-city districts lack the ability that suburbs have to attract and retain teachers with advanced degrees who teach in their areas of certification. In fact, even students in high-ability classes in disadvantaged schools often do not have highly qualified teachers. More low-track suburban students have certified math and science teachers than do high-track students in disadvantaged minority schools.[58] Along with disparities in the quality of teaching come major inequalities in curriculum, both in the breadth of the course offerings and in the availability of advanced courses.[59]

These major inequalities are not addressed in any serious way by federal financial assistance to economically disadvantaged children. The federal policy of assisting economically disadvantaged children through the Chapter 1 program is based on the premise that state and local funds and services are "comparable," and that federal assistance is a supplement to address the special needs of disadvantaged youngsters. State and local fiscal inequities render this notion of a level playing field a fiction, however. Some property-rich districts routinely provide a wide range of services, including preschools, elementary counselors, and social workers, while property-poor districts must rely on Chapter 1 funds to furnish only a fraction of these services. Because the services are interdependent and work most effectively only in combination, and since Chapter 1 provides only $6 of every $100 for public education, state fiscal inequity frustrates the objectives of federal policy.[60]

School Choice and Vouchers

In the continuing and simmering debate over public education, other educational reform proposals have been placed on the table—most prominently initiatives to provide parents with additional options, either within or outside the public school system. While a full examination of these initiatives is beyond the scope of this essay, some brief observations on the likely impact of such measures on the effort to secure equal educational opportunity are in order.

Among the initiatives most commonly proposed are (1) expanded public school choice for parents through devices such as magnet schools, (2) the delegation to private companies of the task of managing some or all of the public schools of a district, and (3) the use of vouchers to give students access to private schools.

Magnet schools—schools with specialized curricular offerings (such as science magnets or schools of the performing arts) or with a particular educational methodology (such as the Montessori school approach)—have been employed increasingly over the past two decades as a means of both improving education and securing school desegregation. The appeal of magnets as a vehicle for desegregation is evident. Rather than simply reassigning students to schools, students and parents in a magnet system are given a choice of schools with special themes. While students may have to ride a bus to get to these schools, this is not regarded as forced busing. Yet, as long as school authorities are committed to juggle the choices made by parents to bring about racial balance at each school, desegregation objectives may be attained.[61]

Although few comprehensive studies are available, magnet schools often are reported to provide positive learning environments for minority and nonminority students alike.[62] The advantages of magnets may stem less from the particular themes of the schools than from the opportunities that they present for talented principals and school leaders to assemble teams of like-minded teachers and imbue them with a new sense of mission.

But while magnets may promote desegregation and other educational improvements, certain concerns remain.[63] Some observers fear that magnets, while promoting racial desegregation, may leave students isolated by socioeconomic status. Such isolation may occur because higher income families may be better informed about their magnet school options than poor families and more motivated to seek these special opportunities for their children, even when magnet schools are located outside their neighborhoods.[64] Efforts have been made in school desegregation decrees, however, to guard against this result—by establishing recruitment and counseling centers to engage in outreach efforts to parents, by locating magnets in all areas of a district, and by forswearing entrance requirements for students except in rare instances (for example, auditions for applicants to schools of performing arts).

Perhaps a greater danger is that the academic and programmatic success of some magnet schools may prompt their proponents to lose sight of their desegregation objectives.[65] Several years ago the Reagan administration proposed federal funding for "nonintegrated magnets"—which should be considered a contradiction in terms. While the initiative was not successful at the time, it would not be surprising to see it arise again.

In contrast to magnet proposals, privatization initiatives are less a means of expanding parental choice than an effort to achieve more effective and efficient operation of schools by contracting the provision of some or all school services out to private organizations. So, for example, Boston University has taken over the administration of the public schools of Chelsea, Massachusetts, and an organization called Educational Alternatives is running nine schools in Baltimore, Maryland, and has recently contracted to run the entire school system in Hartford, Connecticut.

Although little information exists on how to evaluate the success of such initiatives, these privatization arrangements—in theory, at least—may provide useful ways to cut through bureaucratic processes that make school operations more costly and prevent educational needs from being met on a timely basis.

It appears far too early, however, to determine whether such initiatives will result in improved educational opportunities for the minority poor. Since the contracting arrangements are not intended to be permanent, the answer may depend on what the contractors leave behind when they depart. For example, to the extent that the private groups institute strong programs for improving professional development in schools or districts, their efforts may yield dividends of long-term value in improved teaching and student achievement. Less substantive initiatives may yield little educational benefit and may dilute the accountability of public school authorities.

Finally, school voucher programs, which typically provide parents a fixed sum to enable them to enroll their children in private schools, are an educational "reform" that currently is gaining ground in certain policy circles. The two most frequent rationales advanced for such programs are that vouchers will stimulate the private sector, creating competitive pressures that will force public schools to make improvements, and that vouchers will give low-income parents choices that more affluent parents already have.

While the market rationale is dubious,[66] the equity rationale is deceptive. The notion that the poor will benefit from voucher proposals ignores the fact that vouchers are ordinarily not means-tested. Affluent families are eligible to receive funds on the same basis as poor families, and many well-off parents will no doubt use their vouchers to pay the tuition of children already attending private schools or to place them in such schools for the first time. Moreover, the subsidies involved may not cover the entire tuition costs of many private schools, and transportation costs—which are particularly important for the poor—may not be provided. Further, under most voucher proposals, private schools remain free to exclude students who may be difficult or costly to educate and to expel underperforming or misbehaving students, a luxury public schools do not have. Add to this the lack of access that low-income people may have to the knowledge that facilitates the exercise of informed choice, and the result may be a "creaming" process that leaves public schools more economically and racially isolated than before, with disproportionate numbers of students with special needs that are costly to meet. Meanwhile, by depleting the clientele for public education, voucher programs may sap the citizen support for tax levies that most school systems rely on to meet their fiscal needs.

No initiative advanced to benefit the least advantaged students in the nation should be discarded without careful study. But a critical question for any proposal should be what it will do to improve the educational environment for the mass of children locked in racial and economic isolation. By this measure, voucher proposals fall far short and may exacerbate an already grossly inequitable situation.

Conclusion

Two Supreme Court decisions, issued less than a year apart and both decided by a narrow five-to-four vote, thwarted the major legal campaigns for equal educational opportunity of the 1970s—*Milliken v. Bradley* (*Milliken I*), which frustrated the effort to secure metropolitan desegregation across school district boundaries, and *Rodriguez*, discussed above, which thwarted the effort to distribute public resources for education on a more rational, equitable basis. Neither decision, however, withstands careful analysis.[67] Indeed, *Milliken I*, in the words of the late Justice Thurgood Marshall, is "more a reflection of a perceived public mood that we have gone far enough in enforcing the Constitution's guarantee of equal justice than . . . the product of neutral principles of law."[68]

In the case of school desegregation, that perceived public mood undoubtedly incorporates racial fears of ancient vintage, particularly white fears of contact with people who are both nonwhite and poor. Continued racial and socioeconomic isolation allows fears and animosities to grow on all sides. In the case of inequities in educational resources, resistance to change appears to be fed by feelings of entitlement and privilege on the part of suburban residents. The public rebellion against New Jersey Governor Florio's 1990 fiscal reform effort to equalize expenditures through modest tax increases demonstrates how entrenched these feelings of entitlement truly are.

Although the Supreme Court, reflecting divisions in the nation as a whole, was divided closely in the 1970s on school desegregation and school finance reform, it has moved considerably to the right in the intervening years, and there is little prospect that it will reassert its historic role as protector of "discrete and insular minorities"[69] at any time in the foreseeable future. Rather, leadership will have to come from the political branches of government.

During the first two years of President Clinton's term, the administration's educational agenda met with some important successes. The Head Start program was expanded and improved. The Goals 2000: Educate America Act was passed to provide grants to states in return for education improvement plans and pledges to set high standards. The Elementary and Secondary Education Act was reauthorized by the Improving America's Schools Act of 1994, calling for high standards for *all* children, including children in poverty, and establishing accountability on the part of schools and school districts for assuring that students make progress toward these goals. The act also encourages whole-school reform, which has proved most effective in improving the performance of disadvantaged children in high-poverty schools, and devotes increased resources to professional development.[70]

Yet much remains to be done to protect the new reforms against the incursions of the new Congress (many of whose members believe that education should be treated almost exclusively as a local matter), to carry out the hard work of implementation, and to address equal opportunity concerns that have been neglected.

An agenda for educational opportunity is straightforward enough. Its elements should include the following:

1. Establishment by Congress of a right of disadvantaged children enrolled in schools that are not succeeding to transfer to schools—either in the students' district or in adjoining districts—that have a record of success, with transportation provided by the state where needed. Such an initiative would be a form of public school choice that would foster the goals of racial and socioeconomic desegregation and of holding schools accountable for the performance of students.[71]

2. Establishment by Congress of a requirement that each state be held responsible for assuring comparability in the provision of vital educational services in school districts and schools throughout the state. This initiative would translate into national policy the principles of equity established in state courts such as those in Texas, Kentucky, New Jersey, California, and Montana, among others.[72] Only by establishing such national policy can Congress assure that its expenditures truly will serve the purpose of providing special assistance for the needs of economically disadvantaged children.[73]

3. Full funding of the Head Start program so that it will serve all eligible three- and four-year-olds, rather than the three of every ten eligible children who are served currently. Full funding should include assistance to upgrade the quality of the programs and the training and salaries of teachers.

4. A major investment of funds available under Title I in the professional development of teachers. The investment should be accompanied by

a determined effort by President Clinton and other national leaders to make teaching a high status profession and to attract the most able people in the nation to its ranks.[74]

These four proposals by no means exhaust the list of initiatives necessary for educational reform that will benefit all children, including those who are most disadvantaged. The guiding principles of Goals 2000 and the Improving America's Schools Act—that all students can learn and that high standards should be established for all—must be internalized by educators and administrators across the nation and become an operating principle in schools where the assumptions today are quite the contrary. Standardized, norm-referenced tests that compare students only to each other should be replaced by assessments that measure what students actually know and can do. And states should be called on to identify the health and social service needs of students at an early age so that such impediments to learning can be removed.

However, the four initiatives outlined above do go to the heart of long-standing barriers to opportunity. To implement them will require some degree of sacrifice in the form of higher taxes. It also will require, in the words of President Clinton, "the courage to change" by accepting alterations in institutional arrangements that have been comfortable and advantageous to the affluent, much as people in the South ultimately had the courage to accept an end to the legalized caste system. The changes called for, however, do not demand a plunge into the unknown; each is undergirded by enough experience to demonstrate that it can work to the educational advantage of all children.

Over the past decade, some have staked their hopes for educational reform programs on economic self-interest. Business leaders, recognizing the lagging productivity of the economy and the changing character of the workforce, have called for major efforts to bolster the public schools and to invest in the education and training of minorities and disadvantaged youth. These efforts have yielded only modest results, however, and over-reliance on the goal of economic self-interest may be unwise, since business ultimately may fill its needs in other ways—by locating its operations abroad or by importing skilled manpower from other nations.

So, too, it may not be wise to stake one's hopes on public acceptance of the Kerner Commission's warning that continuation of present policies would lead to conflict and a reduction in personal freedom. The accuracy of that warning has been borne out in heightened concerns that many people feel about their personal security, in the abandonment of urban areas, and in the routine adoption of measures such as preventive detention that were controversial two decades ago. Yet many seem to adapt to these changes without great difficulty.

Ultimately, beyond these issues of economic self-interest and peace and good order, we may need to ask, as did the Kerner Commission, what kind of society we want for ourselves and for our children. In personal terms, the most relevant question may be whether, knowing that there are specific effective steps we can take to give a child born into poverty the care and attention that will enable the child to thrive, we can in good conscience fail to take those steps.

Notes

1. *Report of the National Advisory Commission on Civil Disorders* (Washington, D.C.: U.S. Government Printing Office, 1968).

2. *Brown v. Board of Education*, 347 U.S. 483 (1954).

3. Civil Rights Act of 1964, Pub. L. No. 88-352, 78 Stat. 241 (codified as amended at 28 U.S.C. § 1447, 42 U.S.C. §§ 1971, 1975, 2000 [1988]).

4. The Head Start program was created under the Economic Opportunity Act of 1964, Pub. L. No. 88-452, 78 Stat. 508. It was reauthorized under the Head Start Act of 1981, Pub. L. No. 97-35, 96 Stat. 499, and was amended by the Human Services Reauthorization Act of 1984, Pub. L. No. 98-558, 98 Stat. 73, and by the Human Services Amendments of 1994, Pub. L. No. 103-252, 108 Stat. 623 (codified as amended in scattered sections of 20 and 42 U.S.C.).

5. Elementary and Secondary Education Act of 1965, Pub. L. No. 89-10, 79 Stat. 27 (codified as amended in scattered sections of 20 U.S.C.). The act was reauthorized by the Augustus F. Hawkins–Robert T. Stafford Elementary and Secondary School Improvement Amendments of 1988, Pub. L. No. 100-297, 102 Stat. 130, and by the Improving America's Schools Act of 1994, Pub. L. No. 103-382, 108 Stat. 3518.

6. Civil Rights Act of 1968, Tit. VIII, § 812, Pub. L. No. 90-284, 82 Stat. 73, 88 (codified as amended at 42 U.S.C. § 3612).

7. *Keyes v. School District No. 1*, 413 U.S. 189, 207 (1973) (holding that intentionally segregative conduct by a school board in a "meaningful portion" of a school system would require a systemwide remedy); *Swann v. Charlotte-Mecklenburg Board of Education*, 402 U.S. 1, 28–29 (1971) (holding that a district court has broad discretion to administer remedies, including systemwide desegregation through the use of busing); *Green v. County School Board of New Kent County*, 391 U.S. 430, 438 (1968) (holding that a school board has an affirmative duty to eliminate a dual system "root and branch").

8. *Griggs v. Duke Power Co.*, 401 U.S. 424, 429–33 (1971).

9. See, for example, Title IX of the Education Amendments of 1972, 20 U.S.C. §§ 1681–88 (preventing discrimination on the basis of gender in educational programs receiving federal assistance); Americans with Disabilities Act of 1990, Pub. L. No. 101-336, 104 Stat. 327 (codified as amended in scattered sections of 42 and 47 U.S.C. and 29 U.S.C. § 706 [1988]) (providing equal access to persons with disabilities in the areas of employment, public accommodations, and transportation);

Franklin v. Gwinnett County Public Schools, 112 S.Ct. 1028, 1087 (1992) (holding that Title IX remedies include monetary damages); *Lau v. Nichols*, 414 U.S. 563, 564 (1974) (holding that non-English-speaking students are entitled to equal educational opportunity under 42 U.S.C. § 2000d [1988]).

10. See Voting Rights Act Amendments of 1982, Pub. L. No. 97-205, 96 Stat. 131 (codified as amended at 42 U.S.C. § 1973 [1988]) (reversing *City of Mobile v. Bolden*, 446 U.S. 55 [1980]); Civil Rights Act of 1991, Pub. L. No. 102-166, 105 Stat. 1071 (codified as amended in scattered sections of 2, 16, 29, and 42 U.S.C.A. [West Supp. 1991]) (reversing *Wards Cove Packing Co., Inc. v. Atonio*, 490 U.S. 642, 655–58 [1989] and other Supreme Court decisions in 1989); Civil Rights Restoration Act of 1988, Pub. L. No. 100-259, 102 Stat. 28 (codified as amended at 20 U.S.C.A. §§ 1681, 1687, 1688; 29 U.S.C.A. §§ 4, 706; 42 U.S.C.A. §§ 2000–4, 6107 [West Supp. 1991]) (reversing *Grove City College v. Bell*, 465 U.S. 555, 570–75 [1984]).

11. See Bill McAllister, "Call for a Panel on L.A. Unrest Echoes Historical Response," *Washington Post*, May 4, 1992; Carla Rivera, "Riots' Causes Same as in '60s, State Panel Says," *Los Angeles Times*, October 2, 1992.

12. See, for example, John F. Kain, "Housing Segregation, Negro Employment, and Metropolitan Decentralization," *Quarterly Journal of Economics* 82 (1968): 175 (addressing the link between discrimination and segregation in metropolitan housing markets and the distribution and level of minority employment); John F. Kain, "The Spatial Mismatch Hypothesis: Three Decades Later," *Housing Policy Debate* 3 (1992): 371 (reviewing research regarding the impact of housing discrimination on black employment); John D. Kasarda, "Urban Industrial Transition and the Underclass," *Annals of the American Academy of Political and Social Science* 501 (1989): 26 (noting the transformation of cities from "centers of production and distribution of goods to centers of administration, finance and information exchange," and a resulting loss in available blue-collar employment).

13. See, for example, *Abbott v. Burke*, 119 N.J. 287, 355–57, 575 A.2d 359, 393–94 (1990) (discussing the relationship between "municipal overburden" and substandard education in urban areas).

14. Kenneth B. Clark, *Dark Ghetto: Dilemmas of Social Power* (New York: Harper and Row, 1965), 81.

15. NAEP is a congressionally mandated project of the National Center for Education Statistics, U.S. Department of Education. The only ongoing, representative, national assessment of student achievement in various subject areas, it is widely regarded by educators to provide a more reliable indication of students' knowledge and skills than the norm-referenced standardized tests used by most school districts. See Title IV of the General Education Provisions Act, Pub. L. No. 90-247, 81 Stat. 814 (codified as amended at 20 U.S.C.A. §§ 1221–26, 1231–33 [West Supp. 1991]).

16. Marshall Smith and Jennifer O'Day, "Educational Equality: 1966 and Now," in *Spheres of Justice in Education: The 1990 American Education Finance Association Yearbook*, ed. Deborah A. Verstegen and James G. Ward (New York: Harper Business, 1991), 74. The analysis also revealed a reduction in the gap between blacks and whites in mathematics and science (ibid., 76). In addition, the reduc-

tion in racial disparities in reading was accompanied by a closing of the gap between children living in advantaged and disadvantaged homes (ibid., 78). Other analyses of NAEP data have reached similar conclusions. See Gerald David Jaynes and Robin H. Williams Jr., eds., *A Common Destiny: Blacks and American Society* (Washington, D.C.: National Academy Press, 1989) (discerning an "overall pattern . . . of improvement among blacks and decline in the difference between blacks and whites").

17. Smith and O'Day, "Educational Equality," 75. Unfortunately, NAEP data from 1990 show that progress has not been maintained and that there has been a widening of the gap between black and white and advantaged and disadvantaged students (Jennifer O'Day and Marshall Smith, "Systemic School Reform and Educational Opportunity," in *Designing Coherent Educational Policy: Improving the System*, ed. Susan Fuhrman [San Francisco: Josey-Bass, 1993], 250–312).

18. David W. Grissmer, Sheila Nataraj Kirby, Mark Berends, and Stephanie Williamson, *Student Achievement and the Changing American Family: An Executive Summary* (Santa Monica, Calif.: Rand, 1994), 22.

19. National Assessment of Educational Progress, *Three Assessments of Progress in Reading Performance, 1970–1980* (Denver: Education Commission of the States, 1981).

20. Grissmer et al., *Student Achievement and the Changing American Family*, 22–25. "Here's some evidence that some sets of educational and social policies developed over the past twenty-five years look like they're responsible for raising minority test scores," study leader David W. Grissmer was quoted as saying (Debra Viadero, "RAND Documents Academic Gains since 1970," *Education Week*, January 11, 1995, 9).

21. Robert L. Crain and Rita E. Mahard, "Minority Achievement: Policy Implications of Research," in *Effective School Desegregation: Equity, Quality, and Feasibility*, ed. Willis D. Hawley (Beverly Hills, Calif.: Sage, 1981), 55–84. The best progress appears to have occurred where desegregation began in kindergarten or first grade, and where comprehensive programs were instituted that included diagnostic and compensatory services for students and in-service training for teachers (ibid., 67–84).

See also Janet W. Schofield, *Black and White in School: Trust, Tension, or Tolerance?* (New York: Teachers College Press, 1989).

22. James McPartland and JoMills Braddock, "Going to College and Getting a Good Job: The Impact of Desegregation," in Hawley, *Effective School Desegregation*, 141–54; James McPartland, "Desegregation and Equity in Higher Education and Employment: Is Progress Related to the Desegregation of Elementary and Secondary Schools?," *Law and Contemporary Problems* 42 (Summer 1978): 108–32.

23. These findings emerge from a long-term study of some 700 low-income students in Hartford, Connecticut, one group of which began desegregation in the 1960s while the other remained in segregated schools. See "Study Finds Desegregation Is an Effective Social Tool," *New York Times*, September 17, 1985. See also Robert L. Crain and Jack Strauss, *School Desegregation and Black Occupational Attainments: Results from a Long-Term Experiment* (Baltimore: Johns Hopkins Univer-

sity, Center for Social Organization of Schools, 1985) (analyzing the impact of the Hartford desegregation program on occupational outcomes).

24. See, for example, Nancy L. Karweit, "Can Preschool Alone Prevent Early Reading Failure?," in *Preventing Early School Failure*, ed. Robert E. Slavin, Nancy L. Karweit, and Barbara A. Wasik (Boston: Allyn and Bacon, 1994), 58–77.

25. John R. Berrueta-Clement, Lawrence J. Schweinhart, W. Steven Barnett, Ann S. Epstein, and David P. Weinart, *Changed Lives: The Effects of the Perry Pre-School Program on Youths through Age Nineteen*, Monographs of the High/Scope Education Research Foundation, no. 8 (Ypsilanti, Mich.: High/Scope Press, 1984).

26. Ibid., 34–45, 57–60. See also Ford Foundation, *The Common Good: Social Welfare and the American Future* (New York: Ford Foundation, Project on Social Welfare and the American Future, 1989).

27. See Fern Marx and Michelle Seligson, *Public School Early Childhood Study: The State Survey* (New York: Bank Street College of Education, 1988), 3; Fred Hechinger, ed., *A Better Start: New Choices for Early Learning* (New York: Walker, 1986); Sharon Kagan and Edward Zigler, eds., *Early Schooling: The National Debate* (New Haven: Yale University Press, 1987).

Results of the Abecedarian Project at the University of North Carolina indicate that "preschool intervention plus follow-through can result in groups of very high-risk children scoring at or above the national average at the end of the primary grades" (Aletha C. Huston, ed., *Children in Poverty* [New York: Cambridge University Press, 1991], 206). While children from poor families are at high risk for school failure as early in their academic careers as first grade and at increased risk for grade retention, special education placement, and dropping out of school, "the Abecedarian experiment and several other carefully designed interventions demonstrate that early educational intervention can significantly benefit children at high risk for academic failure. . . . Results suggest that educational intervention should begin early in the life span and continue at least into the primary grades" (Huston, *Children in Poverty*, 218).

28. See Kagan and Zigler, *Early Schooling*.

29. Researchers note that the most effective preschool programs are those that last several years (extending into the elementary grades) and include family as well as school interventions (Edward Zigler and Sally J. Styfco, *Head Start and Beyond: A National Plan for Extended Childhood Intervention* [New Haven: Yale University Press, 1993]; Karweit, "Can Preschool Alone Prevent Early Reading Failure?").

30. See Office of Research and Improvement, Department of Education, *National Assessment of Chapter 1 (1986–87)*.

31. U.S. Department of Education, *National Assessment of the Chapter 1 Program: The Interim Report* (Washington, D.C.: U.S. Department of Education, 1992), 28–31; Commission on Chapter 1, *Making Schools Work for Children in Poverty* (Washington, D.C.: U.S. Government Printing Office, 1992). Many of the commission's recommendations for improving the Chapter 1 program were adopted by the 103d Congress in the 1994 reauthorization and were included in the new Improving America's Schools Act. The new Title I calls for challenging state standards for what students should know and be able to do and provides for accountability

through the use of valid and reliable, high-quality state assessments. Moreover, the 1994 act emphasizes strong and effective teaching and professional development and encourages innovation by allowing more funds to be used for schoolwide programs, effective programs to ease the transition from preschool to school, extended day programs, and efforts to increase parental participation.

32. See Robert E. Slavin and Nancy A. Madden, "What Works for Students at Risk: A Research Synthesis," *Educational Leadership*, February 1989, 4–13; Robert E. Slavin et al., "Preventing Early School Failure: What Works?," *Educational Leadership*, December 1992/January 1993.

33. Slavin and Madden, "What Works for Students at Risk"; Slavin et al., "Preventing Early School Failure." Research on the value of other initiatives including reduced class size, the availability of counseling and social services, and the need for experienced teachers teaching in their areas of expertise, is summarized in William L. Taylor and Dianne M. Piché, *Shortchanging Children: The Impact of Fiscal Inequity on the Education of Students at Risk*, Committee on Education and Labor, U.S. House of Representatives, 101st Cong., 2d sess., 1990, 25–32.

34. See Crain and Mahard, *Desegregation Plans That Raise Black Achievement*.

35. See Frederick Mosteller and Daniel P. Moynihan, eds., *On Equality of Educational Opportunity* (New York: Vintage, 1972); James S. Coleman, Ernest Q. Campbell, Carol J. Hobson, James McPartland, Alexander M. Mood, Frederic D. Weinfeld, and Robert L. York, *Equality of Educational Opportunity* (Washington, D.C.: U.S. Government Printing Office, 1966) (the Coleman Report), 21–33; U.S. Commission on Civil Rights, *Racial Isolation in the Public Schools* (Washington, D.C.: U.S. Government Printing Office, 1967).

An ideological debate over desegregation has been waged over the years, with some critics—both black and white—decrying busing on varying grounds. It is the author's experience, however, that parents tend to view the issue in very practical terms—that is, as a matter of whether desegregation in fact will occur and whether it will offer their children greater educational opportunity. In St. Louis, Missouri, for example, the author represented the NAACP and a class of black schoolchildren in helping to negotiate a 1983 settlement agreement under which black city children may attend predominantly white schools in suburban districts. Currently some 14,000 black students have been enrolled by their parents in these schools, presumably because their parents believe the schools offer greater educational opportunity.

36. Dennis W. Brogan, a perceptive observer of the American scene, once pointed out that schools are places students "instruct each other on how to live in America," noting the lessons in practical politics, organization, and social ease that are part of the informal curriculum of high schools (Brogan, *The American Character* [New York: Time, 1956], 174–75).

37. See, for example, *Milliken v. Bradley (Milliken I)*, 418 U.S. 717, 804 (1974) (holding that federal courts lack the power to impose interdistrict remedies for school segregation absent an interdistrict violation or interdistrict effects).

38. See Gary Orfield and Sean Reardon, "Working Papers: Race, Poverty, and Inequality," in *New Opportunities: Civil Rights at a Crossroads*, ed. Susan M. Liss and William L. Taylor (Washington, D.C.: Citizens Commission on Civil Rights, 1992),

17–32. In South Carolina, Georgia, Virginia, Florida, and North Carolina, for example, the percentage of black students in schools that were more than 50 percent white ranged from 40 to 60, whereas in New York, Illinois, and California, fewer than 25 percent of black students are in such desegregated schools (Gary Orfield, Franklin Monfort, and Melissa Aaron, *Status of School Desegregation, 1968–1986* [Alexandria, Va.: National School Boards Association, 1989], 10). In a handful of other situations, areawide desegregation has been obtained through litigation in which courts found that the nature of the government wrongs justified a different result from *Milliken I*. See, for example, *Liddell v. Missouri*, 731 F.2d 1294, 1305–9 (8th Cir. 1984) (St. Louis, Missouri); *United States v. Board of School Commissioners*, 637 F.2d 1101, 1112–14 (7th Cir. 1980), cert. denied, 449 U.S. 838 (1980) (Indianapolis, Indiana); *Evans v. Buchanan*, 555 F.2d 373 (3d Cir.), cert. denied, 434 U.S. 880 (1977) (Wilmington, Delaware).

39. Orfield and Reardon, "Working Papers," 17–18.

40. Norman Krumholz, "The Kerner Commission Twenty Years Later," in *The Metropolis in Black and White: Place, Power, and Polarization*, ed. George C. Galster and Edward W. Hill (New Brunswick, N.J.: Rutgers Center for Urban Policy Research, 1992), 25 (reporting that in 1960 about 2 percent of the black population in the Cleveland area lived in the suburbs, while by 1990 one-third did); Joel Garreau, "Candidates Take Note: It's a Mall World after All," *Washington Post*, weekly ed., August 10–16, 1992 (reporting that by 1992 a majority of all blacks in the Washington, D.C., metropolitan area lived in the suburbs).

41. Children's Defense Fund, *City Child Poverty Data from the 1990 Census* (Washington, D.C.: Children's Defense Fund, 1992).

42. Ibid.

43. Smith and O'Day, "Educational Equality," 63–64. In 1980 21 percent of the African American poor, 16 percent of the Hispanic American poor, but only 2 percent of all white poor in the U.S. lived in high-poverty areas (ibid., 64). To the extent that high concentrations of poverty present special problems, they affect minorities far more than whites (ibid.).

44. See, for example, Frank Clifford, "Rich-Poor Gulf Widens in State," *Los Angeles Times*, May 11, 1992; Shawn Hubler, "South L.A.'s Poverty Rate Worse Than '65," *Los Angeles Times*, May 11, 1992.

45. This figure appears in U.S. Department of Education, *National Assessment of the Chapter 1 Program*, 160 (citing Abt Associates, *Prospects: The Congressionally Mandated Study of Educational Growth and Opportunity* [Washington, D.C.: U.S. Department of Education, 1993]).

46. See, for example, Douglas S. Massey and Nancy A. Denton, *American Apartheid: Segregation and the Making of the Underclass* (Cambridge, Mass.: Harvard University Press, 1993). Massey and Denton assert that "because segregation concentrates any factor associated with poverty [and] because poverty is associated with poor educational performance[,] segregation also concentrates educational disadvantage. . . . By concentrating low-achieving students in certain schools, segregation creates a social context within which poor performance is standard and low expectations predominate" (ibid., 140–41).

47. Orfield and Reardon, "Working Papers," 4.

48. Smith and O'Day, "Educational Equality," 63.

49. See Robert E. Slavin, *Funding Inequities among Maryland School Districts: What Do They Mean in Practice?* (Baltimore: Johns Hopkins University, Center for Research on Effective Schooling for Disadvantaged Students, 1991), 7–8 (demonstrating that districts on the low end of per-pupil funding are also among the lowest in student performance).

Some economists have conducted studies suggesting that few educational expenditures yield significant results. See, for example, Eric A. Hanushek, "When School Finance 'Reform' May Not Be Good Policy," *Harvard Journal on Legislation* 28 (1991): 423–56. But the methodology and claims of such "production function" studies have been sharply challenged. See, for example, Rob Greenwald, Larry V. Hedges, and Richard D. Laine, "When Reinventing the Wheel Is Not Necessary: A Case Study in the Use of Meta-Analysis in Education Finance," *Journal of Education Finance* 20 (1994); Ronald F. Ferguson, "Paying for Public Education: New Evidence on How and Why Money Matters," *Harvard Journal on Legislation* 28 (1991): 465–98; Richard J. Murnane, "Interpreting the Evidence on 'Does Money Matter?'" *Harvard Journal on Legislation* 28 (1991): 457–64.

Moreover, the success of certain relatively costly interventions suggests that money can, indeed, make a difference. See, for example, Robert E. Slavin, "After the Victory: Making Funding Equity Make a Difference," *Theory into Practice* 33 (Spring 1994): 98–103; Slavin, *Funding Inequities among Maryland School Districts*, 26 ("Money itself will not solve all the problems, but it is equally true that any interventions that have a reasonable chance to solve problems will cost money").

50. *San Antonio Independent School District v. Rodriguez*, 411 U.S. 1 (1973). Although *Rodriguez* closed the federal courts as an avenue for school finance reform, cases continued to be brought in state courts based on state constitutional provisions guaranteeing equal protection or a "thorough and efficient" public education. As many as twenty-five states currently are being sued for allegedly operating unconstitutional school financing systems. In the last few years the second wave of state court litigation has achieved some notable successes. Courts in about one-third of the states have held that the state school systems violate their state constitutions. See *Harper v. Hunt*, Appendix to the Opinion of the Justices, 624 So.2d 107 (Ala. 1993); *Roosevelt Elementary School District v. Bishop*, 877 P.2d 806 (Ariz. 1994); *Dupree v. Alma School District*, 651 S.W.2d 90 (Ark. 1983); *Serrano v. Priest*, 487 P.2d 1241 (Cal. 1971); *Serrano v. Priest*, 557 P.2d 929 (Cal. 1977); *Horton v. Meskill*, 376 A.2d 359 (Conn. 1977); *Rose v. Council for Better Education, Inc.*, 790 S.W.2d 186 (Ky. 1989); *McDuffy v. Secretary of Education*, 615 N.E.2d 516 (Mass. 1993); *Committee for Educational Equality v. Missouri*, 878 S.W.2d 446 (Mo. 1993) (state's appeal dismissed on technicality in 1994); *Helena Elementary School District v. Montana*, 769 P.2d 684 (Mont. 1989), mod. 784 P.2d 412 (1990); *Claremont School District v. Governor*, 635 A.2d 1375 (N.H. 1993); *Robinson v. Cahill*, 303 A.2d 273 (N.J.), cert. denied sub nom. *Dickey v. Robinson*, 414 U.S. 976 (1973); *Abbott v. Burke*, 643 A.2d 575 (N.J. 1994); *DeRolph v. Corrigan*, 67 Ohio St. 3d 1477 (Ohio 1993); *City of Pawtucket v. Sundlin*, Nos. 91-8644, 91-0880, 92-0588 (Sup. Ct. March 14, 1994); *Tennessee Small School Systems v. McWherter*, 851 S.W.2d 139 (Tenn. 1993); *Edgewood Independent School District v. Kirby*, 777 S.W.2d 391 (Tex.

1989); *Seattle School District v. Washington*, 585 P.2d 71 (Wash. 1978); *Pauley v. Kelly*, 255 S.E.2d 859 (W.Va. 1979); *Washakie County School District v. Hershler*, 606 P.2d 310 (Wyo. 1980).

Findings of violations, of course, are often only a prelude to long struggles over remedy that take place in the legislative arena and that may delay effective relief for years. Such battles have taken place in New Jersey, Texas, West Virginia, and elsewhere.

51. *Rodriguez*, 411 U.S., 11–13.

52. Ibid.

53. See *Edgewood v. Kirby*, 777 S.W.2d at 392. In *Edgewood*, the Texas Supreme Court ultimately held that "children who live in poor districts and children who live in rich districts must be afforded a substantially equal opportunity to have access to educational funds" (ibid., 397).

54. Ibid., 393.

55. See G. Alan Hickrod and Lawrence E. Frank, "The Forgotten Illinois," in *Witnesses for the Prosecution: Policy Papers on Educational Finance, Governance, and Constitutionality in Illinois* (Normal: Illinois State University, 1989), 23–28.

56. Taylor and Piché, *Shortchanging Children*, 36.

57. Ibid., 37–39.

58. Jeannie Oakes, *Multiplying Inequalities: The Effects of Race, Social Class, and Tracking on Opportunities to Learn Mathematics and Science* (Santa Monica, Calif.: Rand, 1990), 62–67.

59. See, for examples, Oakes, *Multiplying Inequalities*, 26–45.

60. During the 1994 reauthorization process, some lawmakers and education groups spearheaded an effort to force or encourage states to equalize school funding and services from district to district. The effort met great resistance from congressional legislators—both Democratic and Republican—for whom school finance remains a state and local matter, and, ultimately, no interdistrict comparability requirement was included in the reauthorized act.

61. See, for example, Laurie Steel and Richard Levine, *Educational Innovation in Multiracial Contexts: The Growth of Magnet Schools in American Education* (Palo Alto, Calif.: American Institutes for Research, 1994). Equity advocates caution that choice or magnet programs should be "controlled," with racial and ethnic quotas to prevent voluntary resegregation (Richard Rothstein, introduction to *School Choice: Examining the Evidence*, ed. Edith Rasell and Richard Rothstein [Washington, D.C.: Economic Policy Institute, 1993], 22).

62. See, for example, Amy Heebner, Robert L. Crain, David R. Kiefer, Yiu-Pong Si, with assistance from Will J. Jordan and Barbara Tokarska, *Career Magnets: Interviews with Students and Staff* (Berkeley: National Center for Research in Vocational Education, 1992).

63. For example, critics question whether all parents will be equally able to choose the best school for their children, or whether a magnet system will stratify further an already stratified educational system. As Metz explains, "Magnet schools that develop positive reputations often attract more applicants than they can accommodate. Criteria for admission then limit parental choice and raise serious problems of equity" (Mary Haywood Metz, "Magnet Schools and the Reform of

Public Education," in *Choice in Education: Potential and Problems*, ed. W. L. Boyd and Herbert J. Wallberg [Berkeley: McCutchen, 1990], 123–47). Critics fear that magnet schools may draw the best students from other schools in the district, "leaving the weaker students in traditional schools without student leaders or the protection of active parents," and that magnet schools may "become a separate track, bastions of privilege that attract middle class, high-achieving children" and leave regular schools with the least capable students and teachers (ibid., 139–40).

Metz disagrees with such criticisms, however, asserting that magnet schools are more equitable than a traditional school system. "While magnet schools as a class tend to attract student bodies that are slightly more privileged in terms of both class background and prior educational achievement than the overall student population of their districts," she writes, "an absence of magnet schools would not guarantee equitable distribution of these students through the ordinary schools of a city" (ibid., 142). If not for the magnet schools, she suggests, these students might otherwise move to other neighborhoods with better schools or to the suburbs, or transfer to private schools (ibid. 141).

Nevertheless, even in the New York City magnet school system, which reserves places for magnet applicants with low test scores, it has been suggested that more reforms are needed to prevent the remaining neighborhood schools from being "dumping grounds" for the more disadvantaged students whom magnet schools still manage to reject (Robert L. Crain, "New York City's Career Magnet High School: Lessons about Creating Equity within Choice Programs," in Rasell and Rothstein, *School Choice*, 259–68).

64. A Carnegie Foundation study of public school choice programs reports that not only do few parents in general choose to switch their children's schools, but among low-income, minority parents, the less advantaged are also less likely to choose to leave schools close to home (School Choice: A Special Report [Princeton: Carnegie Foundation for the Advancement of Teaching, 1992]). Results of the study suggest that "choice is of greatest benefit to the educationally advantaged," that is, that school choice seems to work best for better-educated parents, who become better informed and are thus more likely to participate in the program. The study noted a correlation between likely participation in choice programs and social class: "The economic status of families . . . seems to be an important variable in determining how well-informed parents become about their options" (*School Choice: A Special Report*, 15).

Even where students and parents are knowledgeable and informed, and students do choose to attend a magnet, low-income students may be at a disadvantage in gaining admission to schools of choice. In New York City, for example, "one-third of students who apply to magnet schools never attend because of limited enrollments, because no magnet chose them, or because they did not receive a place in the lottery where half the seats are assigned. The students who fail in their attempt to attend a magnet are usually from more disadvantaged families" (Rothstein, introduction to Rasell and Rothstein, *School Choice*, 10).

65. Even magnet school proponents such as Metz have suggested that in magnet schools, "racial desegregation, or at least racial integration . . . seems to be the most

easily compromised aim" (Metz, "Magnet Schools and the Reform of Public Education," 130). Likewise, Plank et al., examining public school choice programs using a national data set, report that public schools of choice are not more integrated than assigned schools, and that, for black and Latino students, attending choice schools segregated them somewhat more from whites. Where public school choice programs exist, whites are more likely to remain in their assigned neighborhood schools, while blacks and Latinos are more likely to attend choice schools, particularly magnets and vocational/technical schools (Stephen Plank, Kathryn S. Schiller, Barbara Schneider, and James S. Coleman, "Effects of Choice in Education," in Rasell and Rothstein, *School Choice*, 111–34).

Similarly, in a study of fourteen elementary-level magnet schools in Montgomery County, Maryland, Henig found that despite the magnet program's intent to promote integration, white families tended to opt for schools with lower proportions of minorities, and minority families tended to choose schools in lower-income minority neighborhoods (Jeffrey R. Henig, "Choice in Public Schools: An Analysis of Transfer Requests among Magnet Schools," *Social Science Quarterly* 71 [1990]: 69–82). "Only by directly constraining the choice of some parents—by rejecting about 15 percent of requests for transfer on grounds that they will worsen racial imbalance—have Montgomery County officials been able to keep the magnet program from exacerbating segregation" (Henig, "Choice in Public Schools", 80).

66. In a study of school choice programs in general, Wells, for example, argues that even if it were true that schools would respond to the market pressures of parents' choices, research suggests that parents do not necessarily make choices based on careful evaluation of schools' relative academic quality. Instead, parents and students often choose schools based on nonacademic factors, such as location, racial makeup, family tradition, and familiarity (Amy Stuart Wells, "The Sociology of School Choice: Why Some Win and Others Lose in the Educational Marketplace," in Rasell and Rothstein, *School Choice*, 29–48). Likewise, the Carnegie study found evidence to suggest that academic concerns often are not central to the school choice decision; indeed, more than half of the time, parents made their decisions based on nonacademic grounds (*School Choice: A Special Report*). And John F. Witte, in an ongoing evaluation of the voucher program in Milwaukee for the state of Wisconsin, has found that parents choose schools for a number of reasons besides academic excellence, including location and disciplinary climate (Witte, "The Milwaukee Parental Choice Program," in Rasell and Rothstein, *School Choice*, 69–109).

Another reason that choice or voucher programs may not lead to school improvement is that many students and their parents choose not to participate. Witte has found that the vast majority of eligible parents in Milwaukee choose not to accept vouchers, although the amount of the vouchers is equal to the per-pupil state aid and schools accepting these students are not permitted to charge additional tuition (Witte, "Milwaukee Parental Choice Program").

Finally, as Wells points out, the "economic metaphor" is "based on the assumption that education is much like other services bought and sold in the marketplace and that schools should behave more like private, profit-driven corporations than democratically run public institutions." But we might well ask whether, in a democracy, we think schools should really be thought of as a consumer good. In the words of Ernest L. Boyer, "Adopting the language of the marketplace, school choice advocates portray education as a solitary act of consumerism. To frame the issue in these terms is to distort the vision of public education beyond recognition" (Boyer, foreword to Rasell and Rothstein, *School Choice*, xiii).

67. See William L. Taylor, "*Brown*, Equal Protection, and the Isolation of the Poor," *Yale Law Journal* 95 (1986): 1700–1735; William L. Taylor, "The Supreme Court and Urban Reality: A Tactical Analysis of *Milliken v. Bradley*," *Wayne Law Review* 21 (1975): 751–78.

68. *Milliken v. Bradley* (*Milliken I*), 418 U.S. at 814 (Marshall, J., dissenting).

69. *United States v. Carolene Products*, 304 U.S. 144, 153 n. 4 (1938).

70. Moreover, a school-to-work bill was passed, a federal research agenda was established, the costly and complicated student loan program was streamlined and made more affordable to students, and the Americorps national service program was created.

71. Under the reauthorized Title I program, corrective action against underperforming schools and districts may include the use of student transfers, but coverage of transportation costs is provided only in the case of intradistrict, not interdistrict, transfers (Improving America's Schools Act, Pub. L. No. 103-382, 108 Stat. 3518, § 1116[c][5][B][i][VII] and § 1116[d][6][B][i][VII]).

72. *Edgewood Independent School District v. Kirby* (Tex. 1989); *Rose v. Council for Better Education, Inc.* (Ky. 1989); *Abbott v. Burke* (N.J. 1990, 1994); *Serrano v. Priest* (Cal. 1971, 1977); *Helena Elementary School District No. 1 v. Montana* (Mont. 1989).

73. As noted above, Congress did not, in the latest reauthorization of the Elementary and Secondary Education Act, establish a principle of statewide (interdistrict) equity or comparability but took a small step in Title I to require states to assure that local districts fulfill their obligations with respect to high standards, high quality assessment, and accountability. Section 1111(b)(8) of the new Title I requires that state plans describe (1) how the state education agency will help local districts and schools to comply with the requirements of the act and (2) other factors that the state deems appropriate to provide students an opportunity to achieve the knowledge and skills described in the standards adopted by the state (Improving America's Schools Act, § 1111[b][8][A] and [B]).

74. Section 1119 of the new Title I makes staff development a cornerstone of the Title I program, requiring that all participating schools devote resources from Title I and other sources in amounts sufficient to achieve high-quality professional development, and that districts provide high-quality professional development drawing on resources available under Title I, Title II, Goals 2000, and other sources (Improving America's Schools Act, Tit. I, § 1119[b][1][C]). Despite recommendations from education groups, the act contains no explicit set-aside of Title I funds for professional development, but compliance with the act will require that significant resources be devoted to professional development, including

at least 10 percent of the Title I allocation in schools that do not make adequate progress (Improving America's Schools Act, Tit.I, § 1116[c][3]).

Moreover, Title II of the Improving America's Schools Act appropriates $800 million for fiscal year 1995 and "such sums as may be necessary" for each of the four succeeding years, to provide assistance with professional development activities to state and local education agencies and institutions of higher education (Improving America's Schools Act, Tit. II, §§ 2001–2211).

David Stoesz   # Poor Policy

The Legacy of the
Kerner Commission
for Social Welfare

The legacy of the Kerner Commission for poor, urban African Americans is inextricably connected to the erratic development of the nation's welfare programs. Rather than assure basic guarantees to all as a right of citizenship, following principles of the welfare states of northern Europe,[1] social programs in the United States have been significantly influenced by localism, capitalism, and racism.[2] The consequence of this for African Americans was a marginalization from the cultural mainstream. Instead of extending the social citizenship of African Americans, public social policy was more often crafted in such a way as to minimize the equality sought by racial minorities.[3] At worst the American welfare state excluded African Americans from basic protections against social and economic insecurity; at best it offered promises of full participation in the culture that were to prove largely illusory.

In response to the civil disorders of the mid-1960s, much of the Kerner Commission report chronicled the inadequacy of the American welfare state in remedying the social and economic grievances of African Americans. If social programs of the New Deal and the War on Poverty were to prove disappointing, the reassertion of conservatism during the latter part of the twentieth century cast a pall over the prospects of social justice for African Americans.

The New Deal

To the extent that governmental programs are enacted to ameliorate the social and economic dislocations experienced by citizens, the welfare state serves as a useful point of departure in understanding the events that eventually gave rise to the Kerner Commission. Within the American context, the welfare state has evolved in two major expansions of public policy: the

New Deal and the War on Poverty. A critical assessment of the expansionary eras of the American welfare state reveals that neither program adequately addressed the substantial needs of African Americans. Insofar as public policy skirted the claims of African Americans, programs of the welfare state were implicated in the chaotic events that precipitated the Kerner Commission.

Prior to the New Deal, those in need had little recourse but to rely on family, friends, and neighborhood organizations for assistance. During the Progressive Era, African Americans created their own mutual benefit societies when the many Charity Organization Societies that were emerging in American cities refused to assist them.[4] When Franklin Delano Roosevelt consolidated many of the social programs of the New Deal in the Social Security Act of 1935, agricultural and domestic workers—most of whom were African Americans—were excluded; this exclusion was a tactical concession to southern legislators.[5] Because of the exclusions of agricultural and domestic workers, "more than three-fifths" were denied protections of the Social Security Act.[6]

What benefits were available to African Americans existed in the form of public assistance. Aid to Families with Dependent Children (AFDC) and what is now known as Supplemental Security Income were initially established as state-administered, means-tested welfare programs in the Social Security Act. As state-run programs, public assistance authorized "local welfare authorities [to] determine benefit levels and set eligibility rules."[7] So structured, the public assistance provisions of the Social Security Act allowed state officials to contrive welfare in ways that reinforced low-wage labor and, when desired, the local conventions of Jim Crow segregation. In the South the state administration of public assistance programs meant that benefits would not be provided to agricultural workers during harvest, that welfare workers could use "man-in-the-house" rules to terminate benefits, and that eligibility could be denied African Americans who were involved in civil rights activities, such as voter registration. Under such restrictive and punitive administration, during the 1940s and 1950s public assistance provided negligible economic aid to the poor, particularly African Americans.

The secondary status of public assistance was to change as a result of agricultural mechanization in the South that dislocated millions of African American agricultural workers. With limited employment opportunities in southern cities, millions of families fled north in search of work. Their meager incomes coupled with segregated housing practices in northern metropolitan areas served to populate the black ghettos that became characteristic of older industrial cities. Yet, despite the denial of social and economic opportunity, a nascent civil rights movement made an impression on Democratic politicians who sought to exploit the black vote. Since the earlier decades of European immigration, the conventional political equation for such circumstances was simple: newcomer votes in exchange for governmental assistance. This was not lost on Lyndon Johnson, an unparalleled political opportunist, who saw the equation not limited to municipal politics but applicable to the national polity. Thus, when war was declared on poverty by Lyndon Johnson in the mid-1960s, many poor African Americans who had migrated to urban areas but had not benefited from earlier welfare provisions stood as prospective program beneficiaries—and prospective Democratic voters.[8] In this manner Johnson captured for the foreseeable future the political allegiance of African Americans, sealing off from the Republican Party the earlier generations of blacks who had voted religiously for the "Party of Lincoln." In exchange for their support of the Democratic Party, Johnson mounted a series of programs designed to appeal to poor African Americans—the War on Poverty.

The War on Poverty

The War on Poverty was but one skirmish on a relatively wide front of domestic initiatives. In implementing his Great Society plan, Johnson sometimes advanced proposals of the Kennedy presidency but more often forged boldly ahead with programs of his own. The targeting of welfare-related social programs on the poor, as evident in the Community Mental Health Centers Acts of 1963 and 1965, the Elementary and Secondary Education Act of 1965, Medicaid (passed in 1965), the Food Stamp Act of 1964, the Public Works and Economic Development Act of 1965, and expansion of the Manpower Development and Training Act of 1962, reinforced efforts of the poverty campaign significantly. Thus, although public attention may have been diverted toward the "poverty" programs, in fact, much of the social legislation of the Great Society played a supporting role in combating poverty. In so doing, the many social programs of the Great Society filled a void created by the New Deal: the provision of income and services to the poor, many of whom were African American.

The AFDC program similarly filled a void left by the New Deal. Included in the Social Security Act as a public assistance program, the AFDC provisions were intended to assure income to families whose wage earners had died.[9] Since the inception of AFDC, the makeup of the families sustained by the program has changed considerably. By 1989 only 1.9 percent of families participating in AFDC did so due to the death of a parent.[10] On the other hand, from 1969 to 1989 the percentage of AFDC families on the program as a result of absence of a parent who had "no marriage tie" increased from 27.9 to 52.7 percent.[11] While the characteristics of AFDC families were changing profoundly, as these data indicate, their numbers increased dramatically. Between 1966 and 1971 the number of AFDC recipients more than doubled from less than 5 million to 10 million, causing the cost of operating the program to triple.[12] These data paralleled an emerging stereotype of welfare. The public began to view AFDC as welfare for poor African American women and their children without their father at home.

The main features of the War on Poverty, of course, consisted of the programs enacted by the Economic Opportunity Act of 1964. Among the services to be administered through the Office of Economic Opportunity (OEO) were Head Start, the Job Corps, the Neighborhood Youth Corps, Volunteers in Service to America, and the Legal Services Program. Undoubtedly the most controversial aspect of the War on Poverty was the creation of local Community Action Programs (CAPs) that were to coordinate OEO and other social programs within poor communities. The requirement that CAP boards of directors reflect the "maximum feasible participation" of the poor was seized on by minority militants to confront urban power structures that were already antagonized by OEO's practice of bypassing state and local government in funding CAPs.[13] The wrath brought upon OEO through the hostilities generated by CAPs in major cities led President Richard Nixon to dismantle the agency soon after his election. In the process, specific War on Poverty programs were either terminated or reassigned to more mainstream federal departments.

The War on Poverty bears upon the Kerner Commission in two important ways. First, the failure of the commission to convince the Johnson administration to launch more substantive initiatives to address mounting needs of urban African Americans, particularly in employment and housing, left the minority poor with little choice but to rely on existing welfare programs. Thus, in the period immediately following the hot summers of the mid-1960s, the numbers of people eligible for AFDC and the new, means-tested programs of the Great Society, particularly Food Stamps and Medicaid, skyrocketed. Second, the participatory feature of the CAPs— one of the rare instances in which power was redistributed through public policy—was retracted, and most CAPs were disbanded. While much of the national leadership of the African American community would later be traced to OEO programs, the breadth of that leadership would probably have been greater had the CAPs continued, if only as a coordinative function in poor communities. These factors were to prove instrumental when Ronald Reagan's administration chose to reevaluate welfare policy in the 1980s.

The Reagan Revolution

The 1970s were inauspicious for poor African Americans. The failure of the Kerner Commission to facilitate a comprehensive strategy for urban minorities left them more dependent on existing, means-tested social programs. As the 1980s were to demonstrate, reliance on means-tested programs to accomplish social objectives was flawed because recipients— low-income, poorly educated, and impotent politically—were relatively powerless. In the 1970s when conservatives began to indict the means-tested programs of the War on Poverty for inducing dependency, encouraging promiscuity, and subverting the family, poor minorities for whom these programs had become more important were unable to mount a counteroffensive. Unfortunately, during this period liberal academics who could have stepped into this breach were dissuaded from doing so. The furor following the publication of Daniel Patrick Moynihan's report *The Negro Family: The Case for National Action* in 1965[14] made it emphatically clear to social researchers that investigations of the dysfunctional features of African American families would not go unchallenged. Instead, researchers were encouraged to focus on the strengths of African American families in order to identify how, under the most adverse circumstances, so many had persevered. The consequence of this, as William Julius Wilson argued later, was the failure of the academic research community to chronicle the considerable deterioration of African American institutions in urban areas during the period.[15]

Census data indicate that ghettoization had increased significantly during the 1970s, further isolating poor, urban African Americans from the American mainstream. While the number of AFDC families increased in census tracts that were 20 percent poor as well as those that were 40 percent poor, other social indicators of ghettoization—the unemployment rate of young males, the number of African Americans, and the number of African Americans in poverty—had worsened in the 40 percent poor tracts during the 1970s.

The direction the Reagan "revolution" was to take in welfare policy was evident in the writings of conservative scholars of the early 1980s. On the eve of the Reagan presidency, the Hoover Institution's Martin Anderson claimed that "the War on Poverty has been won, except for perhaps a few mopping-up operations. The combination of strong economic growth and a dramatic increase in government spending on welfare and income transfer programs for more than a decade has virtually wiped out poverty in the United States."[16] Taking a somewhat punitive tack, George Gilder argued that social programs represented "moral hazards," protecting the poor from risks inherent in a market economy. The poor, Gilder contended, needed not government welfare programs but "the spur of their

Table 1. Trends in Social Conditions of Large Central Cities,
1970–1980 (%)

Indicator	Census Tracts with 20 Percent Poor			Census Tracts with 40 Percent Poor		
	1970	1980	Change	1970	1980	Change
Employment rate						
males, age 16+	63.3	56.0	−13	56.5	46.0	−22
AFDC families	19.8	28.0	+40	30.2	42.0	+40
Black persons	27.2	26.5	−3	6.3	8.3	+32
Poor blacks	28.3	30.5	+8	9.4	13.1	+40

Source: Adapted from Sara McLanahan, Irwin Garfinkel, and Dorothy Watson, "Family Structure, Poverty, and the Underclass," in *Urban Change and Poverty*, ed. Michael G. H. McGeary and Lawrence E. Lynn Jr. (Washington, D.C.: National Academy Press, 1988), 102, 130.

own poverty" to improve their plight.[17] Yet the most telling analysis was to come from a previously obscure scholar, Charles Murray, whose *Losing Ground* was to become the conservative statement on welfare of the decade. Welfare programs had become so convoluted, concluded Murray, that the only solution consisted of "scrapping the entire federal welfare and income support structure for working-aged persons, including AFDC, Medicaid, Food Stamps, Unemployment Insurance, Worker's Compensation, subsidized housing, disability, and the rest."[18] Consistent with the tone established by conservative ideologues, the Reagan administration moved swiftly against social programs.

Within seven months after assuming office, President Reagan showed his hand on welfare by signing the Omnibus Budget Reconciliation Act (OBRA) of 1981. OBRA proceeded on a dual track, cutting public assistance benefits while at the same time combining categorical programs into a Social Services Block Grant. The new AFDC eligibility guidelines were particularly punitive, since they were directed at poor families who were participating in the labor force. Suddenly, AFDC family heads who were trying to improve their economic lot found that they could deduct only $160 per month per child for child care, that the deduction for work expenses was limited to $75 per month, and that the earned income disregard (the first $30 per month and one-third of income thereafter) was eliminated after four months.[19] As if to strangle the welfare bureaucracy in paperwork, OBRA required the welfare department to redetermine *monthly* the eligibility of those on AFDC who insisted on working. These, among other measures, had an immediate impact on the AFDC rolls: 408,000 families lost eligibility altogether, and another 299,000 had their benefits reduced.[20]

Federal and state governments realized savings of $1.1 billion in 1983.[21] Significantly, OBRA disentitled working poor families; 5 percent of the total AFDC caseload became ineligible due to OBRA, and "about 35 percent of those who were working were terminated by the legislation." [22]

For most of the families made ineligible for AFDC by the provisions of OBRA, loss of benefits submerged them in poverty. Monthly income loss ranged from $229 in Dallas to $115 in Boston.[23] Former AFDC beneficiaries in these cities had also lost Medicaid coverage. In Dallas 59.2 percent of terminated families could not secure alternative health insurance; in Boston the figure was 27.5 percent.[24] A study of AFDC families in Georgia found that 79 percent fell below the poverty level as a result of OBRA, compared with 70 percent before 1981.[25] An investigation of the quality of life of 129 AFDC families in New Jersey that had lost benefits was Dickensian in its portrayal: "More than half the families were below the poverty level, 4 out of 10 families did not have enough to eat, 2 out of 10 were spending less than the amount required to provide a minimally adequate diet, almost 3 out of 4 had problems paying rent and utility bills, and most significantly, nearly 8 out of 10 families had to forego or delay medical and/or dental care." [26]

Despite changes in tax policy that benefited low-income workers, particularly increased tax expenditures through the Earned Income Tax Credit, the poor fared badly during the 1980s. The tax rebates given the poor through tax policy failed to compensate for the losses of benefits through welfare programs. "Low-income families, especially the working poor, lost appreciably more by cuts in government services than they gained in tax reduction," admitted conservative analyst Kevin Phillips.[27] And since the wealthy continued to benefit from less progressive taxation, the income disparity between rich and poor widened. Between 1980 and 1990 the federal tax burden for the richest quintile of tax filers decreased 5.5 percent, while taxes of the poorest fifth increased 16.1 percent, despite tax expenditures for the poor.[28] Predictably, the rich gained a larger portion of the nation's income during the Reagan era, as measured by changing income distribution.

The Rise of the Underclass

Upward redistribution of wealth was to be of substantial consequence for poor, urban African Americans. Increasingly reliant on public assistance programs that were not indexed for inflation, poor minorities saw their benefits drop precipitously during the 1980s. Between 1972 and 1992 the value of AFDC benefits declined 43 percent due to inflation. Combining benefits for Food Stamps and AFDC left the 1992 median benefit for an

Table 2. Change in Distribution of Total U.S. After-Tax
Income, 1980–1990

Income Quintile	1980 (%)	1990 (%)
Richest fifth	44.8	49.9
Next richest fifth	22.6	21.7
Middle fifth	16.2	14.9
Next poorest fifth	11.4	9.9
Poorest fifth	5.4	4.3

Adapted from Greenstein and Barancik, *Drifting Apart*, 10.

American family of three at $647 per month (28 percent below the poverty level).[29] In 1983 the median worth of nonwhite and Hispanic families was only $6,900, 12.7 percent of that of white families, but by 1989 it had fallen to $4,000, 6.8 percent of that of white families.[30] By the late 1980s the poverty rate of African Americans was three times that of whites.[31]

Compounding the erosion of income and assets, urban African American communities were further disadvantaged by the exodus of middle-income African Americans to the suburbs and the replacement of better-paying, manufacturing jobs with low-wage service jobs. The interaction of middle-class flight and technological transformation proved devastating for minorities residing in older industrial cities. For example, the plight of young African Americans is immediately apparent if the unemployment rate is combined with the labor force nonparticipation rate, as shown in Table 3. By the early 1980s young African American males were not participating to a significant extent in two primary institutions: work and school. Compared with their white counterparts, African American young men were much more likely to be unemployed in every region of the United States. But if they were not working, neither were they in school. This institutional alienation was to portend a rapid escalation of drug-related street violence during the 1980s that continued into the 1990s. By the early 1990s in every region of the United States, more than half of all young African Americans were neither working nor in school.

The consequences of such deterioration in life opportunity are predictable enough. Many urban neighborhoods began to show characteristics that were qualitatively different—and more troubling—than those of communities that were simply poor. "What distinguishes members of the underclass from those of other economically disadvantaged groups," wrote William Julius Wilson, "is that their marginal economic position or weak attachment to the labor force is uniquely reinforced by the neighborhood or social milieu."[32] By the 1990s, areas of many industrial cities had virtually imploded.[33] The "wilding" of New York teenagers who savagely beat a

Table 3. Percentage of Out-of-School Males Aged 16–64 Not Working and Residing in the Central City, by Race, Education, and Region for Selected Metropolitan Areas

Region/Race and Education Level	1968–1970	1980–1982	1990–1992
Northeast			
White			
Less than high school	15	34	37
High school graduate only[a]	7	17	24
Black			
Less than high school	19	44	57
High school graduate only[a]	11	27	31
Midwest			
White			
Less than high school	12	29	34
High school graduate only[a]	5	16	18
Black			
Less than high school	24	52	63
High school graduate only	10	30	41
South			
White			
Less than high school	7	15	18
High school graduate only[a]	3	9	19
Black			
Less than high school	13	29	52
High school graduate only[a]	1	19	22
West			
White			
Less than high school	18	20	26
High school graduate only[a]	10	16	19
Black			
Less than high school	26	44	57
High school graduate only[a]	13	14	43

Source: John Kasarda, "Industrial Restructuring and the Consequences of Changing Job Locations," in *Changes and Challenges: America 1990*, ed. Reynolds Farley (New York: Russell Sage, 1995), tab. 5.15.

Note: Northeast includes Boston, Newark, New York, Philadelphia, and Pittsburgh; Midwest includes Cleveland, Chicago, Detroit, Milwaukee, and St. Louis; South includes Atlanta, Dallas, Houston, Miami, and New Orleans; West includes Denver, Long Beach, Los Angeles, Oakland, Phoenix, San Francisco, and Seattle.

[a] Completed high school, but no higher education completed.

female jogger was replicated when a gang of Boston youth raped and murdered a young mother.[34] Gang killings in Los Angeles soared 69 percent during the first eight months of 1990.[35] Gang-related murders in the nation's capital reached a three-year high, leading the police department's spokesperson to quip, "At the rate we're going the next generation is going to be extinct." [36]

Observers of urban poverty described a serious deterioration in inner-city communities since the 1980s. In an analysis of racial segregation in American cities, Douglas Massey and Nancy Denton developed the concept of "hypersegregation" to refer to those cities in which African Americans tended to live together in separate enclaves. Using a segregation index, Massey and Denton chronicled the experience of larger American cities in which more than 60 percent of the black population lived in a distinct ghetto. In 1970 sixteen cities were hypersegregated; by 1980 the degree of hypersegregation had dropped only 4.4 percent. Between 1980 and 1990 the degree of hypersegregation fell less, 3.2 percent, reflecting further slowing of the already minimal mobility of urban blacks. Despite two decades of social programs following the War on Poverty, most blacks continued to live in ghettos.

Other evidence of the deterioration of urban life was impressionistic. When Claude Brown returned to Harlem twenty years after the publication of his *Manchild in the Promised Land*, he was shocked by the casual viciousness of gang members toward their victims.[37] "In many if not most of our major cities, we are facing something very like social regression," wrote Daniel Patrick Moynihan.[38] "It is defined by extraordinary levels of self-destructive behavior, interpersonal violence, and social class separation intensive in some groups, extensive in others." [39] In the socioeconomic vacuum that had developed in the poorest urban neighborhoods, the sale and consumption of drugs became central to community life. The toll this conversion was to take on young African Americans was astonishing. As of 1988 43 percent of those convicted of drug trafficking were African American. In New York, Hispanics and African Americans accounted for 92 percent of arrests for drug offenses in 1989. In 1990 a criminal justice reform organization, the Sentencing Project, reported that one-fourth of all African Americans between the ages of twenty and twenty-nine were incarcerated, on parole, or on probation. Harvard economist Richart Freeman calculated that 35 percent of all African Americans aged sixteen to thirty-five had been arrested in 1989.[40] By the early 1990s, drug-related pathologies, such as homicide and AIDS, made inner cities an "American nightmare." [41]

In this context the only change in poverty policy that was to emerge during the 1980s, the Family Support Act of 1988, was largely ineffectual.

Table 4. Trends in Black-White Hypersegregation in Sixteen Metropolitan Areas with Largest Black Population, 1970–1990 (%)

Metropolitan Area	1970	1980	1970–1980	1990	1980–1990
Atlanta	82.1	78.5	−3.6	67.8	−10.7
Baltimore	81.9	74.7	−7.2	71.4	−3.3
Buffalo	87.0	79.4	−7.6	81.8	2.4
Chicago	91.9	87.8	−4.1	85.5	−2.3
Cleveland	90.8	87.5	−3.3	85.1	−2.4
Dallas–Ft. Worth	86.9	77.1	−9.8	63.1	−14.0
Detroit	88.4	86.7	−1.7	87.6	.9
Gary-Hammond– E. Chicago	91.4	90.6	−.8	89.9	−.7
Indianapolis	81.7	76.2	−5.5	74.3	−1.9
Kansas City	87.4	78.9	−8.5	72.6	−6.3
Los Angeles– Long Beach	91.0	81.1	−9.9	73.1	−8.0
Milwaukee	90.5	83.9	−6.6	82.8	−1.1
New York	81.0	82.0	1.0	82.2	.2
Newark	81.4	81.6	.2	82.5	.9
Philadelphia	79.5	78.8	−.7	77.2	−1.6
St. Louis	84.7	81.3	−3.4	77.0	−4.3
		Average	−4.4	Average	−3.2

Adapted from Douglas S. Massey and Nancy A. Denton, *American Apartheid: Segregation and the Making of the Underclass* (Cambridge, Mass.: Harvard University Press, 1993), 222.

Under the Family Support Act, $3.34 billion was to be allocated for a five-year period to establish education and job-seeking opportunities—Job Opportunities and Basic Skills (JOBS)—for AFDC recipients. During 1990 and 1991 states would have to enroll at least 7 percent of AFDC parents in workfare; by 1995 the required enrollment would rise to 20 percent. Although two-parent families are covered in the act, beginning in 1997 one parent will be required to work at least sixteen hours a week in an unpaid job in exchange for benefits.[42] The more progressive provisions of the bill included the extension of eligibility for day care grants and Medicaid for one year after a client leaves AFDC for private employment. The bill also mandated the automatic deduction of child support from an absent parent's paycheck.

But the promised savings of workfare soon faded. Two years into the JOBS program, the Congressional Budget Office projected that 10,000 families would be off AFDC by 1991, 20,000 by 1993, and 50,000 by end of the five years of the program—only a 1.3 percent reduction in the number of AFDC families. "The effect of the JOBS program on the number of AFDC recipients or on spending on benefits in welfare programs is thus expected to be modest," concluded the House Ways and Means Committee.[43] In a review of workfare projects, Harvard's David Ellwood calculated increased earnings of $250–$750 per year. According to Ellwood, "Most work-welfare programs look like decent investments, but no carefully evaluated work-welfare programs have done more than put a tiny dent in the welfare caseloads, even though they have been received with enthusiasm."[44]

Policy Options for the Poor

Policy options to address the needs of disadvantaged African Americans have been proposed by liberals and conservatives alike. The plausibility of new initiatives, however, has been constrained by the federal budget deficit as well as by fiscal straits experienced by most states and many local jurisdictions. Many states chose to reduce or eliminate public assistance benefits in order to relieve budget pressures. By 1991 fourteen states had reduced general assistance benefits, the most dramatic example being Michigan's elimination of the program in October 1991, leaving approximately 82,000 beneficiaries without help to face the winter. In addition, nine states cut AFDC benefits for 1991.[45]

Fiscal gridlock reached such an impasse by the early 1990s that liberal and conservative intellectuals in the nation's capital speculated about a "new paradigm" for social policy.[46] Indeed, Bill Clinton's successful bid for the presidency was widely credited to his evocation of a "third way" and a "new covenant" in public policy. Any residual optimism about the Clinton administration unfolding a new direction for social programs was quashed when Republicans won control of Congress in the 1994 midterm elections. Consequently, options in welfare policy have tended toward the right end of the ideological continuum. Republicans have fielded enterprise zones, tax expenditures, and reciprocity of the poor as bases for welfare policy, while Democrats have proposed child support enforcement, civic obligation, and development accounts.

Enterprise Zones

The enterprise zone concept can be traced to the Adam Smith Institute of England, where researcher Stuart Butler elaborated on the work of others who promoted market strategies for community development. Entrepreneurial activity could be promoted in poor areas, reasoned conservatives, by reducing taxes, employee expenses, and health and safety regulations.[47] Imported to the United States by the Heritage Foundation, Butler's ideas came to the attention of then-congressman Jack Kemp, who convinced the Reagan administration to make them the centerpiece of urban policy. Through the 1980s Kemp's Urban Enterprise Zone (UEZ) legislation stalled in Congress. Undaunted, the Heritage Foundation promoted UEZs in states and localities. By mid-decade thirty states and cities had created more than 300 UEZs.[48] Local experimentation notwithstanding, the UEZ concept continued to languish until the Los Angeles riot propelled it to the center of the urban policy debate. Despite the worst civil disturbance in memory, UEZ provisions of the 1992 Urban Aid Act amounted to a modest $2.5 billion for the creation of fifty enterprise zones. Unrelated tax concessions added by the Democratic Congress increased appropriations to $28 billion, an amount unacceptable to President Bush, who vetoed the measure.[49]

Under the Clinton presidency, enterprise zones were relabeled "empowerment zones" and incorporated into the 1994 federal budget. In late 1994 the Clinton White House announced that 106 communities would receive funding to encourage economic development under a multitier arrangement. Six cities—Atlanta, Baltimore, Chicago, Detroit, New York, and Philadelphia—were designated full-fledged empowerment zones and were awarded $100 million each. Four metropolitan areas—Boston, Houston, Oakland, and Kansas City—were to receive $25 million each as "enhanced enterprise communities." Ninety-five smaller cities were allocated $3 million each as "enterprise communities." Finally, three rural empowerment zones were designated—the Appalachian highlands of Kentucky, the delta region of Mississippi, and the Rio Grande Valley of Texas—each to receive $40 million. Cleveland and Los Angeles were assigned "supplemental empowerment zone" status: Cleveland was allocated $90 million; Los Angeles, $125 million.[50]

While big-city mayors chosen for empowerment zone funding expressed relief at the prospects of fiscal transfusions, the prognosis for the poorest urban areas was not good. At $3.5 billion the Clinton empowerment zone initiative represented but a fraction of the revenue loss experienced by cities during the 1980s. At its peak in 1978, HUD funding totaled $57 billion (in 1989 dollars); by 1989 it had plummeted to $9 billion.[51] Former Albuquerque mayor David Rusk was decidedly pessimistic about the White House strategy. Rusk had classified American cities according to three factors that he posited were essential to urban vitality: population loss, minority population, and city-to-suburban income ratio. According to his analysis twenty-four cities had already crossed the point of "no-return," and many of these were targeted for empowerment zone funding. Rusk concluded that "the enterprise/empowerment concept that you're going to

Table 5. Earned Income Tax Credit, Selected Years

Year to Which Credit Applies	Number of Families Receiving Credit (in thousands)	Total Amount of EITC (in millions)	Average Credit per Family
1975	6,215	$1,250	$201
1980	6,954	1,986	286
1985	7,432	2,088	281
1990	12,612	6,928	549
1995	18,411	22,806	1,239

Source: Adapted from Committee on Ways and Means, *Overview of Entitlement Programs* (1994), 704.

reduce poverty by developing the community from within and stimulating the creation of jobs right in the immediate neighborhood" was fundamentally flawed.[52]

Earned Income Tax Credit

In 1975 the Earned Income Tax Credit (EITC) was instituted, whereby low-income taxpayers would be given a rebate from the Internal Revenue Service.[53] Although the EITC was a negative income tax, for conservatives it proved a suitable substitute for welfare. It was paid to those who worked, and it required beneficiaries to participate in the tax system. In fact during the 1980s and early 1990s—the period that direct public welfare expenditures for the poor were under assault—indirect payments under EITC actually increased substantially. In 1987 the EITC was indexed for inflation, and the 1994 Clinton budget included a major expansion in EITC funding. Since its inception the EITC has become an important income maintenance program for the working poor, as shown in Table 5. The rather remarkable growth of EITC tax expenditures suggests that it has become an important option for assuring income security for the working minority poor.

Reciprocity in Public Assistance

A staple of conservative thought on welfare throughout the Reagan era was that welfare programs contributed to dependency and dysfunctional behaviors, especially when benefits were not conditional on reciprocity or, in other words, a standard of conduct expected of recipients. Lawrence Mead observed that "the damage [by welfare programs] seems to be done, not by the benefits, themselves, but by the fact that they are *entitlements*, given regardless of the behavior of clients. They raise the income of recipients, but, more important, free them to behave without accountability to society."[54] Capitalizing on the welfare-to-work provisions of the Family Support Act, conservatives included a number of other desirable behaviors as a condition of receipt of public assistance. By the early 1990s, states were placing new requirements on poor people applying for AFDC, Food Stamps, and Medicaid. Wisconsin introduced "learnfare," requiring beneficiaries to attend school or risk the loss of benefits. In addition to requiring school attendance, Maryland soon made it necessary for parents to assure that their children received preventive health care. New Jersey thereafter denied additional assistance for children born after a grant has been awarded. Not to be outdone, Wisconsin introduced "wedfare," providing incentives for mothers on AFDC to marry.[55]

By the early 1990s, studies conducted by the Manpower Demonstration Research Corporation (MDRC) cautioned against dramatic claims by welfare-to-work advocates, however. A synopsis of selected welfare-to-work programs appears in Table 6. Two elaborations will aid in interpreting the table. First, the Arkansas WORK Program and the San Diego Saturation Work Initiative Model (SWIM) were mandatory and, as a result, served a broad range of AFDC recipients. By contrast, the New Jersey On-the-Job Training (OJT) Program and the AFDC Homemaker–Home Health Aide Demonstrations were voluntary and, as a result, more selective of participants. Second, benefits of welfare-to-work programs are essentially twofold. A successful program would elevate earnings of participants as well as decrease AFDC program costs. Finally, because welfare-to-work programs entail start-up and maintenance costs, independent of the normal operation of AFDC, these administrative costs should be offset by AFDC program savings attributable to welfare-to-work. In the best of all welfare-to-work worlds, earnings would be up, program expenses would be down, and the cost per participant would be low.

The good news is that welfare-to-work programs increase earnings and lower program costs, but not a lot. Only one of the programs increased earnings more than $1,000 for each year after a participant had graduated. As Ellwood had observed, earnings remain too low to vault the typical AFDC mother off welfare. While welfare-to-work did lower AFDC program costs, these savings were also modest; none of the programs realized savings of $1,000 for each year after a participant had graduated. The bad news is that the cost per participant is not realized until well after a participant has graduated from the program and is in the labor market for some time. Only Arkansas's WORK Program recovered its investment per participant in the first year after completion of the program. In most of the

Table 6. AFDC Welfare-to-Work Programs

Program	Type	Cost per Experimental Participant	Outcome	Experimental − Control Difference
Arkansas WORK Program	Mandatory	$118	Earnings	
			Year 1	$167
			Year 2	223
			Year 3	337
			AFDC payments	
			Year 1	$−145
			Year 2	−190
			Year 3	−168
San Diego SWIM	Mandatory	$919	Earnings	
			Year 1	$352
			Year 2	658
			AFDC payments	
			Year 1	$−407
			Year 2	−553
New Jersey OJT Program	Voluntary	$787	Earnings	
			Year 1	n/a
			Year 2	$591
			AFDC payments	
			Year 1	$−190
			Year 2	−238
AFDC Homemaker– Home Health Aide Demonstrations	Voluntary	$9,505	Earnings	
			Year 1	$2,026
			Year 2	1,347
			Year 3	1,121
			AFDC and Food Stamp Benefits	
			Year 1	$−696
			Year 2	−858
			Year 3	−343

Adapted from Judith Gueron and Edward Pauly, *From Welfare to Work* (New York: Russell Sage, 1991), tab. 1.1.

programs, welfare-to-work investments were not recouped until a few years later. Thus, from an administrative standpoint the welfare-to-work payoff is not immediate but long term.

MDRC data do not indicate that welfare-to-work had failed as much as they reflect the incredible inertia that impedes upward mobility of poor families on AFDC. In order to generate earnings sufficient to assure a welfare-to-work program graduate economic independence from AFDC, a huge investment is necessary—on a par with the AFDC Homemaker–Home Health Aide Demonstration's cost per participant of $9,505. It is unlikely that lawmakers would accept this high an investment to help poor families become economically independent of welfare.

The most severe among reciprocity options in welfare reform was the two-year time limit on receipt of welfare advocated by President Clinton. Essentially, the Clinton White House proposed that AFDC recipients receive two years of education, training, and job placement services, after which they would be required to accept private employment, a government-created job, or the termination of benefits. In order to reduce the costs of intensive training and assuring public employment, the administration suggested limiting welfare reform to beneficiaries born after 1971. The Clinton welfare reform plan died from procrastination, however. Saving the proposal for the 104th Congress, Clinton counted on a Democratic Congress to debate welfare reform. The Republican sweep of the 1994 midterm elections, however, made the Clinton plan moot. Instead, Republicans conceived of more radical reforms for welfare. Incoming Speaker of the House Newt Gingrich proposed consolidating AFDC, Food Stamps, and the Women, Infants, and Children Supplemental Nutrition Program into a block grant that would be devolved to the states. Gingrich further suggested transforming funding for the block grant from an open-ended entitlement to a capped entitlement while cutting appropriations 20 percent. In light of the significant decline of the value of welfare benefits during the past two decades and the punitive nature of welfare reform experiments undertaken by many states, the Gingrich proposal would prove devastating for poorest Americans, African Americans being a disproportionate number among them.

Child Support

That so many families on AFDC had outstanding child support orders on absent parents convinced many liberals that public assistance could be enhanced by enforcing child support. Since 1975, child support enforcement has been emphasized in the AFDC program; by 1993 $2.2 billion had been spent to collect $9.0 billion.[56] Enthusiasm about making child support a primary feature of income support for poor women with children led child welfare advocates to propose Child Support Assurance (CSA) as welfare reform. Under the CSA proposal, child support would essentially replace AFDC through three provisions: setting child support as a percentage of the absent parent's income, automatically withholding child support from income as has been done with Social Security taxes, and assuring a minimum benefit to children if the absent parent defaults on payments.[57] CSA would function much like unemployment insurance. For the same reasons that laid-off workers are not presumed to be responsible for their joblessness, CSA presents child support as an assured benefit for the children of irresponsible parents. According to advocates the first two provisions of CSA would increase child support payments, offsetting the third, the assured benefit. Thus, placing the assured benefit at $2,000 per child, the cost of CSA would be about $1 billion, a bargain for removing one-fifth of the families on AFDC from welfare.[58]

Currently two states—Wisconsin and New York—have experimented with the first two features of CSA; but no state has adopted an assured benefit. "The [as]sured benefit is crucial," contended David Ellwood while he was at Harvard's Kennedy School of Government. "Without it, child support reform will mainly benefit upper and middle class single mothers. Child support would then be yet another device that will separate the poor and the non-poor. Middle class women will support themselves with a combination of work and child support. Working class women will be left with only welfare."[59] While Ellwood failed to present a budget for his expanded version of child support, he was willing to set an assured benefit at $4,000 per child, a level that would probably halve the number of families on AFDC.[60] As late as February 1994, child support enforcement and assurance was included in the draft of the Working Group on Welfare Reform, although no assured benefit level was indicated.[61] But when President Clinton announced welfare reform in his address four months later, CSA had been conspicuously deleted.

Except for allowing states, such as New York and Wisconsin, to experiment with CSA, the 104th Congress is unlikely to make it federal welfare policy. As structured, CSA would provide assistance to mothers of children on only one condition: establishing paternity. Conservatives would argue that such a benefit would reward unmarried women for having children and would further erode traditional family structure. For lawmakers obsessed with unmarried parenthood, particularly among African Americans, this would be nothing short of anathema.

Civic Liberalism

Through the 1980s, social philosophers restated the importance of the civic foundations of American culture.[62] The implications of a civic orientation for welfare policy received its most provocative treatment by Mickey Kaus, a senior editor of *The New Republic*. In *The End of Equality*, Kaus contrasts "money liberalism" with "civic liberalism," contending that the latter is a more realistic basis for social policy. Given American antipathy for income redistribution as a goal of public policy, Kaus argues that the creation of class-mixing situations would be more plausible. The classes of American culture tend to diverge and fragment unless public programs are deliberately fashioned to reintegrate them. Thus, Kaus favors a national service that would expose the affluent to circumstances of poorer fellow citizens. But he also suggests a two-year time limit on welfare, much like the Clinton proposal on welfare reform considered above.[63]

If Kaus's notion of civic liberalism was provocative when he introduced it in 1992, the composition of the 104th Congress makes it compelling indeed. A conservative and Republican Congress is likely to retract federal funding commitments for social welfare with urban poverty programs targeted for containment, if not elimination. The challenge for advocates of social justice will be to fashion strategies that enhance race mixing and upward mobility but without the massive infusion of funds associated with social programs. Examples of how civic liberalism might accelerate opportunity for African Americans are varied: inclusionary housing whereby developers must set aside a percentage of units for low- and moderate-income families, school choice allowing parents to select which school their children attend, social service vouchers through which the minority poor would have access to human service providers who have typically served middle- and upper-income clients, and mandatory community service whereby health and welfare professionals must demonstrate community service as a condition for obtaining and maintaining state licensure. Reductions in spending for social programs will require the invention of additional methods for achieving racial justice.

Development Accounts

Recently, "stakeholding"—the substitution of assets for income transfers through social policy—has become an option in poverty policy. Pioneered by Michael Sherraden of Washington University, stakeholding is advocated in response to the realization that the distribution of assets is even more skewed than income, and that the poor can benefit directly from benefits that encourage savings and asset accumulation rather than spending and income distribution. Accordingly, Sherraden has proposed the creation of Individual Development Accounts (IDAs) to bolster assets for the working poor. IDAs would be designated for specific purposes: housing, postsecondary education, self-employment, and retirement. The federal government would simply match IDA deposits made by people in qualifying low-income families. The amount of the federal supplement would vary with the importance of the activity—say $5 in federal match to $1 saved for housing, or $2 in federal match to $1 saved for retirement.[64] One such strategy—the Human Investment Policy for Oregon—is now in a planning phase, having been approved by that state's legislature and governor.[65] Iowa has incorporated development accounts as part of its Family Investment Plan initiative in state welfare reform.

The Prospects for Urban African Americans

The election of Bill Clinton to the presidency offered a measure of optimism for disadvantaged African Americans on what has been an otherwise bleak landscape. Between 1980 and 1992 the number of AFDC recipients increased from 10.1 million to 13.5 million while the purchasing power of benefits remained virtually static.[66] Yet during the same period federal aid to the cities plummeted. From 1980 to 1992 urban aid through General Revenue Sharing, Community Development Block Grants, Urban Development Action Grants, the Economic Development Administration, low-income housing, the Job Training Partnership Act (previously the Comprehensive Employment Training Act), and the McKinney homeless assistance program fell from $41.4 billion in 1980 to $16.9 billion in 1992.[67] The Clinton strategy for redressing federal neglect of cities was a comparatively anemic $3.5 billion for empowerment zones. To make matters worse, the prospects of increased health and welfare aid to poor individuals and families fell, casualties of the ill-fated Health Security Act and the postponement of welfare reform.

Only the naive would be sanguine about any significant improvement in the circumstances of African Americans after the 1994 Republican sweep of congressional elections. The Republican template for social policy reform—consolidating categorical programs into block grants to the states while cutting revenues substantially—will severely attenuate the opportunities of African Americans, particularly those on welfare and the working poor. At best such policies will further segregate African Americans from the social and economic mainstream of the nation; at worst they will be perceived by bigots as tacit assent to race-based hatred. As a result of the former, the tentative progress of African Americans since the War on Poverty will be largely reversed; as a result of the latter, the troubling legacy of racism, evident as far back as the New Deal, will continue to stain domestic policy.

An emerging theme that transcends conservatism and liberalism and that bears particular relevance to African Americans is economic empowerment. During the past two decades progressives have field tested a number of innovative projects. Such endeavors as the Ford Foundation's Local Initiative Support Corporation, James Rouse's Enterprise Foundation, and the Mott Foundation's microenterprise initiative generated an extensive list of successful community development ventures in poor neighborhoods.[68] Among the most significant of these are the Cooperative Home Care Associates of New York City, a worker-owned home health agency that has employed many former AFDC recipients,[69] and Reach Inc., a $20 million network of nonprofit enterprises in Mississippi and Alabama operated by African Americans, many of whom had been dependent on public assistance.[70] What differentiates these initiatives from traditional social programs that have benefited African Americans is that they are a product of the voluntary, nonprofit sector and rely minimally on public funds.

Conservatives, for their part, have conceived of their own empowerment strategy. Prompted by the writings of Robert Woodson, conservative policy institutes, such as the American Enterprise Institute and the Heritage Foundation, have enjoined the debate on racial and economic justice and have fielded proposals of their own. Conservative pronouncements on minority poverty predictably rail against the evils of federal funding and control, but they also evidence constructive suggestions that could benefit poor African Americans. Stuart Butler of the Heritage Foundation, for example, has been a particularly creative thinker, suggesting proposals ranging from enterprise zones to tenant ownership of public housing.[71] On the political front Jack Kemp earned the sobriquet "bleeding-heart conservative" for his willingness to immerse himself in problems of the urban poor, eventually leading to his appointment as HUD secretary under the Bush administration. In the early 1990s Kemp collaborated with former secretary of education William Bennett in founding Empower America, a think tank promoting conservative strategies in domestic policy. These developments are welcome insofar as they reflect a departure from traditional conservative resistance to considering seriously the plight of the minority poor. Economic empowerment may become a common denominator for addressing the increasingly marginal circumstances of poor African Americans.

The urgency of forging a synthesis of left and right cannot be overstated. As the riots that prompted the Kerner Commission so clearly demonstrated, desperate people resorted to civil disorder even as the War on Poverty was unfolding. The lesson is plain enough: the failure to generate a convincing strategy to solve the problems of poor, urban African Americans invites a revisit to the early 1960s. In that eventuality America will be confronted once again with the aftermath of racial injustice. Rising to the top of the list of policy options to aid the minority poor in distressed cities will be economic empowerment of African Americans. Historians will observe that such a strategy was outlined more than three decades earlier by the Kerner Commission.

Notes

1. *Report of the National Advisory Commission on Civil Disorders* (New York: Bantam Books, 1968).

2. For this reason historians have referred to the aggregation of American social programs as the "reluctant" welfare state or the "semiwelfare" state. See Bruce S. Jansson, *The Reluctant Welfare State: A History of American Social Welfare Policies* (Pacific Grove, Calif.: Brooks/Cole, 1993); Michael B. Katz, *In the Shadow of the Poorhouse: A Social History of Welfare in America* (New York: Basic Books, 1986).

3. David Stoesz and Howard Karger, "The Decline of the American Welfare State," *Social Policy and Administration* 3 (1992).

4. John Hope Franklin, *From Slavery to Freedom: A History of Negro Americans* (New York: Knopf, 1980): 287–94.

5. Ibid., 396.

6. Jill Quadagno, *The Color of Welfare* (New York: Oxford University Press, 1994), 157.

7. Ibid., 21.

8. An anomaly in the treatment of African Americans was the brief period of the Bureau of Refugees, Freedmen, and Abandoned Lands (or the Freedmen's Bureau) from 1865 to 1872, during which schools and health facilities were constructed for emancipated slaves in the South following the Civil War. See Franklin, *From Slavery to Freedom*, 235.

9. Katz, *In the Shadow of the Poorhouse*, 237.

10. U.S. House of Representatives, Committee on Ways and Means, *Overview of Entitlement Programs* (Washington, D.C.: U.S. Government Printing Office, 1992), 669.

11. Ibid.

12. Diana M. DiNitto, *Social Welfare: Politics and Public Policy* (Englewood Cliffs, N.J.: Prentice Hall, 1991), 130.

13. The brief and volatile history of CAPs is best chronicled by Daniel P. Moynihan, *Maximum Feasible Misunderstanding* (New York: Free Press, 1969).

14. Daniel P. Moynihan, *The Negro Family: The Case for National Action* (Washington, D.C.: U.S. Department of Labor, 1965).

15. William Julius Wilson, *The Truly Disadvantaged: The Inner City, the Underclass, and Public Policy* (Chicago: University of Chicago Press, 1987), 4.

16. Martin Anderson, "Welfare Reform," in *The United States in the 1980s* (Stanford: Hoover Institution, 1980), 139, 145.

17. George Gilder, *Wealth and Poverty* (New York: Basic Books, 1981), 108.

18. Charles Murray, *Losing Ground: American Social Policy, 1950–1980* (New York: Basic Books, 1984), 227–28.

19. David Stoesz and Howard Karger, *Reconstructing the American Welfare State* (White Plains, N.Y.: Longman, 1992), 51.

20. Committee on Ways and Means, *Overview of Entitlement Programs* (1992), 376.

21. Ibid.

22. Robert Mofitt and Douglas Wolf, "The Effect of the 1981 Omnibus Budget Reconciliation Act on Welfare Recipients and Work Incentives," *Social Service Review* 61 (1987): 247, 248.

23. Committee on Ways and Means, *Overview of Entitlement Programs* (1992), 377.

24. Ibid.

25. John Wodarski et al., "Reagan's AFDC Policy Changes: The Georgia Experience," *Social Work* 31 (1986): 273, 275.

26. Isabel Wolock et al., "Forced Exit from Welfare: The Impact of Federal Cutbacks on Public Assistance Families," *Journal of Social Service Research*, Winter 1985–Spring 1986, 71, 94.

27. Kevin Phillips, *The Politics of Rich and Poor: Wealth and the American Electorate in the Reagan Aftermath* (New York: Random House, 1990), 87.

28. Robert Greenstein and Scott Barancik, *Drifting Apart* (Washington, D.C.: Center on Budget and Policy Priorities, 1990), 17.

29. Committee on Ways and Means, *Overview of Entitlement Programs* (1992), 637, 641.

30. Ibid., 1449.

31. Lawrence Mishel and David Frankel, *The State of Working America* (Washington, D.C.: Economic Policy Institute, 1991), 171.

32. William Julius Wilson, "Public Policy Research and *The Truly Disadvantaged*," in *The Urban Underclass*, ed. Christopher Jencks and Paul Peterson (Washington, D.C.: Urban Institute, 1990), 460, 474.

33. Christopher Jencks, "Deadly Neighborhoods," *New Republic*, June 13, 1988, 23; Juan Williams, "Hard Times, Harder Hearts," *Washington Post*, October 2, 1988.

34. "Eight Boston Teenagers Charged in Savage Slaying of Young Mother," *Los Angeles Times*, November 21, 1990.

35. Louis Sahagun, "Gang Killings Increase 69%, Violent Crime up 20% in L.A. County Areas," *Los Angeles Times*, August 21, 1990.

36. Gabriel Escobar, "Slayings in Washington Hit New High, 436, for 3rd Year," *Los Angeles Times*, November 24, 1990.

37. Claude Brown, *Manchild in the Promised Land* (New York: Macmillan, 1965).

38. Daniel P. Moynihan, *Came the Revolution* (San Diego: Harcourt Brace Jovanovich, 1988), 291.

39. Ibid.

40. Jonathan Freedman, "Targeting the Drugs, Wounding the Cities," *Washington Post*, weekly ed., May 25–31, 1992.

41. Elliott Currie, *Reckoning* (New York: Hill and Wang, 1993).

42. Spencer Rich, "Panel Clears Welfare Bill," *Washington Post*, September 28, 1988.

43. Committee on Ways and Means, *Overview of Entitlement Programs* (1992), 618.

44. David T. Ellwood, *Poor Support: Poverty in the American Family* (New York: Basic Books, 1988), 153.

45. Center on Budget and Policy Priorities and Center for the Study of the States, *The States and the Poor: How Budget Decisions in 1991 Affected Low Income People* (Washington, D.C.: Center on Budget and Policy Priorities, 1991), 23.

46. See James Pinkerton, "Post-Modern Politics: The Search for a New Paradigm" (remarks before the Illinois New Paradigm Society, September 16, 1991); Mickey Kaus, "Paradigm's Loss," *New Republic*, July 27, 1992; Max Sawicky, *The Poverty of the New Paradigm* (Washington, D.C.: Economic Policy Institute, n.d.).

47. George Steinlieb, "Kemp-Garcia Act: An Initial Evaluation," in *New Tools for Economic Development*, ed. George Steinlieb and David Listokin (Piscataway, N.J.: Rutgers University Press, 1981).

48. G. Lewthwaite, "Heritage Foundation Delivers the Right Message," *Baltimore Sun*, December 9, 1984.

49. Art Pine, "President Vetoes Urban Aid Message," *Los Angeles Times*, November 5, 1992.

50. "White House Lists Recipients of Funds for Redevelopment," *Wall Street Journal*, December 12, 1994.

51. U.S. House of Representatives, Committee on Ways and Means, *Overview of Entitlement Programs* (Washington, D.C.: U.S. Government Printing Office, 1990), 1311.

52. Lori Montgomery, "Expert Prophesies Doom for Many Large U.S. Cities," *Albuquerque Journal*, December 25, 1994.

53. Committee on Ways and Means, *Overview of Entitlement Programs* (1992), 1013.

54. Lawrence Mead, *Beyond Entitlement: The Social Obligations of Citizenship* (New York: Free Press, 1986), 65.

55. See Elaine Kamarck, "The Welfare Wars," *New Democrat*, July 1992, 12, 13–15. For a critique of "social engineering," see *Innovations, New Directions, and New Convergences in Poverty Alleviation: Hearing before the Select Committee on Hunger*, H.R., 102d Cong., 2d sess., 1992, 39–48.

56. U.S. House of Representatives, Committee on Ways and Means, *Overview of Entitlement Programs* (Washington, D.C.: U.S. Government Printing Office, 1994), 455.

57. Irwin Garfinkel, "Bringing Fathers Back In: The Child Support Assurance Strategy," *American Prospect*, Spring 1992, 74, 75; David Ellwood, "Child Support Enforcement and Insurance: A Real Welfare Alternative" (unpublished manuscript, Harvard University, Kennedy School of Government, 1992), 9–10.

58. Garfinkel places the cost at $500 million assuming a $1,000 assured benefit level.

59. Ellwood, "Child Support Enforcement and Insurance," 9.

60. Ibid., 8–10.

61. "Welfare Reform Issue Paper" (unpublished paper, Working Group on Welfare Reform, Washington, D.C., n.d.), 36.

62. See Harry Boyte, *CommonWealth: A Return to Citizen Politics* (New York: Free Press, 1989); William Sullivan, *Reconstructing Public Philosophy* (Berkeley: University of California Press, 1986).

63. Mickey Kaus, *The End of Equality* (New York: Basic Books, 1992).

64. Michael Sherraden, *Assets and the Poor* (Armonk, N.Y.: Sharpe, 1991): 220–23.

65. Oregon House of Representatives Legislative Committee, 65th Legislative Assembly, 2d sess., 1990, "Oregonians Investing in Oregonians," committee print, 2.

66. Committee on Ways and Means, *Overview of Entitlement Programs* (1992), 660, 653.

67. Shari Rudavsky, "Financially Taxed Cities Seek Help," *Washington Post*, July 9, 1992.

68. Margaret Clark and Tracy Huston, ed., *Directory of Microenterprise Programs* (Washington, D.C.: Aspen Institute, 1992).

69. Jonathan Rowe, "Up from the Bedside: A Co-op for Home Care Workers," *American Prospect*, Summer 1990, 88–89.

70. William Claiborne, "Mississippi Earning," *Washington Post*, weekly ed., November 2–8, 1992.

71. Stuart Butler and Anna Kondratas, *Out of the Poverty Trap* (New York: Free Press, 1987).

Part Five The Dual Racial Reality
of the Media's Message

Charles Sumner Stone Jr. Thucydides' Law
of History, or,
From Kerner 1968
to Hacker 1992

The doleful prediction of the 1968 National Advisory Commission on Civil Disorders (the Kerner Commission)—"Our nation is moving toward two societies, one black, one white—separate and unequal"[1]—which followed the 1967 racial disorders that scorched America's urban landscape appears to have been documented prophetically twenty-four years later by an impressive array of sociological data in Andrew Hacker's textbook *Two Nations: Black and White, Separate, Hostile, Unequal.*[2] Both the Kerner Commission[3] and Hacker, whose statistical data and sociological analysis updated Gunnar Myrdal's epochal *An American Dilemma,*[4] reached a surprising agreement on the genesis of America's racially dichotomous society:

> [Kerner Commission:] What white Americans have never fully understood—but what the Negro can never forget—is that white society is deeply implicated in the ghetto. White institutions created it, white institutions maintain it, and white society condones it.[5]

> [Hacker:] So in allocating responsibility, the response should be clear. It is white America that has made being black so disconsolate an estate. Legal slavery may be in the past, but segregation and subordination have been allowed to persist.[6]

During the Kerner Commission's hearings on the causes of the 1967 riots, one of the first witnesses was distinguished psychologist Kenneth B. Clark, who bemoaned the Thucydidean nature[7] of prior riot reports that seemed repetitious, primarily because the historical events on which those reports were based had recurred periodically: "I read that report . . . of the 1919 riot in Chicago, and it is as if I were reading the report of the investigating committee on the Harlem riot of '35, the report of the investigating committee on the Harlem riot of '43, the report of the McCone Commission on the Watts riot.[8] I must again in candor say to you members of this Commission—it is a kind of Alice in Wonderland—with the same moving picture reshown over and over again, the same analysis, the same recommendations and the same inaction."[9]

Against this historical backdrop of recurring violent racial clashes, two indexes of black-white progress can be measured: (1) improvement of the media's ability to report a fairer and more balanced story of minority communities, and (2) the extent to which the media's authoritative reporting about democracy has carried over into the media's fairer employment and promotion of minorities. In assigning a sociology of causation for the 1967 riots, the Kerner Commission singled out the media as one of the factors contributing to the racial disorders. Yet the commission did not cite the media as one of the root causes when it answered the three questions that President Johnson asked the commission: "What happened? Why did it happen? What can be done to prevent it from happening again?"[10]

Many black[11] critics and scholars have long insisted that the media's reporting and shaping of images have contributed historically to institutionalized racism because of the press's integral influence as the fourth estate.[12] Based on that contention, the commission logically should have included the media in the first two parts of its threefold taxonomy—"What happened?" and "Why did it happen?"—because of the media's historical role as a cultural refractor and its powerful ability to influence public opinion on critical issues. Instead the commission relegated its analysis of the media to only the third part of its taxonomy—"What can be done?"[13] Jannette L. Dates, a black professor of journalism at Howard University, alluded to the Kerner Commission's inconsistency in acknowledging its criticism of the media while not including the press in its threefold analysis of the causes of the riots: "The report of the National Advisory Commission on Civil Disorders . . . focused on the causes of violence in America and singled out the media as one of the causes of discontent among the black populace."[14]

In trying to assess how the media's influence has changed between 1967 and 1993 and whether its coverage of the black community and its employment of blacks as journalists has improved, remained the same, or worsened during those twenty-five years, we must make analyze five factors: (1) the state of the African American community, (2) the state of race relations, (3) the state of the media, (4) the role of African Americans in the media, and (5) the impact of other minorities on African American progress.

The State of the African American Community

In 1967 only five African Americans were members of Congress. The year began with six members, but on March 1, 1967, the House of Representatives excluded Harlem's representative, Adam Clayton Powell Jr., the flamboyant and controversial chairman of the House Education and Labor Committee, for alleged improper use of committee funds.[15] The vote was 307 to 116,[16] with four of the other five African American congressmen— John Conyers Jr. (D-Mich.); Charles Diggs (D-Mich.); Augustus Hawkins (D-Calif.); and Robert N.C. Nix Jr. (D-Pa.)—all voting against the exclusion. The fifth African American congressman, William L. Dawson (D-Ill.), did not cast a vote.[17]

In comparison, by 1993 forty African Americans, including the first African American women from Florida, Georgia, and North Carolina, had become members of the House of Representatives, and the first African American woman, Carol Moseley Braun, was elected to the Senate from Illinois.

In 1967 there were fewer than fifty African American mayors, and no major city was governed by an African American mayor. By 1991 African Americans had become mayors of more than 300 cities, including Atlanta, Baltimore, Cleveland, Denver, Detroit, Hartford, Kansas City, Los Angeles, New Orleans, New York, Oakland, Richmond, Seattle, and Washington, D.C.[18] In addition, at the present time African Americans are Speakers of the House in two states: Dan Blue in North Carolina and Willie Brown in California. In the last three years African Americans also made history as L. Douglas Wilder became the first African American governor of Virginia and Ronald Brown, who first became chairman of the Democratic National Committee, became the first African American to be appointed as U.S. secretary of commerce in 1993. However, few events in black electoral politics galvanized black voter turnout more than the two presidential campaigns of the charismatic Reverend Jesse Jackson. In 1984 and 1988 Jackson made political history by running for president as a major candidate in the Democratic primaries.

Nonetheless, none of these dramatic gains translated into a significant improvement for African Americans living below the poverty line or for African Americans involved in the criminal justice system. In 1967 34 percent of all African American families lived below the poverty line, compared with 9 percent of all white families.[19] In 1990 the percentage of African American families living below the poverty line had decreased to 29 percent but was still nearly four times that of white families living below the poverty line.[20]

In 1967 the number of inmates in federal and state prisons was estimated to be 204,691.[21] No figures are available on the exact percentage of African American inmates in that year, although one of the nation's most distinguished criminal lawyers who is black, Raymond Brown of Montclair, New Jersey, estimated in an interview with this writer that 15 to 20 percent of the federal and state prison population in 1967 were African Americans. By 1990 the total number of federal and state prison inmates had surged to 738,894.[22] Former Howard University dean Douglas Glasgow estimates that African Americans now comprise 46 percent of all federal and state prisoners.[23]

A pivotal factor in the African American prison population explosion has been the violent confrontations between young African American males and the police. Police brutality between police and African Americans in major cities with large minority populations generally has been viewed as the cause of race riots in New York in 1964, Watts in 1965, Newark and Detroit in 1967, and South Central Los Angeles in 1992. Many African Americans, however, view these confrontations as an ongoing national scandal that is symbolized by the killings of African American motorists by white policemen during high-speed chases in Miami and Detroit and by the secretly videotaped beating of a speeding motorist, Rodney King, in Los Angeles after a high-speed chase and the subsequent acquittal of the policemen involved.

A *USA Today* editorial capsuled the Rodney King beating as the reflection of a national crisis:

"Could this happen in my town?" many asked as they watched over and over the scene videotaped by a witness.

Sadly, the answer for many is yes.

There were 2,500 complaints against Chicago police last year. A probe of police brutality has been demanded in Georgia. There have been problems in Kansas City, Dallas and Miami.[24]

Yet the Kerner Commission Report devoted only two and a half pages to "police conduct,"[25] a euphemism for police brutality and misconduct. In summarizing several national polls and surveys by Gallup, the New York Times, and the Senate Subcommittee on Executive Reorganization, the Kerner Commission concluded that "the 'brutality,' referred to in this and other surveys is often not precisely defined,"[26] despite the commission's own finding that "Negroes firmly *believe* that police brutality and harassment occur repeatedly in Negro neighborhoods. This *belief* is unquestionably one of the major reasons for intense Negro resentment against the police."[27]

Not all pathologies of African American life can still be blamed on white racism, however. In 1967 drugs were not a national menace to the tranquility of African American neighborhoods. In fact, the Kerner Commission mentioned the problems of the street encountered by ghetto children almost as an afterthought. In its analysis of the "jungle" [28] (its official euphemism for the "culture of poverty"), it lumped narcotics addiction with illegitimate births, single-parent homes, and juvenile delinquency.[29] Today, however, law enforcement agencies report that although white Americans comprise over 80 percent of all drug users, black Americans comprise 40 percent of all arrests for drug use.

In addition, even if white police are viewed as what some black rap groups describe as "the gestapo," no police misconduct has devastated black youth with such cruel efficiency as the rate at which young African American males are murdering each other. The Kerner Commission Report's section "Why did it happen?" devotes only four pages to "Crime and Insecurity" as part of its chapter titled "Conditions of Life in the Racial Ghetto." [30] In 1993, however, the widespread criminalization of African American communities by black drug dealers, together with the wanton killings of innocent black bystanders by deracinated black youth in Washington, D.C., Detroit, and Philadelphia provided a competing pathology with white racism in the decimation of African American families. "Experts attribute the rise [in the urban homicide rate] to an increase in drug disputes, deadlier weapons and a tendency among more young people to start careers in crime with a gun." [31]

The extent of black youth responsibility for this urban carnage has been revealed by a report from the U.S. Centers for Disease Control (CDC).[32] Between 1984 and 1988 the murder rate for black men between the ages of fifteen and twenty-four shot up by 67 percent.[33] One of every 1,000 young black men—ten times the number of whites—is doomed to die violently each year, according to Dr. Robert Froehlke, author of the 1990 CDC report. Homicide is now the number one cause of death for black males between the ages of fifteen and twenty-four.[34]

The State of Race Relations

The first defining moment for African Americans in 1967 was the exclusion from the House of Representatives on March 1 of the fiery, flamboyant, and history-making Representative Adam Clayton Powell Jr. Powell, who was from New York City, was only the second African American to chair a congressional committee.[35] In the early years of his ministerial career, when he was leading protest marches in Harlem, Powell was known as "Mr. Civil Rights."

Officially Powell was excluded for misuse of his committee funds, including paying for private trips and putting his wife on the payroll even though she performed no official duties in his congressional district or

Washington office. Privately most of Powell's African American supporters in his Harlem congressional district and a few of his white colleagues charged that racism governed his exclusion because of his sponsorship of the first National Conference on Black Power in August 1966. They pointed to Connecticut's Senator Thomas V. Dodd, whose abuses of office were considered by columnists and editorial writers to be of comparable seriousness but who was merely censured by the Senate in 1966.

When the phrase *black power* first burst onto the national scene in the late spring and early summer of 1966,[36] the social combustibility of white fears and black militancy created such a firestorm of tensions between white and black Americans that many prominent civil rights activists, elected officials, and civic leaders of both races still denounced the phrase and the movement as "divisive." Nonetheless, the phrase acquired a life force of its own. Although violent confrontations between whites and blacks had erupted in 1963 and 1964, before the "black power" movement, in Birmingham, Cambridge, Chicago, Cleveland, Jacksonville, New York City, Philadelphia, St. Augustine, and Savannah, many critics and journalists credited "black power's" influence as the riots' incendiary fuse.

But 1967, when widespread racial disorders resulted in the establishment of the Kerner Commission, was a year of political and racial contradictions. Powell had been excluded in March. Newark erupted with four days of racial rioting on July 11. And the second National Conference on Black Power was held in Newark two weeks later, despite public pleas from New Jersey governor Richard Joseph Hughes that it not be convened. On the day the black power conference ended, Detroit exploded into an orgy of violence rivaling Newark's riots in deadly intensity, racial fury, destruction of property, and loss of lives.

Paradoxically, on June 27, 1967, three weeks before 164 riots and disorders were to engulf 128 cities,[37] President Lyndon B. Johnson announced the appointment of the first African American member of the Supreme Court, the distinguished legal warhorse of the civil rights movement, Thurgood Marshall. On October 2 Marshall was sworn in.

The following year, 1968, may have been one of history's most emotionally convulsive years for African Americans. On April 4, less than one month after the Kerner Commission had issued its report, Martin Luther King Jr. was assassinated in Memphis, Tennessee. Again African American youth went on rampages, burning and looting, particularly in Washington, D.C., forcing President Johnson to call out the national guard to patrol the streets and restore quiet.

On June 5, almost two months to the day after King's assassination, New York senator Robert F. Kennedy was assassinated in Los Angeles while campaigning for the Democratic nomination for president. For African Americans, there was a lonely incandescence in this stygian scenario that had deprived them of a beloved "drum major for justice" and the brother of one of African Americans' most cherished presidential friends. In November Shirley Chisholm of Brooklyn, New York, became the first African American woman to be elected to the House of Representatives, ending the year of the Kerner Commission Report on a moderately positive note.

The following year, 1969, also must be considered historic for two reasons. Although it foreshadowed the beginning of the dissolution of the black-Jewish alliance that had energized the civil rights movement, it also ignited a new political torch that was to light the way to the election of the first African American mayors of major cities.

On January 31 a *Time* magazine cover, under the headline "Black vs. Jew: A Tragic Confrontation," depicted three blacks and three whites grimly facing each other across a split black and white page.[38] The story's headline inside the magazine was less accusatory of African American culpability for the interethnic schism: "The Black and the Jew: A Falling Out of Allies."[39] The conflict revealed, however, a naturally evolving dissolution of the civil rights movement's effectiveness and the inexorable disintegration of the movement's interracial leadership and constituency.

Time's "Black vs. Jew" cover headline also highlighted a pattern of mainstream media reporting that repeatedly has assigned most of the culpability to African Americans for tensions and conflict between the races. Ironically, twenty-three years later, *The Atlantic Monthly* would reprise the accusatory *Time* headline in its October 1992 issue. This time Latinos were assigned as the object of African American hostility: "Blacks vs. Browns."[40]

The year 1969 ended with a small measure of black progress symbolized by the election of African Americans the following year, 1970, when two of America's major cities, Cleveland and Gary, elected their first black mayors.

The era of gradual progress in race relations screeched to a sudden halt in 1970, two years after Richard M. Nixon took office, when the era of "benign neglect" toward black Americans was inaugurated. Urged by Daniel Patrick Moynihan, assistant secretary of labor, as a new policy in a memo to President Nixon, benign neglect was based on the perception that black Americans had made such substantial educational gains that it was no longer necessary for the federal government politically to subsidize civil rights. In the Republican administrations of Presidents Nixon, Ford, and Reagan, the benign neglect rule, which amounted to a political hands-off policy toward civil rights, continued. Between the Ford and Reagan administrations the Democratic administration of President Jimmy Carter briefly interrupted the policy by reviving a mild sensitivity toward civil rights.

By 1992, however, civil rights had been mothballed as an important national issue for both political parties. As both *The Economist* and the *Wall Street Journal* reported in their post-November presidential election stories, neither of the 1992 presidential candidates discussed civil rights during the campaign. "Instead of plain talk about race, the campaign produced an awkward silence," stated the lead editorial in *The Economist*.[41] The *Wall Street Journal* echoed this sentiment: "Eerily missing from the 1992 presidential debate was any mention of civil rights."[42]

Although African Americans can no longer be characterized as Ralph Ellison's "invisible man," the black masses are still disproportionately excluded from the economic mainstream. The resurrection of Malcolm X's charismatic militancy and the seductive influence of his philosophy on young blacks who have retreated from integration has caused radical change: an escalation of black protests on some college campuses in response to white attacks and slurs, an increasing number of applications of black students to black colleges, white resistance to affirmative action, the growth of support for school choice, and an increasing number of African American "immersion schools" in Baltimore, Chicago, Detroit, Los Angeles, Milwaukee, and Portland, Oregon, that are designed specifically for young African American males. Some educators and civil rights activists oppose immersion schools for young African American males as a reinstitution of "separate but equal" and the consequent resegregation of the public school system.[43]

Another new potentially damaging blow to interracial civility is the rise of open conflicts between blacks, on the one hand, and Hispanics and Asians, on the other. For the last fifteen years interethnic conflicts were confined to black-Jewish tensions that had begun smoldering in 1967 after a period of halcyon interracial togetherness during the civil rights movement in which Jews were pivotal to the movement's success. Racial disorders further aggravated black-Jewish relationships because of the larger numbers of Jewish business ownerships vis-à-vis the equally disproportionate numbers of low-income and unemployed African Americans.

In Los Angeles, which has become a classic urban textbook on racial enmities, recurring racial disorders have been in the forefront of the changing relationships between African Americans and other ethnic groups. A comparison of the two riots in Los Angeles—Watts, August 11, 1965,[44] and South Central Los Angeles, April 29, 1992[45]—dramatically illuminates these changes. In 1965 blacks and Latinos were political allies. There were no significant numbers of Korean-American-owned businesses in ghetto communities. When Watts erupted in 1965, the riot was reported and analyzed as a simplistic ethnic algorithm: blacks vs. whites. The media made no socioeconomic distinctions among blacks in reporting on the vandalism and the arrests. Part of this journalistic myopia was caused by a lack of African American reporters. In 1965 the *Los Angeles Times* did not employ a single African American journalist and was forced to send an African

American copy boy into the violence-convulsed community to report the story.

In 1992 a jury's finding that the Los Angeles police and California highway patrolmen were innocent of beating Rodney King triggered a violent outburst in South Central Los Angeles that reflected a more complicated interethnic symbiosis. Lawless African Americans were joined by lawless Latinos in the human tornado that destroyed $1 billion of insured businesses, many of them owned by Korean Americans in an area known as Koreatown.[46] "But state officials believe that at least 30 percent of the approximately four thousand businesses destroyed were Latino-owned."[47] Such anarchical rage at what many perceived as egregiously incomprehensible injustice can be contagious. The day after violence swept areas of Los Angeles, rampaging youths wrecked property and police cars in Atlanta; Compton; Long Beach; Madison, Wisconsin; and San Francisco.

In Los Angeles, where almost only blacks were arrested after the 1965 Watts riots, more Latinos (49 percent) were arrested than African Americans after the 1992 riot.[48] Did this unity of destruction symbolize a strengthened political unity between Latinos and African Americans? Not necessarily. Prior to the momentary Latino–African American unity in destruction, the two groups were becoming more politically estranged. In what reporter Jack Miles called "A New Paradigm: Blacks vs. Latinos," he summed up in one paragraph a prophetic polarization between blacks and Latinos:

> What counts for more, however, than any incipient struggle between older and newer Latino immigrants is the emerging struggle between Latinos and blacks. . . . The terms of engagement, if we take our cue from the rappers, would seem to be black versus white or black versus Asian. But the Korean population of Los Angeles County is just 150,000, a tiny fraction of the Latino population of 3.3 million. Of the 60,560 people in Koreatown itself, only 26.5 percent are Asian; more than 50 percent are Latino. Blacks are the most oppressed minority, but it matters enormously that whites are no longer a majority. And within the urban geography of Los Angeles, African-Americans seem to me to be competing more directly with Latin Americans than with any other group.[49]

This new escalating interethnic conflict may be caused, in part, by the sharp increase of immigrants, the majority of whom are coming from Latin American countries. Miles cited U.S. Census Bureau figures released on May 11, 1992, that reported the admission of 8.6 million immigrants during the 1980s, more than in any decade since 1900–1910. Of that number, over 750,000 indicated to immigration authorities that Los Angeles was their intended destination.[50]

Adding to these burgeoning numbers are the unknown exact numbers of immigrants who enter illegally from Mexico and other Central American countries and who are willing to work at low-paying jobs in order to survive. This illegal influx has only exacerbated the worsening competition between African Americans and Latinos for fewer jobs.

The State of the Media

In 1968 America was a nation of contradictory daily newspaper-reading habits. The 1,438 evening newspapers (including 16 "all day" newspapers) comprised 82 percent of the 1,749 daily newspapers, but their combined circulation of 36,279,265 accounted for 58.9 percent of the total circulation of 61,560,952.[51] The 327 morning newspapers, however, which comprised only 18 percent of the daily newspaper circulation, accounted for 41 percent (25,848,270) of the total circulation. Newspapers were clearly as vital to America's morning reading habits as coffee was integral to the nation's dawning nourishment.

By 1991 the nation's newspaper-reading habits had changed as a result of a national shift to television network news, which, in turn, had begun suffering an ironic loss of viewers to cable television. Twenty-three years after the Kerner Commission Report there were 163 fewer daily newspapers being published. Interestingly, the number of morning newspapers had increased from 327 to 571 (a gain of 244 newspapers), while the number of evening newspapers had decreased from 1,438 to 1,042 (a loss of 396 newspapers).[52]

But the total circulation had held relatively steady at 60,687,125 for a twenty-three-year loss of 1,858,269. Although many publishers have attempted to put the most optimistic face on this comparatively small decrease in readership (2 percent), the decline has serious implications for the nation's reading habits when compared with the increase in U.S. population from 200,706,000 in 1968 to 254,105,000 in 1992.[53] Meanwhile the circulation equation shifted dramatically in twenty-three years. In 1991 the 571 morning newspapers accounted for 68 percent of all newspaper circulation, while the 1,042 evening newspapers accounted for only 31.6 percent of the total circulation of 60,687,125.

America's newspaper readers had irrevocably crossed two informational Rubicons: a change from evening to morning newspaper-reading habits and a shift from newspaper news to television news. Newspaper executives repeatedly have cited the impact of television's evening news as a factor in the decline of afternoon newspapers.

Although 1968—the year of the Kerner Commission—was a year of robust numbers of newspaper readers, it was a year of paucity of jobs for

African American journalists: "Black journalists accounted for less than 1 percent of the United States' working journalists" in 1968.[54] Under the subsequent prodding of the American Society of Newspaper Editors (ASNE), which finally awakened like Rip Van Winkle to the intractable underrepresentation of African Americans in the media, editors—especially those in large metropolitan areas populated by minorities—began the slow process of responding to affirmative action. To encourage further the editors to hire minorities, ASNE set the year 2000 as its goal for achieving demographic parity that would represent the combined proportionate percentages of minorities in the population: African Americans (12.4 percent), Latinos (8.6 percent), Asian Americans (2.8 percent), and Native Americans (.007 percent), for a total of 23 percent.[55]

As of 1992, however, the total percentage of minority journalists—African Americans, Latinos, Asian Americans, and Native Americans—had increased from less than 3 percent in 1968 to 9.3 percent in 1992.[56] ASNE did not begin tracking minority progress in the newsrooms until 1978.

One possible reason for the media's reluctance to increase the numbers and percentage of black reporters has been the media's apparent twofold conviction that it did not need minority reporters to cover the minority community, and that minority reporters were not sufficiently skilled or talented to cover anything else. As a result, one of the biggest cottage industries to develop within the media was the growth of a group of almost exclusively white reporters and editors who achieved national distinction as prize-winning journalistic experts on civil rights, black people, black progress, black pathologies, black culture, black-white relations, black-Jewish relations, black injustices, and black inequalities.

If employment of minorities, particularly blacks, by the mainstream media plodded forward with tortoise-like speed, reporting about blacks came closer to the hare's velocity as a paradigm. Beginning in 1966 blacks were featured almost monthly on the cover of various national magazines or in page-one newspaper features. *Newsweek* was especially solicitous about the state of the black race that antedated the series of urban racial explosions. The *Newsweek* covers are a kind of historical cataloguing of the vicissitudes of the black-white symbiosis that reflected the changing times and America's shifting interests in civil rights. On June 20, 1966 (the year before the riots in Newark and Detroit), *Newsweek*'s cover story on the James Meredith march broke new ground and featured a picture of Martin Luther King Jr. being interviewed.[57] *Newsweek* subsequently featured more cover stories on the black experience than any other mainstream publication:

• August 22, 1966—"Black and White: A Major Survey of U.S. Racial Attitudes Today";

- January 16, 1967—"Must Adam Leave Eden?" (speculating on the possible exclusion of Representative Adam Clayton Powell Jr. from Congress and picturing a saucily grinning Powell in beach attire, leaning on a post);
- November 20, 1967—"The Negro in America: What Must Be Done" (showing two hands, one a clenched fist, the other reaching upward);
- June 30, 1969—"Report from Black America: A Newsweek Poll" (including a collage of black faces);
- May 5, 1969—"Universities under the Gun" (picturing armed black Cornell University students leaving a building);
- February 23, 1970—"The Panthers and the Law" (showing three ominous-looking blacks with a poster of Bobby Seale in the background);
- August 3, 1970—"The Black Mayors: How Are They Doing?" (picturing Kenneth Gibson, the first black to be elected mayor of Newark, New Jersey);
- October 26, 1970—"Angela Davis: Black Revolutionary" (including a picture of the brilliant scholar who had tried to smuggle guns into a courtroom to free the three "Soledad Brothers," who had killed a prison guard);
- June 17, 1971—"The New Black Politics" (depicting twelve black members of Congress, including Shirley Chisholm, on the Capitol steps);
- March 23, 1986—"Brothers: A Vivid Portrait of Black Men in America" (picturing a black man holding his daughter on his lap);
- March 7, 1988—"Black and White: How Integrated Is America?" (showing two five-year-olds, a white boy and a black girl, supposedly hugging each other, but with only the black girl's arm shown draped over the shoulder of the white boy);
- September 11, 1989—"Can the Children Be Saved? One Block's Battle against Drugs" (showing a little black child in Philadelphia. The cover epitomized the stereotype that drugs are a black problem, but more importantly, shifted the emphasis away from civil rights to black-on-black pathologies within the black community.).

During the years of *Newsweek*'s fecund display of black experience covers, *Time,* the *New York Times Sunday Magazine,* and *The Saturday Review* also occasionally featured cover stories on various aspects of the black experience (middle-class blacks, black families, black executives and corporate stress, black studies, and black self-help programs), but none as frequently as *Newsweek*.

During these same twenty-five years, television was adapting, but more slowly, to an awakening moral imperative to report on the black experience. Television was able to dramatize with pictures, perhaps more effectively than newspapers were able to report, the cataclysmic changes of the civil rights movement—from sit-ins, demonstrations, and protest marches to race riots and racial attacks.

In 1993 African American television reporters were no longer an electronic rarity. African Americans reported from Moscow, the White House, the governor's office, the mayor's office, congressional hearings, executive branch departments, theater openings, movies, jazz concerts, and as local weekend anchors. The only regular weekday African American national network anchor person, however, was Bernard Shaw of CNN (Cable News Network).

Despite these historic advances since the year of the Kerner Commission Report, however, African Americans still remain in the back of the electronic bus in numbers, executive positions, and as producers.

The Roles of African Americans in the Media

The Print Media

One of the first casualties of the mainstream media's tepid response to the Kerner Commission Report was its good intentions. Instead of adopting a vigorous equal-opportunity employment program or undertaking a critical self-examination of its reporting on minorities, the media joined journalism schools (some of the more benignly self-exculpatory resisters to equal employment and admissions) to sponsor five-year cyclical seminars, "Kerner Plus 5," "Kerner Plus 10," "Kerner Plus 15," and "Kerner Plus 20." These seminars amounted to nothing more than industry-justifying discussions of reportorial shortcomings, instead of programmatic outlines of methods to incorporate accomplishments and demonstrably successful strategies for the employment and reporting ·of minorities as described in chapter 15 of the Kerner Commission Report, titled "The News Media and the Disorders."[58] Here again, the Kerner Commission Report focused almost solely on African Americans and their Du Boisian "double consciousness"[59] relationship to the media. Seventy-two years after Du Bois's concept of double consciousness had capsuled the African American's historical ethos, a group of African American journalists applied the double consciousness vision to their profession. On December 12, 1975, seven years after the Kerner Commission had issued its report, forty-three African American newspaper, magazine, and electronic journalists met in Washington, D.C., and formed the National Association of Black Journalists (NABJ). Founding members included Mal Goode, the first African American to be hired as a reporter by a television network; the late Max Robinson, the first African American to be hired as a news anchor by a network; Paul Delaney, former deputy national editor of the *New York Times* and now the chairman of the journalism department in the University of Alabama's College of Communication; and this writer, who was then a senior editor at the *Philadelphia Daily News*. I was elected NABJ's first president. With the exception of five journalists from the black media (radio and magazines), the remaining thirty-eight founding members were employed by mainstream newspapers and television and radio stations.

Today, nine NABJ presidents later, including its first woman president, Sidmel Estes-Sumpter, elected in 1991, NABJ has over 3,000 members, a Washington office, ten regional directors, and an operating budget of over $1 million.[60] Of NABJ's twelve objectives, the first was intended to "strengthen ties between blacks in the black media and blacks in the white media."[61] Other objectives intended to "sensitize the white media to the institutional racism in their coverage and employment practices; expand the white media's coverage and balanced reporting in the black community; critique through a national newsletter examples of the media's reportorial deficiencies as they affect blacks; encourage journalism schools to appoint black professors through the work of a liaison committee; work with high schools to identify potential journalists; act as a clearinghouse for jobs; and work to upgrade black journalist in managerial and supervisory jobs."[62]

It is instructive to compare NABJ's 1975 goals with the 1968 recommendations of the Kerner Commission as listed in the report's section, "Negroes in Journalism." Declaring that "the journalism profession has been shockingly backward in seeking out, training and promoting Negroes," the Kerner Commission urged that "the recruitment of Negro reporters must extend beyond established journalists, or those who have already formed ambitions along those lines. It must become a commitment to seek out young Negro men and women, inspire them to become—and then train them as—journalists. Training programs should be started at high schools and intensified at colleges. Summer vacation and part-time editorial jobs, coupled with offers of permanent employment, can awaken career plans."[63]

As did NABJ, the Kerner Commission Report also recognized the equally critical problem of a more balanced, diversified, and accurate portrayal of African Americans in the media if white Americans were to be educated to a more informed appreciation of Negroes as normative American citizens. In the section called "The Negro in the Media," the Kerner Commission Report recommended that "the news media must publish newspapers and produce programs that recognize the existence and activities of the Negro, both as a Negro and as part of the community. It would be a contribution of inestimable importance to race relations in the United States simply to treat ordinary news about Negroes as news of other groups is now treated."[64]

African Americans, however, rarely enjoy the luxury of "ordinary news." As the Kerner Commission documented, African Americans constantly encounter differential and disproportionately malevolent treatment at the hands of an institutionalized white racist system than do whites. It is in the criminal justice system, especially in the hands of the police, where African Americans suffer their most consistent mistreatments.

Yet the Kerner Commission Report seemed to doubt the authenticity or accuracy of reports by African Americans that a double standard is operative in the media and in the criminal justice system. Even worse, the commission seemed unable to make up its mind on just how fair or even-handed the media had been in its reporting. Each of its three conclusions about the media seemed to contradict the others:

> First, despite instances of sensationalism, inaccuracies and distortions, newspapers, radio and television, on the whole, made a real effort to give a balanced, factual account of the 1967 disorders.
>
> Second, despite this effort, the portrayal of the violence that occurred last summer failed to reflect accurately its scale and character. The overall effect was, we believe, an exaggeration of both mood and event.
>
> Third, and ultimately most important, we believe that the media have thus far failed to report adequately on the causes and consequence of civil disorders and the underlying problems of race relations.[65]

Later in its report, however, the commission conceded that its major concern was not with the news media's reporting about the riots, "but in the failure to report adequately on race relations and ghetto problems and to bring more Negroes into journalism."[66] The media leadership infrastructure of African American journalists, civil rights activists, social critics, book authors, entertainers, free lance writers, and members of professional organizations contend that this failure is a direct result of the "white racism" to which the commission alluded in the early part of its report.[67]

Trying to counteract what African American professionals perceive as a white-male-dominated industry with an abulic posture toward racial equality, African Americans have accelerated their efforts in urging the media to hire and promote more African Americans and to be more sensitive to the media's negative racial stereotypes that reinforce racial polarization and that, in turn, provide a fertile pasture for racial hostilities. This two-tier concern is a logical concomitant of Du Bois's double consciousness, which, ninety years later, still determines the operational methods used by African Americans to protest and accommodate the psychic duality of their existence.

Consistent with this two-tier concern is a conceptual dichotomy for the media jointly authored by Clint C. Wilson II, associate dean of the Howard University School of Communications, and Felix Gutierrez, former associate professor at the University of Southern California School of Journalism and current vice-president of the Freedom Forum. In their book, *Minorities and Media*, Wilson and Gutierrez conceptually divide the media into two categories: nonentertainment media (newspapers and news magazines) and entertainment media (movies and television).[68] A case can be made, however, for television's inclusion in the nonentertainment category. Based on television's ubiquitous ability to influence and sometimes even to control the flow of news events, especially elections and the times that important press conferences are called in order to accommodate the six or eleven o'clock news, this medium could also be included in the nonentertainment group. First Amendment issues such as censorship (prior restraint), free press versus fair trial conflicts, access to courtrooms, and trial dispositions affect television as critically as they do newspapers.

Moreover, one of the areas where damaging stereotypes have been employed with pervasive negative impact by both newspapers and television is advertising. In their anthropological assessment of the media's stereotypical imaging of African Americans in news stories and advertisements, Jannette L. Dates, associate dean at the Howard University School of Communications, and William Barlow, associate professor of radio, television, and film at Howard University, authoritatively have summarized the harm inflicted by the media on African American self-esteem and white American respect for African Americans. In the article titled "Split Images and Double Binds" the authors write, "White domination of the mass media, with its pervasive control over the portrayal and participation of African-Americans in those media, has disclosed major cultural contradictions. . . . The black images mass-produced by them . . . have been filtered through the racial misconceptions and fantasies of the dominant white culture, which has tended to deny the existence of a rich and resilient black culture of equal worth."[69]

Alluding to a "schizoid racial representation in the American mass media," Dates and Barlow go on to note,

> More often than not, the images of African-Americans favored by the mainstream media were based on long-standing black stereotypes. These one-dimensional caricatures not only gave white Americans a false impression of black life, art and culture, but they also helped to mold white public opinion patterns, and set the agenda for public discourse on the race issue, thus broadening the cultural gap between black and white America. On the other side of the racial divide, the stereotyped imagery provoked a defiant response from many black image makers, who consciously sought to undermine the prevailing black representations by parodying or negating those stereotypes.[70]

Is this social phenomenon now confined to the pages of African American history,[71] or has significant progress been made in both the nonentertainment and the entertainment media to render obsolete the dialogic concern over harmful African American stereotypes? The question can best be answered by examining the extent to which African Americans have been able to exert control over the merchandising of African American images. Dates and Barlow find "significant inroads" made by some African American entrepreneurs and decision makers, such as Oprah Winfrey and Spike Lee, as television and movie producers.[72]

These authors outline two trends, however, that may retard and even reverse progress in enhancing the media's image of African Americans: first, the failure of minority ownership of media outlets in minority communities to keep pace with changing demographic parity and, second, "the new revisionist black representations in the mass media [that upgrade the black stereotype to] a new 'Noble Negro' stereotype living in an upper middle-class utopia" and whose family has finally become—to use a well-known black expression—"just like white people," as exemplified by the crossover popularity of television's *The Cosby Show*.[73] Some critics, however, still consider Bill Cosby's situation comedy as a more sophisticated, updated, and acceptable version of *Amos 'n' Andy* because both cater to unrealistic image extremes at opposite ends of the entertainment spectrum, and both, paradoxically, are embraced by white conservatives who may not necessarily be enthusiastic proponents of affirmative action.[74] What Harvard University's W. E. B. Du Bois Professor of Humanities and chair of the African American studies department, Henry Louis Gates Jr., who is one of the nation's defining voices of the African American experience, calls a "minuscule integration of blacks into the upper middle class" sows the seeds of its own rejection because "the social vision of Cosby . . . reassuringly throws the blame for black poverty back onto the impoverished."[75]

To what extent does the issue of cinematic racial stereotypes interact with the issue of the news media's employment of African Americans and the news media's reporting of events in the African American community? Are racial stereotypes and, by definition, racism and racial exclusion still as serious a problem in the newspaper industry as the Kerner Commission described in its report? A December 12, 1992, story in *Editor & Publisher* headlined "Tempers Flare: Minority Journalists Tell National Newspaper Association Officials That More Has to Be Done in Diversifying Newsrooms" described an acerbic confrontation during a four-hour meeting between the nearly all-white group of newspaper publishers and representatives of black, Latino, Asian, and gay journalists. According to the *Editor & Publisher* story, all of the minority representatives

> expressed dissatisfaction with the status of minority groups in newspapers and with the Newspaper Association of America's handling of it.

Sidmel Estes-Sumpter, president of the National Association of Black Journalists and a producer at WAGA-TV in Atlanta, saw no improvement over the past year.

"You just don't get it," she said in a 10-minute tongue-lashing of NAA's diversity committee, whose lack of progress left her "angry and very frustrated."

At the close of an afternoon of "talking heads," she called the meeting mostly a wasted effort because she saw little progress in "real solutions."[76]

Estes-Sumpter singled out the warnings of the Kerner Commission Report that the media should begin to reflect the views of minorities if a greater racial amity is to be achieved. In response a few of the executives readily conceded their industry's vulnerability on the charges of racism. "If you don't think there's racism in newspapers today, you're kidding yourself," declared *Seattle Times* publisher and chief executive officer Frank Blethen.[77] Wanda Lloyd, a *USA Today* executive and vice-chairwoman of the National Association of Minority Media Executives, concurred by citing "racism and hostility" at many newspapers. "It may be surprising, but I hear about it all the time," she said.[78]

The ubiquitous "it" (racial hostility) is now being fueled by a double white backlash against the accelerated employment of minorities. "White males consider themselves a threatened group by what we're talking about," declared the *Times Mirror* Company's president David Laventhol to the meeting of the newspaper CEOs.[79] A backlash among white women against the industry's efforts to hire and promote minorities is also increasing, the Quincy, Massachusetts, *Patriot Ledger* editor Bill Ketter told the meeting.[80]

Despite these twin constraints of the white male and white female backlashes, the persistence of racial stereotypes as a hostile impact on public dialogues is one with which newspapers must still cope. Gregory Favre, executive editor of the *Sacramento Bee*, told the groups that newspapers should "audit" their content to ascertain whether they may be inadvertently perpetuating racial and minority stereotypes. By his paper's policy of "exclusion," he realized that the Bee was contributing to the nurturing of "negative" perceptions among minority groups.[81]

But Favre, ironically, has been one of the more enlightened mainstream editors. The problem lay in the profession's historical exclusion of African American journalists. Still, it would be reportorially inaccurate to leave the impression that the mainstream media's major response to the *Kerner Commission Report* with their cathartic seminars, "Kerner Plus 5," "Kerner Plus 10," "Kerner Plus 15," and "Kerner Plus 20," resulted in almost no gains for African Americans after the report had been published.

Gains may have been embarrassingly minuscule, but they did occur. The Kerner Commission overlooked many of the earlier advances by ignoring recurring spasms of African American progress in the mainstream media and by cavalierly dismissing with a footnote[82] the value of the African American press in helping to dismantle racial segregation.

Ironically, a black-owned magazine signaled a change in the mainstream media industry one year after the Kerner Commission had issued its report. *Ebony* magazine photographer Moneta Sleet became the first African American to win journalism's most prestigious award, the Pulitzer Prize. Sleet's honorific "first" may have resulted from the profession's response to the Kerner Commission's public relations pressures, or it may simply have been a harbinger of racially changing times.

Whatever the reason, African American journalists were to bring distinction to their profession between 1969 and 1995 by winning fifteen Pulitzer Prizes for excellence in investigative reporting, international reporting, editorial writing, feature writing, feature photography, spot news photography, explanatory journalism, and commentary.[83] With the exception of the first Pulitzer to *Ebony* magazine's Sleet, the other fourteen were won by African American journalists at mainstream publications such as the *Birmingham News*, the *Boston Globe*, the *Chicago Sun-Times*, the *Chicago Tribune*, the *Miami Herald*, and *Newsday*.

During this same time span, four African Americans won the Alfred I. DuPont–Columbia University Broadcast Journalism Award "for outstanding work in news and public affairs"; six African Americans won the George Foster Peabody Award for distinguished television journalism; and twelve African Americans won the George Poke Award for "courage and resourcefulness in gathering and reporting a story."[84]

Another measure of the media's grudging capacity to change was reflected in the forty-four African "Americans who won the prestigious Nieman Fellowship at Harvard between 1946 and 1994. Fletcher Martin was the first African American Nieman Fellow and later became a USIA [United States Information Agency] official."[85]

These trailblazing awards did not signal the arrival of the racial millennium in equal employment opportunities for black journalists. But they did represent a measure of substantive progress since 1887, when the *New York Sun* employed an African American, T. Thomas Fortune, as a typesetter and part-time reporter.[86] Fortune's employment still represented an aberration for a profession staunchly opposed to employing African American journalists.

Although the Kerner Commission concentrated its 608-page report on the sociology of the 1967 racial disorders, the commission devoted an entire section, chapter 15, to the news media and the disorders in an effort to ascertain the media's impact in answering the report's three major questions: (1) What happened?, (2) Why did it happen?, and (3) What can be done?

Answers to those questions were not necessarily the media's responsibility. Besides, the industry was too busy sponsoring the quinquennial seminars, such as "Kerner Plus 5." At these seminars few presentations documented successful strategies for achieving the equal employment and fair reporting of minorities as urged in chapter 15 of the Kerner Commission Report.[87]

But the Kerner Commission Report had focused almost solely on African Americans and the symbiotic Du Boisian double consciousness[88] with the media. Double consciousness was black America's logical response to white America's double consciousness as defined by Gunnar Myrdal in his epochal work on race relations, *An American Dilemma*.

> The "American Dilemma," referred to in the title of this book, is the ever-raging conflict between, on the one hand, the valuations preserved on the general plane which we shall call the "American Creed," where the American thinks, talks, and acts under the influence of high national and Christian precepts, and, on the other hand, the valuations on specific planes of individual and group living, where personal and local interests; economic, social, and sexual jealousies; considerations of community prestige and conformity; group prejudice against particular persons or types of people; and all sorts of miscellaneous wants, impulses, and habits dominate his outlook.[89]

"Group prejudice," or what the Kerner Commission Report called "white racism," caused the mainstream media to treat the African American as an "invisible man." Repeatedly in *An American Dilemma* Myrdal writes of a "systematic tendency . . . to avoid mentioning anything about Negroes in the press except their crimes."[90] "The white newspapers in the North ordinarily ignore the Negroes and their problems entirely—most of the time more completely than the liberal Southern press."[91]

Myrdal makes a dichotomous distinction in his analysis of the relationship between Negroes and the press. "The press" actually means the "white press" and "the Negro press." But Myrdal does not devote any of the twenty-six pages about the white press to the role of Negro reporters, columnists, or editors in formulating news and editorial policies.

In his twenty-seven-page discussion, "The Growth of the Negro Press," however,[92] he alludes briefly to the early pioneers of Negro newspapers, such as John Brown Russwurm, the Reverend Samuel E. Cornish, Frederick Douglass, William Monroe Trotter, and Robert S. Abbott. As founders, they reacted to the white press's "exclusionary phase"[93] that rejected African Americans as reporters and as subjects of news stories. Meanwhile, the black community was intensifying pressures for a voice that could publicize its struggle for equality.

On March 17, 1827, Russwurm, one of America's first black college graduates, cofounded with Cornish what is generally acknowledged as America's first black newspaper, *Freedom's Journal*. "We wish to plead our own cause," declared the paper's first editorial. "Too long have others spoken for us."[94]

As an early progenitor of the black press, Frederick Douglass, the great abolitionist statesman, was one of the black founding fathers of the civil rights movement who utilized the press to publicize black grievances in the same way that three of the white founding fathers had used the press to argue for the establishment of a United States where only whites were citizens. The distinguished trio of Alexander Hamilton, John Jay, and James Madison, who anonymously authored letters to the editor under the nom de plume "Publius,"[95] were journalistic forerunners of a quartet of four African American civil rights statesmen who either founded or edited black newspapers: Frederick Douglass, W. E. B. Du Bois, A. Philip Randolph, and Adam Clayton Powell Jr.

Douglass founded the *North Star* in 1847 and remained its editor for eight years. Du Bois founded *The Crisis*, a magazine of essays and articles that reflected views of the National Association for the Advancement of Colored People (NAACP). Du Bois served as editor from 1910 to 1934.[96] In the 1920s A. Philip Randolph, founder of the Brotherhood of Sleeping Car Porters, edited *The Messenger*, a socialist magazine that militantly crusaded to improve the working conditions of railway sleeping-car porters.

The Messenger was so widely read and its militant views quoted so often by African Americans that the federal government investigated the magazine for possible seditious articles. After a satirical article, "Pro-Germanism among Negroes," was published in the May–June 1918 issue, the government censored the magazine by suspending its second-class mailing privileges for three years.[97]

In 1942 Powell cofounded the tabloid *People's Voice* with Harlem businessman Charles Buchanan. Powell served as editor in chief and wrote a popular column, "Soapbox." After his election to Congress in 1944, he continued the column, "Soapbox from Washington." Many critics labeled the paper a left-wing front for the Communist Party, and FBI director J. Edgar Hoover issued orders to keep it under surveillance. In 1947 Powell stepped down as editor.

The black press flourished because, as the Kerner Commission documented in its report, the white media had not made much progress in facilitating a dual equality—reporting about black America and hiring black journalists, particularly the latter. "The journalism profession has been shockingly backward in seeking out, hiring, training and promoting Negroes. Fewer than five percent of the people employed by the news business in editorial jobs in the United States today are Negroes. Fewer than one percent of editors and supervisors are Negroes, and most of them work for Negro-oriented organizations." [98]

Despite the near-impenetrability of the mainstream media's glass ceiling, a few African Americans have cracked it and even distinguished themselves nationally as publishers, editors, editorial page editors, columnists, reporters, and photographers.

Carl Thomas Rowan probably merits the accolade of "father of contemporary black journalists." During a lecture to the University of Kentucky journalism department, I proposed a course on the history of African American journalists titled "From Russwurm to Rowan."

After a prize-winning career as a reporter and foreign correspondent for the *Minneapolis Tribune*, Rowan served in several high-level administrative and diplomatic positions in the Kennedy and Johnson administrations before becoming a nationally syndicated columnist. [99] As a result of his door-opening success, major newspapers in Washington, New York, Chicago, and Philadelphia appointed blacks as columnists for the first time. One was *Washington Post* reporter William Raspberry, who later became a nationally syndicated columnist and won a Pulitzer Prize in 1994.

Other African Americans who distinguished themselves in the mainstream media include Theodore Roosevelt Augustus Major "Ted" Poston, whom the *New York Post* hired as a reporter in 1937. Poston later became the first African American to win a George Polk Award (1949). [100]

Robert C. Maynard, a *Washington Post* reporter, started out at age sixteen as a reporter for the African-American-owned *New York Age* and later became the first African American publisher of a major daily newspaper, the *Oakland Tribune*. With his wife, Nancy Hicks, a *New York Times* reporter, Maynard also cofounded the University of California at Berkeley's Institute for Journalism Education, which trained minority journalists. The Berkeley institute was a direct outgrowth of the Kerner Commission's recommendations. [101]

While several African American families have distinguished themselves as publishers and editors in the black-owned press, the Wilkins family has left a legacy in both journalism and civil rights. Roy Wilkins, who was the NAACP's influential voice as executive secretary from 1955 to 1977, started out as a managing editor and columnist for the black-owned *Kansas City Call*. In 1935 he followed Du Bois as editor of *The Crisis* and held that position for fifteen years.

Wilkins' nephew, Roger, served as assistant attorney general for civil rights in the Kennedy administration. A well-regarded writer whose op-ed pieces were frequently published in nationally prominent dailies, Wilkins later became a member of the editorial boards of both the *Washington Post* and the *New York Times*. He is currently a chaired professor of history at George Mason University and appears occasionally on television and radio public affairs programs as a commentator.

Television

Because the phrase *split image* euphemistically encapsulates the double consciousnesses that white Americans and black Americans have internalized, it is especially pertinent to their respective employment and acting roles in the media.

In *Split Image*, a series of essays on African Americans in the mass media, coeditor Jannette L. Dates devotes a lengthy analysis to the television industry's dual treatment of African Americans in programs and in employment.[102] While she delineates the historical range of African American portrayals in television dramas, situation comedies, variety shows, miniseries, soap operas, and talk shows, she ironically offers very little insight into the changing role of African American journalists in television news.

But African American reporters and news anchors are a rising electronic appearance. African Americans are now seen on television reporting for all four networks from the White House, Moscow, Bonn, London, and Paris. Bernard Shaw, CNN's lead anchor and a former CBS correspondent, is the only African American to report network news on a nightly basis.

Ed Bradley is one of the five-person investigative team on CBS's Sunday evening show *60 Minutes*. Carol Simpson is the weekend anchor for ABC News, and Charlayne Hunter-Gault is a national correspondent for PBS's McNeil-Lehrer news show. One of the most impressive national reporters is CBS's Harold Dow. Although Bryant Gumbel, who cohosts *The Today Show*, is not a journalist, the program is frequently a source of news.

But on the three major network Sunday television news shows—*This Week with David Brinkley*, *Meet the Press*, and *Face the Nation*—African Americans are excluded as regulars and appear only occasionally as affirmative-action tokens.

To highlight the dramatic change in television situation comedies, Dates devotes a special section to the sociological impact of the Bill Cosby show, a breakthrough in television comedy for African Americans.[103] For decades, white minstrels or black comedians acting like white minstrels imitating blacks dominated African American comedy. This thespian pattern was evidenced by the spectacular success among both black and white audiences of the white-created and -acted *Amos 'n' Andy* radio show.

The demise of racially stereotypical shows such as *Amos 'n' Andy* and the networks' incremental hiring of African Americans journalists and part-time anchors are dramatic evidence of change in network programming. Even in the South where intractable vestiges of racism and segregation persist in elementary, secondary, and higher education; electoral politics; and employment, some local television stations hire African Americans, particularly women, as news anchors, either for daily (especially morning and noon) or weekend news programs. This exercise in electronic tokenism holds true in cities with numerically significant African American populations, such as Atlanta, Baltimore, Boston, Chicago, Detroit, Durham, Jackson, Los Angeles, New Orleans, New York City, Oakland, Philadelphia, San Francisco, and Washington, D.C.

Because other ethnic minorities are vigorously competing for the prestigious positions of television news anchor, the four major associations for minority journalists[104] try to avoid competing for the limited number of on-camera television jobs in markets where one minority group has the strongest demographic salience. "We would not lobby for an African American news anchor at the risk of displacing a Hispanic news anchor in, say, San Antonio, where there is a dominant Hispanic population," Sheila Stainback, NABJ vice-president for broadcast, told the author during a May 1995 telephone interview.

Although the average white American continues to struggle with the moral conflict inherent in Myrdal's *American Dilemma*, the nation's racial climate continues to change, sometime toward a more enlightened acceptance of African Americans, at other times away from racial collegiality.

The power of television in forming attitudes is a critical catalyst in the changing national climate. At the April 1995 meeting of ASNE, a survey reported that 63 percent of all Americans now get their news from television, a sharp increase from 1984, when fewer than 50 percent of Americans got their news from television.[105]

African Americans have embraced more enthusiastically this national shift to television as a primary dispenser of information and, as a result, have become a more important factor in the advertising marketplace. As Nielsen Media Research has reported, television sets are in use in African American households ten hours and eight minutes each day, compared with six hours and forty-seven minutes daily for white households, a differential of 65 percent more television viewing for African Americans.[106]

This disproportionately higher number of television-watching hours has been cited by educators as one of the factors responsible for the wide discrepancies between black and white achievement levels in school. Taking note of the black propensities for the media's hedonistic massaging, the distinguished black nationalist scholar Maulana Ron Karenga once lamented, "Negroes buy more records than books and are dancing away their lives."[107]

The Impact of Other Minorities
on African American Progress

Alphonse Karr's historical fatalism, *Plus ça change, plus c'est la même chose* (The more things change, the more they remain the same),[108] has a special resonance for the history of African Americans. Not only does history continue to repeat itself in America's recurringly heartless treatment of African Americans, but almost identical negative images repeatedly are resurrected by the media to help the white majority culture enforce the second-class status of African Americans. But things do change, as often for the better as for the worse. Certainly no one would deny that significant progress has been made by African Americans in the media since the publication of the Kerner Commission Report more than twenty-five years ago. The nagging question, however, is how much of this progress is cumulatively irreversible? During the aggressively benign neglect years of the Reagan and Bush administrations, white racism was given presidential byes, and African Americans lost many of the economic and educational gains they had made during the civil rights movement.

Numbers can be seductive. An eightfold increase of minorities in the media in the last twenty-five years may seem, at first blush, impressive. But measured against the disparity between the percentage of minorities in the newsroom vis-à-vis minorities in the national population, that eightfold increase is no cause for celebration. On the other hand, African Americans can see their images every day from early morning (Bryant Gumbel) to midday (Oprah Winfrey) to late night (bandleader Kevin Eubanks on Jay Leno's *Tonight Show*). In between, lugubrious soap operas include occasional African American actors, and television news features African American journalists' reports from around the nation. Most of the major newspapers as well as many smaller newspapers feature de rigueur a syndicated African American columnist.

Still, three-fourths of America's newspapers do not hire African American reporters, and as the recent confrontation between publishers and heads of minority journalists' associations illustrates, white males and females are beginning to protest the expanded hiring of minorities.

Even the enormous success and popularity of the black middle-class-oriented *Cosby Show* had virtually no influence in stopping the escalation of suicidal violence among young African American males. Recognizing this failure, Cosby announced plans to promote a show designed to instill pride in young African American males.[109] As he pursues this electronic vision, however, young African American males appear to be far more interested in the memory of Malcolm X than the existence of Bill Cosby.

In 1993 the racial issue multiplied in competing ethnicities to include not only African Americans but Latinos, Asians, and Native Americans. The rationales for this broadened inclusion and rainbow spectrum of persons are the philosophies of multiculturalism and diversity. But, as the media insist on reporting, competition from minorities for a static piece of the economic and professional pie will continue to aggravate tensions between ethnic groups, despite the acclamation of multiculturalism in some quarters.

At the same time, multiculturalism implicitly threatens the most favored status of white males (MFSWM); hence their disproportionate resistance and the rise of white demigods such as David Duke, who speaks for the smoldering passions of more people than are willing to admit it.

Martin Luther once wrote, "It makes a difference whose ox is gored."[110] Because white males still disproportionately control America's political and economic power structure as well as most of the oxen, they feel more threatened by the vigorous increase of gender and racial political and economic activity. In response to this perceived threat, they can effectively mobilize public opposition to multiculturalism and diversity. As a variation on that defunct E. F. Hutton television commercial would phrase it, when Arthur Schlesinger, George Will, Ross Perot, and Pat Robertson talk, America listens.

Diversity has managed, however, to acquire a cultural cachet that makes it almost fashionable. Only that fashionability prevents diversity from being mothballed over the backlash protests of white males and white females. Fifty years from now, when America commemorates the Kerner Commission Report, it is conceivable that multiculturalism will be so ingrained in America's culture that even a future Asian woman president of the United States will extol its productive felicity as a social permanence. In the year of Kerner plus 25, however, this nation's minorities will continue to debate with their white colleagues the extent to which multiculturalism vitiates our mythical meritocracy after struggling to deny its validity.

Even de Tocqueville, however, saw a kind of tarnished splendor in 1835 in the symbiosis of "The Three Races that Inhabit the United States."[111] One hundred and fifty-eight years ago it would have been almost impossible to conceive of a multicultural society of the national grandeur and demographic complexity that exists today. In all probability "Kerner Plus 50" will celebrate an even more felicitously multicultural and egalitarian society than "Kerner Plus 25." It is always possible, however, as Dr. Kenneth B. Clark lamented before the Kerner Commission about the recurring race riots, that Thucydides' law of history could witness future events that he predicted would "very likely, in accordance with human nature, repeat themselves, if not exactly the same, yet very similar."[112]

Notes

1. *Report of the National Advisory Commission on Civil Disorders* (New York: Bantam Books, 1968) (hereafter cited as *Kerner Report*). This commission was created by Executive Order No. 11365, which was issued by President Lyndon B. Johnson on July 29, 1967 (ibid., 534, Appendix A).

2. Andrew Hacker, *Two Nations: Black and White, Separate, Hostile, Unequal* (New York: Scribner's, 1992).

3. The *Report of the National Advisory Commission on Civil Disorders* eventually became known as the Kerner Commission Report after its chairman, the then-governor of Illinois, Otto Kerner.

4. Gunnar Myrdal, *An American Dilemma: The Negro Problem and Modern Democracy* (New York: Harper, 1944).

5. *Kerner Report*, 2.

6. Hacker, *Two Nations*, 218.

7. "I shall be content if those shall pronounce my History useful who desire to give a view of events as they did really happen, and as they are very likely, in accordance with human nature, to repeat themselves at some future time—if not exactly the same, yet very similar" (George Seldes, comp., *The Great Quotations* [New York: Caesar-Stuart, 1960], 685 [quoting 1 Thucydides, *History*, 22 (411 B.C.)]).

8. After the Watts riots of 1965, the McCone Commission issued a report analyzing the causes of the riots (*Governor's Commission on the Los Angeles Riots, Violence in the City: An End or a Beginning?* [Sacramento: State of California, 1965], 26–80). The commission was chaired by John A. McCone, former director of the Central Intelligence Agency (25 *Facts on File* 447 [1965] [endnote added]).

9. *Kerner Report*, 483 (quoting Dr. Kenneth B. Clark).

10. Ibid., 1, 362–67.

11. The terms *African American, black,* and *black American* are used interchangeably in this essay.

12. In part 2 of the *Kerner Report*, "Why Did It Happen?," no mention was made of the black press and its roles in the making of African American history and in reporting events. In *From Slavery to Freedom*, however, authors John Hope Franklin and Alfred A. Moss Jr., write, "As the Negro community came more and more to take on the attributes of an entirely separate world, the black press performed an increasingly important function" (Franklin and Moss, *From Slavery to Freedom: A History of Negro Americans*, 6th ed. [New York: Knopf, 1988], 378).

Jannette L. Dates, in *Split Image*, also wrote, "The black press . . . deserves special attention . . . because if it had not existed, there would have been no print medium of communications for African Americans that could instill a sense of community, a feeling of self-worth, or keep alive the often muted struggle to escape, first slavery, and then the clutches of segregation and discrimination" (Dates, "Print News," in *Split Image: African Americans in the Mass Media*, ed. Jannette L. Dates and William Barlow [Washington, D.C.: Howard University Press, 1990] 343, 346).

13. *Kerner Report*, 362–89.

14. Jannette L. Dates, "Public Television," in Dates and Barlow, *Split Image*, 303, 304–5.

15. *Congressional Record*, 113:4997–5039 (1967).

16. Ibid., 5037–38.

17. Ibid., 5038.

18. Joint Center for Political and Economic Studies, *Black Elected Officials: A National Roster* (Washington, D.C.: Joint Center for Political and Economic Studies Press, 1991), 21.

19. U.S. Department of Commerce, Bureau of the Census, *Current Population Reports P20-464: The Black Population in the United States, March 1991* (Washington, D.C.: U.S. Government Printing Office, 1992), 24–25.

20. Ibid.

21. U.S. Department of Commerce, Bureau of the Census, *Statistical Abstract of the United States, 1992* (Washington, D.C.: U.S. Government Printing Office, 1992), 197 (citing tab. 329, Federal and State Prisoners: 1960–1990).

22. Ibid.

23. Patrick Welsh, "Young, Black, Male, and Trapped," *Washington Post*, September 24, 1989. Glasgow, author of *The Black Underclass*, "notes that black males are 'unchallenged for last place in every important demographic statistic.' For example: Black men make up only 3.5 percent of the college population but 46 percent of the prison population; a black male has a 1-in-23 chance of being murdered before he is 25" (ibid. [quoting interview with Douglas Glasgow]).

24. "Crack Down Hard on Police Brutality," *USA Today*, March 21, 1991.

25. See *Kerner Report*, 302–4.

26. Ibid., 302 and n. 2.

27. Ibid., 302 (emphasis added).

28. Ibid., 262.

29. Ibid., 262–63 ("Of the 59,720 addicts known to the U.S. Bureau of Narcotics at the end of 1966, just over 50 percent were Negroes").

30. Ibid., 266–69.

31. Michael deCourcy Hinds, "Number of Killings Soars in Big Cities across U.S.," *New York Times*, July 18, 1990. Ironically, some of the cities with the largest increase in homicides have been major cities with African American mayors or large African American populations: Chicago, Detroit, Los Angeles, New York, Philadelphia, and Washington, D.C.

32. Jerry Schwartz, "CDC: Homicide No. 1 Killer of Black Youths," *Philadelphia Daily News*, December 7, 1990 (citing study by CDC epidemiologist Dr. Robert Froehlke).

33. Ibid.

34. Ibid.

35. Chuck Stone, *Black Political Power in America* (Indianapolis: Bobbs-Merrill, 1968), 191.

36. Ibid., 12.

37. *Kerner Report*, 113.

38. "Black vs. Jew: A Tragic Confrontation," *Time*, January 31, 1969, cover, 55.

39. Ibid., 55.

40. Jack Miles, "Blacks vs. Browns," *Atlantic Monthly*, October, 1992, cover, 41.

41. "The Future in Their Past," *Economist*, November 21, 1992, 11.

42. Clint Bolick, "The Great Racial Divide," *Wall Street Journal*, November 30, 1992.

43. On January 7, 1991, the NAACP Legal Defense and Educational Fund, Inc., issued a six-point position paper, "Reflections of Proposals for Separate Schools for African-American Male Pupils," which opposed immersion schools and which was sent to members of the board of directors by Director-Counsel Julius L. Chambers. (The writer is a member of the NAACP-LDF national board of directors.) Citing the "long-term effect," the NAACP-LDF contended, inter alia, that such schools would provide a "new rationalization that could be seized by the majority community to justify racial separatism in the provision of public education, and perhaps ultimately other public goods and services," and that the "overrepresentation" of African American males "in special classes avoids systemic treatment of the problems" (Julius L. Chambers, NAACP Legal Defense and Educational Fund, "Reflections of Proposals for Separate School for African American Male Pupils" [January 7, 1991, position paper on file with author], 1).

In Milwaukee, where two such schools have already been created, Doris Stacy, an eighteen-year veteran of the school board who voted against the plan, said the segregation or isolation of any group of students is "a very dangerous idea. To institutionalize white or black schools in 1990 would be disappointing" (Millicent Lawton, "Milwaukee to Create Two Schools for Black Males," *Education Week*, October 10, 1990, 1–2).

At the same time, immersion schools for young African American males have equally strenuous supporters, some of whom have mixed feelings. "This experiment in Milwaukee must take place," said Spencer H. Holland, director of the Center for Educating African-American Males at Morgan State University (Lawton, "Milwaukee"). Jomills H. Braadock II, director of Johns Hopkins University Center for Research on Effective Schooling for Disadvantaged Students, said he had a "mixed reaction" to the program but saw "a number of potential benefits" (Lawton, "Milwaukee").

44. *Kerner Report*, 38.

45. NABJ Print Task Force, "The L.A. Unrest and Beyond" (August 1992, manuscript on file with author), 2.

46. "Brooms, Buckets, Cooling Embers," *Los Angeles Times*, reprinted in *Understanding the Riots*, ed. Shelby Coffey III (Los Angeles: *Los Angeles Times*, 1992), 130.

47. Miles, "Blacks vs. Browns," 41, 52.

48. Ibid., 41.

49. Ibid., 52.

50. Ibid., 41.

51. Albert E. Weis, ed., *Editor & Publisher International Yearbook* (New York: Editor & Publisher, 1969), 15.

52. Orlando Velez, ed., *Editor & Publisher International Yearbook* (New York: Editor & Publisher, 1992), vi.

53. Bureau of the Census, *Statistical Abstract of the United States, 1992*, 8 (citing tab. 2).

54. Clint C. Wilson II, *Black Journalists in Paradox: Historical Perspective and Current Dilemmas* (New York: Greenwood Press, 1991), 138.

55. Bureau of the Census, *Statistical Abstract of the United States, 1992*, 39–41 (citing tab. 41, Social and Economic Characteristics of the White and Black Population: 1980–1991; tab. 44, Social and Economic Characteristics of the Hispanic Population: 1991; tab. 43, Social and Economic Characteristics of the Asian and Pacific Population: 1991; tab. 43, Social and Economic Characteristics of the American Indian, Eskimo or Aleut Population: 1990).

56. Recent statistics reveal a small gain in minority employment (American Society of Newspaper Editors, "ASNE's 1992 Survey Shows Small Gain in Minority Employment" [April 2, 1992, news release on file with author], 10).

57. "The March Meredith Began," *Newsweek*, June 20, 1966, cover, 27.

58. *Kerner Report*, 362.

59. The phrase *double consciousness* was first used by W. E. Burghardt Du Bois in the epochal essay, "Of Our Spiritual Strivings," in his book *The Souls of Black Folk*, considered a literary classic by most African American scholars. Du Bois, in summarizing the twofold psyche of African Americans, wrote,

> After the Egyptian and Indian, the Greek and Roman, the Teuton and Mongolian, the Negro is a sort of seventh son, born with a veil, and gifted with a second-sight in this American world, a world which yields him no true self-consciousness, but only lets him see himself through the revelation of the other world. It is a peculiar sensation, this double consciousness, this sense of always looking at one's self through the eyes of others, of measuring one's soul by the tape of a world that looks on in amused contempt and pity. One ever feels his two-ness, an American, a Negro; two souls, two thoughts, two unreconciled strivings; two warring ideals in one dark body, whose dogged strength alone keeps it from being torn asunder. (W. E. B. Du Bois, "Of Our Spiritual Strivings," in *The Souls of Black Folk*, ed. W. E. B. Du Bois [Millwood, N.Y.: Kraus-Thomson Organization Ltd., 1973], 3)

60. In this era of moral certitude of ethnic and gender diversity that occasionally is misrepresented as a philosophical perversion called "political correctness," it should be noted that all six NABJ officers in 1993 were women.

61. Chuck Stone, "NABJ's 12 Objectives: A Position Paper" (1975, manuscript on file with author).

62. Ibid.

63. *Kerner Report*, 384–85.

64. Ibid., 385.

65. Ibid., 362–63. In 1968 most African American journalists would have challenged the accuracy of the commission's claim. As further evidence of the dogged persistence of such skepticism, an NABJ task force issued its own report in August 1992 on the 1992 Los Angeles riots and cited "notable failures—stories that were either missed, ignored, underreported or misjudged. Examples include the sparse reporting of Hispanic involvement in the unrest, broad generalizations about the looters and the overemphasis on black-Korean tensions" (NABJ Print Task Force, "L.A. Unrest and Beyond," 2).

66. *Kerner Report*, 385.

67. Often overlooked and frequently omitted from most major papers on the Kerner Commission is one sentence that glowed like a raging forest fire and seared the conscience of many African Americans. In one of the rarest instances in history of a federal document indicting "white racism" as a principal cause of African American subjugation, the commission concluded, "*White racism is essentially responsible for the explosive mixture which has been accumulating in our cities since the end of World War II*" (ibid., 10 [emphasis added]).

68. Clint C. Wilson II and Felix Gutierrez, *Minorities and Media: Diversity and the End of Mass Communication* (Beverly Hills, Calif.: Sage, 1985), 67–109.

69. Jannette L. Dates and William Barlow, "Split Images and Double Binds," in *Split Image*, 455.

70. Ibid., 455–56.

71. Two scholarly books that examine the history of cinematic and racial stereotypes, from diametric positions that may be influenced by the authors' ethnicities, are Donald Bogle, *Toms, Coons, Mulattoes, Mammies and Bucks: An Interpretive History of Blacks in American Films* (New York: Bantam, 1973) (Bogle, an African American, authoritatively analyzes the harmful effects of negative stereotypes that were created and nurtured by Hollywood) and Neal Gabler, *An Empire of Their Own: How the Jews Invented Hollywood* (New York: Anchor, 1989) (Gabler, a Jewish American, examines how Jews became the most powerful ethnic force in conceptualizing and bringing to maturity the movie industry as a fantasized depiction of the American way of life).

72. Dates and Barlow, "Split Images and Double Binds," 457.

73. Ibid.

74. A news editorial cartoon by Steve Benson of the *Arizona Republic* depicted a group of Ku Klux Klansmen about to lynch a black man. One says, "Hey, aren't you Bill Cosby? I love your show" ("Toon Time: The News in Cartoon," *Philadelphia Daily News*, May 27, 1992).

75. Henry Louis Gates Jr., "TV's Black World Turns—But Stays Unreal," *New York Times*, November 12, 1989.

76. George Garneau, "Tempers Flare: Minority Journalists Tell National Newspaper Association Officials That More Has to Be Done in Diversifying Newsrooms," *Editor & Publisher*, December 12, 1992, 14.

77. Ibid., 14.

78. Ibid., 38.

79. Ibid.

80. Ibid.

81. Ibid.

82. "We have not, in this report, examined the Negro press in detail. The thrust of our studies was directed at daily mass circulation, mass audience media which are aimed at the community as a whole" (*Kerner Report*, footnote on p. 384).

83. *Guide to Minority Media Associations, 1994* (Reston, Va.: National Association of Minority Media Executives Foundation), 2.

84. Ibid., 20–22.

85. Ibid., 41.

86. Roland E. Wolseley, *The Black Press, USA: Voice of Today* (Ames: Iowa State University Press, 1989), 48.

87. *Kerner Report*, 382–89.

88. Du Bois, "Of Our Spiritual Strivings," 3.

89. Myrdal, *American Dilemma*, xlvii.

90. Ibid., 104.

91. Ibid., 600.

92. Ibid., 912–15.

93. Wilson, *Black Journalists in Paradox*, 14–15.

94. Wilson and Gutierrez, *Minorities and Media*, 180.

95. Alexander Hamilton, John Jay, and James Madison, *The Federalist*, Modern Library.

96. Wolseley, *Black Press, USA*.

97. James D. Williams, *The Black Press and the First Amendment* (New York: National Urban Leagues, 1976), 14. See also Patrick S. Wasburn, *A Question of Sedition: The Federal Government's Investigation of the Black Press during World War II* (New York: Oxford University Press, 1986).

98. *Kerner Report*, 384.

99. Wolseley, *Black Press, USA*, 223.

100. *Guide to Minority Media Associations, 1994*, 22.

101. *Kerner Report*, 386.

102. Dates and Barlow, *Split Image*, 303–39.

103. Ibid., 280–84.

104. In July 1994 the four minority journalist associations met in a historic "Unity '94" conference in Atlanta. The four associations were the Asian American Journalists Associations, National Association of Black Journalists, National Association of Hispanic Journalists, and Native American Journalists Association.

105. "A Television Trend: Audiences in Black and White," *Washington Post*, November 29, 1994.

106. Ibid.

107. Maulana Karenga, *The Quotable Karenga*. Quoted in Floyd B. Barbour, *The Black Power Revolt* (Boston: Extending Horizons Books, 1968).

108. John Bartlett, *Familiar Quotations: A Collection of Passages, Phrases, and Proverbs Traced to Their Sources in Ancient and Modern Literature*, 15th ed. (Boston: Little, Brown, 1980), 514 (quoting Alphonse Karr, *Les Guêpes*, January 1849).

109. Diane Goldner, "Can TV Help Save Black Youth?: Cosby's New Cause," *USA Today*, October 2–4, 1992 (*USA Weekend*).

110. Bartlett, *Familiar Quotations*, 156 (quoting Martin Luther, *Works*, 62 [1854]).

111. Alexis de Tocqueville, "Some Considerations Concerning the Present State and Probable Future of the Three Races That Inhabit the Territory of the United States," in *Democracy in America*, ed. J. P. Mayer and Max Lerner, trans. George Lawrence (New York: Harper and Row, 1966), 291.

112. Seldes, *Great Quotations*, 685 (quoting 1 Thucydides, *History*, 22 [411 B.C.]).

Part Six

Do We Have the Will to Change?

A Continuing Conversation between Academics and Policymakers

Judith Welch Wegner   Chapel Hill Symposium

Notes and Reflections

On February 12–13, 1993, the contributors to this volume, other noted scholars, and policymakers gathered in Chapel Hill, North Carolina, for a colloquium, "Race, Poverty, and the American City: The *Kerner Commission Report* in Retrospect."[1] Participants sought to refine our understanding of the current status of poor and minority populations living in America's cities and to outline a meaningful agenda, including core recommendations for a national urban policy and identification of related research needs. The colloquium was sponsored by the University of North Carolina Department of City and Regional Planning, the UNC Law School, and the Charles M. and Shirley F. Weiss Fund for Urban Livability.[2]

Conference discussions centered on four major topics: the continued viability of the Kerner Commission's "integration" and "enrichment" strategies; the strategies that developed to provide jobs, boost incomes, and protect families and children; the need for, and characteristics of, a national urban policy; and the political feasibility of a national urban policy that addresses racial and ethnic needs. This essay summarizes the colloquium's principal findings and recommendations.[3]

1. *One core finding of the Kerner Commission—that the nation's cities have been reshaped by an influx of urban African Americans and an exodus of whites and jobs to the suburbs—has proved true, but tells less than the complete story.* The Kerner Commission's model has proved most accurate in describing large cities in the North and Midwest. Cities in other parts of the country, and smaller cities generally, have not developed the same level of hypersegregation envisioned by the Kerner Report. Cities are generally more complex, with multiple metropoles rather than monolithic job centers. Cities exhibit a range of suburbs, including inner-ring suburbs that may be predominantly minority in population. An outmigration of African Americans to some suburban and other rural locales has occurred, along with inmigration of other ethnic minorities. Employment and economic development patterns have also proved more complex. While minority populations remain concentrated in cities, there has been an exodus of job opportunities to the suburbs. Although this has caused a spatial mismatch, more complicated patterns of events may have contributed to employment

problems in the minority community. These problems include a skill mismatch, resulting from inadequate employment training, poor education, and "soft" skills, and a wealth mismatch, with disparities in financial base resulting in broadening inequality in educational opportunities. Further employment problems result from economic restructuring that has caused a reduction in high-paid manufacturing jobs, the creation of low-paid service jobs, and an increased reliance on advanced technology. Entrenched patterns of housing and employment discrimination also contribute to this dilemma.

2. *A complex, interlinked cycle of racial discrimination and economic disparity continues to keep many African Americans from experiencing equal opportunities in the suburbs, and the effects are likely to impede meaningful residential integration in the immediate future.* Economic, educational, and social disparity has resulted from intractable patterns of segregation. As a result of this disparity, it is difficult for many blacks to afford suburban housing. This absence of African Americans from suburban locales feeds white prejudice, which in turn motivates continuing subtle discrimination. Core resistance to integration in the suburbs runs deep and is unlikely to be overcome by increased contact between whites and blacks when strong social and economic disincentives also exist, not the least of which is the lowering of status and property values that may be associated with integration. Faced with these impediments, many African Americans reasonably may choose to live in predominantly black areas in which a sense of community exists and a decent life is available.

3. *Significant reform in traditional antidiscrimination strategies will be needed to bring about residential integration.* Some basic tensions, if not disagreements, exist between those who advocate integration and those who believe that primary emphasis should be placed on an enrichment strategy. Many agree that traditional case-by-case litigation of fair housing complaints has proven ineffective to deter widespread housing discrimination against African Americans. A more fruitful way to identify and redress subtle discrimination in the housing area would be to authorize government agencies to use testers to conduct random "audits" to detect discrimination. It may also be crucial to focus on long-term discrimination through programs sponsored by government agencies themselves (such as the Federal Housing Administration loan system) and to craft institution-based desegregation remedies. Strategies that do not look to litigation as the means of relief may also be needed, such as the use of subsidies to induce integrated neighborhoods, and an emphasis on fostering integration in new housing developments where there is less tendency to defend the legitimacy of preexisting problematic situations.

It will also be important to reexamine fundamental assumptions. "Housing" serves as both shelter and an investment to many people, and it will be necessary to focus on and remove disincentives to integration that stem from investment-related concerns and policies (for example, existing tax policies relating to homeowner mortgage interest). Nonetheless, "integration" should not mean "assimilation," and it is important to realize what is assumed to be the norm. The current moment is one in which the impetus for integration has probably waned, in light of the recent economic downslide and the pattern of further subordinating African Americans in hard times. Integration in other contexts (such as desegregation in education) can make a difference if it takes into account the problems posed by heavy concentrations of poverty.

4. *The Kerner Commission Report's underlying assumptions that the nation's economy would continue to thrive and that cities would continue as "engines of growth" have now been called into serious question.* The Kerner Commission Report was written in a time when national possibilities seemed endless, and it was believed that the War on Poverty could be won. More sobering assessments of the nation's capacity to respond through increased federal expenditures now predominate, and it remains unclear just how the nation's enormous federal deficit can be contained. As a result, realistic prognostication about the future of America's cities and their impoverished minority populations must rest on different economic assumptions, including conservative projections of economic growth and sharply restricted prospects for funds to provide needed remedies. The Kerner Commission assumed that cities themselves would serve as engines of growth capable of generating money as needed. Unfortunately, the globalization of the economy, the increased proportion of jobs that pay poverty wages, the patterns of investment that adversely affect cities (for example, redlining and military spending), and the skepticism about the capacity of municipal governments to remedy urban ills have at least severed the fuel lines to the engines and may have damaged permanently their inner workings. Nationwide economic growth, a shift in national priorities, and the reemergence of metropolitan areas as potent economic forces (drawing on their core resources of people, cultural centrality, and attractive investment opportunities) are critical prerequisites to overcoming the current deficit in needed resources.

5. *The face of urban poverty has changed in recent years, rendering solutions ever more difficult.* The worst levels of poverty are increasingly concentrated in ghetto areas, which are linked with a growing incidence of violence and despair. Many poor families live in single-parent, female-headed households. Multiple problems often affect impoverished populations, including joblessness, drug dependency, and illiteracy. Many of these characteristics of urban poverty reflect deliberate policy shifts in recent years. For example, the deregulation of the business environment has led to an exodus of businesses from inner cities to areas bereft of minorities.

The privatization of public sector employment has resulted in a reduction in the type of civil service job opportunities more readily available to minorities. The assault on job set-aside programs and cutbacks in the social safety net, including cuts in funding for community organizations, have had similarly adverse effects on minorities in our cities. Moreover, the creation of a criminal justice dragnet exacerbated the unemployability of ethnic males, the destabilization of families, and the feminization of poverty, while the adoption of "get tough" education policies, such as tracking, standardized tests, and retention policies, have contributed to increasing numbers of dropouts. Any urban strategy, therefore, must deal with the large and volatile minority male population that is neither in school nor employed.

6. *A reexamination of housing strategies is needed to provide meaningful choice, encourage investment of needed capital, and empower residents.* Housing must remain a central focus, since it affects so many facets of life— access to health care, learning environment, jobs, friendships, and social status. Too little affordable housing is available, low-income families are paying too much of their income for housing, and federal money for housing assistance is far too scarce. Policy differences continue, however, as to whether to place more improved housing in the nation's cities or to focus on assisting minority populations' relocation to the suburbs.

Notwithstanding these dilemmas, a variety of strategies are worthy of exploration. Credit opportunities must be expanded for homeseekers, although that alone will not suffice, since repayment of capital costs and up-keep costs may exceed the income stream of many poor city residents. It is, therefore, important to provide complimentary services, such as consumer counseling, financial management, and educational opportunities, to improve the success of housing programs. The pool of available capital likewise must be enhanced. This goal can be met in a variety of ways: allocation of government funds, creation of public-private partnerships in the aftermath of the savings and loan debacle, creation of joint ventures between entrepreneurs and nonprofit organizations, more broad-based treatment of some forms of housing as a "social good" whose residents enjoy shelter but not investment-related profit, encouragement of individuals' entrepreneurial spirit, and reallocation of existing government subsidies (either by reducing and reallocating benefits associated with home mortgage interest deductions to other forms of housing programs or creating a progressive tax credit mechanism). Another potential source of capital is the "peace dividend" created by the end of the Cold War, provided that the political will exists to earmark these funds and fears of unemployment resulting from reduced defense budgets can be addressed.

7. *Health, education, and welfare policies must also be fundamentally modified to take into account the particular problems of impoverished popula-*

tions, by empowering those in poverty, by focusing on relevant economic incentives, and by helping to build communities. Health care reformers have yet to address the unique problems facing the poor and minority populations, which tend to be sicker, more commonly exposed to environmental hazards, more likely to lack funds and insurance, and more likely to have restricted access to health care providers. Universal access to health care services will provide only a partial solution to these problems. Educational reform must concentrate on early childhood intervention through programs such as Head Start. School finance reform is also needed to level the playing field for impoverished inner-city students. Welfare reform should focus on empowerment of individuals through implementation of the following: (a) raising the minimum wage above the poverty level; (b) relying more heavily on targeted income tax credits and targeted investment tax credits (for example, programs geared toward hiring inner-city youth and providing needed training); (c) matching unemployed laborers with work that strengthens the sense of community (for example, renovation of vacant housing); (d) creating individual human development trust accounts; and (e) providing realistic alternatives that link part-time employment with educational opportunities and child care. Equally important are providing training and role models from the nation's universities, corporations and communities and fostering the growth of community organizations to help individuals form self-help and support coalitions.

8. *America needs a national policy that integrates both economic and social policy and addresses the particular problems of America's cities, while at the same time not undercutting the potential coalition between rural and urban interests.* Although a national urban policy is vitally needed, key aspects of that policy remain subject to debate. The current political climate suggests that such a policy focus on the possible, that it emphasize the importance of partnerships between the public and private sectors and various levels of government, that it encourage mutual responsibility between government and individual citizens, and that it use moral leadership to combat the evils of racism and promote an enhanced sense of community. Since concerns for early educational development, adequate health care, and the creation of investment incentives are shared by both urban and rural interests, perhaps the phrase *national domestic policy* best addresses this concern.

9. *A national domestic policy can only address racial and ethnic needs by not underestimating the prevalence and persistence of racism and by combining incentives with institutional reform.* One of the most important conclusions reached by the Kerner Commission was its recognition that the white society is implicated in the ghetto. It may have become more difficult for American society to acknowledge the truth of this statement and to sustain a commitment to ending racism and its effects. Attention has shifted recently to other economic-related concerns, and government seems to have

reached a stalemate on urban issues, stemming in part from changing patterns of campaign finance and other related factors. A variety of strategies may need to be explored, including reforming the existing bureaucracies that block the pipeline to change. It is important to reexamine federal and state mandates that tie the hands of local governments that seek to take important initiatives. Furthermore, it may be necessary to encourage lawsuits that target historical lending practices and school finance systems on new grounds, emphasize programs that allow members of minority groups to make their own choices rather than pursuing at all costs the goal of integration, and recognize that incremental change through modest experimentation is especially congruent with American political life.

In sum, the problems foreseen by the Kerner Commission have in large measure come to pass. Many forces have exacerbated these problems—the growing complexity of urban ethnic populations, the interrelation of racial discrimination and economic disadvantage, the country's recent economic downturn, policy shifts placing increased pressures on urban unemployed minority males, the changing face of poverty, and the persistence of racism within our society. Nonetheless, as we continue to strive to overcome the nation's tragic legacy of racial discrimination, poverty, and social injustice, new ideas emerge that can result in meaningful improvements in our policies and laws, if only we have the will.

Notes

1. Colloquium presenters included John Charles Boger, UNC School of Law; Nancy Fishman, Northwestern University; John Calmore, Loyola University; George Galster, Urban Institute; Roberto Fernandez, Northwestern University; William Taylor, Washington attorney; Michael Stegman, UNC Department of City and Regional Planning; the Honorable Eva Clayton, U.S. House of Representatives; Peter Dreier, Occidental College; Susan Fainstein, Rutgers University; Chester Hartman, Poverty and Race Research Action Council; Karen Hill, Fair Housing Implementation Office, City of Yonkers, N.Y.; Dennis Rash, president, NationsBank Community Development Program; Dean Emeritus John Turner, UNC School of Social Work; James Johnson, UNC Department of Geography; Paul Leonard, Center on Budget and Policy Priorities; Peter Salsich, St. Louis University; David Stoesz, San Diego State; Sidney Watson, Mercer University; Walter C. Farrell, University of Wisconsin at Milwaukee; Ann Markusen, Rutgers University; Sister Consuelo Tovar, Texas Industrial Areas Foundation Network; Chuck Stone, UNC School of Journalism and Mass Communications; Moses Carey, chair of the Orange County, N.C., Board of Commissioners; and the Honorable David Price, U.S. House of Representatives.

2. The sponsorship of this colloquium was a particularly fitting first project for the Fund for Urban Livability, in light of the lifework of the fund's donors.

Charles M. Weiss is emeritus professor of environmental engineering, UNC School of Public Health. Shirley M. Weiss, a noted scholar who has studied new communities and city centers, is emeritus professor of city and regional planning, UNC Department of City and Regional Planning.

3. The observations offered here are based largely on comments offered by colloquium presenters, essays that appear elsewhere in this volume, and discussions with conference participants. The very nature of the tasks at hand—assimilating themes from diverse essays and presentations and summarizing extensive conversations—has made it impossible for the author to attribute individual ideas to one or more of those in attendance. The reader may assume that the valuable ideas presented here stem from those in attendance as noted in n. 1, above, but that any errors in understanding or explication are the author's own.

John Charles Boger Afterword

A Debate over the National Future

As 1995 draws to a close, the racial and economic issues once so urgently advanced by the Kerner Commission have again moved to center stage, though in a form that would be scarcely recognizable to the framers of that earlier document. While no American president after 1968 fully heeded the Kerner Commission's call for a comprehensive federal strategy to end the isolation of the central-city poor, nonetheless a substantial expansion of federal policies and programs has gradually unfolded, designed to address (albeit inadequately) many of the immediate concerns of African Americans and other urban residents.

In the mid-1990s, however, a bold challenge to that expansion has emerged. Newly invigorated elements within the national Republican Party have launched a multipronged attack not only on the details of these post-Kerner social programs but, more comprehensively, on many core assumptions of Franklin Roosevelt's New Deal. This new initiative calls for the reduction or abandonment of many present federal programs designed to alleviate racial and economic ills. The new initiative is premised on the deeply held conviction that a balanced national budget, a reduced role for federal government, and limited public intervention in economic affairs should become the nation's new priorities. It declares that federal policies designed to assist the urban poor have been, even on their own terms, misguided failures, and that New Deal and Great Society programs now stand as unacceptable impediments to the achievement of the new national priorities.

In this concluding essay, I briefly suggest the terms of the emerging debate and then review their implications for the principal policies—in employment, education, health care, housing, welfare, and political participation—long viewed as crucial to the minority poor within the nation's major cities. Much of the current debate, as framed, centers on budgetary policy, particularly the desirability of curbing the growth of federal spending and, ultimately, reducing the national debt. The racial and poverty implications of those policies have received far less consideration, and their urban impact has been given virtually no public attention at all. Yet an adequate accounting of the long-term benefits of federal budgetary changes must include a fair evaluation of the potentially devastating social and economic costs to be exacted from America's racial and ethnic populations, especially its poor.

The Contemporary Sources of Racial Politics

The New Republican Initiative

A central public statement of the new Republican initiative of the mid-1990s is the "Contract with America," propounded by the Republican congressional leadership during the 1994 congressional campaign.[1] The contract committed its signatories to work for a balanced budget amendment, for congressional term limits, and for federal income tax reductions. Framers of the contract also promised or implied at least five fundamental changes in social welfare policy. First, they have committed themselves to work to curtail or eliminate outright many federal programs (and some federal cabinet offices) in the social welfare area. Second, they have agreed to transfer principal authority for many social programs that remain to state and/or local governments, minimizing federal regulations and relegating the federal role to that of a passive funder. Third, in the name of federal deficit reduction and fiscal responsibility, they have called for substantial reductions in the flow of federal dollars to these programs. Fourth, they have proposed to end the sixty-year federal "entitlements" policy under which income-eligible citizens have been assured of certain federal benefits irrespective of the overall cost to the Treasury. Fifth, they have indicated a marked preference for private or market solutions to most social and economic problems over governmental solutions, whether of federal or state origin.

Although most of these objectives appear race-neutral, in fact they would have a seriously unequal racial impact, since racial and ethnic minorities have disproportionately lower incomes and are disproportionately served by the programs scheduled for revision.[2] This racially unbalanced impact seems to be neither an oversight nor merely an unintended consequence of other Republican priorities. To the contrary, the rhetoric of the new initiative bristles with barely concealed impatience or hostility toward low-income African Americans, Latinos, and recent immigrants to the United States. Moreover, the initiative courts that portion of America's white/Anglo population that is drawn to racial explanations for America's social and economic ills.

While a number of the contract's policies have been dear to conservative Republicans for several decades, their present coalescence into a unified political program and their adoption by the Republican mainstream are distinctly new features on the national political scene. Championing this new approach, Republicans won substantial victories in the 1994 congressional elections, recapturing a majority in both the House of Representatives and the Senate for the first time since 1954.[3] Under the aggressive leadership of Newt Gingrich of Georgia, the new Speaker of the House, the contract has been treated as a mandate from a majority of the nation's citizens. Yet while Speaker Gingrich has achieved significant legislative successes in the House of Representatives, the initiative has, to date, faltered in the more moderate Senate, even as Democratic president Bill Clinton has threatened or asserted his veto authority to stall some of its more radical features.[4] In fact, the real depth of popular support for the new Republican initiative remains unclear. Voter turnout in the 1994 congressional campaigns was low,[5] a substantial percentage of voters professed unfamiliarity with the Republican contract,[6] and public opinion polls in mid-1995 have revealed significant doubts about the desirability of budget cuts deemed essential to implement the contract.[7]

It seems fair to conclude, in short, that a genuine referendum on this major contraction of federal authority has not yet taken place. If Republicans expand on their 1994 congressional successes in 1996 and, most crucially, if a Republican dedicated to these initiatives captures the White House, the nation will almost certainly witness the most profound shift in federal domestic policy since the New Deal of the 1930s. Those policy shifts would, in turn, appear to threaten major economic and social changes for African American and Latino citizens and for the future of America's great but financially troubled cities.

California's Increasingly Racialized Politics

In addition to the new Republican initiative at the federal level, other recent events have also helped to thrust racial issues toward the forefront of the nation's attention. In 1994 citizens in the State of California, laboring under a mounting fiscal burden,[8] debated Proposition 187, a citizen initiative and referendum designed to curtail public benefits and services to immigrants living within the state illegally,[9] most of whom are Hispanics from Mexico or Central America and Asians from Southeast Asia. Proposition 187 received majority support in the November 1994 state referendum,[10] after a media campaign filled with "us-versus-them" rhetoric.[11] Even though enforcement of the proposition was quickly stayed by a federal court, and though constitutionality of the measure remains under court challenge,[12] the campaign succeeded in framing public perception of California's worsening financial problems in racial and ethnic terms.

Californians may soon contribute another issue to the national debate over racial issues if sponsors can obtain sufficient signatures to place the

California Civil Rights Initiatives (CCRI) on the state's 1996 ballot. The controversial CCRI initiative would eliminate virtually all consideration of race or ethnicity in allocating state jobs, admission to state universities and colleges, and other services and benefits.[13] Affirmative action policies have long been viewed with ambivalence by many Americans, and the new California initiative opens a volatile debate at a time when many, especially white males, feel economically vulnerable and view affirmative action programs with increased suspicion or resentment.[14]

Without waiting for a CCRI referendum, the regents of the State of California university system acted preemptively on July 20, 1995, to forbid affirmative action by California colleges and universities in all admissions, personnel, and contracting decisions.[15] President Clinton responded with a well-reported speech the same month, celebrating the value of affirmative action programs that avoid inflexible quotas and the selection of unqualified persons.[16] Congressional Republicans later acted to craft legislation to end affirmative action by the federal government; President Clinton has given strong hints that he would veto any such legislation.[17] Together, these developments suggest that affirmative action programs may well become a partisan campaign issue in 1996.

The Supreme Court's Narrowed Redefinition of the Equal Protection Clause

Californians have not been alone in reconsidering the propriety and reach of racial affirmative action or "racial preference" programs in 1995. During the spring of 1995 the Supreme Court of the United States decided three cases that limited governmental use of racial preferences in different contexts. *Adarand Constructors, Inc. v. Pena*[18] involved federal contracting programs that are authorized to take race, ethnicity, and gender into consideration. The Supreme Court held that all such programs are unconstitutional unless they can survive "strict judicial scrutiny" under the Equal Protection Clause of the Fourteenth Amendment.[19] The *Adarand* majority pointedly refused to limit its rationale to contracting programs; instead, it held that all federal programs will henceforth be subject to the same strict constitutional standards that the Court first applied, in 1989, to curtail the use of affirmative action programs by states and cities.[20]

On the other hand, Justice O'Connor emphasized for the majority in *Adarand* that strict judicial scrutiny did not, and should not, invariably result in the invalidation of race-conscious governmental programs, especially in view of the continued effects of racial discrimination and the special constitutional role assigned to Congress in combating racial discrimination. "We wish to dispel the notion that strict scrutiny is 'strict in theory but fatal in fact,'" Justice O'Connor wrote, adding that "the unhappy persistence of both the practice and the lingering effects of racial discrimination against minority groups in this country" might justify the use of race-based remedial measures in certain circumstances.[21]

In the voting rights area, the 1995 Court likewise displayed deep suspicion of governmental use of racial criteria, irrespective of motives. *Miller v. Johnson*[22] presented the question of how best to accommodate what Professor Lani Guinier has characterized as "the inescapable race consciousness"[23] of the 1965 Voting Rights Act[24] with the imperatives of the Equal Protection Clause.[25] After the 1990 decentennial census, the Georgia legislature met to reconfigure its federal congressional districts and eventually acceded to a plan sanctioned by the Department of Justice to create at least three majority-black districts.[26] Critics of the plan brought suit, contending that the use of race as a districting criterion violated the Equal Protection Clause; defenders insisted that compliance with the Voting Rights Act was a "compelling governmental interest" that justified consideration of black political representation when drawing congressional district lines.[27]

The Supreme Court in *Miller*, as in *Adarand*, condemned Georgia's reliance on race as a "predominant factor" in redrawing its district lines,[28] even though, as Justice Ginsburg pointed out in dissent, state legislatures regularly take a variety of political and demographic criteria—including socioeconomic composition, party affiliation, ethnic identity, gender, and protection of incumbents—into account when redrawing electoral districts.[29]

In a third case, *Missouri v. Jenkins*,[30] the Court extended its doubts about compensatory, race-based governmental actions into the area of public education, where the Warren Court's *Brown* decision first announced the modern principles of Equal Protection that have governed ever since. At issue in *Jenkins* was a federal district court's oversight of a desegregation plan ordered for the Kansas City, Missouri, school district in 1985, after the district court determined that local school board officials and the State of Missouri had acted deliberately to maintain racial segregation.[31] The Supreme Court in *Jenkins* expressed frustration with the district court's ten-year efforts to remedy this segregation, during which time vast sums had been expended for capital improvements within Kansas City schools.[32] Singled out for special criticism was the federal court's effort to order certain educational improvements within the Kansas City school district, ostensibly in order to attract white schoolchildren back into the Kansas City system, thereby increasing racial integration. The Supreme Court held that "the District Court's pursuit of 'desegregative attractiveness' is beyond the scope of its broad remedial authority. . . . The . . . pursuit of the goal of 'desegregative attractiveness' results in so many imponderables and is so far removed from the task of eliminating the racial identifiability of the schools within the [Kansas City, Missouri, school district] that we believe it is beyond the admittedly broad discretion of the District Court."[33]

Seen together, this triumvirate of Rehnquist Court decisions demonstrates a new judicial determination—in sharp contrast to the jurisprudence of the Warren and Burger Court eras—to limit governmental action that would offer 'benign' assistance to racial minorities.[34]

The Impact of Other Public Events on Racial Attitudes

At least two other public events contributed to the renewed national debate over race during 1995. The first was the criminal trial of O. J. Simpson, the African American football player and sports announcer, who was charged with the homicide of his wife, Nicole Brown Simpson, and a companion, Ronald Goldman (both Caucasians), in an exclusive Los Angeles neighborhood.[35] The fully televised criminal proceedings gripped millions of Americans and often dominated daily television and radio news programs.[36] The eventual acquittal of Simpson—after evidence revealed that a prosecution witness, Los Angeles police detective Mark Fuhrman, had long harbored deep hostility toward blacks,[37] and after the defense emphasized broad racial issues during its closing argument[38]—created a sharp national division of opinion, along racial lines, concerning the likely guilt of Simpson, the pervasiveness of discrimination in the criminal justice system, and the propriety of the jury's verdict.[39]

Shortly after the Simpson verdict, national emotions over race were rekindled by the "Million Man March" on Washington, D.C., organized by Louis Farrakan, minister of the Nation of Islam, and the Reverend Benjamin Chavis, former director of the National Association for the Advancement of Colored People.[40] Farrakan's previous support for racial segregation and black separatism, and his frequent charges that Jews especially, and whites more generally, continue to exploit African Americans, made his sponsorship of this event deeply controversial within both the white and the African American communities.[41] The October 16, 1995, march drew perhaps as many as 1 million black men to Washington for a day-long rally[42] built around the themes of the need for atonement by black men for their prior failings to black women, black families, and black communities, and of their need, as black males, to assume greater responsibility for their lives and futures.[43]

The Million Man March prompted President Clinton to present his own address on American racial relations to a Texas audience as a simultaneous counterpoint to the Washington event. In that speech, he spoke of a "rift that we see before us that is tearing at the heart of America." Clinton recalled the famous words of "Abraham Lincoln, [who] reminded us that: 'A house divided against itself cannot stand,'" and he urged Americans to put aside racial grievances and move forward together.[44] Subsequently, several groups put forward the suggestion that "a new Kerner Commission" was needed to examine racial issues in America in the mid-1990s.[45] While the prospects for such a commission seem unlikely at this writing, the request nonetheless underlined the continuing legacy of racial discrimination and the deeply troubling plight of the nation's minority poor, nearly thirty years after the 1967 riots that provoked the initial Kerner Report.

The Contending Public Welfare Policies

The new Republican initiative and the Contract with America have opened an important public debate over questions as basic as the role of the federal government, indeed of government itself, in addressing social and economic problems. Racial and ethnic minorities, and especially the poor, have a deep stake in the outcome of this debate. In this section I examine the racial and economic consequences that may follow from specific policy choices.

Federal Employment Policies and Politics

Both Democrats and Republicans in the mid-1990s have called for able-bodied Americans to make good-faith efforts to provide for themselves; "tough love" and personal responsibility have become mainstream political values. The Clinton administration, however, has strongly supported federal efforts to reward those low-income citizens who do work,[46] both by championing the Earned Income Tax Credit (EITC) program (first adopted in 1975 and expanded in 1986, 1990, and 1993)[47] and by calling for an increase in the minimum wage.[48]

Under the EITC, low-income workers receive supplements to their private wages from the federal treasury, either in the form of tax reductions against income tax otherwise due, or in refundable credits to those low-wage workers who owe no taxes.[49] Under the EITC program, workers with incomes of $8,425 will receive a federal supplement of up to 40 percent of their wages by 1996 (that is, a $3,370 supplement to a family with two children earning $8,425), while workers earning up to $27,000 will receive progressively lesser supplements.[50]

The Clinton administration has also promoted a phased, 90-cent-per-hour increase in the minimum wage, which would rise from the present $4.25 to $5.15 per hour by 1997,[51] contending that this rise is long overdue since the minimum wage has lost 26 percent of its average value in the 1970s, due to intervening increases in inflation.[52]

Because at least 22 million persons, 56 percent of the poor, live in households where someone works during each year, and because 7.4 million live in households where someone is employed full time, the EITC and minimum-wage increases would constitute important antipoverty measures as well as support for the principle of rewarding work.[53]

In addition to income support for low-income workers, the Clinton administration's employment strategy has focused on a School to Work Transition program that would provide federally subsidized training to low-skilled teenaged youths. The Clinton program consolidates and/or supplants dozens of present job training programs from the past decade, including most prominently the Job Training Partnership Act (JTPA). The new objective of the Clinton administration is to avoid the "creaming" so endemic in the JTPA, under which local entities, rewarded for each job placement, tended to confine their training efforts to the most highly skilled and promising youth, avoiding the hard-core unemployed. Since unemployment remains significantly higher among minority youth (18.4 percent of white males aged sixteen to nineteen years, versus 28.1 percent among Hispanic youth and 42.1 percent among black youth), such a program would be especially responsive to minority employment needs.[54]

The new Republican majority, however, has not joined in supporting these Democratic efforts. To the contrary, the Republican-crafted Budget Reconciliation Act of 1995, passed both by the House of Representatives and by the Senate in October 1995, substantially reduced the funds for the EITC; Republican leaders have condemned EITC as a "program out of control," pointing to the increase in federal EITC funding from $3 billion in fiscal 1975 to $9.9 billion in 1992.[55] The future of the EITC program will depend on whether a compromise can be worked out between President Clinton and Republican leaders following the president's veto of the Budget Act.

Republican leaders in Congress also effectively throttled any serious legislative effort to modify the minimum wage; Republicans contended that this substantial increase would have a perverse effect of impelling employers to fire many of their low-wage workers, thereby contributing to greater unemployment.[56] While Secretary Reich and others disputed these dire predictions, the Clinton administration was unable to achieve legislative movement on this issue.

The School to Work Transition and other employment training programs have also been placed on the block for elimination or consolidation by Republicans, who have passed legislation (in the Senate, a Workforce Development Act) that consolidates all present federal education and job training programs into two broad "block grants"—one covering vocational and adult job training, and the other covering workforce preparation for adolescents and other at-risk youth.[57] As part of their massive deficit-reduction efforts, the Republican bills would cut the authorized spending for these programs by 15 percent and would eliminate virtually all of the specific provisions that target certain groups for job training assistance, instead giving broad latitude to the states to decide how to spend their block grant funds.[58] President Clinton and the Democrats have attempted to shape the debate as one about "human capital development"; thus far, the Republicans have retorted by stressing their paramount concern for federal fiscal responsibility.

As noted earlier, some Republicans have also spearheaded an attack against federal and state affirmative action programs, which have accounted for a substantial growth in governmental employment among minority group members since 1970. While the ultimate success of this attack remains uncertain at present, strong constitutional support from the Rehnquist Supreme Court suggests that affirmative action programs are likely to be further curtailed in the coming decade.

Federal Educational Programs

The Democrats under President Clinton have attempted to expand educational programs initially created during the mid-1960s, reasoning that such programs constitute long-range investments that establish a "lifelong learning" agenda benefiting both the individuals involved and the national economy.[59] In 1994 the Clinton administration successfully led an effort to reauthorize Title I of the Elementary and Secondary Education Act, the principal federal program that has, since 1965, channeled funds to schools with high percentages of low-income children.[60] Clinton also sought to expand the Head Start program, another War on Poverty effort, that has since 1965 offered preschool educational activities to low-income children. Presently, Head Start reaches one in five eligible children; President Clinton, declaring that Head Start should be provided to every eligible child, sought a $400 million increase in fiscal 1996 to $3.9 billion, which would constitute an $800 million increase in two years.[61] Finally, President Clinton initiated a new educational program, AmeriCorps, as part of his National Service Corporation, under which students can earn federal funds for college tuition by volunteering their services to designated national public service efforts for a year.[62]

The new Republican initiative, by contrast, has attacked the federal role in education, beginning symbolically with a drive to eliminate (or at least radically modify) the Department of Education.[63] Although that effort has not yet succeeded,[64] the Republicans did manage to pass a bill through the House that would fold major federal educational programs into a single block grant for state distribution, cut back on rather than expand Head Start, restrict federal loan programs for college students and their parents, and kill AmeriCorps entirely.[65] In late 1995 the fate of these initiatives appears to depend on the outcome of negotiations between Republican congressional leadership and the Democratic president, or on the 1996 election. The beneficiaries of these programs have been, disproportionately, low-income black and Latino children.

National Health Care Programs

The most visible failure of the Clinton administration has been the congressional defeat of Clinton's widely heralded national health care reform proposals. President Clinton put the full prestige of his office behind health care reform, allowing First Lady Hillary Rodham Clinton to lead early efforts to draft consensus legislation to assure that all Americans would have access to adequate health care. However, a powerful combination of major private insurance carriers, nervous medical care providers, well-paid lobbyists, and uncertain citizens prevailed on Congress to refrain from adopting any reform legislation.[66] Consequently, late 1995 finds nearly 40 million Americans without any health care insurance at all, one serious bout of illness away from bankruptcy and family ruin.[67] Many are not the unemployed poor, for many of whom Medicaid stands as a health care source of last resort,[68] but the working poor—those employed in jobs that offer no medical benefits and pay too little to allow an employee to purchase private health care insurance.[69]

The uninsured remain disproportionately African American and Latino; 16.2 percent of blacks, 25.3 percent of Hispanics, but only 8.8 percent of whites were uninsured throughout 1990.[70] African Americans below the poverty line are likewise significantly more dependent on Medicaid than are the white poor; 61.5 percent of poor blacks, 47.6 percent of poor Hispanics, but only 42.2 percent of poor whites were covered by Medicaid in 1993.[71]

The new Republican initiative has proposed the most fundamental change in the Medicare program for the elderly and the Medicaid program for the poor since those programs were adopted during the mid-1960s. As part of their comprehensive effort to reduce the federal budget deficit, the Republicans in mid-1995 crafted federal legislation that would slow the growth in Medicare spending in the next seven years and would slow Medicaid growth by $163 billion, with annual federal Medicaid payments some 28 percent less by 2002.[72] Senate Republicans have sought to moderate the initial House version of the bill by guaranteeing continued coverage of young children under age thirteen, pregnant women, and disabled individuals.[73] These assurances would do nothing for other groups, however, and the Urban Institute has estimated that by 2002, between 4 and 9 million persons who are presently covered under Medicaid would be denied coverage if the Senate or House bill were eventually enacted.[74] Moreover, the

Senate bill requires no particular level of medical coverage even for its protected groups (other than mandatory immunizations for children), and thus states might well find themselves financially tempted to deny many important medical services even to pregnant women, children, and the disabled, since the mandatory spending provisions for these groups in the Senate bill are set at levels that are "far below the level of funds currently spent on these groups of people."[75]

Democrats have insisted that the cuts proposed to date are too deep and come at too high a price. Under the Republican initiative, premiums paid by most senior citizens for Medicare, now typically $46.10 per month, would nearly double, to $88.90, by 2002, and the Republican proposal depends on the assumption that millions of senior citizens would abandon federally funded Medicare for private, managed-care providers, who presumably would control costs more carefully and eliminate unnecessary procedures and medical treatment.[76]

Democrats have argued that this assumption is unwarranted, unless citizens agree to accept a lesser standard of health care treatment. Republicans counter that the current Medicare and Medicaid systems cannot continue to be funded at present and projected levels, and that Democrats themselves realize that major legislative changes are necessary to assure the continued survival of a fiscally sound system.[77] While most Democrats and Republicans privately concur that major changes in the shape and funding of health care programs are necessary, a principal question is how heavy a burden should be borne by the poor in any adjustment of spending cuts and access to health services. The stalemate occasioned by President Clinton's veto of the Republican Budget Reconciliation Act in November 1995 has set the stage for crucial negotiations on the future of these central federal health care programs.[78]

Federal Housing Programs

Despite the continued national shortage of decent low-income housing units, especially in many central-city areas, the budget impasse has made any thought of a massive federal building program all but utopian. Thus, the overall federal strategy to assist low-income renters continues to shift from capital expenditures for new buildings and toward greater reliance on subsidization of monthly rental payments to landlords in existing housing units. The 104th Congress has proposed to slash the overall budget for the Department of Housing and Community Development by 20 percent, down from $25.5 billion in fiscal 1995 to $20.4 billion.[79] This proposed cutback, moreover, comes even as the shortfall in low-rent housing units has reached the highest level on record. In 1993 there were 11.2 million low-income renters, but only 6.5 million available low-rent units, a gap of 4.7 million units.[80]

President Clinton, aware of Republican proposals to eliminate the Department of Housing and Urban Development (HUD) altogether, early directed Secretary of Housing Henry Cisneros to propose a series of pre-emptive changes and cutbacks at HUD. Secretary Cisneros complied with that request, but he also lobbied strongly within the administration for a combination of "in-place" strategies, designed to improve housing opportunities and to further community development activities within low-income, central city areas, as well as "mobility" strategies, designed to give low-income families more opportunity to move away from high-poverty neighborhoods to middle-income or suburban locations.[81]

In the view of many Republican spokespersons, by contrast, governmental responsibility for housing and urban development properly should be vested with states and urban areas, not with Congress and the federal government.[82] Secretary Cisneros's ambitious national urban policy strategy has thus found virtually no takers in the 104th Congress.

Once again the stakes in this debate are particularly important for the minority poor, especially African Americans, who have significantly higher participation rates in federally subsidized housing programs. In 1993 33.8 percent of poverty-level black households, 13.8 percent of poverty-level Hispanic households, but only 13.4 percent of poverty-level white households lived in public or federally subsidized housing.[83] Sharp reductions in federal support for these programs will unquestionably affect a higher percentage of the minority poor. Yet political and budget realities jeopardize efforts to address seriously the growing concentration of poor and minority citizens in our nation's central cities.

Public Welfare Transfers

A centerpiece of the new conservative initiative has been the proposal to reform the "welfare system," the complex of federal transfer programs, originally adopted during the 1930s. The special, though not exclusive, focus of the proposed reforms has been on Aid to Families with Dependent Children (AFDC), the program most vividly identified in the public mind with welfare issues.

President Clinton himself promised in 1992 to "transform welfare as we know it," and his administration came forward with a modest proposal to revise that program, including more vigorous enforcement of child support obligations against absent fathers of AFDC children, and the placement of greater responsibility on AFDC mothers to seek remunerative work.[84]

Yet the Republicans seized the legislative initiative after the 1994 elections, passing a Personal Responsibility Act in the House of Representatives (and a similar Work Opportunity Act in the Senate),[85] both of which would eliminate the crucial "entitlement" aspect of the AFDC program that has long assured federal benefits to every income-eligible recipient. The House and Senate bills would replace the entire entitlement approach with federal block grants to each state every year; while these grants would allow states greater discretion in fashioning their own welfare programs, neither the federal government nor the state would be legally obligated under the new legislation to meet the needs of all eligible applicants.[86]

Although the Senate bill includes both (1) a "maintenance of effort" requirement that requires some minimum level of state spending in order to receive federal AFDC funds and (2) a contingency fund in the event of a recession or high unemployment in a particular state, states can comply with the mandatory minimum so long as they spend at least 80 percent of what they spent on AFDC in fiscal 1994.[87] The contingency fund, moreover, is precariously small, comprising only $1 billion for the next seven years. Unless the economy proves remarkably robust, normal downturns could swamp the AFDC contingency fund. (During the two-year recession from 1990 to 1992, resort to AFDC by income-eligible persons forced a $6 billion increase in federal AFDC spending.)[88]

These revised bills have been self-consciously designed by their sponsors to prompt changes in the behavior of the poor, reestablishing moral and "family" values dear to conservative lawmakers. In that regard, the House version of the bill proposes to (1) deny AFDC benefits to any unwed mother under age eighteen; (2) deny AFDC benefits to any additional child, whether legitimate or not, born while a woman is receiving AFDC benefits; (3) impose a five-year cumulative lifetime cap on the receipt of AFDC benefits by any one beneficiary, irrespective of any continuing poverty thereafter;[89] and (4) require mothers of AFDC children to participate in work activities for at least thirty-five hours per week.[90]

The Senate bill, while omitting the mandatory ban on AFDC for children born to underage, single mothers and children born to families while on AFDC,[91] retains the five-year cap and the work requirements. These provisions have been promoted as devices to discourage teenage pregnancy, to encourage AFDC recipients to marry, to compel recipients to use AFDC as no more than transitional aid, and to demand some remunerative work in exchange for AFDC benefits. The likely effectiveness of this approach, of course, depends on a series of untested assumptions about the motivations and behavior of welfare recipients. Critics of this approach suggest that many young woman would not be deterred from early sexuality by these provisions, which would merely have the unintended consequence of punishing innocent children for the choices of their parents. Moreover, other critics have charged that most women want to leave AFDC but discover that there are too few remunerative jobs for AFDC recipients, or that they lack employable skills.[92]

In the drive to achieve additional budget savings, the new Republican initiative has also targeted programs beyond AFDC that provide benefits to low-income citizens, including the Food Stamp program, the School Lunch program, and WIC, the nutrition and health program for women, infants, and children. Although the Senate bill does not require states to end the entitlement status for food stamps, it permits states to do so if they wish, by converting their state food stamp programs into block grant programs without any federal standards on benefits levels or eligibility criteria.[93] States that choose to continue participation under the present approach, however, will face across-the-board reductions in benefits for all recipients and new restrictions limiting those who will be eligible and cutting benefits levels for various subgroups of beneficiaries.[94] The Congressional Budget Office estimates that the cumulative changes included within the Senate version of this proposed legislation would cut food assistance programs by $32 billion over the next seven years.[95]

While the disappearance of federally funded public welfare programs is inconceivable, the mid-range future appears to promise substantial funding cuts in cash and in-kind programs, as well as the crucial loss of any claim of federal entitlement to minimum assistance for the eligible poor. The predicted cumulative effect of these cuts would be over $82 billion between 1995 and 2002.[96] In November 1995 the Clinton administration released an analysis estimating that the welfare provisions of the Republicans' Senate bill would drive 1.2 million more children into poverty, while substantially increasing the degree of poverty endured by children already below the poverty line. The impact of all Senate provisions, including proposed cuts in AFDC, Food Stamps, EITC, and health care programs, was estimated to send an additional 1.7 million children below the poverty line.[97]

The demographic realities of the AFDC and Food Stamp programs, moreover, ensure that, if such cutbacks are carried out, they will fall disproportionately on African American and Hispanic children and their families. While most AFDC families, white or black, use AFDC only during short-term periods of economic instability, over 34 percent of all African American children who received AFDC benefits between 1974 and 1987 stayed on AFDC for more than the proposed five-year maximum; during the same period, only 18 percent of nonblack children received benefits beyond the five-year maximum.[98]

In addition, the bills are especially harsh on legal immigrants to the United States (many of whom are from Mexico, Central America, and Southeast Asia). As the Center on Budget and Policy Priorities reports, "The Senate bill hits poor *legal* immigrants hardest of all. (Illegal immigrants are already ineligible for most benefits.) The bill would deny almost all federal means-tested aid to the large majority of low-income legal immigrants. This includes aid provided under major programs such as SSI [Supplemental Security Income for the elderly poor], Medicaid, and food stamps as well as assistance provided under small programs such as meals-on-wheels to the homebound elderly and prenatal care for pregnant women." [99]

The Struggle over Black Political Representation

The Voting Rights Act of 1965, as reenacted in 1982, has been the principal vehicle for bringing millions of African American and Latino voters to the polls in federal, state, and local elections, especially within the American South. In turn, these new voters have led to dramatic increases since 1968 in the number of minority officials who have reached elected and appointed office. Section Two of the Voting Rights Act has been a major factor in this growth in minority elected representatives, since it encourages the creation of electoral districts that do not dilute minority voting strength. Although the Supreme Court earlier upheld the use of Section Two to avoid "vote dilution" in *Thornberg v. Gingles*,[100] the Court appeared to reverse its basic direction in two recent decisions discussed earlier, *Shaw v. Reno* and *Miller v. Johnson*, both of which seemed to discourage state legislatures from taking race into account in the redesign of legislative districts. Some have predicted that if *Miller* is not itself qualified by subsequent decisions, many of the forty black congressional representatives in the 104th Congress might lose their seats by 1997.[101]

Others, however, have argued that the movement to create "safe" black electoral districts has actually diminished overall black political influence in Congress, since it has necessitated the aggregation of black voters in a few districts, rendering other remaining districts more predominantly white in voter population. In consequence, these critics have observed, congressional representatives in these overwhelmingly white districts have realized that they can cast votes for policies inimical to black political interests without any fear of serious repercussions at the polls. Some have connected the new conservative initiatives outlined above to these emerging electoral dynamics. The Supreme Court heard arguments in two redistricting cases from North Carolina and Texas in December 1995 that may further clarify the permissible limits of race-conscious redistricting.[102]

Professor Lani Guinier and others have argued that black electoral power should be enhanced by electoral reforms, such as cumulative voting, that are novel within the American political context, insisting that "group representation is not only consistent with, but is the very essence of representative democracy." [103] The unpopularity of such proposals among the nation's majority population, however, has been underlined by President Clinton's decision precipitously to abandon his nomination of Guinier to serve as the assistant attorney general for civil rights. President Clinton acted after congressional critics began to challenge Guinier's academic writings on voting reforms.[104]

The demographic realities of minority political status suggest that few legislative changes favorable to African American and Hispanic voters can be expected in Congress or in most state legislatures in the next five to ten years. Eventually, however, the growth in the minority population, especially among Hispanics and Asians in California, Texas, and Florida, may well bring a shift in electoral power in several major states by the early twenty-first century. There does not appear to be a similar increase among the African American population; the fate of African American interests in these states may well depend on whether effective political coalitions can be fostered among America's principal minority groups. Whether these new electoral coalitions, moreover, will be especially inclined toward the minority poor is presently impossible to predict.

The Future of the Minority Poor in Central Cities

The essays in this volume have largely concurred in the assessment that the geographical isolation of low-income blacks and other racial minorities, especially in the central cities of the Northeast and Midwest, has not substantially abated since the Kerner Commission issued its warning in 1968 about the corrosive long-term effects of segregation. No development in the past few years would prompt modification of those sober assessments. Rather, a public mood of weariness with racial striving and scarcely concealed hostility toward the poor has captured many throughout the nation.

President Clinton's recent National Urban Policy Report acknowledges the long-term threat posed by continued neglect:

> For many years, America's cities have been in trouble. Poor families and poor inner-city neighborhoods have become disconnected from the opportunities and prosperity of their metropolitan regions, the nation, and the emerging global economy. A vicious cycle of poverty concentration, social despair, continued outmigration, and fiscal distress in central cities undermines the ability of metropolitan regions to compete in the global economy, threatening the long-term prosperity of the nation. Moreover, the polarization of urban communities—isolating the poor from the well-off, the unemployed from those who work, and minorities from whites—frays the fabric of our nation's civic culture. If these problems continue to go unaddressed, America's future could be severely

compromised, both economically and socially. Simply put, if we do not address the problems of our inner cities, we will not be able to compete and win in the global economy.[105]

Yet the Clinton administration's modest efforts (1) to provide a platform of minimum supports for the poor—national health insurance, earned income tax credits, expansion of educational support for low-income children, and support for increased job training efforts—and (2) to offer some coherent urban strategy have been met with substantial political opposition and widespread public skepticism or indifference. If there is growing income inequality in America as the twentieth century closes, as many economists report,[106] the predominant response among a majority of the electorate seems to be a scramble for a place at the table, rather than advocacy of public policies that might reduce the emerging inequities.

W. E. B. Du Bois, looking forward in 1903, predicted that "the problem" of the still-young twentieth century would be "the problem of the color-line, the relation of the darker to the lighter races of men in Asia and Africa, in America and the islands of the sea." [107] As the century closes, Du Bois's prescience has been confirmed; America' domestic polity and politics have been dominated, especially since 1950, by issues of race, ethnicity, and poverty. The remarkable legal victories won by the civil rights movement against segregation have not overcome the racial divide but instead have disclosed deep and long-lasting economic wounds that accompanied slavery, decades of Jim Crow subordination, and a legacy of overt hostility toward non-European immigrant populations, especially Asians and Hispanic Americans.

To amend Du Bois, one might predict that America's principal domestic challenge in the twenty-first century may well be to transcend the residual economic and social legacies of its past white supremacy and racial subordination. If, indeed, that becomes the nation's chief domestic issue, the contributors to this volume have offered powerful evidence that no national success is likely without far greater governmental attention than has yet been afforded to America's imperiled central cities and to the minority poor within them.

Notes

1. Nancy Mathis, "GOP Signs 'Contract with America,'" *Houston Chronicle*, September 28, 1994 (reporting that more than 300 Republican House candidates signed the contract on September 27, 1994, pledging if elected to work for legislation on ten major points outlined in the contract, including tax cuts, a balanced budget amendment, welfare reform, and increased defense spending); see

also Tom Brazaitis and Sabrina Eaton, "GOP Revels in Possible House Takeover," *Cleveland Plain Dealer*, September 28, 1994 (detailing each of the ten points in the contract).

2. The most recent data on poverty rates reveal a rise in white poverty in 1993 from 10.7 to 12.2 percent, a rise in black poverty from 31.9 to 33.1 percent, and a rise in Hispanic poverty from 28.1 to 30.6 percent (Richard May, *1993 Poverty and Income Trends* [Washington, D.C.: Center on Budget and Policy Priorities, 1995], 11).

The rate of participation in most federal social welfare programs is significantly higher among black and Hispanic households at the poverty level than among white households at the poverty level (ibid., 37–38).

The likely disparate impact of the Contract with America on racial minorities has not been lost on representatives of these groups (Bruno J. Navarro, "Latinos Warned of GOP's 'Contract,'" *Asbury Park Press*, October 8, 1995 [reporting on a warning to delegates to the twenty-sixty annual convention of the Puerto Rican Congress that the "innocuous-sounding goals" of the Contract with America "could create devastating consequences for Latino communities"]); see also Brian Edwards and Orval Jackson, "New NAACP Leader Seeks to Add Voters," *Tampa Tribune*, October 16, 1995 (quoting Florida's new NAACP president as stating, "We believe the Contract with America . . . is anti-black, anti-minority, anti-older people and anti-people who have a need").

3. R. W. Apple Jr., "The 1994 Elections: Congress—New Analysis: How Lasting a Majority?," *New York Times*, November 10, 1994.

4. A number of the more controversial provisions involving health and welfare spending have been folded by Republican congressional leaders into omnibus budget reconciliation legislation that presents President Clinton with the choice of accepting Republican-backed changes in health and welfare policy as the price for budget reductions, or vetoing the legislation and, with it, the federal spending package. President Clinton has declared that he will not accept the Republican changes and will veto the budget package if necessary to forestall their passage (Todd S. Purdum, "President Warns Congress to Drop Some Budget Cuts," *New York Times*, October 29, 1995; Peter G. Gosselin, "Senate OK's GOP Plan on Spending; Measure to Balance US Budget Signals New Era in Social Policy," *Boston Globe*, October 28, 1995).

5. Charles M. Madigan, "Non-Voters Let Anger Rule the Day; GOP Exploited Lack of Focus by Democrats," *Chicago Tribune*, November 9, 1994 (reporting that "low turnout was the issue" on election day and that "the vast majority of the 185.6 million people of voting age in the U.S. avoided politics with a passion" in 1994).

6. Richard L. Berke, "The 1994 Elections: Voters; 'Asked to Place Blame, Americans in Surveys Chose: All of the Above,'" *New York Times*, November 10, 1994 (reporting that most Election Day voters were unaware of either the existence or the contents of the Contract with America).

7. Adam Clymer, "Americans Reject Big Medicare Cut, a New Poll Finds," *New York Times*, October 26, 1995 (reporting that only 27 percent of the public prefers a balanced budget if it means cuts in Medicare or Social Security, compared with

70 percent who prefer the preservation of present Medicare and Social Security benefits over budget cuts).

8. See Iris J. Lav, Edward B. Lazere, and Jim St. George, *A Tale of Two Futures: Restructuring California's Finances to Boost Economic Growth* (Washington, D.C.: Center on Budget and Policy Priorities, 1994) (examining the causes of California's growing short- and long-term fiscal woes).

9. Proposition 187 "amend[ed] California law to restrict access by illegal aliens to state-funded education, medical, and social services" (Cal. Senate Joint Resolution 3, 1995–96 Regular Session, introduced on December 6, 1994).

10. B. Drummond Ayres Jr., "Californians Pass Measure on Aliens; Courts Bar It," *New York Times*, November 10, 1994.

11. See, for example, Lorenza Munoz, "Southern California Voices/A Forum for Community Issues: Platform; Prop. 187: 'Racist Initiative' or a 'Step in the Right Direction?,'" *Los Angeles Times*, August 29, 1994; Patrick J. McDonnell and Chip Johnson, "70,000 March through L.A. against Prop. 187; Immigration: Protesters Condemn the Initiative and Burn an Effigy of Gov. Wilson," *Los Angeles Times*, October 17, 1994; Daniel B. Wood, "California's Immigration Revolt," *Christian Science Monitor*, November 10, 1994. "The so-called 'Save our State' initiative would cut off many public services to illegal immigrants, such as education, welfare, and all but emergency medical care. It would require teachers, welfare workers, and police to report illegal immigrants for possible detention and deportation. . . . Opponents of the measure, who consider it xenophobic and unconstitutional, are not sitting idle. Several groups have filed lawsuits against the initiati[ve]" (Wood, "California's Immigration Revolt").

12. Upon its approval in November 1994, Proposition 187 was promptly challenged in federal court on various constitutional and statutory grounds (James Rainey, "City of L.A. Will Proceed with Legal Challenge to Prop. 187," *Los Angeles Times*, December 10, 1994; see also Lynn Schneiberg, "Approval of Prop 187 Spurs Suits, Protests," *Education Week*, November 16, 1994, 1, 25 [noting that "at least seven lawsuits against various parts of Prop 187 were filed in state and federal courts by various groups"]).

On November 20, 1995, a federal district court granted an injunction against the enforcement of Proposition 187, agreeing with challengers that major portions of the provision violate federal constitutional and/or federal statutory provisions (*League of United Latin American Citizens v. Wilson*, No. CV94-7569 et al., 1995 U.S. Dist. LEXIS 17720 [C.D. Cal., Nov. 20, 1995]; see Paul Feldman, "Lawyers Weigh Options in Prop. 187 Battle; Courts: Measure's Supporters May Seek Early Appeal of Judge's Ruling, but Opponents Could Try to Block That," *Los Angeles Times*, November 22, 1995 [outlining the effect of the district court's ruling on various provisions of Proposition 187]).

13. See Harold Johnson, "Quota Busting: California Civil Rights Initiative," *National Review*, September 25, 1995, 30; Yumi Wilson, "Anti-Affirmative Action Drive Begins, Backers Hope for 694,000 Signatures by February 21," *San Francisco Chronicle*, September 29, 1995. The initial enthusiasm for CCRI and against affirmative action has apparently waned somewhat. California governor Pete Wilson, who openly backed the initiative and launched a national campaign for the

Republican presidential nomination predicated, in substantial part, on his opposition to affirmative action, found little national support and withdrew from the presidential campaign (Cathleen Decker, "Wilson Drops Out of White House Race, Blames Cash Woes," *Los Angeles Times*, September 30, 1995). Moreover, supporters of CCRI announced in mid-November 1995 that their drive for the minimum 700,00 plus signatures was in jeopardy of falling short (Carl Ingram, "Initiative Effort in Cash Bind; Politics: Leader of Anti-Affirmative Action Measure Says Prospects of Qualifying for 1996 Ballot Are in Jeopardy without Immediate Funding," *Los Angles Times*, November 2, 1995).

14. See generally John Riley, "The Great Debate: 3 Decades since Affirmative Action Entered Public Consciousness with Passage of the Civil Rights Act, It Remains a Point of Contention," *Newsday*, June 11, 1995, 4 (reporting mixed results from a recent public opinion poll on affirmative action); Lawrence Bobo and Ryan A. Smith, "Antipoverty Policy, Affirmative Action, and Racial Attitudes," in *Confronting Poverty: Prescriptions for Change*, ed. Sheldon H. Danziger, Gary D. Sandefur, and Daniel H. Weinberg (Cambridge, Mass.: Harvard University Press, 1994), 376–79 and tabs. 14.2–14.4 (reporting changes in attitude between 1986 and 1990, among whites and blacks, on affirmative action programs in education and employment).

15. Margot Hornblower, "Taking It All Back: At Pete Wilson's Urging, the University of California Says No to Racial Preferences," *Time*, July 31, 1995, 34.

In *Podberesky v. Kirwin*, 38 F.3d 147 (4th Cir. 1994), cert. denied, __ U.S. __, 115 S.Ct. 2001 (1995), the Fourth Circuit struck down a minority scholarship program administered by the University of Maryland, holding that without a showing of a governmental interest more compelling than the need to combat "societal discrimination," the university could not justify its sponsorship of race-conscious minority scholarships.

16. "Remarks of President Bill Clinton Regarding Affirmative Action," *Federal News Service*, July 19, 1995.

17. Steven A. Holmes, "Veto Threat on Bill to Ban Hiring Rules," *New York Times*, December 8, 1995 (reporting on congressional testimony by Deval Patrick, assistant attorney general for civil rights, opposing the proposed legislation and indicating that the Department of Justice would recommend that the president veto it if adopted by Congress).

18. __ U.S. __, 115 S.Ct. 2097 (1995). The *Adarand* majority stopped short of invalidating the particular federal highway construction program under challenge; instead, it remanded the case for further consideration by the lower federal courts (ibid., 2113).

19. Ibid., 2113.

20. Ibid., 2117–18. See *City of Richmond v. J. A. Croson Co.*, 488 U.S. 469 (1989). Within a year of the *Croson* decision in 1989, the share of construction dollars from cities and states going to minority contractors reportedly dropped from 41.6 percent to 2.2 percent (Stan Crock and Michele Galen, "'A Thunderous Impact' on Equal Opportunity," *Business Week*, June 26, 1995, 37 [citing figures from the Minority Business Enterprise Legal Defense and Education Fund]).

21. __ U.S. __, 115 S.Ct. 2120 (1995).

22. __ U.S. __, 115 S.Ct. 2475 (1995).

23. Lani Guinier, "[E]racing Democracy: The Voting Rights Cases," *Harvard Law Review* 108 (1994): 109.

24. See Voting Rights Act, 79 Stat. 438, as amended, 42 U.S.C. § 1973 (1982).

25. Ibid., 2483–85. The abstract question initially came before the Court in *Shaw v. Reno*, 509 U.S. __, 113 S.Ct. 2816 (1993), where the Court declared that electoral districting should henceforth be subjected to "strict judicial scrutiny," despite any ostensibly benign purpose of maximizing black political representation. The *Shaw* decision did not clarify how its new holding should be implemented, acknowledging that "application of these principles to electoral districting is a most delicate task" (*Miller*, 115 S.Ct. 2483). Only in *Miller* did the Court begin to reveal its views on how Equal Protection principles should be reconciled with Congress's aims under the Voting Rights Act.

26. __ U.S. __, 115 S.Ct. 2483–84. The Georgia legislature initially devised a plan that created two majority-black districts. The Department of Justice, to whom the plan was submitted for "preclearance" under the Voting Rights Act, objected on the grounds that "Georgia had created only two majority-minority districts, and that the proposed plan did not 'recognize' certain minority populations by placing them in a majority-black district" (ibid.). A second redistricting plan was likewise rejected by the Department of Justice, in favor of alternative plans that would create three majority-black districts (ibid., 2484).

27. Ibid., 2485.

28. The *Miller* Court acknowledged that "redistricting legislatures will . . . almost always be aware of racial demographics" (ibid., 2488), but it held that the crucial question was whether the legislature was "motivated by" such considerations: "A plaintiff must prove that the legislature subordinated traditional race-neutral districting principles, including but not limited to compactness, contiguity, respect for political subdivisions or communities defined by actual share interests, to racial considerations" (ibid.).

29. Ibid., 2504–6 (Ginsburg, J., dissenting).

30. __ U.S. __, 115 S.Ct. 2038.

31. Ibid., 2042.

32. Chief Justice Rehnquist's opinion noted that the district court's plan had required "the renovation of approximately 55 schools, the closure of 18 facilities, and the construction of 17 new schools" (ibid., 2044). "Not surprisingly, the cost of this remedial plan has far exceeded KCMSD's budget, or for that matter, its authority to tax. The State . . . has borne the brunt of these costs. The District Court candidly has acknowledged that it has 'allowed the District planners to dream' and 'provided the mechanism for th[ose] dreams to be realized'" (ibid., 2045). The chief justice emphasized that, on remand, "the District Court must bear in mind that its end purpose is not only 'to remedy the violation' to the extent practicable, but also 'to restore state and local authorities to the control of a school system that is operating in compliance with the Constitution'" (ibid., 2056; citations omitted).

33. Ibid., 2052, 2055.

34. Linda Greenhouse, "The Nation: Gavel Rousers; Farewell to the Old Order in the Court," *New York Times*, July 2, 1995 (summarizing the 1994–95 term of

the Supreme Court, one marked by "a re-examination of basic Constitutional principles . . . about the ability of the Federal Government to take race into account in making public policy"). Greenhouse predicted that *Adarand* would "inevitably curtail programs designed to convey special Federal benefits to members of minority groups," while she saw *Missouri v. Jenkins* as "underscor[ing] the majority's impatience with continued Federal court involvement in school desegregation."

35. Andrea Ford and Jim Newton, "Judge Cites 'Ample Evidence,' Orders Simpson to Stand Trial; Court: Criminalist Testifies That Blood Drop Found at Crime Scene Matches Former Athlete's Type. Defense Attorney Says He Will Push for an Early Trial Date," *Los Angeles Times*, July 9, 1994.

36. James Willwerth, "Dispatches: The Godzilla of Tabloid Stories," *Time*, June 26, 1995, 14.

37. David Shaw, "The Simpson Legacy," *Los Angeles Times*, October 9, 1995 (describing the "Fuhrman tapes . . . [in which] Fuhrman's own voice could be heard uttering the word 'nigger' 41 times").

38. Ronald Brownstein, "Washington Outlook: Simpson Defense's Focus on Racial Identity Further Divides a Nation," *Los Angeles Times*, October 9, 1995 (suggesting that the racial themes in the closing argument of defense attorney Johnnie Cochran "may have inadvertently strengthened the Republican position in national politics" by creating racial polarization among blacks and whites).

39. Richard Morin, "Poll Reflects Division over Simpson Case; Trial Damaged Image of Courts, Races Agree," *Washington Post*, October 8, 1995; Betsy Streisand, "The Verdict's Aftermath," *U.S. News & World Report*, October 16, 1995, 34 (describing wide racial divisions over many issues raised by the Simpson trial).

40. Francis X. Clines, "The March on Washington: Overview; Black Men Fill Capital's Mall in Display of Unity and Peace," *New York Times*, October 17, 1995.

41. Ibid.

42. The National Parks Service's initial estimate of 400,000 participants was sharply challenged by Million Man March organizers, and later estimates suggested that over 870,000 persons participated in the march (Michael A. Fletcher and Hamil R. Harris, "Million Man March Gets Another Head Count; Boston University Researchers Take a Second Look to Try to Establish Final Estimate," *Washington Post*, October 25, 1995.

43. Louis Farrakan, "Excerpts," *New York Times*, October 17, 1995.

44. Todd S. Purdum, "The March on Washington: The President; Clinton, in Solemn Speech, Chides Racists of All Colors," *New York Times*, October 17, 1995; Bill Clinton, "Remarks at the University of Texas at Austin," 31 Weekly Comp. Pres. Doc. 1847, October 16, 1995.

45. Jack Nelson, "Clinton Considers Naming Panel to Study Race Relations Problem," *Houston Chronicle*, October 19, 1995.

46. The Clinton administration's first comprehensive urban policy statement begins with four "guiding principles," the first of which is to "link families to work," aiming to "[reward] work, individual initiative, and family responsibility by reforming welfare, housing and other policies" (Department of Housing and Urban Development, Office of Policy Development and Research, *Empowerment: A New*

Covenant with America's Communities; President Clinton's National Urban Policy Report (Washington, D.C.: U.S. Government Printing Office, 1995), 3.

47. Rebecca M. Blank, "The Employment Strategy: Public Policies to Increase Work and Earnings," in Danziger et al., *Confronting Poverty*, 192; Isaac Shapiro and Sharon Parrott, *An Unraveling Consensus?: An Analysis of the Effect of the New Congressional Agenda on the Working Poor* (Washington, D.C.: Center on Budget and Policy Priorities, 1995), 16.

48. Todd S. Purdum, "Clinton Asks Rise in Minimum Wage," *New York Times*, February 4, 1995 (quoting Clinton, contending that "the only way to grow the middle class and shrink the underclass is to make work pay. . . . In terms of real buying power, the minimum wage will be at a 40-year low next year if we do not raise it above $4.25 an hour"); see also Robert B. Reich and Laura D'Andrea Tyson, "This Is No Way to Reward Work," *Washington Post*, July 25, 1995 (coauthoring a column calling for support for the EITC and an increase in the minimum wage).

49. Blank, "Employment Strategy," 192.

50. Ibid.

51. "Can America Afford $5.15 an Hour?: Clinton's Minimum Wage Hike and the New Politics of Work," *Washington Post*, February 12, 1995; see also Department of Housing and Urban Development, *Empowerment*, 35.

52. Shapiro and Parrott, *Unraveling Consensus?*, 14. Shapiro reported in early 1995 that "the purchasing power of the minimum wage is now at its second lowest level in four decades . . . going back to 1955. . . . If the value of the minimum wage were to have the same purchasing power in 1995 as it averaged in the 1970s, it would need to equal about $5.75 an hour" (Isaac Shapiro, *Four Years and Still Falling: The Decline in the Value of the Minimum Wage* [Washington, D.C.: Center on Budget and Policy Priorities, 1995], 1).

53. Shapiro and Parrott, *Unraveling Consensus?*, 5.

54. Blank, "Employment Strategy," 171, tab. 7.1. The percentages are for 1992. Comparable figures for teenaged women are: white, 15.7 percent unemployed; Hispanic, 26.5 percent; black, 37.2 percent (ibid.).

55. Bill Archer, "Where Credit Is Due; The GOP's Misunderstood Plan to Rein in a Runaway Program," *Washington Post*, October 15, 1995 (urging that Republicans support the EITC, but that, as presently structured, it is "going to families with incomes that are too high" and should also be denied to childless workers); see Gary Burtless, "Public Spending on the Poor: Historical Trends and Economic Limits," in Danziger et al., *Confronting Poverty*, 57, tab. 3.1.

56. "Can America Afford $5.15 An Hour?: Clinton's Minimum Wage Hike and the New Politics of Work," *Washington Post*, February 12, 1995 (quoting House Majority Leader Richard Armey as vowing to fight a minimum-wage increase "with every fiber of my being"). Some economists argue that an increase in the minimum wage "is badly targeted as an antipoverty device. The majority of minimum wage workers are second or third earners in middle-income households" (Blank, "Employment Strategy," 194).

57. *Highlights of Senate-Passed Workforce Development Act* (Washington, D.C.: Center for Law and Social Policy, 1995), 1.

58. Ibid.

59. See generally Mark Pitsch, "Administration Beats Drum for Education," *Education Week*, February 15, 1995, 1 (describing the Clinton administration's fiscal 1996 education budget, which "largely spares education from cuts and seeks big increases for certain programs").

60. Mark Pitsch, "Congress Fends off G.O.P. Attacks, Backs E.S.E.A.," *Education Week*, October 12, 1994, 1 (reporting the reauthorization by Congress of the Elementary and Secondary Education Act, despite efforts by congressional Republicans, "emboldened by the demise of health-care and welfare-reform legislation and Mr. Clinton's waning popularity, . . . [to launch] an all-out effort" to defeat reauthorization).

61. Robert C. Johnson, "Clinton Urges 3.8% Increase for Education Department Programs," *Education Week*, February 15, 1995, 16, 18.

62. Robert C. Johnson, "AmeriCorps Sparks Debate on Federal Service Role," *Education Week*, February 15, 1995, 16 (reviewing the political debate over the National and Community Service Trust Act of 1993).

63. See Millicent Lawton and Mark Pitsch, "Proposal Expected on Merging Education, Labor Departments," *Education Week*, February 15, 1995, 20 (reporting that conservative Republican leaders, including House Speaker Newt Gingrich, want an end to the Department of Education, while more moderate Republican leaders in Congress have suggested a merger of the Departments of Education and Labor); see also Robert C. Johnson, "Budget Plans Put Issues of Process, Politics on Table," *Education Week*, May 24, 1995, 1 (noting that the Republican House budget proposal for fiscal 1996 "call[ed] . . . for killing more than 1900 education programs and abolishing the federal Education Department").

64. See Mark Pitsch, "Education Seen a Litmus Issue in '96 Election," *Education Week*, November 29, 1995, 1, 20 (observing that at least four Republican candidates for president have called for an end to the federal Department of Education).

65. "Status of Federal Legislation," *Education Week*, December 6, 1995, 19; Robert C. Johnson and Mark Pitsch, "Clinton Leads Fight against Budget Cuts," *Education Week*, September 13, 1995, 1.

66. See James C. Jacks and Lillian Jacks, "Chronology of the Birth and Death of a Health Bill: Clinton Administration's Health Care Reform Bill," *Journal of Health Care Finance* 21 (1995): 59.

67. May, *1993 Poverty and Income Trends*, 91 (showing 39.7 million persons with no health insurance in 1993).

68. Medicaid is not a universal health care program even for the poor. "As of 1990, only 45.2 percent of the poor were covered by Medicaid, including about 70 percent of those younger than age six, a bit more than 50 percent of older children up to age eighteen, but only about a third of poor adults aged nineteen to sixty-four" (Barbara L. Wolfe, "Reform of Health Care for the Nonelderly Poor," in Danziger et al., *Confronting Poverty*, 265).

As a result of federal legislation in 1992, however, Medicaid coverage was expanded to include all pregnant women and all children born after September 30, 1983, whose family income is below the poverty line, whether or not the family receives other welfare benefits (ibid., 266). By 1993 47.9 percent of poor persons were covered by Medicaid, and the percentage of poor children under eighteen with Medicaid coverage had jumped from 56.7 percent in 1989 to 67 percent in 1993 (May, *1993 Poverty and Income Trends*, 92).

69. *Number without Health Insurance Remains at Record Level; Long-term Trends Show Decline in Employee-Related Coverage and Growing Importance of Medicaid* (Washington, D.C.: Center on Budget and Policy Priorities, 1995), 1–3 (noting 1995 Census Bureau data that document an increase in those lacking insurance coverage throughout a year, up from 31 million in 1987 to 39.7 million in 1994, and tying that increase to a cutback in coverage of employees by many employer health plans); see also Wolfe, "Reform of Health Care," 255–56.

70. Wolfe, "Reform of Health Care," 256, tab. 10.2. The Current Population Report issued by the Census Bureau in March 1994 found 14.2 percent of whites, 20.4 percent of blacks, and 31.6 percent of Hispanics without insurance at that time (May, *1993 Poverty and Income Trends*, 91). See also Pamela Farley Short, Llewellyn J. Cornelius, and Donald E. Goldstone, "Health Insurance of Minorities in the United States," *Journal of Health Care for the Poor and Underserved* 1 (1990): 9.

71. May, *1993 Poverty and Income Trends*, 92.

72. Richard Kagan and Myra Tanamor, *The Conference Agreement on Medicaid:; How Deep Are Federal, State, and Total Medicaid Funding Cuts?* (Washington, D.C.: Center on Budget and Policy Priorities, 1995). According to Kagan and Tanamor, the $163 billion figure, which is derived from an analysis of the bill approved in the House-Senate Conference Committee in 1995, seriously underestimates the likely total effect set in motion by federal cuts. Although that figure does predict the direct decrease in federal spending if an annual "cap" is placed on federal dollars to each state (as both the House and Senate versions of the bill provide), it does not address the likelihood that states, which have previously been obligated to match federal Medicaid dollars under a Federal Medical Assistance Percentage formula (ibid., 2–3), may not continue to expend unmatched state dollars beyond those necessary to obtain the maximum federal dollars under the cap (ibid.). If fiscally hard-pressed states "matched only to the [federal] cap," an additional $257 billion in state Medicaid funds might disappear over seven years, for total Medicaid losses of $420 billion (ibid.).

73. Cindy Mann, *Can a Medicaid Block Grant Assure People Heath Care Coverage?* (Washington, D.C.: Center on Budget and Policy Priorities, 1995), 1.

74. John Holahan and David Liska, *The Impact of the House and Senate Budget Committees' Proposals on Medicaid Expenditures* (Washington, D.C.: Urban Institute, 1995).

75. Mann, *Medicaid Block Grant*, 3.

76. "Comparison: Highlights of the Plans," *New York Times*, December 8, 1995.

77. Howard Gleckman, Gail DeGeorge, and Sandra Dallas, "The Budget: Talking Turkey," *Business Week*, December 4, 1995, 32; Matthew Miller, "Where It May Really Hurt: The Budget Deal Could Fall Apart over Medicaid—and No Wonder," *Time*, December 18, 1995, 28.

78. Todd S. Purdum, "As Long Promised, President Vetoes the G.O.P. Budget," *New York Times*, December 7, 1995.

79. Joseph P. Poduska, "Senate Passes HUD Money Bill, Would Permit Section 8 Renewals, Delay Fair Housing Transfer," *Housing and Community Development Reporter*, October 9, 1995, 349.

80. Edward B. Lazere, *In Short Supply: The Growing Affordable Housing Gap* (Washington, D.C.: Center on Budget and Policy Priorities, 1995), 2 (citing data from the 1993 American Housing Survey, cosponsored by HUD and the Census Bureau).

81. Barry G. Jacobs, "Cisneros Unveils Budget Signaling 'Dramatic Change' for HUD," *Housing and Community Development Reporter*, February 13, 1995, 636; Department of Housing and Urban Development, *Empowerment*, 39–54 (describing federal initiatives that would assist inner-city residents to choose suburban employment and/or housing opportunities, as well as community development banks, empowerment zones, and enterprise communities programs to provide greater investment in central cities); see generally Alexander Polikoff, ed., *Housing Mobility: Promise or Illusion?* (Washington, D.C.: Urban Institute, 1995) (examining the national experience with, and the promise of, housing mobility programs).

82. See Ted Cornwell, "Dole Wants to Scuttle HUD," *National Mortgage News*, March 20, 1995, 1; "House GOP Freshmen Unveil Proposal to Eliminate HUD, Empower Local Governments," *BNA's Banking Report*, July 10, 1995, 65.

83. May, *1993 Poverty and Income Trends*, 37–38.

84. Mark Greenberg, *New Trees, Same Forest: Despite Changes, the Senate Welfare Bill Remains Flawed* (Washington, D.C.: Center for Law and Social Policy, 1995), 7–8 (contrasting the Clinton administration's welfare proposals with those of the House and Senate Republicans).

85. The House bill passed on March 24, 1995; the Senate bill, on September 19, 1995 ("Senate and House Bill Comparisons Available," in *CLASP Update* [Washington, D.C.: Center for Law and Social Policy, October 19, 1995], 2).

86. Center on Budget and Policy Priorities, *An Analysis of the Senate Welfare Bill* (Washington, D.C.: Center on Budget and Policy Priorities, 1995), 1; see also Greenberg, *New Trees, Same Forest*, 1–3.

87. Center on Budget and Policy Priorities, *Analysis of the Senate Welfare Bill*, 2. By 2000, inflation will likely reduce the minimum state expenditures to no more than 66 percent of 1994, inflation-adjusted dollars (ibid.).

88. Ibid.

89. Under the bill, states may opt to place much shorter cumulative lifetime limits on the receipt of AFDC benefits. States could thus "eliminate cash assistance for families after a year or even a few months" (ibid., 3). Almost half of all children receiving AFDC benefits in 1995, approximately 4.5 million children, live in families that would be ineligible under a five-year-maximum rule. Presumably they would all immediately lose AFDC benefits under the bill (*Summary of Effects of House Bill H.R. 4 on Low-Income Programs* [Washington, D.C.: Center on Budget and Policy Priorities, 1995], 5).

90. "By the year 2003, the adults in 50 percent of AFDC families [in a state] must participate in a work program for at least 35 hours each week" (*Summary of Effects of House Bill H.R. 4*, 6).

91. The Senate bill does not prohibit states from imposing these stricter standards; unlike the House, it merely makes them optional for states (Center on Budget and Policy Priorities, *Analysis of the Senate Welfare Bill*, 3).

92. The Senate bill requires states to achieve a 50 percent work participation rate by the year 2000. However, the legislation does not provide funds to assist states in creating work and training programs for welfare recipients, instead freezing funds for job training programs at the fiscal 1994 level. The Congressional Budget Office has estimated that, by the year 2000, federal funding will fall $3.135 billion per year below that needed by states simply to administer the work provisions of the Senate bill—exclusive of additional funds that will be necessary to assist with child care costs for working mothers (ibid., 2).

93. Ibid., 5.

94. Ibid., 4; *Summary of Effects of House Bill H.R. 4*, 8–9.

95. Center on Budget and Policy Priorities, *Analysis of the Senate Welfare Bill*, 4.

96. "Budget Reconciliation Includes Welfare Worse Than Senate: Veto of Package Expected," in *CLASP Update* (Washington, D.C.: Center for Law and Social Policy, November 20, 1995), 2.

97. *The Administration Releases New Estimates of House and Senate Budget Bills Effects on Poverty and Income Distribution* (Washington, D.C.: Center on Budget and Policy Priorities, 1995), 1.

98. Peter Gottschalk, Sara McLanahan, and Gary D. Sandefur, "The Dynamics and Intergenerational Transmission of Poverty and Welfare Participation," in Danziger et al., *Confronting Poverty*, 95.

99. Center on Budget and Policy Priorities, *Analysis of the Senate Welfare Bill*, 7.

100. 478 U.S. 30 (1986).

101. According to the Congressional Black Caucus, "Thirty-six of [its] 40 members were elected from majority-minority districts" (Brief of the Congressional Black Caucus as Amicus Curiae in Support of Appellees, *Shaw v. Hunt*, __ U.S. __, 115 S.Ct. 2639 [1995] [No. 94-923]).

102. See *Shaw v. Hunt*, 861 F. Supp. 408 (E.D.N.C. 1994), cert. granted, __ U.S. __, 115 S.Ct. 2639 (1995); "Court Considers Race and Politics," *New York Times*, December 6, 1995 (reporting the December 5 oral arguments in which "the Supreme Court came face to face . . . with the implications of its decisions that cast a constitutional cloud over legislative districts drawn to increase black representation, and even over the Voting Rights Act itself").

103. Guinier, "[E]racing Democracy," 125; see also Lani Guinier, *The Tyranny of the Majority: Fundamental Fairness and Representative Democracy* (New York: Free Press, 1994), and "The Representation of Minority Interests: The Question of Single-Member Districts," *Cardozo Law Review* 14 (1993): 1135j.

104. Neil A. Lewis, "Clinton Abandons His Nominee for Rights Post amid Opposition," *New York Times*, June 4, 1993.

105. Department of Housing and Urban Development, *Empowerment*, 2.

106. See generally Sheldon H. Danziger and Daniel H. Weinberg, "The Historical Record," in Danziger et al., *Confronting Poverty*, 21–25 and tab. 2.1 (illustrating the growth of "today's very large gap between those at the top and those at the bot-

tom of the income distribution . . . [and evidence that] those in the middle of the income distribution as well as those at the bottom have fared relatively poorly over the past two decades"); Isaac Shapiro and Robert Greenstein, *Selective Prosperity: Increasing Income Disparities since 1977* (Washington, D.C.: Center on Budget and Policy Priorities, 1991).

107. W. E. B. Du Bois, *The Souls of Black Folk* (New York: Bantam Books, 1989), 10.

Contributors

John Charles Boger is associate dean for academic affairs and professor of law at the University of North Carolina at Chapel Hill, where he teaches courses in constitutional law, race discrimination, poverty, and education law. He holds a B.A. from Duke, an M.Div. from Yale Divinity School, and a J.D. from North Carolina. From 1978 until 1990, Boger was assistant counsel at the NAACP Legal Defense and Educational Fund, Inc., in New York City, where he headed LDF's Capital Punishment Project and, later, LDF's Poverty and Justice Project. He is presently chair of the Poverty and Race Research Action Council.

Alison Brett is a Ph.D. candidate in the Counselling Psychology Program at Northwestern University. She received her B.A. from Cornell in 1985.

John O. Calmore is professor of law and W. Joseph Ford Fellow at Loyola Law School in Los Angeles, where he has taught since 1987. A graduate of Stanford and the Harvard Law School, he served as the director of litigation at the Legal Aid Foundation of Los Angeles and as a staff attorney at the National Housing Law Project and the Western Center on Law and Poverty prior to 1987. On leave from 1990–92, Professor Calmore was a program officer in the Rights and Social Justice Program at the Ford Foundation. Professor Calmore has published numerous articles on housing issues and racial subordination. He is on the board of directors of the New World Foundation and the National Asian Pacific American Legal Consortium, is a member of the Social Policy Advisory Committee to the Bank of America, and is a member of the Working Group of the Institute on Race and Poverty of the University of Minnesota Law School.

Peter Dreier (Ph.D., University of Chicago) is the E. P. Clapp Distinguished Professor of Politics and director of the Public Policy Program at Occidental College in Los Angeles. He previously served for 9 1/2 years as the director of housing at the Boston Redevelopment Authority and senior policy advisor to Boston mayor Ray Flynn. He drafted the Community Housing Partnership Act, which became part of the federal HOME program that, since 1990, has provided federal funds to community-based nonprofit housing development organizations. The Clinton administration appointed Dreier to the advisory board of the Resolution Trust Corporation. He has served as a consultant to the U.S. Department of Housing and Urban Development, the Connecticut Conference of Municipalities, the MacArthur Foundation, ACORN, VISTA, and other government, community, and philanthropic organizations. Dreier has written widely on urban politics, housing policy, and community development. He is a regular contributor to *American Prospect* and the *Los Angeles Times*, and his articles have appeared in numerous other scholarly and public policy journals. He serves on the editorial boards of *Urban Affairs Quarterly*, *Housing Studies*, and *Shelterforce*.

Susan S. Fainstein is professor of urban planning and policy development at Rutger's—the State University of New Jersey. Her teaching and research have focused on comparative public policy, planning theory, and urban redevelopment. She is the author of *The City Builders*, coauthor of *Urban Political Movements* and *Restructuring the City*, and coeditor of *Divided Cities*. She has recently been the principal investigator on a research project, funded by the McKnight Foundation, that evaluated neighborhood-based planning in Minneapolis over a three-year period. In addition, she has published book chapters and articles on a variety of subjects, including race and urban development in the United States, citizen participation, urban social movements, and comparisons of urban policy in the United States and Western Europe.

Walter C. Farrell Jr. is professor of educational policy and community studies in the School of Education at the University of Wisconsin at Milwaukee, where he serves as a member of the graduate and doctoral faculties in urban education and the Department of Curriculum and Instruction. He received his B.S. degree from North Carolina Central University and his M.A. and Ph.D. degrees in urban-social and economic geography from Michigan State, followed by a postdoctoral M.S.P.H. degree from the University of North Carolina at Chapel Hill. He is a consulting senior manager for Coleman & Williams Management Consultants and Certified Public Accountants, Ltd. His research focuses on the race and class underpinnings of the urban underclass, urban education and school privatization, welfare reform, economic and social development in the inner city, and organizational analysis and program evaluation. Dr. Farrell has published over one hundred journal articles, book reviews, scholarly essays, book chapters, research monographs, and technical reports in his field.

Nancy Fishman is a Ph.D. candidate in the Human Development and Social Policy Program at Northwestern University. She received her B.A. from Yale in 1988.

George C. Galster earned his undergraduate degrees from Wittenberg and Case Western Reserve and his Ph.D. in economics from MIT. He has published over seventy refereed articles, primarily on metropolitan housing markets, racial discrimination and segregation, neighborhood dynamics, residential reinvestment, community lending and insurance patterns, and urban poverty. Dr. Galster has been a consultant to the U.S. Department of Housing and Urban Development, numerous municipalities, community organizations, and civil rights groups as well as organizations such as the National Association of Realtors, the American Bankers Association, Fannie Mae, and the Chemical Bank Corporation. Recently he completed an appointment to the Consumer Advisory Council of the Federal Reserve's board of governors. Dr. Galster has held academic appointments at Harvard, the University of California at Berkeley, the University of North Carolina at Chapel Hill, and the College of Wooster. He has been associated with the Center for Public Finance and Housing at the Urban Institute since 1992, serving presently as director of housing research.

Chester Hartman is president/executive director of the Poverty and Race Research Action Council in Washington, D.C. He holds a Ph.D. in city and regional planning from Harvard and has been on the faculty there as well as at Yale, Cornell, the University of California at Berkeley, Columbia, and the University of North Carolina. Prior to assuming his responsibilities at PRRAC, Dr. Hartman was a Fellow at the Institute for Policy Studies. He founded and from 1975 to 1995 chaired the Planners Network, a national organization of progressive urban planners, and he has worked as a community-oriented advocate planner in Boston and San Francisco. Among his books are *The Transformation of San Francisco* and *Critical Perspectives on Housing*.

James H. Johnson Jr. is the E. Maynard Adams Distinguished Professor of Business, Geography, and Sociology at the University of North Carolina at Chapel Hill. He received his B.S. degree from North Carolina Central University, his M.S. from the University of Wisconsin at Madison, and his Ph.D. from Michigan State. His research interests include interregional black migration, interethnic minority conflict in advanced industrial societies, workforce diversity, urban poverty, public policy, welfare reform, and entrepreneurship and minority economic development. For fourteen years before joining the UNC-Chapel Hill faculty, Professor Johnson was the founder and director of the Center for Urban Poverty at the University of California, Los Angeles. He is the 1992–93 recipient of the Center for Advanced Study in the Behavioral Sciences Fellowship from Stanford University. Johnson has published over one hundred scholarly research articles and one research monograph and has coedited four theme issues of scholarly research journals on these and related topics. He is a participating researcher in the Multi-City Study of Urban Inequality funded by the Ford Foundation and the Russell Sage Foundation. He has been a consultant for the U.S. Department of Housing and Urban Development and numerous public and private entities. Professor Johnson's research has been widely cited in major national media outlets, and he has appeared on numerous national television news and policy programs.

Ann Markusen is director of the Project on Regional and Industrial Economics at Rutgers University, where she is State of New Jersey Professor of Urban Planning and Policy Development. She is the author and coauthor of several books on high technology and American economic development. Professor Markusen received her bachelor's degree in foreign service at Georgetown University and her M.A. and Ph.D. in economics at Michigan State University. She has held faculty positions at the University of Colorado, the University of California at Berkeley, Northwestern University, and Rutgers. She has been awarded a Brookings Institution Economic Policy Fellowship and a Fulbright Lectureship in Brazil, and she has been an economic advisor to the cities of Chicago, Cleveland, and Pittsburgh and to the states of Michigan, California, and Ohio. She has served on review panels for the National Science Foundation and the Office of Technology Assessment and is currently on the Committee on Science, Engineering and Public Policy of the American Academy for the Advancement of Science. She serves on the boards of directors of the Economic Policy Institute, Economists Allied for Arms Reductions, and the National Commission on Economic Conversion and Disarmament.

Patricia Meaden is a Ph.D. candidate in the Counselling Psychology Program at Northwestern University. She received her B.A. from Elmhurst College in 1988.

James E. Rosenbaum is professor of sociology, education, and social policy at Northwestern University. He received his B.A. at Yale and his M.A. and Ph.D. at Harvard. He specializes in research on work, education, and housing opportunities. He has published three books and many articles on these subjects. He is directing studies of low-income black families in white suburbs and a study of a mixed-income housing project, Lake Parc Place. His research has been described in the *New York Times*, the *Washington Post*, the *Wall Street Journal*, and *Fortune* and on *Sixty Minutes*, CNN, and NBC's *Today Show*. Rosenbaum's studies of the Gautreaux Program contributed to the federal Moving to Opportunity program, implemented by the U.S. Department of Housing and Urban Development.

Peter W. Salsich Jr. is McDonnell Professor of Justice in American Society and associate dean for academic affairs at Saint Louis University School of Law. He is chair of the American Bar Association Commission on Homelessness and Poverty; a former member of the Council of the Section of Real Property, Probate and Trust Law of the American Bar Association; a Fellow of the American College of Real Estate Lawyers; and a member of the American Planning Association and the Association of American Law Schools. Professor Salsich was the first chair of the Missouri Housing Development Commission and chaired the Board of Directors of Legal Services of Eastern Missouri, Inc., and the Ecumenical Housing Production Corporation of St. Louis. He is the author of several books as well as numerous articles on housing, land use control, local government and property law.

Michael A. Stegman is assistant secretary for policy development and research in the Department of Housing and Urban Development. A nationally known public policy and urban studies academician, he was Cary C. Boshamer Professor and chairman of the Department of City and Regional Planning at the University of North Carolina in Chapel Hill before his HUD appointment. He has been a housing consultant to several states and localities and has led workshops and seminars for elected officials and housing officials throughout the United States. From 1979 to 1981 he served as HUD deputy assistant secretary for research; he chaired the President's Rural Housing Task Force and was a member of the White House Inter-Agency Working Group on Small Communities and Rural Development Policy. His books include *More Housing, More Fairly*; *The Limits of Privatization: A Report of the Twentieth Century Fund Task Force on Affordable Housing*; *The Public Housing Homeownership Demonstration Assessment*; and *Non-Federal Housing Programs: How States and Localities Are Responding to Federal Cutbacks*.

David Stoesz is Samuel S. Wurtzel Chair of Social Work at Virginia Commonwealth University. He has held direct service and administrative appointments in public welfare and mental health services. Dr. Stoesz has written widely about the rise of for-profit health and human service corporations, the role of think tanks in the policy process, social welfare theory, and the development of a postindustrial framework for social policy. He is the coauthor of *American Social Welfare Policy*, *Reconstructing the American Welfare State*, and *The Politics of Child Abuse in America*. His critical examination of the Clinton White House, *Small Change: Domestic Policy under the Clinton Presidency*, was recently published.

Charles Sumner Stone Jr., the Walter Spearman Professor in the School of Journalism and Mass Communications at the University of North Carolina at Chapel Hill, is a former White House correspondent and former editor of three major African American newspapers. The author of three books, Stone is also a former syndicated columnist, a John F. Kennedy Fellow at Harvard, and a former special assistant to the late Rep. Adam Clayton Powell Jr., chairman of the House Education and Labor Committee. Stone holds four honorary degrees.

William L. Taylor practices law in Washington, D.C., specializing in advocacy for the rights of minority and poor children. At the time of the Kerner Commission Report, he was staff director of the U.S. Commission on Civil Rights. Mr. Taylor also serves as vice-chair of the Leadership Conference on Civil Rights and vice-chair of the Citizens' Commission on Civil Rights. He is an adjunct professor of law at the Georgetown Law Center. He received his B.A. degree at Brooklyn College and his law degree at Yale.

Sidney D. Watson is professor of law at Mercer University Law School, where she teaches health care law, bioethics and law, torts, and alternative dispute resolution. She received her B.A. degree from the University of Southwestern Louisiana and her J.D. degree from Harvard. After serving as an attorney with the Louisiana Center for the Public Interest, she became director of the Farmworkers Legal Assistance Project in New Orleans and then a supervising attorney with the Alaska Legal Services Corporation. Professor Watson has directed the clinical education program at Tulane and currently teaches an AIDS law clinic at Mercer.

Judith Welch Wegner is dean and professor of law at the School of Law at the University of North Carolina at Chapel Hill. She received her B.A. degree from Wisconsin and her J.D. degree from the University of California at Los Angeles. After clerking for a federal district judge and serving as an attorney in the Office of Legal Counsel in the U.S. Department of Justice, she served as special assistant to Secretary of Education Shirley M. Hufstedler. Dean Wegner has published and taught widely in the areas of local and state government law, land use planning, property law, and disability law. In 1995 she served as president of the Association of American Law Schools, and she has worked with the American Bar Association and sixteen American law schools to promote cooperative legal programs in eight African nations.

Index of Statutes

General Index